AGING, SPIRITUALITY, AND RELIGION

AGING, SPIRITUALITY, AND RELIGION

A Handbook

Melvin A. Kimble
Susan H. McFadden
James W. Ellor
James J. Seeber
Editors

Foreword by
James E. Birren

FORTRESS PRESS MINNEAPOLIS

AGING, SPIRITUALITY, AND RELIGION
A Handbook

Library of Congress Cataloging-in-Publication Data

Aging, spirituality, and religion : a handbook / Melvin A. Kimble . . .
[et al.], editors.
p. cm.
Includes bibliographical references and index.
ISBN 0-8006-2667-2
1. Aged—Religious life. 2. Aging—Religious aspects—Christianity. 3. Church work with the aged. 4. Aging—Social aspects.
BV4580.A446 1995
208′.4′6—dc20 95-6351
CIP

The paper used in this publication meets the minimum requirements of American National Standard for Information Sciences—Permanence of Paper for Printed Library Materials, ANSI Z329.48-1984.

Manufactured in U.S.A. AF 1-2667

99 98 97 96 95 1 2 3 4 5 6 7 8 9 10

In memory of

Paul S. Maves who pioneered in exploring gerontology
and religion and thereby shaped the exploration of the
unchartered terrain of this emerging field

and Earl D.C. Brewer, whose "Brewer outline"
initially inspired and encouraged the understanding of
a handbook on aging, spirituality, and religion

Contents

Illustrations

Contributors

W.A. Achenbaum
Professor of History and Deputy Director of the Institute of Gerontology
University of Michigan
Ann Arbor

Robert C. Atchley
Professor of Social Gerontology
Director, Scripps Gerontology Center
University of Miami, Ohio
Oxford, Ohio

Thomas Au
Executive Director
United Methodist Homes
Roanoke, Virginia

Andrew Billingsley
Professor and Chair of the Department of Family Studies
University of Maryland
College Park, Maryland

James E. Birren
Founder and Emeritus Director of the Ethel Percy Andrus Gerontology Center
University of Southern California
and Associate Director
Center of Aging, UCLA
Los Angeles

Fredda Blanchard-Fields
Associate Professor of Psychology
School of Psychology
Georgia Institute of Technology
Atlanta

Eugene B. Borowitz
Sigmund L. Falk Distinguished Professor of Education and
Jewish Religious Thought
Hebrew Union College—Jewish Institute of Religion
New York

Marie A. Bracki
Associate Professor of Human Services and Psychology
National-Louis University
Wheaton, Illinois

The late Earl D. C. Brewer
Professor Emeritus of Sociology and Religion
Candler School of Theology
Emory University
Atlanta

Cleopatra Howard Caldwell
Research Investigator, Program for Research on Black Americans
Institute for Social Research
University of Michigan
Ann Arbor

Dosia Carlson
Founder of Beatitudes Center for Developing Older Adult Resources
Pastor for Caring Ministries
Church of the Beatitudes
Phoenix

Linda Chatters
Associate Professor, Department of Health Behavior and Health Education
School of Public Health
University of Michigan
and Faculty Associate with the Program for Research on Black Americans
Institute for Social Research
University of Michigan
Ann Arbor

Drew Christiansen
Director, Department of Social Development and World Peace
Office of International Justice and Peace
United States Catholic Conference
Washington, D.C.

William M. Clements
Edna and Lowell Craig Professor of Pastoral Care and Counseling
The School of Theology at Claremont
Claremont, California

John B. Cobb, Jr.
Professor Emeritus of Theology
the School of Theology at Claremont
and Co-Director of the Center for Process Studies
Claremont, California

Nancy Coleman
Director, Commission on Legal Problems of the Elderly
American Bar Association
Washington, D.C.

Anne Marie Djupe
Director of Parish Nursing Services
Lutheran General Health System
Park Ridge, Illinois

James W. Ellor
Professor of Human Services and Coordinator of Gerontology Programs
National-Louis University
Wheaton, Illinois

David S. Ensing
Assistant Professor of Psychology
University of Toledo
Toledo, Ohio

Dayle A. Friedman
Chaplain
Philadelphia Geriatric Center
Philadelphia, Pennsylvania
and Coordinator of the Rabbinic Program on Aging
Reconstructionist Rabbinical College
Wyncote, Pennsylvania

Lynn W. Huber
Church Consultant and Educator
Little Rock, Arkansas
and former Director of the Office of Affirmative Aging for the Episcopal Diocese of Tennessee

Melvin A. Kimble
Professor of Pastoral Theology and Director of The Center for Aging, Religion, and Spirituality
Luther Seminary
Saint Paul

Harold G. Koenig
Assistant Professor of Psychiatry and Internal Medicine
and Director of the Program on Religion, Aging and Health of the Center for Aging
Duke University Medical Center
Durham, North Carolina

Marc Kolden
Professor of Systematic Theology at Luther Seminary
Saint Paul

Mary M. Knutsen
Associate Professor of Systematic Theology
Luther Seminary
Saint Paul

Jackie C. Lanum
Professor of Behavioral Science
Santa Monica College
Santa Monica, California

Martha Klein Larsen
Doctoral Candidate in Feminist Studies and Theology
Chicago Theological Seminary
and adjunct faculty member
Hartford Seminary
Hartford, Connecticut

Jeffrey S. Levin
Associate Professor of Family and Community Medicine
Eastern Virginia Medical School
Norfolk, Virginia

David Maldonado, Jr.
Professor of Church and Society and Associate Dean for Academic Affairs at Perkins School of Theology
Southern Methodist University
Dallas

Susan H. McFadden
Associate Professor of Psychology at the University of Wisconsin Oshkosh
Oshkosh, Wisconsin

David O. Moberg
Professor Emeritus of Sociology
Marquette University
Milwaukee

Harry R. Moody
Deputy Director
Brookdale Center on Aging
Hunter College
New York

F. Ellen Netting
Professor of Social Work
Virginia Common Wealth University
Richmond, Virginia

Lisa Norris
Ph.D. student in the Department of Psychology
Louisiana State University
Baton Rouge, Louisiana

Rabbi Kerry M. Olitzky
Director of the School of Education and Director of Graduate Studies Program at Hebrew Union College—Jewish Institute of Religion
New York

Omar Otterness
Professor Emeritus of Religion
St. Olaf College
Northfield, Minnesota

Kenneth I. Pargament
Professor of Psychology
Bowling Green State University
Bowling Green, Ohio

Barbara Pittard Payne
Emerita Professor of Sociology and Director of the Gerontology Center
Georgia State University
Atlanta

Jean K. Quam
Director and Associate Professor
School of Social Work
University of Minnesota
Minneapolis

Gary T. Reker
Professor of Psychology
Trent University
Peterborough, Ontario

Stephen Sapp
Professor of Religious Studies
University of Miami
Miami

James J. Seeber
Associate Professor of Sociology at California Baptist College
Riverside, California
and former administrator of the Institute for Religion and Wholeness at the School of Theology
Claremont, California

Henry C. Simmons
Professor of Religion and Aging and Director of the Center on Aging
Presbyterian School of Christian Education
Richmond, Virginia

Lori A. Stiegel
Associate Staff Director of the Commission on Legal Problems of the Elderly
the American Bar Association
Washington, D.C.

Robert Joseph Taylor
Associate Professor of Social Work and Faculty Associate for Research on Black Americans
Institute for Social Work
University of Michigan
Ann Arbor

Jane M. Thibault
Assistant Professor of Family Practice
University of Louisville Medical School
Louisville

Sheldon S. Tobin
Professor in the School of Social Welfare and Research Associate of the Ringel Institute of Gerontology
State University of New York at Albany
New York

Kimberly S. Van Haitsma
Project Director of the Special Care Study
Philadelphia Geriatric Center
Philadelphia

Frederick C. Van Tatenhove
Frank Bateman Stanger Professor of Pastoral Counseling and Chair of the Department of Pastoral Ministry
Asbury Theological Seminary
Wilmore, Kentucky

Linda J. Vogel
Professor of Christian Education
Garrett Evangelical Theological Seminary
Evanston, Illinois

Steven Weiland
Professor, Department of Educational Administration
College of Education
Michigan State University
East Lansing, Michigan

Granger Westberg
Consultant to Parish Nursing Program
Lutheran General Health System
Park Ridge, Illinois

Gary S. Whitford
Assistant Professor of Social Work
Augsburg College
Minneapolis

Anne E. Streaty Wimberly
Associate Professor of Christian Education and Church Music
Interdenominational Theological Center
Atlanta

Edward Powell Wimberly
Jarena Lee Professor of Pastoral Care
Psychology and Counseling
Interdenominational Theological Center
Atlanta

Foreword

What an ideal time for this book to appear. We are nearing the end of a century and a millennium, and we need the best guidance we can get for our journeys through a society that is changing in so many ways, including how many more of us are reaching advanced age. Centenarians are no longer a rarity.

As a turn of the century event, this book is ground breaking because its contributions around the issues of spirituality, religion, and aging are written by so many different specialists. In the past we never had chapters in the same book from theologians and practitioners, chaplains and social workers, social scientists and physicians all directed at a shared goal. Such professionals are usually remote neighbors.

Why did the editors create this volume? A leadership group apparently recognized that there is an age revolution occurring in our society. That there are many more older persons is changing our institutions and our ways of working and serving. For example, both religion and education have had models that an "early dose" or "inoculation" of their teaching would last a lifetime. Are these models valid in an aging and changing society where individuals grope for meaning in their lives as they are challenged by events and relationships? How can our institutions respond creatively both to persons whose lives are expanding as they approach 100 and others who are disabled physically, socially, psychologically, or spiritually in midlife?

As we shift from a primarily youth oriented society toward one of mature balance, new services, new concepts, and new careers will be developed to meet the needs and wants of millions of diverse older persons. Many professionals, including those in religious organizations, have been slow to incorporate findings of modern research in their work, and researchers have been reluctant about collaborating in studying the religious and spiritual experience of growing old. We now have such a collaboration in this book and it is promising.

Clearly social and behavioral scientists are recognizing that important aspects of adult life have been neglected by their not having studied the religious and spiritual concerns of mature and older adults. Nor have religious communities actively embraced knowledge that has accumulated about aging in the last fifty years. I believe that this book is a turning point that will profoundly affect what we think and do about our lives as we grow older and how our institutions will be able to serve us and future generations of older persons to better advantage.

This book is not the last word on a complex subject but it certainly is a strong initiative that will set the stage for collaboration in the service and well-being of our society. It will establish the fact that we need to trade in and trade up our old ideas and knowledge about growing old. In the future, the religious and scientific communities should be more cooperative and less competitive about what we know and don't know.

No book is ever complete and this book stimulates me to think ahead about next editions before the ink is dry. It is expected that gaps in our understanding will occur to us as we direct our attention to how we will serve an older population in the next millennium. I expect more breakthroughs in communication between the research and scholarly communities will result from this publication. What we know and need to know will be shared not only among scholars but among those responsible for congregational life, pastoral care, and training.

What a promising future this book portends!

JAMES E. BIRREN

Preface

This handbook could never have been initiated without the support of a grant from the Lilly Endowment. The Lilly Endowment recognized the importance of bringing together many different voices to reflect upon religion, spirituality, and aging. In addition to supporting the development of this book, the Lilly Endowment underwrote a conference at Luther Seminary, Saint Paul, Minnesota, in October, 1992.

At this meeting chapter authors presented their work and received feedback from people representing the variety of disciplines reflected in this book. These authors, eminent within their own fields, frequently expressed some hesitation about reading a paper on social scientific theory to theologians, or presenting a paper on the theology of aging to psychologists and sociologists. Such interchanges rarely occur in professional settings and yet both those who presented their work as well as those who heard and responded gained fresh insights into their own and other persons' disciplines. The editors hope that interest and excitement similar to that generated in Saint Paul will be experienced by readers of this handbook. The study of spirituality and religion in later life is a complex undertaking but it holds the promise of rich rewards not only for the gerontologists and religious workers who conduct the inquiries but also for elders themselves whose sources of hope and courage are affirmed. Insights into religious and spiritual themes that emerge in later life can also benefit younger persons searching for models of how to maintain a sense of meaning and purpose despite the exigencies of aging.

Many people have made the publication of this book possible. The editors especially want to express their gratitude to three individuals—Earl Brewer, Barbara Payne, and James Birren. About ten years ago, at a meeting of the Association for Gerontology in Higher Education, Earl Brewer held up copies of the other handbooks on aging and asked why none existed to address issues of religion and spirituality. Barbara Payne, in attendance at that meeting, responded by constantly urging authors and publishers to pay more attention to the role of religion and spirituality in older persons' lives. She kept asking why they did not mention these topics in their textbooks. Their claims of lacking access to the information clearly indicated the need for a comprehensive handbook that would represent an authoritative, multidisciplinary resource. Such resources covering other aspects of gerontology have been available for many years, thanks in large measure to the work of James Birren. From the time the editors began to discuss the possibility of a handbook that would address issues in religion, spirituality, and aging, he has been a constant source of support, encouragement, and inspiration. Birren's editorial experience, as well as his kindness and his enthusiasm for the project, has been invaluable.

Supported by the grant from the Lilly Endowment, several assistants at Luther Seminary became involved in the project: Kathryn Werner, Lisa Simonsen, Mary Lewis, Kevin Clark, Anessa Arvin Jorgenson, Julie Clark, Paula Lund, and Melanie Wallschlaeger have provided valuable assistance. Finally, James Wind at the Lilly Endowment has offered guidance and encouragement to the editors. His belief in this undertaking has been greatly appreciated.

Introduction: Beginning the Conversation

The last half of the twentieth century has witnessed a demographic revolution with increasing numbers of persons living longer and better than their ancestors ever could have imagined. These dramatic demographic changes have prompted scholars from disciplines ranging from the biomedical sciences to the humanities to study aging. Ideally, gerontology, the intersection of disparate disciplinary approaches to aging, emphasizes a complex and multi-faceted effort to understand aging persons and aging processes. However, in reality gerontology has focused more on scientific definitions of and solutions to problems of aging and less on humanistic understanding of aging persons. Their lived experiences of aging processes are far more intricate than a list of "problems" might suggest. In addition, until very recently, gerontologists failed to appreciate the ways spiritual yearnings and religious beliefs and practices shape the pathways many older persons traverse through later life.

This situation is changing rapidly, however, with more professionals in gerontology—both those involved with practice and those conducting research in academic settings—willing to entertain questions about the meanings of late life, and the factors that influence how older persons meet potential threats to meaning.

In addition, data from national surveys like the Gallup Polls reveal that a high percentage of the present cohort of older adults attends church or synagogue regularly, engages in private religious practices on a daily basis, and utilizes religious coping strategies. Religious beliefs and behaviors exercise a powerful organizing influence upon the lives of many older persons. Inquiry about variables that shape the subjective experience of aging has led some gerontologists to conclude that the effects of spiritual experience and religious commitments must be acknowledged both in research and in practice.

At the same time as gerontologists are expressing a growing interest in incorporating issues of spirituality and religion into their studies of the aging human, persons working in religious settings are beginning to attend to the special needs and specific situations of older persons. Pastoral care and counseling, program development, worship, and community outreach are all areas requiring attention from persons sensitive to the needs and gifts of older adults. Religious workers—from local parish clergy to the heads of judicatory bodies—who have tended to focus upon the first half of life are now awakening to the rich possibilities for ministry with aging persons.

Until now, few opportunities have been afforded for gerontologists interested in religion and spirituality in late life to exchange insights and questions with persons in the religious sector interested in aging. Clearly, these groups can learn from one another. In the belief that the modern world of scholarship erects too many artificial disciplinary barriers, the editors of this book have undertaken a risky, even audacious, challenge to begin a conversation that includes persons from a wide range of disciplines.

Recent years have witnessed the publication of numerous writings about spirituality, religion, and aging. The problem, however, has been that these writings are often directed to small, particular audiences; it has been extremely difficult to get a larger picture of these issues. Because this handbook represents this needed breadth, it is imperative that it draw upon a wide variety of resources and attempt to appeal to a diverse audience.

The book is divided into six parts. In organizing the chapters, the editors believed it was essential to begin with the aging person. Therefore, Part One addresses the lifespace of the older adult and his or her experiences of spirituality and religion. Questions central to this section of the book include the following: Who are we at the ends of our life journeys? How do we experience ourselves, others, the world, and the Ultimate Other in the face of suffering and loss in later life? How can we maintain the conviction that life is meaningful in old age?

In Parts Two, Three, and Four, attention is drawn to the fact that aging people often find the answers to these questions within communities of faith. These communities care for elders through the activities of clergy (Part Two), corporate worship and education (Part Three), and outreach to the larger community (Part Four). This central section of the book essentially asks: How shall we care for one another? How shall we celebrate together life's journey? How can we work together to find meaning and purpose in old age?

Parts Five and Six move away from the practical and into the theoretical. This third section offers several ways of understanding the questions raised in the other two sections. Contributions from both theologians and social scientists intersect to offer perspectives on these questions: How shall we understand the relation between the individual and the community of faith? What intimations of ultimacy move us in later life? What is involved in the aging process that makes later life such fertile soil for the growth of spiritual and religious consciousness? How have the very ways we have asked our questions about aging and meaning prevented us from discovering their answers?

Within the pages of this handbook are chapters written by physicians, theologians, psychologists, social workers, clergy, chaplains, sociologists, and others. Representatives of these disciplines do not ordinarily meet within the covers of the same book. However, because issues of religion and spirituality arise in nearly all areas of gerontology, from the most theoretical to the most practical, it is appropriate that persons from many disciplines should come together to address these significant concerns.

Participants in this conversation include not only the editors and authors; most important are the readers of this book. As much as possible, we have tried to avoid the specialized jargon of theology and the social sciences. We especially encourage readers to explore topics outside their own areas of expertise. For example, we envision social scientists reading the chapters on theology in order to acquire an appreciation for the similarities and the differences among various theological approaches to aging. The varying theological underpinnings of American religions matter; much significant information is lost when religion is treated as generic. Likewise, we encourage theologians and clergy to read the chapters on social scientific theory and research so that they might begin to understand not only the ways data about aging are accumulated but also the theoretical foundations of sociological and psychological studies of aging processes and persons. The conversation on religion, spirituality, and aging begun in these pages is open to gerontologists and to persons from the religious sector, to researchers and to practitioners, to persons who have studied these issues for many years and to students just beginning to explore the vast array of exciting questions that arise when one contemplates the spiritual motivation to embue life with meaning and the varieties of religious experiences, beliefs, and practices that give shape to that meaning. Many of the authors of these chapters have been pioneers in their various fields. It is hoped that students reading this book will expand upon their insights, ask new questions, and discover other pathways leading toward greater understanding of sources of meaning in later life.

SUSAN H. MCFADDEN

Part One RELIGION, SPIRITUALITY, AND THE AGING PERSON

INTRODUCTION

Much of the impetus to study religion, spirituality, and the aging individual has come from the concern that increasing scientific specialization within gerontology threatens efforts to retain wholistic models of aging. *Harold Koenig* faces this problem directly in the first chapter of this section by proposing a biopsychosocial-spiritual model of health and aging. He examines a number of mental and physical illnesses affecting elders and demonstrates that religion appears to have both a palliative and a preventative effect for older adults. Koenig's own research, described in detail in this chapter, and referred to often by the authors of the next two chapters, represents an important development in gerontology. His scientific work reveals how the religious and spiritual dimensions of human experience interact with the material dimensions. At all times, however, he recognizes that science may not hold all the answers to the hope and strength and courage people find in religion and spirituality.

Although Koenig's research is highly regarded by gerontologists, much of the literature on the relation between religion, spirituality, and well-being is flawed by problems in defining and measuring variables. *Jeffrey Levin* and *Sheldon Tobin* critique this literature and present a number of challenging questions both to researchers and those who would apply research to practice. They urge researchers to explore what older persons' religious beliefs actually mean to them, a task that will require social scientists to understand a wide diversity of beliefs in order to be able to ask the correct questions. Chapters in Part Six begin the kind of interdisciplinary dialogue that Levin and Tobin believe will positively contribute to understanding psychological well-being in later life.

Koenig's chapter demonstrates that religion appears to be related to mental and physical health and Levin and Tobin's chapter offers a critical view of ways of studying this relation. Chapter 3 offers a psychological perspective on *how* and *why* religion enables older persons to cope with the exigencies of their lives. *Kenneth Pargament, Kimberly Van Haitsma, and David Ensing* present a portrait of coping in later life that is much richer than popular views of coping solely as a way of solving problems and promoting positive affect. People cope in order to conserve and transform significance in their lives; coping, therefore, is a response to the fundamental human need for meaning. Like Levin and Tobin, however, Pargament and his colleagues caution against making overly grand generalizations about the effects of religion on people's ability to cope. Certain religious orientations may actually thwart coping efforts; not all older adults will easily come to religion as a source of strength in difficult times; certain kinds of problems may be more suited than others to a religious response.

Chapters 1–4 demonstrate progress in research on religion, spirituality, and the aging person; they also indicate a maturing process in the pursuit of this knowledge by pointing to new questions and by calling for new ways of answering these questions. Many of these issues and methods are examined in later chapters.

With chapter 4, *Robert Atchley* turns this part toward a more global account of how people adapt to their changing life circumstances while maintaining longstanding patterns of relating to the world and of making sense of subjective experience. Less emphasis is given in this chapter to religious practices and beliefs whereas more attention is paid to an inner spiritual continuity that binds a life together.

Atchley's chapter on continuity theory compliments *Linda Vogel's* developmental approach to the ways people construct meaning and nourish their souls across the life span (chap. 5). Like Levin and Tobin, Vogel asserts the importance of recognizing the different life circumstances of elders; she suggests that the able-old may have different approaches to securing meaning in their lives than frail elders. Vogel is also sensitive to how the social construction of gender affects people's experience of spirituality.

Harry Moody, chapter 6, both challenges and supports Vogel. He criticizes much of the work on psychological development described in her chapter by arguing that the highest level of human development may be ego-transcendence and not ego-integrity. In contrast, he portrays the soul-nourishing possible through the transcendence experienced in the practice of mysticism. Further, Moody raises a challenge for the authors of chapters 1 through 3 by suggesting that older people should not always take a Western, rationalistic approach to coping with all difficulties life presents. Perhaps another path would have them accept the mysteries of late life and all its special gifts. The older person may then discover the crazy wisdom of the mystics when the process wisdom resulting from expertise and cognitive insight fails.

Like Moody, *Fredda Blanchard-Fields* and *Lisa Norris* believe that psychological approaches to wisdom have been constrained by too much emphasis on cognition and too little recognition of emotion (chap. 7). After reviewing the recent literature on wisdom as an expert knowledge system, they discuss how thinking and feeling become reunited in late life, their interplay forming the foundation for elder wisdom. Older persons have a greater complexity of emotional understanding; they do not need to find rational answers to all life's challenges; they can journey within to a whole, integrated sense of self where spirituality can flourish. By advocating for the inclusion of emotion in views of wisdom, Blanchard-Fields and Norris turn away from rational, masculine, problem-solving models of wisdom toward a wholistic view of wisdom as an expression of human spirituality.

Finally, chapter 8 straddles both this part and the next one. *David Maldonado* reminds readers not to omit consideration of the socio-historical context in the study of religion, spirituality, and the aging person. He describes the unity between the life circumstances of Native Americans, African Americans, and Hispanic Americans and their experiences of religion and spirituality in later life. He argues that life for the current cohort of ethnic and racial minority elders was shaped in the pre-Civil Rights era when they endured social and economic oppression. In their youth, religion provided a way of coping with a racist society and it continues to offer hope in later life as they struggle with the legacies of that oppression. Maldonado takes as a case example elderly Hispanics living in San Antonio, Texas, and shows how their religious commitments and practices have become even more significant as they have aged.

Part One reveals a continuing struggle to understand the meaning of religion and spirituality. These terms are notoriously resistant to being operationally defined, thus making their study extremely challenging for those taking a strictly empirical approach. Because of the difficulty of even knowing what is being examined, social scientists have neglected the role of religion and spirituality in elders' lives. Clearly, this situation is changing, with researchers like those cited in these chapters accepting the risks of exploring an essential component in the lives of many older persons.

1 Religion and Health in Later Life

HAROLD G. KOENIG

INTRODUCTION

> Even to your old age, I shall be the same
> And even to your graying hairs I shall bear you!
> I have done it, and I shall carry you:
> And I shall bear you, and I shall deliver you. (Isa. 46:4)

What is successful aging? One definition might go as follows: Successful aging is to feel satisfied and fulfilled, to be loved and loving, to have hope and a sense of future. It is to be excited about life, to find meaning and purpose in everyday existence, freely to pursue one's goals until that last moment. An ideal, yes. Achievable, perhaps. A goal worth pursuing, absolutely. Many of the characteristics listed here for successful aging also describe psychological health. Thus, a key to the latter is most certainly related to the former. Another vital aspect of successful aging that cannot be neglected is physical health—the maintenance of physical vigor and the capacity to care fully for oneself and for one's loved ones. Health behaviors (balanced diet, moderation in alcohol intake, avoidance of smoking, prompt and timely health care) play an important role in this respect.

Circumstances in late life, however, often present numerous barriers to the achievement of successful aging. Health problems and a decline in the ability to care for self independently may lead to an ever-shrinking external world over which the elder has control. External stresses from decreased income, increased medical bills, sickness among family members, and so forth, mount up and combine with internal stresses from insults to self-esteem brought on by loss of social roles in family and community. Loss of loved ones through death or relocation in this highly mobile society can adversely affect the elderly person's social network. This can have a devastating impact on the elder's coping ability when he or she had been relying heavily upon the lost person(s) to buffer against stress from other sources.

Clearly, the achievement of successful aging and maintenance of mental and physical health in later life is not an easy task, particularly for those with limited health, financial, and social resources. There is one resource, however, that is available to all regardless of their access to other resources. Throughout recorded history, among virtually all people in every culture, the human response to the problem of helplessness and loss of control has been the same: religion. Religion can offer something that science cannot: it can help persons transcend their situations and can provide hope at a time when science has nothing to offer.

A Biopsychosocial-Spiritual Model

The biopsychosocial model, which operates on a systems approach, seeks to integrate all aspects of the human being and his or her world: the biological, psychological, and interpersonal. Because of the overriding importance of religion in the lives of so many older Americans and the needs that it fulfills, the biopsychosocial model cannot exclude the spiritual and still be called complete; thus, the need arises for a biopsychosocial-spiritual model of health and aging. Such a model simply states that there is a spiritual dimension to humans which is separate from the biological, psychological, and interpersonal dimensions, but which heavily influences each one of these and in turn may be influenced by them. Where the other dimensions of humans end, the spiritual dimension takes off. Religion provides that glimmer of light when circumstances say there is none; it provides a future when all the evidence points to no future; it provides a purpose and direction, when everything in this world appears meaningless; and it provides comfort when there is no one around to comfort.

Reason versus Revelation

The following pages will describe a number of influences that religion may have on the physical and mental health of older persons. This discussion will be based as much as possible on careful, systematic research conducted over the past several decades. A note of caution is in order, however. While research has uncovered much new information, there is much more that is unknown and perhaps unknowable by conventional means of scientific inquiry. There are clear limits on the tools of science which, when it comes to examining the exceedingly complex psychosocial aspects of human behavior, are relatively crude and identify only the most general of trends.

Furthermore, scientific knowledge is only one type of knowledge—that acquired through logic, reasoning, and rational understanding. Indeed, much about the world and about human behavior can be learned in this manner. The claim of many, however, is that *this is the only way of knowing*. Others disagree, arguing that there are other ways of coming into contact with truth. To limit one's understanding solely to the logical and deducible is unwise and perhaps a bit narcissistic.

Virtually all the great religions of the world are based on knowledge that is acquired through intuition, insight, revelation—channels quite different from Western scientific deduction. While there is much that is logical and rational about religion and these other ways of knowing, there is also much that to a purely secular society seems quite foolish. According to St. Paul, "The man without the spirit does not accept the things that come from the spirit of God, for they are foolishness to him" (1 Cor. 2:14). While it is true that religious truths cannot be proven or disproven with the tools of science, their impact on the mental and physical health of people can be studied systematically. That is the goal of much of the research to be described here.

Definition of Religion

Religion as it is used in this chapter is primarily that based in the Jewish and Christian traditions, monotheistic perspectives that see God as distinct and separate from creation, yet immensely interested in this creation and its future. This perspective is primarily based on biblical scriptures and, to some extent, on church and rabbinical tradition. Because the Jewish and Christian perspective is held by the vast majority of older persons in America, it is an appropriate and relevant view of religion to consider for its impact on health.

For the orthodox or conservative Jewish elder, this is a religion where God is a deliverer; through miraculous works God rescued the Jewish people from oppression and slavery in Egypt, guided and provided for them in the desert, and brought them into the promised land. For the traditionally Christian elder, it is a religion where God humbles Himself to become human, experiences and suffers the troubles that humans experience, and then because of love for the men and women God created, willingly takes on the punishment for their sins and dies on a cross. Note the following passage from Psalm 91, which applies to Christian and Jew alike:

> I will say of the Lord, "He is my refuge and my fortress,
> my God, in whom I trust."
> Surely he will save you from the fowler's snare
> and from the deadly pestilence.
> He will cover you with his feathers,
> and under his wings you will find refuge,
> his faithfulness will be your shield and rampart.
> You will not fear the terror of night,
> nor the arrow that flies by day,
> nor the pestilence that stalks in the darkness,
> nor the plague that destroys at midday.
> A thousand may fall at your side,
> ten thousand at your right hand,
> but it will not come near you. (Ps. 91:2-7)

What effects do such religious cognitions and visual imageries have on mental and physical health? Might they motivate and encourage elders to face and overcome the disturbing social and physical changes encountered in later life? Do they provide comfort and peace in circumstances that otherwise should evoke distress? Or, on the other hand as some have suggested, do they hinder the coping process by replacing active problem solving with repression, denial, and fantasy, and thus in the long run exacerbate rather than relieve feelings of frustration, discouragement, depression, fear, insecurity, or disease (Freud, 1927; Rokeach, 1960; Ellis, 1980)?

PREVALENCE OF RELIGIOUS ACTIVITIES

Whatever their relationship to mental health, according to Gallup Polls conducted over the past fifty years, religious cognitions and behaviors are very common in late life (Koenig et al., 1988e). Approximately three-quarters of persons over age sixty say that religion is very important to them (a figure that reaches almost 90 percent in the southeastern United States) (Princeton Religion Research Center, 1982; Koenig et al., 1991). At least half of all older Americans attend church or synagogue weekly or more often, the highest percentage for all age groups, despite having more chronic illness and greater difficulty getting to church. One-third to one-half of all older adults engage in personal prayer (apart from meal times) at least several times per week. No less than 25 percent of adults age fifty or over read the Bible every day, twice as frequently as persons under age fifty. In fact, 60 percent of persons age fifty or over in America believe that the Bible is either the literal or inspired word of God and contains no errors (Princeton Religion Research Center, 1990). Religious television is viewed several times per week by over 40 percent of older Americans, particularly those with disability that prevents church attendance (Princeton Religion Research Center, 1982). It is clear, then, in terms of prevalence of belief and activity, that religion has an enormous impact on the lives of older adults in this country.

RELIGION AND MENTAL HEALTH

> But the fruit of the Spirit is love, joy, peace, patience, kindness, goodness, faithfulness, gentleness, self control. Against such things there is no law. (Gal. 5:22)

Does religion help older persons to cope? The responses one gets depends on how the question is asked. If the question is asked in a direct and straightforward manner to elderly Americans, approximately 90 percent will agree (Americana Healthcare Corporation, 1980–81). Affirmative response rates of this magnitude, however, are probably somewhat inflated by response bias; i.e., it is the "appropriate" response to give when asked such a question. The most reliable, unbiased, but least sensitive way of finding out the extent to which religion helps to cope is simply to ask an open-ended question such as, "What enables you to cope, i.e., what keeps you going?" The respondents' spontaneous response is then recorded and later categorized as religious or not religious in nature. In studies that have used this method, the results have been interesting. In a survey of one hundred middle-class, all white, aged participants in one of the Duke Longitudinal Studies, 45 percent of participants spontaneously noted that religion had helped them to cope during one or more of three stressful life periods (Koenig et al., 1988a). If broken down by sex, about two-thirds of women gave religious responses, compared with only one-third of men. In a study of 339 men age seventy or over consecutively admitted to a VA medical center, 24 percent gave spontaneous religious responses to this open-ended coping question (Koenig et al., 1992a). Finally, in a study of low-income elders in Athens, Georgia, 51 percent of blacks and 28 percent of whites offered religious responses to an open-ended coping question (Rosen, 1982).

Religious coping responses typically involved prayer, Bible reading, trust in the Lord, faith in God, Jesus Christ, going to church, support from their pastor or other members of their congregation. Private religious (prayer, Bible reading) and religious cognitions (trust in the Lord or faith in God) were more likely to be mentioned than organizational religious activities. The reader should recognize that all three of the above-quoted studies took place in the Bible Belt South; both rates and types of religious responses may differ in the West or Northeast. Rates of spontaneous mention of religious coping in this region are probably higher by about 25 percent than those in other areas of the United States (Princeton Religion Research Center, 1987). In any event, there is little question that for a sizable proportion of older Americans, religion is the primary method by which they cope; this is probably more true for women, for blacks, and for those from conservative Christian denominations.

On a related topic, much publicity in the past few years has been given to the protective role that social support plays in buffering against stressful life events in later life (Arling, 1987; George et al., 1989; Haug, Breslau, and Folmar, 1989; Revicki and Mitchell, 1990). Few studies, however, emphasize where this social support comes from. Given that more elders are involved in church groups than all other voluntary community activities combined, it is not surprising that much social support comes from church-related activity (Cutler, 1976). In fact, one of this author's studies of older adults attending a geriatric medicine assessment clinic found that over half of patients reported that all or nearly all of their closest friends came from their church congregation (Koenig et al., 1988d).

Subjective Well-being

Although many older persons claim that religion helps them to cope, does it really? One objective way to answer this question is to evaluate the well-being of religious elders and compare it to that of older adults not involved with religion. This is not as simple as it sounds, however. Elders facing stressful life circumstances will frequently turn to religion for comfort; thus, one may find many persons with great mental distress who are quite religious because of their recently increased activity in that regard. Stress can be a strong force motivating people towards religion. Thus, if one were to find either no relationship or even an inverse relationship between well-being and religiosity in studies of older adults, this would not altogether be unexpected. In a related example, what would happen if one compared the health of older persons living at home with that of elders in the waiting rooms of doctors' offices? Probably one would find much sicker people in doctors' waiting rooms than among those surveyed in their homes; it would be silly, however, to conclude from this observation that going to see the doctor made one sick. The same situation may be occurring in the case of religion and well-being.

It is surprising, then, that so many studies of the relationship between well-being or life-satisfaction and religiosity in later life have found significant positive associations. Both cross-sectional (Beckman and Houser, 1982; Guy, 1982; Hunsberger, 1985; Koenig et al., 1988b) and longitudinal (Blazer and Palmore, 1976) investigations have reported high well-being or life-satisfaction among religiously active older adults; these associations persist even after controlling for health, social support, and financial status. Correlations with well-being are weakest for nonorganizational religious activities such as prayer or Bible reading; however, these are also the activities most likely to be turned to by persons in distress. On the other hand, intrinsic religious commitment and frequency of church attendance bear the strongest relationship with well-being measures. These relationships, in turn, appear strongest in women age seventy-five or over (Koenig et al., 1988).

While some studies have found little or no relationship between religious variables and well-being or life-satisfaction (Barron, 1961; Toseland and Rasch, 1979–80; Markides, Levin, and Ray, 1987), it is notable that no studies have found a significant inverse relationship in older adults between religious indicators and these mental-health variables.

Depression

A number of recent studies have focused on the relationship between religion and geriatric depression. Depressive syndromes may occur in over 25 percent of older adults living in the community (Blazer, Hughes, and George, 1987); among older patients hospitalized with medical illness, the figure exceeds 40 percent (Koenig et al., 1988c; Koenig et al., 1991). Several studies, both cross-sectional and longitudinal, have now reported an inverse correlation between depression and religious variables in older persons. These findings are consistent with the results of studies examining well-being and life-satisfaction reviewed above.

In a sample of thirty elderly women recovering from hip fracture in a Chicago hospital, Pressman and colleagues (1990) report that depressive symptoms (measured by the Geriatric Depression Scale) were inversely related to religiousness at the time of discharge ($r = -.61$, $p < .01$), a relationship that remained significant after severity of illness was controlled for. Among the three religious variables they measured, only "God as a source of strength and comfort" was inversely related to depressive symptoms both on admission ($r = -.39$) and at discharge ($r = -.52$). Functional recovery (measured by meters walked at discharge) was also significantly related to religiousness ($r = .45$, $p < .05$), a finding that also remained significant after controlling for severity of illness. Thus, religious older women both recovered sooner and were less depressed than their nonreligious peers.

Morse and Wisocki (1987) examined depressive symptoms using the SCL-90 and Mood Adjective Checklist in a sample of 156 senior center participants. Elders with high scores on a religion index were significantly less depressed than less religious participants; these results did not change after controlling for a number of chronic illnesses. The investigators also found an inverse relationship between religiousness and anxiety; however, after controlling for a number of chronic illness, this relationship disappeared. Nelson (1990) examined the relationship between religious orientation (intrinsic vs. extrinsic), depression (Geriatric Depression Scale), and self-esteem (Rosenberg Scale) in a sample of sixty-eight elderly participants in a day-care program in Austin, Texas. She also found a significant inverse correlation between intrinsic religiosity and both depression ($r = -.23$, $p < .05$) and poor self-esteem ($r = -.38$). There was a nonsignificant trend for church attendance to be inversely related to both depression ($r = -.08$) and poor self-esteem ($r = -.17$). However, since 88 percent of participants attended church two to three times per week, the sample may have been biased towards religious elders.

In a notable study, Idler and Kasl (1992) from Yale examined the relationship between religious involvement and several aspects of health status, including risk of disability, depression, and mortality, over a three-year period. The 2,812 noninstitutionalized elders composing their sample were enrollees in the Yale Health and Aging project (New Haven, CT); this sample was quite sick and disabled as evidenced by the fact that over one-thousand persons died between 1982 and 1989. Despite this level of disability, 41 percent attended church at least weekly and 38 percent considered themselves deeply religious. Because this sample included high numbers of Catholics (53 percent) and Jews (14 percent), it stands apart from most other studies reported here which have consisted mostly of Protestants. These investigators found a significant protective effect for public religiousness (attendance at services and number of other congregation members known) against disability, and for private religiousness (self-assessed religiosity and strength or comfort from religion) against depression (using the CES-D) among recently disabled men. In studies of hospitalized veterans, an inverse relationship has been found between religious coping and depression both cross-sectionally and longitudinally (Koenig et al., 1992a).

Although the reader should be aware that journals are much less likely to publish "negative" findings (i.e. studies that find no relationship), this review of recent work suggests that beliefs and activities based in the Judeo-Christian religious tradition may buffer against depressive illness in later life.

Suicide

The tragedy of suicide is that it often occurs in the midst of a depressive disorder that is eminently treatable. Almost a century ago (1897), Durkheim reported that suicide rates were highest among persons who were isolated from social contacts; those involved in social groups, on the other hand, had the lowest rates (Spaulding and Simpson, 1951). This was particularly true for groups that shared a common identity and tradition, such as the church. While few studies have examined the relationship between religion and suicide in older populations, some reports are noteworthy. Nelson (1977) examined indirect life-threatening behaviors among fifty-eight chronically ill hospitalized veterans; these behaviors included refusing medications, pulling out IVs, and other self-injurious acts. He found that the intensity of religious belief and commitment varied inversely with these behaviors. In our most recent study of depressed hospitalized men age seventy and over, forty-four of 331 patients were found to have major depressive disorder; of those, 46 percent experienced suicidal thoughts. It was not uncommon for these men to report spontaneously that it was primarily their belief in God that kept them from committing the act. Religion can be a strong deterrent to suicide, particularly for members of traditions whose teachings strongly forbid it (Christianity, Judaism, and Islam).

Anxiety Symptoms

> For God hath not given us the spirit of fear; but of power, and of love, and of a sound mind. (2 Tim. 1:7)

While patients with depression are feeling overwhelmed, defeated, and on the verge of giving up, those with anxiety symptoms—particularly of the more general nature—usually have sufficient energy to function and are not disabled by their illness. Certainly, patients with panic disorder or obsessive-compulsive disorder can be totally incapacitated by their illness, but those with less severe disorder generally do well. In fact, a certain amount of anxiety is necessary in life to keep people motivated and functioning at an optimal level.

What, then, is the relationship between religion and anxiety symptoms in later life? A study of 1,299 older adults surveyed in Wave II of the NIMH Epidemiologic Catchment Area study in the Piedmont area of North Carolina (Koenig et al., 1993) collected detailed information that included six-month and life-time prevalence rates of anxiety symptoms and disorders. In the survey were five questions concerning religion: church attendance, private religious activity (prayer and Bible reading), religious television viewing, importance of religion, and "born again" status. Uncontrolled analyses indicated that anxiety symptoms were more common among those watching religious television and less common among those attending church; they also tended to be more common among elders from fundamentalist or conservative religious denominations. Older adults with no religious denomination at all had surprisingly low levels of anxiety. Once sociodemographic and health factors were controlled, however, these differences all disappeared. Apparently, persons who tended to have high anxiety—women, lower socioeconomic group, less education, chronic illness—were also those more likely to engage in private religious activity (prayer, Bible reading, religious TV), as were those from fundamentalist/conservative religious denominations.

What was learned from the study? A certain level of anxiety may be necessary to motivate persons towards religion; without some anxiety, complacency sets in. It then becomes more and more difficult to put forth the effort necessary to engage in public and private religious activities. The situation is the same in psychotherapy. For constructive change to occur in psychotherapy, there needs to be a certain level of anxiety that keeps patients working on their problems; without this, they tend to drop out of therapy and slide back into old, maladaptive patterns. It appears that religion does provide comfort and relieve anxiety; however, it does not bring total relief, since some anxiety is needed to fuel a continued interest in religion.

Another possible explanation for these findings has become known as Homan's thesis. According to this theory, religion initially increases anxiety and then decreases it (thus, in a cross-sectional study, these factors would tend to balance each other out). By pointing out a person's faults, weaknesses, and the potential repercussions for such sins, religion initially increases anxiety and guilt; later, however, as the person conforms to the new prescribed lifestyle and attitude, anxiety is relieved. This idea has some empirical support (Leming, 1979–80), and is consistent with certain theological and biblical doctrines. Take, for instance, the following words from C.S. Lewis (1943):

> All I am doing is to ask people to face the facts—to understand the questions which Christianity claims to answer. And they are *very terrifying facts*. I wish it was possible

> to say something more agreeable. But I must say what I think true. Of course, I quite agree that the Christian religion is in the long run, a thing of *unspeakable comfort*. But it does not begin in comfort; it begins in the dismay I have been describing, and it is no use at all trying to go on to that comfort without first going through that dismay. (p. 39)

Death Anxiety

Some experts in the field of psychiatry believe that all anxiety derives from a single source: the fear of death. Freud himself was plagued by strong death fears which stirred up superstitious yearnings and ideas, such as attempting to predict the day of his death using a complicated system of numbers. In any case, we know that as people age they become more exposed to death through loss of friends and loved ones; consequently, thoughts of death become more frequent and can be a considerable source of stress. It is easy for young and middle-aged persons to deny their own mortality and repress thoughts of death; however, as the years pass and time grows shorter, as sickness intervenes, as brushes with death occur, the capacity to maintain this denial often weakens. For the elder confronted with the end of life, religion can be an enormous consolation. And why not? There is no scientific proof (nor can there be) that all life and experience cease at death. Belief in an afterlife provides hope for eternal peace and relief from suffering that could not be had on this earth; the medical or psychiatric professional has little to offer as an alternative to simple religious faith. For instance, consider the assurances provided by St. Paul:

> In the same way, our earthly bodies which die and decay are different from the bodies we shall have when we come back to life again, for they will never die. The bodies we have now embarrass us for they become sick and die; but they will be full of glory when we come back to life again. Yes, they are weak, dying bodies now, but when we live again they will be full of strength. They are just human bodies at death, but when they come back to life they will be superhuman bodies. For just as there are natural human bodies, there are also supernatural spiritual bodies. (1 Cor. 15:42-44)

Hence, the religious elder may approach death with equanimity and perhaps even with an excited anticipation. They may long to be rejoined with a loved one (perhaps a spouse or a parent), and the religious view permits this. Some may desire to see and experience directly the God whom they have served throughout their lives, and finally to receive the reward promised for the sufferings they endured while here on earth. On the other hand, this may be a frightening time even for the religious elder. Some religious persons will still fear crossing over that barrier into the unknown, fear leaving their loved ones behind, fear not having accomplished everything they had planned to do during their life, and perhaps even fear that because of real or imagined sins, retribution waits on the other side. Thus, a mix of feelings may be experienced by even the most devoutly religious.

A number of studies report that religious beliefs and attitudes impact positively on feelings about death (Wolff, 1959; Feifel and Nagy, 1981; Koenig, 1988). Nevertheless, a wide spectrum of findings has been reported, from no relationship to a positive relationship between death anxiety and religiosity. Some investigators argue that it is the *certainty* of belief not the content (whether religious or irreligious) that counts (Hinton, 1967; Smith et al., 1983–84). According to this notion, a devout atheist would fare as well as a devout believer. This hypothesis suggests that death anxiety is highest among those who are ambivalent about their beliefs.

Alcohol Abuse

Approximately one in ten older persons abuses alcohol. Two types of alcoholics have been described in the elderly (Gaitz and Baer, 1971). One type has a long history of excessive drinking beginning in early adulthood; this person is usually well-known to social service agencies as a public drunk and has personality characteristics similar to those of younger drinkers. The other type of alcoholic begins drinking heavily late in life, usually after age fifty. Often, this occurs in response to negative life events related to aging (loss of loved ones, poor health, financial insecurity). Late-onset alcoholics rarely drink in public; more often they do so alone in the privacy of their homes. Frequently there is coexistent psychiatric illness, such as depression (Schonfled and Dupree, 1990).

Prior to Alcoholics Anonymous (AA), only 10 percent of alcoholics quit drinking on their own; nearly 30 percent of these cases were a direct consequence of religious experience (Lamere, 1953). According to some, AA's success has been primarily a result of its spiritual aspects (Wilson, 1968). In a study of religious experiences of hospitalized men, about one-third reported a positive change in their feelings about religion at some time in their lives; of that group, over 10 percent related this change to a cessation of addictive smoking or heavy drinking (Koenig, 1994). In an earlier study of elderly outpatients attending a geriatric medicine clinic, intrinsic religiosity was significantly lower among men who used alcohol (Koenig et al., 1988d). Likewise, studies among adults of all ages indicate a moderate to strong negative relationship between religiousness and alcohol abuse (Cahalan, Cisin, and Crossley, 1969; Parfrey, 1976). Religion may offer an alternative to alcohol as a means of coping with life's problems.

Harvard psychiatrist George Vaillant (1982) followed 110 inner-city men with alcohol problems for thirty-three years. He reported that 20 percent achieved three years or more of abstinence, 47 percent achieved abstinence for at least one year, and 33 percent continued to abuse alcohol on a progressive downhill course. Among those achieving abstinence for three years or more, 19 percent of men reported increased religious involvement as a primary factor contributing to abstinence; an additional 38 percent found AA to be a primary factor. Commenting on this finding, Vaillant noted the following:

> . . . it is important to appreciate that a major source of help in changing involuntary habits may come from increased religious involvement. Only recently have investigators like Frank, Bean, and Mack begun to elucidate the nature of this process. Alcoholics and victims of other incurable habits feel defeated, bad, and helpless; invariably they suffer from impaired morale. For recovery, powerful new sources of self-esteem and hope must be discovered. Equally important is the fact that religious involvement facilitates deployment of the defense of reaction formation, wherein an individual abruptly rejects and hates what he once cherished and loved, or vice versa. Reaction formations are essential to abstinence, and they are often stabilized by surrendering commitments to one set of desires up to a 'higher power' that dictates the exact opposite. (p. 132)

RELIGION AND PHYSICAL HEALTH

The evidence linking religious attitudes or behaviors with better physical health in later life is less plentiful than that for psychological health. Nevertheless, a number of studies have suggested such an association. When examining this relationship, however, a number of factors must be considered.

First, as with mental health, religious factors interact with physical health in a dynamic, not static fashion. Both physical health and religiousness may fluctuate over time. According to the "suppressor" hypothesis (Wheaton, 1985), stress from a negative life event such as poor health stimulates an increase in religious activities such as prayer or Bible reading (Krause and Van Tran, 1989). Religious activities then eventually diminish the stress of the negative event and may perhaps even reverse physical disease through neuroendocrine or immunologic mechanisms; this process is not instantaneous, but takes time. Thus, even if religious behaviors did somehow improve physical health, this effect would be difficult to detect since any long-term benefits would be disguised by the short-term association between the acute illness and religious activity. In the absence of longitudinal data, then, either no correlation or a positive correlation with sickness might result. It would be incorrect, based on this data, to conclude that religion was unrelated to health or led to its decline.

On the other hand, a factor that might cause a false positive association between physical health and religion is the interaction between church attendance and functional status (Levin and Markides, 1986). Many earlier studies, among which Comstock and Partridge (1972) is the most renowned, found a strong inverse correlation between mortality and church attendance; this seemed to confirm the long-held notion that going to church led to greater longevity. What they did not consider, however, was that people who were sick, disabled, and at the highest risk for dying were simply *physically unable* to get to church. Without controlling for disability status, this created a false association between church attendance and survival. The confounding effects of physical disability on the relationship between church attendance and health has been thoroughly discussed elsewhere (Levin and Vanderpool, 1987). What must be remembered is that in studying the relationship between religion and health in later life, it is important to include indicators of religiosity other than church attendance (such as intrinsic religiosity, Allport and Ross, 1967), or if church attendance is included, that investigators control for level of physical disability.

Hypertension and Heart Disease

A number of studies have found an inverse association between blood pressure and religious variables. Most commonly, the association has been with church attendance (Scotch, 1963; Walsh, 1980; Graham et al., 1978; Nuckolls et al., 1972; Berkman and Syme, 1979). Scotch (1963) found that women members of the Zulu tribe in South Africa who moved into an urban environment experienced dramatic increases in blood pressure; those involved in church activities, however, experienced no such rise. Walsh (1980) found that among immigrants from nineteen countries, those with higher levels of church attendance had lower levels of blood pressure in the land they moved to. In these studies, church attendance was seen as a stabilizing social factor that buffered against the high levels of stress involved in relocation.

Two studies have now reported lower blood pressures among the religious where an attitudinal variable other than church attendance was measured (Koenig et al., 1988d; Larson et al., 1989); both of these findings, interestingly, were in older men. A study of geriatric clinic patients found a lower level of intrinsic religiosity among men with hypertension than in those with normal blood pressures. In a study that included community-dwelling elderly men without diagnosable cardiovascular disease, Larson and colleagues report lower blood pressure levels among older men who noted religion to be very important compared with those who found it to be only somewhat or not at all important; this difference persisted after controlling for socioeconomic status, smoking, and body size. In contrast, Levin and Markides (1985) found a higher prevalence of hypertension (43 percent) in 203 older Mexican Americans who rated themselves highly religious compared with those considering themselves less religious (30 percent); they hypothesized that increased conflict arising from guilt over pressure to conform to higher behavioral standards was the cause for elevated blood pressures in the religious group.

Benson and colleagues (1977) at Harvard have reported that meditative prayer reduces blood pressure, speculating that a decrease in sympathetic nervous system activity was the mechanism. Likewise, an interesting study by Timio (1985) found virtually no change in blood pressure among a group of cloistered nuns over a twenty-year followup; community-dwelling women, on the other hand, demonstrated a progressive rise in blood pressure during that period. These blood pressure differences were attributed to a number of factors, including an effect of the extended time spent in solitude and meditative prayer by the nuns. Studies have now shown in both men and women that anger and anxiety lead to long-term elevations in blood pressure (Markovitz, 1991). Those who suppress feelings when faced with interpersonal conflict and those who experience higher levels of stress from changes in their environment have a greater likelihood of having hypertension on long-term follow-up.

Because many religious communities have well-established rules for relating to one another and place a heavy emphasis on positive relationships, members may suffer less stress, anxiety, and conflict in this area, and consequently experience lower blood pressure levels. Along a similar vein, after a review of the literature examining religion's effects on the cardiovascular system, Kaplan (1976) concluded that protective effects were mediated through psychological mechanisms that maintain hope and regulate levels of depression, fear, and anxiety.

Recent work by Redford Williams (1989) at Duke University (author of *The Trusting Heart*) has identified the component of Type A personality that is primarily responsible for the increased risk of heart attack in individuals with this personality. Persons with Type A (hard-driving, time conscious, impatient) who have *high levels of anger* are especially likely to suffer heart disease, compared with Type As who are aggressive, competitive, and productive, but have low levels of anger. He has suggested that those who attend church may have lower levels of anger and better interpersonal relations, which thus provides them with some protection from cardiovascular disease. In some way that is not yet known, religious attitudes and behaviors may help to prevent, channel, or sublimate angry feelings in such a way that they do not have physiological consequences. There does not appear to be any data that has been gathered to support this hypothesis.

Cancer

Two studies have examined the relationship between intrinsic religiosity and cancer; neither have found a significant relationship (Acklin et al., 1983; Koenig et al., 1988d). While a lower rate of cancer has been found among various religious groups, this has been largely attributed to dietary and hygienic practices (Mayberry, 1982; Gardner and Lyon, 1982). Dwyer and colleagues (1990) recently reported that religious concentration and denominational affiliation had a significant impact on mortality rates for all malignancies combined, for digestive cancer, and for respiratory cancer after controlling for demographic, environmental, and regional factors known to affect cancer mortality. As noted earlier, an inverse relationship between religiousness and cancer may be disguised in some studies where patients turned to religion for comfort shortly after the diagnosis was made. In a study of over 1,000 hospitalized veterans, however, religious coping was no more common among patients diagnosed with cancer than in those diagnosed with other illnesses (Koenig, 1994).

Cognitively Impaired Elders

Two studies have examined the relationship between cognitive impairment and religiousness. In one study, intrinsic religiosity was found to be higher among patients with dementia than in those without the disorder; the sample size, however, was quite small ($n = 7$) (Koenig et al., 1988d). In another study, an inverse relationship was found between cognitive impairment and religious coping; in other words, patients with early stages of dementia or with delirium were less likely to employ religious coping strategies (Koenig, 1994). One of two possible explanations could account for this. First, religious coping, because of its heavy reliance on religious cognitions such as trust and faith, may require a certain degree of mental alertness to be fully effective. The cognitively impaired, then, may have greater difficulty using religious coping strategies, particularly those that are cognitively based.

A second explanation for this finding attributes it to confounding. Because there is both a negative association between depression and cognitive functioning and a negative association between depression and religious coping, a positive association between religious coping and cognitive functioning would be expected. Religious copers are less depressed; therefore, they also have less cognitive impairment. Both of these explanations, however, are highly speculative, and at this time the relationship between religion and cognitive impairment is poorly understood. Much further work is needed to understand in what way and to what extent patients with Alzheimer's disease and stroke can utilize religious beliefs or behaviors to help them cope with their devastating illnesses.

Emotional memories—often connected with religious experiences among religious elders—are among the last memories to be lost in dementing illnesses. For example, an elderly demented man in his nineties in the author's clinical practice could recall almost nothing about himself or his family, except for his salvation experience; this, with only minimal prompting, he would describe in amazing detail. Marty Richards (1990) has written a beautiful piece on the "spiritual needs of the cognitively impaired." She underscores the fact that many elders with dementia can respond to faith rituals and symbols, noting that communication not requiring the intellect can be used to meet spiritual needs. Often, sharing religious articles, poetry, clothing, relics, or pictures can convey meaning and acceptance to the demented elder. Familiar Bible passages, prayers, and hymns learned in childhood can often be recognized.

From a coping perspective, those with advanced dementia are often more fortunate than those in the beginning stages of impairment, since as the disease worsens patients often experience a lifting of depression as the awareness of their condition diminishes. Nevertheless, in the beginning, patients must be given the opportunity to express their sense of loss and then be given a chance to grieve and work through their feelings (Ellor et al., 1987; Richards, 1990). Because family members may themselves be going through the grieving process, they, too, need comfort and support.

Longevity

As noted earlier, most studies showing a relationship between longevity and church attendance have been confounded by the fact that persons in poor physical health, at high risk of dying, are physically unable to attend to church. Not all studies, however, have used church attendance as their religious variable. In a unique study of 302 adults age eighty-five and over living in the southwestern United States, Hogstel and Kashka (1989) asked in an open-ended question what factors these elders felt were responsible for their long lives. In order of most common response, the following were given: (1) activity ("hard work, exercise, keeping active physically and mentally"), (2) a strong belief in God and "Christian living," and (3) a positive attitude toward self and others.

Likewise, Zuckerman and colleagues (1984) studying four-hundred elderly residents in New Haven, Connecticut, found an inverse correlation between mortality and religiosity. Religiousness was measured by church attendance, self-rated religiosity, and strength received from religion. Interestingly, the strongest predictor of survival was "strength from religion," a variable unlikely to be influenced by functional status. Attempting to replicate these results, 97 religious copers and 165 nonreligious copers were followed over fourteen months; no difference in mortality rate, however, was found between the two groups (Koenig, 1995).

CONCLUSION

Successful aging is a challenge that faces all persons. While there are some very real psychological and physical health barriers that must be overcome for its achievement, it is a goal worth pursuing. Religion may be a key to its realization. In the past five years, evidence among older adults has been accumulating to support a link between mental health and religious attitudes or behaviors based in the Jewish and Christian traditions. Both cross-sectional and longitudinal studies now show that religious elders are less likely to become depressed when confronted with negative life events such as physical illness. Similarly, life-satisfaction and well-being appear to be maintained in many religious older adults despite declines in health, social, and financial resources. The association between physical health and religiousness is weaker than with psychological health. Nevertheless, some studies indicate that religious behaviors and attitudes may at least indirectly (through diet, hygienic practices, enhanced social support, decreased psychological stress) protect against high blood pressure, cardiovascular disease, and perhaps certain types of cancers. Whether the religious perspective adds years to life has not been established; however, it is becoming more and more clear that it may add life to the years that remain.

BIBLIOGRAPHY

Acklin, M. W., E. C. Brown, and P. A. Mauger (1983) "The Role of Religious Values in Coping with Cancer." *Journal of Religion and Health* 22:322–33.

Allport, G. W., and J. M. Ross (1967) "Personal Religious Orientation and Prejudice." *Journal of Personality and Social Psychology* 5:432–43.

Americana Healthcare Corporation (1980–81) *Aging in America: Trials and Triumphs.* Westport, Conn.: U.S. Research and Forecasts Survey Sampling Corp.

Arling, G. (1987) "Strain, Social Support, and Distress in Old Age." *Journal of Gerontology* 42:107–13.

Barron, M. L. (1961) *The Aging American.* New York: Thomas Crowell Co.

Beckman, L. J., and B. B. Houser (1982) "The Consequences of Childlessness on the Social-Psychological Well-Being of Older Women." *Journal of Gerontology* 37:243–50.

Benson, H., J. B. Kotch, K. D. Crassweller, and M. M. Greenwood (1977) "Historical and Clinical Considerations of the Relaxation Response." *American Scientist* 65:441–45.

Berkman, L., and S. L. Syme (1979) "Social Networks, Host Resistance and Mortality." *American Journal of Epidemiology* 109:186–204.

Blazer, D. G., and E. Palmore (1976) "Religion and Aging in a Longitudinal Panel." *The Gerontologist* 16(1):82–85.

Blazer, D. G., D. C. Hughes, and L. K. George (1987) "The Epidemiology of Depression in an Elderly Community Population." *The Gerontologist* 27:281–87.

Cahalan, D., I. H. Cisin, and H. M. Crossley (1969) *American Drinking Practices, A National Study of Drinking Behaviors and Attitudes.* New Brunswick, N.J.: Rutgers Center of Alcohol Studies.

Catanzaro, R.F., ed. (1968) *Alcoholism: The Total Treatment Approach* Springfield, Ill.: C. Thomas.

Comstock, G. W., and K. B. Partridge (1972) "Church Attendance and Health." *Journal of Chronic Disease* 25:665–72.

Cutler, S. J. (1976) "Membership in Different Types of Voluntary Associations and Psychological Well-being." *The Gerontologist* 16:335–39.

Dwyer, J. W., L. L. Clarke, and M. K. Miller (1990) "The Effect of Religious Concentration and Affiliation on County Cancer Mortality Rates." *Journal of Health and Social Behavior* 31:185–202.

Ellis, A. (1980) "Psychotherapy and Atheistic Values: A Response to A. E. Bergin's 'Psychotherapy and Religious Values.'" *Journal of Consulting and Clinical Psychology* 48:642–45.

Ellor, J. W., J. Stettner, and H. Spath (1987) "Ministry with the Confused Elderly." *Journal of Religion and Aging* 4 (2):21–33.

Feifel, H., and V. T. Nagy (1981) "Another Look at Fear of Death." *Journal of Consulting and Clinical Psychology* 49:278–86.

Freud, S. (1953–74) *The Standard Edition of the Complete Psychological Works of Sigmund Freud.* 24 vols. Translated and edited by J. Strachey. London: Hogarth Press.

Freud, S. (1962) "The Future of an Illusion." In Freud 1953–74, 21:3–56.

Gaitz, C. M., and P. E. Baer (1971) "Characteristics of Elderly Patients with Alcoholism." *Archives of General Psychiatry* 24:372–78.

Gardner, J. W., and J. L. Lyon (1982) "Cancer in Utah Mormon Men by Lay Priesthood Level." *American Journal of Epidemiology* 116:243–57.

George, L. K., D. G. Blazer, D. C. Hughes, and N. Fowler (1989) "Social Support and the Outcome of Major Depression." *British Journal of Psychiatry* 154:478–85.

Graham, T. W. et al. (1978) "Frequency of Church Attendance and Blood Pressure Elevation." *Journal of Behavioral Medicine* 1 (1):37–43.

Guy, R. F. (1982) "Religion, Physical Disabilities and Life Satisfaction in Older Age Cohorts." *International Journal of Aging and Human Development* 15:225–32.

Haug, M. R., N. Breslau, and S. J. Folmar (1989) "Coping Resources and Selective Survival in Mental Health of the Elderly." *Research on Aging* 11:468–91.

Hinton, J. (1967) *Dying.* Baltimore: Penguin.

Hogstel, M. O., and M. Kashka (1989) "Staying Healthy after 85." *Geriatric Nursing* January/February: 16–18.

Hunsberger, B. (1985) "Religion, Age, Life Satisfaction, and Perceived Sources of Religiousness: A Study of Older Persons." *Journal of Gerontology* 40:615–20.

Idler, E. L. (1987) "Religious Involvement and the Health of the Elderly: Some Hypotheses and an Initial Test." *Social Forces* 66:226–38.

Idler, E. L., and S. V. Kasl (1992) "Religion, Disability, Depression, and the Timing of Death." *American Journal of Sociology* 97 (4):1052–79.

Kaplan, B. H. (1976) "A Note on Religious Belief and Coronary Heart Disease." *Journal of South Carolina Medical Association* 72 (suppl): 60–64.

Koenig, H. G. (1986) "Shepherds' Centers: Elderly People Helping Themselves." *Journal of the American Geriatrics Society* 34:73.

——— (1988) "Religion and Death Anxiety in Later Life." *Hospice Journal* 4 (1):3–24.

——— (1994) *Aging and God: Spiritual Pathways to Mental Health in Mid-Life and the Later Years.* New York: Haworth Press.

Koenig, H.G. (1995) "Health Care Utilization and Survival of Religious and Nonreligious Copers Hospitalized with Medical Illness." *Journal of Religious Gerontology.* In press.

Koenig, H. G., L. K. George, D. G. Blazer, and J. Pritchett (1993) "The Relationship Between Religion and Anxiety in a Sample of Community-dwelling Older Adults." *Journal of Geriatric Psychiatry* 26:65–93.

Koenig, H. G., L. K. George, and I. Siegler (1988a) "The Use of Religion and Other Emotion-Regulating Coping Strategies Among Older Adults." *The Gerontologist* 28:303–10.

Koenig, H. G., J. N. Kvale, and C. Ferrel (1988b) "Religion and Well-Being in Later Life." *The Gerontologist* 28:18–28.

Koenig, H. G., K. G. Meador, H. J. Cohen, and D. G. Blazer (1988c) "Depression in Elderly Hospitlized Patients with Medical Illness." *Archives of Internal Medicine* 148:1929–36.

Koenig, H. G., and K. G. Meador et al. (1991) "Major Depressive Disorder in Hospitalized Medically Ill Patients: An Examination of Young and Elderly Patients." *Journal of the American Geriatrics Society* 39:881–90.

Koenig, H. G., K. G. Meador, and F. Shelp et al. (1992b) "Religious Coping and Depression in Hospitalized Elderly Medically Ill Men." *American Journal of Psychiatry* 149:1693–1700.

Koenig, H. G., D. O. Moberg, and J. N. Kvale (1988d) "Religious Activities and Attitudes of Older Adults in a Geriatric Assessment Clinic." *Journal of the American Geriatrics Society* 36:362–74.

Koenig, H. G., M. Smiley, and J. P. Gonzales (1988e) *Religion, Health, and Aging: A Review and Theoretical Integration.* Westport, Conn.: Greenwood Press.

Krause, N., and T. Van Tran (1989) "Stress and Religious Involvement Among Older Blacks." *Journal of Gerontology* 44:S4–13.

Lamere, F. (1953) "What Happens to Alcoholics?" *American Journal of Psychiatry* 109:673.

Larson, D. B. et al. (1989) "The Impact of Religion on Blood Pressure Status in Men." *Journal of Religion and Health* 28 (4):265–78.

Leming, M. R. (1979–80) "Religion and Death: A Test of Homans' Thesis." *Omega Journal of Death and Dying* 10:347–64.

Levin, J. S., and K. S. Markides (1985) "Religion and Health in Mexican Americans." *Journal of Religion and Health* 24 (1):60–69.

______ (1986) "Religious Attendance and Subjective Health." *Journal for the Scientific Study of Religion* 25:31–40.

Levin, J. S., and H. Y. Vanderpool (1987) "Is Frequent Religious Attendance Really Conducive to Better Health?: Towards an Epidemiology of Religion and Health." *Social Sciences in Medicine* 24:589–600.

Lewis, C. S. (1943) *Mere Christianity.* New York: Macmillan.

Markides, K. S., J. S. Levin, and L. A. Ray (1987) "Religion, Aging, and Life Satisfaction: An Eight-year, Three-wave Longitudinal Study." *The Gerontologist* 27:660–65.

Markovitz, J. H. (1991) "Anger, Anxiety Found to Raise BP in Women over 40." *Clinical Psychiatry News* 19(6):27.

Mayberry, J. F. (1982) "Epidemiological Studies of Gastrointestinal Cancer in Christian Sects." *Journal of Clinical Gastroenterology* 4:115–121.

Morse, C. K., and P. A. Wisocki (1987) "Importance of Religiosity to Elderly Adjustment." *Journal of Religion and Aging* 4 (1):15–28.

Nelson, F. L. (1977) "Religiosity and Self-destructive Crises in the Institutionalized Elderly." *Suicide and Life Threatening Behavior* 7:67–73.

Nelson, P. B. (1990) "Religious Orientation of the Elderly." *Journal of Gerontological Nursing* 16 (2):29–35.

Nuckolls, K., J. C. Cassel, and B. H. Kaplan (1972) "Psychosocial Assets, Life Crises and the Prognosis of Pregnancy." *American Journal of Epidemiology* 95:431–41.

Parfrey, P. S. (1976) "The Effect of Religious Factors on Intoxicant Use." *Scandinavian Journal of Sociological Medicine* 3:135–40.

Pressman, P., J. S. Lyons, D. B. Larson, and J. J. Strain (1990) "Religious Belief, Depression, and Ambulation Status in Elderly Women with Broken Hips." *American Journal of Psychiatry* 147:758–60.

Princeton Religion Research Center (1982) *Religion in America 1982.* Princeton, N.J.: Gallup Organization and Princeton Research Center.

——— (1987) *Religion in America.* Gallup Report, no. 259. Princeton, N.J.: Gallup Organization.

——— (1990) *The Role of the Bible in American Society.* Princeton, N.J.: Princeton Religion Research Center.

Revicki, D. A., and J. P. Mitchell (1990) "Strain, Social Support, and Mental Health in Rural Elderly Individuals." *Journal of Gerontology* 45:S267–74.

Richards, M. (1990) "Meeting the Spiritual Needs of the Cognitively Impaired." *Generations* 14 (4):63–64.

Rokeach, M. (1960) *The Open and Closed Mind.* New York: Basic Books.

Rosen, C. (1982) "Ethnic Differences Among Impoverished Rural Elderly in the Use of Religion as a Coping Mechanism." *Journal of Rural Community Psychology* 3:27–34.

Schonfled, L., and L. W. Dupree (1990) "Older Problem Drinkers—Long-term and Late-life Onset Abusers: What Triggers Their Drinking?" *Aging* 361:5–11.

Scotch, N. A. (1963) "Sociocultural Factors in the Epidemiology of Zulu Hypertension." *American Journal of Public Health* 53:1205–13.

Smith, D. K., A. M. Nehemkis, and R. A. Charter (1983–84) "Fear of Death, Death Attitudes and Religious Conviction in the Terminally Ill." *International Journal of Psychiatry in Medicine* 13:221–32.

Spaulding, J. A., and G. Simpson (1951) *Suicide* (authors' translation of Emile Durkheim, 1897.) New York: Free Press.

Timio, M. (1985) "Study of Nun Supports Stress Factor in Blood Pressure Increase with Age." *Family Practice News* 15 (9):87.

Toseland, R., and J. Rasch (1979–80) "Correlates of Life Satisfaction: An AID Analysis." *International Journal of Aging and Human Development* 10:203–11.

Vaillant, G. E., and E. S. Milofsky (1982) "Natural History of Male Alcoholism." *Archives of General Psychiatry* 39:127–33.

Walsh, A. (1980) "The Prophylactic Effect of Religion on Blood Pressure Levels Among a Sample of Immigrants." *Social Science in Medicine* 148 59–63.

Wheaton, B. (1985) "Models of the Stress-buffering Functions of Coping Resources." *Journal of Health and Social Behavior* 26:352–64.

Williams, R. (1989) *The Trusting Heart: Great News About Type A Behavior.* New York: Times Books.

Wilson, B. (1968) "The Fellowship of Alcoholics Anonymous." In Catanzaro, 116–24.

Wolff, K. (1959) "Group Psychotherapy with Geriatric Patients in a State Hospital Setting: Results of a Three Year Study." *Group Psychotherapy* 12:218–22.

Zuckerman, D. M. et al. (1984) "Psychosocial Predictors of Mortality Among the Elderly Poor." *American Journal of Epidemiology* 119:410–23.

2 Religion and Psychological Well-Being

JEFFREY S. LEVIN
SHELDON S. TOBIN

Does religion enhance well-being for the aged? While most studies have revealed a positive relationship, associations between religiosity and psychological well-being in samples of older adults have most often been based on simple measures such as frequency of religious attendance. Yet if declining health limits one's attendance at church or synagogue, while also reducing feelings of well-being, then it is not clear that such associations point to a salutary effect of religion on well-being. Rather, it may be that poor health leads to lowered feelings of well-being and also restricts public activities, such as religious attendance. In turn, if ill elderly persons with lowered feelings of well-being due to poor health substitute private religious practices for public attendance, then a paradoxical situation seems to emerge: greater expressions of private religiosity are associated with lower levels of well-being.

Clarification of this paradox and research on the larger scenario described above represent the foci of much recent work in this area and will inform most of the discussion which follows. In this chapter, conceptual, methodological, and theoretical issues related to psychological well-being in older adults will be discussed in detail. The first section will define psychological well-being, comparing it to similar constructs and describing its dimensions, and then review findings on its major determinants, namely, health, socioeconomic status, age, and ethnicity. The second section will describe the state of religious research in gerontology, with an emphasis on recent findings and the limitations of prior studies, and will propose an agenda for future investigations. The third section will offer psychological and philosophical perspectives on the meaning of religion for the well-being of older adults.

PSYCHOLOGICAL WELL-BEING IN OLDER ADULTS

Definitions of Psychological Well-Being

This chapter focuses on the influence of religion on psychological well-being, a component of a broader construct known as subjective well-being. Subjective well-being refers to personal evaluations of self-esteem, morale, psychological well-being, and other related constructs. Psychological well-being, which is believed to comprise several measurable dimensions, has become the construct of choice for assessing subjective well-being in older adults. Objective well-being, on the other hand, refers to observable conditions such as socioeconomic status, functional capacity, and health status, often differentiated into clinical, functional, and subjective dimensions (Whitelaw and Liang, 1991). In turn, both objective and subjective well-being are part of a more encompassing construct known as quality of life, a term more commonly used in clinical medicine and social-indicators research.

Regarding the psychological well-being of older adults, there have been numerous surveys, a proliferation of measurement instruments, and considerable research and theoretical writing on similarities among scales and the dimensions they are believed to measure. Still, disagreement exists on terminology and on dimensions of this construct; moreover, consistent factor structures have not been found for many popular instruments (see George, 1981). Indeed, one authority has observed "a prevailing chaos of conceptualization" characterized by "a variety of ambiguous and poorly differentiated concepts" (Alwin, 1988, 120). It has also been noted that "there is a tendency to regard any psychosocial measurement as an expression of quality of life" (Fava, 1990, 74). Further, the most commonly identified dimensions of psychological well-being (i.e., positive affect, negative affect, happiness, congruence between expected and achieved life goals, life satisfaction, and psychosomatic symptoms) are not necessarily discrete, and, as usually defined, suggest considerable conceptual overlap.

Still, in surveys of older adults, subjective well-being is often assessed, typically by a multidimensional scale of psychological well-being or one of its component constructs, usually life satisfaction (see Kane and Kane, 1981). Among the most commonly used measurement instruments is the Affect Balance Scale or ABS (Bradburn, 1969), which is composed of two self-evaluated dimensions referred to as positive and negative affect. The presence of greater life satisfaction, and thus a higher level of psychological well-being, is inferred from self-assessments of high positive affects coupled with low negative affects.

A concern that simple unidimensional or bidimensional measures such as the ABS leave important factors unaccounted for has led to the development of many additional multidimensional scales, several of which have become extremely popular among researchers. The Life Satisfaction Index or LSI (Neugarten, Havighurst, and Tobin, 1961) in its variant forms (LSIA, LSIB, LSIZ) added the dimension of congruence between expected and achieved life goals, and the Philadelphia Geriatric Center (PGC) Morale Scale (Lawton, 1972, 1975) was created to address adjustment among residential populations in nursing homes. Although developed from different perspectives, these scales share similar foci with each other and with the ABS. In the LSI, for example, the dimensions of zest and mood tone, respectively, are roughly analogous to the dimensions of positive and negative affect. It is not surprising, therefore, that these scales are often highly intercorrelated and that they show similar associations with other variables (Stock et al., 1986). Indeed, efforts have been made to "structurally integrate" or combine these scales into a single multidimensional model, such as an integration of the ABS and the LSI which produced a four-dimensional scale consisting of congruence, happiness, and positive and negative affect (Liang, 1985).

In recent years, a variety of additional scales of psychological well-being have been developed or have had their factor structures confirmed. These include the Older Americans Resources and Services (OARS) mental health instrument (Liang et al., 1989a), the Center for Epidemiologic Studies Depression (CES-D) Scale (Liang et al., 1989b), the General Well-Being (GWB) Scale (Levin, 1994), and the Langner 22-Item Index of Mental Illness (Johnson and Meile, 1981). Typically, these instruments include affective components, positive and negative, as well as some assessment of physical or psychosomatic symptomatology. Nevertheless, an "ultimate" scale of psychological well-being, even if such an instrument could be developed—and this does not appear imminent—might not be desirable. For one, these indices are often developed for different purposes (diagnosis, needs assessment, community survey), have different time referents (currently, in the past week, in the past month, in the past year, ever), and target different populations (all adults, middle-aged and older adults, the old-old).

Determinants of Psychological Well-Being

In light of the structural convergence or overlap of many existing scales of psychological well-being, it is not surprising that some consistency has emerged in published accounts of their significant determinants or correlates among older adults. Although it is premature to state that any definitive consensus exists as to the relative salience of predictors, a few key variables have been found to be strongly and significantly related to indicators of psychological well-being in numerous studies conducted in a variety of settings and with different populations. These predictors include health, socioeconomic status, age, and ethnicity.

The strongest predictor of psychological well-being is typically some measure of *health status* (Okun et al., 1984). Path analyses have identified strong, significant, direct effects on well-being of measures of health, whether indicators of activity or physical functioning or more subjective self-ratings of global health (Markides and Martin, 1979; Chatters, 1988b). Interestingly, a replicated secondary data analysis of findings from thirty-seven studies revealed that self-ratings of health exert more consistent effects on well-being than more "objective," physician-assessed measures of health (George and Landerman, 1984). This strong, predictive effect of health is fairly well accepted and has been highlighted in numerous reviews of the determinants of well-being (Larson, 1978; Diener, 1984; McNeil et al., 1986).

After health status, the most consistent predictor of psychological well-being is *socioeconomic status.* Although the evidence linking income to well-being has been characterized as "overwhelming" (Diener, 1984, 553), the effect of income on well-being is not necessarily great, in that socioeconomic indicators rarely explain more than a negligible amount of its variance (Larson, 1978). It also appears that much of the impact of income on well-being operates indirectly through measures of health (Markides and Martin, 1979), and that the effect of income on well-being is most salient among poorer individuals who are likely to have poorer health than other persons their age (see Larson, 1978).

Age has also been consistently linked to levels of psychological well-being, although existing findings are not entirely clear. In early studies, inverse associations between age and well-being were found (see Diener, 1984), such that younger individuals reported greater happiness than older people. In later studies, however, just the opposite was found or no association at all (see McNeil et al., 1986). More recent findings suggest that well-being does indeed appear to decline with age, probably as a function of age-associated decrements in health status, but also that this finding in cross-sectional studies may be partly spurious due to various confounding factors such as a cohort effect (see Larson, 1978).

Another possibility is that age may be associated differentially with well-being depending upon the particular measure of psychological well-being employed (McNeil et al., 1986). Despite some overlap in measures, the commonly used scales do not equally reflect what is most essential to each person's sense of well-being. For example, two individuals may have the same moderately high level of well-being when assessed by the LSIA, but for quite different reasons. One person may have low congruence but be relatively happy (as reflected, say, in high positive and low negative affect), whereas another person may have high congruence but be relatively unhappy. By similar reasoning, a particular individual may be rated as having both a high and a low level of well-being depending upon the scale or dimension used (e.g., low well-being according to the psychosomatic symptomatology dimension of the OARS, and high well-being according to the adjustment to aging dimension of the PGC). Because these and other constructs (i.e., symptoms, adjustment, morale, happiness, depressed affect) may be age-related in possibly divergent ways, the effect of age on well-being may be entirely a function of the conceptual characteristics of the well-being measure that is used.

Another consistent determinant of psychological well-being is *ethnicity.* Published findings have regularly identified lower levels of well-being for Blacks than for Whites (Larson, 1978; Diener, 1984), but health status, socioeconomic status, and age tend to exhibit the same relationships to well-being among Blacks as among Whites (Chatters and Jackson, 1989), notwithstanding some differences by subgroup membership (see Chatters, 1988a). Unfortunately, the heterogeneity of ethnic minority populations is often disregarded, and considerable diversity is often masked with classifications such as "Black," "White," or "Hispanic."

Finally, in addition to these four main determinants of psychological well-being, several other constructs have been found to predict well-being, particularly in older adults. Foremost among these are retirement, widowhood, and various indicators of social contact and interaction. Findings continue to be published suggesting the effects on well-being of such psychosocial constructs as social support, life events, bereavement, coping, and self-esteem.

RELIGIOSITY AND WELL-BEING

Despite the identification of these consistent predictors, very little of the variance in psychological well-being has ever been satisfactorily explained. Perhaps this result reflects the materialist bias of this tradition of research, whereby one's happiness or satisfaction with life is seen to derive solely from a combination of biological parameters (e.g., age), one's ability to function physically (e.g., health status), potential proxies for social discrimination (e.g., ethnicity), and one's monetary resources (e.g., socioeconomic status). Consideration of additional psychosocial factors is encouraging, but these constructs focus primarily on the interface of the individual and his or her social world; engagement of the "inner" person is largely lacking. That substantive issues related to personality, worldview, meaning, ultimate values, and even the "r" word—religion—might be meaningfully related to one's well-being does not seem to have been considered with any frequency by empirical gerontologists, or, if so, has been deemphasized perhaps due to a perception that measurement of such constructs would present too many challenges relative to measuring health, income, age, and so forth. A recently published report of ethnographic research among yogic renunciates in India concisely underscores this point:

> In talking with these men I had a clear impression of the irrelevancy of much of the research on the correlates of life satisfaction conducted in this country. By any standard, these men were socially disengaged—the number of roles they occupied had shrunk dramatically. Their economic level would place them below the poverty level. Their health ranged from fair to quite poor. They had no support from their families, and they had no personal friends. Despite these and other negative correlates of life satisfaction (at least, as derived from research with Western respondents), these men would have bumped the top of any scale of life satisfaction. (Thomas, 1991, 225)

Until recently, however, when gerontologists and other researchers interested in the construct of psychological well-being would begin exploring its determinants, they typically would not consider the domain of religion. This can be seen in review essays (e.g., Larson, 1978) and empirical studies (e.g., Markides and Martin, 1979) from the 1970s and earlier that summarize or present findings related to many of the constructs outlined earlier. This in no way represents a criticism of these particular reviews and studies; indeed, until such time that a particular set of constructs (e.g., religion) is identified as salient to a particular outcome, it is often hard to justify inclusion of such measures in a study, and thus reviews of current work will fail to conclude that a significant relationship exists. Thus, the tacit assumption that religion, for example, is not related to well-being continues to be reinforced. This seems to be especially the case in studies of health and well-being where the implicit if unspoken materialist bias of epidemiology and biomedicine expresses itself in the selection of particular independent variables believed to be relevant and the exclusion of others, such as religious measures (see Levin and Vanderpool, 1987; Levin et al., forthcoming).

In recent years, this situation has begun to change. Religious involvement, broadly defined, has become more accepted as constituting a set of determinants or correlates of the well-being of older adults due to an accumulation of positive study findings linking a variety of religious indicators to many of the existing scales of well-being. This is reflected in more recent reviews of the well-being literature, which now typically summarize religious findings as an independent domain (e.g., Diener, 1984; McNeil et al., 1986). With the growing interest in religious factors in aging, generally, especially in ethnic-minority populations such as Black Americans (e.g., the work of Taylor) and Mexican Americans (e.g., the work of Markides), coupled with a rediscovery and appreciation of the seminal empirical work of Moberg in religious gerontology in the 1950s and 1960s (see Levin and Vanderpool, 1991), religion is now coming to be accepted more and more as a key component of predictive models of health, well-being, and overall adjustment in older adults.

This growing acceptance of a role for religion in aging and well-being is reflected in the presence of entries on religion (Markides, 1987; Palmore, 1987) in *The Encyclopedia of Aging* (Maddox, 1987), the recent establishment of the *Journal of Religious Gerontology,* and chapters on religion in key gerontological books (e.g., Moberg, 1990; Kart, 1987). This is also reflected in the presence of a Forum on Religion and Aging within the American Society on Aging, and in the publication of the books *Religion, Health, and Aging: A Review and Theoretical Integration* (Koenig et al., 1988b), *Religion and Aging: An Annotated Bibliography* (Fecher. 1982), and *Religion in Aging and Health: Theoretical Foundations and Methodological Frontiers* (Levin, 1994). While chapters on religion have not yet appeared in the *Annual Review of Gerontology and Geriatrics,* the *Handbook of Aging and the Social Sciences,* or the *Handbook of Psychology and Aging,* the increasing number of empirical studies of religion and well-being published in the official journals of the Gerontological Society of America (*The Gerontologist* and *The Journals of Gerontology*) signal a maturation of research in this area and a continued acceptance of religion as a significant factor in the well-being of older adults.

An especially important and encouraging development has been the flowering of several new ongoing programs of research in the area of religion, aging, and well-being, such as the research of Koenig and associates at Duke University (see Koenig et al., 1988b) and of Ellison (e.g., Ellison, 1991; Ellison and Gay, 1990; Ellison et al., 1989), currently at the University of Texas, and the NIA-funded research of Levin, Ainlay, and Idler. These and several other programmatic endeavors have allowed the accumulation of a body of positive findings over the past few years. This in turn has led to the identification of a number of consistent findings and trends and thus to some initial consensus as to how religion influences well-being in older adults.

In the past few years there has been such an accumulation of positive findings linking religion, aging, and well-being that several specialized reviews have been written summarizing results in this area (Levin, 1989; Koenig, 1990; Witter et al., 1985) and outlining key psychometric (Payne, 1982) and conceptual and theoretical issues (Tobin, 1991; Capps, 1985). In a review of published gerontological studies linking religious involvement to health indicators and measures of well-being, Levin (1989) noted several trends consistently supported by empirical findings. First, measures of organizational or public religious involvement (e.g., religious attendance, involvement in church or synagogue activities) are positively related to well-being, whether operationalized as scales or single items, and this association does not appear to decline with increasing age. Second, such measures are positively related to health-status indicators, especially subjective self-ratings of global or overall health (e.g., "In general, how would you rate your health—excellent, good, fair, or poor?") common in aging research. Third, measures of nonorganizational or private religious involvement (e.g., private prayer, reading the Bible, listening to religious programs) may be inversely related to health and well-being, possibly for artifactual reasons. Similar conclusions have been drawn by other reviewers (e.g., Koenig, 1990; Witter et al., 1985).

Despite some consistency in these findings, these findings are not absolutely conclusive for several reasons (Levin, 1989). These include (1) the heterogeneity of well-being measures used in these studies, (2) the preponderance of findings derived from cross-sectional as opposed to panel data, (3) the uninformed conceptualization and operationalization of religious indicators by nonspecialists in religious studies, and (4) the absence of explicit mid-range theoretical perspectives to frame research agendas and specify testable models.

First, numerous indices of well-being have been used as outcome measures in studies identifying salutary religious effects. This heterogeneity in conceptualizing and measuring well-being exerts two conflicting effects on the development of any consensus of empirical results. On the one hand, the variety of single-item measures, multiple-item indices, and multidimensional scales used in this literature seems to suggest that the positive association between religious involvement and well-being is robust; that is, that it does not depend upon the particular measure of well-being that is used. A selective survey of published studies in this area indeed reveals a startling diversity of such measures: ABS, CES-D, GWB, LSIA, LSIZ, Langner, Zung Depression Scale, Beck Depression Inventory, Manifest Anxiety Scale, Geriatric Depression Scale, MMPI, Cavan Adjustment Scale, Cantril Ladder, Gurin Symptom Checklist, Scale of Psychological Distress, Flanagan Life Satisfaction Questionnaire, Diener Satisfaction with Life Scale, DSM-III diagnoses, and lists of items from the General Social Survey and the Quality of American Life Study.

On the other hand, these scales are widely divergent, not just in the wording of items or even in their known dimensionality, but in their conceptual focus as well. As described earlier, well-being is an often vague meta-construct consisting of various affective, cognitive, positive, and negative dimensions or components; add psychological distress and mental illness diagnoses to the mix and it becomes extremely difficult to find much common ground. Therefore, the consistency of positive religious findings linked to an amorphous, general "well-being" may be more apparent than real. The presence of significant findings across this variety of outcomes is nonetheless encouraging, but merely suggestive rather than conclusive of a salutary religious effect.

Second, nearly all extant findings are based on cross-sectional studies. A good deal of published research is even based on nonrandom samples of convenience obtained for clinical or psychological purposes. The requirement of multiwave panel data in order to infer or at least assess the causal criterion of temporality is well-known and need not be discussed further. Much more important for studies of religion and well-being, especially in older adults, is the need to address the much commented upon phenomenon known as the proxy effect whereby associations between religious involvement and well-being may be confounded by functional health or disability. The proxy effect, first identified as such over a decade ago (Comstock and Tonascia, 1977; Steinitz, 1980) and since observed repeatedly by gerontologists, has been examined in a series of papers by Levin and associates (see Levin and Vanderpool, 1989), who have characterized this effect as follows:

> . . . among older subjects, the frequency of religious attendance may be a proxy for disability or functional health rather than an indicator of some influence of religion *per se*. . . . In other words, correlations between health and religious attendance may, in reality, represent correlations between health and functional health (i.e., the capability to get out of bed and go to services). Not surprisingly, such associations between churchgoing activities and health tend to be highly significant in a positive direction. (Levin and Vanderpool, 1987, 593)

To compensate for declining organizational or public religious involvement, older persons may increase their nonorganizational or private religious activities (Mindel and Vaughan, 1978). If so, then functional health may be implicated in the relationship typically found between private religious behaviors and less well-being. That is, rather than private expressions of religion engendering distress, as one might interpret the data, it could be that less healthy older adults turn religiously inward in order to compensate for failing health which has forced them to disengage unwillingly from organized religion. Clearly, this sort of issue can only be resolved completely through the use of multiple waves of panel data whereby the interrelationships of religiosity, health, and well-being may be examined over time.

Third, much of the published research on the impact of religious factors on physical and psychological health outcomes suffers from a number of very fundamental conceptual and operational problems related to the measurement of religiosity (Levin and Vanderpool, 1987). Most commonly, "religion" is treated as an amorphous, singular construct without any attention to defining in theoretical terms whether it is religious attitudes, religious experiences, specific religious beliefs, or religious behaviors (and, if so, whether these behaviors are public or private) that bear on the outcome under consideration. Almost invariably, a single item is used, or perhaps several unrelated items, which are then added together to produce a summary score. When these items that pertain to divergent religious constructs, such as variables addressing a public religious behavior (e.g., religious attendance), a subjective state or attitude (e.g., a self-rating of religiosity), and an instrumental outcome of religious life (e.g., religion as a source of strength and comfort), are added together and labelled "religiousness" (see Zuckerman et al., 1984), the result may be a conceptual "hodgepodge" (Gorsuch, 1984) which makes numerous untenable psychometric assumptions (e.g., content validity, meaningful metric, satisfactory overall fit, parallel measures, perfect reliability).

Rather than representing a single construct, religiosity or religious involvement, broadly defined, is more of a meta-construct or domain of constructs. To treat everything related to religious involvement or containing the term "religion" as if it were an indicator of a singular something called religiosity is a common error, as Talcott Parsons (1961) once noted, and is not unlike adding together items on social support, social skills, and use of social services and labelling the resulting scale "sociality." Fortunately, considerable work over the past thirty years in the sociology and psychology of religion has led to the development and confirmation of a variety of reliable and validated multidimensional measurement instruments addressing the scope of religious life. A special focus has been the confirmation of the underlying factor structure of such instruments, which usually differentiate religious behaviors (both public and private) and subjective religious feelings or attitudes.

Within gerontology, this distinction between public or organizational religious behavior and private or nonorganizational religious behavior (Mindel and Vaughan, 1978) and between religious behavior in general and subjective religiosity (Ainlay and Smith, 1984) has come to be accepted as a useful framework for empirical research into religious effects on a variety of psychosocial outcomes (e.g., Krause and Van Tran, 1989). This tripartite schema appears consonant with the three major conceptual approaches to describing persons, as described by Pattison (1988). Organizational religious indicators measure public universal phenomena from a behavioral perspective, nonorganizational religious indicators measure private unique phenomena from an experiential perspective, and subjective religious indicators measure private universal phenomena from a psychodynamic perspective. None of these perspectives alone is sufficient to capture the richness of religious involvement, but together the breadth of such involvement may be assessed.

What is most critical about this or any other differentiation of religious dimensions is the possibility that certain components of religiosity will be related to certain outcomes but not to others, or that the salience or even direction of religious effects on a given outcome will vary depending upon whether it is organizational, nonorganizational, or subjective religiosity which is the focus (see Koenig et al., 1988a). This seems especially the case with respect to well-being (Levin, forthcoming; Witter et al., 1985). For example, in a study of Black Americans (Levin et al., 1989), organizational religiosity was found to be associated with both health and well-being, nonorganizational religiosity with poorer health but not well-being, and subjective religiosity with well-being but not health.

Fourth, with the exception of those individuals working programmatically in this area, much of the empirical research published on religion and well-being in aging appears to have occurred in a theoretical vacuum. That is, many studies are quite empiricistic in nature and fail to articulate and then test a well-specified theoretical model. Oftentimes, this lack of a theoretical rationale is even acknowledged, and such studies are sanctioned by the belief that a lack of published findings in this area—a mistaken assumption—justifies purely exploratory research. As reviews have shown, there are now dozens of published studies of religion and well-being and, as just noted, some consistency in findings. At this stage in the development of this area, more ambitious hypothesis-testing studies based on theoretically specified research models therefore would be most appropriate. Several useful frameworks have already been tested or proposed, such as social stress or buffering models (Koenig et al., 1988b; Williams et al., 1991), a social networks or social integration perspective (Anson et al., 1991; Ellison et al., 1989), a multidimensional disengagement approach (Mindel and Vaughan, 1978), a confounding or indirect-effects model whereby health status mediates religious effects on well-being (Levin et al., forthcoming), and more eclectic models focusing on health-related attitudes and practices as well as on illness behaviors engendered by religion (Jarvis and Northcott, 1987; Schiller and Levin, 1988).

IMPORTANCE OF RELIGION FOR THE WELL-BEING OF OLDER ADULTS

Earlier in this chapter, we raised the issue of how the diversity of conceptual approaches to psychological well-being can impact the emergence of associations between indicators of religiosity and well-being. For example, if religious involvement is *de rigueur* and universal for members of a particular cultural group and central to feelings of well-being, then an association between religiosity and well-being may not be found. More explicitly, if all or almost all of the members of the cultural group under study strongly value and believe that they have a personal relationship with God, then there may be minimal variance in measures of an intrinsic religious construct. This would necessarily decrease the likelihood of uncovering a significant association between such a construct and well-being. Considering the other side of the equation, if well-being were defined by this group as a harmonious relationship with God, then unless items were included to tap the variability in such relationships, typical measures of well-being might be irrelevant.

Another manifestation of the need to understand meanings is evident when contrasting younger-old to older-old individuals. According to recent national data (Gallup and Castelli, 1989), about two in three Americans believe in life after death. A similar percentage of people typically report that living into one's seventies or eighties represents a blessing from God. Such religious beliefs as faith in a hereafter may be present throughout life but become especially important to the very old as the end of life approaches. These beliefs and feelings in the oldest years may enhance psychological well-being in ways that far outstrip their salience in younger years, when belief in the existence of heaven may impact less on happiness than other more immediate religious expressions such as participating in church groups or boards. The regnancy of more "ultimate" kinds of religious expressions in the very old may explain why studies often find a stronger religious effect on well-being in the older-old than in the younger-old.

Ironically, the presence and extent of these types of beliefs—and indeed religious beliefs in general—have not been assessed in empirical studies in quantity relative to the measurement of more behavioral and attitudinal constructs. One recent descriptive study of older adults examined the prevalence of several religious beliefs including, "Health is a blessing or a gift from God" (Bearon and Koenig, 1990), with which over three-quarters of respondents were in agreement. Sadly, such interesting and much-needed studies are the exception rather than the rule.

In order better to appreciate the meaningfulness of such beliefs among the older-old—principally, that a long and a healthy life is a divine blessing and that in an afterlife awaits a reunion with departed loved ones—a "normative" profile of the psychology of older-old adults should be briefly reviewed (see Tobin, 1991, for a fuller portrait). As this is a normative psychology, it should be kept in mind that the following profile is not necessarily universal, but is typical.

As the end of life draws near and as age-related assaults corrode the sense of self, individuals may begin to perceive themselves as "old." For these individuals, the adaptive task is to preserve the self. Essential to accomplishing this task is the ability to maintain a perception of personal control over everyday affairs, even if this perception is more an inflated misperception than a clear reading of actual control. In turn, connecting the past and present and experiencing vivid remembrance of the past provide validation and continuity to the self. Together, these beliefs in continuity and control provide a sense of wholeness—what Erikson (1982), while in his eighties, termed "integrality." Most sustaining of a feeling of well-being is the conviction of congruence between expected and achieved life goals. This sense of well-being is also achieved and sustained by perceiving oneself as special in surviving to an advanced old age, and is enhanced further if accompanied by the religious belief that this special survival is a personal blessing from God. In turn, the contented acceptance of death is facilitated by the religious belief of a heavenly reunion, as concern shifts from preoccupations and fears of death itself—of nonbeing—to fear of the process of dying—of not wishing to be immobile, in intractable pain, irreversibly confused, or dying alone.

This description of normative aging in the oldest years, before possible gross deterioration becomes overwhelming to the self, has important implications for understanding the well-being of this group. These implications are borne out especially in key conceptual issues pertinent, yet usually unbroached and thus unclarified, in empirical studies. Several examples should help illustrate this point. First, among these oldest individuals, congruence between expected and achieved life goals may be reflected more in life satisfaction than in measures of positive affect or happiness. Second, mood may be impacted deleteriously due to losses such as widowhood and disability, yet this effect on overall well-being may be overcome by high congruence. Third, zest may be high if assessed by the presence of activities that are enjoyed, even if very few, rather than by the amount of enjoyable activities. More to the point, this normative portrait suggests that other, more overlooked dimensions of well-being may be even more relevant to the older old. These might include self-assessments of "specialness," of still being the same person one has always been, of a sense of satisfaction from remaining in control of everyday life, and of the acceptance of one's approaching demise with equanimity. Such possible indicators of psychological well-being—as with congruence—are age-specific; they are tailor-made for a particular group or population.

This specificity in the conceptualization of well-being is important, as one recent study of elderly men in New Delhi and London demonstrated (Thomas and Chambers, 1989). These individuals differed decidedly on what they regarded as central to well-being. The dominant theme among the Englishmen was dread of incapacity—of becoming useless and dependent. For the Indian men there were three interrelated themes: importance of family, salience of religious beliefs, and satisfaction with the present life situation. In the presence of this considerable conceptual divergence between samples, and in light of the substantive content of the well-being "dimensions" for the Indian men, it is not surprising that the association between religiosity and well-being was found to be greater in magnitude among the Indians than among the Englishmen. If in the assessment of psychological well-being greater attention can be paid to developing age- and culture-specific instruments more relevant to the groups under study, then associations of this construct with religiosity may be more likely to emerge and be more meaningful than those associations currently identified.

Paradoxically, this tailor-making of age-specific measures of psychological well-being limits the sort of rigor now expected of empirical research in the social sciences. Standardized measures are preferred, if not necessary, according to the rules of logical positivism, in order to make comparisons among groups. Yet if the conceptual nature of the construct under investigation differs substantively among these groups—as does well-being—then it becomes wise to consider new strategies for assessing levels of this construct, as well as patterns of response in relation to other constructs. Add to this the need to develop and utilize religious measures more pertinent to the salient beliefs and values of older adults, and the study of religious factors in aging and well-being has many frontiers left to approach.

BIBLIOGRAPHY

Academy of Religion and Mental Health (1961) *Religion, Culture, and Mental Health.* New York: New York University Press.

Ainlay, S. C., and D. R. Smith (1984) "Aging and Religious Participation." *Journal of Gerontology* 39:357–63.

Alwin, D. F. (1988) "Structural Equation Models in Research on Human Development and Aging." In Schaie et al., 71–170.

Anson, O., A. Levenson, B. Maoz, and D. Y. Bonneh (1991) "Religious Community, Individual Religiosity, and Health: A Tale of Two Kibbutzim." *Sociology* 25:119–32.

Bearon, L. B., and H. G. Koenig (1990) "Religious Cognitions and Use of Prayer in Health and Illness." *The Gerontologist* 30:249–53.

Bradburn, N. M. (1969) *The Structure of Psychological Well-Being.* Chicago: Aldine.

Capps, D. (1985) "Religion and Psychological Well-Being." In Hammond, 237–56.

Chatters, L. M. (1988a) "Subjective Well-Being among Older Black Adults: Past Trends and Current Perspectives." In Jackson, 237–58.

______ (1988b) "Subjective Well-Being Evaluations among Older Black Americans." *Psychology and Aging* 3:184–90.

Chatters, L. M., and J. S. Jackson (1989) "Quality of Life and Subjective Well-Being among Black Americans." In Jones, 191–213.

Clements, W. M., ed. (1989) *Religion, Aging and Health: A Global Perspective.* New York: Haworth Press.

Comstock, G. W., and J. A. Tonascia (1977) "Education and Mortality in Washington County, Maryland." *Journal of Health and Social Behavior* 18:54–61.

Diener, E. (1984) "Subjective Well-Being." *Psychological Bulletin* 95:542–75.

Eisdorfer, C., ed. (1981) *Annual Review of Gerontology and Geriatrics.* Vol. 2. New York: Springer.

Ellison, C. G. (1991) "Religious Involvement and Subjective Well-Being." *Journal of Health and Social Behavior* 32:80–99.

Ellison, C. G., and D. A. Gay (1990) "Region, Religious Commitment, and Life Satisfaction among Black Americans." *The Sociological Quarterly* 31:123–47.

Ellison, C. G., D. A. Gay, and T. A. Glass (1989) "Does Religious Commitment Contribute to Individual Life Satisfaction?" *Social Forces* 68:100–23.

Erikson, E. H. (1982) *The Life Cycle Completed: A Review.* New York: Norton.

Fava, G. A. (1990) "Methodological and Conceptual Issues in Research on Quality of Life." *Psychotherapy and Psychosomatics* 54:70–76.

Fecher, V. J. (1982) *Religion and Aging: An Annotated Bibliography.* San Antonio, Tex.: Trinity University Press.

Ferraro, K. F., ed. (1990) *Gerontology: Perspectives and Issues.* New York: Springer.

Gallup, G., Jr., and J. Castelli (1989) *The People's Religion: American Faith in the 90's.* New York: Macmillan.

Gelfand, D. E., and C. M. Barresi, eds. (1987) *Ethnic Dimensions of Aging.* New York: Springer.

George, L. K. (1981) "Subjective Well-Being: Conceptual and Methodological Issues." In Eisdorfer, 345–82.

George, L. K., and R. Landerman (1984) "Health and Subjective Well-Being: A Replicated Secondary Data Analysis." *International Journal of Aging and Human Development* 19:133–56.

Gorsuch, R. L. (1984) "Measurement: The Boon and Bane of Investigating Religion." *American Psychologist* 39:228–36.

Hammond, P. E., ed. (1985) *The Sacred in a Secular Age: Toward Revision in the Scientific Study of Religion.* Berkeley, CA: University of California Press.

Jackson, J. S., ed. (1988) *The Black American Elderly: Research on Physical and Psychosocial Health.* New York: Springer.

Jarvis, G. K., and H. C. Northcott (1987) "Religion and Differences in Morbidity and Mortality." *Social Science and Medicine* 25:813–24.

Johnson, D. R., and R. L. Meile (1981) "Does Dimensionality Bias in Langner's 22-Item Index Affect the Validity of Social Status Comparisons?: An Empirical Investigation." *Journal of Health and Social Behavior* 22:415–33.

Jones, R. L., ed. (1989) *Black Adult Development and Aging*. Richmond, Calif.: Cobb and Henry.

Kane, R. A., and R. L. Kane (1981) *Assessing the Elderly: A Practical Guide to Measurement*. Lexington, Mass.: Lexington Books.

Kart, C. S. (1987) "Age and Religious Commitment in the American-Jewish Community." In Gelfand and Barresi, 96–105.

Kent, D., R. Kastenbaum, and S. Sherwood, eds. (1972) *Research Planning and Action for the Elderly*. New York: Behavioral Publications.

Koenig, H. G. (1990) "Research on Religion and Mental Health in Later Life: A Review and Commentary." *Journal of Geriatric Psychiatry* 23 (1):23–53.

Koenig, H. G., D. O. Moberg, and J. N. Kvale (1988a) "Religious Activities and Attitudes of Older Adults in a Geriatric Assessment Clinic." *Journal of the American Geriatrics Society* 36:362–74.

Koenig, H. G., M. Smiley, and J. A. P. Gonzales (1988b) *Religion, Health, and Aging: A Review and Theoretical Integration*. Westport, Conn.: Greenwood Press.

Krause, N., and T. Van Tran (1989) "Stress and Religious Involvement among Older Blacks." *Journal of Gerontology: Social Sciences* 44:S4–13.

Larson, R. (1978) "Thirty Years of Research on the Subjective Well-Being of Older Americans." *Journal of Gerontology* 33:109–25.

Lawton, M. P. (1972) "Dimensions of Morale." In Kent, Kastenbaum, and Sherwood, 144–65.

______ (1975) "The Philadelphia Geriatric Morale Scale: A Revision." *Journal of Gerontology* 30:85–89.

Levin, J. S., ed. (1989) "Religious Factors in Aging, Adjustment, and Health: A Theoretical Overview." In Clements, 133–46.

______ (1994a) "Dimensions and Correlates of General Well-Being Among Older Adults." *Journal of Aging and Health* 6:489–506.

______ (1994b) *Religion in Aging and Health: Theoretical Foundations and Methodological Frontiers*. Thousand Oaks, Calif.: Sage.

Levin, J. S., L. M. Chatters, and R. J. Taylor (forthcoming) "Religious Effects on Health Status and Life Satisfaction among Black Americans." *Journal of Gerontology: Social Sciences*.

Levin, J. S., and J. Liang (1991) "A Measurement Model of the General Well-Being (GWB) Scale." Paper presented at the 44th Annual Scientific Meeting of the Gerontological Society of America, San Francisco, November 24.

Levin, J. S., and H. Y. Vanderpool (1987) "Is Frequent Religious Attendance *Really* Conducive to Better Health?: Toward an Epidemiology of Religion." *Social Science and Medicine* 24:589–600.

______ (1989) "Is Religion Therapeutically Significant for Hypertension?" *Social Science and Medicine* 29:69–78.

______ (1991) "Religious Factors in Physical Health and the Prevention of Illness." *Prevention in Human Services* 9:41–64.

Liang, J. (1985) "A Structural Integration of the Affect Balance Scale and the Life Satisfaction Index A." *Journal of Gerontology* 40:552–61.

Liang, J., J. S. Levin, and N. M. Krause (1989a) "Dimensions of the OARS Mental Health Measures." *Journal of Gerontology: Psychological Sciences* 44:P127–138.

Liang, J., T. Van Tran, N. Krause, and K. S. Markides (1989b) "Generational Differences in the Structure of the CES-D Scale in Mexican Americans." *Journal of Gerontology: Social Sciences* 44:S110–20.

Maddox, G. L., ed. (1987) *The Encyclopedia of Aging*. New York: Springer.

Mangen, D. J., and W. A. Peterson, eds. (1982) *Social Roles and Social Participation: Research Instruments in Social Gerontology*. Vol. 2. Minneapolis, Minn.: University of Minnesota Press.

Markides, K. S. (1987) "Religion." In Maddox, 559–61.

Markides, K. S., and H. W. Martin (1979) "A Causal Model of Life Satisfaction among the Elderly." *Journal of Gerontology* 34:86–93.

McNeil, J. K., M. J. Stones, and A. Kozma (1986) "Subjective Well-Being in Later Life: Issues Concerning Measurement and Prediction." *Social Indicators Research* 18:35–70.

Miller, W. R., and J. E. Martin, eds. (1988) *Behavior Therapy and Religion: Integrating Spiritual and Behavioral Approaches to Change*. Newbury Park, Calif.: Sage.

Mindel, C. H., and C. E. Vaughan (1978) "A Multidimensional Approach to Religiosity and Disengagement." *Journal of Gerontology* 33:103–8.

Moberg, D. O. (1990) "Religion and Aging." In Ferraro, 179–205.

Neugarten, B. L., R. J. Havighurst, and S. S. Tobin (1961) "The Measure of Life Satisfaction." *Journal of Gerontology* 16:134–43.

Okun, M. A., W. A. Stock, M. J. Haring, and R. A. Witter (1984) "Health and Subjective Well-Being: A Meta-Analysis." *International Journal of Aging and Human Development* 19(2):111–32.

Palmore, E. (1987) "Religious Organizations." In Maddox, 561–63.

Parsons, T. (1961) "A Sociological Approach." In Academy of Religion and Mental Health, 9.

Pattison, E. M. (1988) "Behavioral Psychology and Religion: A Cosmological Analysis." In Miller and Martin, 171–86.

Payne, B. P. (1982) "Religiosity." In Mangen and Peterson, 343–87.

Schaie, K. W., R. T. Campbell, W. Meredith, and S. C. Rawlings, eds. (1988) *Methodological Issues in Aging Research*. New York: Springer.

Schiller, P. L., and J. S. Levin (1988) "Is There a Religious Factor in Health Care Utilization?: A Review." *Social Science and Medicine* 27:1369–79.

Steinitz, L. Y. (1980) "Religiosity, Well-Being, and Weltanschauung among the Elderly." *Journal for the Scientific Study of Religion* 19:60–67.

Stock, W. A., M. A. Okun, and M. Benin (1986) "Structure of Subjective Well-Being among the Elderly." *Psychology and Aging* 1:91–102.

Thomas, L. E. (1991) "Dialogues with Three Religious Renunciates and Reflections on Wisdom and Maturity." *International Journal of Aging and Human Development* 32 (3):221–27.

Thomas, L. E., and K. O. Chambers (1989) "Phenomenology of Life Satisfaction among Elderly Men: Quantitative and Qualitative Views." *Psychology and Aging* 4:284–89.

Tobin, S. S. (1991) *Personhood in Advanced Old Age: Implications for Practice.* New York: Springer.

Whitelaw, N. A., and J. Liang (1991) "The Structure of the OARS Physical Health Measures." *Medical Care* 29:332–47.

Williams, D. R., D. B. Larson, R. E. Buckler, R. C. Heckmann, and C. M. Pyle (1991) "Religion and Psychological Distress in a Community Sample." *Social Science and Medicine* 32:1257–62.

Witter, R. A., W. A. Stock, M. A. Okun, and M. J. Haring (1985) "Religion and Subjective Well-Being in Adulthood: A Quantitative Synthesis." *Review of Religious Research* 26:332–42.

Zuckerman, D. M., S. V. Kasl, and A. M. Ostfeld (1984) "Psychosocial Predictors of Mortality among the Elderly Poor." *American Journal of Epidemiology* 119:410–23.

3 Religion and Coping

KENNETH I. PARGAMENT
KIMBERLY S. VAN HAITSMA
DAVID S. ENSING

> When my son was killed in 1975, that was the first time my faith was really tested. Before that everything was just theory. (Cobble 1985, 140)

In times of greatest struggle, religion is often revealed for what it truly is. Perhaps that is why so many of the central messages of the world's religions are embedded in dramas—stories in which the protagonists are put to their hardest tests. Examples include the temptations of Siddhartha Gautama, the response of Abraham to God's request for the sacrifice of his much loved son, and the sufferings of Jesus Christ on the cross. Perhaps that is also why so many of the greatest religious dramas are played out by those in the later years of life. These are pivotal times, when people of greatest maturity meet situations of greatest challenge. It is in these moments that people move from the abstractions of a religion in theory to the concreteness of a religion in action.

Far from historically removed tales, religious narratives capture many of the struggles the elderly face today. Like their biblical counterparts, people in their later years experience widowhood, loss of social status, injustice, a changed network of friends, and the encounter with their own mortality. Painful as they are, these critical moments offer a remarkably open window into human character, faith, and the process of coping with the final transitions of life. This chapter presents a psychological look at the involvement of religion among people in their later years as they come to grips with their greatest trials.

It is important to recognize that when religion is depicted as a way of coping for the elderly, three rich and complex processes are joined: religion, coping, and aging. Each process has a voluminous scholarly literature of its own. This chapter cannot do justice to any of these processes, but it can explore how the three come together. This discussion begins with consideration of some basic assumptions about religion, coping, and aging.

SOME BASIC ASSUMPTIONS

People Cope with Negative Events toward Significance. To many people the concept of coping brings to mind a reactive process, a knee-jerk reflex to the crises encountered in living. It is true that there are times when people have little choice but to react to situations. Illness, accident, and death are events with tremendous power that insist on a response of some kind or another. Yet coping is only partly reactive. Coping also moves to the future. People cope with negative events to achieve something of significance. It may be something material, physical, psychological, social, or spiritual; it may be something good or bad. But regardless of the nature of the significance, coping reaches out to preserve, maintain, or transform values of importance in the face of negative life experience. Coping, in this sense, has a dual character; it embodies both action and reaction. It is a search for significance in stressful times.

The Critical Events of Life Are Constructed with Significance in Mind. The literature on life stress makes clear that events in and of themselves are not very strong predictors of physical or psychological adjustment (e.g., Rabkin and Streuning, 1976). Richard Lazarus and Susan Folkman (1984) have emphasized that the impact of an event is determined in part by the way it is appraised. Events are weighed on the scale of significance. The chronic cough has a very different meaning to the individual who interprets it as the remnant of a cold and to the person who views it as a symptom of lung cancer. The Bible relates the same message:

> How bitter the thought of you, O Death,
> to anyone at ease among his possessions,
> free from cares, prosperous in all things,
> and still vigorous enough to enjoy a good meal!
> How welcome your sentence, O Death,
> to a destitute person whose strength is failing,
> who is worn down by age and endless anxiety,
> resentful and at the end of his patience!
>
> (Ecclesiasticus, XLI)

Events are evaluated against the backdrop of a significance that evolves throughout the life cycle. As Neugarten (1979) notes, the individual does not ask how am I doing, but "how am I doing for my age" (p. 888).

People Do Not Come to Coping Empty-Handed. The early writings on stress presented a pretty grim picture of people tossed about by crisis and trauma. The concept of coping offers a more hopeful point of view. It suggests that people are not ungrounded when they face their most serious challenges in life. They bring to coping an orienting system of resources and burdens which shapes the specific ways they interpret and deal with these situations. Resources and burdens refer to generally helpful and unhelpful beliefs, practices, relationships, and feelings, such as self-esteem, optimism and pessimism, problem-solving skills, social support, and religiousness. Study after study has shown that the character of this orienting system of resources and burdens has important implications for the outcomes of stressful situations (e.g., Gass, 1987; Krause, 1987; Rosik, 1989).

The orienting system is not static; it too changes over time. Part of the challenge in coping for many elderly is that they must grapple with crises as they are accumulating new burdens and losing old resources. But the picture is not altogether bleak. Fortunately, resources can be accumulated as well as depleted. The experiences that come with age may be one such resource. Norris and Murrell (1988) found that, among older adults who encountered serious flooding in Kentucky, those who had been through floods before appeared to be "inoculated" against the effects of the stress. Inexperienced older adults were more strongly affected by the disaster. Religiousness itself is a resource for coping that can be nourished and sustained over the lifespan.

Religion Comes to Life in Concrete Situations. Among psychologists, religion has generally been viewed as a stable dispositional phenomenon, a gradually evolving system of beliefs, practices, and feelings carried over the lifespan. The most central concepts and the most commonly used measures of religiousness deal with orientations—generalized religious approaches that do not speak to the particulars of any situation (e.g., Spilka et al., 1985). There is nothing wrong with studying religious orientations. The problem is that in focusing so heavily on religious dispositions, the way religion comes to life in concrete situations has been largely overlooked. Religion is not only a dispositional phenomena, it is a situational one. In the coping process, the individual must translate his or her general orientational system (religious and nonreligious) into specific coping activities. In the coping literature, brief mention has been made of religion as a defensive strategy, a way of avoiding or denying stress, an emotion-focused method of coping, or a means of secondary control. Religion can be all of these things, but it can assume other specific forms in coping as well. And it is these specific coping activities which have the most critical implications for the outcomes of the event.

In the Project on Religion and Coping, researchers examined how several hundred members of mainstream Protestant and Roman Catholic churches coped with the most serious negative event they had experienced in the past year (Pargament et al., 1990a; Pargament et al., 1992). The members completed measures of religious orientation, situation-specific religious and nonreligious coping, and outcomes of the negative event. Two findings are important to note here. First, the religious orientations were associated with distinctive kinds of situation-specific coping activities. For example, the intrinsic religious orientation was related to appraisals of the event as an opportunity to grow, spiritually-based coping efforts, and a desire to attain closeness with God and a resolution to the problem rather than self-development through religion. Moreover, intrinsicness was tied to generally active problem solving and nonavoidant coping. The extrinsic orientation was associated with a more defensive coping approach. The appraisals of this orientation emphasized the personal threat of the event and the inability of the individual to handle it. In contrast to intrinsicness, the extrinsic orientation was negatively associated with the appraisal of the event as an opportunity to grow. The coping strategies of this orientation emphasized pleading to God for a miracle, doing good deeds, nonreligious avoidance, and a focus on the positive. The more extrinsically oriented also looked to a different set of ends in coping through religion: self-development and emotional-behavioral restraint.

The second noteworthy finding was that the situation-specific religious coping activities predicted the outcomes of the negative life events more strongly than the general religious orientations. (They also contributed unique variance to the prediction of outcomes above and beyond the effects of nonreligious coping activities). Thus, the situation-specific coping activities appeared to be mediators of the relationship between religious orientations and outcomes. To put it another way, they bridged the general to the specific. These findings underscore the importance of the many concrete ways religion expresses itself in specific life situations.

People Try to Cope in Ways That Maximize Significance. How can one make sense of the myriad and at times puzzling ways people cope—religiously or nonreligiously—with adversity? For example, how can one understand the nursing home resident who spends most of her day rocking in her chair, refusing to take part in the social activities in the home? As long as personal definitions of significance and coping are projected on others, the picture is cloudy. But with a different assumption—that people seek diverse ends in diverse ways—the picture becomes clearer. The nursing home resident may spend her time in the rocker reminiscing. Social activities simply get in the way of her coping, as expressed in this excerpt from a poem (Maclay, 1990):

> Preserve me from the occupational therapist, God,
> She means well, but I'm too busy to make baskets.
> I want to relive a day in July
> When Sam and I went berrying. (42)

Everyone tries to maximize personal significance through coping. This is done by selecting ways of coping from the most compelling options available (Pargament et al., 1991a). That people cope in such different ways reflects the diversity of available options and individual motivations.

Lest the coping process appear hopelessly complicated, two functional mechanisms of coping can be distinguished: conservation and transformation. Religion is a part of both. The first and perhaps strongest tendency in coping is to conserve significance—to hold on to the values of greatest importance that have been threatened or harmed. Plagued by chronic pain, one woman tries to draw comfort from the spiritual accounts of fellow sufferers in the Book of Psalms. Another man, recently retired and at loose ends, turns to the church to sustain his sense of self-esteem and identity. Still another prays to God for a miracle to keep her ailing husband alive.

However, when efforts to conserve significance fail or no longer satisfy, the only way to maximize significance may be to transform it. Here too religion is involved. Religious rituals, relationships, and experiences can help the individual relinquish loved objects, as conveyed in the words of one elderly Mormon who describes the car accident that took the life of his wife: "I knew that she was killed. There was a big gash on her wrist, and it wasn't bleeding, and I couldn't get any pulse. And I felt that I could lay my hands on her head and bring her back [a healing practice in the Latter-day Saint church]. And a voice spoke to me and said: 'Do you want her back a vegetable? She's fine. She's all right . . . Let her go'" (Pargament et al., 1990b). Religion can help the individual find a new source of significance, a new mission in life.

Religion Is Not Simply a Way of Coping. There is some danger here in viewing religion as simply a way of coping, merely a tool for dealing with stress. This notion is mistaken in three ways. First, religion is more than a phenomenon of stressful times. As a search for significance in ways related to the sacred (Pargament, 1992), religion has to do with the full range of life experiences, positive as well as negative. When the focus is on religion and coping, it is important to remember that this is only a subset of religious life.

Second, religion is not simply a tool in coping. It has to do with the *ends* of significance in living as well as the *means* for attaining those ends. Religion is intimately involved in the definition of significance. The religions of the world prescribe a vision of the ultimate goals in living. To most faiths the most important goal is a spiritual one, to become close to God. Most faiths do not define the spiritual in narrow terms. Through the process of spiritualization, a number of significant ends become invested with sacred status, from the search for meaning, comfort, and intimacy to the search for self and a better world.

Finally, religion is not only a shaper of coping; it is shaped by coping as well (Pargament, 1990). When religion is brought to bear in times of stress, it too becomes caught up in a maelstrom of forces. It too is changed.

To stress that religion is not simply a way of coping is not to say that there is anything wrong with using one's religion. Perhaps no idea has been derogated so greatly in the literature as this one (e.g., Allport, 1950). Religious instrumentality seems to be a synonym for bad religion. We have a different, somewhat radical point of view—that everyone in one way or another uses his or her religion (Pargament, 1992). A closer look at the criticisms of religious instrumentality shows that what is criticized is not instrumentality per se, but a certain kind of instrumentality: in particular, the use of religion to attain nonspiritual or anti-spiritual ends, as in the case of the minister who preaches to increase his own wealth. Clearly, however, religion can be used in more benevolent ways. Thibault et al. (1991) take an unabashedly instrumental approach to the assessment of the spiritual needs of older adults in nursing homes. How, the authors ask, can the nursing home facilitate the spiritual journey of their residents? Of course there is a great deal of difference between the pastor who professes a faith to bilk his congregation and the nursing home that offers daily worship services to meet the spiritual needs of its members. But this is just the point. The critical question is not who uses religion and who does not, but how religion is used.

DO PEOPLE INVOLVE RELIGION MORE IN COPING AS THEY AGE?

The evidence is clear that the elderly involve religion in coping with life's adversities (Cain, 1988; Conway, 1985–86; Fry, 1990; Koenig et al., 1988; Manfredi and Pickett, 1987; Rosen, 1982). For instance, Koenig and colleagues (1988) interviewed one hundred adults between the ages of fifty-five and eighty and obtained spontaneous reports of the coping strategies they used to deal with the worst events of their lives. Turning to one's religion was mentioned most often, ranking higher than other strategies such as seeking support from family and friends, seeking professional help, and accepting the event. Rosen (1982) noted that 40 percent of a sample aged sixty-five and over spontaneously reported religious coping to deal with life's problems. The percentage of religious coping was higher than any other reported coping mechanism. Conway (1985–86) asked sixty-five black and white elderly women with medical problems to complete a checklist of ways they coped with their difficulties. More respondents prayed (91 percent) than sought information, rested, took prescription drugs, or went to a doctor.

While the evidence from this literature indicates that religion is an important part of the way the elderly deal with difficult times, it does not say that the elderly use religious coping methods more than their younger counterparts. Religious coping strategies may be important to people in all age groups. Unfortunately, although a number of studies have examined the relationship of age to general indices of religiousness (e.g., Ainlay and Smith, 1984; Markides et al., 1987), only a few investigations have focused on the relationship of age to religious coping. In a study of fifty-five elderly adults, age was not related to seeking spiritual support in response to stressful life events (Meeks et al., 1989). Of course the lack of results here could have been affected by the restricted range in ages of the sample. But, in the Project on Religion and Coping no relationship was found between age and the degree of religious involvement in coping with the most negative life event that had occurred within the past year (Pargament et al., 1991a).

On the other hand, a few cross-sectional investigations have provided some evidence of a tie between age and religious coping. In a national sample of adults, Gurin, Veroff and Feld (1960) found that the elderly used prayer more frequently as a way of handling worries than did younger adults. Through factor analysis, McCrae (1984) identified twenty-eight coping strategies used by adults from ages twenty-four to ninety-one for dealing with stressful life events. Of these strategies, the use of faith was the only one associated with age. However, the results of both the Gurin et al. and the McCrae studies could have been due to cohort effects rather than increased religious coping with age.

But perhaps it is the kind of religious coping rather than the amount of religious coping that changes with age. Older people may cope religiously in distinctive ways. The Project on Religion and Coping has found support for this idea. Age was associated with a variety of religious strategies for coping with crisis. Older people were more likely to use spiritually-based ways of coping (e.g., looking to religion for different ways to handle the problem), do good deeds, seek support from clergy or church members, and try to avoid their problems through religion (e.g., pray or read the Bible to take their minds off the problem). Older people were less likely to voice discontent with God or the church and plead with God as ways of coping with their negative events. A cohort effect might also account for these age-related differences. Clearly, more study, particularly of a longitudinal design, is needed to determine whether people are more likely to make use of specific forms of religious coping in their later years.

HOW HELPFUL IS RELIGION TO THE ELDERLY IN COPING?

Studies of the efficacy of religious coping among older adults are relatively few and far between. Most of the available research has focused on the role of religion among the elderly in dealing with three classes of events: illness, the deaths of close family and friends, and their own anticipated deaths.

Religion and Coping with Illness

Only a few empirical studies have examined the role of religion in coping with illness among the elderly. Morris (1982) studied twenty-four sick older men and women who took part in a religious pilgrimage to Lourdes. They found that levels of anxiety and depression declined significantly after the pilgrimage, and these lower levels were sustained over a one-year period. In the Conway (1985–86) study of elderly black and white people facing medical problems, 55 percent reported that they received assistance from God in dealing with their physical concerns. Working with a sample of 162 spouses of cancer patients, Clarke (1989) investigated the degree to which religious factors help in coping with the threat the illness poses to the sense of meaning in life. General religious variables such as church attendance and self-rated religiosity significantly predicted the spouses' ability to find meaning in the event and their satisfaction with the medical treatment. In fact, the religious variables emerged as stronger predictors of these outcomes than a measure of general social support.

Religion and Coping with the Death of a Loved One

A number of studies have investigated the role of religion in coping with the death of a husband. In a study of one hundred elderly widows, Gass (1987) found that the practice of mourning rituals and stronger religious beliefs were negatively related to physical dysfunction and psychosocial dysfunction respectively after the death of a spouse. Similar results were found by Vachon et al. (1982) in one of the few longitudinal studies in this literature. In a sample of younger widows (average age of fifty-two), the perceived unhelpfulness of religion measured one month after the bereavement predicted higher levels of psychological distress two years after the loss. Hansson (1986) examined satisfaction with one's relationship with God as one predictor of adjustment to widowhood. This variable was associated with better adjustment among widows over seventy-five, but not for widows under seventy-five. McGloshen and O'Bryant (1986) interviewed 226 widows between sixty and eighty-nine after their husbands' deaths and found that frequency of attendance at worship services was the strongest predictor of level of positive affect. While these studies generally indicate a positive role for religion in coping with the death of the spouse, questions have been raised about the strength and consistency of these findings (Stroebe and Stroebe, 1987).

Religion and Coping with One's Own Anticipated Death

Because the issue of death looms larger in the lives of the elderly, it might be assumed that they have greater anxiety about death. Generally, however, this does not appear to be the case. In fact, the aged seem to show less fear of death than younger adults (Thorson and Powell, 1990).

What accounts for this finding? Perhaps religious beliefs and practices provide the elderly (who are more religious as a group) with a way of coping successfully with death-related concerns. Koenig (1988) addresses this possibility in his review of the literature on religiousness and death anxiety among the elderly. While the results are somewhat equivocal, most studies support the hypothesis that religious beliefs and practices mitigate death anxiety. For instance, Fry (1990) interviewed 198 home-bound elderly about their death-related concerns and the coping strategies they used to deal with them. Prayer was, by far, the most common coping method. Jeffers and colleagues (1961) interviewed 154 individuals over the age of sixty. Among other variables, they found that belief in the afterlife and more frequent Bible reading were associated with less fear of death. In a study of 152 elderly women and 58 elderly men, Swenson (1961) found significant relationships between more positive attitudes toward death, religious activity, and the MMPI religiousness scale.

Not all studies have yielded similar results. For instance, no relationship was found between measures of religiousness and fear of death in samples of elderly white males (Thorson and Powell, 1989) and elderly psychiatric patients (Christ, 1961). In a relatively small sample (thirty women and ten men), Kurlychek (1976) investigated how belief in the afterlife was related to four dimensions of fear of death: fear of death of self, fear of death of others, fear of dying of self, and fear of dying of others. Belief in the afterlife was associated only with fear of death of others, and this relationship was positive.

The conflicting findings may be partly due to differences in the samples of these studies. Both fear of death and religiousness are generally higher among women than men (e.g., Thorson and Powell, 1990); it may be that religious coping moderates death-related concerns more for elderly women than elderly men. Koenig (1988), for example, found that elderly individuals who used religious beliefs and prayer during stressful situations were more likely to report less fear of death. However, when these data were stratified by gender and age, this pattern of results applied only to women and to the oldest group of elderly (ages seventy-five to ninety-four).

Conclusions

How helpful is religion to the elderly in coping? The weight of the evidence seems to suggest that religious commitment, beliefs, and practices can assist people in troubled times. However, this area of research is still in its infancy. While there appears to be a general relationship between religious involvement and the outcomes to negative events, it seems that (1) religious approaches to coping may be more helpful to some kinds of elderly people than others; (2) religious approaches to coping may be more helpful to the elderly for some kinds of problems than others; and (3) some kinds of religious coping may be more helpful to the elderly than others. Perhaps the next step in this area of research is to go beyond generic studies of religion and coping to finer-grain analyses of particular people coping with particular problems in particular ways.

Distinctions among various types of religious coping are especially important here. Measures of self-rated religiousness, average frequency of church attendance, or religious commitment do not go far enough in specifying the way religion comes to life in coping. Thus, even with significant results, one can only speculate on what it is about the general religious commitment or practice that has made the difference. In the Project on Religion and Coping, some progress has been made in defining and measuring situation-specific measures of religious coping (Pargament et al., 1990a). In a sample of mainstream adult Christians, positive outcomes to negative events were tied to specific kinds of religious coping: beliefs that God was or will be just and loving to the person in stress; experiences of God as a supportive partner in coping; and religious practices, including prayer, church attendance, doing good deeds, and receiving support from the clergy and church members. It was also important to consider what people were looking for in coping. The search for spiritual and personal support was tied to better outcomes, unlike the search for other significant ends. This type of study begins to "flesh out" something of the more concrete operation of religion in critical life events.

Before moving on, it is important to note that even though religion may be helpful to the elderly in periods of stress, it does not necessarily follow that religion is more helpful in extraordinary times than in ordinary ones. Many people may gain just as much strength and support from their faith in daily living as they do in crisis. Only a few studies have examined this complex question, one that deals with the comparative efficacy of religion at different levels of stress among the elderly (e.g., Idler, 1987; Krause and Van Tran, 1989; Siegel and Kuykendall, 1990; Simons and West, 1985). The results have been mixed. For example, Krause and Van Tran (1989) found that religious involvement among elderly blacks was associated with feelings of mastery and self-esteem regardless of the number of adverse life events they had experienced in the month prior to the study. On the other hand, Siegel and Kuykendall (1990) reported that religion had more impact on men under stress than in normal times. More specifically, they found that widowed men who were members of religious congregations were less depressed after the death of their spouses than widowed nonmembers. For men who were still married, congregational involvement was not associated with depression.

The inconsistency in this literature may reflect problems in research design and measurement. However, it may also be an accurate reflection of a basic religious reality—that religion works in different ways for different people. For some, it may operate as a "stress buffer," becoming increasingly effective as stress increases. For others, it may be a "distress-deterrent," proving equally helpful to people regardless of their levels of stress. And for others, religion may a "stress suppressor," with stress leading to increases in religious involvement which, in turn, bolsters the individual in coping (see Ensing, 1991; Krause and Van Tran, 1989). Still another possibility is that religion is helpful in different ways in stressful and nonstressful times. Changing circumstances may dictate changes in what people seek and find from their faith. These are some of the fascinating but still unanswered questions that arise from the examination of the role of religion in coping.

WHAT DOES RELIGION HAVE TO OFFER THE ELDERLY IN COPING?

Although empirical studies have not as yet identified what it is about religion that makes it helpful or harmful in coping to the elderly, certain theoretical speculations can be entertained. This section examines the involvement of religion in four of the key coping tasks of aging: (1) coping to maintain and integrate the self; (2) coping to master the changing environment; (3) coming to grips with the finitude of life; and (4) coping to achieve intimacy.

Coping to Maintain and Integrate the Self

Perhaps the chief task of the old is to achieve integrity of the ego in the face of the assaults that come from within and outside the self (Erikson, 1950). Religious beliefs can contribute to the sense of integrity and continuity between what has been and what is. While other aspects of the self (e.g., physical and social) are often disrupted by disease processes and social events such as widowhood, religious beliefs offer a more stable contextual framework that lends steadiness to the life of the elderly person. This theme is echoed in biblical verses: "Listen to me . . . you whom I have upheld since you were conceived, and have carried since your birth. Even to your old age, and gray hairs, I am he, I am he who will sustain you . . ." (Isa. 46:3-4).

Participation in organized religious life, religious services, and religious rituals can also contribute to the sense of personal continuity throughout the transitions of life. A large portion of today's elderly were raised prior to the Second World War when an individual's identity was tightly bound to the church (Hammond, 1988). Affiliation with a church or synagogue was a "collective expression," largely involuntary and practiced without question, but one that defined who the person was and was not (e.g., I am Jewish not Christian). Participation in organized religious life can sustain this sense of identity. Moreover, it offers the elderly a continuing social role (e.g., religious person, deacon, elder, or child of God) when other roles (i.e., occupational and familial) are lost (Clements, 1990). In some communities aging itself can become a sacrament. Stripped of many external roles and involvements, "The aging person now stands as a sign . . . of what the community always believed . . . the Christian is not justified by work, by achievements, or credentials" but by faith alone (Whitehead and Whitehead, 1979, 189).

Coping to Achieve Mastery of a Changing Environment

The threat or actuality of declining health in old age can lead to the loss of money and home, and dependence on external services. Although the literature is replete with examples of interventions designed to increase mastery of the environment for the elderly, the place of religion has rarely been mentioned. There is, however, some evidence to suggest that the elderly may be empowered by their relationship with God. Higher levels of subjective religiosity among elderly blacks have been correlated with greater feelings of personal control (Krause and Van Tran, 1989). Pargament and colleagues (1988) found higher levels of perceived personal control and self-esteem and lower levels of perceived chance control among church members who indicated that they collaborated with God in solving their personal problems. Those who reportedly deferred their problems passively to God had lower levels of psychosocial competence. Thus, an active partnership with God seemed to bode more positively for these church members than a passive deferring spiritual relationship. However, the sample in the Pargament et al. study was not an exclusively elderly one.

In the face of diminished health, finances, and living conditions, it is possible that an active coping style that may have been adaptive in younger years may now be counterproductive. Among the elderly, a deferring coping style may be more helpful. Deferring to God may offer an opportunity to "gain control by giving up control" (Baugh, 1988). Tremendous energy is required to rage against unchangeable events or to deny their existence, and all of this energy spent may be futile. When the situation is hopeless, the more logical choice may be to give up. But giving up to God places human powerlessness in a broader context, one that says there are larger benevolent forces at play in the universe. By submitting to God's will, people admit their powerlessness, yet rest more easily in the recognition of limitations and weaknesses. Paradoxically then, the surrender to God may be a route to mastery over oneself and one's world. Perhaps that is why Nelson (1977) found religious commitment to be associated with fewer indirectly life-threatening behaviors (e.g., refusing medications, pulling out IVs) in a sample of institutionalized elderly. Through their faith these patients may have been able to transcend the limits of their conditions.

Religious congregations can also serve as resources to the elderly in their search for mastery. Many institutions advocate for and support the elderly. For example, the "Statement on Aging" of the United Methodist Church calls for its congregations to recognize the "sense of personal identity and dignity" of the elderly and to draw on their "experience, wisdom and skills" (Letzig, 1986, 2). Shepherd Centers are congregationally-based senior centers that put this philosophy into practice. Each Center "works with, stimulates, encourages, and supports development of hidden talents and expertise, sees itself as a catalyst, and deals with participants as partners who maintain control and assume responsibility" (Koenig, 1986, 74).

Coping to Come to Grips with Finitude

"Thus was the greatest *Verdrängung* that ever oppressed the human race so completely removed . . . by this most masterly of all psychotherapies" (Hall, 1915, 561). Religion has often been cited as the most productive answer to the fear of death. And, as noted earlier, there is evidence that religiousness is helpful in coping with death anxiety. What it is about religion that ameliorates death-related fears is less clear. Although beliefs in an afterlife may help reframe a death as a time of reward for earthly struggles (Koenig, 1988), these beliefs have not always been tied to a reduction in death anxiety (see Berman, 1974; Thorson and Powell, 1990). Religion may, however, help in other ways. It may assist in the search for meaning by reminding the individual that all experiences, including death, are part of God's plan. It may provide a source of identification with forces outside of the finite, corporal self such that one's personal death is no longer the death of all things of value. Or it may make death easier by providing mechanisms for reconciliation with the community, loved ones, or oneself (Tobin et al., 1986).

More so than the end of life per se, people fear the process of dying (Thorson and Powell, 1990). This is particularly true for the elderly who, when questioned about death, commonly talk about fears of suffering and dying alone (Tobin et al., 1986). But here too religion may be helpful. A person's suffering may be invested with significance from a religious perspective. Pollner (1989) suggests that interaction with a divinity helps people "feel that trivial, painful, or odious activities have significance before an omniscient divinity" (93). From a religious framework pain can also be viewed as a "redemptive and salvific activity for the expiation of sin" (Conwill, 1986, 46). In this vein, Glicksman (1990) reports that white Protestants perceive pain as a moral test of character by God, one that can be passed through endurance, calm, and stoic acceptance. Finally, fears of suffering in death may be alleviated by viewing death as a final act of obedience to God.

Fears of dying alone may also be ameliorated by the experience of an omnipresent God. God offers one supportive relationship that can never be destroyed, a confidante who remains even when friends and family are taken away one by one (Brooke, 1987). Many biblical verses describe God as a comforting presence to the dying, e.g., Psalm 23: "Lo, though I walk through the valley of the shadow of death, I fear no evil, for Thou art with me. . . ." In addition, prayer books are filled with hymns that extol the supportive and comforting relationship with God (e.g., "Abide with me," "What a friend we have in Jesus"). Visitation by clergy and members of the congregation may also be a source of emotional support and comfort to those who are facing death. Sheehan et al. (1988) surveyed over two hundred churches and synagogues and found that the large majority have visitation programs for home-bound elderly (84 percent), for those elderly living in nursing homes (80 percent), and for those in hospitals (70 percent).

Coping to Achieve Intimacy

Intimacy becomes an increasingly precious commodity as social support networks are devastated by the passage of time. Yet, in the midst of these changes, the sense of intimacy can be sustained through the religious community, through closeness with God, and through specific religious beliefs. The church community can act as a "family surrogate," providing regular human contact, emotional comfort, and informal social services (Steinitz, 1981). Johnson and Mullins (1989) found that involvement in the church or synagogue was associated with less loneliness among the elderly. God, a potential parental figure to everyone, can also serve as an important source of intimacy. This view may be particularly helpful to the elderly who can look to God for nurturance and dependence even in their last days. Finally, specific religious beliefs may push the elderly to reach beyond themselves in their increasing isolation. To seek out others and to transcend the self is a virtue extolled by almost every religious tradition. Freed of egoism by faith and hope, says, "the elder can become a 'wounded healer,' whose personal experience of suffering and death unleashes healing compassion and vision for others" (Bianchi, 1987, 185).

WHEN RELIGION FAILS IN COPING

To this point, this discussion has examined how religion is a helpful part of the coping process. This focus contrasts with the critical attention religion has at times received in the literature. However, it is true that religion can play a harmful as well as a helpful role in coping. There is no single key to effective or ineffective religious coping. Instead, one must look at the coping process as a whole and the integration among the elements within it to determine whether religion is a part of the problem or a part of the solution. Theory and research in this area is quite young, but it suggests three potential problems for religion and coping (Pargament, 1992).

A Wrong Direction

Although everyone copes to achieve significant ends, not all ends are alike. As William James (1902) once wrote: "It makes a great deal of difference to a man whether one set of his ideas or another be the centre of his energy" (193). Some destinations are better than others. Yet defining a worthwhile goal can be difficult, even for the religious elderly.

One problem arises when goals are imposed on the individual by others. In this vein, O'Connor and Vallerand (1989) found that elderly French-Canadians who could not describe why they were involved in religious life and those with a non-self-determined extrinsic religious motivation (i.e., participation in religious activities "because one is supposed to") reported lower levels of life-satisfaction, self-esteem, and meaning in life, and higher levels of depression. Heinrich Zimmer spoke powerfully of the importance of a personally defined religion: "The ineffable seed must be conceived, gestated, and brought forth from our own substance, fed by our blood if it is to be the true child . . . we cannot borrow God" (cited in Havens, 1968, 139).

Imbalance among the values of significance represents another hazardous direction in coping. There are many worthwhile goals in living, yet trouble often results when one end becomes an exclusive preoccupation (Pargament, 1992). Even the search for God, unbalanced by other personal and social values, can be destructive to oneself and others. For St. John of the Cross, the sixteenth-century mystic, the sacred and the profane were antithetical values. God was experienced by turning: "Not to what is most easy, but to what is hardest; Not to what tastes best, but to what is most distasteful; Not to what most pleases, but to what disgusts" (cited in James, 1902, 299). History is also replete with religious figures who, in their religious zeal, trampled on the lives and dignity of others. Untempered by values of a different kind, any passion, religious or nonreligious, can lead to the individual in a wrong direction.

A Wrong Road

Another set of problems arises when people take wrong paths to their destinations. For example, the trouble with the much maligned extrinsic orientation to religion is not so much that the individual seeks personal or social gain—goals with which all can identify—but that the goals are sought through the church/synagogue—a system designed with other, more spiritually-based ends in mind. Simply put, the congregation is the wrong road to take for the individual interested in pursuing personal and social ends divorced from anything spiritual (Pargament, 1992). It may not be surprising, then, that measures of extrinsic religiousness relate to poorer adjustment (Donahue, 1985; Payne et al., 1991). These findings hold true for the elderly as well (Rosik, 1989).

In some cases, the individual may take a wrong road because his or her religious system is not comprehensive or flexible enough to deal with the new demands raised by critical life events. Many writers, from William James (1902) to Harold Kushner (1981), have pointed out that religious belief systems may help people as long as their worlds are reasonably predictable and benevolent. However, when crises come crashing down, the same system may be incapable of absorbing and dealing with the events in effective ways. In some cases, the person may be left at a complete loss of understanding. In other cases, the individual may leap to simple but dysfunctional solutions (e.g., God must have sent this illness as a punishment; God would not have taken my spouse from me if she or I hadn't sinned). Conwill (1986) describes the case of a seventy-three-year-old man suffering from pain well after surgery. His physician encouraged him to get re-involved with his life. Buttressed by a rigid and restrictive religious system of belief, the man refused, "because everything is happening like the Bible said it would. With all these wars, and terrible things, the world is going to end soon. Why try? What's there to live for?" (49). Passivity and resignation are not always inappropriate to the situation, but in this case they represented a wrong road.

Against the Stream

Coping occurs in a larger stream of social forces that may support the individual in crisis or make matters worse. This point holds true for the religious world. At times, the individual may find him- or herself struggling with images of a distant, unapproachable God, "a transcendental being, beyond the reach of human understanding," who leaves the believer with a "feeling of unprecedented inner loneliness" (Weber, 1958, 103–4). Others may struggle with images of a harsh, judgmental God. For the elderly, a wrathful view of God may become interwoven into a self-abasing life-review in which suffering is construed as a punishment for sin (Butler, 1963).

The elderly may also find themselves swimming against the current of social religious forces. Throughout history, religious cultures have been known to degrade the elderly (Bianchi, 1987). However, the poor treatment of the elderly by some religious institutions is not a thing of the past. Bianchi (1987) contends that religious systems often unknowingly act on cultural stereotypes against aging and push the elderly to the fringes of their organizations. "Religious institutions seem to corroborate the general attitude that the old have served society enough in the past and are now entitled to retire from social commitment to spend their remaining years in private involvements" (161).

Some congregations may fail to reach out to the elderly or lack the resources to do so. Cluff and Cluff (1983) argue that churches have abrogated their responsibility to serve the community by resisting ecumenically-based social programs and focusing instead on parochial efforts to draw people into the church. Pieper (1981) found that older people were clearly interested in greater church involvement; however, they felt that the church put up barriers to this involvement. For example, activities were often scheduled before or after services—too long a period of time for those elderly who fatigue easily. Similarly, Sheehan and colleagues (1988) discovered that, apart from visitation programs, churches generally did not involve themselves in other elderly-related activities and concerns. Thus, in their later years, many people may find themselves swimming against a strong stream, including a stream of religious forces.

CONCLUSIONS

That people are not helpless in the face of even the harshest life situations has become almost a truism in psychology. How people assess and deal with situations—in short, how they cope—has very important implications for their well-being. This chapter has suggested that religion is often a central part of this process for the elderly. It has offered a conceptual framework that begins to link these three processes: coping, religion, and aging. But this is only a beginning.

Research in this area is just getting under way. The initial results suggest that religious involvement can play an important role in coping for the elderly. Even so, a critical question remains: What is it about religion that makes the difference in coping? We have speculated here on some of the ways religion may be helpful and harmful in the coping process, but these ideas need to be put to further test. Studies of religion "from a distance" will not be sufficient to this task. It is important to get closer to the "nitty gritty" workings of religion as people grapple with changes in status, death, illness, and loneliness. No longer can researchers rely on generic, dispositional concepts and measures of religiousness; instead, we need new methods of looking at the ways religion comes to life in particular situations. This is perhaps the greatest challenge for the psychology of religion and coping. However, promising starts have been made in this direction. With a clearer understanding of the workings of religion in the coping process, we will be in a better position to facilitate the search for significance in the later years.

BIBLIOGRAPHY

Ainlay, S. C., and D. R. Smith (1984) "Aging and Religious Participation." *Journal of Gerontology* 39:357–63.

Allport, G. W. (1950) *The Individual and His Religion: A Psychological Interpretation*. New York: McMillan.

Baugh, J. R. (1988) "Gaining Control by Giving Up Control: Strategies for Coping with Powerlessness." In Miller and Martin, 125–38.

Berman, A. L. (1974) "Belief in Afterlife, Religion, Religiosity, and Life-Threatening Experiences." *Omega Journal of Death and Dying* 5:127–35.

Bianchi, E. (1987) *Aging as a Spiritual Journey*. New York: Crossroad.

Brooke, V. (1987) "The Spiritual Well-Being of the Elderly." *Geriatric Nursing* July/August, 194–95.

Butler, R. (1963) "The Life Review: An Interpretation of Reminiscence in the Aged." *Psychiatry* 26:65–76.

Cain, B. (1988) "Divorce Among Elderly Women: A Growing Social Phenomenon." *Social Casework* 69:563–68.

Christ, A. E. (1961) "Attitudes toward Death among a Group of Acute Geriatric Psychiatric Patients." *Journal of Gerontology* 16:56–59.

Clarke, J. (1989) "Does Religion Help a Person to Cope with a Life-Threatening Illness in the Spouse?" Paper presented at Society for the Scientific Study of Religion, Salt Lake City, Utah.

Clements, W. M. (1990) *Spiritual Development in the Fourth Quarter of Life*. In Seeber, 55–69.

Cluff, C. B., and L. E. Cluff (1983) "Informal Support for Disabled Persons: A Role for Religious and Community Organizations." *Journal of Chronic Disease* 36:815–20.

Cobble, J. F., Jr. (1985) *Faith and Crisis in the Stages of Life*. Peabody, Mass.: Hendrickson.

Conway, K. (1985–86) "Coping with the Stress of Medical Problems among Black and White Elderly." *International Journal of Aging and Human Development* 21:39–48.

Conwill, W. L. (1986) "Chronic Pain Conceptualization and Religious Interpretation." *Journal of Religion and Health* 26:46–50.

Donahue, M. J. (1985) "Intrinsic and Extrinsic Religiousness: Review and Meta-Analysis." *Journal of Personality and Social Psychology* 48:400–19.

Ensing, D. S. (1991) "The Role of Religion as a Stress Buffer: Cross-Sectional and Longitudinal Studies." Unpublished doctoral dissertation, Bowling Green State Univ.

Erikson, E. H. (1950) *Childhood and Society*. New York: Norton.

Fry, P. (1990) "A Factor Analytic Investigation of Home-Bound Elderly Individuals' Concerns about Death and Dying, and Their Coping Responses." *Journal of Clinical Psychology* 46 (6):737–48.

Gass, K. A. (1987) "The Health of Conjugally Bereaved Older Widows: The Role of Appraisal, Coping, and Resources." *Research in Nursing and Health* 10:39–47.

Glicksman, A. (1990) "The Psychological Well-Being of Elderly Jews: A Comparative Analysis." Unpublished doctoral dissertation, Univ. of Pennsylvania, Philadelphia.

Gurin, G., J. Veroff, and S. Feld (1960) *Americans View Their Mental Health: A Nationwide Interview Survey*. New York: Basic Books.

Hall, G. S. (1915) "Thanatophobia and Immortality." *American Journal of Psychology* 26:550–613.

Hammond, P. E. (1988) "Religion and the Persistence of Identity." *Journal for the Scientific Study of Religion* 27:1–11.

Hansson, R. O. (1986) "Relational Competence, Relationships and Adjustment in Old Age." *Journal of Personality and Social Psychology* 50:1050–58.

Havens, J. (1968) *Psychology and Religion: A Contemporary Dialogue*. Princeton, N.J.: D. Van Nost.

Idler, E. L. (1987) "Religious Involvement and the Health of the Elderly: Some Hypotheses and an Initial Test." *Social Forces* 66:226–37.

James, W. (1902) *The Varieties of Religious Experience: A Study in Human Nature*. New York: Modern Library.

Jeffers, F. C., C. R. Nichols, and C. Eisdorfer (1961) "Attitudes of Older Persons toward Death: A Preliminary Study." *Journal of Gerontology* 16:53–56.

Johnson, D. P., and L. C. Mullins (1989) "Religiosity and Loneliness among the Elderly." *The Journal of Applied Gerontology* 8:110–31.

Koenig, H. G. (1986) "Shepherd's Centers: Elderly People Helping Themselves." *Journal of the American Geriatrics Society* 34:73.

——— (1988) "Religious Behaviors and Death Anxiety in Later Life." *The Hospice Journal* 4 (1):3–23.

Koenig, H. G., L. K. George, and I. C. Siegler (1988) "The Use of Religion and Other Emotion-Regulation Coping Strategies among Older Adults." *Gerontologist* 28 (3):303–10.

Krause, N. (1987) "Life Stress, Social Support, and Self-Esteem in an Elderly Population." *Psychology and Aging* 2 (4):349–56.

Krause, N., and T. Van Tran (1989) "Stress and Religious Involvement among Older Blacks." *Journal of Gerontology* 44 (1):S4–13.

Kurlychek, R. T. (1976) "Level of Belief in Afterlife and Four Categories of Fear of Death in a Sample of 60+ Year Olds." *Psychological Reports* 38:22.

Kushner, H. S. (1981) *When Bad Things Happen to Good People*. New York: Schocken.

Lazarus, R. S., and S. Folkman (1984) *Stress, Appraisal, and Coping*. New York: Springer.

Letzig, B. J. (1986) "The Church as Advocate in Aging." *Journal of Religion and Aging* 2 (4):1–11.

Maclay, E. (1990) *Green Winter: Celebrations of Later Life*. New York: Holt and Co.

Manfredi, C., and M. Pickett (1987) "Perceived Stressful Situations and Coping Strategies Utilized by the Elderly." *Journal of Community Health Nursing* 4 (2):99–100.

Markides, K., J. Levin, and L. Ray (1987) "Religion, Aging and Life Satisfaction: An Eight-Year, Three-Wave Longitudinal Study." *The Gerontologist* 27: 660–65.

McCrae, R. R. (1984) "Situational Determinants of Coping Response: Loss, Threat, and Challenge." *Journal of Personality and Social Psychology* 46:919–28.

McGloshen, T. H., and S. L. O'Bryant (1986) "The Psychological Well-Being of Older Recent Widows." *Psychology of Women Quarterly* 12:99–116.

Meeks, S. et al. (1989) "Age Differences in Coping: Does Less Mean Worse?" *International Journal of Aging and Human Development* 28:127–40.

Miller, W. R., and J. E. Martin, eds. (1988) *Behavior Therapy and Religion: Integrating Spiritual and Behavioral Approaches to Change*. Newbury Park, Calif.: Sage.

Morris, P. A. (1982) "The Effect of Pilgrimage on Anxiety, Depression, and Religious Attitudes." *Psychological Medicine* 12:291–94.

Nelson, F. L. (1977) "Religiosity and Self-Destructive Crises in the Institutionalized Elderly." *Suicide and Life Threatening Behavior* 7:67–74.

Neugarten, B. L. (1979) "Time, Age, and the Life Cycle." *American Journal of Psychiatry* 136:887–94.

Norris, F. H., and S. A. Murrell (1988) "Prior Experience as a Moderator of Disaster Impact on Anxiety Symptoms in Older Adults." *American Journal of Community Psychology* 16 (5):665–84.

O'Connor, B. P., and R. J. Vallerand (1989) "Religious Motivation in the Elderly: A French-Canadian Replication and an Extension." *Journal of Social Psychology* 130:53–59.

Pargament, K. I. (1990) "God Help Me: Toward a Theoretical Framework of Coping for the Psychology of Religion." *Research in the Social Scientific Study of Religion* 2:195–224.

______ (1992) "Of Means and Ends: Religion and the Search for Significance." *International Journal for the Psychology of Religion* 2:201–29.

Pargament, K. I., D. S. Ensing, K. Falgout, H. Olsen, B. Reilly, K. Van Haitsma, and R. Warren (1990a) "God Help Me (I): Religious Coping Efforts as Predictors of the

Outcomes to Significant Negative Life Events." *American Journal of Community Psychology* 18:793–824.

Pargament, K. I., J. Kennell, W. Hathoway, N. Gravengoed, J. Newanan, and W. Jones (1988) "Religion and the Problem Solving Process: Three Styles of Coping." *Journal for the Scientific Study of Religion* 27:90–104.

Pargament, K. I., H. Olsen, B. Reilly, K. Falgout, D. Ensing, and K. Van Haitsma (1991a) "Studies of the Ecology of Religious Coping." Unpublished manuscript.

______ (1992) "God Help Me (II): The Relationship of Religious Orientations to Religious Coping with Negative Life Events." *Journal for the Scientific Study of Religion* 31:504–13.

Pargament, K. I., B. J. T. Royster, M. Albert, P. Crowe, R. Holley, R. Schaefer, E. P. Cullman, M. Sytniak, and M. Wood (1990b) "A Qualitative Approach to the Study of Religion and Coping: Four Tentative Conclusions." Paper presented at the American Psychological Association, Boston, Mass.

Payne, R., A. E. Bergin, K. A. Bielema, and P. H. Jenkins (1991b) "Review of Religion and Mental Health: Prevention and the Enhancement of Psychosocial Functioning." *Prevention in Human Services* 9:11–40.

Pieper, H. G. (1981) "Church Membership and Participation in Church Activities among the Elderly." *Activities, Adaptation, and Aging* 1:23–29.

Pollner, M. (1989) "Divine Relations, Social Relations, and Well-Being." *Journal of Health and Social Behavior* 30:92–104.

Rabkin, J. G., and E. L. Streuning (1976) "Life Events, Stress, and Illness." *Science* 194:1013–20.

Rosen, C. E. (1982) "Ethnic Differences among Impoverished Rural Elderly in Use of Religion as a Coping Mechanism." *Journal of Rural Community Psychology* 3:27–34.

Rosik, C. H. (1989) "The Impact of Religious Orientation in Conjugal Bereavement among Older Adults." *International Journal of Aging and Human Development* 28 (4):251–60.

Seeber, J. J. (1990) *Spiritual Maturity in the Later Years.* New York: Haworth Press.

Sheehan, N. W., R. Wilson, and L. M. Marella (1988) "The Role of the Church in Providing Services for the Aging." *Journal of Applied Gerontology* 7:231–41.

Siegel, J., and D. Kuykendall (1990) "Loss, Widowhood, and Psychological Distress among the Elderly." *Journal of Consulting and Clinical Psychology* 58:519–24.

Simons, R., and G. West (1985) "Life Changes, Coping Resources and Health among the Elderly." *International Journal of Aging and Human Development* 20:173–89.

Spilka, B., R. Hood, and R. Gorsuch (1985) *The Psychology of Religion: An Empirical Approach.* Englewood Cliffs, N.J.: Prentice-Hall.

Steinitz, L. Y. (1981) "The Local Church as Support for the Elderly." *Journal of Gerontological Social Work* 4:43–53.

Stroebe, W., and M. S. Stroebe (1987) *Bereavement and Health: The Psychological and Physical Consequences of Partner Loss.* Cambridge: Cambridge University Press.

Swenson, W. M. (1961) "Attitudes toward Death in an Aged Population." *Journal of Gerontology* 16:49–52.

Thibault, J. M., J. W. Ellor, and F. E. Netting (1991) "A Conceptual Framework for Assessing the Spiritual Functioning and Fulfillment of Older Adults in Long-Term Care Settings." *Journal of Religious Gerontology* 7 (4):29–43.

Thorson, J. A., and F. C. Powell (1989) "Death Anxiety and Religion in an Older Male Sample." *Psychological Reports* 64:361–62.

______ (1990) "Meanings of Death and Intrinsic Religiosity." *Journal of Clinical Psychology* 46 (4):379–91.

Tobin, S., J. W. Ellor, and S. M. Anderson-Ray (1986) *Enabling the Elderly: Religious Institutions within the Service System.* Albany, N.Y.: State University of New York Press.

Vachon, J. L. S., R. Rogers, W. A. Lyall, W. J. Lancee, A. R. Sheldon, and S. J. J. Freeman (1982) "Predictors and Correlates of Adaptation to Conjugal Bereavement." *American Journal of Psychiatry* 139 (8):998–1002.

Weber, M. (1958) *The Protestant Ethic and the Spirit of Capitalism.* New York: Scribner.

Whitehead, E. E., and J. D. Whitehead (1979) *Christian Life Patterns: The Psychological Challenges and Religious Invitations of Adult Life.* New York: Doubleday.

4 The Continuity of the Spiritual Self

ROBERT C. ATCHLEY

The continuity theory of aging (Atchley, 1989) was created to help explain a paradox. On the one hand, aging often produces modest physical and mental losses and significant social losses, especially through the deaths of spouse and friends. These losses occur within an ageist society and culture. Older people *as a social category* are set aside; not recruited, wanted, needed, or appreciated by employers or community organizations. The traditional roles that elders can play effectively in human groups have been lost in the modern societies overcome with the desire for techno-scientific "rationality" and the professionalization of everything, including ministry (Cole, 1992). Service programs are paternalistic, often assuming that elders do not know what is best for themselves. Despite all this, most older people are not overwhelmed by this negativity. Most voice a high degree of satisfaction with their lives and display strong self-concepts and high self-esteem. In their private lives, usually lived in a close social circle made up of spouse and/or friends, older people display a quiet dignity that defies society's negative assessments of them. How can this be?

Continuity theory first arose out of an examination of how elders cope with retirement, and how retirement influenced identity and self. Most gerontologists of the early 1960s assumed that in a society that professed loyalty to the work ethic, retirement would necessarily cause upheaval in the person's self-concept. This assumption was challenged by research that established that elders carried their occupational identities and memories of work accomplishments with them into retirement (Atchley, 1971). In retirement their identities contained a strong element of continuity with the self of the past. Long after retirement, people still gained satisfaction from their employment-related accomplishments, and this was as true for telephone company clerks as for school teachers or professors. These observations were the first clues about the processes through which older people create and maintain an interpretive process that uses the past to support life satisfaction in the present. Later, in studies of widowhood, continuity of social support emerged as an important factor in adjusting well to what is for most a very difficult change (Atchley et al., 1979). Widows relied heavily on a small circle of long-standing friends for interaction and activity. Research on how people coped with the time freed by retirement found that continuity of both productive and leisure activities provided the needed structure for a large majority of retirees (Atchley, 1993). In their descriptions of their lives, elders acknowledged that significant changes had occurred, but as they reflected on these changes and fit them into their overview of their life history, they identified significant elements of continuity that transcended and interpenetrated the changes. They interpreted the events of their lives and sometimes reinterpreted their pasts to actively construct images of continuity. This process of integrating life's experiences into a whole generally produced a strong sense of self and satisfaction with the life one has led. It is also usually related to having a positive view of the future as well.

As used here, the concept of continuity implies a vision of one's past, present, and future as interconnected. It is an *evolutionary* theory of the conscious, continuous, intentional development and maintenance of the human personality and self and the external social arrangements that support them. Continuity theory presumes that people invest themselves in the internal and external frameworks of their lives. It also contends that these relatively robust frameworks allow the person to accommodate a considerable amount of evolutionary change without experiencing a crisis. Change is assessed and evaluated in relation to themes of continuity.

Whether evolutionary change involves improvement or growth depends on the person's goals. Simply maintaining adaptive capacity requires evolution in response to an ever-changing environment, but it need not assume growth. On the other hand, many people want to grow and deepen their understanding as they age; and in this case evolution would be aimed at growth.

The central thesis of continuity theory is that in adapting to aging, people attempt to preserve and maintain the long-standing patterns of living and coping that they identify as being uniquely them. They tend to use familiar ideas and coping strategies in familiar environments, activities, and social relationships. Thus, adaptation takes place in ways that preserve the continuity of character, setting, and plot. Change is designed and redefined to be integrated with one's prior history and anticipated future.

Individuals have goals for their developmental direction. Continuity theory assumes that individuals actively seek to achieve their hoped-for selves and avoid their feared selves (Markus and Nurius, 1986). They actively construe their future and organize their choices based on concepts of what has worked for them in the past and where they want to be in the future (Kelly, 1955). As individuals age, their life experiences tend to teach them what aspirations are realistic for them. Therefore, in later life the hoped-for, ideal self tends to be more realistic and, because the gap between the ideal and the real is smaller compared to earlier in life, self-esteem tends to be higher (Atchley, 1991a). Accordingly, specific changes occur in a context that includes ideas about continuing identity and evolutionary direction.

Internal continuity is the persistence of a structure of ideas and memories. The inner structure is formed by the values, beliefs, knowledge, worldview, philosophy of life, and moral framework that are the core of the personality. It also includes the preferences, capacities, coping skills, and abilities that influence how the person interacts with the world. Included here are ontological beliefs, religious beliefs, values, norms, memories of religious experience, religious worldview, and the place of religion and spirituality in the self and identity. Spiritual ideas, identity, and skills are often also an important part of coping. Faith, contemplation, prayer, and trust in God can all be important coping mechanisms (see chapter 3).

To understand how religion and/or spirituality are integrated into ideas and behavior over the life course, one first must know how they fit into the themes the person has used in the past and currently uses to organize self-perception and lifestyle choices. If spiritual identity and religious behavior have been a central theme for the person, then one would expect this emphasis to continue. On the other hand, if religion and spirituality have not been central to the character in the past, one would not expect it to become so.

The direction of evolution depends on the person's goals for development of spirituality and religious behavior. If the goal is to deepen spirituality, the implications are quite different than if the goal is to maintain a sense of spirituality. Likewise, increasing involvement in religious activity is quite different from maintaining a given level of religious involvement.

Knowing the location of religion and spirituality in the individual's personal system can also give important clues for understanding how specific changes would affect the person. For example, when an elder is forced to relocate, if his or her focus is mainly on the inner aspects of spirituality and less on religious participation, then the effects of relocation would probably be less troublesome than for a person whose emphasis was on participation in a particular religious congregation. The degree of upheaval experienced would probably differ considerably.

In general, one might expect that continuity of religious activity is much more vulnerable to changes such as relocation and disability compared to continuity of spiritual self. If, as many researchers have found (Neugarten, 1977), people tend to turn their attention inward in the search for meaning in later life, then one would expect that there would be a general tendency for elders to be less invested in religious activity and more invested in inner spirituality as they age. However, these general aggregate expectations would not hold for a specific individual. What happened to the individual would depend, according to continuity theory, on the nature of that person's inner conception of continuity.

The desire for continuity leads people to seek ways to express old values in new ways. Continuity of spiritual identity may become a more important goal for those who find that they have been immersed during middle adulthood in the secular aspects of their identity. Spiritual beliefs, self, and behavior may also be a very strong channel for giving meaning to life, a goal that grows stronger with aging (Erikson et al., 1986). The spiritual self, especially if it is experiential rather than intellectual, may be less threatened by the infirmity and disability that sometimes comes with advanced age. This is an additional motive for continuity of the spiritual self.

External continuity is the existence over time of geographical location, relationships, and activities. As they develop, people create mental maps of their physical and social environments. These maps serve as an important coping resource, one that most people are motivated to preserve. Relationships are sources for companionship, social support, and a sense of belonging—needs all persons have. Activities provide opportunities to experience competence, contribute to others, and earn respect. Over adulthood, people usually learn which activities provide satisfaction and which do not. Adults generally want to preserve those patterns that have been the most satisfying, and given that social change is constant, they have to conceive of these patterns in ways that allow them to evolve. People also experience pressures from others to maintain continuity in the self that is presented to them.

Participation in religious organizations and activities is an important dimension of external continuity for many people. The external aspects of worship—ceremony, music, and religious symbols—all can provide satisfying continuity. It is a repetition that can produce a feeling of comfort and security. This comfort and security aspect of religious life may be more common among older people. In cases where older people move to a new community, going to church, with its familiar rituals, can provide an important source of external continuity.

Inner continuity offers a solid platform from which people can venture forth to search for meaning. As a result of development, by later adulthood most people have a well-established routine for meeting their basic needs such as food, housing, clothing, and so on. They also are often free of external responsibilities for child-rearing and employment. These changes free aging people to devote more time to issues of meaning.

The simple, close-to-home lives that many older people live may create more space within which to experience spirituality. The simple life has long been a prescription for encountering a greater presence of God, and there are many quiet exemplars among older people. However, they seldom talk much about spirituality or try to intellectualize or convert others. Continuity theory would predict that experiencing spirituality in late life is not a random event but rather an evolutionary outgrowth of years of seeking and contemplation and spiritual development (Atchley, 1991b).

Of course, continuity theory is not designed to explain religious conversion experiences, particularly those that result in a fundamental restructuring of the self that endures over the remainder of a lifetime. To understand these, another kind of theory would be needed. This is an important point. Continuity theory is about people who adapt by actively interpreting their experience and who have persistent goals for developmental direction. There are other types of motives and other dynamics and processes.

It is also important to acknowledge that trying to preserve continuity in the face of fundamental change can sometimes be maladaptive. For example, if a person has been church treasurer for many years, wanting to continue in that role and with that identity is an understandable motive. But if the person has had a stroke and is no longer able to perform basic arithmetic, then trying to preserve continuity is likely to be maladaptive. Unfortunately, in most cases there is no clear line to show when continuity is no longer possible, so the most reasonable course of action is probably to allow the elder to exercise a preference for continuity until there is clear evidence that this is harmful to the elder, for others, or for the organization.

Continuity theory provides a viable framework for looking at how religion and spirituality, however defined, fit into the evolution of a human life. It can help in diagnosing and understanding the adaptive patterns the person has developed and wants to maintain. Continuity theory does not tell deterministically what development leads to in later life. That depends on the individual's developmental goals. Instead, continuity theory gives a set of diagnostic concepts and perspectives that can be used to *discover* where the processes of development have led for a specific person. It helps one discover the symbols and themes that are significant and meaning-giving to the person and that can serve as resources in adapting to changes. The theory also offers insights about when the impulse for continuity may become maladaptive. The goal of continuity theory is to understand the uniqueness of each individual, and as such it supports both empathy and helping. As an evolutionary theory of continuous adult development, continuity theory can be an effective framework for generating and organizing knowledge, interpreting experience, communicating with others, and serving others.

BIBLIOGRAPHY

Atchley, R. C. (1971) "Retirement and Leisure Participation: Continuity or Crisis?" *The Gerontologist* 11:13–17.

______ (1989) "A Continuity Theory of Normal Aging." *The Gerontologist* 29:183–90.

______ (1991a) "The Influence of Aging or Frailty on Perceptions and Expressions of the Self: Theoretical and Methodological Issues." In Birren et al., 1991, 207–25.

______ (1991b) "Detachment and Disengagement: Vedantic Perspectives on Spiritual Development and Wisdom." Paper presented at the annual meeting of the Gerontological Society of America. San Francisco, November 24.

______ (1993) "Continuity Theory and the Evolution of Activity in Later Adulthood." In Kelly.

Atchley, R. C., L. Pignatiello, and E. C. Shaw (1979) "Interaction with Family and Friends: Marital Status and Occupational Differences among Women." *Research on Aging* 1:83–94.

Birren, J. E., J. E. Lubben, J. C. Rowe, and D. E. Deutchman, eds. (1991) *The Concept and Measurement of Quality of Life in the Frail Elderly*. New York: Academic Press.

Birren, J. E., and K. W. Schaie, eds. (1977) *Handbook of the Psychology of Aging*. New York: Van Nostrand Reinhold.

Cole, T. R. (1992) *The Journey of Life: A Cultural History of Aging in America*. New York: Cambridge University Press.

Erikson, E. H., J. M. Erikson, and H. Q. Kivnick (1986) *Vital Involvement in Old Age: The Experience of Old Age in Our Time*. New York: Norton.

Kelly, G. A. (1955) *The Psychology of Personal Constructs*. New York: Norton.

Kelly, J. R., ed. (1993) *Activity and Aging*. Newbury Park, CA: Sage.

Markus, H., and P. Nurius (1986) "Possible Selves." *American Psychologist* 41:954–69.

Neugarten, B. L. (1977) "Personality and Aging." In Birren and Schaie, 626–49.

5 Spiritual Development in Later Life

LINDA J. VOGEL

> How long the road is
> But for all the time the journey has already taken,
> How you have needed every second of it
> In order to learn what the road passes—by.
>
> Dag Hammerskjöld (1964, 81)

Human development is a wondrous and much studied process. The way persons grow and change as they journey through middle age and into old age has been described in both positive and negative terms. Terms like wisdom and maturity may be countered with terms like senility and hopelessness as persons seek to talk about their perceptions of what it means to grow old in today's world.

A review of earlier handbooks on aging suggests that spiritual development was not generally covered. The early literature had to do with self-actualization (e.g., Maslow, 1970) and self-realization (e.g., Allport, 1950); it tended to focus on psychosocial aspects of religion, on participation in institutionalized religion, or on death and dying.

Since 1970 there has begun to be a body of literature on spirituality and aging that has a wider and more holistic approach; this will be the primary focus of this chapter. It will focus on a variety of subjects examined from several angles in order to provide thorough examination of the many ways older adults grow in faith—that is, in love of self and neighbor and God. Faith reflects trust and loyalty, with belief and action. It is a human universal that both forms and is formed by the ways people live their lives. The literature suggests that there is an "intertwining of psychology and theology in our existence" (Fitzgibbons, 1987, 133). This "intertwining" may take different forms at different parts of the life cycle. For this reason, "religious development deserves a central place, alongside moral, personality, and ego development in lifespan psychology" (Benson, 1991, 9).

This chapter will explore ways in which older adults make meaning and ways they nourish their souls. Meaning-making refers to the process through which humans "select information, sort it, filter it, incorporate it according to whether it is interesting or pleasurable or dangerous and painful, to be approached or to be avoided" (Ashbrook, 1989, 19–20). Jones regards *soul-nourishing* as that process that involves persons in finding the "true self in an ever-widening circle, first in the whole and then in God." This process is lifelong with the goal of "solidarity with others" achieved as people become able to expand their worldview and move toward inclusive wholeness (1985, 186–88). Meaning-making and nourishing souls will be explored from the perspectives of psychosocial and structural developmentalists; by examining a process for understanding convictional knowing (Loder, 1989); by hearing the voices of women which provide a counterpoint to predominantly male perspectives on spiritual development; by examining the newly emerging literature on men's spirituality; and by focusing on what it means to make meaning and nourish souls in ways that foster faith.

As persons enter the last third of the life cycle, chronological age is not a helpful guide for understanding human development. Therefore, this chapter will examine issues of spirituality and wholeness as they relate to the able old and the frail old.

The study of spiritual development in later life shows the potential for all persons to grow toward wholeness. Wholeness has to do with "setting one's heart" (a literal translation of *credo* popularly interpreted to mean "I believe") in ways that foster both commitment and connectedness as persons seek to know and live the Truth in relation to themselves, others, creation, and One-Who-Transcends (Little, 1983). Wholeness leads to generative love and an increasing openness to the power of the stories, rituals, and symbols of one's faith tradition as means of both transforming and being transformed (see McFadden, 1985).

DEVELOPMENTAL THEORIES AND SPIRITUALITY

Life phases, seasons, and stages are terms used by psychosocial psychologists to focus on and study human journeys through adulthood. Erikson (1950), Peck (1968), and Levinson (1978) point out the connections between physiological characteristics, personality, the environment, and societal factors which intersect in ways that make it possible to identify and examine developmental tasks which persons experience as they move through the life span. Their work is compared in Figure 5.1, which shows that beginning in middle age, adults must come to terms with new ways of seeing themselves and the world. Wisdom and seeing oneself as a contributing and relating member of society becomes more important than physical power or beauty. Wisdom has more to do with making good choices and being able to use one's imagination to break out of old ways of doing and thinking than it does with intellectual capacity. Being able to envision and try alternative approaches to making meaning indicates that one is able to avoid stagnation and move through generativity toward late-life integrity.

FIGURE 5.1

DANIEL LEVINSON'S ERAS
Erik Erikson's Psychosocial Stages
Robert Peck's Expanded Categories

MIDDLE ADULT ERA
Generativity vs. stagnation
Valuing wisdom vs. valuing physical power
Socializing vs. sexualizing in human relationships
Cathectic flexibility vs. cathectic impoverishment
Mental flexibility vs. mental rigidity

LATE ADULT ERA
Integrity vs. despair
Ego differentiation vs. work-role preoccupation
Body transcendence vs. body preoccupation
Ego transcendence vs. ego preoccupation

These psychosocial developmentalists offer a description (not a prescription) of ways adults in first-world, Western cultures may develop as they move through the life cycle. Knowles' (1980, 29–33) contention that maturing is a lifelong process involving movement from an amorous self-identity to an integrated self-identity and from selfishness toward altruism suggests that there is a significant connection between maturity in later life and issues of spiritual wholeness.

James Fowler's empirical and theoretical work suggests that this process of spiritual maturation can be described through a stage model of faith development. These stages are "not an estate to be attained or a stage to be realized"; rather, they describe "a way of being and moving, a way of being on pilgrimage" (Fowler, 1984, 74). Faith development, as Fowler interprets it, offers a way of understanding *how* persons know, value, and commit; it reveals the processes by which they find and are found by meaning (1991, 17). It also offers clues about how to enter helpfully into relationships and journey together with older adults in ways that nourish souls.

Fowler describes faith as a universal human attribute that transcends the relativity of religious belief systems. It is the "dynamic, patterns process by which we find life meaningful" (Fowler, 1981, 3). Because religious beliefs can be compartmentalized and intellectualized, they need not grasp the whole person. Faith, on the other hand, connotes an "alignment of the heart of will" (3) that represents a person's "way of seeing him- or herself in relation to others against a background of shared meaning and purpose" (4).

According to Fowler's structural theory, faith develops in stages as the whole personality develops. Like Kohlberg and Erikson, Fowler theorizes that an individual can become fixated at one stage or another, unable or unwilling to make the transition to the next stage.

The stages most pertinent to the consideration of older adult spiritual development are Stages 3 through 5. Stages 1 and 2 occur in childhood and Stage 6, "Universalizing Faith," is present only in a very few gifted individuals, if at all. Stage 3, what Fowler calls "Synthetic-Conventional Faith," typically develops in adolescence, although "for many adults it becomes a permanent place of equilibrium" (1981, 172). It is a conventional way of world-orienting because it uncritically reflects the faith system of the community. It is synthetic because it refuses to analyze or understand its constituent parts. Stage 4, "Individuative-Reflexive Faith," may emerge as the young adult gains a sense of identity along with an awareness of a particular ideological loyalty. Persons at this stage appear unable to appreciate ambiguity, complexity, and what Fowler calls the "anarchic and disturbing inner voices" (183) of the unconscious.

Although many aging adults never move beyond Stages 3 and 4 in their faith journeys, beginning in midlife some adults move into the "Conjunctive Faith" of Stage 5. These individuals do not impose their own meanings upon the world but rather remain open to new possibilities and new categories of interpretation. Fowler claims that in order to reach this kind of critical openness to ideas that had formerly been either ignored or rejected, aging persons need to experience a "new reclaiming and reworking" (1981, 197) of their pasts. They need to open themselves up to the "deeper self" in order to achieve "a capacity to see and be in one's or one's group's most powerful meanings, while simultaneously recognizing that they are relative, partial, and inevitably distorting apprehensions of transcendent reality" (198).

Fowler's systematic description of the higher levels of faith development contains a number of the same characteristics attributed to the more general category of "religious maturity" by earlier writers. They, too, declared that the religiously mature person must achieve a critical awareness of the difference between the religious objects of childhood and the experience of the transcendent in maturity (see, e.g., Allport, 1950; Clark, 1958; Strunk, 1965). Fowler's description of Stages 5 and 6 also resembles in many ways the characteristics of wisdom as articulated by psychologists today (see chapter 7).

In a later work, Fowler suggests that cultural paradigm shifts may be in macrocosm what individuals experience in microcosm as they move through the stages of faith. Characteristics of a paradigm shift—both personal and cultural—are (1) the recognition of anomalies—events or experiences that cannot be explained or understood using our current frames of reference and ways of thinking and acting; (2) a crisis that cannot be ignored or explained away and demands a response; (3) a time of transition when people cope as best they can—sometimes using old skills and sometimes risking trying new ways of seeing, thinking, and acting; and, finally, (4) a time of consolidation and reintegration so that the new paradigm becomes integrated into the self (Fowler, 1991,

19–21). The new paradigm frees adults to broaden their perspective as they move more toward inclusivity and flexibility and are able to internalize in new ways the stories and values of their faith tradition (Fowler, 1984, 138–41).

GROWTH THROUGH TRANSFORMATION

Another way of understanding human development is suggested by Loder (1989). He focuses on different ways of knowing by exploring the similarities and differences among scientific knowing, esthetic knowing, therapeutic knowing, and transformational knowing. Regarding the latter, Loder believes that persons may experience transformation in ways that "transcend the stages, reversing arrested development and reinstating repressed structures." He further states that an individual "may leap ahead by passing stages and establish an imaginative basis for development that incorporates but is not restricted to the so-called normal sequence" (141).

Examples of transformative events in Hebrew and Christian scripture that lead to new ways of seeing and acting include Moses's act of killing the Egyptian who was beating a Hebrew (Exodus 2), the experience of the two disciples in Emmaus who only recognized the resurrected Christ in the breaking of bread (Luke 24), and Saul's conversion on the road to Damascus (Acts 9). Transforming moments occur in unexpected times and places—understood by persons of faith as acts of the Spirit of God who blows when and where God wills.

When ways of making sense of experience and faith no longer seem adequate for coping with life's challenges, people may be open to expanding their worldview in order to make room for conflicting and/or new data. This necessitates the discovery of new images and may even require different language in the search for new ways and new metaphors for understanding life and faith (McFague, 1982).

There is risk involved for those older adults willing to visit another's world in order to experience and examine their vision and assumptions (Daloz, 1986, 228). Sometimes this helps one to see one's own vision more clearly. Sometimes it leads to change in that vision or to joining others in creating new visions. However, an alternative in these rapidly changing times is unconsciously and uncritically to hang on to old ways of seeing and doing; this perpetuates the status quo which is like "the water in which fish swim; it is so much a part of our ordering environment that we do not even recognize its existence, to say nothing of its dominating power" (Evans et al., 1987, 268).

Loder describes the "logic of transformation" in a way that has much in common with Fowler's description of paradigm shifts. Transforming moments begin with "conflict-in-context." Old ways of seeing and thinking are not adequate to help people regain a sense of congruence. They then enter into an "interlude for scanning" in order to search for some acceptable way out of the conflicted situation. At this moment, they may be surprised by "insight felt with intuitive force" and find themselves with a transformed context that allows maintenance of integrity while dealing with the conflict. Energy that has been focused on coping with the conflict is now freed up so people experience "release and repatterning" in ways that allow testing of the new "aha" in the context of the original conflict. Finally, there is a period of "interpretation and verification" when people seek to confirm that the new way of seeing and acting does, in fact, resolve the dilemma in personally and publicly acceptable ways (Loder, 1989, 35–44).

As Fox points out, paradigm shifts require reeducation because persons have to learn new roles and new ways of relating with others. They are almost always accompanied by both denial and resistance. They require "generosity, courage, and sacrifice" (1988, 80–81).

Spiritual development incorporates cognitive, affective, and volitional ways of knowing; it is nurtured through education and worship within one's faith community and by reaching out to those in need (see Vogel, 1984). It comes through processes of meaning-making and soul-nourishing that seek to be open to the Transcendent.

For persons of faith who are willing to engage in meaning-making that is open to the Transcendent and to nourish their souls, there is the possibility of joining with others in their faith communities so that "in truthful knowing the knower becomes co-participant in a community of faithful relationships with other persons and creatures and things . . . and knowing becomes a reunion of separated beings whose primary bond is not of logic but of love" (Palmer, 1983, 32). Truth is much more than beliefs or doctrines. It is relational and unfolding. This way of knowing "springs from love [and] will implicate us in the web of life" in ways that "wrap the knower and the known in compassion, in a bond of awesome responsibility as well as transforming joy; it will call us to involvement, mutuality, [and] accountability" (9).

Transformation that results from convictional knowing is one way that older adults may grow toward wholeness. By opening themselves to a process of questioning their assumptions and to the possibilities of seeing the world in different ways, they may be able to understand and experience life more deeply and fully.

SPIRITUAL DEVELOPMENT FROM WOMEN'S PERSPECTIVES

Gilligan (1982) and Belenky et al. (1986) contend that what has been typically offered as generalizations about adulthood does not accurately reflect womanhood. Until attachment, relationships, and interdependence in the human life cycle are valued as much as separation, autonomy, and individuation, understanding of human development will be skewed and less than whole. Miller (1985) suggests that it may be fruitful to follow Perry (1968) and Gilligan and explore the value of relatedness by moving toward a "maturity of interdependence" where connectedness is valued and nonhierarchical images of what it means to be truly human are explored.

As women and others whose voices have not been heard in the places of power and learning begin to speak, the role of hidden curriculum and null curriculum in the development of persons and cultures (Harris, 1989b) becomes painfully clear. *Hidden curriculum* refers to those powerful, implicit values and prohibitions which people take into their being unawares. These are "givens" that perpetuate the status quo without people ever being aware of them. *Null curriculum* forms persons by its absence. People are formed as much by what is never considered as by what is taught.

For older women in particular, the basic assumptions into which they have been inculturated result from a worldview that devalued women and connectedness and that valued independence and power with a white, male base. When those basic assumptions are called into question, family systems and all social systems are called into question. This affects men as well as women as new ways of seeing and understanding develop.

When human vocation is viewed as a partnership with God who invites persons to fashion a community even as they are being fashioned by God, then understanding of what it means to grow and develop and to be transformed takes on new meaning. There is freedom in the discovery that "no one is meant to be the other, the outsider, the not me, the dispossessed. Instead, the me is you, the we is us, the other is myself" (Harris, 1989b, 130).

With this approach, human development can no longer be viewed in only individualistic ways. Human beings can no longer be labeled simply by stages. There is a sense in which all human beings are seen as dancers on the floor of life—each one adding to the beauty and creativity of the dance.

Maria Harris (1988) has suggested that women's development can be seen and experienced as a dance with a variety of steps. It is not hierarchical; rather, it spirals around the dance floor of life as women get in touch with who they are and risk claiming their own ways of being and becoming. Harris explores teaching and learning as a dance "from *Silence,* to *Remembering,* to *Ritual Mourning,* to *Artistry,* and to *Birthing*" (1988, see also Harris, 1989a). These steps in the dance of life can be liberating, especially for older women and others who have been marginalized, and can lead toward wholeness. This becomes one avenue through which older, marginalized persons can grow spiritually.

RECENT DEVELOPMENTS IN MEN'S SPIRITUALITY

Perhaps in response to the emerging literature examining women's spirituality and/or because men are becoming aware of a need to grow spiritually, there is a new body of literature that focuses on spiritual development in men (e.g. Culbertson, 1992; Nelson, 1988). Data from research by The Search Institute "raise important questions about differential patterns of life for men and women, possibly suggesting that the male walk through the middle adult years deflects attention away from things spiritual or away from a sense of connection to energies, passions, and commitments beyond the sphere of self" (Benson, 1991, 7).

Culbertson points to the need for a commitment on the part of men to interdependence which offers wholeness and redemption. He suggests that by reading the Hebrew and Christian scriptures with new eyes, men (and women) will discover that it was

> callous manipulation and fatal competition that marked David's "relationship" with his children; the emotional silence and the failure of nerve that typified Abraham's "relationship" with Ishmael; the accusatory mistrust by which Saul ultimately destroyed his own son's hope for happiness and commitment. (166)

Culbertson goes on to suggest that men must learn "to dance, to laugh, and to lean on both our fathers and our sons in the spirited community of changing men who seek to mirror more truly the full image of God" (167).

Maitland (1987) makes clear that belief in God must be connected to life experience if it is to be more than intellectual assent (83). James B. Nelson (1988) builds on this understanding when he defines spirituality in wholistic ways that claim it is the "ways and patterns by which the person . . . relates to that which is ultimately real and worthful for him or her" (21). Contrary to much in Hebrew and Christian scripture, a kind of dualism became dominant that "came to identify [men] essentially with spirit and mind, while at the same time they identified females with body and matter" (which was seen as "lower") (22). Christian spirituality is now confronted with the critical need to break down this dualistic approach and to embody spirituality in ways that embrace sexuality. Nelson believes that, by engaging in the creation and participation in this new paradigm, men will be more whole and thus more able to be "better lovers" and to "become better friends of God, of our world, and of [them]selves" (132).

In order to explore spirituality, it is necessary to examine the growing body of literature on women's and men's spirituality. This literature offers a liberating word for many older persons—men and women—who have been socialized in religious institutions and the culture of the twentieth century.

MAKING MEANING AND NOURISHING SOULS

Focusing on nourishing souls (Vogel, 1991) represents a way of emphasizing a lifelong process rather than an end product. Coming to understand how older adults develop, learn, think, feel, and act in ways that empower them to make sense of death and life and to grow in love of God, self, and neighbor is the focus of the remainder of this chapter.

At least since the time Horace Bushnell wrote *Christian Nurture* (1988) there has been an ongoing struggle around issues of continuity and discontinuity, of nurture and conversion, of development and transformation. The truth is that there is (some) truth on every side. Persons do develop in predictable ways that can be described and understood. Persons are also transformed in powerful and unpredictable ways. As Fowler asserts, "transformation toward vocation . . . requires not only development but also conversion" (Fowler, 1984, 140).

Because spiritual development often becomes inexorably interconnected with issues of health and role changes in old age, it is important to pay attention to the special circumstances of the able-old and the frail-old.

Soul-Nourishing and the Able-Old

Often at the point of retirement and/or sudden widowhood persons may feel like "a clipped blossom" (Boyle, 1983, 19). This becomes a time for dealing with disengagement from some of the most significant roles and reengagement in roles that offer challenge and opportunities to grow and contribute to the well-being of others and the world. As John Bennett, retired president of Union Theological Seminary, has observed, the time after retirement "should not be a long vacation from responsibility to make contributions to society" (Bennett, 1981, 143). Older persons can and must contribute to personal, family, community, and societal life so that "necessary disengagement need not become apathy or complacency" (Bennett, 1981, 145).

Maves offers a "job description" for those who will to "inherit the life abundant" in their last years. He believes that elders are called to simplify their lives. This is a counterculture act in this consumeristic society, but it is one that can be liberating. To be unwilling to do this can hold persons hostage in places they should no longer be. Elders are also called to accept who they are—as persons created and loved by God. Late life is a time "to heal the bitter memories" that "poison our system, corrode our integrity, and alienate us from others." Coming to terms with "the garbage of unresolved conflict, unfinished grief work, and leftover anger" can be truly liberating. In addition, elders are called "to be good stewards of our health, . . . to reach out to others, . . . to find a reason for being, . . . [and] to see our life in the context of eternity" (1986, 137–41).

For Christians, helping persons understand and reaffirm their baptismal vows (whether they were taken on their behalf by their parents when they were infants or whether they participated in believer's baptism when they could take the vows for themselves) as they move into able-old age means that this is no time to retreat from the world (see Becker, 1986). Their vocation in old age is to continue to grow in faithful discipleship to the living God. It can be a time to focus on "walking the walk" and "talking the talk" of faith in ways that make the world a better place. It is a time for exploring faith issues and questions. No question should be seen as off limits, and *living into the questions* can be experienced as more helpful than being given someone else's answers. It is a time to renew one's commitment to grow in one's understanding of what it means to love God, self, and neighbor.

This can be a time to assume responsibility for sharing family stories and traditions and for *binding the generations.* One such story describes a terrible family conflict that developed when a young man returned home from Vietnam to a small midwestern town. Long hair and an earring in one ear became the focal point of great family battles. It was finally decided that he would move into the nearby farm home with his widowed grandmother. To everyone's amazement, he and his grandmother got along well. When his sister expressed her delighted surprise that things had returned to an even keel at home and that both he and grandmother seemed happy, he said, "We've just agreed that I can have an earring and she can have blue hair!" The grandmother was able to bind the generations in ways that neither the parents nor the son could do.

The able-old are one of the greatest resources families and faith communities have. Here are persons, rich in life experience, who may be able to engage in meaningful ministry both in the congregation and in the world on behalf of their faith community. One of the ways persons grow in faith is to *act their way into believing.* Opportunities to serve that take seriously each one's gifts and the needs of the faith community and world can be paths toward faithful living. Persons who choose to find avenues to care and share will discover, as Sarah Patton Boyle did, that "a sense of belonging goes with putting one's ear to other people's hearts" (1983, 164).

As Fowler observes, older adults can be witnesses to and guarantors of vocation. "Freed from the burden of justifying their lives with their works and liberated from the intensifying cycle of self-absorption that obsessive self-actualization requires, they have the internal freedom to take new risks and to initiate new roles and projects" (1984, 146–47). Old men and women can grow in faith in ways that empower them to become mentors and storytellers for those younger persons who journey with them through life.

Soul-Nourishing and the Frail-Old

Liberating hope must be much more "than simply the projected accumulations of the past." It comes "not out of the past into the future, but from the future into the now, it offers a hope that transcends the accumulation of past mistakes, false turns, missed opportunities, lack of courage, and sin" (Becker, 1986, 93–94). This is not a "pie in the sky" escapism; rather it is a claiming of the promises of a faithful God that the Spirit strengthens persons in their weakness; that nothing can separate the children of God from God's love.

Frailty in later life can prompt a struggle with the meaning of life and the purpose of suffering. Becker shares these thoughts from a frail old woman, Mrs. Raum:

> Sometimes I can't understand why God has not taken me. I keep going in and out of the hospital. I know that my heart will not get any better. My daughter and her family have to do almost everything for me. I just sit in my chair and watch the days go by. I can't read anymore. My eyes are bad. Sometimes I wonder why God waits so long to take me. It's so hard to understand why I have to keep on suffering. I keep praying for God to take me. I've suffered many years, and there is no reason for me to stay on this earth. I've had a good life. If only God would take me. (1986, 96)

The God whom Christians know in Jesus Christ answers human cries of "Why, God?" "Why me?" "Why now?" "Why this way?" "Why, God, why?" with an assurance that no matter what the suffering, God's love is always present. To suggest that suffering is a punishment by God and to fail to proclaim the good news of God's sustaining and caring presence in suffering harms those who desperately need to hear the good news of the acceptance, compassion, and hope offered to all by the Creating/Redeeming/Sustaining God.

Religious hope is grounded in God's promise and in the faith community to which one commits oneself. As Carrigan points out, "The hoping person exists . . . within a wider reality that transcends him or herself. The lone person can only wish, for hope cannot be experienced alone, apart from the hoping community. The community is the sustainer and vehicle of hope, and humankind always hopes *with,* whereas isolation contributes to hopelessness" (1976, 43). Within the bonds of the faith community, frail elders have the potential to realize hope and ultimate meaning. These faith communities, however, must be prepared to respond to elders' particular needs in order to enable them to continue to grow spiritually despite the limitations of frailty (see chapters 16 and 24).

The processes of meaning-making and soul-nourishing are not limited to aging elders able to live active, independent lives in their communities. Spiritual wholeness is available to all persons, although the frail may need special attention to their needs by concerned persons of faith.

Today's aging persons represent a vast, heterogeneous group of many different religious, racial, and ethnic backgrounds. They demonstrate innumerable approaches to spirituality in late life. Nevertheless, it has been the contention of this chapter that all persons, regardless of their individual differences, need to find ways of making their worlds meaningful and of finding wholeness in their lives. Such development may occur in many different forms. The hopeful message, however, is that it does continue throughout old age.

BIBLIOGRAPHY

Allport, G. W. (1950) *The Individual and his Religion: A Psychological Interpretation*. New York: Macmillan.

Ashbrook, J. B. (1989) "Making Sense of Soul and Sabbath: Brain Processes and the Making of Meaning." The First Annual Leroy G. Kerney Lectureship in Chaplaincy and Pastoral Care, The Department of Spiritual Ministry, National Institutes of Health.

Becker, A. H. (1986) *Ministry with Older Persons: A Guide for Clergy and Congregations.* Minneapolis, Minn.: Augsburg.

Belenky, M. F., B. M. Clinchy, N. R. Goldberger, and J. M. Tarule (1986) *Women's Ways of Knowing: The Development of Self, Voice, and Mind.* New York: Basic Books.

Bennett, J. C. (1981) "Ethical Aspects of Aging in America." In Clements, 137–52.

Benson, P. L. (1991) "Patterns of Religious Development in Adolescence and Adulthood." *Psychologists Interested in Religious Issues Newsletter* 17:2–9.

Boyle, S. P. (1983) *The Desert Blooms: A Personal Adventure in Growing Old Creatively.* Nashville: Abingdon.

Bushnell, H. (1988) *Christian Nurture.* New Haven, Conn.: Yale University Press.

Carrigan, R. L. (1976) "Where Has Hope Gone? Toward an Understanding of Hope in Pastoral Care." *Pastoral Psychology* 25:1.

Clark, W. H. (1958) *The Psychology of Religion.* New York: Macmillan.

Clements, W. M., ed. (1982) *Ministry with the Aging.* San Francisco: Harper & Row.

Culbertson, P. (1992) *New Adam: The Future of Male Spirituality.* Minneapolis, Minn.: Fortress.

Daloz, L. A. (1986) *Effective Teaching and Mentoring: Realizing the Transformational Power of Adult Learning Experiences.* San Francisco: Jossey-Bass.

Erikson, E. H. (1950) *Childhood and Society.* New York: Norton.

Evans, A. F., R. A. Evans, and W. B. Kennedy (1987) *Pedagogies for the Non-poor.* Maryknoll, N.Y.: Orbis Books.

Fitzgibbons, J. (1987) "Developmental Approaches to the Psychology of Religion." *Psychoanalytic Review* 74 (1):125–34.

Fowler, J. W. (1981) *Stages of Faith: The Psychology of Human Development and the Quest for Meaning.* San Francisco: Harper & Row.

______ (1984) *Becoming Adult, Becoming Christian: Adult Development and Christian Faith.* San Francisco: Harper & Row.

______ (1991) *Weaving the New Creation: States of Faith and the Public Church.* San Francisco: Harper & Row.

Fox, M. (1988) *The Coming of the Cosmic Christ: The Healing of Mother Earth and the Birth of a Global Renaissance.* San Francisco: Harper & Row.

Gilligan, C. (1982) *In a Different Voice: Psychological Theory and Women's Development.* Cambridge, Mass.: Harvard University Press.

Giltner, F. M., ed. (1985) *Women's Issues in Religious Education.* Birmingham, Ala.: Religious Education Press.

Hammerskjöld, D. (1964) *Markings.* New York: Knopf.

Harris, M. (1988) *Women and Teaching.* New York: Paulist Press.

______ (1989a) *Dance of the Spirit: The Seven Steps of Women's Spirituality.* New York: Bantam Books.

——— (1989b) *Fashion Me a People: Curriculum in the Church*. Louisville, Ky.: Westminster John Knox Press.

Jones, A. W. (1985) *Soul Making: The Desert Way of Spirituality*. San Francisco: Harper & Row.

Knowles, M. (1980) *The Modern Practice of Adult Education: Andragogy Versus Pedagogy*. New York: Association Press.

Levinson, D. J. (1978) *The Seasons of a Man's Life*. New York: Random.

Little, S. (1983) *To Set One's Heart: Belief and Teaching in the Church*. Atlanta: John Knox Press.

Loder, J. E. (1989) *The Transforming Moment*. 2d ed. Colorado Springs, Colo.: Helmers and Howard.

Maitland, D. J. (1987) *Aging: A Time for New Learning*. Atlanta: John Knox Press.

Maslow, A. H. (1970) *Motivation and Personality*. 2d ed. New York: Harper & Row.

Maves, P. B. (1986) *Faith for the Older Years: Making the Most of Life's Second Half*. Minneapolis, Minn.: Augsburg.

McFadden, S. H. (1985) "Attributes of Religious Maturity in Aging People." *Journal of Religion and Aging* 1:39–48.

McFague, S. (1982) *Metaphorical Theology: Models of God in Religious Language*. Philadelphia: Fortress.

Miller, H. (1985) "Human Development: Making Webs or Pyramids." In Giltner, 149–72.

Nelson, J. B. (1988) *The Intimate Connection: Male Sexuality, Masculine Spirituality*. Philadelphia: Westminster Press.

Neugarten, B. L., ed. (1968) *Middle Age and Aging*. Chicago: University of Chicago Press.

Palmer, P. (1983) *To Know as We Are Known: A Spirituality of Education*. San Francisco: Harper & Row.

Peck, R. C. (1968) "Psychological Developments in the Second Half of Life." In Neugarten, 88–92.

Perry, W. (1968) *Forms of Intellectual and Ethical Development in the College Years*. New York: Holt, Rinehart and Winston.

Strunk, O. (1965) *Mature Religion: A Psychological Study*. New York: Abingdon.

Vogel, L. J. (1984) *The Religious Education of Older Adults*. Birmingham, Ala.: Religious Education Press.

——— (1991) *Teaching and Learning in Communities of Faith: Empowering Adults through Religious Education*. San Francisco: Jossey-Bass.

6 Mysticism

HARRY R. MOODY

Why does mysticism have importance for aging and for the role of religion in later life? This question can best be answered with a first-person account, not from a person commonly known as a "mystic" but through an eloquent passage in *The Measure of My Days,* a journal kept by Florida Scott-Maxwell when she was in her eighties and sometimes living in a nursing home. She writes about old people and the special burden and possibility they experience:

> Another secret we [old people] carry is that though drab outside—wreckage to the eye, mirrors a mortification—inside we flame with a wild life that is almost incommunicable. In silent, hot rebellion we cry silently—"I have lived my life haven't I? What more is expected of me?" . . . We have reached the place beyond resignation, a place I had no idea existed until I had arrived here.
>
> It is a place of fierce energy. Perhaps passion would be a better word than energy, for the sad fact is this vivid life cannot be used. If I try to transpose it into action I am soon spent. It has to be accepted as passionate life, perhaps the life I never lived, never guessed I had it in me to live. It feels other and more than that. It feels like the far side of precept and aim. It is just life, the natural intensity of life, and when old we have it for our reward and undoing. . . .
>
> Some of it must go beyond good and bad, for at times—though this comes rarely, unexpectedly—it is a swelling clarity as though all was resolved. It has no content, it seems to expand us, it does not derive from the body, and then it is gone. It may be a degree of consciousness which lies outside activity, and which when young we are too busy to experience. (1979, 32–33)

This passage reveals many of the compelling traits of mystical experience: a miraculous sense of discovery ("a place I had no idea existed until I had arrived here"); an extraordinary energy that transcends "doing" in favor of "being"; above all, a clarity of consciousness in which opposites are resolved. Interesting, too, is that she describes this condition as a distinct gift of old age, reserved for the old because the young are "too busy" to cultivate the quietness and inwardness from which mystical experience becomes possible.

Mysticism has a variety of forms, but through the ages mysticism displays a common core of meaning close to what Florida Scott-Maxwell finds in the distinctive understanding of old age: a detachment from a superficial experience of life in favor of a deeper reality hitherto unknown; dissolving of barriers between the self and the world; and a powerful sense of certainty and existential security that gives meaning to everything. Are there clues to spiritual development in the later years to be found in the literature of mysticism? Does the mystical experience illuminate a deeper role for religion in the last stage of life? These questions demand a closer scrutiny of what mysticism has meant in the past and what it might mean for old age.

WHAT IS MYSTICISM?

The word *mysticism* is difficult to define. It is an ambiguous term often subject to misunderstanding and multiple interpretations. For instance, before 1900, Dean W. R. Inge had already distinguished twenty-five different definitions of "mysticism" (1899), and the number would surely be still larger with the inclusion of the data from comparative religion.

A classic definition of mysticism was given by William James (1901/1958) in *The Varieties of Religious Experience.* James points to four traits of mystical experience: (1) ineffability (the private or incommunicable character of mystical insight); (2) the noetic quality (conveying a distinctive sense of integrating knowledge); (3) passivity (often understood as a grace transcending the voluntary power of preparatory asceticism or meditation); and (4) transiency (the characteristically intermittent or impermanent feature of mystical states).

James's definition, it should be noted, makes no reference to religion or faith traditions. Indeed, it explicitly includes the kind of "cosmic consciousness" described by R. M. Bucke (1931): a feeling of oneness with nature very much in tune with today's ecological consciousness and with "New Age" mysticism signified by interest in meditation, astrology, and higher states of consciousness. Much of today's New Age sensibility actually overlaps with the category of the occult; that is, it amounts to an effort to attain psychic powers or secret knowledge. Enhanced knowledge and power points in exactly the opposite direction from true mysticism, which aspires toward overcoming the ego.

In the present chapter the term "mysticism" will be limited to forms of experience and doctrine found in traditional religion that tend to deepen religion to a point where the religious believer "knows" the truths of faith through experiential knowledge involving the characteristic features of mystical experience identified in William James's definition. The focus of attention in this chapter is on mystical experience conceived in relation to the traditions of the great world religions such as Judaism, Christianity, Islam, Hinduism, Buddhism, and Taoism. It is important to recognize that mysticism is not something alien to the Christian tradition but rather stands at the core of religious renewal in historical figures such as St. Augustine, St. Francis, and St. Theresa. But mysticism also points beyond the Christian tradition and therefore emphasizes an ecumenical aspect of faith. Mysticism, in fact, is that current of religious experience where different faith traditions express themselves in similar terms and can often find common ground. That core of universal mysticism will be the focus of this chapter.

Mysticism does share certain common or recurrent features among all world religions, a fact that has led such interpreters as Aldous Huxley (1945) or Alan Watts (1953) to describe mysticism as the "perennial philosophy." In this view, mysticism appears as a single, distinctive mode of experience, essentially the same the world over, as Bucke meant when speaking of "cosmic consciousness." A sharply different view is expressed by the scholar of Jewish mysticism, Gershem Scholem (1941/1961). For Scholem, there is no such thing as mysticism in the abstract, but, at best, a family resemblance among Jewish mysticism, Christian mysticism, or Hindu mysticism. Still other writers, such as R. C. Zaehner (1957), stress the decisive differences, for example, between Christian mysticism and other varieties of mystical religion.

It is important to remember that not only are there decisive differences in the style and orientation of mysticism manifested in different religions, but there are also profound differences within each of the traditions. These varieties must be kept in mind whenever generalizations are considered. The framework adopted in this chapter is the idea of a "transcendent unity" beyond exoteric religion. According to this view, mystical experience everywhere points toward the same reality, but differing levels of attainment and different forms of expression involve different "truths" arising from interpretations given to the experience. The field of scholarship on mysticism and comparative religion is vast and need not be considered in detail here. In the contemporary American context Christian mysticism offers a useful perspective with which to understand mysticism and late-life spirituality, so Christian mysticism provides the starting point for these considerations.

Maincurrents of Christian Mysticism

Mystical states of consciousness—the plural is used here deliberately—cover a multiplicity of levels or stages recognized in mystical traditions such as Sufism or Tibetan Buddhism, among others. In the Western Christian tradition, too, the stages of mystical experience are recognized but are less explicitly codified or elaborated. At least from medieval times, Christianity has distinguished between the purgative way, the illuminative way, and the unitive way. The last two stages are the locus of mystical experience properly speaking: (1) illuminative experience or infusion of direct knowledge into consciousness through the "eye of the heart" and (2) the ultimate state of union with the Divine interpreted in different ways by the mystics and their followers.

The term *mysticism* goes back to the Greek word *mysterion,* or mystery, as used by the Fathers of the Church. *Mysterion* denotes what is secret and in this sense may refer either to the hidden dimension of scripture, the deep significance of the Christian sacraments, or the knowledge of God through Christ.

The early Fathers understood this "mystic" or hidden sense of scripture as apprehended not through intellect but rather by prayer and love in approaching the Word of God.

The mysticism of the Church Fathers was intimately tied to both scriptural interpretation and mystical theology. A major early influence was Dionysus the Pseudo-Areopagite, who became an authority for both the Eastern and Western Church and whose writings helped transmit the patristic heritage of mystical theology. Dionysius took over scriptural and sacramental dimensions of mystery but identified the ultimate mystery as the surrender of the soul to God in love, always characteristic of Christian spirituality. Dionysius also employed the threefold distinction of purification, illumination, and unification, which dates back still further to the Greek mystery religion.

In the Western Church, Dionysius did not have the same influence that he did for the Eastern Orthodox, which was exemplified by the towering synthesis of St. Gregory Palamas. The Western mystical tradition has tended toward the subjective or individual dimension, a trend that would be accentuated in modern times. This subjective or autobiographical side of mysticism had its origin in St. Augustine, but Augustine's confessional genre had few imitators in the Middle Ages. However, an emphasis on the intensity of individual experience was evident in medieval figures such as St. Bernard of Clairvaux and Richard of St. Victor.

Toward the end of the Middle Ages the trend toward inwardness and pietism became pronounced with the Rhineland mystics such as Tauler and Suso in the generation after Meister Eckhart. The later medieval period was also notable for visionary experience tied to affective mysticism as seen in figures such as Julian of Norwich, Mechtilde of Magdeburg, and Catherine of Siena. This tone is visible, too, in the *devotio moderna* and the *Imitation of Christ.* A characteristically modern approach to mysticism as a state of consciousness was evident in medieval times when Jean de Gerson in the fifteenth century described mystical theology as "experimental knowledge of God through the embrace of unitive love" (Connolly, 1928).

After the Renaissance and the Counter-Reformation, this tendency toward subjectivity was intensified. The Spanish mystics, especially St. Teresa of Avila, placed even greater emphasis on the psychological dimension of mystical experience. St. Teresa distinguished among levels of prayer: the prayer of recollection, the prayer of quiet, and the prayer of union. Her contemporary, St. John of the Cross, is notable for describing the "Dark Night of the Soul," analyzed in terms of theological understanding. This psychological orientation of the Spanish mystics prefigures modern approaches to the subject of mysticism.

Some varieties of traditional Protestantism have been suspicious of mysticism, since their view of monotheism entails a view of God as "utterly Other." A neo-Orthodox writer like Karl Barth would be one example. Any idea of union between God and the soul is suspect. However, the mystical tradition is far from unknown in Protestantism, a prominent example being the Quakers (Fremantle, 1964). Perhaps the greatest contribution of the Protestant spirit to mysticism in the present day is the Protestant primacy of individual conscience or the self as the touchstone for all religious truth and salvation. Even in a secular culture, people with little sympathy for traditional religion may be attracted by mysticism because it speaks to subjective experience and the primacy of self.

In the twentieth century, following the lead of William James, there has been a strong psychological emphasis on mysticism as a state of consciousness. For the modern mind, individual experience characteristically becomes a means of validating or verifying all religious truths. In a scientific world where all ideas must be empirically verified, mysticism becomes legitimated because its claims are presumably confirmed by experience. The fact that such states of consciousness seem recognizable across different cultures and religions adds weight to the epistemic claims for mysticism, although philosophers debate just what those claims might be (Katz, 1978).

Comparative Religious Perspectives

In itself, mystical experience is not linked to chronological age, but ideas about aging and the life course have incorporated the influence of mysticism. Christianity has had relatively little to say about old age, though in the Middle Ages the stages of life were thematized in spiritual terms (Sears, 1986). Other religions have been more explicit in their view about the last stage of life. In the case of Hinduism, for example, late-life development is explicitly tied to ideals inspired by mystical religion. In the Hindu view, aging is conceived as a sequence of progressively higher stages of human activity, or *darshanas,* which parallel Erik Erikson's "Eight Ages of Man" (Kakar, 1986). In contrast to Western psychology, the ultimate goal of these life stages is not individual fulfillment but consciousness of the absolute Ground of Being, called Brahman since the Upanishads (Hume, 1949). Hindu doctrine and tradition recognizes a provisional role for lesser religious goals (ritual, ethics, devotion) up to a point in the life-course where earlier attachments, both sacred and profane, are abandoned.

The Hindu construction of the life-course in effect "maps" the cognitive structure of being onto successively higher stages of life. Relative values of activity or disengagement each have their place, but finally the opposites are united in the mystic vision. In the last stage of life, contemplation or mystical absorption has primacy. In the Hindu model the spiritual seeker in late life leaves society but finally returns, though in a different, transformed state. Coming back to the world, the mystic seeks to be "in the world but not of it," as the Islam mystics have termed it. Islam, unlike Hinduism, identifies entry into the mystical life with the initiatory moment of becoming a dervish or follower of Sufism, which may occur at any age. The life of Muslim mystic and theologian al-Ghazali demonstrates this rhythm of renunciation of the world followed by return to the world, but here the cycle is mapped onto midlife rather than old age (Watt, 1953).

A few empirical studies in gerontology have illuminated the parallels and contrast between Eastern and Western approaches to late-life mysticism. For example, Eugene Thomas and colleagues (Thomas, 1991; Thomas et al., 1991) have collected data from a crosscultural sample of Hindu and Christian elderly people described by their peers as being "spiritually advanced." The data came from interviews with samples of elderly persons in Pondicherry, India, and Birmingham, England, and the findings are illuminating. In contrast to linear stage theories of human development, Thomas and colleagues, like William James, discovered a variety of mystical experiences and spiritual paths among their elderly respondents. Nonetheless, they also found a remarkable qualitative similarity among respondents at the highest spiritual levels. That similarity lends support to claims of a "perennial philosophy" displaying deeper unity among the world's divergent faith traditions.

In both psychology and religion, there are different views on how best to characterize the highest state of human development. From a Western perspective, Erik Erikson (1963), for example, would depict the highest stage of human development as "ego integrity" or the attainment of a fully integrated sense of self. Jung (1971) described the positive tendency of psychological growth as an assimilation of individual self toward the archetypal Self, a paradigm of unity and wholeness found in archetypal imagery in the great world religions.

But can one conclude that mysticism and the language of modern psychology are easily reconciled with one another? The conclusion may be premature. At least on the surface, much of the language and imagery of mystical traditions seems to challenge the Western notion of ideal ego development (Chinen, 1989). Is late-life spirituality to be thought of as a task of integrating the self—aiming at wholeness or the incorporation of the earlier remembered self? Or is it a matter of dropping personal history in favor of self-transcendence? The contrast here recalls the contrast between continuity versus discontinuity theories of aging. The idea of extinction of the self—*fana* for the Sufis, *nirvana* for the Buddhists—seems to suggest the most radical discontinuity imaginable.

Whether the highest stage of human development is best described as ego-integration or as ego-transcendence remains an issue debated by lifespan development theorists and students of comparative religion. The modern psychological goal of ego-integration can perhaps be understood as a secular version of the ideal of salvation or reconciliation with God enunciated by the Western traditions. By contrast, ego-transcendence corresponds to the "no-self" ideal enunciated by many Eastern traditions (Loy, 1988).

There is a familiar geographic dualism summed up in the phrase "East is East and West is West." But the opposition should not be pressed too far. Islam is the classic instance of a "Western" religion where the "personal" God is portrayed in terms that transcend human images (Moody, 1990), while popular Hinduism (e.g., the cult of Krishna) contains strong currents of devotional mysticism (Thursby, 1992). In the Christian tradition, a towering figure like Meister Eckhart speaks in a language that resembles the "no-self" ideals of Vedantic Hinduism or Zen Buddhism (Suzuki, 1971). Eckhart's idea of detachment (*Gelassenheit*) here is fundamental: "He who would be serene and pure needs but one thing, detachment. . . . The heart detached has no desire for anything nor has it anything to be delivered from. So it has no prayers at all; its only prayer consists in being uniform with God" (Eckhart, 1924, 341). This condition of detachment can be correlated with a distinctive "late freedom" to be found in the last stage of life (Rosenmayr, 1983).

Framed in this way, the ideal of detachment pushes the gerontological notion of "disengagement" beyond all sociological categories and instead gives it a positive content as the overriding spiritual goal of life itself. Here one can see how mysticism can help to challenge and reframe ideas in gerontology, such as earlier debates over disengagement theory. The mystical tradition may give an unexpected perspective on the virtues of disengagement. A new validation of disengagement would mean to see it not primarily as abandonment of social roles or as desolate aloneness. Whitehead defined religion as how the human being makes use of aloneness (1960). The paradox is that in this condition of aloneness the mystic experiences union with all creation.

Something of this same sentiment is found in the twentieth-century Hindu Master Ramana Maharshi, who articulated the wisdom of the Vedanta: "Retirement means abidance in the Self. Nothing more. It is not leaving one set of surroundings and getting entangled in another set, nor even leaving the concrete world and becoming involved in a mental world" (Ramana Maharshi, 1955, 299).

Contemporary Approaches to Mysticism

The contemporary mind, preceded by William James, is often inclined to approach mysticism from the standpoint of psychology. Here Ramana Maharshi's point serves as a reminder of the limits of all psychological methods and ideals. Human development is not necessarily the same thing as intellectual development, not even if reframed as dialectical development, as Klaus Riegel (1976) and psychological theorists of cognitive development sought to do. Mysticism does not involve an enlargement of "the mind" but the overcoming of everything taken to be the familiar mind or self. Seen in this way, the goal of spiritual growth in later life has nothing to do with "late life learning" or enlarging the mind through travel, study, reflection, or even psychotherapy. All such activities may represent new ways of getting entangled or involved in a "mental world." The "anti-intellectual" stance of Ramana Maharshi obviously represents an implicit critique of ideals of cognitive development that depict "growth" in terms of ever more refined intellectual operations. On the contrary, Maharshi's ideal of "retirement" has much in common with Zen Buddhist skepticism (Suzuki,

1971) about the intellect and also with the traditional Christian mystical primacy of Divine Love, from Hildegard of Bingen to Teilhard de Chardin.

What about the idea that mysticism and perhaps late-life spiritual development represent a fruition of "wisdom?" Is late-life mysticism simply a "feeling" without cognitive content or claims? The answer depends on how one thinks about the essential content of wisdom: Is it a matter of worldly judgment ("shrewdness") or metaphysical insight into the nature of things? Process wisdom, as demonstrated in the recent work of Paul Baltes and colleagues (1990), represents a refinement of cognitive processes of adult judgment. Psychologists today might describe such wisdom in terms of "expert systems," an important and legitimate research enterprise. But process wisdom does not go so far as the "crazy wisdom" urged by mystics. Baltes's cognitive research, like the psychology of Erikson or the epistemology of Aristotle, constitutes the highest of humanistic culture. But cognitive development understood through this model is not the same thing as the mystical way of knowing.

In many respects, mysticism is committed to modes of knowing that are subversive for dominant modes of rationality. The rational spirit tends toward predictability and control, whether through science or religious dogma. By contrast, the mystical spirit tends toward dissolution of the self that seeks control. This opposition explains the conflict between mystics and established orthodoxy, a conflict that recurs periodically in Jewish, Christian, and Islamic traditions. However often mysticism becomes reconciled with orthodox rationality, as it did for St. Thomas and al-Ghazali, nonetheless the way of the mystics remains apart: "The Spirit bloweth where it listeth" (John 3:8). Mysticism constitutes what might be called a "countertradition" because it insists on a radical discontinuity between what is known and what is unknown: for example, the Unknowable Godhead (Eckhart) or the ineffable "suchness" experienced in Enlightenment (Zen Buddhism).

Yet, human beings seek ways to integrate this mystical countertradition into the framework of aging and the life course, to make the mystical way part of an ongoing life story. A common approach to late-life mysticism takes the form of autobiography where the mystical quest is part of a spiritual journey. Today there is growing interest in reminiscence and life-review; some writers even speak of "spiritual life-review" in the sense of an examination of conscience or repentance. The idea of life-review must be traced back originally to Protestant spirituality, and the spiritual significance of life-review has clear importance for aging. Yet, few writers on reminiscence have understood or recognized the religious origins of the idea of life-review, which was put forward originally by Robert Butler (1963) in purely psychodynamic terms and has largely remained bounded by psychology.

The power of life-review today cannot be appreciated without understanding its covert religious appeal and its historical roots in spiritual autobiography. By origins the literary genre of autobiography is a distinctively Protestant idea: it is part of the examination of conscience displayed in *The Pilgrim's Progress* (Bunyan, 1987). Autobiography has few parallels in other great civilizations such as the Chinese, Hindu, or Islamic. Even in the West during the Middle Ages, St. Augustine's *Confessions* (Augustine, 1963), as an autobiographical work, had no serious imitators. The popularity of life-review today corresponds to a need to find meaning in the last stage of life, a meaning now defined in psychological rather than religious terms. The two strands of psychology and religion can of course be successfully combined as they are in such popular books as *The Road Less Traveled* (Peck, 1978).

But is this rise of "psychological mysticism" an altogether positive phenomenon? In a culture where religion is constantly in peril of becoming converted into a vehicle for psychological self-help, mysticism stands in a peculiar position. On the positive side, it is one means by which the secular mind can be attracted to religious ideas. Yet contemporary psychology tends to accept religion and mysticism only on its own terms, which typically amounts to some form of therapy in which assumptions about the normal life-course, not to mention metaphysics, are simply taken for granted. In actual practice, the mystical path, whether in youth or age, calls all assumptions and consolations into question. It offers not reassurance but radical examination of the self.

For instance, in considering the psychology of late-life mysticism, it is important to appreciate the role of negative emotions: for example, guilt and remorse over the past (often an issue in life-review), fear of death, or loss of cognitive functions that support the sense of self. Nouwen (1986) has focused on the phenomenon of loneliness, usually thought of as a deficit, which nonetheless has a certain relationship to solitude, conceived as deep solitude and the basis for spiritual growth in later life. The danger in American culture is that mysticism may too easily become identified, in a onesided way, with the "pursuit of happiness" or "life-satisfaction," as gerontology would have it. But this approach is contrary to the central traditions of mysticism, which is, above all, a stripping away of illusion or consolation in favor of divine reality itself: "Not my will, but yours be done" (Luke 22:42b).

The mystical tradition forthrightly accepts the validity of emptiness, aloneness, passivity, and the loss of the self—qualities usually thought of as negative—as states to be avoided. From a psychological standpoint these experiences are seen as strictly pathological or defective. But the mystical traditions have always insisted on the need for a "dark night of the soul" before there can be a celebration of luminous or joyous experience. In traditional terms, the purgative way necessarily precedes the illuminative or unitive way.

The point here is that even a seemingly "negative" psychological state—such as loneliness or abandonment—takes on a different meaning when considered in light of mystical ideas about the purpose or meaning of late-life development. Viewed in developmental perspective, the "Dark Night of the Soul" (St. John of the Cross, 1958) would correspond to a stage of transitional "regression in the service of transcendence." The great contribution of mysticism to late-life development could be to help reclaim ideas such as "retirement" or "disengagement" by giving them a positive meaning that challenges the idolatrous worship of activity for its own sake that is so characteristic of the present age.

The study of late-life mysticism is a case where psychological theory can be brought to bear on religious phenomena so that psychology and religion become complementary, not antagonistic ways of approaching late-life development. There is a great need to move beyond the point where Freud, for instance, could simply dismiss religion as an "illusion" of immature minds incapable of facing reality. Fortunately, contemporary psychiatry is more open-minded toward spiritual concerns. Important contributions have been made by transpersonal psychology, an outgrowth of humanistic psychology inaugurated by Maslow (1971), and developed in different ways by writers like Washburn (1988, 1990) and Wilbur (Wilbur et al., 1986). For example, as Washburn sees it, the Dark Night of the Soul is an essential stage in moving toward the trans-ego state. Writers who come from a more orthodox religious perspective might take a different view. They would interpret these states of consciousness in keeping with their own doctrine and symbols. But the point is that a genuine conversation between psychology and religion around late-life spirituality seems feasible and stimulating. The subject of mysticism will surely occupy a central place in that discussion.

Mystics have always understood their experience as a supreme insight into the meaning of human existence; those, like Viktor Frankl, who are concerned with late-life meaning, must take account of mystical experience, whether or not they agree with the interpretation given by the mystical traditions. Similarly, most mystics have described their consciousness in ways that point toward wisdom as an integration of thought and feeling, and wisdom remains an important emerging topic of interest in lifespan development psychology. Finally, the popularity today of New Age ideas and charismatic Christianity in America will continue to raise questions about how traditional mysticism can be understood in relation to contemporary and future religious trends.

THE RELEVANCE OF MYSTICISM FOR AGING

Taking mysticism and aging seriously would mean a very far-reaching reassessment of the possible meaning of old age. One can think of old age as a kind of "natural monastery" in which earlier roles, attachments, and pleasures are stripped away. From the monastic viewpoint, isolation is not "loneliness," nor is "disengagement" a lack of charitable concern for the world, as the career of Thomas Merton demonstrated. To think of aging in this way is very different from the celebratory revisioning of the life-course so common today as gerontologists try to remake the condition of the "young-old" into a kind of extended middle age full of vigor, sexuality, curiosity, contributive roles, and all the rest.

The mystical tradition offers a very different language and a very different ideal for the second half of life.

The mystical tradition provides the basis for a regulative ideal—a sense of purpose and meaning—for the last stage of life. The difficulties of incorporating a mystical approach to late-life meaning into present society should not, however, be underestimated. To recover that basis of meaning in postmodern culture is not easy because, in different ways, mysticism poses a challenge to both science and religion. In fact, as has been suggested here, mysticism is best thought of as a countertradition standing in opposition to both ecclesiastical authority and to the tendency of the religious life to reduce faith to the purely cognitive element ("belief"). The Western rationalistic tradition in mainstream theology has long had its countertradition in the form of mysticism, which includes not only a theory of reality but specific forms of practice that aim to transform being. Those practices are linked not just to individual ecstasy but to a tough-minded moral discipline required for self-transcendence. Here is where past traditions are crucial for guidance. Spiritual seekers today are inclined to embrace certain antitraditional aspects of mysticism while overlooking the distinctive moral preparation required in all genuine mystical paths.

For secular minds in this culture, mysticism represents a subversive countertradition in still other ways. In this civilization, elite intellectual groups typically do not believe in religion or afterlife; yet they do believe in the personal or societal future—most prominently in the ideal of progress (Lasch, 1991). At the individual level, the idea of progress is often translated into some version of "successful aging": essentially the "modernization" of old age and the rejection of traditional contemplative ideals (de Beauvoir, 1972). Modern life is characteristically teleological and purposive, always oriented to the future. But mysticism stands in contrast to contemporary ideals such as "successful aging," "productive aging," and so on. The mystical ideal helps one reimagine the "journey of life" in a very different way (Cole, 1992). Instead of trying to remake old age based on the image of youth or midlife, mysticism offers a way of glimpsing the special gifts reserved for the last stage of life. "The last years may matter the most," as Florida Scott-Maxwell (1979, 33) put it. The reason why they matter is to be found in "a degree of consciousness which lies outside activity, and which when young we are too busy to experience"—in short, the mystical experience.

Above all, taking mysticism seriously amounts to a radical revision of everything one knows or believes one knows about the world, about what "reality" finally consists of. Mysticism involves fundamental *cognitive* claims about the world. The mystics say, in effect, "Now I know." Taking mysticism seriously means accepting, at least in phenomenological terms, that mysticism is a noetic process. That is, the mystics themselves believe that they have come to know something, indeed something more important than anything else about the world. Mystical experience is not a matter of sentiment: not an "oceanic feeling" (Freud, 1989), a state of being reconciled, of having positive "object relations," (Winnicott, 1986) or even simply being at peace with others. Taking mysticism seriously would be something quite different from psychological reductionism which collapses the noetic claims of mysticism into psychological explanations of one kind or another.

Of course, taking mysticism seriously will not be persuasive or even intelligible to everyone. Those without any direct access to mystical experience can only approach the depth of these experiences by thinking in analogical terms of profound moments in their personal lives: the birth of a first child, the death of a parent, a time standing atop a mountain at sunset or listening to music when at that moment the ordinary self is forgotten or transcended. These are precisely the "peak experiences" that Abraham Maslow (1971) pointed to when seeking a definition of self-actualization. Interestingly, Maslow believed that self-actualization was more prevalent among the old than among the young, and he may have been right. The exploration of this question is one that deserves attention from those investigating religion and aging. In looking into the question, it may be that attention to mysticism can open up new ways of thinking about what spiritual growth in later life might mean.

Very old people—centenarians, for example—are often surprised or puzzled at why they have lived so long. What does it mean that they have lived so long? Still other elderly people, weighed down by suffering, experience this question of meaning as a challenge to faith: Why is God keeping me alive? In Scott-Maxwell's (1979, 32) words: "I have lived my life haven't I? What more is expected of me?" The mystical response to the condition of old age does not directly answer this question "Why survive?" so much as it offers a way of transcending the question, as the philosopher Wittgenstein suggested in the concluding passage of his *Tractatus Logico-Philosophicus*:

> To view the world *sub specie aeterni* is to view it as whole—a limited whole. Feeling the world as a limited whole—it is this that is mystical. When the answer cannot be put into words, neither can the question be put into words. . . . The solution of the problem of life is seen in the vanishing of the problem. . . . There are, indeed, things that cannot be put into words. They *make themselves manifest*. They are what is mystical. (1947, 149–51)

"The solution of the problem of life is seen in the vanishing of the problem." The traditional mystics would agree: people know more than can be said in words.

The problem of course is that the silence of mystical experience seems to preclude further investigation or perhaps even shared understanding. Is mysticism, late-life or otherwise, then just an individual option, perhaps an individual withdrawal from the claims of society? Does the mystical life have any benefit or value for old people or others in society? The mystical tradition in all faiths would insist on some wider benefit. The invisible work of contemplation has value for society, not just for the individual mystic. This intimation of intangible grace from contemplation is reminiscent of the Jewish tale of the forty righteous believers whose work is not seen in the world and whose names are known only to God. But, the tale goes on to say that if these forty righteous ones ceased to exist, the world itself would perish.

This same sentiment is shared by the Christian contemplative tradition. In the Trappist monastic practice, as in the ancient monasteries on Mount Athos, the work of the contemplative may consist entirely in perpetual prayer and remembering God, without any obvious or tangible "benefit" for worldly humanity. The presence of these contemplative souls, even in limited numbers, can be thought of as acting something like vitamins in the human body: small trace elements make the whole organism healthy in ways unrecognized in everyday life.

Is it possible, then, that contemplative prayer could be a form of "productive aging"? The meaning of productivity or helping the wider community may be much deeper and more mysterious than we know, just as the human self is deeper and more mysterious than we know. It is this deeper dimension of life that the mystics can help people to recover as they try to discover what the last stage of life may offer.

This chapter has asserted that mysticism is the deepening and intensification of the spiritual life to its utmost point. Mysticism finally is inseparable from the life of sanctity or perfection of faith: to "love the Lord your God with all your heart, and with all your soul, and with all your might" (Deut. 6:5). It is a summit of perfection symbolized by the Buddhists in the ideal of *nirvana,* by the Muslims in the ideal of complete submission (*Islam*) to God, and by the injunction of Jesus in the Gospels: "Be perfect, therefore, as your heavenly Father is perfect" (Matt. 5:48).

On a human level, this perfection or visible manifestation of grace is seen in the fulfillment of virtues: concretely, in love and compassion visible in the lives of the saints. The realized mystic, then, is not to be recognized by special states of consciousness but rather by humility and self-effacement, which is, after all, the final goal of the mystic quest. Indeed, the main characteristic of such people is quietness, inwardness, empathy and kindness toward others, and, above all, gratitude. "Gratitude is heaven itself," as William Blake put it. But the attainment of this state is not easy, as mystics the world over have always insisted. Ultimately, it is a gift, not an achievement. In T. S. Eliot's phrase it is "a condition of complete simplicity, (costing not less than everything)" (1952, 1450). And perhaps in the words of the Gospel, it is also "the one thing needful" (Luke 10:42) not only for the old but for all persons whatever their age.

BIBLIOGRAPHY

Augustine (1963) *The Confessions of St. Augustine.* Translated by Rex Warner. New York: New American Library.

Baltes, P. B., J. Smith, U. M. Staudinger, and D. Sowarka (1990) "Wisdom: One Facet of Successful Aging?" In Perlmutter, 63–81.

Bucke, R. M. (1931) *Cosmic Consciousness: A Study in the Evolution of The Human Mind.* 7th Ed. New York: E. P. Dutton.

Bunyan, J. (1987) *The Pilgrim's Progress.* London: Penguin Books.

Butler, R. N. (1963) "The Life Review: An Interpretation of Reminiscence in the Aged." *Psychiatry* 26:65–76.

Campbell, J., ed. (1971) *The Portable Jung.* New York: Viking.

Chinen, A. B. (1989) *In the Ever After: Fairy Tales and the Second Half of Life.* Wilmette, Ill.: Chiron.

Cole, T. R. (1992) *The Journey of Life: A Cultural History of Aging in America.* New York: Cambridge University Press.

Cole, T. R., David D. Van Tassel, and Robert Kastenbaum (1992) *Handbook of the Humanities and Aging.* New York: Springer.

Connolly, J. L. (1928) *Jean Gerson: Reformer and Mystic.* Louvain: Librairie Universitaire, Uystpruyst.

de Beauvoir, S. (1972) *The Coming of Age.* Translated by Patrick O'Brian. New York: Putnam.

Eckhart, M. (1924) *Meister Eckhart.* Vol. 1. Translated by B. Evans. London: Watkins.

______ (1981) *Meister Eckhart: The Essential Sermons, Commentaries, Treatises and Defense.* Translated by E. Colledge and B. McGinn. New York: Paulist Press.

Eliot, T. S. (1952) *T. S. Eliot: The Complete Poems and Plays.* New York: Harcourt, Brace and Company.

Erikson, E. H. (1963) *Childhood and Society.* 2nd rev. ed. New York: Norton.

Fremantle, A., ed. (1964) *The Protestant Mystics.* New York: New American Library.

Freud, S. (1989) *The Future of an Illusion.* Edited by J. Strachey. New York: Norton.

Hume, R. E., trans. (1949) *The Thirteen Principal Upanishads.* 2nd ed. Madras: Oxford University Press.

Huxley, A. (1945) *The Perennial Philosophy.* New York: Harper and Bros.

Inge, D. W. R. (1899) *Christian Mysticism.* Bampton Lectures. London: Methuen.

James, W. (1958) *The Varieties of Religious Experience. A Study in Human Nature.* New York: New American Library.

Jung, C. G. (1971) "The Stages of Life." In Campbell, 3–22.

Kakar, S. (1986) "The Human Life Cycle: The Traditional Hindu View and the Psychology of Erik Erikson." *Philosophy East and West* 18:127–36.

Katz, S. T., ed. (1978) *Mysticism and Philosophical Analysis.* New York: Oxford University Press.

Lasch, C. (1991) *The True and Only Heaven: Progress and Its Critics.* New York: Norton.

Loy, D. (1988) *Nonduality: A Study in Comparative Philosophy.* New Haven, Conn.: Yale University Press.

Maslow, A. H. (1971) *The Farther Reaches of Human Nature.* New York: Viking.

Moody, H. R. (1990) "The Islamic Vision of Aging and Death." *Generations* 14 (4):15–18.

Nouwen, H. J. (1986) *Reaching Out.* New York: Doubleday.

Peck, M. S. (1978) *The Road Less Traveled.* New York: Simon and Schuster.

Perlmutter, M., ed. (1990) *Late Life Potential.* Washington, D.C.: Gerontological Society of America.

Ramana Maharshi (1955) *Talks with Sri Ramana Magarshi.* 3 Vols. Edited by T.N. Venkataraman. Tiruvannamali, S. India.

Riegel, K. (1976) *The Psychology of Development and History.* New York: Plenum Press.

Rosenmayr, L. (1983) *Die Späte Freiheit: Das Alter, ein Stuck Bewusst Gelebten.* Berlin: Severin und Siedler.

St. John of the Cross (1958) *Ascent of Mount Carmel.* Translated and edited by E. Allison Peers. 3rd rev. ed. Garden City, N.Y.: Doubleday.

Scholem, G. (1961) *Major Trends in Jewish Mysticism.* New York: Schocken Books.

Scott-Maxwell, F. (1979) *The Measure of My Days.* New York: Penguin.

Sears, E. (1986) *The Ages of Man: Medieval Interpretations of the Life Cycle.* Princeton, N.J.: Princeton University Press.

Suzuki, D. T. (1971) *What is Zen?* New York: Harper & Row.

Thomas, L. E. (1991) "Dialogues with Three Religious Renunciates." *International Journal of Aging and Human Development* 32 (3):211–27.

Thomas, L. E., J. S. Brewer, P. A. Kraus, and B. L. Rosen (1991) "Two Patterns of Transcendence: An Empirical Examination of Wilbur and Washburn's Theories." Paper presented at the Annual Meeting of the American Psychological Association, San Francisco.

Thursby, G. R. (1992) "Islamic, Hindu and Buddhist Conceptions of Aging and Death." In Cole, Van Tassel, and Kastenbaum, 175–96.

Washburn, M. (1988) *The Ego and the Dynamic Ground: A Transpersonal Theory of Human Development.* Albany, N.Y.: State University of New York Press.

______ (1990) "Two Patterns of Transcendence." *Journal of Humanistic Psychology* 30 (3):84–112.

Watt, W. M. (1953) *The Faith and Practice of al-Ghazali.* London: Allen and Unwin.

Watts, A. (1953) *Myth and Ritual in Christianity.* New York: Vanguard Press.

Whitehead, A. N. (1960) *Religion in the Making.* New York: Meridian.

Wilbur, K., J. Engler, and D. P. Brown (1986) *Transformations of Consciousness: Conventional and Contemplative Perspectives on Development.* Boston: Shambhala.

Winnicott, D. W. (1986) *Home Is Where We Start From: Essays in Psychoanalysis.* New York: Norton

Wittgenstein, L. (1947) *Tractatus Logico-Philosophicus.* London: K. Paul, Trench, Tubner.

Zaehner, R. C. (1957) *Mysticism, Sacred and Profane: An Inquiry into some Varieties of Praeter-natural Experience.* Oxford: Clarendon Press.

7 The Development of Wisdom

FREDDA BLANCHARD-FIELDS
LISA NORRIS

Recently the popular literature has become increasingly concerned with self-development and the inner personal journey toward health and wholeness (e.g., Keen, 1991; Murdock, 1990). This has resulted in a number of books affirming the difficult yet fulfilling process of self-growth. This process is difficult in the sense that it can be extremely painful with "no recognizable guideposts nor recognizable tour guides . . . [and] seldom receives validation from the outside world" (Murdock, 1990). The lack of social validation is particularly evident in the psychiatric community's tendency to pathologize this process and characterize the pain involved in growth as a "disorder." For example, the description of an "identity disorder" in the DSM III-R Manual (American Psychiatric Association, 1987) is almost completely identical to what others describe as a quest for meaning in life or the inner journey toward wholeness with its uncertainty, painful self-consciousness, and loneliness (for example, see Keen, 1991).

This interest in issues of self-development has also been the focus of a number of current theories of adult development in the scientific discipline of psychology. In particular, there has been a growing interest in the area of wisdom. Similar to these popular writers, some theorists have examined the development of wisdom as related to and perhaps even a vehicle of the process of integrating the divided self (e.g., Chinen, 1989; Jung, 1933; Kramer, 1990; Labouvie-Vief, 1990). However, they have also noted that this is not a common occurrence among growing and aging adults. Before examining why this is so, we will first discuss selected attempts by psychological researchers to conceptualize wisdom and related empirical findings. Next, we will focus on a particular conceptualization of wisdom: the balance between emotion and cognition which is related to the "journey within" and the difficulty individuals have on this pathway of self-integration. In this case, both the scientific psychological literature and recent popular writings on this topic will be examined. Finally, the issue of wisdom and spirituality will be addressed as a critical component of the integrated adult and wisdom.

CONCEPTUALIZATIONS OF WISDOM

Although the concept of wisdom is an ancient one (wisdom was reported in Egyptian hieroglyphics written soon after 3000 B.C.; cf. Birren and Fisher, 1990), for a long period of time this topic was neglected as psychology began to define itself as a scientific discipline. The long-standing association among wisdom and philosophy and theology, as well as its "mentalistic" qualities, were deemed incompatible with scientific investigation by the behaviorist school of thought, which dominated psychological views during the mid-twentieth century. However, with current interest in research on the positive aspects of aging in adult cognition, this elusive concept has recently enjoyed a rebirth.

One of the earliest papers to emerge during this rebirth is Clayton's (1975) attempt to operationalize the concept of wisdom. She views wisdom as a construct that describes a way of thinking and places it in the domain of the interpersonal (Clayton, 1982). Accordingly, wisdom involves the ability both to make and to accept compromise when confronting difficult, real-world problems concerning human nature (i.e., social, interpersonal, and intrapersonal problems). Clayton differentiates the concept of wisdom from intelligence by describing it as the ability to deal with the paradoxes, changes, and contradictions encountered in social situations, and asserts that wisdom focuses on the solution of societal problems in the face of uncertainty.

Similarly, Meacham (1983, 1990) views wisdom not as an accumulation of facts or abilities, but as an attitude about knowledge, the manner in which this knowledge is applied, and the ability to evaluate the veracity and limitations of this knowledge. In this case, the wise person accumulates information while at the same time being aware of her or his limitations in knowing. Two extremes may arise from an imbalance between knowing and not knowing. First, overconfidence in the knowledge one possesses may result in closed-mindedness, rigidity, and a lack of curiosity. Second, extreme insecurity (i.e., doubt) about what one knows will likely lead to feeling cautious and uncertain in acting. The wise individual has reached a balance between "knowing" and "doubting"; the actual amount of information is of secondary importance.

Meacham (1990) further suggests that all people are wise to begin with, but most lose wisdom as they age. As one accumulates knowledge, success, and power, it is easier to move away from the balance between knowing and doubting. One may develop overconfidence in knowing through the age-related accumulation of power, information, etc., or when immersed in an intellectual climate that discourages open-mindedness and encourages stereotyping and intolerance. Conversely, rapid cultural and technological changes or major tragedies may shake one's confidence, propelling one toward the doubting extreme. Meacham asserts that supportive interpersonal relations, in which individuals feel free to express doubts and uncertainties, are necessary in the maintenance of wisdom. Therefore, the goal of wisdom is to construct new uncertainties, doubts, and questions as one accumulates information, and this is fostered in a supportive, nonjudgmental environment. Given that wise individuals have a greater insight into the limitations of knowing, Meacham (1983) feels that they will be proficient at asking questions. This ability to construct uncertainties, doubts, and questions (i.e., moving beyond the problem at hand) is also discussed extensively in Arlin's (1990) conceptualization of wisdom.

While Arlin (1990) and Meacham (1983) emphasize problem expansion in wise individuals, Kitchener and Brenner's (1990) Reflective Judgment model defines wisdom as the ability to make good judgments and decisions when faced with uncertain life problems. In this case, the wise individual possesses a large store of information (e.g., expertise) as well as the awareness of the limits of human knowing. The Reflective Judgment model outlines a stage development of seven forms of epistemic cognition concerning one's assumptions of what can and cannot be known, how one knows, and one's certainty in his or her knowing. Early stages (stages 1–3) are irrelevant to the understanding of wisdom as individuals in these stages deny the existence of real uncertainty. What makes stage 7 most likely to foster wisdom is that not only does one acknowledge the uncertainty of knowing, but one also acknowledges the uncertainty of knowledge in general and considers and synthesizes many perspectives. Whereas a wise person understands that his or her judgments may not be the final answer, he or she recognizes that the best solution available must be chosen. In other words, the wise person is not caught up in the multiplicity of perspectives where commitment to one point of view is impossible given that there is no absolute right or wrong. Instead, the wise person has learned the necessity to make commitments within relativism (Perry, 1970).

Kitchener and Brenner (1990) administered the Reflective Judgment Interview in the context of four problem situations to individuals of varying age and educational levels. Older more highly educated participants scored at higher levels. In addition, adults at stage seven were rare prior to age thirty, which suggests that more wisdom-related responses occur in the latter half of adulthood.

Overall, past research on wisdom has been characterized by sporadic attempts at theoretical speculation on what constitutes wisdom (e.g., Clayton, 1982; Meacham, 1990) and isolated empirical studies that reflect agreed-upon components of wisdom, i.e., problem finding or reflective judgment. One of the few systematic attempts to develop a program expressly to study wisdom is reflected in the work of Baltes and his colleagues, who have developed a comprehensive model of wisdom (e.g., Baltes and Smith, 1990; Baltes et al., 1984; Staudinger et al., 1992). Their model incorporates many of the previously discussed components, with an emphasis on the expertise and use of an individual's knowledge systems in the fundamental pragmatics of life. Additionally, they indicate that wisdom is multidimensional in nature and implemented in the resolution of ill-defined interpersonal problems.

Within this framework, five wisdom-related criteria have been proposed: rich factual knowledge about fundamental life pragmatics; rich procedural knowledge about fundamental life pragmatics (i.e., strategies for decision making and action planning); knowledge about the differing contexts of life (e.g., timing of child-rearing, change in women's roles, financial situation, etc.); knowledge about cultural and individual differences in values, goals, and priorities; and recognition of as well as strategies to deal with the uncertainties in life (Baltes and Smith, 1990).

In a number of empirical studies assessing these wisdom-related criteria, Baltes and his colleagues found that adults' "wise" responses to life-planning and life-review problems did not differ across age (Smith and Baltes, 1990; Baltes et al., 1990). They concluded that wisdom-related knowledge may better reflect individual and specific life experiences. However, older and middle-aged adults did display greater "awareness of uncertainty" (Baltes et al., 1990).

The research reviewed thus far suggests that wisdom is most evident in the interpersonal/social domain and it involves the recognition of uncertainty in life situations, the ability to make good judgments and/or give good advice, and the ability to take relativistic perspectives in reasoning. The translation of these qualities of wisdom into an empirical framework has focused on knowledge, knowing, and doubting knowledge. However, as noted by a number of these researchers, wisdom is multidimensional. Thus, it is important to recognize that wisdom is not simply one aspect of knowledge, but knowledge is only one aspect of wisdom.

This "expert" knowledge system approach has been fruitful in initial investigations of wisdom. It is the component of wisdom that is most easily operationalized empirically, given the current principles, methodology, and technology of cognitive psychology, specifically "knowledge in expert systems" research. When psychology was in its infancy, it struggled to become a legitimate scientific discipline by borrowing from already established scientific techniques in the physical sciences. Similarly, wisdom has been legitimatized in the science of psychology by operationalizing it into a knowledge system framework, i.e., borrowing from an established scientific approach. Although much empirical work has been generated from this approach, the limits of wisdom as acquired knowledge about the human condition have not been tested. It is now time empirically as well as theoretically to move beyond the limits of focusing on the knowledge component of wisdom. Other aspects merit closer attention.

The theorists reviewed above note the importance of wisdom in the domain of interpersonal relations (e.g., Baltes and Smith, 1990; Clayton and Birren, 1980; Clayton, 1982; Meacham, 1990), and/or the importance of understanding the emotions of individuals in the context of wisdom (Baltes and Smith, 1990). Although several of these positions have emphatically made the point that emotion is involved with wisdom, they fail to elaborate on or demonstrate the role emotion plays in wisdom. The following section will discuss recent positions that have incorporated the interface between cognition and emotion into the conceptualization of wisdom and related empirical work.

THE INTEGRATION OF EMOTION AND COGNITION

Awareness of the uncertainty or the limitations of our knowledge has been offered as an important aspect of wisdom. Researchers have demonstrated that the wise person recognizes and effectively manages uncertainty in a problem context (Baltes and Smith, 1990) or has the sensibility to admit not knowing (Meacham, 1983, 1990). The "management of uncertainty" has been described as the ability to estimate the occurrence of events; to give advice regarding the risk of success or failure of uncertain decisions; or, since what can be known will always exceed what one knows, to realize that knowledge must be constructed through synthesizing opposing views. In other words, past research has focused on the outcome of decisions made in the face of uncertainty. Such successful outcomes involve objective judgment that takes into consideration the inherent subjectivity of an interpersonal situation. The focus is on synthesizing multiple perspectives with cognitive processes seen as of primary importance. Although these researchers do not claim that affective processes are not involved in wisdom, they do not examine affect as a basis for making wise judgments. This is similar to the judge in the courtroom who must make a dispassionate, "objective" ruling although still retaining her empathy for the individuals involved.

Some cognitive psychologists have openly questioned whether emotion can be separated from cognition, either theoretically or empirically, and have instead represented emotion as an important influence on cognition in the laboratory and in everyday life (e.g., Lazarus, 1984; Zajonc, 1984; Buck, 1985). In the psychological study of wisdom, the primary importance of an interface between emotion and cognition has only recently surfaced (e.g., Blanchard-Fields et al., 1987; Kramer, 1990; Labouvie-Vief, 1990). Affect is viewed as playing a critical role in wisdom, for it contributes to the ability to recognize subjective biases in thinking and feeling so that the artificial polarity created between them can be transcended. In other words, emotional regulation in the face of uncertainty is seen as central to wisdom.

Although related, this notion of emotional regulation is different from the "management of uncertainty" described above. Here, the individual attains a balance between emotion and cognition and can simultaneously embrace both. Thus, emotions are not set aside or repressed in order to make a "rational" decision. Instead, both analytic processes and emotional experience are equally weighted in importance in the process of decision-making, judgment, advice-giving, problem-solving, and in the search for meaning and purpose in life.

This integrative perspective on wisdom has been elegantly presented in the theoretical and empirical work of Gisela Labouvie-Vief (1990). She takes a life-span developmental perspective in assertions that self- and emotional regulation continue to develop through adulthood and aging. In particular, she and her colleagues (Labouvie-Vief et al., 1989a; Labouvie-Vief et al., 1989b) have examined adult age differences in the developmental complexity of emotional understanding. As an extension of cognitive development beyond adolescence, Labouvie-Vief (1990) contends that there is a dissociation between context-sensitive, personal, and organismic systems (e.g., affect/emotion), and stable, abstract, and impersonal systems (e.g., cognition or the "rational" self) which continues into adulthood. The childhood socialization process has resulted in the "emotional" self being hierarchically subordinated under the "rational" self. In other words, it is more "valid and acceptable" in our society to be rational and objective than emotional or "irrational." She further proposes that a major achievement of mature adulthood (i.e., wisdom) is the integration of these systems, when the individual experiences them as lateral or equal in importance rather than hierarchically organized. For example, a person comes to recognize that concrete sensations and feelings interact with rather than are subordinate to the logical, rational, abstract mind in producing more mature and flexible coping.

The reintegration of emotion and cognition in later adulthood also fits nicely into a framework incorporating the long-standing ontogenetic view that development proceeds from a state of global organization to differentiation, finally evolving into a state of hierarchic integration (Werner, 1957). Thus, development is characterized by a dialectical synthesis of two opposing processes, differentiation and integration. An example of this process is found in biology. Cellular development in utero begins with an oversupply of cells that are unspecialized and nonfunctioning, i.e., a state of globality. As development progresses, a process of selective depletion takes place. Certain cells begin to differentiate or specialize while excess cells are eliminated. However, the process does not end with cellular specialization. In order for the organism to function effectively, these specialized cells must be integrated into a functioning system; thus, hierarchic integration occurs.

Analogously, the affective and cognitive systems go through a process of differentiation as a function of childhood socialization. This process of dissociation and devaluing of the emotional self is important in early development, permitting the individual to categorize (i.e., differentiate) experience in a stable and reliable manner (e.g., Labouvie-Vief, 1990). There is evidence to suggest that later on in adulthood the urgency to integrate these systems is more likely to emerge (Blanchard-Fields, 1986; Labouvie-Vief, 1990; Neugarten, 1968; Pascual-Leon, 1990). It may be that at this point in development the individual is ready for this interface, because as noted in the very beginning of this chapter, it may involve the painful journey of confronting one's own emotions and stories about the self. Perhaps this can be reframed in terms of a developmental task or milestone, for it is in middle age and older adulthood that individuals are more prone to reflect inward and confront the personal meaning of life (Erikson, 1978b; Neugarten, 1968). It should also be noted that this does not mean that there is no interplay between differentiation and integration or emotion and cognition in childhood and adolescence. The human life cycle is characterized by their continual interplay. It may be more a distinction between conscious and nonconscious awareness of the interplay between cognition and emotion in adulthood and childhood, respectively.

As the young adult matures, she realizes that resolution of uncertainty or crises based on an imbalanced interpretation often gives rise to further crises. If emotional reactions to a situation are suppressed or repressed, to our own chagrin, they have a way of reemerging into a new yet familiar crisis. When the adult reaches the point of urgency to confront these crises, it can lead to a process of integration or growth in consciousness resulting in a harmonized and balanced construction of reality that can be characteristic of the second half of the life span. For example, the divorcee who suppresses her feelings of anger and fear of abandonment regarding the breakdown of her marriage plunges her energy into building a successful career. However, five, ten, maybe fifteen years later, life has a way of once again presenting a situation where fear of abandonment resurfaces in a new relationship, offering a new chance to resolve these repressed but burning issues.

It is at this point that the individual has the opportunity to become aware of the societally-imposed polarization of emotion and cognition and can transcend it through conscious integration of the self. Resolving uncertainty is no longer seen as the primary motivation. Instead, there is an increased tolerance for uncertainty and a deepening in the search for meaning and purpose in life. Awareness of the paradoxical and contradictory nature of reality facilitates transcendence needed to embrace the uncertainty. It is this self-guided search through the expansion of consciousness that provides the interface between current thinking in adult developmental research and current writings on spirituality and the "journey within." To understand this, it is necessary to explore the questions empirical researchers have asked with respect to this developmental journey and then examine their research attempts to answer these questions.

What is the nature of the interface between emotion and cognition as defined by empirical researchers who come from an adult developmental and aging perspective? Most of research in this area has focused on a number of areas of functional significance in everyday living, including everyday problem-solving, social judgment, coping with stress, and everyday decision-making.

In several recent studies, Blanchard-Fields (1994; Blanchard-Fields and Norris, 1994) examined the qualitatively different ways that adolescents, young adults, middle-aged adults, and older adults construe what caused certain event sequences to occur. In this case, participants were presented with event sequences that represented interpersonal dilemmas as well as achievement situations. Event dilemmas varied in the degree to which factors that caused the situation were clearly presented or ambiguous. After reading each event sequence, participants were asked to rate the degree to which the primary character was responsible for the outcome, other situational factors were responsible for the outcome, and both the primary character and situational factors were jointly responsible for the outcome (1994). In a subsequent study (Blanchard-Fields and Norris, 1994), in addition to these ratings, participants were asked to provide their reasoning behind each of the ratings in essay form. Both studies demonstrated that adolescents were consistently lower in their ability to coordinate multiple perspectives, especially in emotionally laden and ambiguous social dilemmas, as compared to middle-aged and older adults.

Other researchers as well have suggested that with adulthood comes an integration and consistency in reasoning across cognitive and affective domains. These studies suggest that the coordination of cognition and affect represents a critical element for further progression in adult development. For example, Kramer, Goldston, and Kahlbaugh (1989) demonstrate that older adults with high emotional intensity demonstrate more mature dialectical thinking. Both my own research (Blanchard-Fields and Irion, 1988) and that of Labouvie-Vief et al. (1989a, 1989b) have demonstrated that higher levels of emotional regulation and openness to affective experience relate to more mature coping mechanisms and social cognitive reasoning. Lawton and Albert (1990) also have demonstrated that older adults are more effective in regulating their emotions. They suggest that there are qualitative changes in the way the individual perceives and structures everyday problems, as well as increased efficacy in regulating affective responses with increasing age.

In another study, Blanchard-Fields and Camp (1990) assessed the relationship between emotional saliency and qualitatively different styles of everyday problem-solving. Participants were presented with twenty-four problem situations reflecting consumer problems (e.g., returning merchandise), home management problems, and family/friend issues. They rated the degree to which they would use the following problem-solving strategies in each of these situations: planful problem-solving (i.e., very instrumental and directly confronting the situation), cognitive analysis (i.e., cognitively appraising the situation), passive-dependent (i.e., accepting the situation, and not attempting to change it), and avoidance/escape (i.e., actively removing oneself from the situation). They found that low emotionally salient problems (e.g., consumer situations) yielded no age differences in problem-solving style, whereas high emotionally salient problems produced increased variability in responding between older adults. In high emotionally salient problem domains (e.g., family and relationship issues), older adults displayed an awareness of when to "avoid," "passively" accept, or use more instrumental modes of responding in a situation that cannot be controlled. Younger adults opted more for a problem-focused or cognitive analytical approach to all problems.

It is interesting to note that past conceptualizations of effective problem-solving have promoted direct, planful problem-solving as the strategy of choice. Again, this corresponds to our societally-imposed values that cognitive-analytical and instrumental modes of functioning are highly rational and favorable. From this perspective, the Blanchard-Fields and Camp (1990) results could be interpreted as evidence for older adults' adherence to "less effective" strategies such as passive-dependence and avoidance. However, from the perspective of equal importance of cognitive and emotional strategies, older adults can be seen as having a larger repertoire of problem-solving strategies to draw upon as well as the "wisdom" to know in which context each strategy would be most effective.

The latter interpretation is further supported in a study conducted by Blanchard-Fields and Irion (1988). In assessing the extent to which they were responsible for a personal stressful situation, older adults rated themselves as responsible for the cause of the stressor whereas younger adults were more likely to rate themselves as responsible for the outcome of the stressor. In addition, the young adults blamed themselves for the stressful outcome and consequently were more likely to avoid or become hostile with respect to coping with the stressful event. Older adults tended to perceive the source of stress as located in the self which, alternatively, caused them consciously to reflect upon and reappraise the situation. Older adults were more likely to achieve control over the situation through "lack of instrumental control," self-reflection, and acceptance.

Labouvie-Vief and her colleagues have also found evidence for this developmental progression in terms of (a) emotional regulation and (b) the relationship between emotional understanding and coping. Where the language of self-regulation in youth is focused on conscious control of the outer world (e.g., the need for confirmation in more powerful, external authority), older adults exhibit a "richer language of self-regulation" integrating inner expression with outer presentation (Labouvie-Vief et al., 1989a). In addition, older adults exhibit increasing levels of complex emotional understanding. In turn, greater emotional understanding predicts more mature and efficacious coping strategies (Labouvie-Vief et al., 1989b).

What has been learned from these empirical studies with respect to the interface between emotion and cognition? They suggest that emotional regulation plays a critical role in effective functioning in particular and wisdom in general. The "balanced" individual (a) is open to affective experience without judgment and the need for certainty, (b) exhibits a reflective understanding of personal emotional reactions, and (c) is able to look inward for guidance, rather than resort to societally-prescribed external regulation. This research also suggests the need for more research on the dynamic interaction between emotion and cognition in order to understand effective functioning as well as the "wise" adult.

These studies on everyday problem-solving and coping have only begun to demonstrate the ways in which individuals represent and take account of emotions of self and others involved in these problems. There is a need to move beyond the simple manipulation of emotional tasks in order to assess emotional "understanding" of the individual towards a more experiential, process-oriented approach to the study of the emotion-cognition interface. In other words, more research is needed examining the individual's phenomenological experience of emotion in the context of wisdom.

Another literature in adult development that has focused more on these issues is personality change in adulthood. Without going into too much detail in this vast area of research, some pertinent theoretical perspectives and findings will be reviewed that relate directly to recent popular writings in this area.

PERSONALITY CHANGE IN ADULTHOOD AND THE JOURNEY WITHIN

A number of theorists have focused on the development of self in adulthood as a function of personality change (i.e., growth in consciousness and awareness) rather than as the development of effective functioning, such as coping and problem-solving (Erikson, 1978; Jung, 1933; Loevinger, 1976). Orwoll and Perlmutter (1990) feel that the personality component of wisdom is exemplified in theories such as those of Erikson and Jung. Erikson views wisdom-related personality growth in older adulthood as associated with virtue: accepting life as it was lived, positively adapting to physical deterioration and impending death, and relinquishing leadership to the future (Orwoll and Perlmutter, 1990). Jung sees wisdom-related growth as confronting progressively deeper aspects of the self: accessing the personal unconscious, integrating the dark side of the self, and balancing opposing forces such as inner and outer reality, good and evil, male and female (Orwoll and Perlmutter, 1990). Orwoll and Perlmutter conclude that advanced personality development yields individuals who experience their affect in undefended and open ways, fostering self-awareness. As discussed earlier, this self-insight is facilitated by the synthesis of affective clarity and cognitive complexity.

Recent research has explored the relationship between personality factors and wisdom-related responses. For example, Maciel et al. (1991) found that wisdom (defined in terms of the responses reported above in the Baltes et al. studies) was related to openness to challenging experiences throughout the lifespan. Similarly, Kramer et al. (1989) indicate that an important task for later-life development may be to maintain a degree of openness to affective experience, which requires the discarding of immature defense mechanisms.

In contrast to this emphasis on late-life openness to affect, some research reports quantitative loss or decline (e.g., reduction in affect intensity or diminution of emotional resources) in older adulthood (eg., Diener, Sandvik, and Larsen, 1985). However, these deficit and compensatory views of affect neglect to address the issue of the universality of such changes across individuals and within individuals across contexts as well as the ways in which emotion may change qualitatively and adaptively across the lifespan. What appears to be a deficit in affect intensity or emotional resources may instead represent effective self-regulation, without precluding the possibility of intense emotional responses under specific conditions. Thus, the inward turn that aging brings—the return to one's organic basis in the body and the letting go of the need to seek societal approval—may be mistaken for emotional disengagement from society. Instead, it may represent a heightened sensitivity and intensity to one's own emotional self. This type of growth cannot be assessed in terms of "how many" relationships an individual is engaged in or a global personality scale of affect intensity, but in the quality and honesty the individual has acquired in relationship to the self.

A number of recent popular writings in both women's and men's development have also discussed this "journey within" towards an integrated and whole self. The "wise" message of this journey that is common to most of these writings is the importance of resolving the great polarities of life by "living the moment." This is elegantly expressed by June Singer (1989) who writes:

> A wise person once said that the goal of the masculine principle is perfection and the goal of the feminine principle is completion. If you are perfect, you cannot be complete, because you must leave out all the imperfections of your nature. If you are complete, you cannot be perfect, for being complete means that you contain good and evil, right and wrong, hope and despair. So perhaps it is best to be content with something less than perfection and something less than completion. Perhaps we need to be more willing to accept life as it comes. (32)

These polarities can be resolved by embracing the possibility of being perfectly perfect in imperfection. However, "accepting life as it comes" is not the entire story. The message moves beyond accepting the moment to embracing the total experience of the moment—the pain as well as the joy. Murdock (1990) calls this mindful suffering and return. Instead of blaming others for pain, people can be with the suffering and heal naturally. To be with the pain, or whatever emotion is felt, allows movement through it and prevents aborting the process. In this way, people can become whole (Murdock, 1990). Thus, we again come full circle in this chapter, reframing the descent into pain in terms of "positive disintegration" in service of further growth and wholeness.

Wholeness or unity as wisdom is echoed in Hermann Hesse's classic novel *Siddhartha* (1951). Siddhartha's mentor in the meaning of life leaves him, having fulfilled his mission. At this point Siddhartha's wound heals and the pain flows from his being, his self merged into unity. Hesse writes:

> From that hour Siddhartha ceased to fight against his destiny. There shone in his face the serenity of knowledge, of one who is no longer confronted with conflict of desires, who has found salvation, who is in harmony with the stream of events, with the stream of life, full of sympathy and compassion, surrendering himself to the stream, belonging to the unity of all things. (136)

However, the paradox of this "knowledge" acquisition is illuminated when Siddhartha's lifelong friend, Govinda, implores Siddhartha to reveal this knowledge of life that he has acquired. Siddhartha replies:

> Yes, I have had thoughts and knowledge here and there. Sometimes, for an hour or for a day, I have become aware of knowledge, just as one feels life in one's heart. I have had many thoughts, but it would be difficult for me to tell you about them. But this is one thought that has impressed me, Govinda. Wisdom is not communicable. The wisdom which a wise man tries to communicate always sounds foolish. . . . Knowledge can be communicated, but not wisdom. One can find it, live it, be fortified by it, do wonders through it, but one cannot communicate and teach it. (142)

Again, it is through living the moment, surrendering to oneself without judgment, letting go of the inner critic that wisdom may be achieved. This is reflected in Siddhartha's proclamation that "everything is necessary, everything needs only my agreement, my assent, my loving understanding; then all is well with me and nothing can harm me" (144).

The lesson of wisdom from Siddhartha is learning by being. Wisdom is seen as incommunicable and cannot be completely achieved in that it is a process. It is through the experiential mode of existence and not via society's "wise one" teachings that this seasoning occurs. Lessons can be taught, to a certain degree, by those who impart knowledge and direction. This has led to a proliferation of self-help books proffering self-affirmation, including books on the women's or men's movement and codependency, among others. However, at best, such books and related teachings and therapies serve to stimulate the journey, not complete it. Indeed, there is always the danger that external teachers and guides may foster dependency. In this case, the individual relies on the "teacher" for self-growth. Instead, the responsibility for self-growth comes from within the individual, which, again, can be seen as a major task in the second half of the lifespan. This is substantiated in the move from external to internal regulation in older adulthood demonstrated in empirical studies of cognitive-emotional understanding.

This journey inward—this move toward internal regulation and wisdom—consists of an important component illuminated in the more popular writings, yet still lacking in the scientific investigation of wisdom: spirituality. Spiritual growth is intertwined with self-development, the growth of wisdom and the journey inward.

A CONCLUSION, NOT AN ENDING: SPIRITUAL GROWTH AND WISDOM

In each of the areas of wisdom discussed throughout this chapter a consistent theme emerges: the personal quest for meaning of life or finding meaning and purpose in life in order to become whole. The developmental psychology literature suggests that genuinely to encounter these existential questions one must reclaim the emotional self so that both emotion and cognition are seen as valid and important in problem-solving and daily living. This same observation appears in the philosophical and spiritual literature. However, the spiritual nature of the development of wisdom has received little attention in the scientific psychological literature (see Kramer, 1990 as well). Psychologists, in general, are hesitant to embrace the notion of spirituality. This may be partly because spirituality not only represents the developing emotional and cognitive self, but also the transpersonal self.

Regardless of the reluctance of research psychologists to study the transpersonal component of spirituality, a common ground already exists in the two literatures, i.e., in the interpersonal domain regarding issues of intimacy, finding meaning and purpose in everyday experience. Both literatures discuss the journey into the self, guiding and nurturing one's spiritual consciousness. The developmental move from the unconscious and passive role the emotional self plays earlier in the lifespan (i.e., external regulation) to the development of emotional awareness through self-reflection and consciousness in the latter half of the lifespan (i.e., internal regulation), is a spiritual pathway. Thus, the process described throughout this chapter under the label of wisdom and adult development is essentially a spiritual process. Both adult developmental and spiritual orientations agree that individuals are struggling with the process of becoming whole, of transforming a fragmented self into a balanced and harmonized being.

The role of religion has been to guide and nurture this developmental process, ultimately to transform human consciousness into a self-oriented spiritual consciousness. However, some religious figures suggest that organized religion runs the danger of becoming another societally-prescribed, external regulation authority. Perhaps, there should be more reliance on the self, in addition to authorities from organized religion, in this journey. This, indeed, corresponds more to the original goal of world religions. For example, Matthew Fox (1990) proclaims that the spiritual pathway is an awakening to the consciousness of the intrinsic divinity in all things and that spiritual poverty is a result of being dissociated from one's own divinity. He also laments that individuals are kept out of touch with their inner selves through addictions to drugs, alcohol, television, shopping, religion, work, etc. Fox depicts the need to become aware of the mystical natures or the divine element inside all persons. Again, this echoes the adult developmentalists and investigators of wisdom in their characterization of adult development and aging.

The common problem that keeps reappearing in this prototype of healthy adult and spiritual development is that a sizeable portion of the population does not necessarily exhibit these qualities. As noted earlier in this chapter, a consistent finding is that the majority of middle-aged and older adults do not necessarily display wisdom-related responses nor manifest a healthy integration of emotion and cognition or between their feminine and masculine selves. Popular writers have lamented the basic tendency in society to deny such personal and/or spiritual development in adulthood, leaving many individuals separated from and out of harmony with their true self. Many individuals, therefore, have adapted to the world by means of societally-imposed certainties. They do this because of how they have been socialized.

Socialization teaches people to value the masculine, instrumental, agentic mode of functioning as echoed in the old adage, "A man is his works." This product-oriented society measures an individual by her or his accomplishments in life to the neglect of embracing the process of living. However, this perspective is changing. As Keen (1991) suggests, today's overdeveloped societies contrasted with underdeveloped nations at the beginning of industrialization have encouraged great numbers of individuals to become more reflective about values and visions by which they are living. "We have entered a time of great turmoil and creativity; the 'normal' majority is becoming increasingly reactionary in an effort to conserve the values of a passing era, and the hero's path is becoming crowded with individuals looking for a way into a more hopeful future" (Keen, 1991, 126). This is particularly illuminated in the recent book by Gloria Steinem, *Revolution from Within*. A staunch leader of the feminist movement, she takes the needed step beyond advocating an all-encompassing "masculine" or instrumental/aggressive mode of adaptive functioning for both females and males and, now, urges all persons to have the courage to take the journey into self-enlightenment. In other words, we need to reclaim the feminine, our emotional selves.

And so, there are several lessons for psychologists attempting to study and conceptualize wisdom. First, they need to be careful in interpreting deficits in older adult functioning, for they may be overlooking a stylistic difference that reveals much wisdom. Recall that what may look like withdrawal in older adults, i.e., decreased emotional intensity, may actually represent increased sensitivity to one's own emotional self, or what may look like passive acceptance of problems may be an understanding of when passivity as opposed to instrumentality is effective.

Second, philosophers and psychologists have specified awareness of uncertainty as well as tolerance for uncertainty as important components of wisdom. Scientific psychology has translated these philosophical components of wisdom into research. Perhaps it is time to take a lesson from writers of a nonempirical nature and embrace the affective components. In the words of Rainer Maria Rilke (Mitchell translation, 1984), it may be time to "live the questions." Wisdom, in this sense, is living the uncertainty and celebrating it.

BIBLIOGRAPHY

American Psychiatric Association Staff (1987) *Diagnostic and Statistical Manual of Mental Disorders.* (3rd ed., rev.). Washington, D.C.: American Psychiatric Association.

Arlin, P. K. (1990) "Wisdom: The Art of Problem Finding." In Sternberg, 230–43.

Baltes, P. B., and O. G. Brim, Jr., eds. (1984) *Life-Span Development and Behavior.* New York: Academic Press.

Baltes, P. B., F. Dittmann-Kohli, and R. A. Dixon (1984) "New Perspectives on the Development of Intelligence in Adulthood: Toward a Dual-Process Conception and a Model of Selective Optimization with Compensation." In Baltes and Brim, 6:33–76.

Baltes, P. B., and J. Smith (1990) "Toward a Psychology of Wisdom and Its Ontogenesis." In Sternberg, 87–120.

Baltes, P. B., J. Smith, U. M. Staudinger, and D. Sowarka (1990) "Wisdom: One Facet of Successful Aging?" In Perlmutter, 63–81.

Birren, J. E., and L. M. Fisher (1990) "The Elements of Wisdom: Overview and Integration." In Sternberg, 317–32.

Blanchard-Fields, F. (1986) "Reasoning on Social Dilemmas Varying in Emotional Saliency: An Adult Developmental Perspective." *Psychology and Aging* 1:325–33.

______ (1994) "Age Differences in Causal Attributions from an Adult Developmental Perspective." *Journal of Gerontology: Psychological Sciences* 49:43–51.

Blanchard-Fields, F., J. R. Brannan, and C. J. Camp (1987) "Alternative Conceptions of Wisdom: An Onion-Peeling Exercise." *Educational Gerontology* 13:497–503.

Blanchard-Fields, F., and C. Camp (1990) "Affect, Individual Differences, and Real World Problem Solving Across the Adult Life Span." In Hess, 462–97.

Blanchard-Fields, F., and J. C. Irion (1988) "Coping Strategies from the Perspective of Two Developmental Markers: Age and Social Reasoning." *Journal of Genetic Psychology* 149:141–51.

Blanchard-Fields, F., and L. Norris (1994) "Causal Attributions from Adolescence through Adulthood: Age Differences, Ego Level, and Generalized Response Style." *Aging and Cognition* 1:67–86.

Buck, R. (1985) "Prime Theory: An Integrated View of Motivation and Emotion." *Psychological Review* 92:389–413.

Chinen, A. B. (1989) *In the Ever After: Fairy Tales and the Second Half of Life.* Wilmette, Ill.: Chiron.

Clayton, V. P. (1975) "The Meaning of Wisdom to Young and Old in Contemporary Society." Paper presented at the meetings of the Gerontological Society, Louisville, Ky.

______ (1982) "Wisdom and Intelligence: The Nature and Function of Knowledge in the Later Years." *International Journal of Aging and Human Development* 2:315–21.

Clayton, V. P., and J. W. Birren (1980) "The Development of Wisdom Across the Life Span: A Reexamination of an Ancient Topic." In Baltes and Brim, 3:103–35.

Diener, E., E. Sandvik, and R. J. Larsen (1985) "Age and Sex Effects for Emotional Intensity." *Developmental Psychology* 21:542–46.

Erikson, E., ed. (1978a) *Adulthood*. New York: Norton.

Erikson, E. H. (1978b) "Reflections on Dr. Borg's Life Cycle." In Erikson, 1–32.

Fox, M. (1990) "Toward a Spiritual Renaissance." *Common Boundary* July/August: 14–20.

Harris, D. B., ed. (1957) *The Concept of Development*. Minneapolis, Minn.: University of Minnesota Press.

Hess, T. M. (1990) *Aging and Cognition: Knowledge Organization and Utilization*. New York: North-Holland.

Hesse, H. (1951) *Siddhartha*. New York: Bantam.

Jung, C. G. (1933) *Modern Man in Search of a Soul*. New York: Harcourt, Brace and World.

Keen, S. (1991) *Fire in the Belly*. New York: Bantam.

Kitchener, K. S., and H. G. Brenner (1990) "Wisdom and Reflective Judgment." In Sternberg, 212–29.

Kramer, D. A. (1990) "Conceptualizing Wisdom: The Primacy of Affect-Cognition Relations." In Sternberg, 279–313.

Kramer, D. A., R. B. Goldston, and P. E. Kahlbaugh (1989) "Age, Affect Intensity, and Dialectical Beliefs." Unpublished manuscript.

Kuhn, D., and J. A. Meacham, eds. (1983) *On the Development of Developmental Psychology*. Basel, Switzerland: Karger.

Labouvie-Vief, G. (1990) "Wisdom as Integrated Thought: Historical and Developmental Perspectives." In Sternberg, 52–83.

Labouvie-Vief, G., M. DeVoe, and D. Bulka (1989a) "Speaking about Feelings: Conceptions of Emotion Across the Life Span." *Human Development* 32:279–99.

Labouvie-Vief, G., J. Hakim-Larson, M. DeVoe, and S. Schoeberlein (1989b) "Emotions and Self-Regulation: A Life Span View." *Psychology and Aging* 2:286–93.

Lawton, M. P., and S. Albert (1990) "Affective Self-Management Across the Lifespan." Paper presented at the *American Psychological Association Convention*, Boston. August.

Lazarus, R. S. (1984) "On the Primacy of Cognition." *American Psychologist* 39:124–29.

Loevinger, J. (1976) *Ego Development: Conceptions and Theories*. San Francisco: Jossey-Bass.

Maciel, A., U. Staudinger, J. Smith, and P. Baltes (1991) "Which Factors Contribute to Wisdom: Age, Intelligence, or Personality?" Paper presented at the *American Psychological Association Convention*, San Francisco. August.

Meacham, J. A. (1983) "Wisdom and the Context of Knowledge: Knowing That One Doesn't Know." In Kuhn and Meacham, 111–34.

______ (1990) "The Loss of Wisdom." In Sternberg, 181–211.

Murdock, M. (1990) *Heroine's Journey.* Boston: Shambhala.

Neugarten, B. L. (1968) "The Awareness of Middle Age." In Neugarten, 93–98.

Neugarten, B. L., ed. (1968) *Middle Age and Aging.* Chicago: University of Chicago Press.

Orwoll, L., and M. Perlmutter (1990) "The Study of Wise Persons: Integrating a Personality Perspective." In Sternberg, 160–80.

Pascual-Leone, J. (1990) "Wisdom: Toward Organismic Processes." In Sternberg, 244–78.

Perlmutter, M., ed. (1990) *Late Life Potential.* Washington, D.C.: Gerontological Society.

Perry, W. (1970) *Forms of Intellectual and Ethical Development in the College Years.* New York: Holt, Rinehart, and Winston.

Rilke, R. M. (1984) *Letters to a Young Poet.* Translated by S. Mitchell. New York: Vintage Books.

Schaie, K. W., and M. P. Lawton (1991) *Annual Review of Gerontology and Geriatrics.* Vol. 11. New York: Springer.

Singer, J. (1989) "A Silence of the Soul: the Sadness of the Successful Woman." *The Quest,* 3.

Smith, J., and P. B. Baltes (1990) "Wisdom-Related Knowledge: Age/Cohort Differences in Response to Life Planning Problems." *Developmental Psychology* 26:494–505.

Staudinger, U., J. Smith, and P. B. Baltes (1992) "Wisdom-Related Knowledge in a Life-Review Task: Age Differences and the Role of Professional Specialization." *Psychology and Aging* 7:271–81.

Steinem, G. (1992) *Revolution from Within: A Book of Self Esteem.* Boston: Little.

Sternberg, R. J., ed. (1990) *Wisdom: Its Nature, Origins, and Development.* Cambridge: Cambridge University Press.

Werner, H. (1957) "The Concept of Development from a Comparative and Organismic Point of View." In Harris, 125–48.

Zajonc, R. B. (1984) "On the Primacy of Affect." *American Psychologist* 39:117–23.

8 Religion and Persons of Color

DAVID MALDONADO

Religious faith and religious institutions have played crucial roles in the lives of racial and ethnic minority elders in the United States. As a result of their cultural heritages and socio-historical experiences, religious faith, practices, and communities were central to their survival in this country. The current generation of older racial and ethnic minority persons, African Americans and Hispanics in particular, reflect high levels of religiosity, including both private and public dimensions. These persons report that their religious faith and their churches aided them in coping with historical challenges to their well-being, and even today serve as critical resources for coping with the challenges of old age.

This chapter begins by briefly examining the historical and cultural forces that have contributed to the significance of religion in the lives of older Native Americans, African Americans, and Hispanics. Because this volume addresses the African American experience in several other chapters (see, e.g., chapters 11 and 20), the discussion here will focus upon the religious lives of elderly Hispanics.

Racial and Ethnic Minority Elderly: A Definition

For the purposes of this chapter, the phrase "racial and ethnic minority" refers to the ethnic populations of *color.* This includes the African American, Hispanic, Native American, and Asian American populations. This is to distinguish them from the European ethnic populations, which traditionally have been known as "white." In essence, racial and ethnic minority populations of color are distinguished from the dominant population by their racial and cultural differences. However, it is important to note that racial differences alone are not the basis for understanding religious faith or practices among these populations; race per se does not determine religious practice. Nonetheless, racial factors have played important roles in shaping the context, social status, and experiences of the various racial populations in the United States, and such social experiences are important for understanding the roles and significance of religion.

Reference to "racial minority" is to call attention to the particular significance of the racial element in the historical experiences of these populations.

Because they are Negroid, Asian, Hispanic/Mestizo, or of some variation, these populations have been recognized and treated as different from the white/Caucasian population. Race has been a key factor in the social structures and processes of this society in such a way that those who are considered nonwhite have been the subject of differential treatment. To be Black, Hispanic, Asian, or Native American is to be considered nonwhite and not a member of the dominant population.

The term "minority" is also used with reference to the numerical status of these populations in relationship to the dominant European American (white) population within the United States. The populations of color have been in the numerical minority in general. It needs to be kept in mind, however, that there are regions of this country—especially urban areas—where these populations are in the majority. Nonetheless, on the whole, they have been in the numerical minority.

The term "minority" is also used as a reminder that these populations have historically been distinguished by their cultural differences. Their African, Asian, Native American, and Hispanic cultures are quite different from the culture of the dominant European American population. As such they are minority cultures in a context in which another culture is the dominant and normative culture. Thus, the term "minority" recognizes historical cultural relationships.

COMMON EXPERIENCES IN THE PRE–CIVIL RIGHTS ERA

Although each minority population has had its own distinctive history, many have emerged through similar socio-historical experiences. Among the historical elements shared by the racial and ethnic minority populations of color is that of an initial experience of domination and disadvantage in this society. For example, the African American population's entry was predominantly through enslavement. The Native Americans were the target of attacks and persistent persecution until they were confined to reservations or annihilated. The Mexican American population of the Southwest and the Puerto Rican population became part of this country as a result of war or the threat of war. The initial Asian immigrants were brought in as controlled labor groups.

The current generation of older racial and ethnic minority persons was born or immigrated during an era in which these populations were still struggling with the social, economic, and political consequences flowing from enslavement, conquest, or oppressive labor conditions. This generation of older persons was born into households and communities whose statuses and conditions were rooted in their historical predicaments. Whether they were native born or immigrated, as culturally and racially different populations, they share the experience of being nonwhite in a society dominated by the white population. This was particularly significant during the pre–Civil Rights era. That era was a period in the domestic history of the United States when racial segregation and discrimination were openly practiced and tolerated by the various social and public structures. For the persons of color, this produced several important experiences: (1) racially based attitudes and treatment; (2) cultural biases; and (3) separation based on race and ethnicity. These factors affected their social status, mobility, and access to resources.

More concretely, the pre–Civil Rights era meant that the current generation of older racial and ethnic minority persons were reared in racially segregated housing and neighborhoods. Racial separation was a fact of life. The Black ghettos, Hispanic barrios, Chinatowns, and Indian reservations were their homes. Segregated neighborhoods generally meant poor housing and inferior public services, such as sanitation and other public health services (Maldonado, 1989).

Segregated schools did not affirm their cultural or historical roots; rather, they tended to alienate, marginalize, and poorly prepare the present cohort of ethnic and racial minority elders for a competitive economic system. As a result, many dropped out of school quite early and were poorly prepared for the job market. Their only option for employment were those jobs at the lower skill and economic levels. With limited educational foundations, the current generation of older racial and ethnic minority persons was limited to domestic, farm labor, blue collar and other limited employment careers. Most of these employment settings did not provide health care or retirement programs.

Limited employment opportunities meant economic marginality and limited economic resources. Most of the income earned by these elders of color was used to rear their families, which tended to be large and the only real blessing they knew. As products of the pre–Civil Rights era, this generation entered old age with broken bodies and empty pockets.

An important question that the pre–Civil Rights experience raises is in regards to the skills and resources these ethnic minority populations were able to utilize in order to maintain their dignity and mental health, and to survive such difficult and challenging living conditions. Religious faith and the minority churches are among the various resources being explored by scholars studying this era.

Religious Roots of Three Minority Populations

Native Americans. An example of how intergroup contact resulted in a variety of religious adaptations is the religious experience of the diverse tribes and nations of the Native American populations. These possessed various forms of religious practices and native religions. Needless to say, these were not Jewish or Christian, but rather reflected the worldviews and experiences of the diverse Native American populations. These were in place and deeply ingrained in the life and cultures of this population at the time of the conquest (Hultkrantz,

1987). The Anglo invasion meant the introduction of Christian religious forces, especially through the work of white missionaries, which aimed at converting and christianizing these native populations.

The christianization of the Native American population has had a peculiar outcome. There is great variety of religious practices among these native populations. For example, some have become totally Christian in their theology and practice while others have maintained their traditional native religions. Also, many have merged Christian and Native American religious beliefs.

In all cases, the Native American population has traditionally been highly spiritual and religious. The elderly have held special places in the cultures and religions of the Native American populations; this has involved honor, respect, and leadership as elders of the tribe and clan. The old ones are expected to possess wisdom and a connection to the past (Arden and Wall, 1990). In essence, the role and status of the elderly in their communities have been closely connected to religious tradition and practices. The current generation of elderly Native Americans was reared in such religious and cultural contexts. Many of them still live in reservations. Such religious forces played important roles in their early years and helped to shape their lives, worldviews, and expectations.

African American. It has been suggested that religion among the African American population needs to be understood as flowing from both its African origins and the enslavement experience in the new world. For example, Africans forcibly transported to America brought deeply ingrained notions of communality and kinship, spirituality and a sense of oneness with nature, and a belief in ancestral worship and reverence for the elderly (Carter, 1982). These African religious roots point to an understanding of religion that is not restricted to traditional forms such as religious structures and practices, but rather suggests a broader view that incorporates the total tribal life and experience.

Enslavement likewise served as an important formative context for African American religious expression and experience. The dehumanizing and oppressive nature of enslavement generated a need for coping if the tribe was to survive. In such a context, religion—even the forced adoption of the white masters' religion—became an important source of coping. Religious expressions, such as Negro spirituals, clearly pointed to the enslaved conditions and the desire and hope for freedom. The constant threat of death and the imposed confinement made freedom and liberation a common theme in the Negro spirituals which emerged during slavery. These expressed psychosocial needs of a people wanting to be free are manifested in religious terminology and point to the importance of religious faith in their coping and survival (Frazier, 1974).

The emergence of the Black church as a central institution within the African American community indicates the importance of religion within this population. Next to the family, the Black church is probably the most important social institution within this community. It contributed to the ability of the

African American community to cope with its oppressive conditions; it also provided for its many social needs. The Black church not only functioned as an important source of religious and spiritual strength but also as an essential center of community and social life (Taylor and Chatters, 1986a, 1986b, 1991). Its role in the Civil Rights era is a clear sign of its centrality in the African American community (King, 1986).

Hispanic. The religious heritage of the Hispanic population traces back to the Spanish conquest over the native Indian populations of Mesoamerica. This resulted in the domination of Spanish Catholicism over the native Indian religions, although recent research indicates a syncretistic confluence of religious motifs (Carrasco, 1990). The Spanish conquest over the Indian population reflects the conquest of a theocratic society and culture by a population equally driven by religious motives. The outcome has been the emergence of Hispanic populations with cultures manifesting strong religious foundations. A strong identification with the Catholic Church has been a historical reality; however, an increasing Protestant presence can be noted (Maldonado, 1991).

The current generation of older Hispanics grew up in a time when discrimination and segregation were openly practiced against non-Anglo peoples. Because of their racial and ethnic difference, this generation of Hispanics paid a heavy price. They were denied a quality education which resulted in limited employment and career opportunities. This is evident in employment histories reflecting unskilled or semiskilled employment. Many worked in temporary, agricultural, or domestic jobs. As might be imagined, this type of position did not provide much in the way of income, health benefits, or retirement plans. Their experience was one of pervasive marginality—social, economic, and political. They were excluded from participation in the core institutions of society and are now paying the price of that exclusion (Maldonado, 1989).

Although their status and treatment was related to their racial and ethnic composition, Hispanics did not necessarily view their culture as the source of their problem. In fact, their racial roots and cultural heritage provided an important sense of peoplehood and important resources for addressing their life situation. Within their culture this generation of older Hispanics found an important source of strength, meaning, and support in their religious faith and the church. Next to the family, the church was probably the most important social institution in their lives and communities, and their religious faith the most important source of support and coping resources.

Religion in the Lives of the Hispanic Elderly

The study of religious factors in the lives of older Hispanics has been a major gap in the research on older Hispanics. Only recently has attention been given to this important aspect of their lives. Of significance is research conducted by

Markides and Martin (1983) which gives major attention to this topic, and the study by the National Hispanic Council on Aging (Gallego, 1988) which included aspects of religion in its study of four sites in the United States.

Because of the lack of information about the role of religion in the lives of older Hispanics, this discussion will be based primarily upon unpublished data gathered from interviews recently conducted with 178 older Hispanics (mostly Mexican American) living in San Antonio.[1] This sample resembles the national profile of older Hispanics (see Andrews, 1989) in that it is predominantly poor, of limited educational attainment, and female. In addition, of the 107 women interviewed for this study, 56 percent were widowed. These data, along with the reports of Markides and Martin (1983) and Gallego (1988), provide a portrait of the private religious practices as well as the public religious participation of older Hispanics.

Religious Affiliation. Because of the critical role of the Catholic Church in the development of this population, it is not surprising that empirical studies have found that the vast majority of this population is Christian with 85–89 percent reported to be Roman Catholic (Andrews, 1989; Gallego, 1988; Lacayo, 1980; Markides and Martin 1983). However, these studies also report that from 9 to 13 percent of all Hispanics are affiliated with the Protestant church, which reflects a recent phenomenon in this country and in Latin America.

The interviews in San Antonio revealed a somewhat different picture. Although 74 percent of these elders identified themselves as Roman Catholic, 24 percent claimed affiliation with a Protestant church. Surprisingly, 22 percent of the entire sample of 178 said they did not belong to any particular congregation.

Public Religious Practices. Church attendance appears to be a weekly activity for a high percentage of older Hispanics. Three-fourths of the persons surveyed in San Antonio indicated that they attend a religious activity once a week. In fact, over 80 percent had attended such an event during the week of the survey. Overall, women report higher rates of attendance, while a higher proportion of males report that they almost never attend (10 percent).

Attending worship services is the primary public religious activity for older Hispanics. Prayer meetings and senior groups are the second major types of activity in which they participate. The older persons surveyed in San Antonio are more likely to attend prayer meetings than church school; this might reflect a greater need for spiritual nourishment than for religious education in older age. An interesting variation, however, is the difference between men and women on this issue. While women are twice as likely to attend prayer meetings (46 percent) than church school (23 percent), men are more likely to attend church school (54 percent) than prayer meetings (39 percent).

[1]A detailed report of this study can be obtained from the author.

The previous section pointed to a fairly high attendance profile for older Hispanics. When asked to compare their current level of participation in church activities to previous periods in life, four out of ten (43 percent) indicated that they were more active in old age than before. Males reported a greater level of continuity ("about the same: 37 percent") than females (24 percent), and females reflect a slightly higher level of most active (35 percent–28 percent). This suggests that older Hispanics perceive themselves as more active in religious activities in their older years, and in fact one-third of all would like to be even more active, especially women (42 percent).

It is well known that public religious participation is not a good indicator of religiosity in elders due to the number of obstacles they face in getting to these religious activities. In response to a question regarding the problems they face in attending public worship and other religious activities, the majority (59 percent) of these older Hispanics, especially women (68 percent), indicated that health is the number one problem. The second most important obstacle they perceive is that of transportation. This is particularly a problem for women, 29 percent of whom noted that a lack of transportation prevented them from participating in public religious activities.

Religiosity. Self-understanding in regard to religiosity offers an important insight to how people perceive their religious lives. In assessing his or her own religiosity, the individual might consider both private and public aspects of religiosity or just one aspect. What is important is how the individual views himself or herself overall. Markides and Martin (1983) reported that a majority of elder Hispanics in their study described themselves as religious (very religious + quite religious = 52 percent; somewhat religious = 38 percent), with women in the majority of the group who called themselves very religious. Only 8 percent of that sample saw themselves as "not very or not at all religious." Similarly, Gallego (1988) reported 5 percent as "not religious," 35 percent as "quite religious," and 43 percent as "average religious." Among those interviewed in San Antonio, 63 percent claim a high sense of religiosity (quite religious and very religious); within this subgroup females report higher levels of religiosity, especially among the "very religious." Only 3 percent of the total sample view themselves as not at all religious, with males reporting the highest level in comparison to females (7 percent to 1 percent). It could be concluded that a majority of older Hispanics view themselves as religious, with females showing the highest levels of self-perceived religiosity.

Within the literature on religion and aging, there has been a perennial discussion about whether people become more religious as they age or whether high levels of religiosity among older persons is a cohort phenomenon. The interviews in San Antonio revealed that among this group of elder Hispanics, there is a strong perception of experiencing a closer relation with God in old age as compared to other periods of life. In addition, when asked whether their faith was stronger at this time in comparison with the past, 51 percent of the sample said that it was. As can be seen in Table 8.1, far more women than men reported that they felt closer to God and stronger in their faith in later life than they had in younger days.

Private Religious Practices. In addition to religious self-understanding, the private practice of religion is an important aspect of religiosity. Although these actions may be in concert with a broader network of believers via prayer links or through organized reading programs, for the most part, the private practice of religious faith refers to those actions taken individually as part of a personal spiritual discipline. The most commonly used spiritual discipline among older Hispanics is prayer. Markides and Martin (1983) found that most older Mexican Americans pray on a daily basis (82 percent), and only few never or almost never pray daily (2 percent). The survey of elders living in San Antonio shows that 92 percent of the women and 77 percent of the men pray one or more times per day. Only 6 percent indicate that they almost never pray. Among these elders, the second most commonly used spiritual discipline is meditation. A majority of both males and females report that they meditate daily, although it is unclear exactly how they define meditation. Bible reading, however, does not appear to be a part of daily religious practice as less than a third of this group engage in this private religious activity.

The elders interviewed in San Antonio were asked about the frequency of their use of religious electronic media. Less than 10 percent watch religious television programs daily, although up to 70 percent watch occasionally. For this

TABLE 8.1
Closeness to God and Strength of Faith Compared to Other Periods of Life

	Males	*Females*	*Total*
Closeness to God:			
Closest ever (now)	46%	67%	59%
Closer now than in the past	26%	15%	20%
As close as ever	23%	12%	17%
Not as close now	3%	2%	2%
Much further than in the past	1%	3%	2%
Never felt close to God	1%	0%	1%
Strength of faith:			
Strongest faith now	37%	60%	51%
Stronger now	21%	16%	18%
Same strength as ever	34%	17%	24%
Weaker faith now	7%	5%	6%
Weakest faith now	1%	2%	2%

population in which 43 percent have less than $4,788 annual income, it is important to note that 13 percent of the men and 22 percent of the women contribute money to support the religious media. It is not known how many of this sample contribute to their own churches, nor is it known what percentage of total income is contributed.

Religious Faith and Practice as Forms of Coping. Other chapters in this volume support the observation that older adults turn to religion in times of physical and mental distress. The elder Hispanics studied in San Antonio are no different. A large percentage (82 percent) describe their religious faith as very helpful to them and prayer tops the list of their preferred coping strategies, with 76 percent of the men and 96 percent of the women saying they turn to prayer when they are feeling stress and/or sadness.

CONCLUSION

Although this chapter has focused primarily upon the elderly Hispanic population, it should be noted that Native Americans, African Americans and Hispanic elders can all claim rich religious traditions. Whether Roman Catholic, Protestant, or some combination of traditional religion with Christianity, these populations reflect a clear sense of religious identification and religious self-understanding. Their public and private religious activities suggest active religious lives. Data seem to indicate that at least among the Hispanic group, religion has become a more salient force within their lives as they have aged. Perhaps this is due to their marginal status within the wider society. Further research on this question with Hispanics and other ethnic and racial minority elders is clearly needed.

Religion and religious life, both public and private, have represented important sources of strength, support, and identity in the lives of racial and ethnic minority elderly (Maldonado, 1990). This brief review of their histories and social experiences suggests difficult journeys, ones in which religion and the church have played significant roles. This generation of older racial and ethnic minority persons reflects that challenging history and the religious faith that helped them cope, survive, and reach old age.

BIBLIOGRAPHY

Andrews, J. (1989) *Poverty and Poor Health among Elderly Hispanic Americans.* New York: Commonwealth Fund Commission on Elderly People Living Alone.

Arden, H., and S. Wall (1990) *Wisdomkeepers: Meetings with Native American Spiritual Elders.* Hillsboro: Ore.: Beyond Words.

Carrasco, D. (1990) *Religions of Mesoamerica.* San Francisco: Harper San Francisco.

Carter, A. C. (1982) "Religion and the Black Elderly: The Historical Basis of Social and Psychological Concerns." In R. C. Manuel, 103–9.

Frazier, E. F. (1974) *The Negro Church in America.* New York: Schocken.

Gallego, D. T. (1988) "Religiosity as a Coping Mechanism among Hispanic Elderly." In Sotomayor and Curiel, 117–35.

Hultkrantz, A. (1987) *Native Religions of North America.* San Francisco: Harper & Row.

King, M. L. (1986) *Stride Toward Freedom.* San Francisco: Harper & Row.

Lacayo, C. A. (1980) *A National Study to Assess the Service Needs of The Hispanic Elderly.* Los Angeles: Asociacion Nacional pro Personas Mayores.

Maldonado, D. J. (1989) "A Framework for Understanding the Minority Elderly." In Schuster, 8–29.

______ (1990) "The Minority Church: Its Roles and Significance for the Minority Elderly." In Stanford, 25–31.

______ (1991) "Hispanic Protestants: Historical Reflections." *Apuntes* 11:3–16.

Manuel, R. C., ed. (1982) *Minority Aging: Sociological and Social Psychological Issues.* Westport, Conn.: Greenwood Press.

Markides, K., and H. W. Martin (1983) *Older Mexican Americans.* Austin, Tex.: Center for Mexican American Studies.

Schuster, E., ed. (1989) *Low Income, Minority and Rural Adult Population: Issues for the Future.* Ypsilanti, Mich.: Geriatric Education Center of Michigan.

Sotomayor, M. and H. Curiel, eds. (1988) *Hispanic Elderly: A Cultural Signature.* Edinburg, Tex.: Univ. of Texas—Pan American Press.

Stanford, E. P. et al., eds. (1990) *Ethnicity and Aging: Mental Health Issues.* San Diego: San Diego State University Center on Aging.

Taylor, R. J., and L. M. Chatters (1986a) "Religious Participation among Elderly Blacks." *The Gerontologist* 26:630–36.

______ (1986b) "Church Based Informal Support among Elderly Blacks." *Gerontologist* 26:637–42.

______ (1991) "Nonorganizational Religious Participation among Elderly Black Adults." *Journal of Gerontology* 46:S103–11.

Part Two PASTORAL CARE IN AN AGING SOCIETY

INTRODUCTION

Pastoral care occurs within the context of a faith community. As the chapters in Part Two demonstrate, pastoral care also must be understood as embedded in a sociocultural context that confers meager meaning on the aging process.

Unfortunately, by providing scant education in pastoral care with older adults, seminaries participate in the social marginalization of aging persons. In chapter 9, *Melvin Kimble* notes the slow growth of literature on pastoral care with elders and the even slower response of seminary curricula to an aging society. Adopting a model of the whole person, not unlike that presented by Koenig (chap. 1), Kimble shows how the "double-edged nature of aging"—its positive and its negative characteristics—creates a crisis of meaning for many older persons. Kimble argues that pastors not only have a responsibility to care for older persons but also to speak with a prophetic voice to a society that invests little or no meaning in aging. One of the contributions clergy can make through their pastoral care activities is to encourage elders to tell their stories, both for their own benefit and the good of the larger society. Further, clergy need to understand that pastoral care involves much more than hospital and home visitation. Pastoral care of older persons includes the development of rites and rituals so elders together with their faith communities can articulate the meaning of the long journey through life.

Continuing the theme that pastoral care cannot be undertaken in isolation from the broader community, *James Ellor* and *Marie Bracki* point out how clergy need practical information about referrals to community agencies (chap. 10). Clergy must cooperate with these agencies because older persons not only have spiritual needs to be addressed in pastoral counseling sessions, but also may need meal delivery, home maintenance assistance, and transportation provided by various private and public organizations. But how will a pastor know what an older person needs? Ellor and Bracki argue that clergy should understand approaches to assessment so they can respond to the older person as an individual with particular needs—spiritual and religious as well as social, psychological and physical—and not as a generic old person for whom a smile, a prayer, and a few words about the weather will suffice.

Furthermore, ministers need to understand that the life circumstances of elders vary widely. In particular, when dealing with racial diversity, pastors must attend not only to the needs of the individual but also to the ways the wider society shapes the aging process. *Anne Wimberly* and *Edward Wimberly* address this issue with regard to pastoral care with African Americans (chap. 11). They offer insights into the pastoral care process applicable to all older persons but they are especially concerned to point out the special needs of older Blacks. Like Maldonado (chap. 8), Wimberly and Wimberly note how racism and economic disadvantage have conspired to create difficult conditions for older African Americans; in contrast, support from the church and strong family ties provide resources that create unique opportunities for pastoral care with this group of elders.

As Ellor and Bracki noted, pastoral caregivers often find themselves dealing with the vagaries of the everyday life of older persons. For example, ministers sometimes receive calls from the attorneys, trust officers, and children of older people perceived as needing special assistance. In the area of legal matters, clergy may feel particularly ill-equipped to be helpful. *Lori Stiegel* and *Nancy Coleman* provide in chapter 12 practical information on a broad array of topics that pastoral caregivers may encounter. The legal issues raised in this chapter—from health care decision-making to housing—all support the contention that pastoral caregivers must understand their work as integrated into the wider community.

The topic of health care decision-making and health care provision concerns *Stephen Sapp* as he addresses the many ethical dilemmas clergy encounter as they care for aging persons (chap. 13). Sapp begins by addressing how Judaism and Christianity have traditionally understood aging. After grounding his argument in the Bible, Sapp considers contemporary ethical concerns related to old age. Throughout his discussion, he evokes a theme that quietly reverberated through earlier chapters by Moody (chap.6) and Vogel (chap. 5) and that will be directly addressed in later chapters on theology: old age evokes human reflection on the socially-enforced dichotomy between being and doing. Recognition that the "being" of elders constitutes their essential value must not, however, produce an image of passivity in old age. Sapp cites numerous Scriptural references to the obligations of elders to the community as well as obligations of the community to elders. Finally, echoing Kimble's concern for the wider dimensions of pastoral care, Sapp argues that clergy must become advocates for the ethical treatment of older persons.

9 Pastoral Care

MELVIN A. KIMBLE

INTRODUCTION

The gerontological revolution with its dramatic increase in the number and percentage of persons over the age of sixty-five provides challenging opportunities to reflect upon the nature and scope of pastoral care and ministry. It is estimated that older adults represent a disproportionately large percentage of members in most faith communities—from 20 to 40 percent—and that half of the clergy's pastoral work is directly related to this population (Moberg, 1980, 286). Clergy have the pastoral responsibility to be helpful and supportive guides in the older adults' exploration of the unchartered territory of living out their vocation in a longer life that continues to have meaning and purpose.

The vigor of pastoral care and its authentic relevance for ministry with older adults depends upon its continuing closeness to and creative engagement in the specific life and functions of congregational-based ministry. The ministry of nurturing and shepherding that characterizes pastoral care assumes the setting of a gathered community of faith. Clinebell pointed out that " . . . no other helping profession has a comparable, supportive fellowship available year-in, year-out, to undergird its work" (1966, 51). The continuing involvement in organized religious life and practice of present cohorts of older adults provides a foundation and starting point for meaningful pastoral care ministry.

This chapter will discuss some of the ways in which pastoral care is accomplished in ministry with older adults. It includes a brief review of the literature of pastoral care with the aging. Both the need for a multidimensional model of aging that encompasses the whole person and also the double-edged nature of aging are examined. Aging and the crisis of meaning are discussed, followed by a discussion of life-review as a method of pastoral care and mutual ministry. Perspectives on ministry with the suffering and dying are presented as an essential function of pastoral care. Finally, the chapter concludes with an exploration of three additional examples of pastoral care areas with older adults: gerontological gender issues, the family surrogate model, including ministry to an increasingly diverse membership that includes a variety of frameworks and life patterns, and pastoral care as advocacy.

THE LITERATURE OF PASTORAL CARE

A brief review of contemporary literature of pastoral care reveals that surprisingly few pastoral theologians have examined the pastoral care implications of older adulthood. Not until mid-century did significant writings began to appear intermittently that addressed the pastoral needs of older adults. In 1949, Paul Maves and J. Lennart Cedarleaf coauthored *Older People and the Church*. The 1950s resulted in a rash of pamphlet publications, especially from religious boards and agencies, that introduced congregational issues related to the older adult which included some implications for pastoral care ministry (Gray and Moberg, 1962, 119). In 1954, Paul B. Maves edited an issue of *Pastoral Psychology* that focused on older persons and the church and marked a significant recognition of the pastoral care dimensions of older adulthood. In 1962, Robert Gray and David Moberg published *The Church and the Older Person,* which provided information and insights for pastoral care ministry.

A promising collection of essays edited by Seward Hiltner with provocative pastoral care inferences appeared in the Winter 1976 issue of *Pastoral Psychology* and was later published as a collection with the title *Toward a Theology of Aging.* William Clements' *Care and Counseling of the Aging* (1979) and *Ministry with the Aging* (1981), which he edited, further extended the dialogue of pastoral care ministry. Several other works appeared in the 1980s that continued to introduce pastoral care issues, sometimes implicitly but more often explicitly; e.g., *Aging as a Spiritual Journey* (Bianchi, 1984), *Faith for the Older Years* (Maves, 1986), and *Ministry with Older Persons* (Becker, 1986). *Toward a Practical Theology of Aging* (Lyon, 1985) is a provocative work that explores a viable theological context for pastoral care with older adults. Individual essays have also begun to appear with greater frequency in journals or pastoral care collections (Lapsley, 1985; Buxbaum, 1987; Kimble, 1987) and have contributed pastoral care insights to the growing body of literature in this field. In 1988, the Interreligious Liaison Office of the American Association of Retired Persons (AARP) compiled a collection of essays (Powers, 1988) that reflect perspectives on aging from eight disciplines central to theological education, including essays on pastoral care (Spangler) and pastoral theology (Kimble). *Spiritual Maturity in the Later Years* edited by James Seeber (1990) represents a collection of papers presented at a conference convened at Claremont School of Theology in 1987 and contains a rich source of pastoral care insights. Thomas Robb's *Growing Up: Pastoral Nurture for the Later Years* (1991) sets forth helpful suggestions for shaping pastoral care ministry.

Although not pretending to be complete, the abbreviated review of the literature suggests some of the pastoral care theologians and practitioners who have specifically addressed aging and older adulthood. The *Journal of Religious Gerontology* currently introduces many facets of ministry with the aging that manifest pastoral care dimensions of aging.

Course offerings in pastoral care and ministry with the aging in theological education curricula, however, have been conspicuous by their absence. Theological education has yet to take seriously its responsibility to equip candidates for the ministry with skills and understanding of aging and older adulthood. Thomas Cook (1980) summarized the National Interfaith Coalition on Aging's (NICA) program of Gerontology in Seminary Training (GIST), which sought to introduce gerontology more fully into theological curricula. Citing Project GIST as a good beginning, Cook urged the religious sector ". . . to become self-directing to insure that there is continuing and continuous upgrading" of theological curricula to "include and enhance gerontology" (279). Barbara Payne and Earl Brewer (1989) conducted a project entitled *Gerontology in Theological Education* (GITE) under a grant from the Administration on Aging in 1986 that focused on introducing aging content into seminary education in the Atlanta, Georgia area. Their report (1989) also includes responses from a questionnaire sent to 153 seminaries in the United States accredited by the Association of Theological Seminaries (ATS) that confirmed the dearth of curricula offerings in aging. The unavoidable conclusion is that theological curricula do not reflect a high priority for equipping students for creative and responsible pastoral care ministry with older adults. This lacuna is present despite the fact that pastoral care is increasingly carried on in the context of an aging society.

NEED FOR NEW METAPHORS

In their ministry with the aging, clergy encounter pervasive medical metaphors that view aging as disease and deterioration. Clearly, ministry with the aging requires more than a biomedical paradigm. Aging touches all of the basic questions of life and impacts all dimensions of being. It is a multidimensional reality that demands an interdisciplinary approach. Many quarters of the gerontological enterprise increasingly recognize that a wider frame of reference in gerontology is required to allow and encourage the full exploration of questions about old age and its meaning. Natural science has in many respects served gerontology well, but not well enough. It is too exclusive, narrow, and unidimensional in its biological definition of aging.

Insights of the medical and behavioral sciences must be brought into dynamic dialogue with the humanities, including religion and theology, if the phenomenological structure of later life and the profound multidimensional issues of aging are to be understood and responded to. This is beginning to happen. For example, the Conference of Religion, Spirituality and Aging held in 1992 at Luther Northwestern Theological Seminary sought to facilitate and advance this dialogue by bringing together a distinguished group of scholars, researchers, and practitioners representing disciplines of medicine, biology, psychology, sociology, history, nursing, chaplaincy, and theology.

A dimensional ontology (Frankl, 1967b) that recognizes the rich and varied multidimensionality of human persons while still preserving their anthropological unity is required. Any examination of aging and aging persons should reflect an understanding that it is the *whole* person who is aging and aged. This wholeness is a blend of spiritual, physical, mental, emotional, and social dimensions of human growth and development. The social and spiritual dimensions of the individual as well as the physical need to be acknowledged and valued in any definition of human existence (Davidson, 1991). A segmental approach to the aging process will only result in a reductionistic, restrictive, one-dimensional caricature of the older person.

A paradigm that uses a phenomenological approach to aging and its processes and moves beyond an empirical research model limited to a positivistic focus in biomedical and social conditions of aging is needed. Such an approach to gerontology could proceed fruitfully with recourse to hermeneutical and semiological methods. The human experience of aging and growing older requires a hermeneutic, a means whereby it may be interpreted and given meaning.

James Birren has been at the forefront in issuing a call for gerontologists to move beyond disciplinary boundaries by introducing new metaphors to integrate and bridge islands of knowledge in the multidiscipline of gerontology. He contends:

> Metaphors provide a medium for creating *missing links* among disciplines; they function in a *no man's land,* beyond the traditional disciplinary boundaries, but within the common territory of concern. One example of the potential integrative role of metaphor is seen in reference to spirituality in aging. Traditionally, this aspect of human nature has been the domain of such disciplines as theology, philosophy, literature and cultural history. However, insofar as a very significant part of gerontology is the study of *human* development and aging, there are important concerns for science and practice, particularly pertaining to such issues as wisdom and meaning. Discussion of such topics involves socio-cultural and psychologic discourse, as well as theological and philosophical discourse. These perspectives require integration with biological metaphors of aging, for example, in the area of health. Further, all of the foregoing have implications for the quality of life of older persons, and for ethically informed intervention in the field of aging, because appropriate involvement with another person or group of persons presupposes the best available knowledge base. It is possible that the pursuit of metaphors can provide a kind of *Ariadne's Thread* through this labyrinth of disciplinary orientations and issues, toward a comprehensive understanding of human aging. (Birren, 1991)

Armed with such a wholistic understanding of the whole person, pastoral care can go about its shepherding ministry with older persons avoiding the Scylla of biologism or the equally dangerous Charybdis of spiritualizing the aging process. Pastoral care needs to reflect on its own methodological focus in its concern to bring healing to the concrete and personal experiences of the human life cycle, including old age, and thereby establish itself as an integral partner in interdisciplinary practice with older adults.

DOUBLE-EDGED NATURE OF AGING

Examples of the double-edged nature of aging are abundant in the gerontological literature (Atchley, 1983; Butler and Gleason, 1985). The negative, pessimistic view of aging, for example, is emphasized by researchers who focus on sickness, isolation, poverty, and enervation and see growing old as an unmitigated series of defeats and losses. The language of medicine itself perpetuates metaphors of health and aging that paint a picture of "aging as disease, decline and deterioration" (Davidson, 1991, 177). Such metaphors and paradigms describe a pattern of aging that weaves theories and conclusions out of the fabric of human diminution and decrement. These "ain't it terrible" theorists (Robb, 1991) often include in their bleak tapestry of growing old colors that depict aging as a "social problem" and older persons as a drain on the resources of family and society.

Still other metaphors emphasize an "ain't it wonderful" viewpoint, and researchers of this persuasion paint rosy pictures of aging and being old that are unrealistically positive. They depict the elderly as a population who have a lifestyle that is comfortable and healthy with high levels of life-satisfaction.

Obviously, neither of these theories is adequate or accurate, because the aging process and being aged are far too complicated to be treated so simplistically and categorically. Certainly aging can and does have positive features, but it also has negative ones. Many elders, for example, can document negative losses such as health, income, role, status, competency, autonomy, and significant others in their lives. But this is not the whole picture. Loss is not the unqualified experience of aging and becoming old, nor is diminution and depreciation. Human documents through the ages have attested to the growth of human character and sensibilities and the maturation of the spirit that represent the fruits of a long life. Neither the exclusivistic positive or negative characterization of this last stage of life will suffice.

Erikson's Developmental Theory. Erik Erikson's work provides a helpful representation of the double-edged nature of aging. He describes the psychosocial conflicts of middle age as "generativity vs. stagnation" and those of the later years as "integrity vs. despair" (Erikson, 1959, 1982). The many ways people attempt to resolve these conflicts confirm the multifaceted, complex and overlapping issues that are part of the human life cycle.

In the eighth and final stage of life there is personal mourning "not only for time forfeited and space depleted but also . . . for autonomy weakened, initiative lost, intimacy missed, generativity neglected" and "identity potential by-passed or, indeed, an all too limiting identity lived" (Capps, 1987, 65–66). Wisdom, one of the virtues of adulthood, enables persons to view their lives with all their diminishment and losses in a more wholistic manner. As Capps insightfully observes:

> The melancholic represent . . . a fragmented life, because melancholics are essentially at odds with themselves, viewing their inevitable losses as grounds for self-contempt. But older persons who possess the human strength of wisdom can continue to exemplify a living sense of the whole of life in spite of their losses and can thereby instill in younger persons a confidence in the way of life that both generations, with some variations, share. . . . A biblical example of the dialectic between wisdom and melancholy is Job, a man whose name is now synonymous with suffering. . . . Job's story suggests that the wholeness of life is a matter not of finding quiet retirement but of finding the necessary strength to confront the deadly threat of melancholy. And that means having the wisdom to see human problems, including our own, in a more holistic way, maintaining a vigor of mind and accepting the gift of responsible renunciation. (Capps, 1987, 113, 115)

Older Adulthood as Dynamic Process of "Becoming." It is important to remember that, although aging is largely a positive experience for most persons, it is unpredictable and unique for each person. There are always many variables in each person's life that shape and determine health and quality of life. Human life with all of its individual uniqueness and diversity nevertheless continues to the very end to be characterized by opportunities for personal development and growth. One of the many challenges for older persons is to engage fully the present—in order to offset what Alfred North Whitehead called our "human style," which is "to mourn the past and worry about the future, while all the time the Sacred Present is passing us by, half-used, half-enjoyed" (McLeish, 1983, 37). Each person's life history with the singular and distinctive events and experiences that have shaped it results in an older person who is remarkably and wonderfully individualized.

In spite of the variety of physical, psychological, and social changes that occur as one ages, acquired skills enable most persons to function with amazing effectiveness. Researchers have demonstrated that as persons grow older they develop a valuable reservoir of patterns with which to organize their experience (Kalish, 1982; Kastenbaum, 1979). This allows persons to evaluate their experiences and crises and to make decisions about how best to respond to them. Having experienced some of the sadness and sorrows of life, they have learned something about how to grieve, adjust, compensate, and rebuild. They are truly "survivors." In addition, the awareness of their lifelong experiences of God's presence and love in their lives provides them with a sense of trust and hope as they move into the uncertain future. In all of this, the challenge of the "double-edged" nature of aging and growing old is to be aware of the dialectical forces that hold negative and positive aspects of aging in creative tension and to maintain the capacity to be "in process" throughout one's lifetime.

AGING AND CRISIS OF MEANING

Albert Camus once contended, "There is but one truly serious problem, and that is . . . judging whether life is or is not worth living" (1955, 3). Pastoral care addresses the crisis of meaning. That basic, fundamental "problem" emerges with considerable urgency as persons become aged. Questions arise: "Is growing old worth one's whole life to attain?" "What is the meaning of life when one is elderly?" "Can the meaning of who I have become be sustained in this last stage of my life?" To respond to these questions requires more than a medical paradigm, for such a model is powerless to reveal to us the meaning of our lives (Kimble, 1990a).

There is an increasing body of evidence to suggest that the crisis of aging and being old is a crisis of meaning (Moody and Cole, 1986). It has been observed that the enormous gains in longevity as the result of medical and technological progress have been accompanied ". . . by widespread spiritual malaise . . . and confusion over the meaning and purpose of life . . . particularly in old age" (Cole, 1984, 329). Increasingly more people today have the means to live, but no meaning for which to live. An individual throughout her or his lifespan is motivated to seek and to find personal meaning in human existence. Ross Snyder agrees and further states:

> Meaning formation is a central activity of the species Human Being. The vitality—and graciousness—of a person's life depends upon their supply of meanings. Particularly in the second half of life, meaning formation is not a fringe benefit, but a major ministry to people in the last half of life. A major way these years stay freshly human. (Snyder, 1983)

The shockingly high suicide statistics among older adults provide a disturbing commentary on the apparent "existential vacuum" (Frankl, 1967) that many older adults experience in their last stage of life. Suicide has become a solution for some elderly people for whom life no longer has meaning when losses and changes occur with bewildering and sometimes overwhelming frequency and intensity. This state of inner emptiness appears to be one of the major causes of depression and despair. In one study a research team emphasized that in order effectively to help depressed people *". . . the answer would be for old age itself to offer the elderly something worthwhile for which to live"* (Miller, 1979, 19).

Elaine Ramshaw has helpfully written:

> The human need to make sense of experience is universal and fundamental. Faced with the biggest questions of life and death, love and evil, the origin and destiny of the human race and the universe, we cannot pin down an answer in logical formulas. We turn to symbolic expressions of our trust in that which grounds the goodness in our experience and shapes the tradition in which we make our meanings. The need for the ritual expression and reinforcement of the symbolic world view is intensified in situations which threaten meaning or coherence. (Ramshaw, 1987, 25)

Contributing to the pervasive grimness about aging and growing old is this lack of symbols and appropriate rituals to mark and give positive meaning to the passing of lifetime. Devoid of transcendent symbols that facilitate confrontation with and acceptance of the natural process of aging and dying, persons frantically search for deliverance in the latest medical messiah or technology. The present crisis of meaning calls for relevant symbols that sustain meaning as individuals live out their longer life expectancies. Faith communities have a responsibility to introduce such transcendent symbols in the ritual and rites of worship as well as pastoral care. As Kathleen Fischer reminds us, "Ritual is one of the paths of integrity as we age" (Fischer, 1985, 50).

A symbol system that is impoverished results in expressions of guilt without absolution, of isolation and alienation which have forgotten God's covenant promise and relationship as well as its expression in the household of faith, and of suffering that is void of meaning and only devalues and debases the sufferer. Responsible and creative pastoral ministry using the healing and salvific symbols of the Jewish and Christian tradition, for example, incorporates understanding of guilt, suffering, and death. The introduction of such symbols of meaning in the midst of suffering does not deny the inevitable reality of suffering, but rather transcends it.

Pastoral care and nurture of the elderly most efficaciously enters into their lives not with polished techniques and slick programs but with an insightful understanding and communication of the source of meaning rooted in God's grace. Salvific symbols are rich sources of meaning in the praxis of faith and formulation of the existential order.

A responsible and nurturing ministry with the elderly explores the human dimensions and contours of the aging experience. It probes the interior as well as the exterior dynamics of the aging process. The goal is to examine the unique personal experience of aging with its increasingly narrowing boundaries and the cascade of changes and losses that mark one's passage through lifetime. The ministry of nurturing the elderly includes those occasions in which God's love most poignantly interfaces with a person's life and when a sense of life's ultimate meaning is introduced. James Birren has reminded the religious sector that its primary purpose is to be a generator of personal and social meanings (Birren, 1984). The religious community in its ministry with older adults has an extraordinary opportunity to claim this primary role as an affirmer of the value and worth of all persons at every stage of life and to implement its role as a generator of personal and social meaning. Older persons need a sense of meaning in order to continue to struggle and cope with the eroding and debilitating diminishments that aging and growing older eventually introduce. As a covenant community of believers, the religious community has the source and center of the ultimate meaning of life in the proclamation of God's sustaining love. In a society that measures the value of life in ways that often devalue and dehumanize, this message with its recreative power confronts persons at whatever stage with a destiny and a purpose. The faith community is the proclaimer of that message concerning the meaning of life in and through pastoral care ministry.

LIFE-REVIEW

Life-review appears to be one of the developmental tasks of the last stage of life and serves a positive function. There is a sense of urgency for the elderly to share their life story. One of the developmental tasks of aging is to maintain a past scanning function that reclaims the past. Personal experiences are always located in time. Memory implies time elapsed. The fear of forgetting and the need to remember both mark the last stage of life. Memory enables persons to hold fast to their identity and to shape and interpret it in new ways. People do not merely have these memories; they are these memories. By remembering connections can be made and the patterns and designs of our lives can be discovered. Life-review provides a configuration, a mosaic of meaning in our lives, and facilitates the next stage which includes death. Life-review, in other words, helps older adults tell their story, who they are and where they have been. Frankl poignantly observes:

> Nothing and nobody can deprive us of what we have safely delivered and deposited in the past. In the past nothing is irretrievably or irrecoverably lost, but everything is permanently stored. Usually people see only the stubblefield of transitoriness—they do not see the full granaries into which they have brought in the harvest of their lives: the deeds done, the works created, the loves loved, the sufferings courageously gone through. (Frankl, 1978, 38–39)

Life-review is a normal activity that persons in every culture have engaged in and valued, for reminiscing by way of oral histories has recounted the past and provided cultural wisdom through the ages. Robert Butler, beginning with a seminal article in 1963, introduced reminiscence in the form of life-review as a therapeutic tool in the service of ego integrity for older people. Butler suggested that life-review is a universal experience shared by older persons, albeit with different intensities and results. Butler described the process:

> As the past marches in review, it is surveyed, observed, and reflected upon by the ego. Reconsideration of previous experiences and their meanings occurs, often with concomitant revised or expanded understanding. Such reorganization of past experiences may provide a more valid picture, giving new and significant meanings to one's life. It may also prepare one for death. (1963, 68)

Life-review has proven to help maintain a higher level of functioning, an increase in mental alertness, a greater sense of personal identity, and a reinforcement of coping mechanisms (Burnside, 1984). A word of caution is in order concerning life-review. Proper training should be given to anyone who is practicing life-review with others. There also needs to be careful monitoring of persons participating in life-review. Persons who reflect deep feelings of being depressed, for example, should not engage in this process, but be referred to an appropriate professional counselor (Birren and Deutchman, 1991, 98–100; Coleman, 1986, 153–58; Shute, 1986, 57–58). It is generally recognized that life-review needs to be further investigated with the aim of better understanding its content, function, and process as an adaptive mechanism of the elderly (Thornton and Brotchie, 1987, 102; Haight, 1989).

The implications of life-review for pastoral care and nurturing the elderly are obvious and myriad. Memory reveals God's presence in people's lives. Faith is the recounting of God's presence and love in the journey through time. Skilled pastoral care that understands the dynamics of life-review can help older persons retrieve events from their memories that mediate God's graciousness to them. Furthermore, through their ability to convey the healing word of God's forgiveness, clergy can address the sense of despair of old guilts and failures that have continued to fester through time. Because emotional and spiritual options remain open until death, as Butler has reminded us, reconciliation and healing remain viable possibilities.

Life-review is a phenomenological approach in seeking to understand the "lived world" of a person. In pastoral counseling it represents a shift away from crisis intervention that is intent on analysis that sometimes becomes reductionistic. Life-review is a process that requires responsive listening as a person shares the story of his or her life. More than a sentimental journey back through time, it helps that person identify meanings in his or her life. It means gently nudging persons to reflect on what a joyful or sorrowful event meant in their lives. It chronicles not only a person's encounter with life, but also with God.

Evelyn and James Whitehead further illustrate the possibilities of the use of life-review in mutual ministry:

> . . . Such powerful self-awareness can be a gift to the community of believers as well as a force for personal integration. This recovery of memories, this recollection of one's past, can be understood religiously as *anamnesis*. . . . Believers of every faith are empowered by the memories, made present, of God acting in their past. The recollections recover the gracefulness of past events and serve to integrate the many parts of a person's life with the present.
>
> In those cases where the believing community (the family, the parish, the prayer group, the religious house) can support its older members in their life-review, can share in the experience with them, and proclaim its religious significance, the community is itself enlivened by the witness of faith. The personal past of those who believe with us and before us is the "deposit of faith" of our community. It is a record of God's action and provident care among us, concretely, in the world today. (Whitehead and Whitehead, 1979, 186)

The skillful use of life-review assists clergy in engaging in a ministry that enriches their communication with older adults by validating that "having been" is a valued mode of being (Frankl, 1978). It utilizes reminiscence as a pastoral tool in assisting persons to become aware of the continuity and meaning of their lives. The patterns of life are shaped by the meaning given to what is remembered.

PASTORAL CARE WITH THE SUFFERING AND DYING

Suffering and dying belong to the human condition and are inescapable. Suffering is a universal theme present at every stage of the life cycle. Both Judaism and Christianity hold to the conviction that suffering and dying are potentially meaningful.

Persons who suffer from some incurable disease or illness are not morally or spiritually inferior. One can be plagued by life's diminishments and still maintain human worth and dignity. More than that, it is possible to fashion positive meaning out of unavoidable suffering, meaning that even ennobles the sufferers. Testimonies of those suffering from incurable leukemia, for example, have spoken concerning "this grace-filled time" of their lives. The Apostolic Letter *On the Christian Meaning of Human Suffering* contends that "when the body is gravely ill, totally incapacitated, and the person almost incapable of living and acting, all the more do interior maturity and spiritual greatness become evident . . ." (John Paul II, 1984). It is this challenge of faithful endurance and patience in suffering that clergy are sometimes called upon to introduce in their ministry with suffering persons. It may well be that the most sublime and profound lessons about human suffering and its meaning are reserved for the frailties and limitations of the final years of life.

Rites and rituals, including sacraments and sacramentals, may help many persons to experience healing of body, mind, or spirit. Examples of sacramentals used in healing include prayers, anointing with oil, and blessings of healing and reconciliation. Pastoral care that offers support, encouragement and realistic hope are some of the appropriate and effective ways of rendering pastoral care to the sick and suffering.

The sacred writings of different religious traditions speak to the meaning of life and death as well as the mysteries of love and healing. Responsible and creative ministry of pastoral care utilizing the healing and salvific symbols of a faith tradition incorporates understanding of suffering within declarations of God's sustaining love.

Facing one's own personal death is the final developmental task of old age. Aging, with its narrowing boundaries, reminds persons that they are all death-bound creatures. Indeed, to live in time is to live toward death. As a final challenge, older persons confront their own dying and death. Faithful pastoral care is rendered if it helps persons to view death as a natural part of the created order of life.

Dying and death are largely, although not exclusively, thought of as being the business of the elderly. Approximately three-fourths of all deaths today occur among those who are over the age of sixty-five. Although it is important to be careful about equating aging and growing old with death, it is certainly obvious that death for most persons these days comes during the stage of older adulthood. As a final stage of growth, older persons confront and experience their own dying and death (Kimble, 1990b, 70–81).

It may well be that one of the essential pastoral skills for doing ministry will increasingly be assisting frail older adults to prepare spiritually for death. While not advocating the return to the somber, often morbid *De arte moriendi* (*On the Art of Dying*) of the Middle Ages, clergy will need more carefully to examine their own feelings and fears concerning dying and death as well as to develop attitudes and skills that enhance and equip them for ministering to the dying and their families.

Pastoral care ministry with older adults and their families often means becoming involved in the avalanche of pre-mortem questions that have been introduced in present-day health care. As more persons live longer lives and reach crisis points where they become vulnerable and can no longer care for themselves, massive perplexing questions are introduced into their lives. Complex ethical questions concerning the quality of life and the danger of either overvaluing or undervaluing it emerge with confounding dimensions. Such questions as the use of modern life-sustaining technology, the economics of health care, the allocation of resources, and other unresolved substantive and procedural issues are but a few that they must often confront (see Sapp, chap. 13). Pastoral care has a challenging role of engaging in ministry with older adults and their families facing such agonizing and bewildering decisions. Thoughtful and responsible pastoral care can increase the possibility that the conclusion of life not be a destructive negation of its meaning.

ADDITIONAL PASTORAL CARE OPPORTUNITIES

Gerontological Gender Issues and Pastoral Care. Women comprise the surviving majority in our society. In the present "graying of America," women will be culturally defined as *older*—and *elderly*—over a longer period of time than men. For example, white females have the longest life expectancy, 78.6 years, followed by black females, 73.5 years. White males have a life expectancy of 71.8 years, and black males of 64.8 years (Taeuber, 1992). These approximately seven additional years or more of life expectancy compound the double jeopardy of ageism and sexism that challenge and confront the older woman. In addition, women of color have racism added to their trajectory of aging and growing old, and are three times as likely as white women to be living in poverty when they are elderly. Women predominate in the grim statistics of one-person households, reduced income, increased poverty, and greater risks of ill health, death and institutionalization (Markson, 1983). Because the average age of the onset of widowhood is fifty-six years of age, for many women widowhood and poverty are always on the horizon.

Because of the disproportionately large representation of women who are members of a faith community and throughout their lifespan often maintain a higher involvement than men, it is mandatory that clergy acquaint themselves with the demographics and issues of aging women and their implications for relevant and innovative pastoral care (Kimble, 1985).

Older women are not a homogeneous population. Although there is a danger of generalizing from the demographic data and viewing all older women as disadvantaged and even victimized, there is no one pattern of experience of aging for either men or women. If there is one thing characteristic of the elderly population, it is heterogeneity. But there remains an undeniably obvious higher degree of vulnerability for older women in the present society that tragically is deeply ingrained in the present social-cultural-economic system. Questions concerning the meaning of life and suffering, self-definition and worth, sexual and family roles, and attitudes toward caregiving and care-receiving are among the challenging questions that confront older women and those who would render pastoral care to them.

Pastoral Care as Family Surrogate Model. A recent report to the United States House of Representatives Select Committee on Aging (1980) identified the faith community as a preeminent representative of the voluntary sector that should be encouraged and enabled by the federal government and other concerned groups in this society to assume a more primary role with respect to the elderly. Faith communities use a formal/informal family surrogate organizational model, offer multiple educational counseling and social support programs, and utilize a mixture of volunteers of all ages, including the current elderly, as well as professional staff. These characteristics are organizational advantages that are distinct and essential to meeting the needs of an increasingly aging population.

The theological and biblical resources for ministry and for the expression of the caring community are made visible in the local congregation where the whole family of God is gathered. Here the intrinsic dignity and value of each person regardless of age is affirmed and honored (Kimble, 1981). In such a supportive atmosphere, creative pastoral care encourages the sharing of strengths and weaknesses, joys and sorrows, and talents and limitations of all age groups. In such a ministry, the faith community follows a historically rich tradition in which the congregation as the household of God becomes the context for loving service to one's neighbor and engages in pastoral care tasks (Laporte, 1981).

Pastoral Care as Advocacy. The faith community is called to provide a vision of society in which there is justice for young and old. A prophetic perspective for pastoral care that introduces a concern for justice and human rights and that insightfully and responsibly focuses on issues of equity, power, autonomy, and dignity is required if the unique issues and needs of older persons are to be addressed.

The elderly need people willing to stand up for them and with them to seek the necessary changes that will assure them adequate income, housing, food, and health care. In an age-segregated society, the faith communities must be an advocate for the maintenance of programs and policies that will secure benefits to older adults, especially to the elderly poor, older adults with physical or developmental disabilities, the elderly minorities, the homebound, and the isolated. Legal assistance, law enforcement that protects rights and guards safety, supportive services that assist in maintaining independent living, laws that eliminate age discriminatory employment and retirement practices, and nursing home regulations that assure quality care at the end stage of life are but a few of the areas that need to be addressed in pastoral care ministry with the elderly. If the faith community intends to be an advocate for older adults, it must work both locally and nationally for appropriate legislative action and act as a sentinel in fighting cuts in those programs and services which are beneficial and essential to an older person's well-being. Clergy must avoid modeling passivity, indifference, and hopelessness if they are to affirm the contribution of older adults to our society and to secure for them more equal access to its goods and services.

CONCLUSION

The task of pastoral care is to set forth a comprehensive view of life that is neither escapist nor evasive, but confronts life with all of its growth and fullness as well as its limitations and finitude. Clergy become vessels of that care in their ministry as they participate in those pivotal events at every point of the human life cycle which provide the occasions for "helping encounters in the dimension of ultimate concern" (Tillich, 1984, 126). Ministry with older adults presents the challenge to be a faithful guide as well as a supportive resource in their quest for wholeness that enlarges and enriches their experiences of grace and meaning in all stages of life, including old age.

BIBLIOGRAPHY

Atchley, R. C. (1983) *Aging: Continuity and Change.* Belmont, Calif.: Wadsworth.

Becker, A. H. (1986) *Ministry with Older Persons.* Minneapolis, Minn.: Augsburg.

Bianchi, E. (1984) *Aging as a Spiritual Journey.* New York: Crossroad.

Birren, J. E. (1984) "Gerontology: A Scientific and Value-laden Field of Inquiry." Lecture delivered at Luther Northwestern Theological Seminary, St. Paul, Minn., May 4.

______ (1991) "Preface" in Kenyon, ix-x.

Birren, J. E., and D. Deutchman (1991) *Guiding Autobiography Groups for Older Adults: Exploring the Fabric of Life.* Baltimore: Johns Hopkins University Press.

Burnside, I. (1984) *Working with the Elderly.* 2nd ed. Monterey, Calif.: Wadsworth.

Butler, R. N. (1963) "Life Review: An Interpretation of Reminiscence in the Aged." *Psychiatry* 24:65–76.

Butler, R. N., and H. P. Gleason, eds. (1985) *Productive Aging.* New York: Springer.

Buxbaum, R. E. (1987) "Coming Issues in the Pastoral Care of the Aged." In Oliver, 33–45.

Camus, A. (1955) *The Myth of Sisyphus.* New York: Vintage Books.

Capps, D. (1987) *Deadly Sins and Saving Virtues.* Philadelphia: Fortress Press.

Clements, W. M. (1979) *Care and Counseling of the Aging.* Philadelphia: Fortress Press.

Clements, W. M., ed. (1981) *Ministry with the Aging.* San Francisco: Harper & Row.

Clinebell, H., Jr. (1966) *Basic Types of Pastoral Counseling.* New York: Abingdon.

Cole, T. R. (1984) "Aging, Meaning and Well-Being: Musings of a Cultural Historian." *International Journal of Aging and Human Development* 19:329–36.

Cole, T. R., and S. Gadow, eds. (1986) *What Does It Mean to Grow Old: Reflections from the Humanities.* Durham, N.C.: Duke University Press.

Coleman, P. G. (1986) *Aging and Reminiscence Processes: Social and Clinical Implications.* New York: Wiley.

Cook, T. C. (1980) "Gerontology in Seminary Training: Introduction and Overview." *Theological Education,* 16 (3):275–79.

Davidson, W. A. S. (1991) "Metaphors of Health and Aging: Geriatrics as Metaphor." In Kenyon et al., 173–84.

Erikson, E. H. (1959) *Identity and the Life Cycle.* New York: Norton.

______ (1963) *Childhood and Society.* 2d rev. ed. New York: Norton.

______ (1982) *Life Cycle Completed: A Review.* New York: Norton.

Fischer, K. (1985) *Winter Grace, Spirituality for the Later Years.* New York: Paulist Press.

Frankl, V. (1967) *Psychotherapy and Existentialism: Selected Papers on Logotherapy.* New York: Washington Square Press.

______ (1978) *The Unheard Cry for Meaning.* New York: Simon and Schuster.

Gray, R. M., and D. O. Moberg (1962) *The Church and the Older Person.* Grand Rapids, Mich.: Eerdmans.

Haight, B. (1989) "Life Review: A Report of the Effectiveness of a Structured Life Review Process: Part II." *Journal of Religion and Aging,* 5 (3):31–41.

Hiltner, S., ed. (1975) *Toward a Theology of Aging.* New York: Human Sciences Press.

John Paul II (1984) Apostolic Letter: *On the Christian Meaning of Human Suffering* (Salvifici Doloris). Washington, D.C.: U. S. Catholic Conference.

Kalish, R. (1982) *Late Adulthood: Perspectives on Human Development.* 2d ed. Monterey, Calif.: Brooks-Cole.

Kastenbaum, R. (1979) *Growing Old: Years of Fulfillment.* San Francisco: Harper & Row.

Kenyon, G., J. E. Birren, and J. J. F. Schroots, eds. (1991) *Metaphors of Aging in Science and the Humanities.* New York: Springer.

Kimble, M. A. (1981) "Education for Ministry with the Aging." In Clements, 209–19.

______ (1985) "The Surviving Majority: Differential Impact of Aging and Implications for Ministry." *Word & World* 5(4):395–404.

______ (1987) "Pastoral Care of the Elderly." *The Journal of Pastoral Care* 16, (3):270–79.

______ (1988) "Pastoral Theology." In Powers, 43–50.

______ (1990a) "Aging and the Search for Meaning." In Seeber, 111–29.

______ (1990b) "Religion: Friend or Foe of the Aging?" *Second Opinion* 15:70–81.

Laporte, J. (1981) "The Elderly in the Life and Thought of the Early Church." In Clements, 37–55.

Lapsley, J. N. (1985) "Pastoral Care and Counseling of the Aged." In Wicks, 245–66.

LeFevre, C., and P. LeFevre, eds. (1981) *Aging and the Human Spirit.* Chicago: Exploration Press.

LeFevre, P., ed. (1984) *The Meaning of Health.* Chicago: Exploration Press.

Lyon, K. B. (1985) *Toward a Practical Theology of Aging.* Philadelphia: Fortress Press.

Markson, E. W., ed. (1984) *Older Women: Issues and Prospects.* New York: Free Press.

Maves, P. B. (1966) *Faith for the Older Years.* Minneapolis, Minn.: Augsburg.

Maves, P. B., ed. (1954) *Pastoral Psychology* 5, (46).

Maves, P. B., and J. L. Cedarleaf (1949) *Older People and the Church.* New York: Abingdon-Cokesbury Press.

McLeish, J. A. B. (1983) *The Challenge of Aging: Ulyssean Paths to Creative Living.* Vancouver, B.C.: Douglas and McIntyre.

Miller, M. (1979) *Suicide after Sixty.* New York: Springer.

Moberg, D. O. (1980) "Aging and Theological Education." *Theological Education* 16 (3) (Special Issue):283–93.

Moody, H. R., and T. R. Cole (1986) "Aging and Meaning: A Bibliographic Essay." In Cole, 247–54.

Oliver, D. (1987) *New Directions in Religion and Aging.* New York: Haworth.

Payne, B., and E. Brewer, eds. (1989) *Gerontology in Theological Education.* New York: Haworth.

Powers, E., ed. (1988) *Aging Society: A Challenge to Theological Education.* Washington, D.C.: American Association of Retired Persons.

Ramshaw, E. (1987) *Ritual and Pastoral Care.* Philadelphia: Fortress Press.

Robb, T. (1991) *Growing Up: Pastoral Nurture for the Later Years.* New York: Haworth.

Seeber, J. J., ed. (1990) *Spiritual Maturity in the Later Years.* New York: Haworth.

Shute, J. C. (1986) "Life Review: A Cautionary Note." *Clinical Gerontologist* 6 (1):57–58.

Snyder, R. (1983) "Meaning Formation and Significant Survival." Handout at a workshop on Meaning and Senior Adults, San Francisco Theological Seminary, San Anselmo, Calif.

Spangler, J. (1988) "Retired Care." In Powers, 29–36.

Taeuber, C. M. (1992) "Sixty-Five Plus in America." Washington, D.C.: U.S. Department of Commerce, Economics and Statistics Admin., Bureau of the Census.

Thornton, S., and J. Brotchie (1987) "Reminiscence: A Critical Review of the Empirical Literature." *British Journal of Clinical Psychology* 25:93–111.

Tillich, P. (1984) "The Theology of Pastoral Care." in LeFevre, 125–30.

Tobin, S., J. W. Ellor, and S. Anderson-Ray (1986) *Enabling the Elderly: Religious Institutions within the Community Service System.* Albany, N.Y.: State Univ. of New York Press.

U.S. Congress. House Select Committee on Aging (1980) "Future Directions for Aging Policy: A Human Service Model." 96th Congress. Washington, D.C.: U.S. Government Printing Office.

Whitehead, E. E., and J. D. Whitehead (1979) *Christian Life Patterns: The Psychological Challenges and Religious Invitations of Adult Life.* New York: Doubleday.

Wicks, R. J., R. D. Parson, and D. P. Brown, eds. (1985) *Clinical Handbook of Pastoral Counseling.* New York: Paulist Press.

10 Assessment, Referral, and Networking

JAMES W. ELLOR
MARIE A. BRACKI

INTRODUCTION

The need has been well documented for clergy to be trained to respond adequately to the problems of older adults and their families. The types and complexity of problems faced by older adults and their families has proliferated. The range of services that might be helpful has grown at a corresponding rate. Clergy hear about and become involved in many of the problems of their older members. While some of these problems and concerns can be addressed by calling on members of congregations to assist one another, other problems are not as easily addressed.

The helping process is a natural part of the role for most clergy in light of their theology and personal concern for persons. However, few have received formal training in the processes of assessment and referral. Given the complexity of many of older adult needs and the increasing number of elderly, the need for clergy skills in this area has never been greater. This gap in training reflects a major problem in light of research findings that suggest that, particularly among older adults, clergy are the first persons outside of the family who are sought out for assistance.

Furthermore, as many issues are intergenerational in nature, requests for help may come not from older persons, but from their children or younger friends who are aware of the possibilities for services, including counseling. Referrals made "across the miles" via EAPs (Employee Assistance Programs), managed care, or other related sources can be anticipated to increase. As the baby boomers age they will request services and will be clear about what they expect not only for themselves but also for their aging parents. This article discusses the role of clergy in assessment and referral. It will address some specific concerns about assessment and referral. Finally, ethical issues related to assessment and referral will be noted and suggestions made regarding the value of collaborative consultation.

ROLE OF CLERGY IN ASSESSMENT AND REFERRAL

Clergy often play a vital role in the panorama of sources of assistance for older adults. Studies by Veroff et al. (1981) have suggested that when a problem arises, outside the family clergy are the most likely to be contacted before even the family physician or a social service agency. This pattern is undoubtedly more true for nonmedical than for medical issues. Pruyser (1976) offers three reasons why persons contact clergy. They may do so because clergy have an historical tradition of helping. Second, the helping patterns of clergy have included a concern with physical as well as emotional and spiritual healing. Third, individuals, both in a congregation and in the community, turn to clergy because they know them. Clergypersons might be contacted then for emotional support or assistance or for counsel on a religious matter that bothers them. One study suggests that "one-fifth of the clients of a pastoral counseling center gave religious reasons for choosing the center" (Posavac and Hartung, 1977).

Clergy play an important role in the greater network of mental health. If pastors are the first professional contacted outside the family, then clergy are on the front line of the mental-health continuum of services. Such counseling, however, is but one of many tasks in the life of busy pastors. A study of clergy in British Columbia found that the average clergyperson spends seven hours per week providing counseling (Wright, 1984). Assuming that pastors work a forty-hour week, counseling constitutes 17.5 percent of their work week. The actual percentage would vary, of course, depending on the nature of the congregation, availability of family and other sources of support, as well as the available counseling skills of pastors. However, clergy roles involve numerous other tasks from preaching to teaching during the remainder of the week. Part of the unique role of clergy is that they frequently relate to many more aspects of the lives of people they help than simply providing counseling.

Clergy become involved in counseling and helping persons in many different ways. For some it is an application of their advanced training in counseling. Many clergy, however, become involved because they come into contact with persons in need in much the same way that family members respond when a relative has a problem. At times, clergypersons may get involved whether or not they have the necessary expertise to help, simply because they are the only ones available at that moment.

THE ASSESSMENT—NOT DIAGNOSIS—PROCESS

Why should clergypersons engage in any assessment at all? The simplest answer is that the more information that is available about individuals and their situations, the more appropriate and effective the helping response can be. People engage in assessment all the time, but usually with little specific direction about what to do or how to do it. Involvement with a person in need implies that the clergyperson will make an assessment. Sometimes this is a matter of listening to the individual describe his or her need. If the request is for a ride to the doctor, the rabbi, priest, or minister becomes a broker of services by calling another parishioner to assist the caller. At other times the concerns or problems may be more complex. Emotional problems may be more severe or health problems more complex. At these times the clergyperson needs to be able to assess the situation. Assessment under these circumstances focuses on how the concern or request for assistance should be handled.

What should be assessed is the next logical question to face. Often mental-health problems come to the attention of clergypersons as noted above. Occasionally the problem is obvious, such as in psychosis or acute depression. More often, however, the problem is more subtle and requires a greater exploration of different facets of the individual's life, behaviors, physical health, etc. Additionally, illness may not be evident, although it may be affecting the person's mental health and the person's overall physical well-being.

An assessment process by clergypersons should emerge from those paradigms or professional points of reference with which clergy are familiar. Within the social sciences social workers, psychologists, and counselors approach the task in similar ways. For these mental-health professionals, the emphasis is on clinical assessment. Clinical assessment involves exploration with the client of the various issues and concerns presented. During this process, the clinician along with the client draw some conclusions as to what is needed and how to approach any future counseling sessions or a pending referral. While mental-health clinicians do not start from a single model, they do start with a similar set of tools to work with clients. Psychologists may add formal testing to the assessment process. These objective measures may contribute specific information to the clinical judgment of the clinician.

For clergy, there is no single approach recognized in the literature. Some clergy rely entirely on clinical judgment; others may include testing in the process of assessment. Two variables make clergy somewhat different from other therapists. First, clergy are associated with the supernatural. It has been suggested that two types of therapists are sought out for their ability to perform magic, the psychiatrist with pills and clergy for their relationship to the divine. Regardless of the extent to which the client or parishioner ascribes a greater relationship with the divine to the pastor, he or she may seek a pastor to invoke or reflect the will of God in the counseling process. The second variable suggests an investment in the spiritual dimension. Holistic assessment as understood by Alfred Adler and other existential psychologists includes an understanding that persons are made up of physical, social, and emotional aspects. An important part of this concept is that these elements cannot be artificially separated within persons. Therefore, the connection among these various aspects of persons presents human nature as a single, unified being.

Granger Westberg offered the addition of the "w" to holism, suggesting the inclusion of the spiritual aspect of persons. Most clergy would heartily agree with this addition. The investment in and ability to speak with authority about the spiritual aspect of the whole person suggests a unique relationship between the clergyperson and the parishioner or client.

The unique position of clergy in the continuum of mental health professionals implies the potential for a distinctive approach to assessment. Hunt et al. (1990) note, "The word *assessment* implies that a comparison is to be made between 'what is' and some specified standard or set of criteria" (13). In formulating a view of human nature for assessment, pastors must question what aspects of the traditional paradigms from psychology inform their understanding of human nature as well as what theological principles are also implied by their statement of faith. Within the realms of psychology, the view of human nature and approach to the client are defined by the paradigm that is followed. This paradigm dictates the types of questions and even how the questions are asked within the context of assessment. Clergy modify such paradigms by inclusion of a theological position that reflects personal and/or denominational preferences.

Examination of the literature on what to assess yields numerous perspectives (and opinions) on the spiritual element. For some clergy, spirituality is important, but not well integrated into their understanding of counseling. For others, the spiritual is a primary focus. Indeed, one of the complaints articulated by many mental-health professionals is that some clergy only wish to discuss the spiritual and ignore the other aspects of the person.

It is important to note that all assessment involves an interpretation based on a particular view of the human nature of the client. For a person who utilizes the behavioral paradigm, behaviors are the products of learning. Therefore, what is to be addressed in assessment are the antecedents and consequences for the behaviors in question. For the psychoanalytic therapist, the problems of the individual are rooted in unconscious conflicts. Therefore, assessment entails a process of identifying the conflicts in order to promote insight into the unconscious. An eclectic professional may seek to elicit information regarding the problem as perceived by the individual and pursue the issues in whatever way appears appropriate for the situation. The field of gerontology has not developed a single paradigm. Rather, it has sought to enhance the existing paradigms or views of persons with additional information about the aging process.

The Importance of a Religious Dimension

Perhaps clergypersons would feel most comfortable trying to understand the meaning that religion has for the person who has come seeking assistance. But this seemingly simple concept is more complicated than it appears. Does religion mean the participation in a church service or attendance at a social event or a discussion of one's relationship with God? Research literature identifies the multidimensionality of this subject and suggests that it would be useful to understand individual differences in order better to intervene in multiple areas if necessary.

The need to understand the role of religion for older persons has been documented extensively. Moberg (1986) notes:

> Ninety-five percent of those aged sixty-five or more who participated in a 1982 poll said they pray, and more than four-fifths claimed their religious faith was the most important influence in their lives. . . . Despite greater incidence of health and mobility problems, the elderly had higher rates of attendance at a church or synagogue, with forty-nine percent attending in an average week, compared to forty-one percent for all adults (13).

The 1987 Gallup poll (Princeton R. R. C., 1987) found that older adults were more likely to be members of a religious congregation and participate in groups for Bible study or prayer. Sixty-seven percent of persons aged sixty-five or over felt that religion was very important in their lives. Numerous surveys have demonstrated the comparative importance of religion to the current population of seniors. These studies note that people do *not* seem to become more religious as they age; rather, as a society we have become less religiously oriented. Thus, future elderly may be less religious.

One approach to religion has been the sociological perspective which, among other things, deals with the religious role in various subcultures and denotes sex differences in church attendance and general participation (Birren and Schaie, 1990; Kane and Kane, 1981). Palmore (1980) stated that the church is in a unique position to assist seniors since it is the single organization to which more seniors may belong than any other. He attributed this phenomenon to the fact that these elders were raised in a more religious era and have retained that part of their lives. It stands to reason, then, that this cohort may be more inclined to talk with a minister than with a traditional mental-health professional. If religion is important, a reasonable understanding as to how it affects individual lives would be important to many research and practice studies. Historically this has been addressed using three primary constructs: religiosity, spiritual well-being, and spirituality.

Religiosity. Barbara Payne (1982) delineates the three main categories of the methodological use of religious variables used prior to 1976 as "(1) organizational participation; (2) religiosity, including privatized religious behavior; and (3) religious activities, practices, and personal adjustment" (344). During that time, two significant questions consumed most of the emphasis of study. "Do persons become more religious as they age?" and "What do these religious variables correlate with?".

E. D. Starbuck (1911), a pioneer in the field of psychology and religion, concluded that "faith and belief in God grow in importance as the years advance." This study initiated the debate as to whether or not change in religious practice was an aging effect or more of a cohort effect. More recent studies by Orbach (1961) and Cavan et al. (1949) reached similar conclusions. In 1922, G. Stanley Hall concluded that persons do *not* grow more religious as they age. This particular issue was addressed by the Duke University longitudinal studies. Blazer and Palmore (1976) concluded that religious attitudes and satisfaction tend not to change significantly after the age of seventeen. Little further inquiry has been made since 1976.

A second theme incorporated religious variables as correlates. Some of the variables researched were militancy (Alston et al., 1972), disengagement theory (Cook, 1971), fear of death (Feifel, 1974), and religious practice (Lazerwitz, 1961). Payne (1982) notes that "measures used for studies of religion and aging between 1948 and 1976 . . . reflect a theoretical absorption with disengagement theory and its counterpart, activity theory" (343).

Two basic problems emerge with these religiosity-based studies. The first is a problem of definition. The term *religiosity* is generally used for the approach employed by these studies. However, the term itself is frequently not defined. In much of the literature the terms *religion, religious,* and *religiosity* are used indiscriminately to refer to some type of behavior or feeling that can be associated with religion.

Persons who were trying to understand religious variables were social scientists, most often sociologists. For a social scientist to study a phenomenon, it must have a definition that reflects a quantifiable object, or behavior. Scientific study of religion suggested that for any observation to be objective, it must be verifiable by other researchers. Thus, such items as, Do you attend a religious worship service? or How often do you pray? became common indicators of religion. Most clergy or philosophers would note that while these religious factors reflect the activities of religion, they fail to examine faith. Somewhat closer to a discussion of faith or belief were questions that asked, How strongly do you believe in . . . ? Unfortunately, these items continue to defy philosophical continuity, since asking any group of persons, How strongly do you believe in God? without asking for a definition of God makes the data less useful.

A second problem raised by the first is that defining and understanding religion varies according to the professional orientation of the individual. Persons who are philosophers and theologians would suggest that focus on primary observable variables fails to capture the internal metaphysical ramifications of faith. Social scientists, on the other hand, often suggest that one's behaviors are reflective of one's beliefs. Once again, the failure to put forward a viable set of definitions weakens the ability to work with the outcomes of study. The assessment of religiosity is important but, taken alone, is far from sufficient to understand religion in the lives of older Americans.

Spiritual well-being, modeled after the Life Satisfaction Indexes of the 1960s, provided a valuable stepping stone for research to assess the spiritual domain. Moberg and Brusek (1978) and Moberg (1984) as well as others have attempted to develop scales for spiritual well-being, using them both as free-standing instruments and as insertions into other instruments. This concept also provided a useful paradigm for the development of programs utilizing a holistic philosophy during the 1970s and early 1980s.

In an effort to define spiritual well-being, the National Interfaith Coalition on Aging (1975) suggested that "spiritual well-being is the affirmation of life in a relationship with God, self, community and environment that nurtures and celebrates wholeness." This definition contained the elements of Moberg's concept, but in language that did not lend itself to the development of a measurement tool.

Moberg (1971) conceptualized spiritual well-being as having both a horizontal and a vertical component. Ellison (1983) notes, "The vertical dimension refers to our sense of well-being in relation to God. The horizontal dimension refers to a sense of life purpose and life satisfaction, with no reference to anything specifically religious" (331).

Spirituality. There have been many attempts to define and measure spirituality. Paloutzian and Ellison (1982) constructed a religious well-being scale and an existential well-being scale. It has been used by numerous researchers and clinicians since its development (Ellison and Smith, 1991). Gleason (1990) has suggested that spirituality exists on a continuum between literalism and symbolism. He points out the utility for clergy to understand where their parishioners' views fall in order to be able to respond in a more meaningful way to them. Elkins et al. (1988) developed a "nonreligious approach to the therapeutic treatment of clients suffering from spiritual distress" (16). Fitchett and Burck (1990) used a multidimensional model to understand spirituality. It is the only tool that has been developed by chaplains, rather than by psychologists and sociologists. However, it employs a sophisticated theological paradigm, not applicable to psychosocial assessment.

Other instruments include the Contemporary Spirituality Inventory (CSI) developed by Trent and colleagues (1991). In this inventory spirituality is defined by the use of factor analysis of a series of questions. Religious or spiritual behaviors or religiosity do not seem to be included. McFadden and Falck (personal correspondence) have designed an instrument to measure spiritual integration. The SPIN is an instrument recently developed and based on a theoretical model originally conceptualized by Thibault and colleagues (1991). It employs a wholistic approach to understanding the spiritual dimension. Critical to any understanding of wholism is not that there are multiple dimensions, but how the dimensions come together. Holistic and wholistic theorists agree that the various dimensions cannot be separated. However, if we conceive of them as pieces, then we can treat them separately. Spiritual well-being added the concept that the role of the spiritual is to be an integrative element in the life of the individual. Thus, the spiritual is not one dimension, but an integrative dimension. The developers of the SPIN see the potential for any of the dimensions of the person to perform integrative functions. This includes the various subdimensions of spirituality. Within the SPIN reside three subdimensions: the cognitive, affective, and behavioral. These dimensions are not dissimilar from those found in Glock or implied by some of the concepts involved in the work of the authors of spiritual well-being. However, in the SPIN, the integrative dimension is not a part of any one dimension, but rather seen as the life force of the individual.

Spiritual assessment is not an activity to be engaged in only by clergy, nor should it be viewed in isolation as another personal attribute to be studied. Recent literature affirms that spiritual well-being increases personal adjustment, can improve physical health, and can improve quality of life (summarized in Bracki et al., 1990). The assessment of spiritual needs can give a clinicians, clergy persons, or well-trained volunteers important information for planning and intervention on behalf of the client population for whom they intervene. This is especially significant when the broader concept of spirituality is used. A simple tally of church attendance or belief in a specific dogma or system does not give much information about what a person might find useful to deal with unmet spiritual needs. For example, viewing beauty in nature may be considered an expression of spirituality *and* may also have been used as a comfort during previous times of adversity. If it can be determined that a resident has had little opportunity for this, some resource might be made available to that individual. No single instrument can identify all needs and beliefs, but it *can* be used as an entree to a more careful and focused discussion.

The efforts to understand spirituality and to contribute to both clinical and research activities have become somewhat more sophisticated in the past several years. We have clearly moved beyond religiosity as too narrow an approach. Religiosity should not be completely discarded, however, as it is one aspect of spirituality. The greater depth meaning of faith and the spiritual aspect of persons needs to be explored.

The initial assessment to be done by clergypersons may include, but should not be limited to, an examination of the role of religion in the client's life, but it should also look at the broader domain of spirituality. It is the authors' position that this could be a highly significant part of a comprehensive approach in understanding an individual who has presented him- or herself for help. For the senior population especially, this variable may be critical in identifying strengths and coping mechanisms to assist in all levels of intervention.

Referral

While clergy may not be experts in diagnosing physical or emotional problems, they can certainly recognize that a problem may exist. It is at that point that a referral is in order to a more appropriate source to clarify the problem. All of the disciplines in the health and mental-health fields advocate referral to someone with more expertise when more information is essential or when the client is unresponsive to treatment. This principle is expressed in various codes of ethics. Clergypersons should consider this practice and take the initiative in forming collaborative relationships with service providers in other disciplines in the best interest of the client/parishioner.

Once an assessment is completed it may become clear that a pastor/therapist is not able to offer all of the services necessary. Under these conditions a referral is warranted. A referral is defined as offering the client/parishioner other options for services beyond those offered by the referring pastor or counseling center. In some cases this may be as simple as suggesting that the individual see his or her physician, or it may involve a more complex effort to engage multiple services.

A study by Wright (1984) suggests that social workers and physicians are the most common professions referred to when clergy make referrals. Wright goes on to note that referrals between clergy and community agencies are usually one way—to the agency. The range of needs to be addressed should be reflected in the range of services or referral sources known to clergypersons. The first step is to establish who the resources are within the community. When working with older adults, one important place to begin is with the local area agency on aging. The 1973 Amendments to the Older Americans Act established the area agency on aging to provide information and referral and to coordinate services for older adults. While the mandates have changed somewhat since 1973, these agencies continue to be the lead agency in assuring information availability to older people. All fifty states are served by area agencies on aging.

It may be useful for persons establishing referral resources to visit the local area agency on aging and any other primary referral sources in their community. Face-to-face contact with persons who can respond to the needs of persons in the parish can set the stage for a more personalized response at the time of need. A wide range of community services may be available from nutrition services and transportation to home health and recreational services. Even mental-health and social work specialists in gerontology are developing. Some agencies offer consultation and training for professionals and the general public.

Once referral sources are established, a system to keep track of the information is needed. Various systems for this, from a rolodex or card file to a computerized data set, can be employed. The most important factor in any referral program is to keep it current. This will include the types of services offered, criteria for eligibility, and financial arrangements that are possible to pay for the services. The more detailed the information obtained, the more detail there is to keep up to date. For many religious organizations, this may mean that simply keeping primary resources on file such as the area agency on aging or the state department on aging is more functional than trying to keep up with all of the details involved in a comprehensive system of referral.

Once the therapist or pastor finds a resource and determines the agency to which he or she wishes to refer, the next step is to make the referral. It is usually best to assist the parishioner/client to talk directly with the agency. If the individual needs assistance in the process, a release may be used for exchange of information. The referring person will need to know some basic information about the client/parishioner (age, gender, marital status, possibly information about income and assets), as well as information about the condition or problem that is prompting the referral. In cases where a guardian, close relative, or some other third party is involved in the decision, he or she will also need to give consent for exchange of information and should be involved in the referral process.

The legal and ethical rules of confidentiality must be carefully observed. Depending on the state, there are generally laws governing the types of information that can be transmitted to whom. For example, if a patient leaves the hospital, extensive records can be forwarded to a home health agency with the approval of the patient. However, even with the patient's approval, many hospitals cannot forward the same information to a clergyperson.

Studies by Tobin et al. (1985) suggest that when mutual respect is established between referral sources and clergy, problems of distrust between professionals from different disciplines can be avoided. The clergyperson can take initiative by demonstrating the need to care for the whole person in a comprehensive manner. In so doing, the process of collaborative consultation may be established. In this context, various professions may share their expertise to develop a common treatment plan that is inclusive and thorough.

Resources to provide for religious and spiritual needs should be included in the treatment plan if it is a wholistic response to individuals. Traditional spiritual practices may be highly relevant to the person, or possibly what is needed for spiritual sustenance is not very traditional at all. Clergy may find themselves advocating for persons on the basis of what those persons' needs seem to be rather than what a religious congregation might believe is needed.

SUMMARY

Clergy are often the first line of response to the needs of older adults. In this role they must be able to respond personally and/or by making a referral. This requires careful, whole-person assessment that allows pastors to obtain enough information to decide either how to help individuals or how to make appropriate referrals.

One of the key factors that clergy can effectively assess is the domain of religion and spirituality. This can be a significant part of understanding the whole person and should provide much needed information for identifying strengths and coping mechanisms. Clergy can also take the initiative to form collaborative consultative relationships with other caregivers in order to provide comprehensive treatment approaches that involve professionals from other disciplines.

BIBLIOGRAPHY

Alston, J. P., C. W. Peek, and C. R. Windgrove (1972) "Religiosity and Black Militants: A Reappraisal." *Journal for the Scientific Study of Religion* 11:252–69.

Birren, J. E., and K. W. Schaie (1990) *Handbook of the Psychology of Aging*. 3d ed. New York: Academic Press.

Blazer, D., and E. Palmore (1976) "Religion and Aging in a Longitudinal Panel." *The Gerontologist* 16 (1):82–85.

Bracki, M. A., J. M. Thibault, F. E. Netting, and J. W. Ellor (1990) "Principles of Integrating Spiritual Assessment into Counseling with Older Adults." *Generations* 14 (4):55–58.

Busse, E., and D. Blazer, eds. (1980) *Handbook of Geriatric Psychiatry*. New York: Van Nostrand Reinhold.

Cavan, R. S., E. W. Burgess, R. J. Havighurst, and H. Goldhamer (1949) *Personal Adjustment in Old Age*. Chicago: Science Research Associates.

Cook, J. (1971) "An Application of the Disengagement Theory of Aging to Older Persons in the Church." Ph.D. dissertation, University of Michigan.

Elkins, D., L. Hedstrom, L. Hughes, J. Leaf, and C. Saunders (1988) "Toward a Humanistic Phenomenological Spirituality: Definition, Description and Measurement." *Journal of Humanistic Psychology* 28 (4):5–18.

Ellison, C. W. (1983) "Spiritual Well-Being: Conceptualization and Measurement." *Journal of Psychology and Theology* 11 (4):330–40.

Ellison, C. W., and J. Smith (1991) "Toward an Integrative Measure of Health and Well-Being." *Journal of Psychology and Theology* 19 (1):35–48.

Feifel, H. (1974) "Religious Conviction and Fear of Death among the Healthy and the Terminally Ill." *Journal of the Scientific Study of Religion* 13:353–60.

Fitchett, G., and J. R. Burck (1990) "A Multi-Dimensional, Functional Model for Spiritual Assessment." *The Care Giver Journal* 7 (1):43–61.

Gleason, J. J. (1990) "Spiritual Assessment and Pastoral Response: A Schema Revised and Updated." *Journal of Pastoral Care* 44 (1):66–75.

Glock, C. Y. (1962) "On the Study of Religious Commitment." *Religious Education* 57 (Research Supplement): S98–110.

Hall, G. S. (1922) *Senescence, the Second Half of Life*. New York: Appleton.

Hunt, R. A., J. E. Hinkle, Jr., and H. N. Malony (1990) "Overview of Dimensions and Issues." In *Clergy Assessment and Career Development*. Edited by R. A. Hunt, J. E. Hinkle Jr., and H. N. Malony, 13–18. Nashville: Abingdon Press.

Kane, R., and R. L. Kane (1981) *Assessing the Elderly: A Practical Guide to Measurement*. Lexington, Mass.: Lexington Books.

Lazerwitz, B. (1961) "Some Factors Associated with Variation in Church Attendance." *Social Forces* 39:301–9.

Magan, G. G., and E. L. Haught, eds. (1986) *Well-Being and the Elderly: An Holistic View.* Washington, D.C.: American Assn. Homes for the Aging.

Mangen, D. J., and W. A. Peterson, eds. (1982) *Social Roles and Social Participation.* Vol. 2 of *Research Instruments in Social Gerontology.* Minneapolis, Minn.: University of Minneapolis Press.

Moberg, D. O. (1971) *Spiritual Well-Being.* Washington, D.C.: White House Conference on Aging.

______ (1979) *Spiritual Well-Being Sociological Perspectives.* Washington D.C.: University Press of America, Inc.

______ (1984) "Subjective Measures of Spiritual Well-Being." *Review of Religious Research* 25 (4): 351–64.

______ (1986) "Spirituality, Aging, and Spiritual Care." In Magan and Haught, 11–22.

Moberg, D. O., and P. M. Brusek (1978) "Spiritual Well-Being: A Neglected Subject in Quality of Life Research." *Social Indicators Research* 5:303–23.

National Interfaith Coalition on Aging (1975) *Spiritual Well-Being: A Definition.* Athens, Ga.: National Interfaith Coalition on Aging.

Orbach, H. L. (1961) "Aging and Religion." *Geriatrics* 16:530–40.

Palmore, E. (1980) "The Social Factors in Aging." In Busse and Blazer, 222–48.

Paloutzian, R. F., and C. W. Ellison (1982) "Loneliness, Spiritual Well-Being, and Quality of Life." In Peplau and Pelman, 224–37.

Payne, B. P. (1982) "Religiosity." In Mangen and Peterson, 343–87.

Peplau, L. A., and D. Perlman, eds. (1982) *Loneliness: A Sources Book of Current Theory, Research and Theory.* New York: Wiley Interscience.

Posavac, E. J., and B. M. Hartung (1977) "Exploration into the Reasons People Choose a Pastoral Counselor instead of Another Type of Psychotherapist." *Journal of Pastoral Care* 31:23–31.

Princeton Religion Research Center (1987) *Religion in America.* Princeton: Princeton Religion Center.

Pruyser, P. W. (1976) *The Minister as Diagnostician.* Philadelphia: Westminster Press.

Renetzky, L. (1979) "The Fourth Dimension: Applications to the Social Services." In Moberg 1979, 215–28.

Starbuck, E. D. (1911) *The Psychology of Religion: An Empirical Study of the Growth of Religious Consciousness.* 3d ed. New York: Charles Scribner's Sons.

Stark, R., and C. Y. Glock (1966) *American Piety.* Los Angeles: Univ. of California Press.

Thibault, J. M., J. W. Ellor, and F. E. Netting (1991) "A Conceptual Framework for Assessing the Spiritual Functioning and Fulfillment of Older Adults in Long-Term Care Settings." *Journal of Religious Gerontology* 7 (4):29–45.

Thorson, J. A., and T. C. Cook, Jr., eds. (1980) *Spiritual Well-Being of the Elderly.* Springfield, Ill.: Charles C. Thomas Publisher.

Tobin, S. S., S. M. Anderson-Ray, J. W. Ellor, and T. Ehrenpreis (1985) "Enhancing CMHC and Church Collaboration for the Elderly." *Community Mental Health Journal* 21 (1):58–61.

Trent, D. D., J. Mouriz, C. Helberg, and J. H. Garner (1991) "Contemporary Spiritual Inventory." Unpublished Paper. Department of Counseling Psychology, Univ. of Kansas, Lawrence, Kansas.

Veroff, J., R. A. Kulka, and E. Douvan (1981) *Mental Health in America: Patterns of Help-Seeking from 1957 to 1976.* New York: Basic Books.

Wright, P. G. (1984) "The Counseling Activities and Referral Practices of Canadian Clergy in British Columbia." *Journal of Psychology and Theology* 12:294–304.

11 Pastoral Care of African Americans

ANNE STREATY WIMBERLY
EDWARD P. WIMBERLY

Older African Americans are often considered to be survivors and effective life copers. This derives from the assumption that their advancement to old age is, alone, an accomplishment in personal coping (Chatters and Taylor, 1989). There is no denying the coping skills and the moral and spiritual strengths of African Americans who have reached the older adult life stage. However, these persons often need assistance in their movement through the life stage and turn to others for it. They seek support that can help and sustain them as they face the tasks associated with their life stage and stress-producing issues. Their faith community plays a significant role in this regard.

The supportive networks and the spiritual and religious functions of the church are key elements for coping used by older African Americans (Chatters and Taylor, 1989, 313; Taylor, 1986, 635). Pastoral care and nurture are part of the church's ministry that assist in the provision of resources for older African Americans. The purpose of this chapter is to show how pastoral care and nurture function as part of the church's response to older African Americans. Attention will be given to: (1) the meaning of pastoral care and nurture, (2) life-stage tasks and issues of older African Americans addressed by pastoral care and nurture, and (3) approaches to care and nurture.

THE MEANING OF PASTORAL CARE AND NURTURE

Pastoral care and nurture of African American older adults constitute a way of caring that is consistent with the overall understanding of African American pastoral care. Specifically, pastoral care and nurture are contextual responses of *agape* love by caring others who understand themselves to be related significantly to God. They are direct contextual responses to the needs of older African Americans for resources found within the faith community. They are also mediators of needed resources found outside the church. Both pastoral care and nurture are intricately related. Yet, they are distinct and have their own unique foci. Nurture refers to creating a caring environment within which care can occur. It also refers to educational and advocacy initiatives with and on behalf of older persons. Pastoral care refers to the actual direct caring response by others to persons facing life transitions and life crises.

Effective pastoral care and nurture for African American older adults are responses to specific needs of these persons within their specific sociocultural context. This emphasis means that a contextual or indigenous model of pastoral care and nurture is preferred. A model is needed that responds to these persons' preferences for diverse types of support including material aid, information, and emotional support. It also takes into account their preference for informal network helpers.

It is important to recognize that the indigenous model necessarily differs from the model undergirding much of the counseling and care taking place in the United States. That is, its dominant focus is not on individualized formal therapeutic settings often found in current models (E. Wimberly, 1990, 98). Communal relationships and the church as a healing entity provide the normative framework within which solicitous care and support of African American older adults take place. Within this framework, persons can share the life issues they face. Through this framework, the sources of these issues are located and ways of addressing issues are found. Moreover, focus is on assisting older African Americans to affirm a lasting and transcendent foundation for their lives that goes beyond what everyday societal roles and activity can provide.

In short, the indigenous model of pastoral care and nurture embraces a worldview or overarching meaning system that emphasizes a communal and wholistic orientation toward care and nurture. It includes a collective group orientation compared to an individualistic orientation. It also emphasizes the use of oral-auditory aspects of perception that are distinct from a visual or a written cultural orientation. At the center of the model is a vital support network, needed resources, and storytelling and story-listening approaches (E. Wimberly, 1990, 97). The caring and nurturing model must be built on the strengths of the cultural context of African American elders.

Importance of Caring Others and Resources

Pastoral care and nurture of African American older adults are responses of *agape* love undertaken by a network of caring others (E. Wimberly, 1983, 4). This network of caring others is understood to include the clergy and the faith community, family members, and extended family members. In pastoral care and nurture of older African Americans, these people comprise a communal network of relationships that reflect the quality of God's *agape* love.

Through the network of caring others, resources are mobilized that are aimed toward assisting older persons in confronting life issues that are painful, troubling, or unexpected. This network is also aimed toward helping persons find a basis for ongoing life meaning in the face of difficult life issues.

Within the African American church and experience, resources refer to cultural, spiritual, emotional, social, and interpersonal supports on which older adults rely. These resources need to be explored further.

Cultural Resources. Cultural resources are embodied in the historical African American worldview. A worldview is an overarching meaning system that informs the entire life of a particular community. The worldview provides stories on which older adults draw for sustenance. Included among the stories are ones focused on cultural heroes and heroines of the past and present, particularly persons who have come through great adversity. There are also nurturing stories associated with family and friends. The worldview also provides values from which older adults draw to make meaning in their lives. The contents of this value orientation include (1) the inherent worthiness of each person as unique, (2) the inner potential for growth and development in relationship to God and others, (3) the primacy of caring and supportive relationships in community, and (4) the power of God working through the community to build up the lives of persons (E. Wimberly, 1982, 32; Lincoln and Mamiya, 1990, 2–7).

African American elders view as important their transmission of stories and values of the worldview to the next generation; and they revere opportunities to do so. This place of elders in the transmission of the worldview is captured in the following:

> But, with specific reference to the black church, there exists a world view that undergirds its past religious life and that has come to us by the way of a tradition of the elders. This tradition includes recorded and oral affirmations of the faith of slaves and ex-slaves. (Wimberly and Wimberly, 1986, 14)

As custodians of the worldview, elders passed on the tradition of caring as well as the values that undergird the tradition. In pastoral care, then, they become the carers as well as the recipients of care.

Spiritual Resources. Spiritual resources take the form of nurture through prayer, Bible reading and study, and participation in the ritual life of the faith community and other religious activities. These resources are important means of coping and are ways by which older adults form and reaffirm attitudes, values, and skills needed for deepening their faith (Chatters and Taylor, 1989; Taylor, 1986, 636). Through these resources they are opened to God's ever-present love and forgiveness and the enlivening of the inner life. They are also placed in touch with a normative framework that serves as a guide for making critical decisions.

Emotional, Social, and Interpersonal Resources. Emotional, social, and interpersonal resources emerge out of available patterns of meaningful ties and relationships that help people maintain emotional and spiritual well-being. These patterns of relationships are evidenced by the ongoing expressions of care, comfort, and support of older adults by clergy and natural support groupings. These patterns also involve structured responses by clergy to the needs and requests of older adults and their family members for guidance and help. Through caring relationships, persons maintain a sense of wholeness amidst the challenges of older adulthood.

LIFE-STAGE TASKS AND LIFE ISSUES OF OLDER ADULT AFRICAN AMERICANS

Pastoral care and nurture are needed to assist older African Americans in addressing specific life-stage tasks and life issues. The term "life tasks" refers to actions undertaken by persons that are aimed toward attaining positive resolution of challenges associated with life transitions as one moves from one life stage to another.

The term "life issues" refers to situational needs, demands, problems, and concerns of older African Americans that require coping resources and strategies. Life issues hold potential for threatening the well-being of persons. When life issues go unresolved, they make the positive outcome of life tasks difficult. In this way, life tasks and life issues are related. The network of caring others must be aware of both the life tasks and the life issues facing older African Americans. Resources must be mobilized that can assist in addressing both. The intent here is to explicate key life tasks and life issues of older African Americans.

Life Tasks and Life Issues of Older African Americans

Erik Erikson's life cycle theory has been influential in pastoral care and nurture through focus on tasks associated with each life stage (see chap. 7). Seen as applicable across cultures, Erikson's developmental theory provides a helpful starting point for understanding tasks confronting African American older adults. That is, his conceptual framework is helpful in setting the stage, as it were, for looking at contextually specific tasks and issues (Erikson, 1985).

Erikson proposes that developing a sense of ego-integrity is contingent on a person's strong sense of identity developed earlier in the life cycle. But, the concern for identity is not confined to earlier stages. Affirming a valued identity continues over the life course and must be considered a central task during older adulthood (Gordon et al., 1976, 323; Bianchi, 1982, 137–38, 178–79). This is particularly true with African American older adults whose self-image is deeply affected by their experiences as part of an ethnic minority group in America and by losses and diminishments related and unrelated to this status (Bianchi, 1982, 137).

In addition to ego-integrity, generativity is another life task that older African Americans face. For Erikson the task of generativity involves developing and sustaining care for future generations (Erikson, 1985, 266–68). Failure to develop this capacity is called stagnation.

For older African Americans, there is the need to contribute to the welfare of others and to be needed by others. Fulfillment of the generativity task sometimes evokes issues that call for special care and support. For example, older adults sometimes find it difficult to express their feelings about negative consequences of caring for younger family members. As a result, their personal needs may go unmet. They also sometimes find it difficult to give up activities and responsibilities within the faith community that have had great meaning for them. This is because they experience the relinquishing of revered roles as the relinquishment of their need to be generative as well as their access to mutual support. Care must be taken to create an environment where the advantages and disadvantages of generative roles can be explored.

Persons involved in pastoral care and nurture of African American older adults need to take into account the very real reference points that impact their attaining a sense of ego-integrity, affirming a valued identity, and developing generativity. A key reference point is life experiences, past and present, within larger society. Another key reference point is those experiences, past and present, within the various arenas of African American culture. Cognizance of these reference points is helpful in deciding specific pastoral care and nurture initiatives that help persons to address wholistically and positively life tasks and life issues (Moseley, 1991, 59; Chatters, 1988, 246–47).

Larger Society as a Reference Point

The life tasks of older adulthood cannot be divorced from the minority status of older African Americans in larger society. Indeed, use of this experience as a reference point is essential because persons bring into older adulthood feelings about their experiences. They confront ongoing effects of assaults to identity and of limitations imposed by their stigmatized status. This presents a crisis for many and a block to their ability to live life with meaning and integrity and to affirm within themselves a valued identity.

It is only when ministries of pastoral care and nurture take into account larger society as a reference point that the life tasks and life issues of older African Americans can be addressed from their specific contextual vantage point.

Context-Specific Life Tasks and Life Issues

This section will present a case study as a way of illustrating what is meant by life tasks and life issues from a context-specific perspective using larger society as a reference point. The case illustration is as follows:

> Mrs. R. is seventy-six years old. She began to talk about some of her experiences when she was younger. She recalled going to a public school for African Americans where the books she and the other students used were outdated and stamped with the name of the white school up the road. She remembered being dead earnest about finishing high school. But she felt forced to quit school after the ninth grade because the income she could make by going to work was needed to add to already meager family resources.
>
> The only work she could find was as a domestic worker with no social security and no other benefits. She said she didn't really understand the importance of social security then, but she does now.
>
> Off and on she had done domestic work after she married in order to add to her husband's janitorial work income and to provide for their children. Her husband died some years ago. Her income now is very meager and she covers up her feelings so others can't tell, because she feels that it does not do anybody any good to complain. But, sometimes she said she feels like giving up. She said that remembering all those years of hard work with so little to show for it is depressing, especially because of the situation she is in now. She said she would still be doing that work, but she had to quit recently because of health problems.
>
> She stated that she wishes things could have been different. But, the way things were "for our people," there wasn't much else to do but to make the best out of a bad thing. She said that among her biggest regrets is that she never got to finish high school. This was in spite of her telling about friends who did finish, but who still were not able to get jobs other than domestic work.

Mrs. R's story highlights the assault to the ego-integrity resulting from earlier experiences as an African American in larger society. Her references to "giving up," "depressing" memories, and "regrets" about unfinished business emphasize the presence of a crisis that calls into question her attainment of a sense of ego-integrity.

The stories of other older African males and females are similar to Mrs. R's. But, often, when asked about life satisfaction, these persons will respond that their lives are satisfying. When their disclosure of their story is sought, it is discovered that some have resigned themselves to their life situation. This resignation becomes translated into "life-satisfaction." Others celebrate whatever they have been able to do with meager opportunities and resources. Their celebration becomes translated into their self-assessed life-satisfaction.

There are, of course, older African Americans who have achieved high educational attainment and occupational position. However, many speak of their journey toward accomplishment as a struggle that sorely challenged their sense of self. It is important, therefore, that their stories be heard as a means of identifying feelings and disappointments.

From a contextual viewpoint, affirming a valued identity and attaining a sense of ego-integrity are interrelated tasks. Both of these tasks have to do with persons seeing their lives as having positive value in spite of their minority status and experiences associated with it. These tasks also entail older adults coming to grips with their feelings about their experiences and what they were or were not able to do about it. Moreover, persons must be able to envision options for coping with current and future consequences related to their past and present status in larger society. It is at this point that specific life issues become connected with the fulfillment of life tasks.

There is need for many older African Americans to confront the impact of status-related economic, health-care, and housing limitations. Like many older African Americans, Mrs. R. faced an issue of material well-being that was related to her work history. This required Mrs. R's participation in the workforce after the normal retirement age. Pastoral care and nurturing ministries are often called upon to respond to the material needs of older adults and to assist them in negotiating structures and services that can help meet dire material need.

An additional point can be made regarding the relationship of life tasks to life issues emanating from older African Americans' status in larger society. Harmful stereotypical images of old age are found in the larger youth-oriented society. These images become issues of older African Americans to the degree that older African Americans have been identified as having a double jeopardy of being African American and being old. Older African American women are said to have a triple jeopardy of being African American, old, and female. Limitations in the basic necessities of life are associated with these jeopardies and interfere with well-being. Indicators of income and economic well-being have consistently shown African American older adults as a particularly disadvantaged group. Moreover, poor health and inadequate housing tend to be correlates of income and economic disadvantage (Manuel, 1988, 44–46). These give cause for care.

Because the issue of insufficient basic supplies of life is of great concern for African American older adults, divesting themselves of negative stereotypes of what it means to be old is not overemphasized, as Bianchi suggests (Bianchi, 1982, 178). It is not the negative image of old age that requires pastoral care and nurture. Indeed, because of repeated hardships older African Americans face through a lifetime of economic and social disadvantage, they tend to perceive themselves as "old" at an earlier chronological age than dominant society members (Bengtson, 1979, 25). Many accept becoming old, socially, as a natural consequence of life. Being old is not necessarily associated with forced retirement and the loss of the work role. In fact, for many, the issue has to do with needing to work or feeling the necessity of work in order to supplement inadequate incomes resulting from discontinuous work histories (Gibson, 1988, 315–19). This issue is compounded for those who find employment in old age impossible either because no job is available or because of health or other reasons.

The key point of this section is that experiences, past and present, of older African Americans within larger society are important for understanding context-specific tasks and issues these persons face. Persons involved in ministries of pastoral care and nurture need to consider this reference point when attempting to assist older African Americans in addressing life tasks and issues.

African American Culture as a Reference Point

The tasks of attaining ego-integrity versus despair, affirming a valued identity, and developing generativity by African American older adults are informed not only by their experiences in larger society, but also by experiences in African American culture. Dominant among these experiences are those emanating from family networks and from religious environments and religious orientations.

Family Networks. Throughout their lives, older African Americans have been typically participants in a cultural ethos within which beliefs in the institution of the family are very strong. Within the cultural ethos, the family is regarded as the greatest source of life-satisfaction (Staples, 1991a, 29). Composed of circles of kinfolk, including blood kin and a fictive kin network not related by blood, the family functions as a mutual support network. Its function is that of a social and psychological refuge for persons.

Emphasis on family-oriented values has had much to do with the high proportion of older African Americans residing in the community. Government data show that only 3 percent of the total population of African American older adults are institutionalized, compared to about 5 percent of white elderly. Among the oldest old (age 85-plus) who are generally more likely to be widowed and needful of care, only 12 percent of African Americans are in nursing homes, compared to 23 percent of white Americans (U.S. Department of Health and Human Services, 1990, 195).

A common living arrangement of older African Americans is the intergenerational household where there are children of various ages. This household is often an economic package that entails sharing expenses. Elders have also been found to be directly involved in caring for their own children and frequently assuming primary care of grandchildren as well (U.S. Department of Health and Human Services, 1990, 195, 213; Flaherty et al., 1991, 193; George, 1988, 113, 118; Chatters, 1988, 244–45). The following case illustration is indicative of elder functions in intergenerational family settings:

> Mrs. M is a seventy-year-old widow who lives in a small bungalow in a low-income area of a big city. Living with her is her nine-year-old granddaughter whom she has cared for since the child was about four years old. Mrs. M and her thirty-one-year-old adult daughter, who is the child's mother, agreed that the child would be better off with her grandmother because of the difficult circumstances of her mother during and following her divorce and because of her changing work schedule.
>
> Mrs. M is on a low fixed income. This income is supplemented from time to time by a small amount of money from her daughter and gifts of money sometimes given

by her other children. But, she said that even with the added sum, things are tough. She said, "There's not a lot to go around, and there's not much time for me. But, I don't like to complain." She also said that there are times when she does feel as if she can't continue. But, she quickly added that she's glad she's alive to raise her granddaughter and that her granddaughter brings her joy and is good company for her.

The intergenerational household offers elders an important avenue for fulfilling generative needs and for carrying out mutual support. Older African Americans seek to contribute to the welfare of others and need to be needed by others. But, this is the case whether they are living in intergenerational households or in other living arrangements. To the extent that this happens, they fulfill the historical understanding of elders as "guardians of generations" (Flaherty et al., 1991, 193). For many, this generative role contributes to the affirmation of a valued identity and the fulfillment of ego-integrity necessary for life meaning during older adulthood.

The generative needs of older African Americans must be understood, encouraged, and affirmed by persons in ministries of pastoral care and nurture. At the same time, there must also be understanding that older African Americans experience very real family and personal-related issues that take on crisis proportions when they go unresolved. These issues include finances, health concerns, troubling marital and family relationships, changes or the potential need for changes in living arrangements, illness, death of loved ones, grief, and loneliness. Of particular importance for pastoral care and nurture is the recognition that caring support, guidance, and advocacy may be warranted as older African Americans address these matters.

It needs to be added here that older African Americans are a diverse group. Besides intergenerational family settings, there are a variety of types of living arrangements, including nuclear family settings, elders living alone, institutional settings, and other variations of extended and augmented households. Even though a disproportionate number of older African Americans are poor, African American elders are represented across the various socioeconomic levels. They also represent widely diverse educational backgrounds. Those in ministries of pastoral care and nurture need to be aware of this diversity and alert to differences in needs and issues.

The Church as a Resource. The church also is a resource along with the family network for responding to the life tasks and life issues of older African Americans. It helps persons develop a sense of ego-integrity by providing a meaningful worldview that helps the African American elder to establish a meaningful philosophy of life. As the faith community, the church provides a means of affirming the identity of African American elders as persons related significantly to God and to others. It also provides a context for them to contribute to the growth and development of the next generation. The church functions in a similar manner to the family through its presence as an extended family to elders (Chatters, 1988, 245). This role of the church is illustrated in additional information given by Mrs. M. whose case example appeared earlier.

> Mrs. M is a regular attending member at her church, where she takes her granddaughter. At one time, she attended midweek Bible study classes. She gave this up because it is held at night, but she continues as one of the communion stewards. She has lifelong friends in the church, and she expressed her feeling that the church is good for her and good to her. She said that she didn't know what she'd do without it.
>
> She summarized her life journey by saying that life had been anything but easy, but that the Lord has seen fit to hear her prayers and to bring her this far. She said, "I don't expect I'll be able to keep on doing what I'm doing now forever, but I intend to go on as long as the Lord lets me."

Of particular import for pastoral care and nurture within church settings is the recognition that the African American church provides older African Americans with a religious worldview that they find sustaining. Also, like Mrs. M., many find prayer and Bible study to be key means of addressing the issues of life. Moreover, the church is often able to function as a liaison between older adults, their families, and community agencies. Finally, within the church opportunities for elders to tell their stories and for these stories to be heard by caring listeners are needed.

Church and Family Partnerships. Both the family and church contexts are settings in which older African Americans engage in life-review. For them to engage in this process in any meaningful way, caring others must display willingness to hear the life story and to support the elder's struggle with that story. In this way, older adults are helped in their attaining ego-integrity and in affirming a valued identity.

While the African American church and family network have provided significant arenas for the addressing of life tasks and issues of older African Americans, these supportive networks and their functioning cannot be taken for granted in the future. There is increasing evidence that these supportive networks will continue to be challenged by the uprooting of supportive networks in technological society. Consequently, there is need for pastoral care and nurturing ministries to be more intentional in the training of persons within supportive networks for their caring response to older African Americans. This happens best when churches and families are in partnership.

APPROACHES TO MOBILIZING RESOURCES FOR CARE AND NURTURE

The main goal of pastoral care with African American older adults is to bring the cultural resources and resources of the social and religious support network to bear on life issues and tasks of old age. The resources should assist with the healing, sustaining, and guiding of African American older adults. The concern is for healing of psychosocial and spiritual wounds related to past and present experiences. Focus is also on sustaining health and wholeness to the maximal degree possible. And, the intent is to offer guidance that can help elders to continue to make informed decisions about their ongoing lives as long as possible.

Pastoral care is aimed toward mobilizing resources that can help older adults find a sense of ego-integrity when they face major life crises, issues, and events. This involves helping them regain a sense of worth and value in the midst of losses. This also means helping them to develop a perspective that enables them to see themselves as valuable despite the circumstances and crises they face. The religious support system often becomes particularly essential at this point because it offers a transcendent perspective on life situations that brings hope.

Specific resources needed by elders within the African American church and family include (1) a cultural and religious worldview that affirms their worth before God, (2) the uses of prayer, Bible reading, and other educational supports that inform life meaning and decision-making, (3) wholeness-producing participation within communal particularly generative activities and storytelling and story-listening, (4) maintaining an atmosphere of care that facilitates the life-review process, and (5) the availability of support systems in the face of conflict, change, and crisis.

Nurture as Assuring Basic Supplies

Nurture is an important dimension in the preparation of the congregation for its role in supportive networks. As part of this task, the church must educate persons to understand the role of support systems in the lives of elders. Moreover, these persons need to be trained to respond to the needs of elders and those that have been outlined. Seminars and workshops for these purposes will be important.

Another important task of nurture is to help those in the networks to create environments where life-review through storytelling and story-listening can take place. Life review through storytelling can be healing when there is a caring other who takes the time to listen (A. Wimberly, 1981, 67–69; see chap. 9, this volume). It is important to create an environment where they can have the time and are encouraged to do life-review within the context of caring others. Life-review is very personal and requires an accepting environment, and members of congregations and family members need to be encouraged to continue to create this kind of environment.

In addition to the training and education role, nurture also involves advocating with and on behalf of African American elders relative to economic needs, housing, and health care (see chap. 9). Pastoral care and nurturing ministries need to function out of an awareness of the various programs and benefits for the elder and of how to access information and referral. These ministries also need to be cognizant of legislation involving the elderly and to advocate on the elder's behalf. Moreover, these ministries can play a pivotal role in consciousness-raising that helps inform the church and the community about stereotypical images of elders that jeopardize their well-being.

Pastoral Care Intervention Strategies

Within the model of pastoral care, the role of the pastor is central. This section is concerned with specific strategies for helping elders face crises evolving from life issues and events with which they need the help of others. Key roles that the pastor performs are the following: (1) visitation and continued contact with the elders to know their needs, (2) ministering to those who are in crisis by helping them to review the crisis and potential means of addressing it, (3) accepting their feelings associated with the crisis, (4) assisting the fulfillment of tasks they are confronting, and (5) mobilizing and aiding the caring network to assist persons in addressing life tasks and issues.

While attending to the feelings that the elder might be expressing, it is important to be cognizant of possible concrete actions and behaviors that the elder can take to resolve the crisis. The resources for assisting in resolving the crisis rests somewhere in the support network, in either the elder's family, extended family, church, or community agency. The next role of the caregiver is to mobilize the support network so that its resources can be brought to bear on the crisis. The goal is to help the elder maintain ego-integrity and a sense of worth and value through this process. The caregiver realizes that somewhere within the support network there are healing, sustaining, and guiding resources. Pastoral care of older African Americans takes place when these resources are made available to older adults in need.

SUMMARY

In this chapter the nurture and pastoral care dimensions of African American elders have been presented. The emphasis has been on the use of natural support networks existing in the African American church and family for the caring of the African American elder. The use of these support systems constitutes an indigenous approach.

BIBLIOGRAPHY

Bengtson, V. (1979) "Ethnicity and Aging: Problems and Issues in Current Social Science Inquiry." In Gelfand and Kutzik, 9–31.

Bianchi, E. (1982) *Aging as a Spiritual Journey.* New York: Crossroad.

Binstock, R. H., and E. Shanas, eds. (1976) *Handbook of Aging and the Social Sciences.* New York: Van Nostrand Reinhold.

Chatters, L. (1988) "Subjective Well-Being among Older Black Adults: Past Trends and Current Perspectives." In Jackson, 237–58.

Chatters, L. M., and R. J. Taylor (1989) "Life Problems and Coping Strategies of Older Black Adults." *Social Work* 6:313–19.

Erikson, E. H. (1985) *Childhood and Society*. New York: Norton.

Flaherty, M. J., L. Facteau, and P. Garber (1991) "Grandmother Functions in Multigenerational Families." In Staples 1991b, 192–200.

Gelfand, D., and A. Kutzik, eds. (1979) *Ethnicity and Aging: Theory, Research and Policy*. New York: Springer.

George, L. K. (1988) "Social Participation in Later Life: Black-White Differences." In Jackson et al., 99–126.

Gibson, R. (1988) "The Work, Retirement, and Disability of Older Black Americans." In Jackson et al., 304–24.

Gordon, C. et al. (1976) "Leisure and Lives: Personal Expressivity across the Life Span." In Binstock and Shanas, 310–41.

Hunter, R., gen. ed. (1990) *Dictionary of Pastoral Care and Counseling*. Nashville: Abingdon.

Jackson, J. S., ed. (1988) *The Black American Elderly: Research on Physical and Psychosocial Health*. New York: Springer.

Lincoln, C., and L. Mamiya (1990) *The Black Church in the African American Experience*. Durham, N.C.: Duke University Press.

Manuel, R. C. (1988) "The Demography of Older Blacks in the United States." In Jackson et al., 25–49.

Moseley, R. (1991) *Becoming a Self Before God: Critical Transformations*. Nashville: Abingdon.

Staples, R. (1991a) "Changes in Black Family Structures: The Conflict between Family Ideology and Structural Conditions." In 1991 ed., 28–36.

Staples, R., ed. (1991b) *The Black Family: Essays and Studies*. 4th ed. Belmont, Calif.: Wadsworth.

Taylor, R. J. (1986) "Religious Participation among Elderly Blacks." *The Gerontologist* 26:630–36.

U.S. Department of Health and Human Services (1990) *Minority Aging*. Washington, D.C.: U.S. Department of Health and Human Services.

Wimberly, A. (1981) "A Conceptual Model for Older Adult Curriculum Planning Process." Atlanta: Ph.D. Dissertation, Georgia State University.

Wimberly, E. (1982) *Pastoral Counseling and Spiritual Values*. Nashville: Abingdon.

______ (1983) "Contributions of Black Christians to the Discipline of Pastoral Care." *Reflection* 80:4–8.

______ (1990) "Black Issues in Psychology." In Hunter, 96–98.

Wimberly, E., and A. Wimberly (1986) *Liberation and Human Wholeness: The Experiences of Black People in Slavery and Freedom*. Nashville: Abingdon.

12 Legal and Financial Concerns

LORI A. STIEGEL
NANCY COLEMAN

INTRODUCTION

Legal problems of older persons may be intertwined with matters of a religious or spiritual nature—they may affect a person's spiritual well-being; they may prevent participation in religious services or activities; they may serve as the basis for sermons, congregation-sponsored lectures, or social service programs designed to help address law-related problems. Some individuals may want to discuss issues of faith before signing a living will or health-care power of attorney. Another may be unable to attend services because of the unlawful denial of transportation services. A congregant may have to move far from the congregation because of eviction from an apartment or foreclosure on the home. A couple may think they have to divorce in order to obtain Medicaid payment of nursing home care for the ill spouse. Another couple may be reluctant to marry because of the feared financial impact on their children from previous marriages. A congregation may want to sponsor an education program about obtaining government benefits or about health-care decision-making. A religion-affiliated social services agency may find that some of its clients have problems managing their incomes or obtaining services they need to live independently.

Clergy, their staff, and lay volunteers do not need to act as lawyers and paralegals in order to help older congregants and community members with legal problems. They simply need to be able to recognize when a congregant *might* have a legal difficulty and to refer that individual to an appropriate source for assistance. They should also be aware of the law-related issues facing older persons and their families as the twenty-first century draws near, so that those concerns may be addressed through sermons, educational programs, and service programs offered within a congregation and as part of its community ministry to the elderly and their families. This chapter will educate clergy, staff, and lay volunteers about some of those issues through brief discussions of legal problems and the resources available to provide education about or assistance in resolving them.

GUARDIANSHIP AND ITS ALTERNATIVES

Guardianship

This section will use *guardianship* generically. State terms vary; court-appointed surrogate decision-makers also may be called conservators, committees, curators, or fiduciaries.

Guardianship is a legal relationship in which one person (the "guardian") is appointed by a court to act for another person (the "ward" or "incapacitated person") who is incapable of making personal or financial decisions.

While guardianship is sometimes necessary, it should be used as a last resort. Appointment of a guardian may deprive the ward of significant legal rights and personal autonomy, reducing the ward to the legal status of a child. Guardianship is costly—emotionally, psychologically, and fiscally. Judicial oversight of guardians often is lacking, at times resulting in abuse or neglect of the ward by the guardian or others.

Congregations can sponsor programs about guardianship and encourage planning to avoid it. Also, congregants can volunteer to serve as guardians or as monitors of guardians and the courts.

Alternatives to Guardianship

Guardianship should be used only when less restrictive legal measures and social service programs have been considered or attempted and found to be unsuitable.

A *durable power of attorney* (DPA) may be used by a legally capable person ("principal") to grant another ("agent" or "attorney-in-fact") authority to act on his or her behalf. A DPA generally remains valid until a guardian is appointed for the principal, so it is used to plan for the possibility of incapacity and avoid the need for a guardianship.

A *trust* enables a person ("grantor," "settlor," "creator," or "trustor") to transfer money or property into a trust, which is then managed by a "trustee" for the benefit of the grantor or other "beneficiaries" in accord with the trust document. Many types of trusts can be created, depending upon the grantor's intent, the beneficiary's needs, and the amount of available money or property. Trusts may be used to plan for property management in the event of the grantor's incapacity.

Joint ownership of real estate or bank accounts may meet an incapacitated person's need for money or property management and thus obviate the reason for a guardian's appointment.

Some states allow persons to seek *voluntary guardianship* by asking courts to appoint guardians over their property. These laws enable an individual who is aware of, or concerned about, loss of capacity to plan for property management with judicial oversight prior to becoming incapacitated.

A *health-care power of attorney or proxy* (HCPA) allows a person ("principal") to name another ("agent" or "proxy") to make health-care decisions for the principal if he or she is unable to do so. HCPAs may address everyday health-care decisions, not just those relating to life-prolonging procedures in the event of terminal illness. HCPAs may include instructions or guidelines to the agent about the type and extent of health care desired by the principal. HCPAs may negate the need to appoint a guardian to make health-care decisions on the principal's behalf.

A *living will* is used by someone to express directions about the treatment desired in the event he or she has a terminal illness, is near death, and cannot make or communicate health-care decisions. Generally, living will laws limit the decisions that can be directed through a living will to those concerning the use, withdrawal, or withholding of "life-sustaining" or "life-prolonging" procedures. A living will may circumvent the need for appointment of a guardian to make those health-care decisions on behalf of an incapacitated, dying person.

Daily Money Management (DMM) refers to a broad group of services designed to assist older persons or persons with disabilities who need help managing their financial affairs. These services usually include check depositing, check writing, checkbook balancing, bill paying, insurance claim preparation and filing, tax preparation and counseling, investment counseling, and public benefit applications and counseling. DMM may prevent the appointment of a guardian to manage a person's finances.

A *representative payee* (RP) is a person or organization authorized to receive, manage, and spend government benefits for a person deemed incapable of doing so due to mental or physical incapacity. The RP's authority is limited to the specific government funds, so an RP may be an alternative for people with few resources and little income other than that benefit.

Health-care or family consent statutes generally allow specified persons or classes of persons to make health-care decisions for an adult who cannot make or communicate such decisions due to disability, illness, or injury. The laws rank those allowed to make decisions for the incapacitated adult; if the highest-priority person is not available, the next highest is chosen and so forth. Close family members (e.g., spouse, parent, or child) are usually ranked the highest. Some statutes include friends or others in the priority list. Some laws restrict the type of health-care decisions that may be made by the substitute decision-maker; others contain no restraints. Health-care consent statutes offer an alternative to guardianship by allowing the timely designation of a substitute decision-maker without court proceedings to appoint a guardian.

In a *limited guardianship,* a judge gives the guardian authority only over those matters which the ward is incapable of handling. Thus the ward is allowed to retain some rights and autonomy. Limited guardianship, although more restrictive than other alternatives, is less so than a full guardianship.

Religious organizations and congregations can readily become involved in education and services related to alternatives to guardianship. For example, topics such as living wills and health-care powers of attorney lend themselves to sermons and lectures, and representative payee and money management programs are often run by denomination-sponsored social service agencies. Clergy or congregants may also serve as agents under a durable or health-care power of attorney for older persons without family or friends willing or able to act as agents.

MEDICARE

Medicare is the federal health insurance program for (1) persons over age sixty-five who are eligible for (even if they are not yet receiving) Social Security, Railroad Retirement, and Civil Service retirement benefits and (2) persons under age sixty-five who have received Social Security or Railroad Retirement disability benefits for at least twenty-four months. Persons with end-stage kidney disease may obtain Medicare benefits after only a three-month waiting period; some widows and widowers with disabilities may receive Medicare after a year. Persons over age sixty-five who are not eligible for retirement benefits may be eligible to enroll in Medicare by paying additional monthly premiums.

Medicare is divided into two parts. Part A covers hospital, skilled nursing home, home health, and hospice services. Part B covers doctors, therapists, ambulance, diagnostic services, prostheses, and durable medical equipment. The amount of coverage, copayments, and deductibles varies for each service.

Many important health-care services are not covered by Medicare. These include routine physical examinations, eye examinations and glasses, dental care (unless hospitalization is required), and drugs that are not administered as part of covered treatment in a hospital, nursing home, or hospice.

Hospital Services

Medicare Part A covers ninety days of hospital services per "spell of illness," which begins when a person is admitted to a hospital or skilled nursing facility and ends when the person has been out of the hospital or nursing facility for sixty consecutive days. Medicare beneficiaries have sixty "lifetime reserve" days which may be used only once to supplement the ninety days of coverage. Beneficiaries must pay certain costs in connection with a hospital stay: (1) a deductible per spell of illness; (2) a daily copayment if the beneficiary is in the hospital between sixty-one and ninety days; and (3) a copayment for each "lifetime reserve" day used. The deductible and copayment figures change each year. Hospital services covered include bed and board, routine nursing services, drugs prescribed for use in the hospital, medical appliances and equipment, services of residents and interns, and inpatient physical therapy.

Nursing Home Services

Medicare Part A covers up to one hundred days of nursing facility care in each "spell of illness." To be eligible, the beneficiary must have been in a hospital for the three days prior to nursing home admission. Beneficiaries are responsible for a copayment after the twentieth day of covered nursing home care; the copayment is generally about the same as the charge for a day of nursing home care. Nursing homes must accept the Medicare payment (including any copayment) as full payment. The services covered are generally the same types as those covered in a hospital.

Home Health Services

These services will be discussed later in this chapter.

Hospice Services

Medicare Part A covers up to 210 days of hospice care for persons who are certified to be terminally ill and who indicate in writing that they wish to receive hospice care rather than other Medicare benefits. Hospice beneficiaries pay 5 percent of the charge for drugs up to $5.00 per prescription, and 5 percent of the cost of respite care up to a maximum equal to the amount of the inpatient hospital deductible. The hospice is reimbursed for all services, up to a cap established by law. Hospice services include: skilled nursing care; physicians' services; medical social services; home health aide and homemaker services; physical and speech therapy; medical supplies and appliances; counseling; and short-term inpatient care (including respite care) in an institutional setting.

Physicians' Services

Medicare Part B covers physicians' services that are "reasonable and necessary." Beneficiaries must pay a $75 deductible each year and a 20 percent copayment for most services. The "allowed charge" paid by Medicare is often lower than the amount charged by the physician, so beneficiaries actually have to pay more than the copayment. To alleviate this problem, Congress created a category of "Medicare participating physicians" who "accept assignment"—meaning that they accept 80 percent of the allowed charge as full payment from Medicare and bill the patient for only the 20 percent of the allowed charge. Non-participating physicians may "accept assignment" on an individual basis.

A recent change in the Medicare law prohibits non-participating physicians from charging more than the "limiting charge" for services provided to

Medicare Part B beneficiaries. Questions about whether the amount charged by the physician exceeds the limiting charge should be directed to the local Medicare Part B carrier or a lawyer or advocate.

Additional Services

Part B also covers the following: outpatient hospital services; rural health clinic services; physical and occupational therapy and speech pathology services; comprehensive outpatient rehabilitation facility services; prosthetic devices and durable medical equipment; x-ray and other diagnostic tests; ambulance services; and some vaccinations.

Health Maintenance Organizations (HMOs)

Medicare reimburses HMOs for treatment of beneficiaries as long as the HMO qualifies to participate in the program by meeting a number of rules. Medicare qualifying HMOs often cover services that are not paid for by Medicare (e.g., vision or dental care, routine check-ups) and thus are often appealing to beneficiaries. In exchange for additional coverage, however, beneficiaries encounter significant restrictions on their right to choose their own health-care providers.

Appeals Procedures

Medicare Parts A and B provide different schemes for challenging decisions regarding coverage or levels of reimbursement. These procedures are quite complicated. Clergy and lay volunteers should simply be aware that most unsatisfactory decisions may be challenged, and that there are lawyers and other advocates familiar with the procedures for these appeals. Time frames are often restrictive, so immediate referrals are critical. Congregations can establish a Medicare advocacy program, relying on trained volunteers to assist persons with filing for benefits, assessing the accuracy of coverage levels, and challenging incorrect coverage decisions.

Medigap Insurance and Qualified Medicare Beneficiaries

The cost of Medicare deductibles and copayments may be daunting to older persons in need of health care. Medigap policies covering these deductibles and copayments are available for purchase from private insurance companies. Many older people have been taken advantage of by Medigap policy salespeople. To help alleviate this problem, a new system to educate consumers about the benefits of various Medigap policies has been created.

Low-income older persons may be able to benefit from the Qualified Medicare Beneficiary (QMB) program. The QMB law requires state Medicaid programs to pay the Medicare premiums, deductibles, and copayments for older persons and persons with disabilities who are poor, even if they are not poor enough to be eligible for Medicaid. Income and asset criteria vary annually.

MEDICAID

The Medicaid program, governed by both federal and state laws and regulations, pays for the provision of health-care services to poor older persons who meet stringent income and asset eligibility criteria. In most states, Medicaid is linked to eligibility for Supplemental Security Income (SSI)—meaning that an individual must be over sixty-five or blind or disabled, and poor, to receive benefits. Twelve states use even more restrictive criteria. There are, however, certain classes of persons who have lost entitlement to SSI because of unusual circumstances but who are allowed by law to retain their Medicaid benefits. States also may provide Medicaid coverage to eleven optional categories of persons who fall within parameters established by federal law. Eligibility criteria are so complex that it is advisable for all older persons with low incomes and assets to apply for Medicaid even if they are not on SSI.

States must provide Medicaid recipients with at least the following services: inpatient and outpatient hospital services; skilled nursing facility services for people over age twenty-one; x-ray and laboratory services; early and periodic screening, diagnosis, and treatment for people under age twenty-one; family planning services and supplies for individuals of child-bearing age; physicians' and some dental services; and midwife services. States may provide any of the other twelve services authorized by Medicaid law.

Medicaid payment of nursing home care is critical to many older persons. States may provide Medicaid coverage for persons with incomes up to 300 percent of the SSI level; each state's income cap varies. Most states have flexible programs, allowing a person to "spend down" income on certain items to fall below the cap. Complex laws govern the "transfer of assets" in order to become eligible for Medicaid, as well as the division of income and assets between spouses when one needs nursing home care.

The Medicaid program provides rights to administrative and judicial review, as does the Medicare program, for denials or terminations of coverage. Services of a lawyer or other advocate are critical, given the complexity of the Medicaid program.

ACCESS TO HEALTH CARE

Older persons who are not eligible for Medicare or Medicaid often have trouble obtaining or paying for health care. There are a variety of federal and state laws and programs that may help alleviate this problem. Under the "COBRA health insurance continuation law," persons who would otherwise lose their employer-provided health insurance because of job termination, divorce, or death of a spouse are entitled to purchase that health insurance at the group coverage rate for either eighteen or thirty-six months, depending on the reason why insurance was lost. After the conversion period ends, persons are entitled to purchase their insurance at the individual coverage rate. A federal law known as the Hill-Burton Act requires health-care facilities that received federal construction funds to provide a certain amount of free care each year for twenty-five years to poor persons. While the free care obligation of many of these facilities is ending, they have an ongoing obligation to provide treatment in medical emergencies regardless of a person's ability to pay. Federal "anti-dumping" laws mandate that hospitals that did not receive Hill-Burton funds also provide treatment in medical emergencies to persons who cannot pay. Some states have health insurance pools for persons at high risk of illness who otherwise cannot obtain insurance; participation is expensive, however. Poor older persons without insurance or with large medical bills should be urged to contact a lawyer or advocate to determine whether there is some source of coverage or payment, and for advice about bill collection by health-care providers.

HOME CARE FOR THE ELDERLY

An older person in need of long-term care does not always have to enter a nursing home or board and care-type facility to receive it. A number of programs allow frail elders to receive appropriate care in the community.

Medicare Home Health Program

This program is available to persons eligible for Medicare who are (1) confined to home or to an institution that is not a hospital or primarily engaged in the provision of skilled nursing or rehabilitation services; (2) in need of intermittent skilled nursing or therapy services; and (3) determined by a physician to need such care, as established by a care plan reviewed every two months. The program provides skilled nursing; home health aide services; physical, speech, or occupational therapy; medical supplies; and medical social services. Medicare covers these services if they are (1) "reasonable and necessary," (2) "non-custodial," and (3) "part-time or intermittent."

Eligibility and coverage for Medicare home health services are governed by extensive and complicated rules and regulations. Most decisions denying eligibility or limiting coverage may be challenged through Medicare's appeal process. It is advisable to have a lawyer or other advocate assist in this complex process.

Medicaid Home Care Programs

These programs are available to Medicaid recipients who are eligible for Medicaid coverage of skilled nursing services under their state's plan. Federal law requires states participating in the Medicaid program to cover the following services: private duty nursing (unlike Medicare, these do not have to be "skilled" services), home health aid services, and medical supplies, equipment, and appliances. Coverage of physical, speech, and occupational therapy is optional, but most states provide these services. Medicaid home health services are available to those who are: (1) homebound or in a facility that is not a hospital or nursing care facility, (2) in need of "part-time or intermittent" care, and (3) determined by a doctor to need such care, subject to a written plan reviewed periodically. Some states have "waiver programs" that provide additional services (e.g., homemaker, personal care, adult day care, respite care).

Medicaid home care programs are governed by federal and state laws, regulations, and rules. Every state must establish an appeal process for persons whose claims for assistance are denied, not acted upon promptly, or terminated. As with Medicare, the appeals process is quite complicated and the services of a lawyer or advocate are beneficial.

Older Americans Act Programs

Home delivered services are offered by Older Americans Act (OAA) programs. These services usually include home delivered meals, chore and homemaker services, or adult day and respite care. OAA programs serve persons age sixty or older. OAA programs have no income eligibility guidelines, but are supposed to be targeted to those in greatest economic or social need. There is no appeals process if OAA services are denied or terminated.

Veterans Programs

The Department of Veterans Affairs covers some home health care through its outpatient medical program, and it also provides an additional payment to cover such care for a veteran or a veteran's surviving spouse who is "housebound" or who needs "aid and attendance." The veterans program is governed by complicated laws, regulations, and rules. The program provides some measure of review of its decisions denying or terminating services. Assistance from a lawyer or advocate who is knowledgeable about this program may be critical for gaining appropriate benefits.

LONG-TERM CARE

Criteria for Medicare and Medicare coverage of nursing home care were discussed earlier. The Department of Veterans Affairs also provides nursing home care to veterans and their dependents if certain criteria are met. Additionally, private long-term care insurance is developing as another source of nursing home payment. These policies are complex and expensive. A number of advocacy organizations have developed informational materials on purchasing a long-term care insurance policy.

Older persons may experience many problems related to admission and access to nursing homes and to receipt of quality care. These can include discrimination in admission against Medicaid recipients and other poor persons; limited access to the nursing home resident by family, friends, and the public; involuntary transfer of the resident to another facility; loss or theft of the resident's property; illegal charges for personal items or care; and inadequate care and medical treatment. There are numerous federal and state laws and regulations addressing these and other problems, and federal and state regulators should investigate and assist in resolving these problems. Each state has a long-term care ombudsman program responsible for advocating on behalf of nursing home residents. Public interest lawyers often address legal problems of nursing home residents, and an increasing number of private lawyers are involved in this area.

Similar problems arise in other long-term care facilities that provide lower levels of care, e.g., board and care and assisted living facilities. These facilities are subject to less regulation and government oversight, however.

SOCIAL SECURITY

Social Security is a social insurance program; eligibility is based on work history and status, rather than income and asset levels. Retired or disabled workers or their dependents or survivors are eligible for benefits if they have worked the required number of quarters in covered employment. Benefit levels are based on the average amount earned by the worker.

Workers may continue to earn income while collecting Social Security benefits; however, their benefits will be reduced according to the level of their income. That "earnings test" is changed annually, and there are regular attempts to reduce or eliminate it altogether.

There is a complex administrative and judicial review process for Social Security decisions. Two areas that are often the subject of review relate to the determination of eligibility based on disability and the overpayment of benefits. These are problems for which the services of a lawyer or advocate are useful; statistics indicate a greater degree of success for persons with these problems who have some representation.

SUPPLEMENTAL SECURITY INCOME

Supplemental Security Income (SSI) is a "means-tested" program intended to provide a minimum level of income (still below the poverty line) for those persons with extremely low income and asset levels who are either over age sixty-five, disabled, or blind. The income levels change annually. The rules governing what is counted as income and assets are extremely complex. As the receipt of one dollar in SSI usually entitles a person to Medicaid benefits, SSI can be extremely valuable. Nevertheless, many older people will not apply for SSI because they think it is welfare or they are confused by or afraid of "the system."

As with Social Security, common problems with SSI relate to eligibility assessments and ongoing determinations of income, assets, and disability; work incentives; and overpayments. The administrative and judicial review process for SSI is similar to that for Social Security. Due to the complexity and constant change of the SSI laws and rules, it is critical that persons challenging an SSI decision have legal representation.

HOUSING

While it is clear that older persons who are being evicted for failure to pay rent or whose homes are the subject of foreclosure proceedings should be referred to a lawyer, there are other housing issues that have less obvious legal remedies.

Increasing numbers of older persons risk eviction from rental housing because of their alleged inability to continue living independently. The Fair Housing Amendments Act was amended to require that anyone providing private or subsidized housing must make "reasonable accommodation in rules, policies, practices, or services" to allow a person equal opportunity to live in a dwelling. An example of reasonable accommodation is allowing the use of a guide dog without charge in a building that prohibits pets. What constitutes a reasonable accommodation is decided in each case, so clergy and volunteers should be aware that a situation in which eviction seems imminent may be resolved through the help of a lawyer or advocate.

Older persons with limited incomes often find it difficult to pay property tax bills as their homes appreciate in value and their tax rates increase. Many local and state governments provide tax deferral and tax exemption programs to alleviate that problem. Deferral programs allow qualified individuals to postpone payment of property taxes until they move, sell their home, or die. Generally, the deferred taxes are treated as a lien on the home, with payment due when the property is transferred through sale or probate. Exemption programs establish a set amount of a home's value that is not subject to tax, thus lowering the amount of taxes due. Some jurisdictions offer tax exemptions to all homeowners; others create or expand an exemption for certain classes of people, such as the elderly.

Older persons with limited incomes experience difficulty paying for many items and services in addition to property taxes. Through "home equity conversion" (also referred to as a "reverse mortgage"), older persons can turn their home's equity into a cash resource. The money borrowed through the reverse mortgage is generally repaid from profit earned when the home is sold or from the homeowner's estate after his or her death. Although reverse mortgages are becoming more widely available, there are still many areas in which no mortgage lenders participate in home equity conversion. Reverse mortgages are quite complicated and may affect one's eligibility for government benefits or one's plan for distribution of property after death. A lawyer is necessary when one is considering a reverse mortgage.

These and other housing problems are common among the elderly; thus, they provide many opportunities for pastoral counseling and referral and for educational programs.

AMERICANS WITH DISABILITIES ACT

Persons with physical or mental disabilities, regardless of age, often experience discrimination because of their disability by employers, state and local governments, and public services and accommodations. The Americans with Disabilities Act (ADA), effective on January 26, 1992, prohibits discrimination on the basis of disability by state and local government programs, private employers, public accommodations and services operated by private entities, public services, and telecommunications relay services. The ADA mandates access to buildings, activities, jobs, and services of public and most private entities.

While religious organizations and entities controlled by religious organizations are exempt from the ADA, it is useful for providers of pastoral care to be aware of the legal protection available to persons with disabilities under the ADA. The topic is excellent for educational programs. Congregants with disabilities who believe they are the victims of discrimination should be referred to a lawyer who specializes in disability law.

LEGAL RESOURCES FOR OLDER PERSONS

The law and aging network is comprised of many entities helping older people prevent or respond to legal problems. These are entities to which you can refer older clients with problems that are or seem to be legal in nature or that can assist your congregation or organization in planning legal programs for the elderly. Your local area agency on aging or state unit on aging can help you find the legal organizations serving your community.

Legal assistance projects funded under Title III of the federal Older Americans Act provide free legal help to persons age sixty or above. They have no financial eligibility guidelines, but must serve persons in greatest social or economic need. The types of problems handled and services provided depend on each program's funding, staffing, and case priorities.

Legal Services Corporation/Legal Aid programs provide free help to people of any age who meet financial eligibility guidelines and have problems in the program's priority areas.

Legal hotlines, now in Arizona, the District of Columbia, Florida, Maine, Michigan, New Mexico, Ohio, Pennsylvania, and Texas, offer a toll-free number for free advice and referrals to legal services programs or attorneys who charge reduced fees.

Pro bono panels, administered by legal services programs and bar associations, offer volunteer lawyers who represent people of any age meeting financial eligibility and case guidelines.

Law school clinical programs allow law students, supervised by attorneys, to provide free legal help to eligible persons.

Reduced fee panels of state and local bar associations provide names of private lawyers who take cases for reduced fees.

Lawyers referral services, sponsored by state or local bar associations, maintain a panel of private attorneys who handle specific problems. The service may charge a fee for the referral, but initial consultation with the attorney is free.

Private elder law practices have burgeoned in recent years. The National Academy of Elder Law Attorneys (NAELA) distributes a pamphlet on selecting an elder law attorney (contact NAELA at 1604 N. Country Club Rd., Tucson AZ 85716, 602/881-4005).

State and local bar association elder law committees and sections provide materials, training, and advocacy.

State legal services developers, through the state office on aging, develop, train, and provide technical assistance to legal assistance programs for older persons.

National legal organizations, such as the ABA Commission on Legal Problems of the Elderly, provide training, materials, technical assistance, and referrals to local legal resources.

13 Ethical Perspectives

STEPHEN SAPP

This chapter addresses the relationship between ethics and aging. Most people have an intuitive understanding of what the word *aging* means, but the definition of the term *ethics* is neither so obvious nor universally agreed upon. For the purposes of this chapter, ethics will be defined as the systematic analysis of what things are right or wrong, good or bad, virtuous or evil; and of specific decisions, actions, and policies based upon the determination of right/wrong, good/bad, virtuous/evil. Note that sometimes *ethics* is limited to the first part of the definition and the second part is said to define *morality,* but such a distinction is not necessary in a general treatment like this. Although one's ethics do not have to be rooted in theological belief, the ethical analyses of this chapter will take place from the perspective of religious values.

The relationship between aging and ethics, though a relatively new area for serious examination in American religious scholarship, is hardly a novel sphere for human inquiry. For example, the emphasis of Chinese religion on respect for, even veneration of, and thus proper treatment of the elderly is well known. Also, as will be noted shortly, the foundational documents of the dominant religions in the United States, Judaism and Christianity, address the subject quite clearly.

Why, then, has this concern become so prominent recently in this country? The demographic realities reported elsewhere in this volume are the most obvious answer. The increasing number of older people who are themselves living longer is raising issues and prompting questions that have been largely ignored in the recent youth-oriented culture of the United States. When as many as one out of four citizens of this country may be "old" by the middle of the next century, it is impossible not to take seriously the ethical implications of such a situation. Not incidentally, the median age of many congregations is sixty or higher and can be expected to rise.

Ethical issues that arise with regard to aging can be broadly divided into two categories: first, those that result from one's own aging; and second, those that concern one's responsibilities to others who are elderly. Overlaps exist between these two categories because any schematization oversimplifies and makes distinctions that are simply too neat and clean for real life. Nonetheless, this approach can serve to put some order into a complex topic.

Before turning to a consideration of these two areas, a word is in order concerning the importance of this issue for religious institutions and their leaders. This chapter will assert that the meaning of human aging is at its heart a *religious* issue, and so, logically, are appropriate responses to it. For this reason, to paraphrase Georges Clemençeau, "Aging is too important to be left to the gerontologists." In the Jewish and Christian traditions, the role of the religious leader is not merely to tell people what they *want* to hear but to make sure they hear what they *need* to hear and to get them thinking within the framework of the values of their particular belief system about the things they ought to think about. The churches and synagogues of this country, therefore, need to become proactive in aging issues, not reactive as they have been on so many other matters of great social import. The many ethical issues raised by the aging population need to become not just a pastoral concern, but a central aspect of the teaching mission of religious institutions. Furthermore, clergy not only are the "point persons" within these institutions but also have the opportunity to wield considerable influence in the broader community, where the ethical issues of aging often are neglected or addressed from value perspectives inimical to the true welfare of older persons. This chapter suggests some of the directions religious leaders can take in addressing these issues within their congregations and beyond.

ETHICAL ISSUES ARISING FROM ONE'S OWN AGING

During a lecture T. S. Eliot was asked, "Mr. Eliot, what are we going to do about the problem you have discussed?" Eliot's response was to tell the student that he had asked the wrong question: "We face two types of problems in life. One kind demands the question, 'What are we going to do about it?' The other raises the altogether different question, 'How do we behave toward it?'" Aging is clearly a problem that forces the question of how to behave toward it, certainly a legitimate concern for ethics. And in order to behave properly toward aging, one must admit that it is not a problem to be solved by medical, technological, political, or any other means; that is, there is really nothing one *can* do about it.

Regarding an individual's own aging, then, one issue is critical, both in its own right and because of its fundamental significance for proper behavior toward others. In fact, arguably underlying every other issue of ethics and aging is the necessity of coming to grips with one's own aging and thus one's mortality, of deciding what the inevitable process of growing older means to each individual and therefore how to behave toward it. Although admittedly a very difficult task, without this first step, one's attitudes and actions with regard to aging and the elderly will never reflect truly personal integration and acceptance of God's basic plan for humankind.

On the surface, this matter may appear to be a spiritual/developmental issue rather than an ethical one, and most recent works that deal with personal concerns of aging (as distinguished from public policy matters) have tended to focus not on ethical issues but on spiritual aspects of growing older (see, e.g., Bianchi, 1982; Nouwen and Gaffney, 1974; Turnage and Turnage, 1984). The literature that does exist on ethics and aging has concentrated, not surprisingly, on social ethics, that is, public policy concerns raised by the aging of the population of the United States (Binstock and Post, 1991; Callahan, 1987, 1991; Moody, 1992; Sapp, 1992). A failure to deal with the fact and meaning of one's own growing older, however, will have significant ramifications not only for oneself but also for those with whom one interacts. Human beings are social creatures, and even decisions and actions that appear intensely "personal" must take into account their effect upon others.

As suggested above, it is important to note that a person's basic view of aging—what one understands to be the meaning of growing older and the proper approach to it—is not the medical, scientific matter that it is often thought to be in this country, although obviously the basic processes that bring about aging are. The question of attitudes toward aging, of what growing older means to the individual, is a philosophical/theological question, that is, a question of *value* and therefore of ethics. Modern medical science can describe better and better the biological processes that bring about the aging of the human organism, but the question of what aging means and how a person should respond to it, both in oneself and in others, simply goes beyond any scientific description to a fundamental understanding of the meaning and purpose of human life itself.

In the Western religious tradition, guidance about the meaning of life (and death) comes from a number of sources, but ultimately the major religions that have shaped American culture, Judaism and Christianity, have located the foundation of their belief and teaching in the Bible, a set of writings that they consider in some special way authoritative. In trying to understand one's own aging and to find meaning in it, these documents can provide a sound starting point for those who stand in this religious tradition, and it is clearly the role of religious institutions and their leaders to do a better job of interpreting the rich resources at their disposal concerning the meaning of aging.

From the Hebrew scriptures, several concepts are useful in addressing this issue (for fuller discussion of biblical material relevant to aging, see Sapp, 1987). These include a frank recognition of the inevitability of aging as part of God's plan for the human race, illustrated in all genres of Old Testament literature (e.g., Gen. 3:19; 1 Kings 2:2; Isa. 40:6-7; Ps. 39:4; Eccl. 3:1-2), as well as an acknowledgment of the various losses that accompany growing older (see, e.g., Gen. 27:1; 1 Kings 1:1-4; 2 Sam. 19:35; Eccl. 12:1-8). Offering some counterbalance (albeit imperfect) to the losses of old age is the association of age with increased wisdom (e.g., Deut. 32:7; Job 12:12, 32:6-7), also suggested by use of the term *elder* to describe those particularly suited to lead the community.

In the Christian tradition that builds upon this Hebrew heritage, several more ideas offer guidance about appropriate attitudes toward one's own aging.

For example, in Paul's writings the Apostle articulates an understanding of the *soma* (body) of the believer in terms of the whole person as created by God for fellowship with God, in contrast to the *sarx* (flesh) as the person attempting to live self-sufficiently without acknowledgment of his or her dependence upon God. This view offers a starting point for moving beyond this culture's identification with personal worth of external characteristics usually associated with youth, such as physical appearance, agility, strength, and the like. The centrality in Christian thought of reliance upon God's grace for salvation (see, e.g., Rom. 3:24) instead of upon one's own talent, strength, and ability speaks directly to the increasing dependence that becomes such a problem for most Americans as they age. Paul's teaching in 1 Corinthians 1:18-31 about the radically different standards that God uses to judge personal worth also has direct relevance for a person's attitude toward his or her own aging. It is not the qualities that are important by "worldly standards" that God values but precisely those that the world disparages.

Several important ethical implications that clergy need to communicate to their congregations flow from this religious perspective. Those who share it can more easily acknowledge their increasing dependence upon others as they grow older, thus more readily accepting needed assistance as they become less able to "go it alone." They should have a greater appreciation for the fact that human worth derives not from what one does and certainly not from what one has but rather from who one is. This knowledge can again permit an easier acceptance of some of the changes that accompany aging, both physically and in terms of role and status attrition within the community. Another result is an increased willingness to let go of those things that age inevitably takes from a person, leading to a diminished desire to "stay young" in the various senses that society says give one value but that cannot in reality be achieved. Especially instructive in this regard is the biblical image of coming to one's death "full of years," like a vessel that has fulfilled the purpose for which it was created and therefore can gain nothing of value by trying to contain more than was intended for it. Such an attitude can truly contribute to a "good old age" (Gen. 25:8) and can help older persons accept their approaching death without excessive and ultimately futile attempts to prolong life beyond a reasonable point.

Although responsibilities *to* the elderly will be the focus of the next section, this examination of ethical issues arising from a person's own aging cannot conclude without a brief comment on responsibilities *of* the elderly. Former Governor Richard Lamm of Colorado created quite a controversy several years ago when he stated that older persons have an obligation to "get out of the way" in order to make resources of various kinds available to younger people. Lamm's recommendation deserves more discussion than this brief chapter allows, but here it can be stated that traditional Jewish and Christian ethics will not facilely accept his suggestion. Indeed, older individuals, while not becoming exempt from responsibilities incumbent upon all believers, also acquire others more specific to their age. Both the Hebrew and Christian scriptures, for example, place emphasis upon the "elders" as leaders of the community (at least in part because of the wisdom they supposedly have acquired during their long lives), and the New Testament adds some particular responsibilities for widows as well.

Although the exact nature of the responsibilities will vary with the older person's situation, it is quite clear that in the Jewish and Christian religious traditions age alone does not relieve a person of his or her obligations to other individuals in particular and to the community at large (cf. the discussion below of "rational suicide"). For example, given the many difficulties of various types experienced at the end of life, a case can be made that older people have an ethical obligation to plan for their aging in order to minimize the burden on those who must assume responsibility when the elders can no longer care for themselves. Such an obligation certainly entails the execution of advance directives such as living wills and the designation of health-care surrogates so that one's wishes will be clearly known, and to the extent that one's means allow, financial arrangements should be made to provide the level and quality of care desired. A question that deserves intense scrutiny is the ethics of transferring assets to adult children or others in order to become eligible for Medicaid, thus shifting the financial burden of one's later years to the state. On a more personal level, an older parent should consider whether it is ethical, for example, to make children promise never to put him or her in a nursing home or to carry out some other "last request" that will impose an undue burden on younger family members. Again, clergy are especially well placed to raise these issues with their congregations and to make available resources and guidance for exploring them.

Before turning to look at ethical issues that arise in connection with responsibilities to the elderly, two further considerations can serve as a bridge between the major sections of this chapter. Highly influential (many would argue determinative) in the development of individual attitudes toward growing older is *society*'s attitude toward aging (as distinguished from its more specific responsibility to and for those who are older). That is, what does society teach its members—through both formal and, perhaps even more important, informal channels—about what it means to grow old and to be old? Much has been written in recent years about the devaluation of the elderly in contemporary American society and the virtual obsession with youth as the only valuable period of life (see, e.g., Butler, 1975; Rosow, 1985). Although such views have been effectively rebutted and may be on the wane (at least in part because of the aging of the powerful baby boom cohort), the crucial question of what Daniel Callahan (1990) has called the "public meaning" of aging remains to be addressed adequately. For the sake of those already old and perhaps even more so for those not yet old, this country must do a better job of helping people prepare for this inevitable aspect of human existence by finding ways to restore meaning to old age and to allow older persons to rediscover worthwhile roles in society. Without such an effort, the "good old age" mentioned earlier will remain out of reach for millions of the citizens of the United States. In this regard, clergy can exercise both their pastoral function—helping their congregants come to healthier understandings of their own aging—and their prophetic calling—demanding that society work to discover ways to utilize the experience and wisdom of older persons rather than continue to waste this valuable resource.

This discussion raises a final point in this consideration of the ethical implications of one's own aging. Because of the role and status attrition the elderly have suffered in contemporary American society, perhaps coupled with the frequently overused ability of modern medical technology to prolong life well beyond the point of being "full of years," an increasing number of older people appear to be choosing to end their own lives in what has come to be called "rational [or, tellingly, 'preemptive'] suicide." Although no one can know what another person is suffering, many cases of this kind seem to reflect not intractable pain but rather an emptiness, a sense of having lost any meaning in one's life, and a desire to perform one final act of "rational" self-direction. From the viewpoint of Western religious tradition, this approach is not acceptable because it subverts such biblical values as the worth of each individual as a being created in God's own image, the importance of community, and one's obligations to others in favor of such secular values as autonomy and the illegitimacy of all suffering. Clearly, a more positive "public meaning" of aging, greater efforts to avoid or overcome the isolation and loneliness too many older people suffer, and more effectively articulated presentations of the views of the dominant religions on the worth of all persons regardless of age would offer the elderly who see little point in continuing to live a more hopeful image of the later years of life.

ETHICAL ISSUES ARISING FROM RESPONSIBILITIES TO THE ELDERLY

Ethical considerations that grow out of responsibilities to the elderly can be divided into two major categories: obligations that devolve mainly upon the individual, and those that seem more properly to belong to society as a whole. The responsibilities of individuals, though broader than a single concern, focus on one central issue: the obligations of adult children to their aged parents, with regard to support in general and personal care in particular. Clearly this is an issue of considerable moment for the older members of families, who understandably have serious concerns about their security in old age, especially in the face of rising costs and projected problems with publicly provided support. Caring for elderly parents creates difficulties for younger family members also. Often compounded by the needs of one's own children (the so-called "sandwich-generation" syndrome), financial costs associated with elder care can be significant, as can conflicts with career goals and demands on personal time; however, the failure to provide needed care for elderly parents will not only burden adult children with the knowledge of their parents' unmet needs but also set a rather poor example for their own children of the care the middle generation will likely expect when they get old. Clergy can make a significant contribution in this regard by educating congregations about these matters and offering guidance within their particular faith traditions concerning the difficult decisions that must be made. In addition, many congregations have great opportunities to relieve some of the elder-care burdens of their community through creative respite and daycare programs utilizing volunteers drawn from among their older members, many of whom themselves desperately need some meaningful activity to restore their sense of self-worth.

Although prospects of caring for elderly parents certainly do not brighten many people's thoughts of the future, it is hard to claim that the Jewish and Christian religious traditions see such care as anything but obligatory. This obligation is based primarily on the fifth of the ten commandments in the Hebrew scriptures, "Honor your father and your mother" (Exod. 20:12; cf. Deut. 5:16), which was originally understood to demand not only respect and reverence throughout life but also material support in old age as well (for a thorough treatment of this matter from a Jewish perspective, see Blidstein, 1975). The Christian tradition finds further backing for such a view in Jesus' controversy with the Pharisees over Corban (Mark 7:1-23), in which he makes clear that financial support of one's parents cannot be neglected even to fulfill a religious vow, and in his own provision of care for his mother while he hung dying on the cross (John 19:26-27). In addition, 1 Timothy 5:3-16 contains explicit directives concerning the care of widows, with primary responsibility placed upon children, grandchildren, and apparently even other relatives.

The exact nature of the care required, and the avenues by which it may be provided, are of course dependent on the particular circumstances of the elder and family, and the motivation for choosing certain types of care also must be considered. In some situations, for example, providing financial support for care actually given by others may better meet the needs of all parties than trying to care for an elderly parent oneself, and the motive for choosing one over the other should be a genuinely self-giving concern for the welfare of the older person. Even if an adult child is unable to provide a certain type or level of care for legitimate reasons, such inability does not excuse that person from offering whatever kind of help is possible, at the very least expressions of affection and emotional support.

The last area to be considered in this consideration of ethical perspectives on aging is society's obligations to its older members, clearly a matter of primary significance for public policy and unquestionably the topic that is attracting the most attention today because of the growing number of frail older persons in this country and the anticipated increase in the burden they will place upon society. A whole complex of ethical issues here includes such matters as income security in old age; gross inequities in the treatment of older women and minorities (especially those who fall into the so-called "multiple jeopardy" groups); practices related to work, retirement, and leisure; and, inseparable from all these matters, the overarching concern about the cost and availability of health care.

Garnering considerable attention in this arena is the debate prompted by the "generational equity" movement (Marmor et al., 1990), worthy of examination in some detail because its members are so vocal in raising a number of difficult ethical questions concerning the elderly (Longman, 1987). One of the major assertions of proponents of generational equity is that benefits for the elderly are responsible for the deplorable situation of many of this nation's children, the very future of our society. They claim that through unfair and excessive intergenerational transfers to the elderly—many of whom are much better off than children and the younger workers who are being heavily taxed to provide the benefits to the older retirees—current aging policy thus creates inequity between the generations that can be remedied only by such actions as reducing non-means-tested entitlements and increasing private responsibility for income security in old age.

Underlying much of this critique of current aging policy by advocates of generational equity is an abiding antipathy to government involvement in practically any area of life. In fact, the movement appears to have seized upon the issue of equity between generations as a way to attack government programs that benefit *all* age groups. Rather than urging the dismantling of what is perhaps the only public program that has widespread support and has in large part accomplished its goal—Social Security—a worthier aim might be to encourage its use as a model for attempts to improve the situation of children without returning older people to their pre–Social Security levels of poverty. It is interesting that the proponents of generational equity, who decry the plight of this nation's children, do not offer any specific policy proposals for improving it. In short, the real issue appears to be not one of age at all but rather the ageless problem of unequal distribution of resources in general, with all the accompanying inequities between rich and poor of all ages. This is an issue that the deep ethical tradition of biblical religion addresses unwaveringly. Beginning with the concern for the disadvantaged articulated so clearly in Torah, continuing in the demands of the prophets for justice, and culminating in the regard of Jesus and the early church for those in need, the Jewish and Christian traditions agree on this point to a degree difficult to find on most others.

Another critical concern for ethics with regard to society's responsibility to the elderly has to do with decisions about health care, significant if for no other reason than the fact that people over sixty-five (roughly 12 percent of the population of the United States) account for about one-third of all health-care expenditures annually while many children and young adults suffer from a lack of adequate care. Proposals by respected commentators such as Daniel Callahan (1987, 1991) and Norman Daniels (1988) for allocating health-care resources (many advocates for the elderly contend the proper term is "rationing") raise some very serious ethical questions about the use of age as a criterion. Daniels, for example, advocates an approach he calls the "prudential lifespan account." By this he means that in a situation of limited health-care resources, prudence requires that such resources be utilized in ways that reflect the specific needs of particular age groups, which will likely be unequal. Thus individuals of different ages may well receive unequal treatment at a given time, but over the course of their entire lifespans they will be treated fairly.

Daniel Callahan's recent writings on the topic have generated the greatest response, and a more detailed look at his position can serve further to illustrate this issue. In his widely noted (and perhaps unfairly criticized) book *Setting Limits: Medical Goals in an Aging Society* (1987), Callahan proposes that medical care be limited for people who have reached a "natural life span," that is, one that has allowed for encountering, if not fully achieving, "life's possibilities" (66). The criticism of Callahan has focused on two points. First, he suggests an age of the "late 70s or early 80s" as the natural lifespan for most people, prompting the response by many critics that chronological age is a poor predictor of the completion of a person's life. Second, he recommends implementing this concept through three governmental responsibilities: a duty to help people attain their natural lifespan but not exceed it; an obligation to finance only that life-extending technology that allows a natural lifespan; and the provision beyond the natural lifespan of only palliative and not life-extending care (137–38). To Callahan's critics, this is nothing short of age-based rationing, however he tries to rationalize it. Not surprisingly, therefore, numerous responses have been forthcoming to Callahan's proposal and similar ones offered by others (see, e.g., Binstock and Post, 1991), and without question this issue will continue to be a critical one in coming years. The religious institutions of this country offer an ideal setting within which to explore these matters, and clergy need to educate themselves and their congregations in this crucial area.

One concluding comment is in order. Although the present volume is intended primarily for those of Jewish and Christian background, it is important to call attention to the growing importance of other religions for a full understanding of this critical area. It is undeniable that Judaism and Christianity have provided the framework for the ethical values of this nation; furthermore, it is persons either actively practicing one of these religions or generally influenced by their worldview who have been most influential in setting the ethical tone of this culture. Nonetheless, the numbers of adherents of other religions have been increasing recently and will continue to do so, and both researchers and practitioners in the field of gerontology need to take this change seriously. For example, Islam currently numbers some six million adherents in the United States and will soon replace Judaism as the second largest religion in this country. As was suggested earlier, from a religious point of view aging is first and foremost a question of *values,* which is precisely what religion is all about. Thus, knowledge of the beliefs of Islam and other traditions such as Hinduism, Buddhism, and native Chinese religions—and especially of the actions demanded by those beliefs (which is what ethics really is)—will become increasingly important for those who are genuinely interested in the critical relationship between religion and aging (see, e.g., Clements, 1989; Nakasone, 1990; Tilak, 1989).

BIBLIOGRAPHY

Bianchi, E. (1982) *Aging as a Spiritual Journey.* New York: Crossroad.

Binstock, R. H., and S. G. Post, eds. (1991) *Too Old for Health Care? Controversies in Medicine, Law, Economics, and Ethics.* Baltimore: Johns Hopkins.

Binstock, R. H., and E. Shanas, eds. (1985) *Handbook of Aging and the Social Sciences.* 2d. ed. New York: Van Nostrand Reinhold.

Blidstein, G. (1975) *Honor Thy Father and Mother.* New York: Ktav.

Butler, R. N. (1975) *Why Survive? Being Old in America.* New York: Harper & Row.

Callahan, D. (1987) *Setting Limits: Medical Goals in an Aging Society.* New York: Touchstone Books.

______ (1990) "Can Old Age Be Given a Public Meaning?" *Second Opinion* 15:12–23.

______ (1991) *What Kind of Life? The Limits of Medical Progress.* New York: Simon & Schuster.

Clements, W. M., ed. (1989) *Religion, Aging and Health: A Global Perspective.* New York: Haworth.

Daniels, N. (1988) *Am I My Parents' Keeper? An Essay on Justice between the Young and the Old.* New York: Oxford.

Longman, P. (1987) *Born to Pay: The New Politics of Aging in America.* Boston: Houghton Mifflin.

Marmor, T. R., J. L. Mashaw, and P. L. Harvey (1990) *America's Misunderstood Welfare State: Persistent Myths, Enduring Realities.* New York: Basic Books.

Moody, H. R. (1992) *Ethics in an Aging Society.* Baltimore: Johns Hopkins.

Nakasone, R. Y. (1990) *Ethics of Enlightenment: Essays and Sermons in Search of a Buddhist Ethic.* Fremont, Calif.: Dharma Cloud.

Nouwen, H. J. M., and W. J. Gaffney (1976) *Aging: The Fulfillment of Life.* Garden City, N.Y.: Doubleday Image.

Rosow, I. (1985) "Status and Role Change through the Life Cycle." In Binstock and Shanas, 62–93.

Sapp, S. (1987) *Full of Years: Aging and the Elderly in the Bible and Today.* Nashville: Abingdon.

______ (1992) *Light on a Gray Area: American Public Policy on Aging.* Nashville: Abingdon.

Tilak, S. (1989) *Religion and Aging in the Indian Tradition.* Albany, N.Y.: State University of New York Press.

Turnage, M., and A. Turnage (1984) *Graceful Aging: Biblical Perspectives.* Atlanta: Presbyterian Office on Aging.

Part Three CONGREGATIONAL MINISTRY IN AN AGING SOCIETY

INTRODUCTION

Readers of Part Three would do well to reflect upon the issues raised about well-being in Part One. Chapters 14–19 focus upon ways the well-being of aging persons can be nurtured within the faith community. These chapters also reveal how the well-being of the faith community itself is shaped by its response to aging persons.

W. Andrew Achenbaum observes that religious ritual can counter the social marginalization of older adults as long as the rituals intentionally incorporate images of aging (chap. 14). However, Achenbaum's survey of American religious practices uncovers few rituals directly related to experiences of late life, although there are many that celebrate the milestones passed by the young. This chapter provides an important supplement to the contextual concerns raised in Part Two because it offers insights into the historical origins of current religious practices that are oriented toward youth. Achenbaum suggests that meaningful new rituals that lift up the concerns of aging could be incorporated into religious observances. Further, he observes that older persons have much to contribute to the rituals that mark the journey of youth. Generational conflict, a social problem directly addressed by Sapp (chap. 13), might be ameliorated if religious institutions provided leadership in the development of ritual forms of celebrating the entire life span.

Achenbaum amply demonstrates that religion confers no special immunity to institutional ageism. Not only have religions failed to honor aging in ritual, but they have also failed to acknowledge the aging process in their educational ministry. In chapter 15, *Henry Simmons* asserts that the lack of religious curricula about aging results from contextual forces that have shaped thinking about religious education. For too long, education was viewed as the province of the young. The lessons learned in youth, however, may no longer represent adequate resources for older adults attempting to come to terms with the religious and spiritual meanings of aging. Therefore, argues Simmons, faith communities need a new approach to selecting curricular materials for older adults. He employs the metaphor of art as a way of integrating ideas about the potential transformative power of religious education. He also provides valuable insights that can be applied to many different kinds of interactions with aging persons.

Faith communities not only must meet older adults' spiritual needs through their ministries of education; they also must insure that the worship experience itself—the very heart of the faith community's life—includes elders. *Dosia Carlson* reviews the meaning of worship to elders from different faith traditions (chap. 16). She describes types of worship, its varied settings, and the specific needs of elders that sometimes require special attention from worship leaders. Like Achenbaum, Carlson calls for intergenerational religious ritual. She suggests a number of celebrations and ceremonies that churches and synagogues could institute in order to restore meaning to the aging process.

The attenuation of the social meanings of aging functions as a subtext in many of the chapters in this section with authors calling for religious institutions to find creative ways to combat ageism in this society. Writing from a feminist perspective, *Martha Klein Larsen* (chap. 17) addresses the problem of ageism directly by arguing that ageism—like sexism—results from deeply ingrained patriarchal assumptions about power and authority. She calls upon congregations to contradict cultural messages about female aging in order to affirm the value and vital roles of women in their midst. Religious institutions must provide older women with more opportunities for study, service, and spiritual growth and in doing so, these institutions must be self-critical about their own participation in reinforcing cultural stereotypes about age and women. Using the metaphor of the exodus, Larsen urges faith communities to journey into a promised land where all persons regardless of age or gender may participate fully. She calls for liturgies that include feminine images of God and for educational programs that encourage all persons to reject ageism and sexism.

Worship, preaching and education are but three examples of the ways faith communities convey a sense of meaningfulness about aging to all their congregants. In addition, congregational life involves fellowship and service. *James Seeber* has studied many programs sponsored by churches and synagogues across the nation and describes them in chapter 18. Here Seeber details how local congregations have addressed the concerns of older persons—both members and nonmembers. He notes that congregations need to become more intentional about their ministries to elders because the congregations themselves are aging. Programs designed for youth that once attracted the majority of the congregation may no longer be appropriate for most of the members. In other words, congregations must be open to change.

Change is the theme of chapter 19 in which *James Ellor* addresses the issue of parish revitalization. Like other authors in Part Three, he notes how religious communities often accept the ageist stereotypes promulgated in the culture. For example, many people erroneously conclude that older adults resist all change, that they are rigid, and that they tenaciously cling to "the way we have always done things." Faith communities that embrace this attitude deprive themselves of the considerable energy that can flow from the wisdom of elders who understand the creative potential found in the tension between stability and change. Other ageist attitudes lead church and synagogue leaders to conclude that membership dominated by elders signals the death of the religious institution. This leadership may then assume that the only way to resuscitate the community is to orient programs toward youth. Ellor argues against such a narrow conceptualization of revitalization and notes how congregations can become more vital by actively including older persons in all aspects of the community's life.

Each of these chapters asserts that the ministries of congregations can become more vital, more meaningful, and more true to their calling when they intentionally acknowledge the elders in their midst. That is, the well-being of the institution may depend upon the way it addresses the well-being of elders. Unfortunately, out of fear of rejection by the one institution with which they have identified across the life span, older people may be reluctant to speak up when their religious and spiritual needs are not being met. In addition, older adults are not immune to ageist attitudes and often fall prey to the belief that faith communities must devote all their energies to the young. It is incumbent upon persons joined in communities of faith to work to overcome these attitudes so that all persons—young and old—can experience religious and spiritual growth in their worship and learning, their fellowship and service.

14 Age-Based Jewish and Christian Rituals

W. A. ACHENBAUM

> For everything there is a season,
> and a time for every matter under heaven:
> A time to be born, and a time to die;
> a time to plant, and a time to pluck up
> what is planted. (Eccl. 3:1-2)

> From one ancestor he made all nations to inhabit
> the whole earth, and he allotted the times of their
> existence and the boundaries of the places where they
> would live, so that they would search for God and
> perhaps grope for him and find him—though indeed he is
> not far from each one of us. For "In him we live and move
> and have our being." (Acts 17:26-28)

Time in the Bible operates on three planes (ideas here adapted from Green, 1987). First, at the core is the sacred—God's eternal kingdom. Divine interventions into human affairs, as the passage from Acts declares, manifest themselves in diurnal as well as epochal encounters. Humans, moreover, come to know God in divergent ways at successive stages of their growth. Various age groups react differently to God's revelatory spirit, Joel (2:28) claimed: "Your sons and your daughters shall prophesy, your old men shall dream dreams, and your young men shall see visions."

Human time, in contrast, is measured differently. Children are born on a certain date; they grow in accordance with biological time clocks, usually dying before their 120th birthday. Nations rise and fall according to rhythms of their own. "Time is the messenger of the gods," James Birren puts it, "a messenger who passes through space, matter, energy, and minds" (Birren and Cunningham, 1985, 153). Though he occasionally writes about aging and spirituality, Birren here wants to explicate the significance of changes in the speed of biological mechanisms, improvements and decrements in cognitive processes, and varieties and variations in social interactions—phenomena operating on a second temporal plane. Time as messenger of the gods is explored further elsewhere (Achenbaum, 1991, 83–102).

God and humans also meet on a third plane, in institutional time—in giving bread, in public worship, in theophanic moments dimly understood amidst joy, struggle, or fear. Peter L. Berger offers a useful theoretical perspective in *The Sacred Canopy.* Rituals, he hypothesizes, enable individuals to grasp the broader purposes of their unfolding lives, to see their spiritual journeys in broader context. "The social ritual transforms the individual event into a typical case. . . . The individual is seen as being born, living and suffering, and eventually dying, as his ancestors have done before him and his children will do after him" (1967, 54). Private celebrations paradoxically become more intimate by acknowledging through ritual participants' links to a larger worship community.

This essay addresses the covenantal bonds forged on this third mediating, institutional plane, in the sanctuary of time. It focuses on certain age-based rites that provide common ground for encounters between God and humans in the Jewish and Christian traditions. Greater attention to the importance of rituals might counterbalance the marginalization of the old (cf. Simmons, 1990). Yet rites and rituals are not the only institutions that mark familiar turning points in people's lives in religious settings.

Jewish and Christian congregations also have established organizations and procedures for socializing members of different ages into their networks and for dealing with some of the inevitable vicissitudes of human existence from womb to tomb. "Israel legitimated its institutions in terms of the divinely revealed law," Berger elaborates. "The historically crucial part of religion in the process of legitimation is explicable in terms of the unique capacity of religion to 'locate' human phenomena within a cosmic frame of reference" (Berger, 1967, 35). Unlike the objectives set forth in governmental policies or the program statements enunciated by private groups, religious welfare institutions underscore covenantal bonds in declaring their missions:

> The institutions are magically lifted above these human, historical contingencies. They become inevitable, because they are taken for granted not only by men but by the gods. Their empirical tenuousness is transformed into an overpowering stability as they are understood as but manifestations of the underlying structure of the universe. They transcend the death of individuals and the decay of entire collectivities, because they are now grounded in a sacred time within which merely human history is but an episode. In a sense, then, they become immortal. (Berger, 1967, 37)

Age-based rituals and organizations have a temporal dynamics of their own. They are adapted to respond to changing human needs and aspirations over successive generations. By the same token, their very perdurance affirms fundamental continuities in human aging.

Given the scope of the present volume, "modern" examples of age-based rituals and institutions in the U.S. will be the focus. In several instances, ancient practices, now discarded, will be cited to urge the renewal of old customs in order to meet the spiritual and social needs of older members of congregations. A modern-day feast of fools for elders may not be desirable, but we might, as did the medieval Boy Bishops and Mock Kings, "imagine, at least once in a while, a wholly different kind of world" (Berger, 1969, 3), through celebrations that challenge the ageist assumptions pervasive in secular society. That this survey reveals in American religious practices a certain blindness to late life provides grounds for constructive action. Lively traditions for our aging society can emerge from seemingly obsolescent rites and institutions if their essential purposes speak to current needs.

AGE-BASED JEWISH AND CHRISTIAN RITUALS

Jewish congregations, differences among U.S. Conservative, Orthodox, and Reform branches notwithstanding, have maintained a more elaborate set of rites and rituals marking stages of the human life than have Christians in America. "For every matter has its time and way, although the troubles of mortals lie heavy upon them," opined the Teacher in Ecclesiastes (8:6), who in chapter 12:1–8 offers an allegorical interpretation of the journey of life. Paul, in contrast, stressed that Christians aspired to an age-irrelevant maturity: "Brothers and sisters, do not be children in your thinking; rather be infants in evil, but in thinking be adults" (1 Cor. 14:20). He looked forward to the time when "all of us come to the unity of the faith and of the knowledge of the Son of God, to maturity, to the measure of the full stature of Christ" (Eph. 4:13). U.S. Christians, more than their Jewish contemporaries, still downplay age-specific differences and rituals (cf. Christiansen [chap. 27] and Van Tatenhove [chap. 28], in Achenbaum, 1985).

Number Our Days

Almost without exception, the birth of a child is a joyous occasion. Among Jews, it is also a moment celebrated within the religious community: "Blessed shall you be in your coming in" (Deut. 28:6). Nowadays, specific observances reflect customs passed down from different locales over the centuries, without necessarily coinciding or complementing one another. In accordance with a Palestinian practice, for instance, relatives of a newborn sometimes have a tree planted in Israel. A Jewish American baby girl is often named in the synagogue at the first Sabbath services following her birth. Naming boys in the U.S. generally occurs at circumcision, although practices vary. Scripture provides countless examples of names that invoke a child's relationship to God (Gen. 4:25; Gen. 30:24) or animals that God has created (Jonah—dove, Rachel—ewe, Deborah—bee). Descendants of Eastern European Jews are often named for a recently deceased patrilinear relative. The custom of "redeeming" the *first-born* son is still observed by Orthodox Jews. In adherence to Scripture (Exod. 13:12-13; Num. 18:14-16), the father gives money to a leader, which later is returned or given to charity. This ritual is not performed on Caesarean babies (Birnbaum, 1979, 18, 49; *Encyclopedia Britannica* 1985, 22:445; Schauss, 1950, 12–13, 21, 27; Donin, 1972, 271–79).

Jews throughout the ages have considered circumcision, long deemed part of their covenant with God (Gen. 17), an outward sign of communal solidarity. Hence the ancient benedictions and tools. Circumcision is not an exclusive cultic rite, however, and some concessions have been made to modernity. The *mohalim* who cuts the foreskin is now licensed; rather than waiting until the eighth day after birth, some Jewish (and, for several decades, many Christian) boys are circumcised before they leave the hospitals (Schauss, 1950, 13–14, 18, 79–81; Birnbaum, 1979, 103). In earlier periods, additional ceremonies for newborn Jewish children included throwing raisins and coins in a child's cradle or giving the child's weight in gold to charity as well as festivities upon the weaning of children.

Nearly every Jewish congregation in America today provides special religious training for their young. Jewish parents have always been expected to instill reverence, love, and fear of the Lord. "Recite [God's words and commandments] to your children and talk about them when you are at home and when you are away, when you lie down and when you rise" (Deut. 6:7; see also Prov. 4:1, 3). Usually at age six (though sometimes at age five), boys were sent to primary schools (or occasionally to private residences) to learn about the Bible and how rabbis interpreted it. Girls are still segregated in some Orthodox facilities, but they are not excluded from learning Hebrew or the fundamentals of their faith. A major objective of this education is to prepare children for their Bar Mitzvah or Bat Mitzvah. Once that goal is accomplished, however, attendance falls precipitously. Fewer than 3 percent of all high school students are enrolled in religious education programs (Birnbaum, 1979, 223–26; Schauss, 1950, 97).

At age thirteen, Jewish American boys are called upon to recite Torah benedictions. After 1963, when a chief rabbi in Israel declared that twelve-year-old girls should rejoice attaining religious maturity, there have been greater opportunities for young women to participate in services. A bar/bat Mitzvah (literally "Son/Daughter of the Commandment") has, in terms of the religious community, come of age. Henceforth, they bear responsibility for observing and fulfilling God's will. The age of majority, preparations for the ritual, and the actual ceremony itself have changed over time. During the nineteenth century, Reform Jews in Europe instituted a solemn rite of confirmation as an alternative to the wearing of the *t'flin* and the *talis* so visibly featured in the older ceremony. Confirmation was first introduced in New York City's Temple Emanu-el in 1847, and it became an integral part of synagogue services in Reform congregations thereafter (Birnbaum, 1979, 94–95; Schauss, 1950, 112–21). Much importance is ascribed to confirmation and Bar

Mitzvah services in Jewish American communities today. Distant relatives and Christian friends as well as immediate family and members of the congregation attend the ritual. The festivities can rival weddings in terms of lavishness, conspicuous consumption, and warm feelings.

Because of the centrality of the family in Judaism, marriage is viewed as the most significant ceremony in the lives of adult Jewish Americans. Jews in ancient times allowed a year to pass between the reading of the marriage contract and the giving of the ring. Nowadays, the two parts of the ceremony are performed together. Opinions about the "best" ages to marry have fluctuated. As is the case with Protestants and Catholics, Jewish men and women are older when they marry today than even a few decades ago (Schauss, 1950, 143, 148, 179; Birnbaum, 1979, 94). Parental dictates or pregnancy determine the timing far less often than one's personal desires, educational plans, and concerns over interfaith marriages, attitudes toward divorce, and peer pressure. Still, given the drama of the ceremony itself, getting married in accordance with Jewish customs is hardly the same as going to a justice of the peace. The vows made between husband and wife are made in the context of the covenant between God and humankind. Surrounded by families and friends, reminded that only the restoration of Jerusalem will bring true joy to all, the rite involves more than two people affirming their love. The community itself is strengthened by a new conjugal unit, with the attendant expectation of continuity in generations.

Some rites and duties that Judaism has created to mark turning points in the prime of life do not depend on chronological age per se. Responsibility for raising and educating young children typically fall on men and women between the ages of eighteen and sixty. So do many household and temple tasks, which reflect one's commitments and obligations more than age-consciousness. Mosaic law declared that a woman is ritually unclean for a week after giving birth to a son (a fortnight for a daughter). Only Hasidic Jewish congregations still practice ritual cleansings in the U.S. (Schauss, 1950, 18, 50) Similarly, it takes years to pass qualifying rabbinical examinations, but young scholars are sometimes called *zaken,* literally "elder," by fellow rabbis (Herr, 1963, 2:346; Ben-Sasson, 1971, 2:346–48).

Because of the honor accorded elders and the concern Jews express for maintaining dignity in old age, Judaism has over the centuries developed certain age-specific rituals to attend to people's needs in late life (Philipson, 1901, 1:231). Some Essene groups make it a goal to honor the old and the Talmud sets no limit to the number of times a responsible Jew should visit the sick. To attend to the needs of the chronically ill and those close to death, many congregations after the sixteenth century began to rely on the *Chevro Kadisho,* originally a burial society that had two ranks of membership, with full status being reserved for elderly, dignified men (Schauss, 1950, 256–59; Birnbaum, 1979, 93). Surplus income from burial plots was often used for charity, including orphan care. Contemporary American funeral customs vary, but older members of the synagogue figure prominently in the ways that Jewish congregations bury their dead.

Judaism, in short, makes a concerted effort to dramatize the range of human encounters with the Ultimate One. Many age-specific rites do not take place in a temple or synagogue: it is the youngest who raises the first question at the Passover meal; the elders of the family sit in places of honor. "So teach us to count our days that we may gain a wise heart," the psalmist entreated (90:12). For Jews, reaffirming their covenantal relationship with God has been the privilege and responsibility of the children of Israel of all ages in every era.

"To Mature Manhood, to the Measure of the Stature of the Fullness of Christ"

The RSV translation of Eph. 4:13 conveys the extent of age-irrelevance in Christian ideas of human development. All ages are invited to follow Christ. Over the centuries Christian rituals have been reinterpreted and modified to accommodate the needs of people of very different ages and readiness. Children are to be assured access; nor is forgiveness denied to sinners in the eleventh hour.

One is a Jew at birth, but only the rite of baptism signifies membership in the Christian Church. Scholars have disagreed over the centuries about whether it was necessary to be "born again" to be counted as a Christian. Tertullian's objection to infant baptism suggests that the practice occurred early on. Current Roman Catholic views of baptism self-consciously distance themselves from earlier church views and distinguish themselves from Protestants. The church no longer follows literally the teaching of Pelagius or Augustine, which claimed that infants that die before being baptized were consigned to limbo or damned to hell. Pastoral urgency may prompt baptizing infants near death, but grace is present to all from the moment of conception. In the reformation, Lutherans and members of other new Protestant groups generally accepted Catholic attitudes toward infant baptism. Anabaptists (literally, "baptized again"), in contrast, insisted on adult baptism; they were convinced that people should become Christians voluntarily, when they were mature enough to understand what was entailed. Baptism is the only requirement for receiving holy communion in the Episcopal Church, though people do not need to have been baptized in accordance with the liturgy of the Anglo-Catholic tradition. Sacraments like baptism "establish a relationship ultimately with God and with Christ but immediately with the church" (McBrien, 1981, 738, 746–47, 1154–55; *Encyclopedia Britannica,* 1985, 1:877; Episcopal Church, 1977, 299–315). Practices vary greatly among other U.S. Christian churches. Baptists and members of the Disciples of Christ perform the rite on adults. Some fundamentalist groups also reserve baptism for adults and then opt for full immersion.

The ritual of confirmation is intertwined with the history of baptism, with variations in practices increasing among Christian bodies since World War II.

Bishops confirm in the Roman Catholic and Episcopal churches. In the former, confirmations rarely take place before age seven and now are likely to occur between the ages of twelve and fifteen. Most Roman Catholic children, however, receive First Communion in the second or third grade. Special catechism classes are offered for children (and occasionally their parents) to prepare them for rites that connote fuller membership in the Church. In the Episcopal Church, confirmation earlier in the century took place around age thirteen, followed a week or so later by Eucharist. The current *Book of Common Prayer* now gives directions for a confirmation service "with forms for reception and for the reaffirmation of baptismal vows" (Episcopal Church, 1977, 412). Lutherans, unlike Roman Catholics and Episcopalians, do not consider confirmation a sacrament, although like the latter they view the public profession of faith as an important step in Christian maturation. When other Protestants use the term "confirmation," they refer not to a special service, merely to the fact that baptism has occurred. The Eastern Orthodox generally perform baptism, confirmation, and communion in the same service.

Unlike Jewish rituals, Christian rites and sacraments of initiation do not follow the natural course of human development. Initiatory rites acknowledge but do not underscore a person's age. Adolescents and older adults alike are encouraged to renew promises made on their behalf when they are ready and willing to do so. The emphasis on "maturity" does not mean that Christians emphasize adult education more than Jews, however. For Roman Catholics before Vatican II, "adult religious education was regarded as the exception, and the religious education of youth the norm" (McBrien, 1981, 747). No dramatic innovations have occurred during the past two decades. There are Protestant "inquiry" classes but, compared to youth programs, most adult religious programs are halfhearted affairs.

It is only slightly overstating the irony to note that, for all of their emphasis on "maturity," Christian churches do not presently have special rituals and rites for adults. Clergy perform more than half of the marriages in the U. S. today, but wedding rituals reflect as much about American popular culture as they do religious traditions. Churches have pastoral offices to deal with the reconciliation of a penitent person, or ministration to the sick, or the ministration at the time of death. Merely to the extent that many served by these offices are elderly might it be said that, by ministering to the needy, Christian churches are taking ritualistic account of age and old age.

Older people have long held positions of leadership and honor in the Christian community. The Greek word *presbyteros* denoted a position of authority between a deacon and a bishop. "Elders" play an important role in many Protestant denominations and Christian sects today. Similarly, most Roman Catholic and Episcopal bishops and prelates are elected when they are mature; most serve until they die or are required to retire. A man at twenty becomes an elder in the Mormon Church. Boys worthy of the honor and responsibility become deacons at twelve and priests before twenty. High priests tend to be old: All Mormon presidents—and most of their counselors—during the twentieth century have served past their eightieth birthday (Arrington and Bitton, 1979; *Encyclopedia Britannica,* 1985, 4:420, 9:678). Methodists call fully ordained ministers "elders." Lutherans use the terms "deacon" and "elder" interchangeably. Most elders are men, but women have played important roles. Eldresses managed most Shaker Communities during their heyday between the 1830s and 1880s, into their decline in the twentieth century. Mary Baker Eddy headed the Christian Science Church well into advanced age.

Older women historically played a greater role in church affairs than they do today. Without identifying my source, I once presented the text of 1 Timothy 5:3-16 to a group of gerontologists and policy makers as a "radical" new way to relieve poverty among older women. I stressed the reasonableness of its age/needs-based means test, its insistence that women be empowered to make contributions throughout their lives, as well as the positive benefits to be gained from their good works. The early church made such use of the Order of Widows until their responsibilities were reassigned to deaconesses and nuns as the numbers of older women become too large to maintain (Thurston, 1989). To the best of my knowledge, no Christian body has tried to revive this lost tradition.

AGE-BASED RELIGIOUS INSTITUTIONS

Anyone who has thumbed through the yellow pages of any metropolitan center or driven through the neighborhoods of any large community has to be impressed by the contributions that religious congregations have made to U. S. education and social welfare. Children who do not go to public schools attend parochial schools, Christian academies, yeshivas, or prep schools with chapels on campus. Many hospitals bear the names of saints or of Protestant denominations. Jewish benefactors typically ensure that their local old-age home has the most up-to-date facilities available. More often than not, the oldest orphanage in town was founded by a local church or as an interdenominational venture. This is no accident: responsibility for educating the young and for providing care to the sick and needy of all ages is deeply embedded into both Jewish and Christian traditions. The ways that religious groups chose to fulfill these obligations greatly affected institutional arrangements over time. Europeans transplanted their diverse ideas and institutions to the new world.

Thus American religious bodies took care of children in need not simply because the public sector was laggard, but because it was an historic part of their institutional mission. Church groups had founded orphanages as early as the fourth century. By the Middle Ages monasteries took charge of this function. Some city governments assumed care in the late 1400s. The Roman Catholic

Church shared responsibility with Protestant groups for caring for orphans and foundlings in early modern Europe. In the 1600s August Hermann Francke connected orphanages with a new arrangement for secondary-school education. His scheme was adopted in England and later replicated in North America (*Encyclopedia Britannica,* 1985, 16:306; Pullan, 1989, 7, 23).

The Ursulines established a children's asylum in New Orleans in 1727 to care for children whose parents were killed in an Indian raid. The Rev. George Whitfield, the most famous preacher in the Great Awakening, started an orphanage in Savannah in 1740. Fifty years later, Charleston erected the first public institution for children. As states assumed greater responsibilities for institution building, religious groups opted for strategic interventions. The Rev. Charles Loring Brace established the Children's Aid Society in 1853 to move urchins from the corruptions of New York City to homes in the west. To prevent the proselytizing of Irish and German youth, the Catholic Church created urban shelters. Religious groups thereafter also provided resources for handicapped children (Trattner, 1984, 113–18).

Education. Just as church leaders early on took responsibility for orphans, so too church fathers such as Justin Martyr, Tertullian, and St. Augustine laid the foundations for elementary and secondary educational systems in Western civilization that remain viable today. Initially, schools were to teach the principles of Christian faith and ethics to those not yet ready to receive the eucharist. During the early Middle Ages, bishops started schools for training future clergy. The Reformation and Counter-Reformation sparked waves of innovations, spearheaded by Germans (such as Luther, Franke, and Melanchthon) and Moravians on the Protestant side and by the Jesuits on the Catholic. Only in the eighteenth century did support for state control of public education rise, during the period in which North America was settled.

Educational systems established in colonial America reveal the variety of their European backgrounds (cf. Cremin, 1970–88, for the history of elementary education presented here; cf. Anglican Board of Social Responsibility Social Policy Committee, 1986, for a European perspective). Sometimes investors made proprietary arrangements. Elites on both sides of the ocean bequeathed land and personality. The Jesuits took matters into their own hands, supporting a school in seventeenth-century Maryland through mission funds, tuition, and bequests. Two colonial temples ran schools. Although most colonial schools were designated as "public" or as "free," the path toward public elementary education accessible to all was tortuous and twisted. Pieties, though rarely dogma, pervaded every curricula. Religious influence, if not church control, was evident throughout.

The percentage of Americans between the ages of five and nineteen enrolled in primary and secondary schools rose from 38 percent to 61 percent between 1840 and 1870. States during the period assumed primary responsibility for managing "public" schools. To the extent that religious training directly or indirectly insinuated itself into the curriculum, the practice was defended as part of a larger effort to socialize young Americans to the virtues of a liberal, democratic, capitalist, Protestant republic. The stress on "Americanism" threatened the identity and values of many religious bodies. Hence, three decades after St. Peter's Church opened the first parochial school in New York (1801), Roman Catholic authorities were engaged in political warfare with the governor of New York, legislators, and the mayors of its major cities. As a result of documents promulgated between the American Roman Catholic Church's first and third Plenary Councils (1852–84), every parish had to build a school; unless dispensed by the bishop, all Catholic parents had to send their children to a parochial school. Nor were Roman Catholics alone in this impulse: between 1847 and 1870, the Presbyterian (Old School) Church tried in vain to establish its own parochial system.

Although the Presbyterians could not lure students from the public system during school days, Protestant denominations were successful in launching a Sunday School movement. Lay people in Britain established the first classes in 1780 to teach people how to read and study the Bible. The Philadelphia Sunday School Union, an interdenominational organization concerned with the religious education needs of children and (to a lesser degree) senior adults, was established in 1791. As the program grew in size and quality, so did its teacher-training programs and educational materials. In the antebellum period religious officials joined with community leaders to foster the lyceum movement, town meetings of the minds. Methodist Bishop John Vincent and philanthropist Lewis Miller held the first Chautauqua session for the Sunday School Teachers' Assembly in upstate New York in 1874. Chautauqua remains the prototype for educational ventures that combine religion and recreation (Bode, 1968; Morrison, 1974; Ahlstrom, 1972; *Encyclopedia Britannica* 1985, 11:392–93). An International Council of Religious Education, founded in 1921, merged with the National Council of Churches in 1950.

Despite the missionary spirit of most Christian educational ventures, some groups were ignored. Christians might have reached out more to black children who were treated as second-class citizens in public schools—if they attended. There were only thirty high schools in the South for blacks in 1910. Black congregations contributed what they could for education. Some northern congregations gave funds to train teachers, but most religious institutions had other priorities. Southern Baptists were often apathetic or hostile (Ahlstrom, 1972, 710, 720).

Religious institutions today play a valued if diminished role in U.S. education. During the twentieth century roughly 90 percent of America's youth were enrolled in public schools. Hasidic Jews, the Amish, and fundamentalist groups teach their own. Catholics supported 5,000 parochial schools in the 1920s. Parishes have difficulty maintaining the system now, yet they still enroll 3 million children. Separate academies for high school boys and girls, first established by the church in the 1700s, remain an important alternative to public high schools (Dolan, 1985, 242–50).

Higher education in America also has religious roots. Puritans established Harvard (1636) and Yale (1701). Anglicans founded William and Mary (1693) and led efforts to put Penn (1754) and Columbia (1758) on sound footing. Less than 200,000 U.S. Catholics were maintaining fourteen colleges and universities by 1830. The names of places founded in the nineteenth century, such as Southern Methodist, Eastern Baptist, and Midland Lutheran, reveal their denominational origins. Founded in 1948, Brandeis quickly became a major research university. Some religious institutions, such as Oral Roberts University, have thrived because of their sectarian orientations; most, however, open their doors to students of all (or no) faiths and offer curricula similar to their secular counterparts in the public and private spheres.

Welfare. The church long has given high priority to caring for the sick and needy. Like orphanages, almshouses date back to the fourth century. Monks and nuns established hospitals in the Middle Ages. Quakers, Baptists, Methodists, and Lutherans became pace-setters in welfare institution building in Europe and America. Religious influences spurred Henri Durant to found the Red Cross in 1859. Homes for the aged have existed for at least a millennium (LeFevre and LeFevre, 1981, 28; Rothman, 1971; *Encyclopedia Britannica* 1985, 16:305; Gold and Kaufmann, 1970, 264).

More than other groups before the enactment of Social Security in 1935, however, U.S. religious organizations assumed most of the institutional responsibility for the aged. In the first quarter of the nineteenth century, Protestants groups on the eastern seaboard began to build facilities for "indigent widows, single women," and "gentlemen"; the former servants of middle-class often were admitted. The Sisters of the Holy Family, an African American order, opened the first Catholic old-age home in New Orleans in 1842. Within three decades, the Little Sisters of the Poor alone were running thirteen homes. Jewish institutions, such as New York's Home for Aged and Infirm Hebrews, established a reputation for comprehensive, community-based programs that it still enjoys (Dorff, 1987, 14–20; Reuben, 1987, 117–22). By the turn of the century, contributions from churches and synagogues represented two-thirds of the funds for elder care. Most of the 1,200 benevolent homes operating in the U.S. in 1929 were established by Protestants, Catholics, and Jews (Gold and Kaufman, 1970, 271–72; Achenbaum, 1985, 108; Haber, 1983).

Thereafter, a variety of public and private secular institutions began to address the economic, health-care, and social needs of our aging population. Religious groups still play a vital role in this "aging enterprise." Even small Black congregations provide home-care assistance for frail, elderly African Americans (cf. Caldwell, chap. 20). Increasingly after World War II, activities have been undertaken at (inter)denominational headquarters. The National Conference of Catholic Charities commissioned case studies of care for the aged in various cities. The Federal Council of Churches sponsored a survey, published as *Older People and the Church* (Maves, 1949, 715–20). White House Conferences on Aging have occasioned concerted effort. The National Interfaith Coalition on Aging, formed in 1972, quickly served as an umbrella for more than one hundred Protestant, Catholic, and Jewish organizations (Cook, 1977). Its affiliation with the National Council on the Aging in 1991 should facilitate its outreach mission. The American Society on Aging in 1988 created the Forum on Religion and Aging to share models of spirituality and ministry (Seeber, 1990a, 195).

Amidst recent efforts to promote intergenerational exchanges in the religious sector has been a call by and to some older Americans to bear witness to events earlier in their lifetimes. In 1980 Congress established the U.S. Holocaust Memorial Council to oversee "a permanent living memorial museum to the victims." Opening in 1993, the museum is designed to remind people of all ages of the horrors done and permitted by those willing to pervert and forsake Jewish and Christian traditions. Concurrently, survivors' accounts reaffirm the virtues of a spiritual developed sustained by covenantal bonds.

RE-CREATING RITUALS AND INSTITUTIONS FOR AN AGING SOCIETY

This survey indicates that there are more age-specific rituals and institutions designed for younger people than for older Jews and Christians. This pattern is not common to all world religions. Hinduism, in contrast, divides the ideal lifecourse into four stages, each with a distinctive set of privileges, interdictions, and duties (Zimmer, 1964, 155). In addition, there seem to be fewer opportunities for girls and women than for males at similar ages to participate as fully in the liturgical and institutional life of the religious community. The gender bias is not inevitable: lately, scholars have generated considerable interest in recovering women's voices and orders in ways that will be faithful to Jewish and Christian traditions as they seek to respond to modern dictates (Achenbaum, forthcoming). A recent trilogy of books by Miriam Therese Winter, *WomanWord, WomanWisdom,* and *WomanWitness*(2) provide lectionaries of women's place in Hebrew and Christian scriptures.

In fostering the renewal of older members of congregations, greater advantage should be taken of age-based rituals and religious institutions. Recent surveys indicate that the old are at least as earnest in their beliefs and regular in their attendance as younger people (Moberg, 1990; Gallup, 1984). Acknowledging their eldership in some public way might reinforce among young and old alike the view that experience is an important guide on the path to wisdom. Just as rituals such as circumcision, communion, and marriage bring all age groups together, so too intergenerational complementarity (in the spirit of Malachi 4:6 and Luke 1:17) might be promoted in rehabilitation or literacy programs. At a time in which Federal commitments to welfare have been eviscerated, churches and synagogues must do more than their current resources could possibly allow. It should empower its "gray heads" to use their gifts as they enable rising generations to find theirs. As T. S. Eliot noted, such a conscious effort to (re)create late-life tradition might facilitate peoples' search for wisdom as they grow older:

> Men's curiosity searches past and future
> And clings to that dimension. But to apprehend
> The point of intersection of the timeless
> With time, is an occupation for the saint—
> No occupation either, but something given
> And taken, in a lifetime's death in love,
> Ardor and selflessness and self-surrender.
> For most of us, there is only the unattended
> Moment, the moment in and out of time,
> The distraction fit, lost in a shaft of sunlight,
> The wild thyme unseen, or the winter lightning
> Or the waterfall, or music heard so deeply
> That it is not heard at all, but you are the music
> While the music lasts. These are only hints and guesses,
> Hints followed by guesses; and the rest
> Is prayer, observance, discipline, thought and action.
>
> T. S. Eliot, "The Dry Salvages" (1952, 136)

Not surprisingly, it is often the old themselves who are suggesting ways to recognize late-life transitions in meaningful ways.

In 1922, for instance, twelve-year-old Judith Kaplan became the first bat mitzvah in a Reconstructionist Jewish congregation. Seventy years later, seventy prominent women (including Betty Friedan) watched Judith Kaplan Eisenstein mark her second bat mitzvah, which she viewed as "a statement to something larger than oneself" (*New York Times* 1992, A16). Christian congregations often encourage the same sort of recognition. Churches formally salute members on their seventy-fifth, eightieth, or ninetieth birthdays. Parties are held to honor rabbis, priests, and ministers on the twenty-fifth or fiftieth anniversary of their ordination or installation as senior religious official. Anecdotal evidence suggests that other celebrations are crafted to affirm continuities of faith over the lifecourse. A Catholic parish in Wisconsin, for example, holds an annual pot luck dinner to honor couples who have been married forty or fifty years.

In recent years, clergy and lay people have developed rituals and customs expressly designed to draw attention to the distinctive features of being old. Demographics often is the primary engine driving this "invention of tradition."

Few once lived past seventy-five. Now, the median age of most U.S. religious bodies approaches or exceeds forty-five. Clergy are ministering to more and more older people in aging congregations. Thus, just as many Orthodox newlyweds have their first home blessed, so too more and more spiritual leaders are requested to bless homes in retirement communities and rooms in nursing homes.

More innovative are calls for some "official" recognition of changes in (self)-identity. William Clements suggests that more attention needs to be paid in religious settings to recognizing the status of grandparents (1990, 60–65). Even more daunting is the challenge of finding ways to acknowledge the shedding of earlier roles in life as a natural, theologically grounded response to the finitude of life. Selling the family home, transferring property to children, retiring are no less momentous events than graduating from school, getting married, or other events of youth now often celebrated in religious as well as social ways. Synagogues and churches need "to devise rites for losses," claims Henry Simmons. Such rituals would "make public what society sees as increasing marginalization in a context where there will be some incentive to struggle together to common wisdom . . . small signs of hope to be shared and fostered" (Simmons, 1990, 163).

Trying to invent age-based religious "traditions," some will object, is oxymoronic. Traditions may be reworked to meet changing circumstances, but they cannot be created *de novo*. Rituals should be inspired by the human desire to be open to God's love; they symbolize "social events" in a liturgical act, not a sociological process. In principle, this "conservative" position has merit, with two caveats to be added. First, as responses to obscene tragedies such as the Holocaust and to extraordinary triumphs such as Vatican II attest, there is ample precedent in both Jewish and Christian traditions to effect changes in "prayer, observance, discipline, thought and action" in radical ways. The graying of America in the twenty-first century will force members of faith communities to rethink their practices. Second, it is possible through grafting variations on ancient rites and customs to bring into existence new rituals and practices that utilize older people's talents more effectively.

It is not too difficult to imagine ways to incorporate age-relevant sensitivities into rituals and spiritual gatherings. In my family, for instance, the responsibilities of godparents pass from generation to generation. My older daughter's godfather was an eighty-one-year-old Peruvian patriarch; when Señor Mujica died, Elias IV took on the task of helping my wife and me ensure that our older child was raised in the faith. Since there is no limit to the number of sponsors at a baptism or conformation, it might make sense to underscore the faith community's stake in these events by having a "stranger," an older member of the congregation, serve in this capacity. Conversely, even those whose cognitive capacities have been deadened are able to respond to ancient, and familiar, cues. Hence those who work in Alzheimer's units report that older people respond to

"That Old Wooden Cross" as readily as "Silver Threads among the Gold"; they can repeat the Lord's Prayer even as their memory fails in other domains (Richards and Seicol, 1991, 30–31).

In addition to using and finding the wisdom of old age through age-old rituals, it makes sense to revive biblical customs to meet the needs of an aging society. Acts 6:1-6 suggests that elders in the early Jesus movement took charge of welfare activities. Shepherd's Center, established in 1972 as a site for Meals on Wheels, has evolved into a prototype for this sort of opportunity for volunteerism and for personal growth, as do Senior Friends and "contemplative communities" (Ellor, 1990, 108).

"These are only hints and guesses," Eliot would say. Other precedents surely can be mined from our immensely diverse heritage. When age-specific rituals and institutions seem inappropriate, then religious leaders should opt for the "basics," which stress the fundamental calling to serve, and to celebrate the presence of God at every stage of life. This is, after all, one reason for time's repetitiveness on the institutional plane: for those who failed to get the point early on, hope remains for future maturity. And the familiar commandments to respect life, to empower people to love God, themselves, and their neighbors, surely include the old as well as everyone else. Thoughts about age-based rituals and institutions thus end where they began: Jewish and Christian religious bodies probably are less ageist than other secular organizations, but they can better meet the needs of older people through traditions at their disposal.

BIBLIOGRAPHY

Achenbaum, W. A. (forthcoming) "Lost Traditions/Horizons Reclaimed." In Bass et al.

______ (1991) "'Time is the Messenger of the Gods': A Gerontologic Metaphor." In Kenyon, Birren, and Schroots, 83–102.

______ (1985) "Societal Perceptions of Aging and the Aged." In Binstock and Shanas, 129–48.

Ahlstrom, S. (1972) *A Religious History of the American People*. New Haven, Conn.: Yale University Press.

Anglican Board of Social Responsibility, Social Policy Committee (1986) Social policy statement. London: Church House.

Arrington, L., and D. Bitton (1979) *The Mormon Experience*. New York: Vintage Books.

Bass, S. B. et al., eds. (forthcoming) *Productive Aging*. New York: Springer.

Ben-Sasson, H. H. (1971) "Care for the Aged." In *Encyclopedia Judaica*. Vol. 2:346–67.

Berger, P. L. (1967) *The Sacred Canopy: Elements of a Sociological Theory of Religion*. Garden City, N.Y.: Doubleday Anchor.

Binstock, R. H., and E. Shanas, eds. (1985) *Handbook of Aging and the Social Sciences*. 2d ed. New York: Van Nostrand Reinhold.

Birnbaum, P. (1979) *Encyclopedia of Jewish Concepts.* New York: Sanhedrin Press.

Birren, J. E., and W. Cunningham (1985) "Research on the Psychology of Aging: Principles, Concepts, and Theory." In Birren and Schaie, 3–34.

Birren, J. E., and K. W. Schaie, eds. (1985) *Handbook of the Psychology of Aging.* 2d ed. New York: Van Nostrand Reinhold.

Bode, C. (1968) *The American Lyceum.* Carbondale, Ill: Southern Illinois University Press.

Clements, W. M. (1990) "Spiritual Development in the Fourth Quarter of Life." In Seeber, 55–69.

Cook, T. C., Jr. (1977) *The Religious Sector Explores Its Mission in Aging.* Athens, Ga.: National Interfaith Coalition on Aging.

Cox, H. (1969) *The Feast of Fools.* Cambridge, Mass.: Harvard University Press.

Cremin, L. A. (1970–88) *American Education.* 3 Vols. New York: Harper Torchbooks.

Dolan, J. P. (1985) *The American Catholic Experience.* New York: Doubleday.

Donin, H. H. (1972) *To Be a Jew.* New York: Basic Books.

Dorff, E. N. (1987) "Honoring Aged Fathers and Mothers." *Reconstructionist* 53:14–18.

Eliot, T. S. (1952) "Four Quartets." In *The Complete Poems and Plays,* 1909–1950, 115–45. New York: Harcourt, Brace and World.

Ellor, J. W. (1990) "Wholistic Theology as a Conceptual Foundation for Services for the Oldest-Old." In Seeber, 99–110.

Encyclopedia Britannica (1987) *Encyclopedia Britannica.* 15th Edition. 32 vols. Edited by P. W. Goetz et al. Chicago: Encyclopedia Britannica.

Encyclopedia Judaica (1971–72) *Encyclopedia Judaica.* 16 vols. Edited by G. Wigoder et al. Westport, Conn.: Ktav.

Episcopal Church (1977) *Book of Common Prayer.* New York: Seabury Press.

Ferraro, K., ed. (1990) *Gerontology: Perspectives and Issues.* New York: Springer.

Gallup, G. (1984) *Religion in America, 1984.* Princeton, N.J.: Princeton Religion Research Center.

Gold, J. G., and S. M. Kaufman (1970) "Development of Care of Elderly." *Gerontologist* 10:264.

Green, E. (1987) *Time's Covenant: The Essays and Sermons of William Clancey.* Pittsburgh: Univ. of Pittsburgh Press.

Haber, C. (1983) *Beyond Sixty-Five.* New York: Cambridge University Press.

Herr, M. D. (1963) "Old Age." *Encyclopedia Judaica.* Vol. 2:343–46.

Jewish Encyclopedia, The (1901) *The Jewish Encyclopedia.* 12 vols. Edited by Isidore Singer et al. New York: Funk and Wagnalls Company.

Kenyon, G. M., J. E. Birren, and J. J. F. Schroots, eds. (1991) *Metaphors of Aging in Science and the Humanities.* New York: Springer.

LeFevre, C., and P. LeFevre, eds. (1981) *Aging and the Human Spirit.* Chicago: Exploration Press.

Maves, P. B. (1960) "Aging, Religion and the Church." In Tibbetts, 698–749.

Maves, P. B., and J. L. Cedarleaf (1949) *Older People and the Church*. New York: Abingdon-Cokesbury Press.

McBrien, R. P. (1981) *Catholicism*. San Francisco: Harper & Row.

Moberg, D. O. (1990) "Religion and Aging." In Ferraro, 179–205.

Morrison, T. (1974) *Chautauqua*. Chicago: Univ. of Chicago Press.

New York Times (1992) "Bat Mitzvah Pioneer Looks to her 2d." *New York Times*. March 19: A-16.

Philipson, D. (1901) "Old Age." In *The Jewish Encyclopedia*. Vol. 1:230–31.

Pullan, B. (1989) *Orphans and Foundlings in Early Modern Europe*. Stenton Lecture. University of Reading, Reading, Pa.

Reuben, S. C. (1987) "Old Age: Appearance and Reality." *The Journal of Aging and Judaism* 2:117–22.

Richards, M., and S. Seicol (1991) "The Challenge of Maintaining Spiritual Connectedness for Persons Institutionalized with Dementia." *Journal of Religious Gerontology* 7 (3):30–31.

Rothman, D. (1971) *The Discovery of the Asylum*. Boston: Little.

Schauss, H. (1950) *The Lifetime of a Jew*. Cincinnati: Union of American Hebrew Congregations.

Seeber, J. J. (1990a) "Postscript." In 1990b, 195–96.

Seeber, J. J., ed. (1990b) *Spiritual Maturity in the Later Years*. New York: Haworth.

Simmons, H. C. (1990) "Countering Cultural Metaphors of Aging." In Seeber, 153–65.

Thurston, B. B. (1989) *The Widows*. Minneapolis, Minn.: Fortress Press.

Tibbetts, C., ed. (1960) *Handbook of Social Gerontology*. Chicago: Univ. of Chicago Press.

Trattner, W. I. (1984) *From Poor Law to Welfare State*. 3d ed. New York: Free Press.

Winter, M. T. (1990) *WomanWord: A Feminist Lectionary and Psalter on Women of the New Testament*. New York: Crossroad.

______ (1991) *WomanWisdom: A Feminist Lectionary and Psalter on Women of the Hebrew Scriptures, Part 1*. New York: Crossroad.

______ (1992) *WomanWitness: A Feminist Lectionary and Psalter on Women of the Hebrew Scriptures, Part 2*. New York: Crossroad.

Zimmer, H. (1964) *Philosophies of India*. New York: Meridian Books.

15 Religious Education

HENRY C. SIMMONS

INTRODUCTION

Given the disproportionately large number of older adults in local congregations compared to the general population, the case for religious education for older adults seems clear: (1) there are developmental tasks of older and late adulthood that need to be addressed (for example, Erikson, 1963 and Havighurst, 1972); and (2) for people of religious faith, the wisdom of the religious community, including its interpretation of the Bible, is needed to shed light on these tasks. One author states the case with refreshing directness: "The message of the Bible may be the same in words, but it is different in interpretation and application with each changing phase of life. Not to realize this is to run the risk of coming to the end of life on the road that leads to disappointment and failure" (Dobbins, 1959, 36). This matching of human tasks and the worshipping community is the responsibility of religious education; and such systematic religious education depends in large part on formal religious education programs or instructional materials. Without resource materials to support their efforts, even the most conscientious educators will be hard pressed to sustain programs for the religious education of older adults.

With the large numbers of older adults in churches and synagogues, one may reasonably expect that this chapter would have as a principal task an examination and analysis of resources. Such is not the case. A recent comprehensive study of literature in the area of religion and aging from 1876 to 1992 (Simmons and Pierce, 1992, 34–42) shows a clear lack of religious educational resources for older adults or their teachers. Of the thirty-two items listed in the study (twenty books, nine articles, three dissertations), only three directly address the issue of the religious education of older adults for enrichment or awareness (in distinction to programs oriented to issue or task, e.g., lay ministry training, retirement planning, death preparation).

Instructional materials, that is, explicitly curricular resources, are few and far between. Reichert and Reichert (1976) offer five units on spiritual disciplines and sacraments assuming that older people need to understand life experience in light of faith. Johnson (1981) plans twelve units of explicit religious content, some directed toward life-change stages. *Affirmative Aging* by the Episcopal Society on Aging (1985) has ten chapters on a series of spiritual and life issue areas. Mulhall and Rowe (1988) present six discussion topics on human issues in aging.

The lack of adequate religious education resources for older adults and the clear need for instructional materials are our two starting points. The first part of the chapter will analyze the social context in which the lack of religious educational resources occurs. It will be argued that social context and curriculum are inextricably intertwined and that the lack of resources is an educational issue. The second part of the chapter proposes that an aesthetic approach to curriculum can provide criteria for the creative adaptation of other materials as instructional resources. Age seen as art provides a basis for social critique, for the enhancement of immediate experience, and for the religious transformation of person and community.

THE SOCIAL CONTEXT

The lack of instructional materials for the religious education of older adults occurs within a social context. As early as 1790, there were notable shifts in the social perception of white older adults in the U.S.: the human ideal became not maturity and old age, but youth. D. H. Fischer notes a simple but significant aesthetic instance of this shift, namely, costume: "From about 1790 to our time, fashion has attempted in its endless variety of ways to make old men look young again" (1978, 87). Between 1865 and 1914, there were important transitions in the perception of the old that made old age obsolete. In *Old Age in the New Land,* Achenbaum (1978, 39–54) notes several of importance. (1) A medical view of old age now saw it as a time of incurable pathological disorders and as a time of weakness and decrepitude. (2) The earlier assumption that surviving to old age was a sign of God's predeliction or proved a person's inherent goodness and wisdom was increasingly challenged. The ills of the old—of morals or of temperament—were attributed to their declining abilities. (3) The growth of large-scale business and rational bureaucratic principles, combined with an increasing belief that the roles of a new society required youth, led to an "unprecedented devaluation of older workers' usefulness" (Achenbaum, 1978, 50). The young represented the progress of evolution; the old were a symbol of the lack of fitness needed to ensure survival. Theirs was a demoralizing presence. (4) An increasingly laissez-faire economic philosophy virtually guaranteed that the old would be poor and dependent on younger workers. (5) With advances in health and sanitation, and a concomitant decline in the death rate for all but the old, death was increasingly associated with old age. Death was not part of inevitable and successful progress; nor were the old. The old were social misfits who stood in the way of the new.

In 1975, Robert Butler wrote a widely acclaimed book whose title implied that little had changed in a half-century: *Why Survive? Being Old in America.*

Butler contended that to be old in America was to be poor, to depend on inadequate and unsecured pensions, to be the victim of marginal housing, to be isolated and lonely, to be the victim of discrimination. Some years later, Laura Katz Olson argued that

> the situation of disadvantaged sectors of the older population stems from market and class relationships, along with racist and sexist institutions, that negatively affect workers and families, to varying degrees, throughout their life cycle. Such forces engender even more oppressive conditions during old age. (1982, ix)

In stark contrast to these views stands *Age Wave: the Challenges and Opportunities of an Aging America* (Dychtwald and Flower, 1989). This book grew out of an invitation to Dychtwald, then twenty-three, to write a human-potential program for senior citizens, and is thus marked by its origins. This book has become a sort of symbol and rallying point for a new view of aging. Many people today advocate its perspective—that old age is now a time of new promise, a time to redesign America for a maturing market. This positive image of old age is widespread and is vigorously defended by those who oppose "ageism."

How we see the issue of religious education for older adults will depend in large measure on our vision of the old. During the last decade, the world has changed in many ways for the better for those who are old. Yet, the world of the old is best understood if we recognize that earlier negative attitudes are still powerful social forces that shape our perception of the old and account in part for the absence of formal instructional materials for those who grow old in our midst. This argument is based on simple observation, i.e., most old, and not exclusively the frail and poor old, are still seen through negative stereotypes. As Wear and Nixon state, ". . . after a certain age persons are perceived to become dependent, less intelligent, nonsexual, excessively cautious—just less *interesting*" (1991, 118). The argument is also based on a conviction that stereotypes are culturally embedded notions intrinsic to present understanding of the human.

Splitting the Positive from the Negative

The distance between positive views of aging (e.g., *Age Wave*) and the more negative views of aging is great. The positive view splits off all negatives and presents a lovely, affluent, "air-brushed" picture of old age. This splitting of the positives from the negatives of old age is not neutral in its impact on the old and on the development of religious education resource materials for the old. Among a wide variety of possible explanations for the splitting of positive from negative views of aging, two are germane to our inquiry.

The "Enlightened" View of Aging. Any attempt to understand the religious education of older adults needs to take into account an evolving understanding of aging. There have been formidable (and well-intentioned) efforts over the last decade to eliminate negative stereotypes of and prejudices about older people. These efforts have historical antecedents that make today's efforts more fully comprehensible. In the last century,

> Impelled by their perfectionism in physical and spiritual matters, and by their belief in the power of individual will, Victorian moralists dichotomized and rationalized experience in order to control it. . . . Rather than acknowledge ambiguity and contingency in aging, Victorians split old age into: sin, decay, and dependence on the one hand; virtue, self-reliance, and health on the other. (Cole, 1986, 123)

This "enlightened" view retains much of its power in an altered form today. Today's popular images of older people as healthy, sexually active, engaged, productive, and self-reliant may counteract negative stereotypes. However, they effectively ignore the probable losses—the intractable vicissitudes—of age and mask the need for public support for old, sick, and often poor people. The splitting off of negative from positive realities of aging has a direct effect on religious education: if the old are imaged as healthy, sexually active, engaged, productive, and self-reliant, instructional materials geared to their needs will be profoundly affected by this onesided image. Though many older persons do live the kinds of lives described so positively, yet, barring sudden and early death, even they will not end their days without experiencing some of the losses of age.

The Belief in a Just World. This splitting off of negative from positive realities of aging must meet some social or psychosocial need in order to maintain its power. One disturbing analysis of the dynamic underlying this splitting off is found in Melvin Lerner's award winning book, *The Belief in a Just World: A Fundamental Delusion*. For Lerner, a just world is one in which people get what they deserve. "People want to and have to believe they live in a just world so that they can go about their daily lives with a sense of trust, hope, and confidence in their future" (Lerner, 1980, 14). In its briefest form, this belief or fundamental delusion allows us to deal with the harsh realities that afflict so many because we accept that the world *is* just and people must be getting what they deserve. If the world is just, if people get what they deserve, those who have less and suffer more must be in some way responsible for their own fate. People who occupy minority statuses (e.g., people on welfare, the mentally ill, women, the sick old) are judged to be worse and different—"potentially dangerous, inferior, undesirable in important ways. . . . [They] therefore deserve less, and, indeed, deserve punishment at times" (Lerner, 1980, 16).

Those who suffer the losses of age must, in a world that is just, deserve what they suffer. To cast them off into the darkness, then, is not inappropriate. It is economically and socially appropriate. In this analysis, the splitting off of negative from positive realities of aging has another direct effect on religious education: if the now healthy old are also imaged as *potentially* unhealthy, frail, poor, weak, and dependent, the lack of instructional resources to address these probable losses is further justified.

The Social Context as Framework for Curriculum

While this analysis of the social context of curriculum is necessarily selective and brief, it should be clear that social context and curriculum are inextricably intertwined. The absence of formal instructional resources for older adults is not a value-neutral oversight. Rather, it indicates in profound and disturbing ways that the religious sector has bought into one view of aging that is inimical to the complex reality of aging—probable losses, possible gains. ("Bought into" is meant quite literally: denominational instructional material production is a multi-million dollar business in the U.S.) The worshiping community must take responsibility for dictating what are appropriate curricular materials for the religious education of older adults. While the issues of aging and death are common to all humans, the ways in which aging and death are lived out are stamped and shaped by a particular social context. Ours is a context that devalues the old, splits the negatives of aging from the positives, and sees the lot of the old who are not healthy, sexually active, engaged, productive, and self-reliant as "fair"—they get what they deserve.

These are educational issues. The growing field of "Critical curriculum inquiry" seeks to "challenge directly underlying human interests and ideology. . . . It is based on a commitment to social justice" (Sirotnik, 1991, 245). Basic questions need to be asked and asked again: What are we doing now? How did it come to be this way? Whose interests are and are not being served by the way things are? Any discussion of curricular materials should hold in mind these questions and the social context in which they are asked.

These issues can and must be named with religious language by the worshiping community. Who is God? What does it mean to be human? To what are humans called? How does the community of faith create a more human world?

"IF AGE WERE ART . . .": ADAPTING MATERIALS FOR CURRICULAR USE

Experienced educators know that almost anything can, whether deliberately or "in a pinch," serve as instructional material. How may we identify and order materials that in substantial ways are client/audience focused (Marsh, 1991, 272) and that address the social context described above? What kinds of instructional materials and approaches are likely to provide a basis for social critique, for the enhancement of immediate experience, and for the religious transformation of persons and community? To sort through these issues and find a basis for judgment, we turn to aesthetics, the study of the perceived qualities of art, as applied to curriculum. Some salient features of art and aesthetics are sketched out very briefly to guide our inquiry.

Art, Transformation, and the Religious

Our analysis of social context shows a culture that "has a vacuum at its heart" (Gilkey, 1984, 188) and that deals with humans as means to its technical ends. In this technical culture, art can be used technically—to create an ad that will sell something. But art can also have vast creative power. "Art opens up the truth hidden behind and within the ordinary; it provides a new entrance into reality and pushes us through that entrance" (Gilkey, 1984, 188). Some art is outraged at the dehumanization of people, at the emptiness of their lives, at suffering and marginalization. Such outrage can be the starting point for social critique.

At more personal and communal levels, art can reshape "immediate experience to make it . . . an event of intrinsic worth, that is an event which, in and of itself, in and through its own taking place, creates immediate and experienced *meaning*" (Gilkey, 1984, 188). When an experience *is* on its own terms, when there is immediate and experienced meaning that is not that of the culture, there is change.

Art and religion both have the power to transform lives because both deal with the mythic-symbolic. "The symbol captures something of the essence of the human experience of this unknown and thus suggests there is more to be explored" (Slusser, 1979, 206). Although religious communities often *de facto* side with the prevailing technical culture, there is in religious symbols something that is always potentially disruptive. The resistance to change is great. The weight of culture is massive. But change can come from within. "Those who are still under the sway of the old . . . have not made peace with the deep creative aspects of the psyche, the Myth-Maker within" (212). But change does occur, and transformation is a goal of religious education *and* art.

Aesthetic Inquiry: "If Age Were Art . . ."

Issues of aging are extraordinarily complex, and the complexity is not simply technical. It is the rich complexity of human life itself that technical, nonimaginative language cannot capture. Thus we look to the perspective of art to understand better the concreteness of human life, to break the power of a merely technical society, to ground individual experience, to shape meaning, and to transform.

These sound like lofty aims—and indeed they are. But they are not removed from the absolute everydayness of ordinary human lives. The human response to old humans is an aesthetic response. What we are trying to establish is that old human beings are not to be judged by the standards of a technical culture.

They—these old women and men—are themselves the works of art that can transform. They are the art when they refuse to be treated as functions of something else; they are the art that is immediate and bodily (often to our discomfort); they are the makers of their own meanings when, in growing old, they become like themselves . . . only more so.

Elizabeth Vallance, writing about aesthetic inquiry, says:

> the aesthetic response provides, in effect, a moment of repose, a break from our normal practical way of valuing our environment, a chance to be impressed or amused by seeing things in a new way. . . . As we "bracket" our everyday experiences, . . . placing temporary fleeting frames around parts of it to isolate images or feelings or sounds and make them accessible to this aesthetic response, we create a story of memorable moments that tacitly shape our future responses. (1991, 159)

The aesthetic response breaks in on complacency and sees the world in new ways. It "brackets" everyday experiences to see new totalities and disturbs culturally sanctioned routines.

The aesthetic approach offers guidelines for selecting materials, for organizing them and for their use. Instructional materials in religious education for older adults, like art, are products of human construction; they are means of communication. If they are adequate to the religious task, they transform knowledge to make it accessible to the learner. They produce a problem-solving process and they make meaning in an encounter with an audience. They provide "brackets" or boundaries to the audience's experience. They can provoke strong reactions. They can be placed within a religious history of tradition and change. They are open to criticism and assessment.

The comparison between art and religious education for older adults does more justice to the field than other images. Recognizing the complexity of the lives and realities of older adults, some authors have approached their subject with materials that evoke an aesthetic response, in the hope of shaping future responses (cf. Nouwen and Gaffney, 1974; Folliet, 1983; Fine, 1987; Kugelmass, 1986; Miller, 1990; Pierskalla, 1992). Characteristic of these works and of this approach to religious education is a recognition that art, including the art of living, is a human construction, open to inquiry, malleable. These authors produce problem-solving processes that work in interaction with an audience. Their works let the audience put "brackets" or boundaries around ordinary experience to see with new eyes. Their materials, like all art, only make sense in historical context. And finally, they invite strong reactions, criticism, and assessment because their final goal is transformation.

All this describes the best of the materials that can be used for curriculum for older adults. The reader will observe in this contention a judgment that the more technical "how to . . ." materials have limited worth or appeal. Given the earlier analysis of the social forces at work, it will be clear that only a transforming vision can provide the shock needed to budge the overwhelming inertia of social fact.

With these admittedly soft criteria in mind, we turn now to four areas in which exist materials that may be shaped into instructional materials for older adults: empowerment, worship and ritual, personal spiritual life, and reminiscence. Each of these areas is selected because of openness to understanding with aesthetic criteria. Each should be approached with the theme in mind: "If age were art . . ."

Empowerment. The title of Maitland's recent book (1991) articulates a vision of empowered aging as understood in this essay: *Aging as Counterculture: A Vocation for the Later Years.* In this section, we inquire about the function of the group in helping people who no longer can embrace social values uncritically.

In a pioneer work on older people and the church, Paul Maves noted the *group* as the place where power and creativity are born.

> Human beings are inescapably social and have a need to associate themselves meaningfully in groups. There are certain satisfactions, such as companionship, common commitment, a sense of belonging, and an experience of participation, that can be achieved in no other way. There is also a creative element in group interaction that cannot otherwise be had. (Maves and Cedarleaf, 1949, 156)

The focus on the group as the means of empowerment highlights that curricular materials may be not print or electronic media but the interaction over time of human persons. The curriculum may be lived together, lived artfully, remembered and reconstructed. Novels, plays, and poetry, though not referenced here, are also invaluable resources for the interaction of human spirits. In the work of Maves and others (e.g., Maggie Kuhn), it is the group itself which is the place of release of power. In "Discovering the Public/Private World: A Research Note" (Simmons, 1993a) a method is offered for understanding individual lives at the point where they intersect with social settings. This method may be of particular value for research based on age-specific religious education. Maxwell Jones states in his *Growing Old: The Ultimate Freedom:*

> We have stressed the importance of group interaction among motivated people as a prelude to social change. In retrospect I now realize how the energy liberated in such a setting had a peculiar fascination for me and sharpened my awareness so that at such times I seemed to think and interact far beyond my usual level. (1988, 58)

In some cases, while the group is the place of release of power, it is the participant-observer (or perhaps educator) who notices and records the transformations that occur. Three quite different instances of this—each powerful in its own way—are Barbara Myerhoff's *Number Our Days* (1978b), Natalie Rosel's "Growing Old Together: Neighborhood Communality among the Elderly"

(1986), and Susan Perlstein's "A Stage for Memory: Living History Plays by Older Adults" (1984).

The transformation that occurs in a group may be intensely personal; it may also serve for communal transformation from the control of cultural norms. This may be fostered by learning the skills of peer reflection even before any personal experience of the oppression of old age. "Those who live in an 'extended middle age' are still rewarded for conforming to the norm, rather than for developing a unique self. The task is to engage this group in a sort of readiness program" (Simmons, 1989, 51). Transformation from the power of cultural norms may also occur as there is developed a sense of solidarity with others who suffer the oppression of a culture that slowly but surely relegates the old person to the status of a marginalized nonentity. The group, working together, may develop an emerging sense that a new order is possible and that personal and collective agency will truly lead to change. Together, older persons must make a collective counter-judgment about the nature and worth of old age (Simmons, 1988). This is empowerment. Everyday experience is "bracketed." The promised awkward, troubling turn-around begins.

Worship and Ritual. An author writes about two retired friends, one of whom was so completely deaf that communication was almost impossible. Earlier he had wondered what pleasure they found together; now he has begun to understand.

> These two friends visited each other regularly and spent hours together, smoking their pipes, drinking the local wine, and not speaking a word to each other. . . . The mere presence of the other enabled friendship to be expressed and . . . God was also present in their presence with each other. (Folliet, 1983, 150)

In these few images we see ordinary experience "bracketed" as the author sees with new eyes.

The dynamics of ritual include these factors:

> Ritual inevitably carries a basic message of order, continuity, and predictability. . . . Ritual always links participants to one another and often beyond, to wider collectivities that may be absent. . . . Religious rituals go further still, connecting humankind to the forces of nature and the purposes of the deities, reading the form of the macrocosm into the microcosm. (Myerhoff, 1984, 306)

These more abstract images name a very human reality—two old men, one deaf, sitting together daily, smoking their pipes, sipping wine. This analysis points out that by their rituals these old men are linked to each other, to wider collectivities, and to God. At some level it is the task of religious education that uses worship and ritual as the stuff of its curriculum both to sharpen our attention to the ordinary and to name this mysterious reading of the macrocosm into the microcosm.

The events that are ritualized may be secular: birthdays, the arrival of the Social Security check, reunions (cf. Troll, 1988), giving up the family home, accepting a hearing aid, making it safely one more time to the senior center (cf. Myerhoff, 1978a, 1978b, 1984; Robb, 1991; Simmons, 1990). It is *socially* unacceptable to ritualize negative events, but the need to ritualize these is real. As Myerhoff notes: "While these are undeniably negative and painful events, the clear public acknowledgment of them by others who accept and care about them has clarifying, healing consequences that redefine relationships and identities for all those involved" (1984, 312). It may be a function of a religious community to take leadership in this. For the religious person, these events can become the stuff of a curriculum for aging. In events such as these, named, celebrated, ritualized, the individual finds not an isolating moment, but a link to a common humanity. The art of ritual lets us see ordinary experiences with new eyes.

Liturgy or public worship that is inclusive of the old in explicit ways is rare (cf. Carlson, chap. 17 and Friedman, chap. 24). Retirements may be marked; deaths certainly are. In between, in those twenty-five or thirty years of human life, "there is a universe of differentiation that remains a cultural wasteland for each to calculate and navigate alone, without the aid of ritual, ceremony, or symbol" (Myerhoff, 1984, 312). In the religious community it is uncommon to bring the lives, the experiences, the challenges, the tasks, and the gains of the old into the life of public worship. Worship and liturgy in real ways signal the true curriculum of the group; changes in this area may have powerfully transformative effects.

Personal Spiritual Life. Given the perspectives already developed, it should be clear that the notion of a "*personal* spiritual life" stands at a point of tension. There are powerful social forces for the individualization of meaning; thus a "*personal* spiritual life" may be purely individual. But the individual who is within supportive groups, whose life experiences are ritualized, who is part of common worship, may find a place in the fellowship of believers where the personal and the public come together and nourish each other. Religious education curriculum has a necessarily public face and "personal spiritual life" is part of the group's curriculum for older adults only to the extent that this public dimension is maintained. This does not exclude some intensely personal dimensions of prayer; yet it does not allow for God ever to become simply a private fact or construct.

A review of the 130 items under the heading "Personal Spiritual Life" in Simmons and Pierce (1992) notes several categories: meditations, the devout life, spiritual development and growth, and spiritual well-being. A note of caution is well taken in this context:

> There is a great deal of guidance for a devout old age. Devotional literature is clearly an important part of the response of the religious community, particularly Christian,

> to and by the elders in our midst. The quality of the guidance is varied. . . . The best of these materials are extraordinarily good, but identifying the best and even the adequate requires considerable discretion. (Simmons, 1993b, 151–52)

In this area, personal and denominational preference, individual and group need, a sense of timeliness, and the fact that an item is still in print are all important factors in the decision about use of material within a curriculum. In addition, the criteria developed from aesthetics are helpful in establishing a range of characteristics of this approach to curriculum. At least cumulatively, what we select in this area ought to cover all criteria and counter or violate none.

Examples clarify these principles of selection. Chinen (1989) uses fairy tales, supplemented with analysis, to address issues of transformation in late life. Fairy tales "bracket" ordinary experience and establish boundaries so that the daily can be seen with new eyes. The protagonists can succeed only through transformation; the reader must struggle to resist that seductive argument that this, not business-as-usual, is the way life really is. *In the Footsteps of the Mystics* (Simmons, 1992) makes clear that the articulation of the spiritual life is, like art, a human construction. Readers are invited to identify their preference in prayer and meditation according to one of four "ways," to retell the story of their personal journeys, and to engage in conversation, through brief excerpts, with Muslims, Jews, Christians, and Native Americans who have been intimate with God in very distinctive ways. Kathleen Fischer (1985) addresses the spiritual life of elders in ways that produce problem-solving processes in interaction with her readers. Fischer shows how faith can transform the later years of life through spirituality:

> the ultimate ground of all our questions, hopes, fears, and loves: our efforts to deal creatively with retirement and to find purpose for our lives after our family has been raised; our struggle with the loss of a spouse or the move from a home of many years; questions of self-worth and fear of reaching out to make new friendships; the discovery of new talents, deeper peace, wider boundaries of love. (1985, 9)

Coupland (1985) addresses a specific problem-solving process in interaction with her readers, namely the special concern of parishioners who seek to begin or renew their lives of prayer later in life.

These few examples indicate how the criteria developed from an aesthetic approach to curriculum may give guidance to the selection of materials for use in a curriculum with older adults.

Reminiscence. In Erikson's widely accepted schema of the critical periods of development in the life cycle, the final stage is Ego-integrity vs. Despair. Ego-integrity is marked by a "post narcissistic love of the human ego—not of the self. . . . It is the acceptance of one's one and only life cycle as something that had to be" (Erikson, 1963, 268). Most people who are familiar with Erikson's schema will accept this description as fairly representing his point of view. This is yet another indication of a widespread privatization of meaning. What Erikson goes on to say is integral to his understanding of Ego-integrity: "The style of integrity developed by his culture or civilization thus becomes the 'patrimony of his soul.' . . . In such final consolidation, death loses its sting" (Erikson, 1963, 268).

Reminiscence can function as an element of a public curriculum (as understood in the context of this chapter) only if the cultural "patrimony of the soul" is present. In large measure, however, that cultural framework is missing today in the wider culture. Within the context of the religious community it may still be present and even powerful, although this should not be presumed. "The bankruptcy of privatism becomes all too evident in old age. But by that point individuals alone cannot invent meanings to save themselves from despair" (Moody, 1986, 13).

If meaning is anchored in a reality larger than the individual, reminiscence and life-review may be useful elements of a curriculum and may meet all the aesthetic criteria developed above. If human life is art, the telling of that life as located in history may also be a work of transforming art as "we create a story of memorable moments that tacitly shape our future response" (Vallance, 1991, 159). The *Annotated Bibliography* (Simmons and Pierce, 1992, 139–148) gathers thirty-five items that in some manner or other focus on finding patterns in and making sense of memories.

> Memories are key to all these writings, with memory understood in a dynamic way as open to reinterpretation and reintegration into the person's present. A variety of approaches emerge: story-telling, journal writing, logotherapy, structured life-review processes, self-narratives. (Simmons and Pierce, 1992, xxviii)

The selection and use of these materials should be governed by the criteria elucidated; too often, unfortunately, older adults are, within the context of an intergenerational educational event, asked to "tell the youth what it was like in the old days." This uncritical use of reminiscence is not likely to yield much that is positive.

CONCLUSION

The first part of this chapter has been a reflection on the social context of old age and its implication for the religious education of older adults. Social contexts shape human beings; this is both an educational and a religious issue. One can only wonder about the human cost—the disappointments and failures—of the general inattention by the religious community to the particular tasks of old age and late life. "The message of the Bible . . . is different in interpretation and application with each changing phase of life. Not to realize this is to run the risk of coming to the end of life on the road that leads to disappointment and failure" (Dobbins, 1959, 36). The second part of this chapter has laid out some criteria for educators and elders to adapt materials for curricular use. These criteria, from art and aesthetic curricula, are starting points for organizing and evaluating existing materials. The task is urgent.

BIBLIOGRAPHY

Achenbaum, W. A. (1978) *Old Age in the New Land: The American Experience since 1790.* Baltimore: Johns Hopkins University Press.

Apostolos-Cappadona, D., ed. (1984) *Art, Creativity, and the Sacred.* New York: Crossroad.

Armstrong, J., and F. R. Johnson (N.d.) *Study Guide for Affirmative Aging.* Bethlehem, Pa.: Episcopal Society for Ministry on Aging Office.

Butler, R. N. (1975) *Why Survive? Being Old in America.* San Francisco: Harper & Row.

Chinen, A. B. (1989) *In the Ever After: Fairy Tales and the Second Half of Life.* Wilmette, Ill.: Chiron.

Cole, T., and S. Gadow, eds. (1986) *What Does It Mean To Grow Old?* Durham, N.C.: Duke University Press.

Cole, T. R. (1986) "The 'Enlightened' View of Aging: Victorian Morality in a New Key." In Cole and Gadow, 115–30.

Coupland, S. (1985) *Beginning to Pray in Old Age.* Cambridge, Mass.: Cowley.

Dobbins, G. (1959) *The Years Ahead.* Nashville: Convention.

Durka, G., and J. Smith, eds. (1979) *Aesthetic Dimensions of Religious Education.* New York: Paulist Press.

Dychtwald, K., and J. Flower (1989) *Age Wave: The Challenges and Opportunities of an Aging America.* Los Angeles: J. P. Tarcher.

Episcopal Society for Ministry on Aging, ed. (1985) *Affirmative Aging: A Resource for Ministry.* Minneapolis, Minn.: Winston Press.

Erikson, E. H. (1963) *Childhood and Society.* 2d rev. ed. New York: Norton.

Fine, I. (1987) *Midlife: A Rite of Passage* and *The Wise Woman: A Celebration.* San Diego, Calif.: Woman's Institute for Continuing Jewish Education.

Fischer, D. H. (1978) *Growing Old in America.* New York: Oxford University Press.

Fischer, K. (1985) *Winter Grace: Spirituality for the Later Years.* New York/Mahwah, NJ: Paulist Press.

Folliet, J. (1983) *The Evening Sun: Growing Old Beautifully.* Chicago: Franciscan Herald Press.

Gilkey, L. (1984) "Can Art Fill the Vacuum?" In Apostolos-Cappadona, 187–92.

Havighurst, R. J. (1972) *Developmental Tasks and Education.* 3d ed. New York: McKay.

Johnson, C. (1981) *The Second Half.* Chicago, IL: Convention Press.

Jones, M. (1988) *Growing Older: The Ultimate Freedom.* New York: Human Sciences Press.

Kaminsky, M., ed. (1984) *The Uses of Reminiscence: New Ways of Working with Older Adults.* New York: Haworth.

Kertzer, D. L., and J. Keith (1984) *Age and Anthropological Theory.* Ithaca, N.Y.: Cornell University Press.

Kugelmass, J. (1986) *The Miracle of Intervale Avenue.* New York: Schocken.

Lerner, M. (1980) *The Belief in a Just World: A Fundamental Delusion.* New York: Plenum Press.

Maitland, D. J. (1991) *Aging as Counterculture: A Vocation for the Later Years.* New York: Pilgrim Press.

Marsh, C. J. (1991) "Interactive Inquiry: The Research Synthesis." In Short, 271–74.

Maslow, A. H. (1954) *Motivation and Personality.* New York: Harper.

Maves, P., and J. L. Cedarleaf (1949) *Older People and the Church.* New York: Abingdon-Cokesbury Press.

Miller, W. (1990) *Promised Land.* Nashville: Winston-Derek.

Moody, H. R. (1986) "The Meaning of Life and the Meaning of Old Age." In Cole and Gadow, 9–40.

Mulhall, D., and K. Rowe (1988) *A Time For . . . .* Los Angeles, CA: Franciscan Communications, 83.

Myerhoff, B. (1978a) "A Symbol Perfected in Death: Continuity and Ritual in the Life and Death of an Elderly Jew." In Myerhoff and Simic, 163–206.

______ (1978b) *Number Our Days.* New York: Simon and Schuster.

______ (1984) "Rites and Signs of Ripening: The Intertwining of Ritual, Time, and Growing Older." In Kertzer and Keith, 305–30.

Myerhoff, B., and A. Simic, eds. (1978) *Life's Career-Aging:Cultural Variations on Growing Old.* Beverly Hills, Calif.: Sage.

Nouwen, H., and W. Gaffney (1974) *Aging: The Fulfillment of Life.* New York: Doubleday.

Olson, L. K. (1982) *The Political Economy of Aging.* New York: Columbia University Press.

Perlstein, S. (1984) "A Stage for Memory: Living History Plays by Older Adults." In Kaminsky, 37–52.

Pierskalla, C. (1992) *Rehearsal for Retirement: My Journey into the Future.* Valley Forge, PA: National Ministries, American Baptist Churches.

Reichert, S., and R. Reichert (1976) *In Wisdom and the Spirit: A Religious Education Program for Those over Sixty-five.* New York: Paulist Press.

Robb, T. B. (1991) *Growing Up: Pastoral Nurture for the Later Years.* New York: Haworth Press.

Rosel, N. (1986) "Growing Old Together: Neighborhood Communality Among the Elderly." In Cole and Gadow, 199–234.

Short, E., ed. (1991) *Forms of Curriculum Inquiry.* Albany, N.Y.: State University of New York Press.

Simmons, H. C. (1988) "Religious Education of Older Adults: A Present and Future Perspective." *Educational Gerontologist* 14: 279–90.

______ (1989) "Ministry with Older Adults: Freedom in Old Age." *Professional Approaches for Christian Education* 19:45–53.

______ (1990) "Ministry with Older Adults: Rites and Signs of Ripening." *Professional Approaches for Christian Education* 19:83–86.

______ (1992) *In the Footsteps of the Mystics.* Mahwah, N.J.: Paulist Press.

______ (1993a) "Discovering the Public/Private World: A Research Note." *Journal of Psychology and Theology* 21:(4) 319–22.

______ (1993b) "Review Essay: When You Can't Find a Copy of *Blasting the Rock of Ages* Is There Any Guidance for a Devout Old Age?" *Religious Education* 88:(1) 149–153.

Simmons, H. C., and V. Pierce (1992) *Pastoral Responses to Older Adults and Their Families: An Annotated Bibliography.* New York: Greenwood Press.

Sirotnik, K. (1991) "Critical Inquiry: A Paradigm for Praxis." In Short, 243–58.

Slusser, G. (1979) "Language and Symbols in the Human Psyche." In Durka and Smith, 202–18.

Troll, L., ed. (1988) "Rituals and Reunions." *American Behavioral Scientist* 31:619–720.

Vallance, E. (1991) "Aesthetic Inquiry: Art Criticism." In Short, 155–172.

Wear, D., and L. Nixon (1991) "Try Thinking about It This Way: Redescribing Women and Aging." *Journal of Women and Aging* 3:117–25.

16 Worship, Traditions, and Settings

DOSIA CARLSON

WHAT IS WORSHIP?

Introduction

Participating in time-honored rituals that are imbued with a sense of the transcendent, singing beloved hymns of praise, sharing traditional prayers, seeking God's guidance through sacred writings—all these can be pathways to worship. In addition to introducing basic concepts of worship, this chapter will discuss the basic needs, challenges, and opportunities posed by helping adults nourish and sustain their faith in corporate and private worship.

Basic Understandings

For many older adults, spiritual well-being is related to their participation in worship services. John McGee states that worship is "the celebration of ultimate concern" (1967, 461). It is this recognition and experience of the numinous and the transcendent in religious ritual and worship that renders life meaningful and significant. Worship is seeking and apprehending the presence of God. It is a bridge both to Divine Presence and to self-understanding (Carlson and Seicol, 1990, 65). It is the expression of one's self as one seeks to know God and know one's life in God. Worship is both corporate and private and involves both the individual and the community.

According to Fischer (1987, 69), wonder is the basis of worship. This quality of awe and mystery, often apparent in young children, can continue nourishing spiritual openness throughout life. Although senses may become somewhat dulled with age, a healthy curiosity can add zest to living and keep alive that sense of wonder, an important ingredient in worship experiences.

Too often worshipers, including clergy who may be the primary designers and leaders, presume worship is simply something that one does. However, in his book *Paths in Spirituality,* Macquarrie (1972, 15) states that worship actually is the human responding to what God has already done and is still doing. According to Macquarrie, God has implanted in human beings the desire to worship God and grow in likeness to the Divine. "It is God's Spirit working in us that first brings us to worship the mystery of Holy Being and to seek God's grace."

Jewish and Christian Worship Approaches

An increasingly pluralistic society requires a deepened sensitivity to diverse expressions of faith. Although there is a steady increase within North America of the religious communities of Islam, Buddhism, and Hinduism, worship practices in those religions will not be discussed here. Rather, the major emphasis will be on Judaism and Christianity. Even within each of these faith communities which share a common foundation in biblical tradition, there are differences in ways that the presence of God is represented and experienced in worship.

For devout Jews, the whole of life is worship. Central to the Jew's life of faith is the acknowledgment of God as creator and Lord of life. Elderly worshipers in Jewish temples or synagogues may find a sense of security through following traditional patterns of worship. Thus, they anticipate that every service will include at least three basic elements: the Jewish affirmation of faith known as *Shema,* the period of prayer or *tefillah,* and teachings from the Torah which have been given to Israel as both gift and task. Within Judaism, significant variations occur depending on whether the believer follows orthodox, conservative, or reformed traditions.

For some Jewish people, especially those identified with Hasidic spirituality, every action of the day from waking to sleeping is accompanied by prayer. Prayers, cleansing rituals, work routines, and meals all become functions of faith (Buxbaum, 1990, 8) and occasions for praising God.

During the 2,000 years of Christian history, many primary patterns of worship have persisted. Both Pope Pius X and Pope Pius XII spoke of worship as the glorification of God and the sanctification and edification of human beings (Willimon, 1983, 42). A primary means of supporting those goals is through word and sacrament, as gathered people move in time and space in timeless worship. Deeply rooted in New Testament teachings, the sacraments of baptism and the Lord's Supper have remained essential for all of Christendom. Participation in the Holy Eucharist, for example, is vital for Catholics as well as many Protestants, and failure to be able to receive the sacrament can cause genuine distress.

In many Protestant worship traditions, there is a strong emphasis on proclamation and a scripture-centered sermon. In all its various forms and expressions, in a cross-section of ethnic and cultural communities, glorifying and praising God remain paramount.

Corporate and Private Worship Experiences

Most often worship suggests the gathering of a community of believers such as during a Jewish *shabbat* service or a Catholic mass. Depending on the particular tradition, there is usually a combination of adoration, confession, thanksgiving, supplication, and dedication. Because expressions of the Jewish and Christian faith are based on sacred writings, most worship times incorporate readings from Holy Scripture. Addressing God through prayers is also a basic ingredient in worship. The singing of hymns is another bonding element in worship. Frail elderly persons unable to attend church or synagogue services often comment that they particularly miss the hymn singing.

Coming together for worship with those sharing similar faith commitments can promote feelings of strength and support. As men and women, usually of mixed ages, pray, sing, and confess creeds together, a solidarity develops that can enhance not only spiritual but also total well-being. When temporary or permanent disabling conditions prevent persons from continuing to participate in corporate worship, they may feel an acute sense of loss. Clergy need to be sensitive to those feelings and seek ways to help people compensate for such losses.

Whether or not older persons are able to participate actively in corporate worship services, they always have the possibility of engaging in worship privately. This devotional approach, found in all religious groups, is for many an essential part of their religious experience. If there has been a lifelong cultivation of personal prayer life, this practice can continue to thrive in more mature years.

Although prayer life can become ingrown and focused only on self-centered desires, the full range of prayer includes a compassionate concern for needs of the wider world. It can foster a responsible interrelationship with life in its many dimensions. Nurturing such a connectedness helps older people grow in integrity. In developing his spiritual guide for aging, Missinne (1990, 85) stresses the value not only of prayer but also of reading, meditation, artistic creation, and enjoyment of the beauty of nature and other people.

SETTINGS FOR WORSHIP

Synagogues and Churches

Although older persons may in later years have their first encounter with organized religion, it is more likely that they have been active in synagogues and churches and bring with them a history of affiliation. That very rootedness often represents years of membership including an accumulation of cherished memories of worship. The experience of worship needs to build upon a lifetime of ritual and memory. As Holmes (1981, 92) contends, "Worship requires an accumulation of memories." It is not something that the faith community ". . . can 'invent' for those who are aging. It is meant to be built within a lifetime."

When encouraged to reminisce creatively, most elders can recall high moments of personal and family history centered in worship: circumcisions, baptisms and infant dedications, bar mitzvahs, first communions, weddings, rites of burial or memorial services. In reciting memories to younger generations, the elders help pass on religious symbols of ultimate meaning and values. Carlsen (1991, 130) stresses this need for intergenerational interaction within congregations. She frames this need in the context of finding meaning-making perspectives. Although she does not deal with worship as an expression of meaning, it often serves that role for young and old.

Candles, statues, vestments, postures and gestures during the service, and liturgical music all combine to create an atmosphere that cannot be replicated outside the special setting. This has important implications for frail elderly who may be limited in their ability to go to the worship setting of their choice.

Private Worship in Home Environment

Common worship with a body of like-minded believers can nurture strength and hope. On the other hand, personal devotions become a healthy balance to the group experience. The Latin root for "devotion" is the word for "vow." Basic to all worship must be an individual intention or vow to respond to God. An interesting observation from White (1980) is that individuals engaging alone in personal devotions can determine their own pace and content. This is in contrast to using a prescribed structure or liturgy during corporate worship.

Some older persons may have to rely primarily on private worship experiences. Consequently, congregations that regularly distribute devotional materials, usually on a periodic basis, are performing an important ministry. Better than mailing such materials to homebound men and women is having a member of the congregation deliver them. This direct social contact assures the elder that he or she is still in touch with other worshipers and an integral part of the faith community.

Within Roman Catholicism as well as some Protestant denominations there is growing use of eucharistic ministers. *An Important Office of Immense Love: A Handbook for Eucharistic Ministers* by Champlin (1984), for example, outlines for Roman Catholics, in helpful detail, the significance of this ministry and precise ways of taking holy communion to members unable to attend mass.

Another way to keep strong bonds between homebound people and those able to be more active is to develop prayer chains. By designating an appointed time to be in prayer with others, each participant knows there is an invisible bond linking people together around prayer concerns. Telephone chains can communicate a sense of caring and enrich personal devotional life.

Worship in Other Institutional Settings

The growing number of retirees choosing to live in retirement communities presents a challenge to developing meaningful worship for this population. The advantages of intergenerational celebrations of faith may be somewhat difficult to cultivate in such a setting. Simply importing youth choirs or children to help usher is little more than a token approach. Some retirement communities have selected mission projects involving children, such as tutoring at grade schools or assisting with scout troops. However, these activities cannot replace the values that may be present in intergenerational worship.

On the other hand, many retirement facilities develop a genuine sense of cohesiveness that is enhanced by corporate worship. If no chaplain resides in such settings, retired clergy may volunteer to develop opportunities for worship.

Nursing home residents in one study (Thibault et al., 1991, 38) were asked to respond to the question "What do you want the staff to know about your spiritual needs?" Their strongest reply was in wanting an opportunity for liturgical worship in their own denomination, especially on Sunday. This finding implies the importance of helping people worship in the language and setting most familiar to them.

Another setting for a very simplified form of worship can be at a patient's bedside in an acute care hospital. In times of serious illness, surgery, trauma, or impending death, clergy and their commissioned representatives can provide a hopeful presence. Prayers of the faith, administration of the sacraments, and words of reassurance can all contribute to the inner wholeness of the elder.

Additional Settings for Worship

Wherever older adults gather in the name of their faith there may be an opportunity to join in thanksgiving, to seek guidance, to acknowledge the presence of their divine Creator. Worshipers do not always need a lofty cathedral or an elaborate temple to be aware of the Holy in their lives. Creative worship can abound in camps, retreats, even trips planned by fellowship groups.

Advanced technology brings fresh possibilities within the worship arena. Some homebound older adults find substitute church communities through weekly programs beamed into homes via television or radio. Likewise, many congregations are making audiotape recordings of their services. Still others are able to video record weekly or special services. Such innovations must be taken seriously weighing both the advantages and disadvantages they offer.

WORSHIP THROUGH CELEBRATIONS AND CEREMONIES

Significance for Older Adults

As implied earlier, worship, whether corporate or private, can encompass a variety of moods and occasions. From penitence to jubilation, from confession to adoration, the many ways worshipers relate to God involve a kaleidoscope of emotions.

Religious festivals as well as historic events, such as family or institutional anniversaries, connect us with the past. According to Hulme (1986, 86), these times of remembrance reinforce our awareness of the eternal dimensions in our present moments so that our hope for the future is strengthened. Even the anticipation of events to be observed can, for older people, add meaning to the passing of what otherwise might be colorless days.

In addition to bringing a sense of expectation to calendars, celebrations can help reinforce family bonds and deepen religious traditions. Thus, events surrounding the sacred ceremony of a wedding often bring together family members who may have been separated for years. Grandparents, great-grandparents, and other older relatives find much mental and emotional stimulus even in the act of preparing for such events.

Categories of Celebrations and Ceremonies

In describing two important acts of domestic worship for Sabbath days and festival days, Millgram (1971, 297) first addresses the *Kiddush*. This is a ritual recited over a cup of wine immediately before the family Sabbath meal. The second is *Havdalah* which declares that God has made a distinction between the holy and the profane. This is pronounced at the end of the Sabbath or festival.

Persons of any religious persuasion may choose to celebrate God's presence at each meal by offering prayers of gratitude. Lifetime patterns of daily observances, such as reciting the rosary, should be respected by family members or professional caregivers. Continuing firmly established practices may bring a sense of stability and continuity to aging people.

Significant transitions in life take on heightened meaning when acknowledged in the context of worship. Some older couples choose a particular wedding anniversary, for instance, the fiftieth anniversary, as a time to renew marriage vows. Home dedications may be customary at the time a family first inhabits a house. A natural variation on that is to have a home benediction when the inhabitants are about to move out. This is especially impressive when the dwellers have lived in one location many years and may be moving to a retirement facility.

The fact of retirement itself can give rise to celebrations. Some congregations incorporate this into public worship. Simmons (1990, 163) urges religious communities to publicly ritualize retirement in ways that will emphasize what the retiring person has to offer society. There is need for ritualizing some of the unique experiences and moments of transition in the lives of older adults.

No doubt the ultimate life passage is death. Rites and rituals that assist and strengthen dying persons and their families should be introduced creatively and meaningfully. In some situations, the dying person may contribute ideas about what to include in his or her memorial service. In any case, the funeral service or other worship experience accompanying death offers a natural opportunity to proclaim dimensions of faith as well as to remember the life of the deceased.

In institutional settings, staff members often become deeply related to persons for whom they are caring. Thus, employees, such as those in nursing or food service departments, benefit from sharing in services of remembrance. Chaplains do well to devote special attention to spiritual needs of staff members.

Continuing to celebrate holy days, as mentioned earlier, contributes to a sense of continuity and rootedness. The Jewish calendar, complete with its own numbering of the years, offers adherents a faith-filled way to mark the change of seasons. As the blast of the shofar ushers in each new year in the fall, so other festivals mark historic events and the passing of the months (Knobel, 1983, 5). Similarly, the rhythm and cycle of the Christian calendar offers rich opportunities for creative and meaningful worship.

Role of the Arts

Throughout the ages, the arts in their many forms and expressions have been called upon "to serve the beauty of holiness." Music, sculpture, painting, and architecture have all contributed richly to the experience of worship. As Collins maintains: "Art is not some kind of decoration layered upon ritual action and ritual word. Art is the very core of the expressive forms that comprise liturgy" (1983, 13). Older persons may contribute of their talents, whether that be in the arena of music, visual art, dance, drama, or other artistic expressions that enhance worship.

ADAPTATIONS FOR OLDER WORSHIPERS

As men and women move into their later years, they may experience some physical changes that can affect their participation in worship. Changes involving diminishing eyesight, hearing, and ambulation can often be corrected by adequate lighting, large-print worship materials, adequate sound systems, signing, and removal of architectural barriers. Innovations in technology related to aging losses and disabilities often enable older adults to cope with and compensate for physical changes.

Older persons who are cognitively impaired bring with them special needs. Some with Alzheimer's disease can respond to faith symbols and rituals. In her book *Ritual and Pastoral Care,* Elaine Ramshaw suggests the impact of ritual sharing with the cognitively impaired:

> Ritual is a cognitive as well as an affective experience; it can involve both our thinking and our feeling on many levels. People who have not developed or have lost certain cognitive capacities, such as long-term memory or abstract conceptual thought, will apprehend ritual somewhat differently. Such cognitive impairment can come with many conditions: mental retardation, senility, brain disease or injury. Most people who are cognitively impaired can still participate in ritual and find it meaningful, and in fact many experience it more intensely through its

affective and concrete-symbolic dimensions than do most cognitively "normal" people. (1987, 77–78)

Persons who are markedly confused in the present may respond surprisingly well to familiar ritual, music, prayer, or lifelong patterned liturgical symbols (Richards, 1990, 63).

There is no single experience in worship that has the same meaning for all people. The importance of acknowledging individual differences certainly pertains to the choices people make as they participate in personal or corporate worship. A task for leaders in churches and synagogues is to keep persons of all ages vitally involved in worship that is grounded in the faith tradition and speaks to the whole person, thus fostering spiritual growth and meaning.

BIBLIOGRAPHY

Buxbaum, W. (1990) Jewish Spiritual Practices. Northvale, NJ: Aronson Press.

Carlsen, M. B. (1991) *A Meaning-Making Perspective.* New York: Norton.

Carlson, D., and S. Seicol (1990) "Adapting Worship to Changing Needs." *Generations* 14 (4):65–66.

Champlin, J. M. (1984) *An Important Office of Immense Love: A Handbook for Eucharistic Ministers.* New York: Paulist Press.

Clements, W. M., ed. (1981) *Ministry with the Aging.* San Francisco: Harper & Row.

Collins, P. W. (1983) *More Than Meets the Eye: Ritual and Parish Liturgy.* New York: Paulist Press.

Fischer, E. (1987) *Life in the Afternoon.* New York: Paulist Press.

Holmes, U. T. (1981) "Worship and Aging: Memory and Repentance." In Clements, 91–106.

Hulme, W. E. (1986) *Vintage Years: Growing Older with Meaning and Hope.* Philadelphia: Westminster.

Knobel, P. S., ed. (1983) *Gates of the Seasons: A Guide to the Jewish Year.* New York: Central Conference of American Rabbis.

Macquarrie, J. (1972) *Paths in Spirituality.* New York: Harper & Row.

McGee, J. (1967) *Religion and Modern Man: A Study of the Religious Meaning of Being Human.* San Francisco: Harper & Row.

Millgram, A. E. (1971) "Private and Home Worship." In *Jewish Worship,* 289–319. Philadelphia: The Jewish Publication Society.

Missinne, L. E. (1990) *Reflections on Aging: A Spiritual Guide.* Liguori, MO: Liguori.

Ramshaw, E. (1987) *Ritual and Pastoral Care.* Philadelphia: Fortress.

Richards, M. (1990) "Meeting the Spiritual Needs of the Cognitively Impaired." *Generations* 14 (4):63–64.

Simmons, H. C. (1990) "Countering Cultural Metaphors of Aging." *Journal of Religious Gerontology* 7 (1–2):153–65.

Thibault, J. M., Ellor, J. W., and Netting, F. E. (1991) "A Conceptual Framework for Assessing the Spiritual Functioning and Fulfillment of Older Adults in Long-term Care Settings." *Journal of Religious Gerontology* 7 (4):29–43.

White, J. F. (1980) *Introduction to Christian Worship*. Nashville: Abingdon.

Willimon, W. H. (1983) *The Service of God: How Worship and Ethics Are Related*. Nashville: Abingdon.

17 A Feminist Perspective on Aging

MARTHA KLEIN LARSEN

Religious communities need to address issues of aging that are relevant for older adult women, because women over fifty comprise the majority of their memberships. This chapter is intended to aid religious communities as they struggle with their ministries to older adult women; it therefore is oriented to an interfaith perspective. This "feminist theology" would need to include other issues if it were intended for a Christian audience only, and it would look different again if the paper were addressed to the author's own Lutheran community.

When one begins to struggle with what aging means for women, it becomes clear that aging and our social construction of images of beauty affect women at a very early age. To address the topic of aging, therefore, is to address an issue that is timely for virtually for all female members of our society. When women are central to one's critique of ageism, one begins to notice aspects of aging that have previously gone unnoticed.

AGEISM AND SEXUAL DUALISM: THE FEMINIST CHALLENGE

Getting older is less profoundly wounding for a man, for, in addition to the propaganda for youth that puts both men and women on the defensive as they age, there is a double standard about aging that denounces women with special severity. Society is much more permissive about aging in men, as it is more tolerant of the sexual infidelities of husbands. Men are "allowed" to age, without penalty, in several ways that women are not (Sontag, 146).

Ageism is at root more devastating for women than for men. The source of ageism lies in the sexual dualism of Western culture, which dates back to Plato's division of reality between mind and body. The body is the source of evil, subject to change and decay; physical sensations and emotions are to be mastered by the mind. The mind or consciousness is immortal, godlike, and alien to earth and body. This hierarchy of mind over body is duplicated in the hierarchy of male over female: the masculine is identified with mind and female is equated with body (Ruether, 1993, 24).

For Rosemary Radford Ruether, all dualisms find their source in this hierarchial sexual dualism (Ruether, 1975, 3). Hence, Western culture is characterized by racism (white persons over persons of color), militarism (strong over weak), an ecological crisis (humanity over creation), sexism (male over female), and ageism (young over old). In each dualism the more powerful element is identified with masculinity and maleness; the "less powerful" is identified with a feminine, passive, and weaker side. Older adult women are in a double bind in that they not only experience sexism but sexism in the context of ageism.

Sexual dualism has characterized much of Western history and is being challenged by the modern women's movement. Patriarchy is that system of power (primarily white and male in our Western culture) that perpetuates sexual dualism and other forms of oppression. Feminists vary in their definitions of patriarchy, but most essentially agree that it is a system beneficial to those in power to keep certain groups disadvantaged and subordinate: women, economically disadvantaged classes, and persons of color.

Feminist analysis seeks to understand the subtle and insidious ways in which women and other oppressed groups are kept subordinate. Ageism is one of those ways. Feminism attempts to provide a vision of a new humanity characterized by mutuality and nonhierarchial relationships, and it offers strategies for transforming society along these lines. Feminist theology focuses on an analysis of the ways in which religious belief systems have contributed to and legitimated patriarchal forms of power. Like secular feminists, feminist theologians critique male systems of power that keep women and other groups subjugated. Feminist theologians vary widely on their strategies for achieving a more just and egalitarian society. Some advocate revising and reforming religious institutions and "traditional" theology; some claim that leaving the church or synagogue (separatism) is the only viable alternative. Others have envisioned a combination of these two alternatives in ways that also invite dialogue with those whose voices have rarely been heard, for example, women of color, economically disadvantaged classes, and lesbians.

The challenge of patriarchy and a critique of it is central for all feminists. Rosemary Radford Ruether writes:

> We must do more than protest against the old. We must begin to live the new humanity now. We must begin to incarnate the community of faith in the liberation of humanity from patriarchy in words and deed, in new words, new prayers, new symbols, and new praises. This means that we need to form gathered communities to support us as we set out on our exodus from patriarchy. (Ruether, 1986, 5)

The question of ageism and its adverse affects upon women cannot be separated from a critique of patriarchy. As ageism has its roots in sexual dualism (whereby older adulthood is identified with a more feminine social construction characterized by weakness, dependency, passivity, and vulnerability), a theology that challenges commonly held notions of aging must address this issue of sexual dualism as well.

THE SOCIAL CONSTRUCTION OF AGING

In addition to recognizing its source in sexual dualism, a beginning step in addressing ageism is to expose its socially constructed nature. Any ideology tends to mystify us into thinking that it is "natural." Aging and interpretations of biological processes associated with it are now being challenged by some social scientists as socially constructed:

> Several biologists have argued that the human life span may soon be closer to 120 or 130 years than to the 90 to 110 years previously estimated. Such an increase in life span with, presumably, an equivalent increase in years of physical vigor makes an examination of age as a social construction both timely and important. (Turner, 16)

Feminist philosopher Alison M. Jaggar has cautioned against any form of biological determinism that can be used to attack or justify a particular form of social organization, to diagnose the causes of human discontent, or to set the limits of social change. Such theories tend to encourage fatalism and suggest to some that society must adapt to these unchangeable human propensities or resign itself to the inevitable existing one (Jaggar, 107). Many ideas about aging are based on biological determinism.

Views on aging are socially constructed. If these views work to the disadvantage of women, what reconstruction of aging is more life-enhancing? Feminist critique is not value neutral; no theory is. Feminist theory/theology is done on behalf of women. Yet totalizing, universal systems are exclusive and often deny the reality of other perspectives. Can we come up with a reconstruction that is not class-oriented or racially biased and that takes into account the diversity of women's experience? The following theological reflections attempt to make a beginning in this direction. It is a beginning that recognizes the author's context as a white, middle-class woman approaching forty and that her knowledge of aging and other racial and class realities is limited. Nevertheless, some of what follows may be applicable to most women, because to some degree they share a struggle to overcome the sexism inherent in the dominant class-treatment of women. As Ruether observes:

> We must say that there is no final and definitive feminist theology, no final synthesis that encompasses all human experience, criticizes what is sexist, and appropriates what is usable in all historical traditions. This book, therefore, represents not *the* feminist theology but *a* feminist theology. (Ruether, 1983, 20)

Hence a beginning is made toward *a* feminist theology for aging.

Religious communities need to participate aggressively in the social construction of aging in a way that advocates for the full humanity of women. If communities are to be a life-giving resource for women of all ages who struggle with growing older, this task is essential. Religious communities must be involved with the construction of aging in a way that has implications for what it means to be physically attractive in our society. Susan Sontag observes that

> the reason that women experience aging with more pain than men is not simply that they care more than men about how they look. Men also care about their looks and want to be attractive, but since the business of men is mainly about being and doing, rather than appearing, the standards for what is attractive in men are permissive; they conform to what is possible or "natural" to most men throughout most of their lives. The standards for women's appearance go against nature, and to come anywhere near approximating them takes considerable time and effort. Women must try to be beautiful. At the least, they are under heavy social pressure not to be ugly. . . . Good looks in a man is a bonus, not a psychological necessity for maintaining self esteem. (Sontag, 1979, 472–73)

In order to reconstruct notions of aging, ideas about beauty and physical appearance must be reconstructed. This goal will contribute to the full humanity of all women, from the older adult woman who has been through face lifts and a tummy tuck to the very youngest child who puts on her mother's spiked heels and wants to look like her Barbie doll.

Is this goal an appropriate one for religious communities? Congregations have many women who suffer from negative body images that result from comparison to socially constructed images of the ideal woman. Some of these issues may not be as oppressively poignant for economically disadvantaged women. As Sontag points out, one needs to have a certain amount of leisure time and money to "fight the cosmetic battle," long and tenaciously (Sontag, 1979, 466). Nevertheless, these are oppressive forces indeed at work in our society; many women feel in bondage to their weight problems and to a certain ideal of what a woman should look like. As women age the oppression of these forces does not seem to diminish. Society negatively stereotypes older adult women as characterized by grey hair, sagging breasts, double chin, wrinkles, and "crow's feet."

Bondage is a good word to describe the degree to which women have internalized the mind/body dualism, a dualism integrally connected to negative body images and, hence, to aging. Susan Bordo makes a comparison between anorexia and the internalized metaphysics of the body/mind dualism. The body becomes a separate entity from the self: alien, a prison, the enemy that must be controlled by the mind. Anorexics speak of the body as something one learns to master and over which one achieves intellectual independence from its lure and distractions. The ultimate goal of an anoretic is to cease to experience hungers and desires (Bordo, 1993, 145–46). It is as if two selves are at war with one another: the male side—with its associated values of greater spirituality, higher intellectuality, and strength of will—with the female side—characterized by uncontrollable appetites, impurities, taints, and voracious hunger (Bordo, 1993, 155). Bordo believes that the psychopathology of anorexia nervosa is far from an anomaly or an aberration and is a characteristic expression of our culture, one that crystallizes much of what is wrong with it. Indeed, some feminists hold that "anorexia represents one extreme on a continuum on which all women today find themselves, insofar as they are vulnerable, to one degree or another, to the requirements of the cultural construction of femininity" (Bordo, 1993, 47). As women age, the struggle to transcend society's dualistic notions of ugly/beautiful, young/old, and vital/frail over-weight/slim remains difficult and usually becomes exacerbated as one advances in years. This results from internalizing a notion of the body as separate from one's essential self. Just as the anorexic experiences bodily betrayal and an on-going battle with the body's hungers and desires, aging women may feel as if they are at war with their bodies and its inevitable aging process. It is a "race against time," a time for strategically planning a method of attack designed to forestall the body's natural movement toward older adulthood.

If women internalize cultural notions of beauty and, therefore, aging, and if they participate in the cultural construction of femininity in a way that conforms to a male-defined identity, how can women in conjunction with their religious communities begin the process of allowing women to view themselves as created in the image of God/ess?[1] Depending on the context of a particular religious community, the focus of what this means will vary. The needs of lower-class working women who are struggling with economic survival are not the same as those of a more affluent white widow. Because they both experience the sexism of the dominant ideology, however, perhaps one place to begin is for women to affirm that side of their humanity which has been historically consigned to (white) men: autonomy, self-control, independence, exercise, and the development of the physical body. This task may be easier for women of color or working-class women, as their circumstances have necessitated fortitude and self-reliance in order to survive emotionally and economically. These women have often had to exhibit characteristics often considered "unfeminine" (that is, male) by the dominant class if they and their families were to continue.

Some feminists question the possibility of being completely divorced from the context that has so essentially created identity. Bordo views women's bodies as a site of struggle "where we must *work* to keep our daily practices in the

[1]I use Rosemary Radford Ruether's term *God/ess* to indicate that the taking of one human image literally, for example, God as male, is idolatrous. Male language for the divine must lose its privileged place. She writes, "Images of God/ess must include female roles and experience . . . [and] cannot validate the roles of men or women in stereotipic ways that justify male dominance and female subordination." See *Sexism and God-Talk,* p. 69.

service of resistance to gender domination, not in the service of docility and gender normalization" (Bordo, 1993, 184). For Ruether such a task cannot be completed until a nonsexist society comes into being:

> What women might be like, how we would symbolize the polarities of self and other, thinking and feeling, activity and receptivity outside these traditions of male domination is something that we cannot know until a nonsexist society is created where women are recognized as full human persons, with a right to develop their potency not only for others, but for their own self fulfillment. (Ruether, 1975, 159)

The affirmation of these human characteristics, heretofore discouraged by the dominant class as being unfeminine, will aid in transforming society's ageism. Women will begin to challenge their participation in a system which dictates that they remain "girlishly" incompetent, helpless, passive and noncompetitive. Women will affirm their humanity and, as Sontag points out, become adults:

> They [women] can aspire to be wise, not merely nice; to be competent, not merely helpful; to be strong, not merely graceful; do be ambitious for themselves, not merely for themselves in relation to men and children. They can let themselves age naturally and without embarrassment, actively protesting and disobeying the conventions that stem from this society's double standard about aging. . . . Women should allow their faces to show the lives they have lived. Women should tell the truth. (Sontag, 1979, 478)

Some gerontologists who have studied gender in later life have noted a reversal of roles in older adulthood. Women seem to become more autonomous, less submissive toward and dependent on their husbands and begin to exhibit a more dominant role in the marital relationship. Women become caretakers of the frail male. We need to question, however, whether such studies have adequately taken into account racial/ethnic differences among aging couples. For example, how does one account for the African American families who have long histories of being headed by single, strong, autonomous women? Where is a role reversal evident in these families? And in a two-parent black family, are female dependency and submission to a male member similar to what one might find in a white, middle-class, nuclear family? Or are these power relations and male/female relationships characterized by a dynamic other than submissive female/dominant male?

In addition to racial and ethnic differences among aging couples, we need to analyze whether in fact a substantial role reversal is taking place or we are observing a continuation and disproportionate assumption of caretaking and nurturing tasks by the dutiful wife. Is there a substantial increase in the woman's real power in the home and in society? Does her status in relation to her husband qualitatively change? Is a man's position in the social hierarchy suddenly changed? Sandra Bartky asked these questions with regard to women and their emotional nurture of men in general (Bartky, 1990). In regard to older adulthood one might apply a similar analysis: Is a man's superordinate position abandoned and his male privilege relinquished in older adulthood? Vulnerability and frailty are not necessarily a prelude to a loss in male privilege or to an elevation in the status of women. These factors need to be considered when studying whether role reversals in older adulthood are actually an intergender process or a continuation of gendered expectations.

THE EXODUS AND RELIGIOUS COMMUNITIES

The costs for women who begin the task of affirming their full humanity (and for the men who support them) can be very great. On one's exodus from patriarchy a woman at any age may be placing herself at great risk within her family system and in regard to other social and work relationships. The material losses and emotional conflict are very real. Women need attentive support as they individually work out the ramifications of this journey and the rate at which they will embark upon it.

A beginning needs to be made in challenging patriarchal notions of beauty and aging, power relations in older adulthood, and oppressive influences that prevent women from becoming fully human. In order to begin the corresponding process of reconstruction, religious communities in conjunction with women can determine forms and structures to accomplish this end. Some of these structures may need to exclude male participation at some point(s) in their formation in order to allow women the necessary space and freedom to explore issues in safety and without inhibition. Women's auxiliaries and other such groups may give women the opportunity to explore and redefine feelings in a context in which they do not perceive themselves as crazy, maladjusted, hormonally imbalanced, bitchy, or ungrateful (MacKinnon, 1989, 100). Women's groups intentionally designed to promote such exploration might show women their situation in a way that affirms that they can act to change it (MacKinnon, 1989, 101).

Empowering women in context of such groups is an essential step in the exodus out of patriarchy. Such empowerment is the work of the divine. Rita Nakashima Brock speaks about the presence of Christ in a community that is the "whole-making, healing center of Christianity" (Brock, 1988, 52). In the context of such a community individuals share their pain and woundedness in a safe context of mutual vulnerability. The heart's search for healing from suffering and brokenness in the midst of this sharing happens "heart to heart" through intimate connections with others. Brock calls this healing the presence and revelation of erotic power, the divine dimension of human existence (Brock, 1988, 45–52). Women's groups in the context of religious communities can be a source of empowerment and healing that embody and manifest the presence of

God/ess. They can be a source not only of empowerment but of the beginning of a new vision for humanity—a vision in which women are fully human and in which they can begin to imagine new identities and self-definitions. The role of men in this process will need to be worked out in individual communities. Informal sharing opportunities in the context of shared meals, adult forums, or the formation of a committee on gender and aging are some possibilities.

Integral to the above process is a multi-racial, multi-class identity. This is a more difficult task for many of our religious communities. A multi-racial and multi-class dialogue is essential within the context of the religious community if women are to struggle successfully with a reconceptualization of reality in a way that overcomes "the typically feminine set of attitudes and modes of perception that have been imposed on women in a male dominated world" (Jaggar, 1988, 383). Power relations need to be transformed across age, class, gender, and racial lines.

Women's perceptions of reality are distorted both by male dominant ideology and by the male-dominated structure of everyday life (Jaggar, 1988; Bartky, 1990). One way to struggle effectively with this dilemma is through mutual dialogue. Not all women are involved in an exodus from patriarchy. Women's perceptions of reality can be distorted by male-dominant ideology and by the male-dominated structure of everyday life (Jaggar, 1988, 371). Religious communities can prophetically call women away from patriarchy in order that they might realize their full humanity and work to revolutionize those systems of power that, contrary to the will of God/ess, oppress women and others. Religious communities can be a resource for all women and men who age.

The above process must not only include women of different races and class backgrounds; it is imperative also that the complexion of such a group be intentionally intergenerational. The decade of the eighties saw a rapid growth of interest in the impact of ethnicity on the process of social aging; yet this field needs additional research on the ways in which gender impacts upon aging in different ethnic contexts (Barresi, 1990, 247). It is therefore, imperative that all women be included in the task of reconstructing what the full humanity of women might envision.

Alison Jaggar points out that men and women will need to learn each other's "texts": men need to learn women's and white/Anglo women need to learn to understand the experience of women of color. Everyone also needs to learn the text of older adulthood. Such a prerequisite to collective dialogue involves commitment, humility, and willingness to understand and become familiar with an alternative way of viewing the world (Jaggar, 1988, 386–87). Leaders of religious communities need to become passionate listeners and examples for the congregation by taking seriously experiences they do not necessarily share.

How can religious communities be of assistance to women as they age? Can these communities be a source of encouragement in the process outlined above? For communities that do not allow women in leadership positions the possibility of affirming women as competent, wise, and strong is jeopardized. A religious community in its exodus from patriarchy must affirm women in leadership positions (and this does not mean tokenism) and must reform its doctrine of God to include all of human experience, one that is not just a reflection of an all-powerful, controlling, male figure. This latter construction has historically defined what it means to be human and has legitimated male power.

Likewise, a religious community that gathers for worship and uses liturgies that reflect only a "male" theology of God as a patriarchal figure are not affirming for women who need to identify with feminine imaging of the divine in a way that does not devalue femaleness. The Jewish and Christian Scriptures contain images of God as a woman in the throes of childbirth (Isaiah 42:14), as the all-encompassing womb who births creation (Job 38:8, 29), and as a nursing mother (Numbers 11:12-13). Moreover, in I Peter 2:2-3 we find an image of Christ suckling newborn Christians:

> Like newborn infants, long for the pure, spiritual milk, so that by it you may grow unto salvation—if indeed you have tasted that the Lord is good. (NRSV)

Theologians like Virginia Ramey Mollenkott (1990), Phyllis Trible (1978), and Brian Wren (1989) have explored the many biblical images of God depicted in feminine terms. Such imaging of God in a liturgical context can be life-giving for women whose roles and life experiences have been ignored or devalued. In addition the Jewish and Christian Scriptures contain examples of strong women who remained childless, such as the widow and prophetess Anna, who became a model for the first community of disciples (Thurston, 1989), and other significant leaders such as Miriam, Deborah, and Huldah. The biblical account of Ruth and her mother-in-law Naomi and their loyalty and love is an empowering example for women facing widowhood or who have chosen to remain unmarried. These scriptural resources can be an important influence as woman age in the context of their religious communities.

As with any liturgical change like the feminine imaging of God, sensitivity to one's tradition, the history of a particular congregation, and knowledge of the particular women involved determines how one proceeds pastorally in this regard. Change can be liberating for some members and absolutely appalling to others. Meeting the needs of all women and men and their corresponding intergenerational concerns must be prayerfully kept in life-giving and mutually challenging tension.

Religious communities in their exodus from patriarchy will need new rituals to strengthen, nurture, and empower the men and women on this journey. These rituals need to incorporate life-cycle events such as the ones included by Ruether in *Women-Church:* a puberty rite for young women, a birthing preparation liturgy, lesbian and heterosexual covenant celebrations, and menopause and croning liturgies (Ruether, 1986). These liturgies are ritual events during which religious communities experience the transforming presence of the divine in the context of intimate togetherness. They can be powerful vehicles of consciousness-raising and consciousness-changing—essential moments and movements in which a shared vision of a full humanity for men and women begins to break through to historical reality. Women of all ages struggle with aging. "Nothing more clearly demonstrates the vulnerability of women than the special pain, confusion, and bad faith with which they experience getting older" (Sontag, 1979, 477). Older adult women need a context in which notions of beauty include gray hair, changes in mobility and energy level, facial lines of aging, and weight gain or weight loss. Women of all ages need religious communities that embody the unconditional grace of God/ess for them. Women need to hear that they are loved, accepted, cherished, and beautiful in a way that is communicated to and affirming of *all* (girls and) women. Perhaps then they can start believing that as they age they are truly valued—an indication that the exodus is nearing its completion.

BIBLIOGRAPHY

Barresi, C. M. (1990) "Ethnogerontology: Social Aging in National, Racial, and Cultural Groups." In K. F. Ferraro, (ed.) *Gerontology: Perspectives and Issues.* New York: Springer.

Bartky, S. L. (1990) *Femininity and Domination: Studies in the Phenomenology of Oppression.* New York: Routledge.

Bordo, S. (1993) *Unbearable Weights: Feminism, Western Culture and the Body.* Los Angeles: University of California.

Brock, R. N. (1988) *Journeys by Heart: A Christology of Erotic Power.* New York: Crossroad.

Jaggar, A. M. (1988) *Feminist Politics and Human Nature.* Totowa, N.J.: Lowman & Littlefield.

MacKinnon, C. A. (1989) *Toward a Feminist Theory of the State.* Cambridge, Mass.: Harvard.

Mollenkott, V. R. (1990) *The Divine Feminine: The Biblical Imagery of God as Female.* New York: Crossroad.

Ruether, R. R. (1975) *New Woman/New Earth: Sexist Ideologies and Human Liberation.* San Francisco: Harper & Row.

______ (1983) *Sexism and God-talk: Toward a Feminist Theology.* Boston: Beacon.

______ (1986) *Women-Church: Theology and Practice.* San Francisco: Harper & Row.

______ (1993) *God & Gaia: An Ecofeminist Theology of Earth Healing.* San Francisco: Harper.

Sontag, S. (1979) "The Double Standard of Aging." In J. S. Williams ed., *Psychology of Women: Selected readings.* New York: W. W. Norton.

Thurston, B. B. (1989) *The Widows: A Women's Ministry in the Early Church*. Philadelphia: Fortress Press.

Trible, P. (1978) *God and the Rhetoric of Sexuality*. Philadelphia: Fortress Press.

Turner, B. F. (1994) "Introduction." In B. S. Turner and L. E. Troll eds., *Women Growing Older: Psychological Perspectives*. Thousand Oaks, Calif.: Sage.

Wren, B. (1989) *What Language Shall I Borrow?: God-Talk in Worship: A Male Response to Feminist Theology*. New York: Crossroad.

18 Congregational Models

JAMES J. SEEBER

INTRODUCTION

What are congregations typically doing to meet the specific needs of older members? This chapter describes a wide range of senior ministries developed in congregations across the nation. A survey done through the Forum on Religion, Spirituality and Aging of the American Society on Aging and the National Interfaith Coalition on Aging, identified more than sixty congregations that have outstanding senior ministries. Additional information about several congregations in the southeast drawn from a study by Dr. Al Dimmock, formerly professor at the School of Christian Education, Union Seminary, Richmond, Virginia, is included, as well as descriptions of congregations studied by the author in California during Religion and Aging Seminars taught at California Baptist College.

The Context

It is important to think of congregational programs for older people within the larger context of American religious life. Congregations always operate in two environments—the external and the internal. The external environment includes the immediate social and physical community where the church or synagogue is located. It also includes the larger denominational and interdenominational communities with which a religious group is identified. The internal environment includes the self-image and customs of the local congregation. All of these influence what types of ministry congregations choose to emphasize. Key internal and external environmental factors are shown in Figure 18.1 (adapted from Tobin et al., 1986). The outer circle shows specific external factors affecting the development of congregational programs. The inner box notes internal factors that shape a congregation. Probably the most influential external factors are recognition of a need and the awareness of a model, whereas the crucial internal factors appear to be interest by clergy and a felt need within the congregation.

The recognition of a need for senior ministries in many congregations began in the 1970s. This followed ten years of public aging programs developed through the Older Americans Act passed in 1965. Prior to that time, older persons unable to care for themselves were either cared for by their families or

FIGURE 18.1
The Environment of Congregations

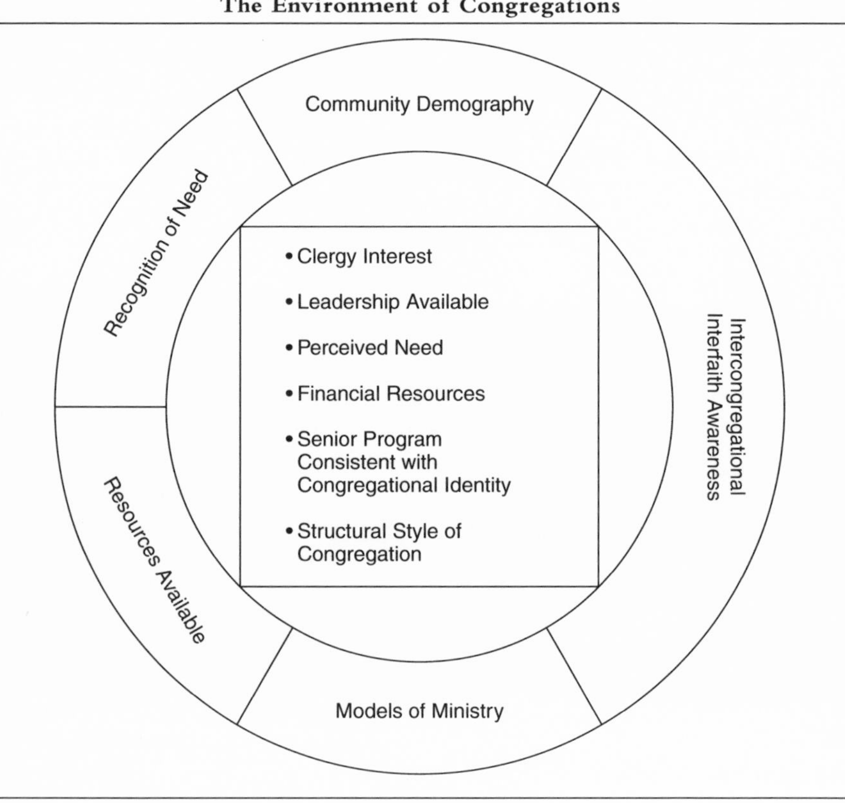

placed in nursing homes. From the mid-1970s forward, there has been a growing interest in how congregations can effectively minister to older people has developed. Persons over sixty-five do, after all, constitute from 15 to 50 percent (or more) of most congregations' members.

Diversity

Gerontologists frequently comment on the diversity of life found among America's elderly today. Wide variation exists in education, income, health, interests, abilities, and attitudes. There has never been a senior population so varied. In fact, numerous scholars have introduced several subsets of the older population to help make general statements more accurate. Neugarten speaks of the young-old and the old-old. A functional way to group persons together for discussion purposes is that of the active-elderly, transition-elderly, and frail-elderly.

Clements (1992) recently suggested that we refine our subsets into the young-old (60–75), the old (75–99), and the very old (100+) about whom our knowledge is extremely sketchy. While chronological age may not be the best basis for classification, Clements's series recognizes the phenomenal increase in the number of centenarians in American society. Increasing from 12,000 in 1980 to over 24,000 in 1990, they will swell to 108,000 at the turn of the century and will expand to approximately 1,000,000 by the year 2055 when baby boomers hit the century mark. While the continued contribution to society by these long-living seniors will be remarkable, so will the possible need for support services.

Elements in Successful Programming

In analyzing data from over nine hundred parishes with active senior ministries drawn from some thirteen Roman Catholic dioceses nationwide, Fahey and Lewis (Lewis, 1989, 29–31) concluded that a cluster of organizational and attitudinal factors were the keys to successful congregational programs. These were as follows:

a. *Intentionality.* Wherever comprehensive program planning and development was followed, special services for the frail elderly were included. Conscious planning may be helpful to move a congregation into new program areas on a continuing basis.

b. *Rootedness.* Initial interest was most often followed by clearly tying the program into some ongoing program or regular committee, council, or board within the congregation. This would link the senior ministry to some group in the parish and would place it in a position to receive both leadership and funding.

c. *Need assessment.* Knowledge of the type and extent of need in the congregation and in the neighborhood helps to justify and direct the program to be developed.

d. *Records.* Information to justify and support the program is always valuable.

e. *Identifiable leadership.* Volunteer versus staff leadership is not as important as having a clear person or, better yet, group of persons who oversee and keep the program moving.

f. *Training in gerontology.* Better quality sustained leadership develops with good training in and knowledge of gerontology.

g. *Financial and volunteer support.* The strength of a program is carried by adequate manpower and funding, both of which trace back to a congregation's support for a program.

h. *Community service ties.* While very few parishes had links with the social service network, programs were benefitted for those who did. Huber (chap. 19) likewise found an amazing lack of linkage to service agencies among congregations of various denominations.

i. *Neighborhoodness/interreligiousness.* The geographic ties to an area (parish concept) contributed to a number of local area cooperative programs. Both ecumenical (with other Catholic parishes) and interreligious programs were common, suggesting a readiness to work together when a need is recognized.

Lewis (1989) found in studying Catholic parishes that most congregations carry on multiple senior ministries (average three), not just one. In examining the current survey of congregations identified as outstanding, the program types were also varied and can be grouped into three general categories, namely, religious, fellowship/educational, and social service ministries.

RELIGIOUS MINISTRIES

Spiritual Nurture via Regular Worship and Outreach

Do congregations meet the spiritual needs of their older members in the course of regular ministries such as particular worship and related activities? David Oliver has suggested that congregations should not overlook or denigrate what they may already be doing in serving older members (Oliver, 1986, 2). Primary participation as well as major leadership at every level is common among retired persons in many congregations. When persons retire from external careers, they are actively sought out to accept voluntary roles in the congregation. Seniors serve as trustees, choir members, ushers, group officers, teachers in educational programs, and as clergy in many cases. As the proportion of working women continues to increase in the 1990s, congregations will welcome active seniors into leadership roles. Gray and Moberg (1977) and others have long taken note of ministries *by and with* older persons as an important part of ministry *to* older persons.

Some congregations in high older-age density communities have mostly older membership. When seen as opportunities for significant ministry, such congregations often thrive; when viewed as a reason for alarm because "the church is dying," congregational life usually suffers (cf. chap. 18). Legitimate "neighborhood ministries" will serve mostly older people in areas adjacent to retirement homes and retirement communities, in certain central city districts and in many rural areas of the upper midwest. In these settings, to cater to and to serve a predominantly younger population is "not normal" and should cause some questioning as to the goals of the congregation.

An older Baptist congregation in Long Beach, California faced a struggle after an unpleasant division within the congregation in which several younger families withdrew upon the resignation of a pastor. The congregation called a pastor who saw the strength of the elderly core in the congregation and built the church around an intergenerational appeal in which senior ministries was a major goal. A new bussing ministry was instigated primarily for seniors, and a new church bus was purchased and dedicated using memorial funds. Participation reportedly rose steadily.

Many congregations, including the Baptist church noted above, recognize senior members for their important contributions in worship services from time to time. Such lifting up of valued service is an important antidote to the ageism discussed earlier and models positive spiritual maturity as a role for seniors. *Senior* adult educational groups, *senior* adult choirs, and *senior* Bible studies are common in many places. One Baptist church in Atlanta includes a special quarterly altar call for seniors to renew their dedication to serve God in the later years.

A range of architectural and technological aids can make such participation by older people far more valid. Congregations can model for the larger society access by the handicapped through ramps instead of steps, wide doorways, and equally wide entrances to rest rooms, classrooms, etc. Quality sound equipment and hearing aids, large-print materials, and good lighting in all areas are now commonplace knowledge. Some denominations, including United Methodists, offer incentive "access" grants to congregations who remodel to accommodate the elderly and handicapped.

A major area of potential senior ministry for congregations in the United States is that of outreach to the religiously unattached, what is commonly called evangelism. Older people pose an important challenge for outreach because they often are experiencing major changes in a short time and thus are in need of spiritual resources that can help them to find meaning in these changes. Social science has shown that religion traditionally provides a sense of identity and meaning in the face of life's many changes and comfort or solace in the face of life's uncertainty and/or losses. Many older people living in mobile home parks, publicly subsidized housing for the elderly, single-room occupancies, board and care homes, and retirement homes are functionally alienated from congregations. Due to relocation into a strange community, change in economic situation, limiting health condition, or other problems, these persons are not served by religious groups. However, they are people with needs whom caring communities can serve (cf. Ellor, chap. 19).

Some religious groups have reached out to these unique populations. In Rialto, California, a Baptist church has begun a home Bible study for persons in a publicly owned mobile home park who are interested in learning and sharing the Christian message. The group was begun with the agreement that it *not* include door-to-door visitation and that it not be for recruiting persons to any congregation. The group has supported older persons through the illness and death of their spouses, has helped acquaint new residents with one another, and has brought love and meaning into the homes of many. As in many actions by religious groups, it not so much *what is done* as *how it is done*. Spiritual resources are needed by all, especially in later life. A nun in Fond Du Lac, Wisconsin leads a Bible study group in a senior housing project in her city. The class is part of a Spiritual Aging program in her parish.

Visitation to Hospitalized and Homebound Seniors

Probably the most active senior ministry by congregations large or small of all denominations is visitation of nonactive elderly. Hospital visits by both clergy and lay visitors are appreciated by all ages of patients and especially by older patients. Older persons may be fearful that the new health problem encountered may be one that will seriously limit their lives. Amid such anxious concerns, a friendly familiar face is often welcome medicine!

In some rural settings where distances for visitation are significant, cooperative ecumenical hospital visits are done. In rural southwest Iowa, Catholic and Protestant clergy from thirteen churches shared in hospital visitation on a weekly schedule with different clergy making the trip to the county seat hospital on different days. Numerous hospitalized persons reported receiving a visit by one of the local clergy each day that they were in the hospital!

Home visits are also important. A Chicago study that included ministry to the homebound found that a considerable number of older people, particularly in colder weather climates, while not bedfast, are certainly limited to their own homes and functionally shut in for much of the year. In good weather, occasionally such persons might attend church or a favorite social club, but only under ideal conditions. Such housebound persons, estimated at 8 percent of all elderly in the Chicago study, make up four distinct groups—the temporarily homebound due to illness, a fall, etc.; the service shut-ins who lack access to, funds for, or, perhaps, familiarity with social support services that would enable them to remain somewhat active outside the home; the chronically sick and bedfast; and the caretakers of the elderly isolated by their role as caretaker of a shut-in person (Tobin, Ellor, and Anderson-Ray, 1986, 76–78). This 8-percent homebound, combined with the 4 to 5 percent of older people in nursing homes, account for about 3.6 million or 12 percent of all older Americans.

Such programs can be led by part-time Ministers of Visitation, often older retired clergy or trained lay persons. One visitation program that reaches out to parishioners, whether young or old, in many denominations is that of the Stephen Ministry, in which lay visitors are trained to provide comfort and care. Under regular supervision, Stephen ministers provide a variety of spiritual and social services.

Various technological supports are utilized as well. Some congregations broadcast their services over local cable TV or local radio stations in order to reach the homebound and others. Some congregations audio- or even videotape the main Sabbath worship service and carry the tapes to those shut-ins who want to receive them. A retired school principal in a small Kansas county seat distributed the audio tape, a Sunday bulletin, and a hymn book to shut-ins over a four- or five-day schedule each week for his church. Thus a weekly visit *and* a worship service was shared with each person. Even a "Traveling Bible Study" is carried to homebound persons through one type of senior ministry carried out by the Senior Friends. A core group of persons moves from one shut-in household to another with each meeting (Ellor, 1990, 108–9). This allows visitation, spiritual care, and fellowship all to be extended to the older homebound person.

In all of these settings, regular visits and the sacramental/symbolic bond of communion would also seem to have appreciable value. A five-year shut-in from a small Kansas town was rather proud that throughout her long illness, the elders in her Presbyterian church had brought communion to her home each quarter when communion was served at church. In many nursing home ministries, communion services are gladly received by all, and persons writing about worship with dementia-afflicted older persons have observed that such persons often respond appropriately and actively to such liturgical acts as communion. This suggests the lasting value of religious symbolism in worship with older people (discussion of worship and aging: Achenbaum, chap. 14; Carlson, chap. 16; and Friedman, chap. 24).

Nursing Home Ministries

One widespread program of congregations is that of some type of ministry to nursing home residents. Though typical, such programs are often undertaken with minimal enthusiasm and an equal level of training. However, these experiences *can* become an enriching part of the pastoral care and even of the social ministries of a congregation.

Typical of nursing home ministries are occasional visits and leading of worship services; providing "care" boxes and reading material for members in homes; helping to lead Bible study classes or other sharing groups; and carrying communion to members in nursing homes. A practical guide for effective nursing home visitation is *Healing with Time and Love* by Sister Patricia Murphy (1979).

In some cases, professional chaplains serve several homes on a full-time basis, providing a continuity much needed for beneficial ministry. One such program serves residents in thirty convalescent hospitals in San Mateo County, California (unpublished brochure). It is supported by the Presbyterian churches of the county and provides for a variety of clergy- and laity-led spiritual care, education, and fellowship programs. Another interdenominational ministry has been led by a Protestant chaplain in the Los Angeles area. Over a period of twenty-five years, Rev. Edward Schulz has provided weekly religious services and spiritual care in about twenty non-church-related nursing homes, employing professional helpers and filling a critical need for thousands of older people. Dr. Schulz has developed a portable altar/sound system that can be rolled into almost any physical setting for worship. His broadly ecumenical ministry includes Catholic and Protestant leaders (from personal conversation). In Wausau, Wisconsin, twelve Lutheran congregations cooperated to provide spiritual care to nearly seven hundred older people in six nursing homes. The program is guided by a full-time chaplain and augmented by an active Stephen Ministry of volunteer visitors (Schwanke, 1986, 57–64). In Tucson, religious services and spiritual care are provided regularly in seventeen nondenominational nursing homes by a nun through Catholic Community Services. In Belleville, Illinois, two priests under the sponsorship of the Catholic Diocese of Belleville and more than seventy volunteers provide religious services and a variety of spiritual and personal care to residents in thirteen nursing homes. One Catholic parish in Chicago offers twice-yearly anointing services for nursing home residents as well (Retirement Research Foundation, 1989, 6).

In many communities across America, neighborhood churches have essentially "adopted" a nursing home in the area and provide some degree of spiritual care on an ongoing basis. Such ministries are vital to the elderly served but should be carefully related to the life and mission of the congregation to ensure continuation should current leaders move on. They also suffer from a lack of trained leadership to provide spiritual care to the elderly.

The general approach to spiritual care in the nursing home should be sensitive to the life-situation and religio-cultural backgrounds of the participants. Some variety in worship styles is appropriate; However, endless variety satisfies no one. In many places, "ecumenical" worship includes Protestant-Catholic-Jewish participants. It has the advantage of a broad range of religious resources but carries the responsibility to avoid sectarian messages. The more frequently worship or other forms of spiritual care can be related to the religious background and interests of worshipers, the more valued it will be by all. Liturgy means "work of the people," and even in the nursing home, individuals have something to contribute to the worship experience, from passing out songbooks to sharing a story to leading in singing familiar old hymns. Developing religious rituals specific to the settings and to the persons can be a valued part of spiritual care (cf. Friedman, chap. 24).

Memorial services are often poorly handled or ignored in nursing homes. Some homes do not allow them on the grounds that a morbid atmosphere would be the result. Residents are usually aware of the death of other residents and staff clearly are aware. A spiritually uplifting memorial service allows persons to express the loss and to let go of the grief. Morbid atmospheres are the result of denial, not of positive spiritual care. A Jewish nursing home in Phoenix observes a memorial service once each week and will remember all who have died in that week, be it one or several.

Funeral or Memorial Services in the Congregation

An area in which clergy are thought to be skilled is that of grief support and comfort at the time of death. With rare exception, clergy are the ones called upon in our society to conduct funeral or memorial services—even for persons they never knew or families who have no known tie with their congregations. Unfortunately, only a small percentage of clergy have ever had any training in pastoral care with the bereaved and only a fraction of those received specific skill training in grief counseling. This is somewhat comparable to hiring a chef for a restaurant who doesn't know how to cook.

Every congregation is going to have numerous cases of grief work to attend to, whether due to death or other major losses such as job loss, marital breakups, or chronic physical disabilities. Howard Clinebell, internationally known professor of pastoral care and counseling, has said repeatedly, "We are experiencing an epidemic of grief in our society and don't know it" (unpublished speech), nor, one might add, do we know what to do about it!

Virtually all congregations are called upon to respond in times of loss or of death. Many congregations have committees that will help to provide funeral or memorial service assistance, including serving meals or refreshments to those attending the service, distributing or disposing of flowers afterward, or simply sending a note on behalf of the congregation recognizing the loss and offering written comfort. Funeral or memorial services are, in fact, senior ministries today, because 75 percent of those who die are sixty-five or older. For older persons in their eighties or nineties, the children as well as any remaining siblings and friends are older adults.

Hospice: A New Direction

A new program that is helping individuals and their families to cope with the dying process in a more humane and personal way is that of Hospice. These programs, either residential or carried out in the home, are an alternative to dying in the hospital. Hospice programs are exploding in number across America—there are over one thousand such programs, and hospice did not begin in the U.S. until 1974. With a few exceptions, hospice has developed with little or no leadership from parish clergy or congregations, but instead has come mostly from within the medical community. This trend would suggest that there is a widespread need, apparently crossing all denominations, for much better education for pastoral care of the dying and bereaved.

FELLOWSHIP/EDUCATIONAL MINISTRIES

Many congregations studied listed major senior activities that can perhaps best be described as educational fellowship-building programs. Whether the topical focus of the groups is religion, as in many Sunday School classes, or other topics, as with special senior groups in the congregation, or Shepherd Center models in which both education and a variety of social services are also undertaken, the common ingredient that was described over and over was fellowship-building among older people. Ongoing educational groups are second only to attendance at principal worship events of congregations with regard to the involvement of older people. Such groups include "Religious School," women's or men's groups, Bible study, or similar groups. In many congregations, such settings are where the closest fellowship among members is experienced. Many groups within congregations have experienced "aging in place" (cf. Ellor, chap. 19). Typical of this trend is an active senior adult class called the Twigbenders in one California United Methodist church. It was formed in 1949, when a requisite to join the class was to have *pre-school* children in the home. The class has been a key leadership group in the large congregation over the years and continues to be so but now comprises mostly retired grandparents. Many class members know one another as "extended family" and have shared spiritual care through the class and its activities.

The demographics of aging suggest why these groups are important. After retirement, the work associations of many people are effectively cut off and community status may change as well. In addition, many persons, especially women, experience the loneliness of becoming widowed. Congregations provide a first-line chance to maintain meaningful ties with persons who are often long-term acquaintances. It isn't strange, then, that well over half of the congregations studied had programs in which friendships and fellowship were a primary part of the experience and were a major purpose for gathering in the first place. A number of scholars have identified religion and religious ties as common to the existence of social support relationships in later life (Freed, 1990, 36–56; Hatch et al., 1991, 144–70; Huber, 1985; Lubben et al., 1992, unpublished research; Sotomayer and Curiel, 1988; Steinitz, 1981). Such support contributes to personal well-being and to receiving assistance when needed in the later years. The programs identified can be listed in three categories: fellowship, education, and practical service.

Fellowship. Programs in this area typically include meals together, recreational activities, shopping and fun trips, seasonal cards, presents, and remembrances, various intergenerational activities, and formal or informal visitation.

An example of this variety of program is seen in the "Not Done Yet" Club at First Baptist Church in Barstow, California. A recently retired public school teacher is the full-time director of the group. The stated purpose is to have fun, fellowship, and be an outreach to new people for educational purposes of the church. There are three older adult Sunday School groups and the monthly NDY Club meetings which include many non–church members. Through the varied activities, members try to keep each other active and involved and give a sense of being useful in church and community.

Fellowship is also served by specialized senior programs such as a dance/exercise class in one congregation. Creative and fun trips spark interest for the Silver Saints at All Saints Catholic Church in Dunwoody, Georgia. In nearby Atlanta, a nun at the Cathedral of Christ the King has woven a beautiful tapestry of fellowship times—luncheons, visits, birthday cards, and practical service, as well as spiritual ministries to older parishioners and especially to the frail elderly.

Education. Educational programs abound among senior ministries. Arts and crafts classes as well as informative classes taught through community recreational or adult educational agencies are offered for seniors in churches and synagogues. One example of cooperation between community agencies and a congregation is the Concord Adult Activity Center at the First Presbyterian Church of Concord, California. Once a week classes of all sorts, as well as speakers and discussions, are presented. A commitment to lifelong learning as well as fellowship has developed. A similar weekly program at the Senior Center in the Fruitvale Presbyterian Church in Oakland, California offers classes including French lessons and a hot meal together for a nominal fee.

Several congregations with multifaceted programs were identified. While such programs tend to be found in large congregations or cosponsored by several groups, smaller congregations may respond in multiple ways to older people, although the programs may not be as visible as larger ones are. One United Methodist church in East Point, Georgia provides transportation, periodic brunches, and regular visits, while bringing church seniors into community senior groups and also blending church seniors into congregational programs and activities. The Fourth Presbyterian Church in Chicago (Retirement Research Foundation, 1990, 7), Calvary Baptist Church in Salem, Oregon, and First Presbyterian Church in Burlingame, California all have programs that combine fellowship activities and information about services as well as direct services to help older persons. In Chicago, informative programs about health and wellness are central, while in Burlingame a seven-part program reaches out to shut-ins and nursing home residents and serves active church elders with weekly fellowship programs.

One model of educational fellowship-building is the Shepherd Centers concept of senior ministries. Shepherd Centers began at Central United Methodist Church in Kansas City in 1972, when a Meals-on-Wheels project was started which grew to nineteen services serving 4,000 persons by 1980 (Cole, 1981, 250–65). Dr. Elbert Cole, the founding pastor, has now assisted over 1,000 other congregations or groups of congregations to establish Shepherd Centers in the U.S. and abroad. Factors that have made Shepherd Centers successful are that leadership is vested in older persons, and programs are community focused and centered in faith communities (congregations), privately supported, and cooperative, nonduplicative, and service-providing in nature (Akins, 1989, 13).

Shepherd Centers are most successful among middle-class people of some means, although large networks of support groups allow lower-income people to be served as well. Life Enrichment Services in Decatur, Georgia is supported by forty-six congregations and a number of community groups. It offers what older persons in that community need through a multifaceted services program. At the Mack Love Senior Center, classes are taught, support groups are formed, and a variety of in-home services are offered. One advantage of such programs is that through intercongregational and community cooperation older persons are able to help themselves and others.

Practical Service. As a part of the fellowship-building function of senior ministries, helping persons out develops as groups become aware of the needs of older people. In the case of Shepherd Centers, such practical service is reflected in the initial purpose of preventing institutionalization, hence the fostering of a variety of in-home services such as handyman, homemaker assistant, or volunteer transportation. In many congregations it appears that a range of practical help develops from the friendships that arise in fellowship-building experiences. Visitation and/or telephone reassurance to the housebound often leads to practical services and would seem to be a major bridge to the recognized need for social support services.

SOCIAL SERVICE MINISTRIES

Congregations have a long history of providing social services to needy groups, dating from biblical times when there was an understood responsibility for the widow and the orphan. Since the development of the welfare state over the past fifty years, religious groups tend to see their role more in terms of providing short-term assistance or offering gap-filling services that are not available through public channels. Congregations have, in a number of instances, been innovators of new forms of service for those in need, including the elderly. A recent example is the development of adult day-care centers. Congregations have been among the first to offer such services (Negstad and Arnholt, 1987, 27).

A variety of different social services were being provided by congregations that were named as outstanding in senior ministries. Among the various services are what might be labelled general assistance/case manager, voluntary caregiver, support groups, and health-care services.

General Assistance/Case Management. A range of general assistance was identified and probably other kinds of assistance are given that were not mentioned. From visitation or telecare to learn of needs (noted above in relation to fellowship-building), to informing people about services available in the community through various informal and formal information and referral processes, older people are linked to social services. St. Andrew's Church in Roswell, Georgia is a younger congregation in an older population area. Seeing the need for help among the older residents, a hotline for information was established which has been a blessing to many people. St. James Catholic Church in Chicago, through a consortium of congregations, provides not only information and referral and advocacy assistance, but two nuns offer a range of direct personal assistance as well, from managing funds to planning moves to making funeral arrangements for people (Retirement Research Foundation, 1989, 6). Such proactive service, unusual a few years ago, is becoming increasingly common as the system of human services becomes more stressed and more complex. There are also parishes that provide direct financial aid to help with food or rent; others offer classes or guidance in money management, as noted earlier. Some parishes even offer case management, a new, comprehensive style of social work, for older persons. St. Matthew's Lutheran Church in Charleston, South Carolina has an organized Guardianship Program that help older members who need help with their bills and also offers a variety of recreational and fellowship activities. St. Thomas More Catholic Parish in Decatur, Georgia and two Catholic parishes in North Miami, Florida all provide case management services to older client/parishioners, the latter parishes by working through a local nursing home. In each setting, a licensed social worker or a volunteer under a social worker's supervision works with an older person to assess what services are needed and then helps to secure such services in the community service system. The Florida parishes serve a largely Hispanic population and offer in-home services and financial guidance as well as case management.

Together with Catholic Community Services, the North Miami program has created services ranging from home repair to adult day-care to "a scripture-model reflection program on dealing with aging issues for elderly persons and their middle-aged children" (unpublished literature describing program). Another program in Florida is the Volunteer Guardianship Program of Lutheran Ministries of Florida, a service available as guardian of last resort for older persons. Prescreened volunteers assist persons who have no one else. They are committed to at least biweekly visits with clients to check needs and to provide long-term help. Paid staff supervise volunteers and their work (Keyser, 1986, 41–46).

Volunteer Caregivers. In 1983, through grants from the Robert Wood Johnson Foundation, twenty-five projects in seventeen states were established to provide first-level intervention into the lives of older persons in need by using volunteers for in-home services and assistance. These Interfaith Volunteer Caregiver Programs were founded based upon needs identified from earlier studies of older peoples' problems with independent living (Sherwood and Bernstein, 1985–1986, 55–67). All twenty-five projects were still operating and financially viable two years after the three-year grants ended. In 1987, the National Federation of Interfaith Volunteer Caregivers was founded to offer assistance to these and other projects. By 1992 the federation had grown to nearly two hundred organizations including seventy-two new IVCPs between 1989 and 1992. Well over 1,200 congregations now are actively involved in one of these projects.

An outstanding example of one such project *not* funded by the RWJ Foundation is Center D.O.A.R. in Phoenix, Arizona. The program began in 1978 with the formation of a senior adult group, Friendly Adults at the Church of the

Beatitudes. The interfaith caregivers program began in 1984. It has grown to have 1,900 volunteers from seventy-five congregations in the Phoenix area. Later, Generations, a program of support and information for caregivers that includes ten support groups in the city, was established. Finally, the Flinn Learning Resource Center, housed at the Church of the Beatitudes, provides a library, workshops, and seminars for older people or church leaders.

Support Groups. Congregations host or sponsor a variety of support groups for seniors. Issues include grief, substance abuse, being single, and being primary caregiver for another older person. Such sponsorship is valuable. More intensive services such as adult day-care or respite care for older persons and caregivers are offered by some groups. Valley Center at Grace Presbyterian Church in Walnut Creek, California, for example, is supported by several agencies and churches. The center provides adult day-care for frail and impaired clients, including recreational and educational programs one day each week on campus. A Respite Center for persons with Alzheimer's and related disorders is also available three days each week. The latter program incorporates education and support groups for family and caregivers. Such efforts are of inestimable help to families in caring for their aging relatives. In-home respite care is provided through Holy Communion Lutheran Church in Racine, Wisconsin, thus relieving caregivers for a few hours each week. Workshops, support groups, and other information is also provided to families.

Health-Care Services. More than one thousand parish nurses today offer a range of health education and health-care services in congregations of many denominations nationwide. Such services include health information fairs, exercise and nutrition education classes, and clinical services, such as blood pressure screenings, consultations, home visits, and referrals. Programs of that type are summarized by Djupe and Westberg (chap. 21 in this volume).

BARRIERS TO AND FUTURE POTENTIAL OF SENIOR MINISTRIES

What impediments exist to the growth of senior ministries in any congregation with many older members? The primary impediment is not lack of funding. Rather, it is the lack of vision and awareness of how widely-embedded ageism prevents leaders of congregations from seeing the need for and value of such programs. *First,* many older members are "invisible" in congregations. As noted in the Chicago study of housebound elderly, they are present occasionally and not missed between times. Many other elderly are, in fact, a quiet part of the regular participants. It is relatively easy to miss the needs of older persons who look no different than they have looked in years. *Second,* opportunity is a major key to program development, and the lack of linkage with service agencies, documented by Huber (chap. 19) and by Lewis (1989, 31), often results in congregations either trying to do all things alone or not doing much at all. *Third,* one face of ageism is seen when the instant response to the discovery that a large number of elderly are members of a congregation is an effort to recruit younger families. Looking only to younger families as "tomorrow's church" overlooks older persons as part of "today's church." A better response would be to develop intergenerational programs that serve both younger and older people. *Fourth,* since senior ministries are often a new form of ministry and require both time and budget, there may arise a "Back-to-Egypt" Committee, i.e., a group that sees no need for the program since "we never did it that way before." Sadly, footdraggers at times are the elders themselves who have a satisfactory lifestyle and fail to see why more is needed.

Many reasons for hope for senior ministries also exist. These include, *first,* that awareness of the graying of America is becoming widespread, from classrooms to mass media to consumerism, so that the graying congregations do not seem out of step. *Second,* religious groups are publishing materials to help groups relate to the service sector of communities. One example is *Linking Your Congregation with Services for Older People* (Stensen, 1992). It describes community aging services and what congregations can expect to receive from them. *Third,* a decrease in youth and younger persons as volunteers means that programs must increasingly turn to older people who have time, resources, and skills to volunteer as part of a vital congregation. *Fourth,* an increasing number of stimulating models of senior ministry are emerging as congregations begin seriously to ask how they can serve an aging population. Awareness of such options heightens interest in senior ministries. This chapter and book are an effort to enhance those options.

SUMMARY

Congregational programs for older people are an increasing part of the American religious scene. Because a common general understanding of aging people is lacking, the program forms vary greatly. However, theologies of compassion and concern in all denominational traditions recognize the desirability of serving elderly in need.

Most congregational programs in the Seeber survey can be classified as (1) *spiritual ministries* in which religious rites are shared with older people in regular congregational settings, or pastoral care and outreach are extended to reach isolated groups; (2) *fellowship/educational ministries* in which a variety of activities are offered in order to build friendship and meaningful contact between people in the congregation or community, so that a basic function of religious groups is met, i.e., to offer meaning and identity to people; and (3) *social service ministries* in which an astonishing array of social support relationships are nurtured and actual social services delivered.

What the religious community is currently doing to serve older persons should not be overlooked. However, with the rapidly growing number of older Americans and especially of frail older Americans, the hidden potential for many thousands of congregations to engage in meaningful ministries should also not be ignored.

Every indicator of social need and economic/political culture suggests that the voluntary sector of America is needed to help ensure a reasonable quality of life for older people. Congregations are already a part of older people's lives and can potentially assist with many of the programs and services needed today.

BIBLIOGRAPHY

Akins, T. E. (1989) "Shepherd's Centers Promote Meaning in Life." *Aging Network News* July, 13.

Clements, W. M., ed. (1981) *Ministry with the Aging*. San Francisco: Harper & Row.

______ (1992) "Issues from the Fourth Quarter of Life." Unpublished address.

Cole, E. C. (1981) "Lay Ministries with Older Adults." In Clements, 250–65.

Ellor, J. W. (1990) "Wholistic Theology as a Conceptual Foundation for Services for the Oldest Old." In Seeber, 99–110.

Freed, A. O. (1990) "How Japanese Families Cope with Fragile Elderly." *Journal of Gerontological Social Work* 15 (1–2):39–56.

Gray, R. M., and D. O. Moberg (1977) *The Church and the Older Person*. Grand Rapids, Mich.: Eerdmans.

Hatch, R., and L. Hatch (1991) "Informal Support Patterns of Older African-Americans and White Women: Examining Effect of Family, Paid Work and Religious Participation." *Research on Aging* 13:144–70.

Huber, L. (1985) "Connections: A Study of the Church in the Personal Networks of the Aging." Ph.D. dissertation, Case Western Reserve University, Cleveland, Ohio.

Keyser, A. W. (1986) "Legal Guardianship for the Elderly: A Volunteer Model." *Journal of Religion and Aging* 2:41–46.

Lewis, M. A. (1989) *Religious Congregations and the Informal Supports of the Frail Elderly*. New York: Third Age Center, Fordham University.

Lubben, J., F. DeYoung, and J. J. Seeber (1992) Unpublished research.

Murphy, P. (1979) *Healing with Time and Love*. Los Angeles: Andrus Gerontology Center, Univ. of Southern California.

Negstad, J., and R. Arnholt (1986) "Day Centers for Older Adults: Parish and Agency Partnership." *Journal of Religion and Aging* 2 (4):25–32.

Neugarten, B. L. (1974) "Age Groups in American Society and the Risk of the Young-Olds." In Eis, F. (ed.) *Political Consequences of Aging*. Philadelphia: American Academy of Political and Social Sciences.

Oliver, D. (1986) "Reflections on the Role of the Church, Synagogue, or Parish in Developing Effective Ministries with Older Persons." *Quarterly Papers on Religion and Aging* 2 (4):1–7.

Retirement Research Foundation (1989) "St. James Church." *ENCORE: Encouraging Community Response to the Elderly,* 6–7. Park Ridge, Ill.: Retirement Research Foundation.

______ (1990) "Fourth Presbyterian Church." *ENCORE: Encouraging Community Response to the Elderly,* 7–8. Park Ridge, Ill.: Retirement Research Foundation.

Schwanke, E. R. (1986) "Providing Pastoral Care for the Elderly in Long Term Facilities without a Chaplain Utilizing Coordinated Congregational Responses." *Journal of Religion and Aging* 2:57–64.

Seeber, J. J., ed. (1990) *Spiritual Maturity in Later Life.* New York: Haworth.

Sherwood, S., and E. Bernstein (1985–86) "Informal Care for Vulnerable Elderly: Suggestions for Church Involvement." *Journal of Religion and Aging* 2 (1–2):55–68.

Sotomayer, M., and H. Curiel, eds. (1988) *Hispanic Elderly: A Cultural Signature.* Edinberg, Tex.: Univ. of Texas, Pan American Press.

Steinitz, L. Y. (1981) "The Local Church as a Support for the Elderly." *Journal of Gerontological Social Work* 4 (2):44–53.

Stensen, J., and G. Gibson Hunt (1992) *Linking Your Congregation with Services for Older Adults.* Alexandria, Va.: Catholic Charities.

Tobin, S., J. W. Ellor, and S. M. Anderson-Ray (1986) *Enabling the Elderly: Religious Institutions within the Community Service System.* New York: State Univ. of New York.

19 Elements of Parish Revitalization

JAMES W. ELLOR

Congregations, like other groups or organizations, go through life cycles. They have a beginning, a period of maturity, and then generally decline with the hope for living again. As a diagnostic indicator that suggests the ability of a religious group to understand itself, the life-cycle model is useful. Unfortunately, the parallel to the human life cycle can include the myths of aging in the discussion. A search of the literature on parish revitalization and renewal reveals little directly noted about older adults. However, embedded in both the institutional life cycle and the change literature often utilized in revitalization is the concept that "old" is the enemy of revitalization. This would suggest that older adults resist change and frequently inhibit renewal.

In this chapter, the concept of change in relation to parish revitalization is reviewed in light of the gerontological literature. The author finds that older adults are experts at change. However, at a time of life when loss is the predominant source of change, change is not enthusiastically embraced. The author suggests an alternative approach to planned change that utilizes systems theory, assessment, and planning as a positive approach to revitalization. This approach reflects community demography as well as the history and needs of the congregation.

INTRODUCTION

When religious congregations evolve into groups primarily of older adults, the congregation is often thought to be dying. Both the seniors themselves and the younger members of the congregation seem to believe that the vitality of the congregation is reflected in the growth of younger families. The graying of the congregation may be due to a variety of factors. At times, congregations grow older as a reflection of the aging of the community at large. Congregations in transitional neighborhoods are, at times, made up of the seniors who can not afford to leave the area as younger families may try to do. At other times, older adults are survivors of a religious tradition in an area where that group no longer lives in large numbers. For a variety of reasons, then, congregations may grow older across time. Traditional approaches to the revitalization of congregational systems treat "old" as the enemy. Old buildings, old worship styles, old clergy, and at times the old members are treated as if they are the source of the problem. In this chapter, the author will examine parish revitalization in light of the contributions of the field of gerontology. A discussion of change theory in light of the needs of older congregations will be concluded by a discussion of a wholistic method of revitalization that can build on the strengths of congregations.

DEFINING THE PROBLEM

Various groups and academic centers have contributed to the development of a body of literature for persons attempting to help congregations grow. The oldest group are those involved in evangelism. Evangelization, or the act of reaching out to persons who have not known the truth as it is seen by the evangelist, can be an effective approach to parish revitalization as long as the congregation is inclined toward this type of outreach and as long as there are persons in the community open to hearing this new truth. Congregations with active evangelism programs will grow, both because they are reaching out and because the act of reaching out engenders the type of enthusiasm needed to facilitate the bonding within congregations. Authors of parish revitalization literature have noted that some parishes simply cannot bring together the necessary organization or enthusiasm to reach out to new members. In this case, it is necessary to find a different approach.

Numerous approaches to revitalizing local congregations have been developed. Some employ the use of educational programs within the congregation, some work to develop clergy in a new direction, some seek to change the boards and committees of congregations. Worley suggests that the distinctions between the various approaches are reflected in "the content of its educational resources and in its design or plan" (1978, 7).

Also at the root of the concept of revitalization is some type of theory or understanding of change. Three of the most common approaches include evangelism (a term used by Christian churches), parish revitalization, and parish renewal. These three concepts are structurally different as to who is targeted for change.

Evangelism and Outreach. The traditional concept of evangelism focuses on the "nonbeliever," a person who has not heard the message of a particular congregation or theological position. Congregations employing evangelism send out individuals and/or groups of individuals to reach out to persons generally within the surrounding community. Evangelism has also been the fundamental skill employed by missionaries for thousands of years.

FIGURE 19.1
The Congregation as a System

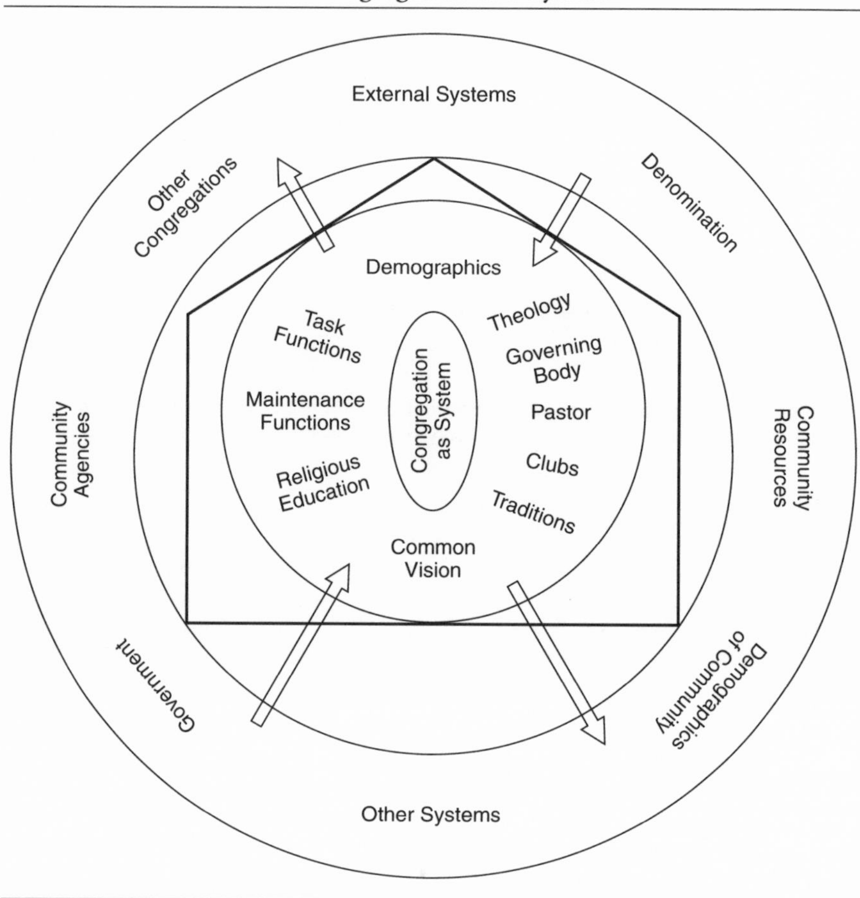

Parish Revitalization. Parish revitalization seeks to promote growth in congregations by changing elements of congregations. This may include the pastor, the lay leadership, the religious education program, or some combination thereof. An important structural component of this approach is its focus on congregations and on the larger community context in which they reside. In parish revitalization, the nature of all of the systems involved in the congregation is taken into consideration. This is particularly true of Worley's Wholistic (1978, 17).

Parish Renewal. The concept of parish renewal has been the focus of a recent national program in the Roman Catholic Church. The primary focus of parish renewal is congregations. In this approach, small groups, study of religious materials, and alternate forms of worship come together to attempt to bring renewal to the life of congregations.

ORGANIZATIONAL CHANGE

The concept of the life cycle of organizations offers a useful analogy for some aspects of parish revitalization. Clearly, organizations have a beginning and, in some cases, an ending. Congregations may experience this. They may also experience maturity as a group. These facts are noted in both group dynamics and organizational behavior literature. Unfortunately, the parallel to the human life cycle can be applied with misleading implications. Wagner (1979, 41) notes that "old age, as we will define it in this chapter, leads to a natural death." Such is the logical conclusion if a human life-cycle analogy is followed. Yet, Wagner goes on to note that "the percentage of senior citizens in a congregation may have nothing to do with church old age" (1979, 43). Wagner deals with this problem by talking about older adults in the church and distinguishing between the "disease of old age" and having a large population of older adults. Gerontologists point out that aging *is not a disease!!* Rather, it is a normal part of life.

Adizes (1988) offers an important redefinition of the "aging" process of the corporation which is applicable to congregations. He points out that "young" means the organization can change relatively easily, although what it will do, because it has a low level of control, is rather unpredictable. "Old" means there is controllable behavior, but "the organization is inflexible; it has little propensity for change" (2). By this definition the issues of growth are *flexibility* (younger organizations are more flexible) and *controllability* (mature organizations are more stable or controllable), not *youth* or *old age.* Adizes has suggested that the optimum situation for an organization is one in which flexibility and controllability are in tension with each other. Further, he notes that an organization does not need to pass into "old age," and that in "old age" the organization can be brought back or revitalized. Death, for organizations, is not inevitable.

The first issue, then, to be encountered in parish revitalization depends upon the organizational stage, whether primarily one of flexibility or one of controllability. Put in these terms, the negative stereotypes of aging are less likely to influence congregational decision-making. In some communities, the demographic characteristics are such that older adults may be the majority of persons available to be the congregation. In such cases, a congregation can become more vital by involving seniors. As noted by Tillapaugh (1982), programs that facilitate the outreach of the congregation into the community will foster growth. If the concept of a "maturing" congregation can be separated from reference to a congregation of elderly persons, then it can be expected that a congregation can be revitalized by involving more older adults.

Whether the approach to renewal is within congregations, within persons outside of congregations who need to hear a new message, or a combination of various systems within and outside of congregations, older adults will inevitably be involved. Older adults are a part of the system and membership of their own congregations and are frequently approached by persons from other religious groups in their evangelistic efforts.

One significant influence on congregations is the ecological nature of the community in which they reside. To some extent, the age make-up of the surrounding community, whether central city, suburban, or rural, will correlate with that of congregations. If the congregation is in an older community, it is likely to have more older members. Two common types of older communities are the intentional communities of older adults and communities where numerous older adults have aged in place.

Throughout the United States, but particularly in retirement states such as Florida and Arizona, communities such as Sun City have sprung up to provide seniors with places to retire. In some instances, communities were originally designed for retirees. In other cases, significant in-migration by older adults has occurred. In either case, congregations in such communities will find that seniors are demographically the largest available constituency.

In far more cases, seniors predominate in a community, not because the community was designed for retirement, but because the seniors moved into the area when they were younger and never left. This phenomenon is referred to as aging in place. The concept is applied to persons who have not moved but continue to live in the same place. When an entire community or portion of a community experiences this phenomenon, congregations are again faced with the reality of older adults as a predominant constituency. This happens in many different types of settings. It happens in rural areas where the younger persons have moved out, leaving only the older adults. It happens in central cities and small towns where younger persons have moved to the suburbs, leaving seniors in their home communities.

A third scenario finds seniors as the group who are less mobile. As communities experience ethnic or racial transition, they may come to be inhabited by younger persons of one racial or ethnic group and seniors of another. This will impact congregations if the two groups tend to worship in different types of congregations. In these cases, one congregation may find its membership dwindling while another may be growing.

These are not the only scenarios, but they are three common, albeit very different phenomena that can impact the make up of congregations. In some instances seniors are the victims of the changing dynamics of the community. In other cases, seniors may be the source of these dynamics.

Change theory, however, suggests that change is stressful. Communities that come to be made up predominantly of older adults reflect demographic changes that may not be welcome. Change is a significant concern for parish revitalization. In order for congregations to revitalize, they must in some way change. Even desirable changes will be accompanied by some amount of stress.

Change is a complex process. For individuals, change is often the result of loss. While not all changes involve losses, for older adults, most of the common changes do involve some type of loss. Often older adults, particularly those over seventy-five years of age, experience changes in health, reduction in income, and reduced mobility for travel. Many seniors experience some shrinking of their social world as friends move to other climates to be near family or in warmer environments, or as some die. The predominant theme in this type of change is that the senior will feel out of control of the change. The types of changes that lead to loss are those things which are unanticipated or unpreventable.

For some seniors, the only aspect of life that can be held on to as not changing is their faith. Within the various religious traditions, the concept of the reliability and unchanging nature of God are important themes. It is important to note that it is God, not the religious congregation, that is cited as not changing. Yet, at a time of change when individuals feel out of control in other aspects of their lives, it is not inconsistent to desire that the form of religious faith also be nonchanging.

Payne (1990, 31–34) describes the case of "Patty" who began a new life in late-middle adulthood in a new city. She found that the churches, even one of her own denomination, were changing in both form and belief from her background and that without knowing her or her professional past, they only saw her as one of those "oldpeople" (one word). The disillusionment of so much change and alienation was unnerving until she found social ties of meaningful exchange with persons and eventually reintegrated into the church congregation as the "new" Patty.

Unfortunately, nonchange may not be realistic. Institutions need to change, to reflect new circumstances, to move in innovative directions that allow for growth and development. At these times, seniors may find themselves obstructing change rather than supporting it, out of a need to control the one type of change that is within their control. This, however, leaves seniors with the image of being against change in the church or even labeled as the enemy of growth and renewal.

For many seniors, part of the need to prevent change may come from the memories that are attached to the congregation. Wind and Lewis (1991) discuss the observation that congregations are places of memories. James M. Gustafson (1961, 73) notes, "Common memory makes possible common life." Wind and Lewis point out that shared memories take a group of individuals and bring them together as a group with "shared understanding and perceptions" (1991, 16). In older congregations it is not unusual to find that the keepers of the memories are the older members. A new member may be able to observe the Rose Memorial Window, but it is an older member who knew the Rose family and the circumstances around which they donated the window. Congregations as well as other types of voluntary organizations live in paradoxical circumstances, on the one hand seeing the importance of the memories that continue to define the group and on the other hand manifesting "the quintessential American penchant for freedom from constraints of the past and openness to new possibilities of the present and future" (Wind and Lewis, 1991, 15).

The need for renewal brings this paradox into focus. On the one hand, some seniors may be holding on to the memories of the congregation, trying not to allow it to change at the pace at which everything else in their lives is changing. On the other hand, those same seniors may be the very ones that want the congregation to survive in order to continue to be the place of their memories. Clergy frequently report feeling caught in the middle of these feelings, trying to promote growth while preserving memories. At times this leads to confrontation between the older and younger members of the congregation, and at times it leads to alienation of the older congregants.

PROCESSES OF RENEWAL OR CHANGE IN CONGREGATIONS

Step A. While each type of renewal offers a different approach to renewal, the first step in most types is to create a committee to develop the approach. As with any committee offering leadership in a religious congregation, this committee should be made up of persons who are respected by the congregation and who reflect the demographic make-up of the congregation. This group should be empowered to study and propose an approach to revitalization that seems appropriate for the congregation. Worley (1978) emphasizes that as this group develops, it will need to reach a consensus as to the dynamic nature of the congregation as well as to the process of revitalization to be employed. This consensus he refers to as a "common vision" for planning. Each member of the planning group needs to have the same vision for change.

Step B involves assessing the congregation and community in order to understand who they have been (the corporate memory), who they believe they are (the corporate myth), and who they want to become (the corporate vision). This assessment should include both the strengths and weaknesses of the congregation as well as a realistic perspective as to what the congregation can and cannot do for itself and its community. This assessment should include an examination of all of the various systems that impact the congregation.

Step C is a plan that is developed and brought to the congregation. Through an educational process a common vision for the entire congregation is developed, and the congregation is ready to embark on the revitalization process. Some plans may directly involve the role of the clergy, some involve the religious education program, some involve community program development.

One myth to be disposed of is that congregations primarily made up of older adults cannot grow. Numerous examples of older congregations are available in the literature (Tilberg, 1984, 57). For older congregations to grow, several things must be addressed. Congregations must understand that the traditional target of growth, younger families with younger children, may not be available. In older communities, persons who are available are older persons, not young families. It is possible for congregations to grow by attracting other older persons. The purpose of growth and revitalization is to address a primary goal of the congregation. Generally, in religious groups, that is to reach out to persons who would like to be a part of a faith community.

Parish renewal need not have age limitations. Unfortunately, older members of congregations often are the first to insist on bringing in more young people, even at the expense of reaching out to older adults. This phenomenon often comes from the memory of the congregation. Too often the assumption is that a revitalized congregation is one just like it used to be when the congregation had many families with children. Often that reflected a different demographic era for the congregation. Many times seniors hold a "snapshot" or picture in their memory of what the congregation used to look like when it was a "vital group" and they want to recapture that picture. A key to change, then, is to accept the fact that if the demography has changed, the vision also must change.

Step D involves the identification and addressing of some of the concerns of the older members. Older adults are often perceived as set in their ways. "Rigidness and conservatism vs. flexibility and liberalism are functions of personality structure and social environment rather than of age" (Maves, 1981, 15). Many older adults are actually experts at handling change. Historically, persons who reach an advanced age have successfully survived many changes. However, congregations wishing to change need to be careful not to perceive that the old ways were always bad or wrong and the new ways always good and positive. For example, when new liturgical procedures or new programs or the use of new hymnals need to be introduced, the manner in which such changes are introduced is crucial to their acceptance. Opposition may arise from the unexpected changes or from changes that are too briefly explained or justified. One week the congregation is doing something the old way, the next they are doing it the new way. The longer the old procedure has been in place, the greater the need to grieve the loss before changing to the new procedure.

Parish renewal then involves a congregation-wide process of assessing and envisioning the potential ministry to be developed. It is implemented by recognizing and interweaving past programs with new forms of ministry. Such change is not age-related. It can be inclusive of all in the congregation.

Butler (1961) introduced the concept of reminiscence therapy that has become extremely important in counseling with seniors. This concept also offers congregations an approach to promote change. The concept of reminiscence or life-review suggests that there can be therapeutic value in remembering the past as long as it is held in tension with the present. To employ reminiscence in working to create change in a congregation—for example, the initiation of a new hymn book—the group leader, clergy person, or other facilitator would begin by bringing together the congregation or at least key elements of the congregation if size prohibits full participation. The purpose of this meeting is twofold. The first is to remember the significance of the old hymn book. What did it mean to the members of the congregation? What were their first experiences of this hymnal? Is it associated with people, events, or other significant memories? It is often helpful to write down all of the memories that are shared in this event. By so remembering, the congregation is experiencing with the person or persons who remember these events, and in remembering, honors them. It may be that part of the problem in this transition is that some of the old books were dedicated to persons who have died and whose memory is kept alive for some persons through these books. In such a case, it may be helpful to dedicate some of the new hymnals to these persons in order to retain their memory in the congregation.

At times it may be helpful to find a symbolic way of capturing the memories shared. This may be done by transcribing those memories and placing the document in a special place of honor, or it may be done by taking a historic picture of the group being remembered and finding a place to display it. In any case, the purpose is to create a transcendent symbol of the older memorials in order to honor their meaning and yet offer that meaning to the newer memorials. By honoring the memories rather than shunning them, the congregation then can move to the new books without conveying the message that the old is no longer wanted or useful. Yet another symbolic act could be to donate the old texts to a congregation that is less fortunate and could make good use of them.

This process was dramatically illustrated after the merger of two denominations resulted in two congregations being located within a block of each other, each determined to survive. It was logical to combine these two struggling congregations into one, but each had a rich heritage with cultural uniqueness. When it was finally decided which building to sell, they discovered that the property was of greater value than the building. Since the building would be torn down, they gained permission to take a few treasured items from it. The congregation began by creating a scrapbook about each church. Included were old pictures of the buildings and people involved. They also made two patch quilts, one for each congregation.

On the day of the celebration of the merger and the initiation of services in one combined church, both congregations came together and walked over to the old church. Congregants were instructed to bring hammers and screwdrivers if they wished to. They were then encouraged to remove any item of significance to themselves or their families. Once all of the items were removed, they were carried to the new church. Electric socket plates, pictures, pull cords for signalling the choir, and numerous odd objects were collected. They were then placed on display at the new church where the two groups together offered ideas as to how the various items could be employed. The church leadership, together with appropriate tools and technical expertise, then set about incorporating each object in the new building. Once this task was completed, the two quilts were sewn together and placed prominently in the sanctuary. Care was taken in the process not to cover some treasured memory of the old church building with a new item.

Once a group has decided how to create change, some type of outreach is generally needed. In some congregations that may mean the development of groups or social programs for older adults. In others it may mean reaching out to older adults in the community. This process may encounter a myth that all older adults are already members of congregations. Tobin et al. (1986) found that in one community in which 60 percent of the residents were over the age of sixty-five, almost 30 percent of the persons attending senior centers and clubs were not members of local congregations. An important question to be explored regarding these nonmembers was whether they were in fact spiritually-oriented persons and, if so, whether they would be interested in joining local congregations but had not been asked. In many instances they were in fact members of distant congregations that no longer listed them as members or even congregations that had been dissolved.

Reaching out to this group is a process of listening to them and offering them a new congregation. The concept of evangelism, often employed in these instances, suggests that the evangelist is going to offer the senior some new theology or idea. For many seniors, there is very little that they have not already heard. The approach that might prove more productive would be to sit and listen to seniors and hear why they became unattached from the congregation to which they had belonged. In some instances there may have been a disagreement with a clergyperson, in other cases a failure to be responded to in a time of great need. Whatever the reason, it needs to be heard and healed. Such healing comes not by condemning the offending congregation but acknowledging the pain. Finally, an invitation to a new congregation can then offer the senior a new option.

Numerous approaches to revitalization are offered in the literature. No matter which method is selected, "growth = change" (Schaller, 1984). Change is not new to older adults. However, they may find themselves opposing change, when in light of all of the other changes in their lives that are beyond their control, they must face new change in the very institution where they sought continuity and permanence. By listening to seniors, honoring the valued older process or object, and then creating a transcendent symbol, seniors may become allies in the process of change. Growth is possible in older congregations and communities. Such growth may best occur where there exists a vision of reaching out and sharing what the congregation has to offer.

BIBLIOGRAPHY

Adizes, I. (1988) *Corporate Life Cycles: How and Why Corporations Grow and Die and What to do about it.* Englewood Cliffs, N.J.: Prentice Hall.

Butler, R. N. (1961) "Re-awakening interest." *Nursing Homes* 10:8–19.

Dudley, C. S., J. W. Carroll, and J. P. Wind, eds. (1991) *Carriers of Faith: Lessons from Congregational Studies.* Louisville, Ky.: Westminster/John Knox.

Gustafson, J. M. (1961) *Treasure in Earthen Vessels: The Church as a Human Community.* New York: Harper & Row.

Maves, P. B. (1981) *Older Volunteers in Church and Community: A Manual for Ministry.* Valley Forge, Pa.: Judson.

Payne, B. P. (1990) "Spiritual Maturity and Meaning-Filled Relationships: A Sociological Perspective." In Seeber, 25–39.

Schaller, L. E. (1984) *Growing Pains: Strategies to Increase Your Church's Membership.* Nashville: Abingdon.

Seeber, J. J., ed. (1990) *Spiritual Maturity in the Later Years.* New York: Haworth.

Tilberg, C. W. (1984) *Revolution Underway: An Aging Church in an Aging Society.* Philadelphia: Fortress Press.

Tillapaugh, F. R. (1982) *Unleashing the Church: Getting People out of the Fortress and into Ministry.* Ventura, CA: Regal Books.

Tobin, S. S., J. W. Ellor, and S. M. Anderson-Ray (1986) *Enabling the Elderly: Religious Institutions within the Community Service System.* Albany, N.Y.: State University of New York Press.

Wagner, P. C. (1979) *Your Spiritual Gifts Can Help Your Church Grow.* Ventura, CA: Regal Publishers.

Wind, J. P., and J. W. Lewis (1991) "Memory, Amnesia, and History." In Dudley, Carroll, and Wind, 15–17.

Worley, R. C. (1978) *Dry Bones Breath!* Chicago: The Center for the Study of Church Organizational Behavior.

Part Four COMMUNITY OUTREACH IN AN AGING SOCIETY

INTRODUCTION

Central to both the Jewish and Christian faith traditions is an ethic of care for others. In Part Two on pastoral care and Part Three on congregational life, emphasis was placed upon the ways religious institutions care for members or adherents. The chapters in Part Four demonstrate that the ethic of care does not stop at the walls of the church or synagogue. Rather, Jews and Christians are called to care for persons within the larger community where political institutions greatly affect decision-making about service.

Tracing the historical roots of the imperative to seek justice for all persons, *Lynn Huber* begins with an examination of the types of services that have been offered to older adults by various faith communities (chap. 20). Although all affirm the ethic of care, religious institutions vary widely in their approaches to service. Huber notes a number of variables that affect the kinds of outreach programs churches and synagogues undertake. Size of the institution, ethnicity and class, and denominational differences all combine to prompt unique ministries to elders. Huber points out how controversies have arisen over the types and appropriateness of social action; she also notes the vast differences among religious bodies in beliefs about their relation to the political domain. Although there are often tensions between the two, Huber maintains that there are numerous benefits of cooperation, particularly in an age when political institutions lack both the resources and sometimes the will to meet the needs of older persons. She also describes the positive results accruing from interfaith coalitions and she provides information about several potent models of such cooperation. Partnerships, whether between religious and secular agencies or between religious bodies themselves, can provide creative solutions to many of the issues facing older persons today.

Because of their importance within black communities, African American churches have a long history of providing these kinds of creative solutions. *Cleopatra Caldwell, Linda Chatters, Andrew Billingsley,* and *Robert Taylor* have in recent years provided much valuable data regarding the role of the black church in meeting the needs of aging individuals. In chapter 21, they describe the kinds of services offered by these churches in their outreach to African American families. Their detailed presentation of information gleaned from the Black Church Family Project clearly demonstrates the depth of commitment by black churches to aging persons.

One of the most critical needs facing older persons of all races is health care. For many years, *Anne Djupe* and *Granger Westberg* have challenged faith communities to attend to the physical, mental and spiritual health concerns of older adults (chap. 22). They describe three types of congregation-based health programs and in so doing, they insist that ministry to the whole person must include care for the body as well as the spirit. In a time of political uncertainty regarding health care, it is imperative that religious bodies reassert their call to healing. By forging links with community-based health care institutions, congregations can provide leadership in creating a vision of health and well-being that affirms the whole person.

Besides health care, another pressing problem facing older adults today is housing. Caldwell and her colleagues present data in chapter 21 showing that home care services are the most common type of outreach to elders by black churches. Older people value their autonomy and want to remain in their homes as long as possible. Sometimes independent living becomes impossible, however, and alternatives must be sought. Again, because of limited public resources and more importantly, because of their calling to care for others, churches and synagogues often find themselves in the business of providing housing for older persons. Religious groups have a long tradition of providing housing of all kinds, as *Ellen Netting* notes in chapter 23. She cites information about the many different types of housing religious bodies have sponsored and she offers practical advice for congregations that feel called to this kind of ministry.

For many years, faith communities have been instrumental in supporting residential retirement complexes, continuing care retirement communities, low-income rental housing, and nursing homes. Looking ahead to the needs of elders in the twenty-first century, *Jane Thibault* believes another model is needed (chap. 24). Congregations will have to attend not only to providing safe, affordable, supportive housing, but they also must create living environments that encourage spiritual growth. She argues that gerontology's affirmation of the increasing interiority of later life calls for a new type of living arrangement for aging persons. Various levels of commitment to spiritual development already exist among religious congregations but none, according to Thibault, have taken the risk of establishing contemplative communities where aging persons can pursue spiritual growth. Given the yearning for meaning articulated by contemporary middle-aged persons increasingly frustrated by a materialistic culture, Thibault's model provides a vision of old age enriched by intentional commitment to spiritual values.

Many aging persons of faith will never live to see the time when congregations create spiritual communities. They spend their days in nursing homes whose practices and policies kill the spirit long before the body dies. To these persons, *Dayle Friedman* offers hope by showing how long-term care facilities can become more sensitive to the spiritual challenges residents face every day: the empty and burdensome time, the meaninglessness of daily routines, and the disconnections resulting from isolation from the familiar world outside the nursing home (chap. 25). Religion, says Friedman, can give time back to nursing home patients. Religious practice nurtured in long-term care institutions structures the days, weeks, months, and years. It restores meaning by affirming the essential value of all old people. It makes connections through time by reaching into the past and projecting into the future. Friedman shows how congregations can work with long-term care facilities to provide truly meaningful ministries that will enhance the spiritual lives of elders.

Another kind of ministry that challenges faith communities in an aging society is prompted by emerging awareness of the ways gay men and lesbians experience the aging process. Because a vital part of their identity has long been regarded as taboo, aging gays and lesbians may have felt marginalized or even actively rejected from participation in congregational life. As a result, many of these persons create their own communities which often have little contact with religious institutions. However, as *Gary Whitford* and *Jean Quam* (chap. 26) note, there are many opportunities for bridge-building between the gay and lesbian community and religious congregations that affirm human value regardless of age or sexual orientation. Faith communities committed to ministry to aging persons need to examine whether their forms of service inadvertently or deliberately exclude persons on the basis of their sexual orientation.

Whether they provide hot meals, housing, health care, ministries of visitation, or any of the other kinds of service described in Part Four, congregations are finding ways to enact the ethic of care. As they have done through the centuries, these bodies of faithful people are demonstrating to the wider world that religion not only enhances the individual's well-being but it also empowers persons to nourish the well-being of others.

20 The Church in the Community

LYNN W. HUBER

By 2030, when all the baby boomers have entered the ranks of older adults, more than one in five Americans will be over the age of sixty-five. How is the church (this term will be used in the sociological sense to include temple and synagogue as well as church) addressing the needs of older adults, both within its own walls and in the community? How does it work with other organizations on behalf of older adults?

This chapter will (1) briefly examine the historical roots of older adult ministry in the local congregation; (2) describe congregational differences that influence their willingness and capacity to work with older adults; (3) examine interchurch and church-agency relations, including attitudinal barriers to their cooperation, and related conceptual issues.

AN HISTORICAL INTRODUCTION

The early prophetic stream in Judaism proclaimed a responsibility to care for the poor, orphans, widows, and strangers as a mandated religious obligation to God. Maves (1981), Kemp (1960), and the Synagogue Council of America (1975) highlight Hebraic scriptural themes of love of neighbor, tithing for the poor, leaving grain in the fields for gleaners, and other forms of obligatory charity. In fact, the very word for *charity* in Hebrew also means *justice;* the two concepts are inseparable.

First-century Christianity created the office of deacons specifically for the purpose of working with those in need (Acts 6). The medieval church, particularly the monastic communities, expanded this tradition of hospitality, both as a religious obligation and as a means of achieving grace. The medieval synagogue also generated "shelters for the sick (*bikkur cholim*) . . . [and] homeless (*hekdesh*)" (Synagogue Council of America, 1975). Such practices were widespread but not well coordinated. By the eighteenth century, fairly well-organized approaches had emerged and led to the development of many formalized social welfare activities.

Both Jewish philanthropists and Christian proponents of the Social Gospel of the nineteenth century built on this religious concern for justice for the oppressed, and our own century has seen a flowering of both sectarian and denominational missionary efforts, overseas and domestically, that was previously unmatched. Moberg (1962, 151) reported that "in 1903 fully one-third of the nation's benevolent institutions were church-connected" (see also Synagogue Council of America, 1975).

The American church served many functions in its local community (Holmes, 1968). In the eighteenth and nineteenth centuries it was often the "village center": a meeting place, an educational resource, a political meeting hall, and a social center. The church more or less took for granted that it was a community-based and neighborhood-serving facility, and it often provided a variety of health, social, recreational, and educational services, and sometimes even such infrastructures as roads (see Felton, 1920).

While most of these community functions have since been transferred to secular institutions, some are still performed by the church. They are more likely to be found in rural churches, in those located in and serving discrete neighborhoods, in ethnically homogeneous congregations, and in lower- and working-class congregations. The African-American church has been a major social support for its members throughout its history (see chap. 11). The recent phenomenon of the mega-church (serving ten thousand or more persons) has also brought a renewal of the church's role as a center for social and educational enrichment, a sort of "one-stop shopping center."

To focus more particularly on social services for older adults, we note that prior to the passage of the Older Americans Act in 1965, the role of the church in programming specifically designed for the aged was significant. In many communities, congregationally sponsored "Golden Age" programs were the only organized older adult services, other than public assistance and Social Security. Subsequent to the passage of this act, many recreational and other service programs were developed under secular auspices and funding, although in some cases (particularly in small communities) the church continued to house or sponsor such programs (United Presbyterian Church, 1967; Bachman, 1955–56; Cayton and Nishi, 1955; Moberg, 1972; Synagogue Council of America, 1975).

With the current emphasis on private initiative and with decreased governmental funding of social services in general, it is not surprising that we are seeing a renewal of demand for church-sponsored programs for older adults.

THE LOCAL CONGREGATION AS SERVICE PROVIDER FOR THE OLDER ADULT

Types of Services

The services offered by congregations to older adults are varied. Several studies have attempted to catalogue and categorize the services offered by religious congregations. The first of these projects was completed by the National Interfaith Coalition on Aging (NICA, 76). This study examined data from a national survey of congregations and provided the earliest list of programs and services available. Tobin et al. (1986) did a three-year study of six communities in one metropolitan area. The researchers interviewed all of the clergy in these six communities. They concluded that the services provided in local congregations could be divided into four groups: (1) *religious programs* or services that directly address the spiritual concerns of members of the congregation; (2) *pastoral care programs* that address the one-to-one or small-group needs of parishioners; (3) the *church-as-host* programs which are run by an outside agency but rent space in a local congregation; and (4) the *church-as-service-provider* programs that reflect formal social service provision provided through the auspices of the local church, often in conjunction with a local denominational social service agency. More recently, a study by Mary Ann Lewis (1989) of a national sample of Roman Catholic parishes employs four categories. Her categories were: (1) *programs that are part of the life of the parish,* including Holy Communion, religious counseling, and prayer; (2) *programs that provide social and recreational services,* including bingo, recreational activities, and visits to seniors in their own home and in nursing homes; (3) *services providing emergency and emotional assistance,* including counseling, bereavement support, and emergency meals; finally, (4) *assisting the older person with daily living,* including cooking, shopping, and cleaning. Dr. Lewis notes that this last category is rarely provided in her sample.

These two studies are unique because they began their observations from systematic study of the types of programs offered in congregations. The first study by Tobin et al. (1986) provides a useful schema of programs found in the communities studied by the authors. Unique to this schema is the category "The Church as Host." This schema conceptually mixes program content with program auspices. However, by doing so, it points out the movement from informal church-based programming to externally supported formal service provision. The schema provided by Lewis (1989) offers a different way of examining the types of programs that were found in the congregations that her research team examined.

Elbert Cole (1991), founder of the Shepherd's Centers of America (which will be discussed below), provides a schema that is conceptually useful. It divides such services into four categories:

1) *Life maintenance:* designed to meet survival needs, with programs such as meals on wheels and chore services, housekeeping assistance, emergency food and clothing and financial assistance, transportation, and information and referral. Life maintenance is certainly at least as much the province of social service agencies as it is of the church and is often better managed there. If services are not otherwise available, however, the congregation must help to make them so; if they are, it needs to know about them in order to make appropriate referrals.

2) *Life enrichment:* designed to meet educational and recreational needs, with programs such as continuing education, social events, and travel. Such services are offered in numerous senior centers and other secular settings, but also frequently in churches.

3) *Life reconstruction:* designed to provide assistance in dealing with life's transitions (such as bereavement and illness), with programs such as support groups and peer counseling. These functions are shared among family and friends, church, social agencies, and private therapists. The major stress in times of life transition often comes from questions of meaning, from trying to make sense of the experience. This task certainly is appropriate to the church, but many congregations do not have structures in place, or personnel with competence, to address these issues.

4) *Life transcendence:* designed to provide assistance in dealing with theological and spiritual issues through such activities as worship and study. This is clearly a church function; in fact, it is seen by many as the primary (sometimes even the only appropriate) task of the church.

A complementary perspective is offered by Ellor and Coates (1985–86), who describe three possible levels of congregational advocacy efforts: (1) to meet the needs of individual clients; (2) to meet the needs of all seniors in the community; and (3) to meet the needs of all older people through state or federal legislation.

This third level, addressing the needs of all older persons, involves more than strategic planning. It raises a philosophical question, however, namely, whether it is the prerogative (or responsibility) of the church to become involved in political affairs. There is currently a great diversity of opinion on this issue in the religious community, as is evident in the controversies over abortion. The position taken on the overall question of church involvement in political affairs will affect the ways congregations (and national and judicatory church bodies as well) decide to approach services for older adults.

Five "styles of ministry" were described by Steinitz (1980) in her study of forty representative churches in a large midwestern suburb. These were: (1) spiritual/evangelistic; (2) theological/intellectual; (3) social activist; (4) congregation-focused: bureaucratic style; and (5) congregation-focused: family style. These styles of ministry correlated with the congregation's emphasis on religious experiences, education, and social action; with the congregation's willingness to provide direct services to older adults; and with the type of services they were most likely to provide (See Figure 20.1).

Social activists were most likely to see political involvement as an appropriate church-related activity, congregation-focused churches the least likely to adopt that position. It was a goal of the Moral Majority to convince the evangelistic churches to adopt a more social activist position. We are not likely to see an end to this controversy in the near future.

Figure 20.1
"Styles of Ministry . . . and Their Apparent Relation to Church-Provided Social Services to the Elderly" (Steinitz 1980, 98)

Style of Ministry: Name	*Description of Emphasis*	*Denominations and Church Size Where Predominantly Found*	*Apparent Relation to the Provision of Social Services to Elderly Congregants*
Spiritual/ Evangelistic	Personal religious experience	Conservative Protestant denominations. Mostly medium-sized and small churches	Few formally organized services. Reliance on informal social support networks generated according to patterns of friendship and a notion of religious duty within the church. Many opportunities for spiritual enrichment and the development of friendships among parishioners.
Theological/ Intellectual	Building knowledge and understanding. Includes many educational opportunities	Mainstream Jewish congregations and among some Protestant and Catholic clergymen. Mostly medium-sized churches	Older people expected to return to the church for intellectual enlightenment and spiritual enrichment. Otherwise they should seek out community agencies for the provision of most social services.
Social activist	Pursuit of social justice	Liberal Jewish and Protestant congregations. Medium-sized churches	Notion of other people in the world being worse off than elderly members of the church. Main services available: opportunities for part-time (voluntary) work and fellowship through the provision of social services outside the church.
Congregation focused: bureaucratic style	Emphasis on the needs and concerns of church members	Catholic churches. Mainstream Protestant denominations. Large and medium-sized churches	High value on formally organized social services to elderly congregants.
Congregation focused: family style	Emphasis on the needs and concerns of church members	Mainstream Protestant denominations. Small churches	High value on social services to elderly congregations. Most services are informally organized (i.e., like an extended family).

Formal Services Likely to Become Freestanding. As congregationally-based services become formalized, there is a tendency for them also to become secularized or at least separated from sponsorship by a particular congregation. Andron (1982) studied the relationships between synagogues and Jewish federations in twelve communities and found that "with a few notable exceptions, programmatic contacts between the synagogues and federation constituents . . . were virtually nonexistent" (205; also see Synagogue Council of America, 1975; Netting, 1987; Ellor and Tobin, 1990). While this may lead to efficiency of operation, it deprives service recipients of the benefits of strengthened ties to their own congregations, just when such ties may be most needed.

Intergenerational Approaches. The church is virtually the only institution in our society that is consistently intergenerational. Schools, the workplace, and often residential areas tend to be age-segregated. Quality of life for persons of all ages is enhanced by intergenerational contacts. Particularly in the church, which exists to help people come to grips with values and the meaning of life, such contacts are needed. Elders, sharing the story of the place of God and the church in their lives, can be models for younger adults and children, and having someone to whom to pass on the story can enrich their own lives as well.

Elders can also both give and receive services that enrich the entire congregation. In a day when many families are divided by divorce or geography, the church can become a place for "artificial extended families" to meet each other's social and emotional needs. Furthermore, providing intergenerational programming reduces the stigmatizing that persons of different ages may otherwise do to each other. Creative resources for intergenerational programming are available, and more are being developed all the time (see Presbyterian Publishing House, 1987).

Congregational Differences Affecting Older Adult Ministry

Several factors are involved in determining what services churches provide. Some important factors are congregational size, the degree of clergy/lay leadership support, and denominational affiliation. We will briefly discuss these variables.

Church Size. The size of the congregation is related to the likelihood of services being made available for particular groups within the congregation, including older adults. The larger the church, the broader and more diverse the program offerings are likely to be. In addition, the larger the church, the more likely it is that staff members with specialized training will be available. Even in those large churches that do not have programs specifically designed for older adults, there almost always is someone with a specialization in pastoral care, who usually ends up, *de facto,* working with older adults.

Smaller churches are more likely to have higher concentrations of older adults but also to have lower income, less training, and less staff time available to work with them (Steinitz, 1981; and Ellor and Coates, 1985–86). They are also less likely to provide formal social services, but will help to meet the needs of older and other members on an ad-hoc basis. The available services are likely to be intergenerational rather than specialized by age group.

In a study of 212 churches and synagogues in a northeastern state, Sheehan et al. (1988, 236) found that the "size of the congregation was [positively] related to the likelihood that clergy made referrals to social service agencies on behalf of older persons." Larger churches or synagogues were also more likely to be the "site for community programs serving older persons."

Degree of Clergy/Lay Leadership Support. An essential factor in successful programming for older adults is the active support and cooperation of the clergy and lay leadership of the congregation (Haber, 1984). This is the case with all congregational programming in churches. Needed *at a minimum* from the clergy is "benign neglect"—publicizing, authorizing, and publicly recognizing the work being done. Needed *at a minimum* from laity is a small cadre of interested persons who will maintain the effort.

Social Class, Denominational, and Ethnic Differences. In a study of the place of the church in the personal networks of older adults (Huber, 1985), three like-sized but otherwise very diverse congregations were compared as to the degree to which they provide support to their aged members. Implications of these findings can be used to reflect on differential approaches to working with congregations and to linking them with social services.

One was a middle- and upper-middle-class, largely white, Episcopal congregation, with extensive ties to the social service network in its community. A second was a Black Baptist church in which an enormous amount of informal helping went on all the time (see chap. 11). Third was a very traditional, Polish, Roman Catholic working-class congregation with little linkage to the social service network or to other outside organizations.

Different congregational strengths were found to be important in these churches. Churches like the Episcopal congregation can easily educate their members about social services and how to connect with them. This population group also has a great deal of experience and skill to offer the community, and the church can be utilized as a vehicle for recruiting older adults to meet needs for volunteers both within and outside of the congregation.

Such congregations might also be the place from which to draw leadership for the development of interfaith programs such as a Shepherd's Center or an interfaith volunteer caregiving program (see descriptions below).

Churches like the Black Baptist congregation are already doing a great deal of informal helping. They also are in a potentially very good position to provide linkage and

> advocacy services for their congregants when needs exceed the ability of the natural helping system to meet them. This function might well be performed by tapping the skills of younger leaders of the congregation, many of whom have vocational ties to the social service system. (Huber, 1987, 70)

For congregations without a tradition of defining mutual help as an appropriate church-related activity, there would clearly need to be a change in the underlying values presented by clergy and accepted by laity in order for the congregation to be drawn into community organization activities.

Wilson and Netting (1988, 59), in an exploratory study of differences between Black and Anglo congregations, developed two hypotheses for future research that were supported by data from Huber's study. These are: (1) the Black elderly tend to accept services from the church more readily than from formal social service agencies; and (2) the church will be the major source of informal support for the Black elderly more often than for the Anglo elderly.

However, both Black and Anglo clergy viewed themselves as effective referral agents for their congregants. While this was also the view of the clergy in Huber's study, such a perspective was not held by congregants themselves. Out of 124 instances of social service usage by study respondents, only three were church-facilitated. Thus, although much of the literature indicates that the church performs a referral role, since most of these responses come from clergy, we cannot be sure that such linkage actually takes place for most church members needing services. This is a topic needing further exploration.

INTERORGANIZATIONAL EFFORTS INVOLVING THE CHURCH

Let us consider (1) some attitudinal barriers to church-agency cooperation; (2) theoretical models that address it; and (3) some models of cooperation that have proven successful.

Attitudinal Barriers to Church-Agency Cooperation and Efforts to Overcome Them

Social service personnel and church workers often suffer from mutually nonproductive attitudes. In a real way, we are dealing with two cultures. Neither may be aware of the resources available through the other, of shared values (which are often couched in different language), or of how to negotiate the other's system. Both churches and social agencies are arenas full of minefields in which, if you do not know the rules, it is difficult to make things happen (Ellor, 1983). The result is a much less than ideal system of information, referral, and service delivery.

One example: The strong value placed by social service workers on clients' self-determination may constrain them from cooperation with religious organizations, based on the false assumption that discussion of religion necessarily interferes with clients' free choice. On the contrary, helping people connect their life issues with their faith may actually be a vehicle to enhance self-determination. In order for that to happen, there needs to be an attitudinal change on the part of many professionals.

Another part of the problem may be due to misunderstanding of the constitutional mandate for separation of church and state. The constitution precludes *both* state establishment of religion *and* state interference with its free practice. However, there is *no* prohibition on mutual cooperation between public and church employees, as long as those limitations are observed.

From the congregation's perspective, there may be reluctance to go into a secular world in which members are uncertain of being well received and unsure about how their religious values will be respected and supported. Although social services are rooted in the religious tradition, when they became secularized they often tended to exaggerate the battle between science and religion and to feel that adherence to the former required a break with the latter. At its extreme, a social service professional with a Freudian background may view religion as a dysfunctional defense system, while a traditionalist adherent to a religious faith may have equally great suspicions about the integrity of the "godless" therapist or social worker (Marty, 1980).

There are some interesting exceptions to the dearth of linkages between religious and social service systems. One such exception is the CRANECE Project (Church in Rural Aging Networks: Education and Collaborative Efforts), funded by the Administration on Aging through the West Virginia University Gerontology Center. CRANECE was a cooperative effort among the university, the statewide Council of Churches, the statewide Area Agency on Aging, and many denominational and social agencies, to facilitate these groups working together to meet the needs of older adults.

Regional workshops were held throughout West Virginia to train social service and church personnel together. This resulted in several collaborative projects: (1) development of resource directories; (2) provision of regional seminars; (3) creation of "new organizations to provide one-stop shopping service for older adults"; and (4) development of "community-based alternatives to institutional care" (Schneider, 1992, 7).

More extensive cooperation among these three major sectors—education, social services, and the church—seems essential if real progress is to be made in developing collaborative approaches to working with and on behalf of older adults.

An example of this is an interesting new local effort started in Kansas City in 1990 by Dr. Elbert Cole—the Congregation Resource Center (CRC). The CRC is designed to connect the social welfare and church systems, organize services, and maintain service delivery in the local congregation; it links over 1,300 congregations in a ten-county area around Kansas City. It provides library services and training for congregational programming and sponsors projects such as a congregational nurse program (called parish nursing in other locations) and an extensive friendly visiting program for older adults under the state's guardianship.

Should the Church Be More Involved in Older Adult Programming?

We are facing a demographic and economic revolution, with rapidly increasing numbers of elders on the one hand, and a decreasing resource base with which to meet their needs on the other. Even were it desirable, it is totally improbable that the religious sector will ever have the resources to help the bulk of older adults in need, particularly in cases where requisite services are costly (for example, income, housing, medical care, and the like). The church is, however, an important resource to be used "in bridging the gaps that will be inevitably left between growing numbers of old people and shrinking public support" (Morris, 1986).

Theoretical Considerations. A basis for this perspective is offered by Berger and Neuhaus (1977), who discuss the church as one of a number of "mediating structures," organizations that interface on the one hand with the individual in rather informal (even intimate) ways, and on the other hand with the larger structures of which the whole social order is composed.

Marjorie Cantor (1991) describes the social support system for older adults. Midway between the individual and the formal system are quasi-formal "tertiary" supports that come from "mediating support elements." While care given by formal social services and governmental agencies and by family, friends, and neighbors is mediated through such support elements, most of the theoretical materials that address appropriate role division omit attention to them.

Primary groups and bureaucracies carry different but complementary roles. Litwak and Szelenyi (1969) looked at the tasks best suited to each system. Nuclear family members can handle repetitive tasks that demand long-term commitment and proximity but little expertise. Extended kin can help with those which require long-term commitment but less proximity. Friends can provide emotional support over the long haul. Neighbors can help in emergencies and with things requiring a short-term commitment. Formal agencies are needed for expertise, capital investment, and logistical support.

Given that the church can be so important in supporting persons, it is interesting that Litwak and Szelenyi did not even mention this resource. Nevertheless, the church in many cases can fulfill any of these functions. In a study of the religious patterns and participation of older adults, Payne (1988, 263) found that "receiving assistance from the church when they have needs in late life is next in preference to receiving from the family." The church is unique as a mediating institution; it has several characteristics that differentiate it. First, the church has a clear value base that places persons above profit or other organizational goals. Thus, in attempting to engage the church on behalf of those in need, including the elderly, it is possible to appeal to the church's own value base, rather than attempting to convince it of a new one (Wood, 1981; Wilson and Netting, 1988).

Second, the church is uniquely free from external prescription about the form and content of its organizational structure. Churches vary from denomination to denomination in the type and amount of structure they manifest. But even given denominational guidelines and more unofficial local norms, there is great room for diversity. Thus, an individual congregation is free to develop ad-hoc structures to achieve its goals.

Third, the church is an organization with open boundaries. Unlike many social service agencies and most other bureaucracies, the church is continually recruiting new members and is open to their having varying levels of participation.

The Roman Catholic Church has made some progress in developing social service delivery systems at the neighborhood level. This is made somewhat easier by the fact that the parish is defined as a neighborhood. Joseph and Conrad (1980, 427) describe the primary service offerings of such programs as "access services; individual, group and family counseling; volunteer activities; and work with the aging . . . [through services such as] meals on wheels, telephone networks, self-help programs, home visiting, . . . chore services and home repairs."

Benefits of Cooperative Efforts. Given overlapping goals and values, churches and social agencies can benefit in many ways from cooperative efforts, and, perhaps more important, so can those they serve. Some of these benefits are (cf. Tobin et al., 1986, 144–45; Biegel and Naparstek, 1981; S. L. Hendrickson, 1986):

1. Pooling and expanding resources such as space, volunteers, expertise, and finances.
2. Reaching the unreached. The church may provide a more accessible setting for providing services to persons with stigmatizing social or health problems.
3. Identifying gaps in service.
4. Facilitating information and referral.
5. Coordinating services (for example, to hospice patients who need both medical and religious services).
6. Gaining community acceptance through the multiple channels of communication available.
7. Increasing the skills of potential natural helpers by offering professional training.
8. Decreasing unneeded duplication of services. (In some instances, duplication of services is advisable; for example, provision of ethnic-religious nursing homes allows for maintaining dietary and other cultural components.)

9. Increasing service accessibility through utilizing neighborhood-based locations.
10. Reducing the sense of isolation of both agency and church workers.

Thus, an effective liaison among and between churches and the social service sector is very important if we are to meet the needs of older adults effectively.

A Model for Interagency Cooperation

The nature of the relationship between the church and the social service sector can vary enormously. Tobin et al. (1986) provide a comprehensive schema for examining the cooperative efforts of two or more organizations:

- *Communication:* Verbal, written, or other forms of communication between two or more organizations. Limited to sharing information or ideas between groups. This would include consultation.
- *Cooperation:* Two or more separate organizations plan and implement independent programs but work toward similar, nonconflicting goals. The organizations share information but act on it independently. Organizations advertise for each other and try to avoid unnecessary duplication of services.
- *Coordination:* Two or more separate organizations work together as they plan and implement separate programs. Efforts are made to ensure the programs interact smoothly and avoid conflict, waste, or unnecessary duplication of services. Organizations share information, advertise for each other, and make referrals to each other.
- *Collaboration:* Two or more separate organizations join together to provide a single program or service. Each organization maintains its own identity, but resources are jointly shared.
- *Confederation:* Two or more organizations merge to provide programs or services. None of the participating organizations maintains a separate identity or separate resources (149).

Steinitz (1980) described four types of linkages found in the churches in the community she studied: "occasional joint church-agency programs, the use of church space by agencies, information and referral contacts and contacts made to churches by social agencies involved in outreach to the elderly" (136). All of these would fit into the above framework.

We would expect to find numerous examples of all of Tobin's (1986) categories in church-church and church-agency collaborative efforts, except for the last (confederation), although an interesting example of confederation of multichurch services was found in Nashville. There, three separate intercongregational service efforts were merged in order to provide administrative and public relations efficiency, both resulting in more services and expanding them to the entire metropolitan area (Webb, 1992).

Categorizing Services by Auspices

Services can also be categorized in terms of their sponsorship. A typology of such auspices would include:

I. Denominational efforts
  - Congregational
  - Judicatory
  - Independent, denominationally-sponsored social services

II. Interfaith models
  - Services exclusively for older adults
    - Shepherd Centers
    - Interfaith voluntary caregiving
    - Interfaith coalitions
    - Miscellaneous others
  - General social services agencies
  - Council of Churches spin-offs
  - Ad-hoc grassroots organizations

III. Social service efforts (private and/or governmental)
  - Area agencies on aging
  - Councils on aging
  - Elder-care initiative

IV. Private national organizations
  - The American Association of Retired Persons (AARP)
  - National Interfaith Coalition on Aging (NICA)
  - American Society on Aging (ASA)

Denominational Efforts. To date only one nationwide study of denominational efforts on behalf of older persons has been undertaken (Lewis, 1989), but such organizations as the National Interfaith Coalition on Aging (since 1991 a constituent member of the National Council on Aging) and the Forum on Religion, Spirituality and Aging (of the American Society on Aging) have provided vehicles for sharing information about what is going on in this field.

The Presbyterian Church, one of few national denominations with full-time older adult ministry staff, has developed a network of "Older Adult Enablers," who work throughout judicatory and congregational bodies to promote older adult ministry.

The Roman Catholic Church has been a leader nationally in development of a model respite care program. Church members are recruited, trained, and placed to give substitute care to the frail elderly in order to provide temporary relief to the primary caregiver (Eastman and Kane, undated).

As indicated earlier, a number of denominations have independent social service programs that serve older adults. Primary leaders in this endeavor are Roman Catholics, Lutherans, and Jews. Presbyterian, Baptist, and Episcopal bodies have also been leaders in the development of retirement facilities.

Judicatory bodies vary enormously in what they are willing and able to do. Blessed by a trust fund with a specific mission in older adult ministry, the Episcopal Diocese of Tennessee has been able to recruit and train "Affirmative Aging Advocates" in almost all of the congregations in the diocese to do education and other programming on a congregational level. Further, it has facilitated interfaith and social service connections for its congregations. The program, called "Affirmative Aging," is based on the assumption that older adults are at least as much doers of ministry as they are receivers. It attempts to empower older adults to have a positive impact on their congregations and communities.

Interfaith Models. Among the more interesting examples of interfaith collaboration are the Shepherd's Center movement and the National Federation of Interfaith Volunteer Caregivers (and their local affiliates). The former is a multipurpose organization begun as a local effort in Kansas City, whereas the latter is a single-function network funded by the Robert Wood Johnson Foundation to support volunteer caregiving efforts. We will describe each of them in some detail.

The Shepherd's Center movement, begun in Kansas City in 1972 by Dr. Elbert Cole, has spread throughout the country and elsewhere. There are now ninety-six centers serving over 200,000 participants. A Shepherd's Center is a nonprofit corporation, designed "to empower older adults to develop and provide programs with services which improve the quality of life for older adults in their communities" (Shepherd's Centers of America). It is based within and serves a clearly defined neighborhood, within which all religious congregations are invited to participate.

Shepherd's Centers do not duplicate already existing services, but work with them and fill in service gaps. Members determine their own priorities, and programs are undertaken only when there are volunteers willing to staff them. Most have educational programs. Many have meals on wheels, chore services, and other life maintenance programs. Each center sets its own priorities and determines its own programs.

Shepherd's Centers have few paid staff members (usually only one); they depend entirely upon the members to research, plan, develop, and deliver their services. Thus they are really services "by, with, and for" older adults. Shepherd's

Centers use existing space within member congregations, both in order to save costs and to maintain the interfaith character of the program. The national Shepherd's Centers of America organization provides technical assistance and training to those interested in forming new centers.

The National Federation of Interfaith Volunteer Caregivers (NFIVC) had its roots in a Robert Wood Johnson Foundation grant for the founding of twenty-five local Interfaith Volunteer Caregiving (IVC) organizations. NFIVC developed linkages among these and other interfaith programs to provide technical assistance and a clearinghouse capacity to member organizations, and to encourage the development of additional centers. Currently there are over two hundred IVCs in the United States. While they differ greatly in structure and programming, all attempt to reach out to the frail elderly and their caregivers and support them through services of the interfaith community.

One innovative program began recently in New Haven, Connecticut as a joint effort of the IVC of Greater New Haven and the Yale University School of Nursing, supported by a grant from the Kellogg Foundation. Called BEST (Better Elder Services Today), this IVC has the ambitious goal of improving the system of health-care delivery in the community. "The program is unique in bringing together the natural, volunteer, and professional caregivers as well as community living elders . . . to make community living possible for frail elders" (NFIVC, 1992).

The Robert Wood Johnson Foundation also has funded six sites around the country to test the idea of *service credit banking* (variously known as Time-Dollar, Credits for Caring, and Samaritans' Cooperative Bank). Such projects recruit elderly volunteers to help other elders remain in their homes for as long as possible.

One of the sites, Grace Hill Neighborhood Services in St. Louis, Missouri, is sponsored by an interfaith organization, two sectarian hospitals, and a number of individual church congregations ranging from Roman Catholic to Baptist. An interfaith coalition in Miami is also developing a multiple-sponsor model.

One of the difficulties in recruiting volunteers is coordinating efforts among religious congregations and potential recipients of help; the NIVFC approach may provide a viable intermediary, interfacing the formal and informal caregiving sectors of the community. It also allows for persons with an interest in serving others to make provisions for the time when they may not have sufficient resources to meet their own needs.

Although not designed specifically for the religious community, this model can be used by congregational and interfaith groups. It can easily be run (using the Ellor and Coates typology) as a cooperative or a collaborative program.

Intergenerational Efforts. There is increasing concern that intergenerational conflict may result from competition for scarce public resources, and there is increasing recognition that both older adults and children benefit from intergenerational programs. As a result, a number of groups and coalitions are being formed to promote intergenerational activities.

Perhaps the most significant of these is Generations United (GU), a coalition of over one hundred national organizations. Among its leaders are the American Association of Retired Persons, the Child Welfare League of America, the Children's Defense Fund, and the National Council on the Aging. One program sponsored by GU is the West End Intergenerational Residence in New York City, which "provides transitional housing to a mix of seniors, mothers and children, who support one another through social, recreational and grandparent programs" (Generations United, 1992).

Social Service Efforts. Since the passage of the Older Americans Act in 1965, Area Agencies on Aging (AAAs) have been charged with overall planning for services for older adults. AAAs are varied in their sponsorship, with some receiving public funds and others relying on private resources. They are varied in their jurisdiction (ranging from subcounty through regional to statewide); and varied in whether they run, supervise, or only attempt to coordinate programs. Some administer funding while others do not. Likewise they vary in the degree of their cooperation with the religious sector.

Joyce Berry, Commissioner of the Administration on Aging under President Bush, set in motion what is called the "Eldercare Campaign." This effort stems from a number of changed conditions, including the rapidly increasing number of older adults (especially in the group over eighty-five, the "oldest old") and the decreasing availability of funding for all social programs, including those for older adults. The campaign attempts to involve sectors other than social services in addressing the problems of older adults. Thus, business and industry, the private nonprofit sector, the religious community, civic organizations, and government are attempting to build partnerships together.

The three goals of the Eldercare Campaign are (1) to expand resources by involving nontraditional players; (2) to increase public awareness of the demographics and of the needs of frail older adults; and (3) to put the emphasis on the local level by creating coalitions to identify and meet local needs.

The Tennessee Eldercare Corps Advisory Committee, for example, has put together a plan to help localities recruit and equip community members to participate in the campaign. Using personnel from the state Commission on Aging, regional Area Agency on Aging leaders, local and judicatory church staff with responsibilities in older adult ministry, and others knowledgeable about the aging network, it has begun pilot work in four diverse geographic areas. The Administration on Aging has funded this project to provide staffing and training support. Initial results look promising for creating a new partnership to improve services for older adults in that state.

Private National Organizations. The Interreligious Liaison Office (IRLO) of the American Association of Retired Persons (AARP) is charged with providing technical assistance, conferences, publications, and volunteer consultation to the religious community (local, state, and national) in addressing issues of older adults. The IRLO also works in the religious and aging networks to help in bridging the gap between the two.

The National Interfaith Coalition on Aging was founded after the 1971 White House Conference on Aging to address the spiritual needs of older adults and to provide linkage between religious organizations and the aging network. Since 1991 NICA has been a constituent member of the National Council on Aging. NICA is involved in research and provides resources to congregations, denominational bodies, and local and regional interfaith coalitions.

The Forum on Religion, Spirituality and Aging (FRSA) of the American Society on Aging was developed to meet the needs of practitioners working with older adults. Its membership includes social service, medical, and religious professionals. FRSA is a resource for educational programs, conferences, and publications on issues of religion, aging, and spirituality.

SUMMARY AND CONCLUSIONS

The last decade has seen the emergence of a new era in regard to social services and aging. No longer are funds available in almost unlimited quantities; no longer are we able to envision meeting basic needs of most older adults through government programs alone. Rather, we are facing on the one hand a tidal wave of older adults, and on the other a dearth of resources to meet their needs. The widening gap is a major challenge. The church, academia, government, business and industry, and the civic sector all are affected, and they will be even more so in the next forty years. All will be called upon to work together in new and innovative ways.

In this chapter we have examined theoretical and practical links and barriers to such cooperation and have noted a variety of efforts to address these problems under a range of auspices.

The potential of the church to work in such partnerships should not be either over- or underestimated. It is not possible for the church to be the primary resource to meet many of the needs of tomorrow's older adults; but in cooperation with the other sectors mentioned, the church can be (and often already is) a major player in linking these sectors and in improving the quality of life for older adults.

In all such efforts, we should keep in mind the diversity of the older adult population. While the concern of some programs, such as the Eldercare initiative, is primarily for the frail, care-needing population, most older adults are actually active volunteers contributing to the solution of social problems. A study commissioned by the Administration on Aging found that 41 percent of older adults (15.5 million) are currently volunteering and that there is a potential pool of another 14.1 million who are potential volunteers (Berry, undated).

The church is the one institution in our society charged with addressing issues of meaning and purpose. All the rest of the current and potential aging network members may touch on these issues peripherally, but it is the church which must face them head on. Serving as a vehicle for recruiting older adults, and plugging them into "vocations," callings, which provide opportunities to be of service, may well be the most important function of the church in community organization. The challenge to help make these connections confronts us all.

BIBLIOGRAPHY

Adams, R. G., and B. J. Stark (1988) "Church Conservatism and Services for the Elderly." *Journal of Religion and Aging,* 69–85.

Andron, S. (1982) "Synagogue-federation Relations: An Empirical Assessment." *Journal of Jewish Communal Service* 58 (3):199–207.

Bachmann, T. (1955–56) *The Churches and Social Welfare: Proceedings of the First Conference on the Church and Social Welfare.* Vol. 3. New York: National Council of Churches in the U.S.

Berger, P. L., and R. J. Neuhaus (1977) *To Empower People: The Role of Mediating Structures in Public Policy.* Washington, D.C.: American Enterprise Institute for Public Policy Research.

Berry, J. (N.d.) *In Touch with Commissioner Berry.* Undated pamphlet. Washington, D.C.: U.S. Administration on Aging.

Biegel, D. E., and A. J. Naparstek (1981) "The Neighborhood and Family Services Project: An Empowerment Model Linking Clergy, Agency Professionals and Community Residents." In Jeger and Slotnick, 303–18.

Bonnyman, G. (1992) Speech, "The Role of the Church in the Health Care Crisis," a conference of the Office of Affirmative Aging, Episcopal Diocese of Tennessee; Nashville, May 2.

Cantor, M. H. (1991) "Family and Community: Changing Roles in an Aging Society." *The Gerontologist* 31:337–46.

Cayton, H. R., and S. M. Nishi (1955) *The Churches and Social Welfare.* Vol. 2: *The Changing Scene, Current Trends and Issues.* New York: National Council of the Churches of Christ in the U.S.A.

Cole, E. (1991) "Church and Community, Partners in Service." Workshop at McKendree Village, Nashville, September 6.

______ (1992) Personal communication.

Cook, T. C., Jr. (1977) *The Religious Sector Explores its Mission in Aging.* Athens, Ga.: National Interfaith Coalition on Aging.

Eastman, P., and A. Kane (N.d.) *Respite: Helping Caregivers Keep Elderly Relatives at Home.* Washington, D.C.: National Council of Catholic Women.

Ellor, J. W. (1983) "Bridging Churches and Social Service Agencies: Value Conflicts and Program Potential." *Social Work and Christianity* 10 (1):21–39.

Ellor, J. W., and R. B. Coates (1985–86) "Examining the Role of the Church in the Aging Network." *Journal of Religion and Aging* 2:99–116.

Ellor, J. W., and S. S. Tobin (1990) "Serving the Older Person: The Church's Role." In Garland and Pancost, 184–93.

Felton, R. A. (1920) *Serving the Neighborhood.* New York: Inter-church World Movement of North America.

Garland, D. R., and D. Pancost, eds. (1990) *Marriage and the Family.* Granada Hills, Calif.: Baker.

Generations United (1992) Generations United. Brochure.

Haber, D. (1984) "Church-based Mutual Help Groups for Caregivers of Non-institutionalized Elders." *Journal of Religion and Aging* 1 (1):63–69.

Hendrickson, M. (1985–86) "The Role of the Church in Aging: Implications for Policy and Action." *Journal of Religion and Aging* 2 (1–2):5–16.

______ (1986a) *The Role of the Church in Aging.* Vol. 2: *Implications for Practice and Service.* New York: Haworth.

______ (1986b) *The Role of the Church in Aging.* Vol. 3: *Programs and Services for Seniors.* New York: Haworth.

Hendrickson, S. L. (1986) "Churches as Geriatric Health Clinics for Community Based Elderly." *Journal of Religion and Aging* 2:13–24.

Holmes, W. A. (1968) *Tomorrow's Church: A Cosmopolitan Community.* Nashville: Abingdon.

Huber, L. W. (1985) "Connections: A Study of the Place of the Church in the Personal Networks of the Aged." Ph.D. dissertation, School of Applied Social Sciences, Case Western Reserve University, Cleveland, Ohio.

______ (1987) "Connections: Congregational Differences in the Place of the Church of the Personal Networks of Elderly Members." *Journal of Religion and Aging* 4 (2):59–73.

Jeger, A., and R. Slotnick, eds. (1981) *Community Mental Health: A Behavioral Ecological Perspective.* New York, Plenum Press.

Joseph, M. V., and A. P. Conrad. (1980) "A Parish Neighborhood Model for Social Work Practice." *Social Casework* 61:423–32.

Kemp, C. F. (1960) *The Pastor and Community Resources.* St. Louis: Bethany.

Lewis, M. A. (1989) *Religious Congregations and the Informal Supports of the Frail Elderly.* New York: Third Age Center, Fordham University.

Litwak, E., and I. Szelenyi (1969) "Primary Group Structures and Their Functions: Kin, Neighbors and Friends." *American Sociological Review* 34 (4):465–81.

Marty, M. E. (1980) "Social Service: Godly and Godless." *Social Service Review* 54:463–81.

Maves, P. B. (1981) *Older Volunteers in Church and Community: A Manual for Ministry.* Valley Forge: Judson Press.

Moberg, D. O. (1962) *The Church as a Social Institution: The Sociology of American Religion.* Englewood Cliffs, N.J.: Prentice Hall.

______ (1972) "Religion and the Aging Family." *Family Coordinator* 21 (1):47–60.

Morris, J. N. (1986) "Issues in Publicly Subsidized Long Term Care Systems and Implications for the Religious Sector." *Journal of Religion and Aging* 2 (1–2):151–63.

National Federation of Interfaith Volunteer Caregivers, Inc. (1992) *Annual Report.*

National Interfaith Coalition on Aging (1976) *Survey of Programs for Aging under Religious Auspices.* National Interfaith Coalition on Aging, Inc., Grant Report AOA # 93-HD-57390/4-03.

Negstad, J., and R. Arnholt (1986) "Day Centers for Older Adults: Parish and Agency Partnership." *Journal of Religion and Aging* 2 (4):25–31.

Netting, F. E. (1987) "Spinning Off: A Case Study of the Secularization of Church-related Social Services for the Elderly." *Journal of Religion and Aging* 3 (3–4):115–25.

Payne, B. P. (1988) "Religious Patterns and Participation of Older Adults: A Sociological Perspective." *Educational Gerontology* 14:255–67.

Piedmont, E. B. (1968) "Referrals and Reciprocity: Psychiatrists, General Practitioners, and Clergymen." *Journal of Health and Social Behavior* 9 (1):29–41.

Presbyterian Publishing House (1987) *Older Adult Ministry: A Resource for Program Development.* Atlanta, Ga.: Presbyterian Publishing House.

Robert Wood Johnson Foundation (1990) "Service Credit Banking." Project Site Summaries. University of Maryland Center on Aging.

Schneider, V. et al. (1992) "CRANECE—Church in Rural Aging Networks: Education and Collaborative Efforts." Unpublished manuscript, West Virginia University Gerontology Center, Morgantown, W. Va.

Schoenberg, S., and P. Rosenbaum (1980) *Neighborhoods that Work: Sources for Viability in the Inner City.* New Brunswick, N.J.: Rutgers University Press.

Schwanke, E. R. (1986) "Providing Pastoral Care for the Elderly in Long Term Care Facilities without a Chaplain Utilizing Coordinated Congregational Resources." In Hendrickson 1986a, 57–64.

Sheehan, N. W., R. Wilson, and L. M. Marella (1988) "The Role of the Church in Providing Services for the Aging." *Journal of Applied Gerontology* 7:231–41.

Shepherd's Centers of America (N.d.) In-house brochure.

Sherwood, S., and E. Bernstein (1985–86) "Informal Care for Vulnerable Elderly: Suggestions for Church Involvement." *Journal of Religion and Aging* 2 (1–2):55–67.

Steinitz, L. Y. (1980) "The Church within the Network of Social Services to the Elderly: Case Study of Laketown." Dissertation, School of Social Service Administration, University of Chicago.

______ (1981) "The Local Church as Support for the Elderly." *Journal of Gerontological Social Work* 4:44–53.

Synagogue Council of America (1975) *That Thy Days May Be Long in the Good Land: A Guide to Aging Programs for Synagogues.* New York: Synagogue Council of America.

Tobin, S., J. Ellor, and S. Anderson-Ray (1986) *Enabling the Elderly: Religious Institutions within the Community Service System.* Albany, N.Y.: State University of New York Press.

United Presbyterian Church (1967) *The Church and Aging.* New York: United Presbyterian Church in the U.S.

Webb, D. (1992) Personal interview with the director of FOCUS, Nashville.

Wilson, V., and F. E. Netting (1988) "Exploring the Interface of Local Churches with the Aging Network: A Comparison of Anglo and Black Congregations." *Journal of Aging and Religion* 5 (1–2):51–60.

Wood, J. R. (1981) *Leadership in Voluntary Organizations: The Controversy over Social Action in Protestant Churches.* New Brunswick, N.J.: Rutgers University Press.

Young, K. R. (1954) "Social Services Provided by the Congregations of the Lutheran Church—Missouri Synod, in Saint Louis During 1953 to their Aged Members." Ph.D. dissertation, George Warren Brown School of Social Work, Washington University, St. Louis.

21 Church-Based Support Programs for Elderly Black Adults: Congregational and Clergy Characteristics

CLEOPATRA HOWARD CALDWELL
LINDA M. CHATTERS
ANDREW BILLINGSLEY
ROBERT JOSEPH TAYLOR

INTRODUCTION

The prominence of religious and church involvement in the lives of African Americans has prompted a number of writers to suggest that Black churches could constitute an organizational base that would encourage and actively promote the provision of social service and public health programs to various constituent groups (e.g., older adults, children, and youth). The development and effective implementation of health and social service programs within the context of Black churches requires the consideration of several questions that address basic issues concerning the nature of Black religious involvement, organizational traits, and factors affecting the operation of Black churches and the relationship of the church to the African American community as well as to the instititutions of wider society. The present chapter reviews the relevant literature on these topics and explores these issues in relation to church-based supportive programs that serve older adults. In addition, this study utilizes data from the Black Church Family Project to explore these questions among a sample of northern Black churches.

The chapter begins with a review of what is currently known regarding the religious participation of older Black adults and the determinants and characteristics of religious-based support networks. Following this, we review the role that Black churches have played in African American communities more broadly and their specific relationship to older Black adults. A description of the Black Church Family Project introduces the conceptual model that serves as a foundation for the study and discusses the methodology that was employed, characteristics of the Black church sample, and the major study variables. Following this, a profile of general church-based outreach programs is presented, along with a description of the types of elderly support programs that are offered. Next, congregation and clergy characteristics are used to differentiate between churches with and without elderly support programs. Finally, the concluding section discusses these findings more broadly and provides a profile of the congregation and clergy characteristics that are associated with supportive programs for older adults.

Religious Participation among Elderly Black Adults

A general profile of religious involvement among elderly Black adults indicates that religion and religious institutions play a primary role in their lives. Studies based on the National Survey of Black Americans data support a picture of an extensive degree of religious involvement among this group (Chatters and Taylor, 1989; Taylor, 1988a, 1988b). In comparison to their younger counterparts, older Black adults had a higher probability of being a religious affiliate (Taylor, 1988a), of having attended religious services as an adult (Chatters and Taylor, 1989; Taylor, 1988b), and of being a church member (Chatters and Taylor, 1989; Taylor, 1988b). In addition, older persons engaged in nonorganizational religious behaviors on a more frequent basis (e.g., reading religious materials, listening or watching to religious broadcasts, praying, requests for prayer) (Chatters and Taylor, 1989; Taylor, 1988b) and expressed a higher degree of subjective religious involvement (Taylor, 1988b). Collectively, these findings indicate that religion assumes a prominent position in the lives of older Black adults.

An analysis of denominational affiliation among older Black adults revealed that over half of this population was Baptists (54.7 percent), 13.6 percent were Methodists, 5.7 percent were Roman Catholic, and the remaining percentage of respondents were distributed across twenty-five different religious affiliations (Taylor, 1993). With regard to religious participation, only 3.4 percent of elderly Black adults indicated that they had not attended religious services since they were eighteen years old (other than weddings or funerals). Half of all elderly Blacks attended religious services at least once a week, and eight of ten attended at least a few times a month. Three out of four (77.6 percent) elderly Blacks were church members, almost half (43.9 percent) read religious books nearly every day, one-third (33.8 percent) watched or listened to religious programming nearly every day, and nine out of ten (93.6 percent) indicated that they prayed nearly every day (Taylor, 1993). Analysis of the demographic correlates of these religious behaviors revealed significant gender, age, marital status, urbanicity, and health differences. One of the largest and most consistent differences was gender, whereby older Black women displayed significantly higher levels of religious participation than did elderly Black men. With regard to marital status differences, divorced and widowed respondents exhibited lower levels of religious involvement than married respondents (Taylor, 1986a; Taylor and Chatters, 1991). In addition, age was positively associated with the frequency of prayer.

Taylor and Chatters's (1991) examination of nonorganizational religious involvement among older Black adults found that demographic factors and health disability predicted levels of nonorganizational religious participation. Although health disability was positively associated with frequency of watching or listening to religious programs, it was not significantly related to other religious variables (prayer, reading religious materials, requests for prayer). These findings, in conjunction with other work using the NSBA sample (Taylor, 1986a), suggest that rather than substituting nonorganizational practices for organizational religious activities, persons in poor health engage in both types of behaviors simultaneously. Although they are comparable to their healthier counterparts with regard to church attendance, their higher rates of viewer/listenership suggest that they use broadcast religious programming to supplement rather than substitute for formal activities.

Determinants and Characteristics of Religious-Based Social Networks

Although it is generally accepted that church members are important sources of assistance to Blacks, this issue has received surprisingly little systematic attention and scrutiny. Recent analyses have examined the role of church members as a source of informal social support to elderly Black adults (Taylor and Chatters, 1986a, 1986b) and Black adults across the entire age range (Taylor and Chatters, 1988a). The primary emphasis is on examining the social structure determinants of church-based support networks and their functional role in providing social support. Taylor and Chatters (1986a) found that church members provided a variety of forms of social support. Frequency of church attendance as a form of public commitment was a critical indicator of both receiving assistance and the amount of support provided. An examination of different sources of aid (Taylor and Chatters, 1986b) demonstrated that older adults received concomitant support from family, friends, and church members. Eight of ten respondents received support from either a best or a close friend, about six in ten received support from church members, and over half received support from extended family members. Analysis of type of support received indicated that advice, encouragement, and help during sickness were the most frequently reported forms of assistance.

Analyses involving the full adult age range found that socio-demographic and religious factors were predictors of the receipt of support from church members (Taylor and Chatters, 1988a). Overall, two out of three respondents (64.2 percent) indicated that church members provided some level of support to them. Church attendance, church membership, subjective religiosity, and religious affiliation were all significantly related to the receipt of support. The salience of network involvement variables as determinants of the receipt of assistance is congruent with research suggesting that level of support is linked to degree of network participation and integration.

The Role of Churches in African American Communities

Black churches traditionally have played an important role in the evolution of African American family and community life. Black Americans have relied upon churches to provide not only religious and spiritual guidance, but also emotional, economic, and social support. Further, churches constituted the institutional foundations for various educational, civic, and political enterprises (Lincoln and Mamiya, 1990). These roles and functions of the Black church were critical, given the economic hardships and social inequalities that resulted from the African American's denial and exclusion from fully active and effective participation within larger society (Williams and Williams, 1984). Lincoln and Mamiya's (1990) exhaustive and perceptive analysis of Black churches argues that African American religious traditions emanated from the unique and dynamic social, political, and historical contexts that characterized the position of Blacks within American society. Because Black religious traditions occur within the context of a larger society that was frequently overtly hostile to Blacks, the aims and purposes of religious belief and expression were uniquely oriented and adapted toward the betterment of the life circumstances that affected this group.

Since their inception, Black churches have provided various forms of support and services to their individual members and the broader Black community (Frazier, 1974; Lincoln and Mamiya, 1990; Mays and Nicholson, 1933; Taylor and Chatters, 1986a; Roberts, 1980). Independent Black churches in the north began their rise to prominence as early as 1740 and were fully developed as an institutional segment of African American communities by 1800 (Smith, 1988). It was not until the outbreak of World War I and the mass migration of African Americans from southern to northern cities, however, that the Black church developed its present preeminence as a community center (Frazier, 1974). Major Black churches in northern cities, headed by leaders such as Adam Clayton Powell in New York City and Leon Sullivan in Philadelphia, broke new ground in their secular community outreach mission during the 1960s (Lincoln, 1973). By 1979, community outreach had become a major activity of many urban Black churches (Lincoln and Mamiya, 1990).

Early efforts to examine the community functions of Black churches include Mays and Nicholson's (1933) empirical investigation of the importance of religion to African Americans and the community outreach role of Black churches in the late 1920s. Researchers have since documented the contributions of contemporary Black churches as: (1) political agents for social change (Harris,

1987); (2) sponsors of educational programs for children and youth (George et al., 1989; Billingsley and Caldwell, 1991); and (3) providers of social service programs involving families and the community (Billingsley et al., 1991; Lincoln and Mamiya, 1990). Finally, Eng et al. (1985) suggested that the development of church-based support programs provides a unique outreach opportunity and encompasses a number of distinct benefits. They concluded that the effectiveness of community-based service delivery is, in large measure, contingent upon the status of the provider organization. Given the high regard and allegiance that the Black church continues to possess among many African Americans, religious institutions are in an ideal position to assess and provide needed services and, further, to encourage participation in the wider formal service delivery system. These advantages are particularly salient for African American elderly, given possible decrements in informal social supports (Chatters et al., 1985, 1986; Taylor and Chatters, 1986b).

Black Churches and the Elderly

It is estimated that roughly 78 percent of elderly African Americans belong to a church (Taylor, 1986a). A general profile of church functions indicates that they promote contact and social integration among members that contribute to the emotional well-being of the elderly (Johnson and Barer, 1990; Taylor et al., 1987; Steinitz, 1981). Further, churches provide concrete help in the form of Day Centers for older adults (Negstad and Arnholt, 1986) and medical screenings for various diseases and conditions (Tobin et al., 1986; Eng et al., 1985). Others (Taylor et al., 1990; Tobin et al., 1986) have emphasized the importance of outreach programs that are jointly sponsored by a group of churches and the role that churches can play in establishing linkages to social service agencies as a means of expanding services to the elderly.

Against this backdrop of current information about churches and their relationships to older Black adults, we can estimate the future growth in the size of the older Black population and consider the extent and nature of their projected social welfare needs and requirements. The number of persons aged sixty and over is expected to increase to 500 million by the year 2025 (Letzig, 1986). Since 1930, the African American population over sixty-five has been increasing at a considerably faster rate relative to the older White population (Manuel, 1988). Clearly, demographic changes of this magnitude will require a major reappraisal of the nature, variety, and breadth of services that will be necessary to meet the needs of older citizens. Given the many challenges (e.g., greater poverty, lack of affordable housing, limited access to medical care) facing African American elderly today (Taylor and Chatters, 1988b), it is essential that we develop a more comprehensive understanding of those community-based support services that maintain and enhance their social well-being as well as their mental and physical functioning.

Previous research documents that, prior to entering the formal service delivery system, African American elderly will engage assistance from Black churches (Taylor and Chatters, 1986a; Walls and Zarit, 1991). However, very little is known about the types of services that are provided in this context. Those few studies that have examined this issue directly focus on one or more of the following dimensions of church-based aid: emotional support, spiritual guidance, social integration, or instrumental support (Haber, 1984; Steinitz, 1981; Taylor et al., 1987; Taylor and Chatters, 1986a; Walls and Zarit, 1991). Further, the majority of work in this area has concentrated solely on the social support that only the members of a church receive. Many churches, however, extend their mission and responsibility beyond the borders of their congregational membership to address the needs of the community at large. In an effort to further delineate and understand the roles that Black churches can play in the provision of social services for the elderly, we must first assess the characteristics of those particular churches that are currently involved in offering these services to members and nonmembers alike.

The purpose of this chapter is to examine the types of outreach programs that are sponsored by contemporary Black churches to meet the needs of elderly adults. We will highlight a number of characteristics that distinguish churches that, as a part of their mission, sponsor programs that provide both instrumental assistance and emotional support to elderly persons who are not congregational members. This chapter relies on information from 635 Black churches in the northern portion of the United States that are part of a larger study, "The Black Church Family Project." The purpose of this project was to examine the outreach programs that Black churches sponsor to assist families in need. The methodology for the Project is described below.

The Black Church Family Project

The Black Church Family Project is designed to identify and describe family and community support programs that are available within a nationally representative sample of Black churches. The specific outreach programs of interest are those that satisfy the requirements that: (1) their programmatic objectives and activities are designed to enhance and support the functioning of African American families; and (2) they include an identifiable outreach component that offers services to persons who were *not* church members. Based on the assumption that Black churches are distributed in a manner similar to that of African American households, the church sample was drawn using the basic sampling strategy developed for the National Survey of Black Americans (NSBA) at the Institute for Social Research. The NSBA sample itself was drawn according to a multistage area probability procedure designed to ensure that every Black household had an equal chance of selection for the study. Based on the 1970 census distribution of the Black population, seventy-six primary sampling areas were selected to represent the nation. These areas were stratified by racial composition and geographic areas called "clusters" (Chatters, Taylor, and Jackson, 1985).

For the Black Church Family Project, the desired total sample size of 1,500 churches was allocated across the four geographic regions of the country (i.e., northeast, north central, south, and west) in proportion to the number of African American households in each region. In addition, faith tradition was used as a major stratifying variable for the Black church study. Due to the uncertainty in estimating eligibility and response rates for Black churches, a replicated sampling procedure was used. This resulted in a final sample of 315 churches in the northeast and 320 churches in the north central region. This chapter presents results from the 635 northern Black churches that reflect the combined data from the northeastern and north central regions of the country. Each of the interviews were taken with the senior minister or a knowledgeable informant designated by the minister. Interviews were conducted by telephone and were approximately thirty minutes in duration. The overall response rate for the study in the North is 57 percent.

To date, this is the most extensive and systematic study focusing on the outreach efforts of Black churches. The study builds on other pioneering work that, in conjunction with this effort, documents that the Black church is a well-established and independent mainstay within the African American community. Further, the Black church possesses the economic, political, and social potential to provide major leadership in the next era of social reform (Billingsley et al., 1991).

The Black Church Family Project's Conceptual Model

The basic conceptual model of the Black Church Family Project assumes that the family comprises the first level of the social environment (see Table 21.1). The African American family is encompassed by a number of social forces and community-level institutions located in varying degrees of proximity to the family (Billingsley, 1993). The Black church, as one of these community-level institutions, is positioned between the family and formal service delivery systems that are organized at the society level. Thus, the Black church is in an optimal position both to provide assistance to families and to serve as a referral network to formal social service institutions when necessary. In essence, a reciprocal relationship exists between families and churches and, in turn, churches constitute a primary conduit or mediating structure (Lincoln and Mamiya, 1990) between families and the formal service delivery system. This arrangement provides a foundation and opportunity for the church to assist and nurture the family as an autonomous primary support provider, as well as through participation in cooperative efforts with other community institutions and agencies and the larger social system.

TABLE 21.1
Types of Community Outreach Programs Provided across the Life Cycle

Program Type	*% of Programs*	*% of Programs*
Children and Youth	31.3	566
– Child Welfare		
– Scouting		
– Parenting/Sexuality		
– Mentoring		
– Teen Support		
– Recreational		
– AIDS Awareness		
– Substance Abuse		
– Head Start		
– Basic Education		
– Academic Support		
Adult Family Support	51.2	923
– Family Counseling		
– Child Care		
– Adult Literacy		
– AIDS Awareness and Support		
– Substance Abuse		
– Food Distribution		
– Clothing Distribution		
– Shelter		
Elderly	8.5	153
– Home Care		
– Fellowship/Social		
– Meals-on-Wheels		
– Housing		
– Multi-services		
– Financial		
– Medical		
Community Development—All Groups	9.0	162
– Community Housing		
– Economic Development		
– Health-related Services		
– Community Development Corps		
– Social Action Activities		
Totals	100	1804

Employing this conceptualization, our focus is on the specific types of assistance programs that northern Black churches provide for community elderly through their organized outreach efforts. This chapter will provide baseline data on the nature of church-based services to the elderly and the characteristics of churches that sponsor such support programs. Our particular focus is on the Black church as a service delivery system. As such, we are interested in examining: (1) whether and to what extent Black churches operate in this manner; and (2) whether they possess a number of indigenous organizational characteristics that may be attractive to elderly persons who need assistance and that, in addition, facilitate the church's functioning in a service delivery capacity.

Description of Churches in the Sample

The churches in this sample range in age from one to 203 years, with a median age of 37 years. Most churches are stable fixtures in their communities; half have resided at the same location for twenty years or more and 74 percent have moved two or fewer times in their history. The majority of churches (75 percent) are located in neighborhoods that are described as mostly Black or all Black. A variety of faith traditions are represented in the sample. As the majority of Black churches are Baptist (Jacquet, 1989; Payne, 1991; Taylor and Chatters, 1991), it was anticipated that the largest portion of the 635 churches would be Baptist (44 percent). The second largest group is Methodist churches (13 percent), followed by Pentecostal (11 percent), Church of God in Christ [COGIC] (7 percent), and Apostolic (4 percent) churches. The remaining faith traditions include a variety of other Christian religious groups such as Episcopalian, Presbyterian, and Seventh-Day Adventist. Worship services are held on at least a weekly basis in virtually all of these churches (99 percent); 63 percent of churches indicate that they occasionally or frequently sponsor nonreligious activities at the church.

Fifty-eight percent of respondents report that their congregations are comprised of both working- and middle-class persons, 31 percent state that their congregation is working-class exclusively, and only 8 percent indicate that their congregation is middle-class. A diversity of congregational sizes are represented in the study, with memberships ranging from as few as six to as many as 5,000 members; approximately half of the churches have 162 members or more. As with most churches in this country, the vast majority (88 percent) of churches in the sample have congregations in which greater than 50 percent of the members are female. Clergy positions within the Black church remain very much male-dominated; 93 percent of the senior ministers are men and only 7 percent are women. Seventy-five percent of these ministers are between the ages of thirty-five and sixty-four years and 90 percent are married. The senior ministers of northern churches are highly educated, with 68 percent possessing some level of college training or more. Additionally, 80 percent of the senior ministers have received seminary or Bible College training.

Slightly more than half of the churches (56 percent) have one paid minister, 30 percent have no paid clergy at all, and the remaining 14 percent of churches have two or more paid clergy. Interestingly, 65 percent of the senior ministers of these churches have no employment outside the church. Roughly half (51 percent) of the churches have paid staff other than the senior minister. Finally, an impressive 62 percent of these congregations entirely own their church structure and an additional 28 percent are in the process of purchasing their building. Only 8 percent of the churches in this study are renting their church home. Sixty-seven percent (n = 426) of the churches in this sample sponsor at least one outreach program in the wider community and, of these, 28 percent or 120 churches offer support programs for the elderly.

Types of Church Outreach Programs

Table 21.1 presents the types of outreach programs that northern churches sponsor. A total of 1,804 community outreach programs are provided by the 426 churches that have such activities. The majority (51.2 percent) of these programs are family support programs that address the needs of the family as a unit (e.g., family counseling, food and clothing distribution programs) or adult family members (e.g., adult literacy, support groups for men and women). Demonstrating a substantive commitment to children and youth, roughly a third (31.3 percent) of the churches' programs target this population specifically. The majority of these programs are basic educational and academic support, recreational, or cultural awareness programs. Community development programs comprise 9 percent of church activities and include community-based projects designed to improve the economic condition of the community or to provide communitywide services such as health, housing, or social action.

Church-based programs for the elderly account for 8.5 percent of the 1,804 available programs. This percentage of programs is small, given that adults over the age of sixty-five years comprise roughly 12 percent of the entire Black population (Taylor, 1986b) and older persons are more likely than younger groups to be church members (Chatters and Taylor, 1989). A number of churches in the sample offer more than one type of senior citizen program, so that those 120 churches with elderly support programs provide a total of 153 senior services. Additionally, churches with three or more general family support or community development programs are more likely to sponsor elderly support programs than those with two or fewer programs [$X^2(4) = 298.81$, $p<.001$, $CV = .69$]. Table 21.2 provides the percentage distributions for specific types of elderly support programs offered. As indicated, the most frequently sponsored programs are home-care services (39 percent) that are designed to assist the elderly with household cleaning and related tasks. Fellowship activities account for 18 percent of church-based senior programs and are intended to maintain the seniors' involvement in the community. Daily home delivery of meals is the next most common program offered (10 percent), followed by

TABLE 21.2

Types of Elderly Support Programs Offered by Churches

Program Type	%	*N*
Home Care	39	60
Fellowship/Social	18	27
Meals-on-Wheels	10	16
Housing	9	14
Multiservices	5	7
Financial	2	3
Medical	2	3
Other	15	23
Totals	100	153

senior citizen housing (9 percent) and multiser0vices (5 percent) programs. The multiservices programs are typically designed to refer senior citizens to a variety of formal service agencies that they routinely need, such as social services, medical care, and legal aid. Direct financial assistance (2 percent) and medical screening (2 percent) programs are also offered by churches, though much less frequently.

Programs such as home care and meals on wheels are critical types of formal support programs because they reduce the likelihood that elderly adults will be placed in nursing homes or other long-term care facilities. Past efforts have demonstrated that providing people with some level of assistance with the routine activities of daily life, such as cooking, shopping, and cleaning, can delay or avert institutionalization. Available research indicates that for every health-impaired person residing in an institution, there are at least two equally impaired older adults who still live in the community (George and Maddox, 1989). Consequently, health impairment, per se, is not the exclusive predictor of institutional placement.

Probably the most important factor predicting the likelihood of nursing home placement is the absence of a caregiver (George and Maddox, 1989). Absence of a caregiver is defined as the unavailability or unwillingness of family members to take on or continue caregiving responsibilities (George and Maddox, 1989). Consequently, formal services that are provided by churches may help a frail elderly person live independently or provide needed assistance to family caregivers by alleviating, in some measure, the burden and stress of their caregiving responsibilities. Formal services that are focused on elderly adults, then, may reduce the likelihood of nursing home placement among this group.

Characteristics of Churches with Elderly Support Programs

This preliminary information indicated that only a small proportion of the churches in the sample sponsor outreach programs for the elderly. Consequently, we decided to investigate the organizational characteristics of churches that provide these programs as a way of identifying other churches that may be responsive either to initiating or to expanding such efforts in the future. Based on previous analyses of the characteristics of churches that provide community outreach programs (Billingsley, Caldwell, Hill, and Rouse, 1991), as well as those that sponsor family support programs (Caldwell and Greene, 1992), we were able to identify a number of distinctive characteristics of these churches. The results of the present analysis revealed a specific cluster of church attributes that were related to the provision of elderly support programs.

Church Demographics. The results of our analyses suggest that churches that sponsor elderly support programs have several distinct characteristics (see Table 21.3). These churches themselves tend to be older, with those that are over seventy-five years old most likely to offer programs for the elderly. Churches with congregational memberships of more than four hundred are more likely to have such programs compared to congregations of lesser size, while small congregations of seventy or fewer members are least likely to provide programs for the elderly. Further, congregations that are perceived as being mostly middle-class or a combination of both working- and middle-class are more likely to sponsor elderly support programs, compared to mostly working-class churches.

Church Staffing Patterns. The staffing pattern of the church also emerges as an important determinant of whether or not a church provides elderly support programs. The staffing patterns of churches seem to represent a rough approximation of the economic condition of the church. When possible, churches with adequate financial resources provide a salary, home, car, and benefits for the senior minister. Although associate and assistant ministers are often not compensated, the staff positions of church secretary, musicians, and/or janitor are typically paid in an economically stable church. We find that churches with no paid clergy, including the senior minister, and those with no paid staff other than the senior minister are the least likely to offer elderly support programs.

Church Activities. Past research has highlighted the prominent role of the church as a focal center for a number of community activities (Mays and Nicholson, 1933; Frazier, 1974). More recent studies indicate that for the contemporary Black church this role has been curtailed to some degree, as African Americans have gained greater access to the resources of the larger society following the Civil Rights movement (Lincoln and Mamiya, 1990). Nevertheless, many churches continue to open their doors to community groups when needed. The results of this study indicate that churches that sponsor nonreligious activities on a frequent basis and congregations that allow their church buildings to be used as meeting places for community groups are also those that are more likely to provide elderly support programs for the community than are churches that do not engage in these activities.

TABLE 21.3
Characteristics of Churches with Elderly Support Programs

	% Yes	*% No*	*N*	X^2	*Cramer's V/Phi*
Demographics					
Congregational Age					
<1–40 years	14.5	85.5	339	16.93***	.16
41–75 years	19.2	80.8	156		
76+	31.1	68.9	132		
Membership Size					
1–70	5.5	94.5	146	51.93***	.29
71–175	13.0	87.0	185		
176–400	22.3	77.7	157		
400+	36.6	63.4	145		
Social Class of Congregation					
Working-Class	12.4	87.6	194	13.82**	.15
Both Working and Middle	21.6	78.4	370		
Middle-Class	30.6	69.4	49		
Other	5.3	94.7	19		
Staffing Patterns					
Number of Paid Clergy					
None	9.6	90.4	188	27.08***	.21
One	19.6	80.4	352		
Two+	35.6	64.4	90		
Other Paid Staff					
No	10.5	89.5	305	27.82***	.21
Yes	27.0	73.0	322		
Frequency of Nonreligious Activities					
Rarely	11.6	88.4	233	32.16***	.23
Occasionally	15.2	84.8	217		
Frequently	32.4	67.6	185		
Building Used as Meeting Place					
No	22.4	77.6	156	4.28*	.10
Yes	31.8	68.2	267		
Cooperation with Social Agencies					
No	20.8	79.2	120	5.01*	.11
Yes	31.8	68.2	299		
Financial Status					
Building Ownership Status					
Renting	1.9	98.1	52	11.23**	.13
Buying	18.9	81.1	180		
Own	21.3	78.7	394		

*$p<.05$
**$p<.01$
***$p<.001$

Additionally, churches that have an established working relationship with social agencies in the community tend to offer support programs for the elderly, compared to churches that do not work with community agencies. The exact nature of the causal relationship, however, is not clear. That is, it is not known whether churches that already have a working relationship with agencies tend to initiate elderly programs or whether the elderly support programs (and contact with community agencies) originate out of a recognition of the expressed needs of elderly persons within the congregation. It is important, however, to recognize that social service agencies have program development expertise that could be very useful for churches that are working with the elderly. Even fellowship programs and activities that are primarily social in nature may require some assistance from agencies such as the local transportation department or recreational agencies.

Church Financial and Denominational Status. One of the best indicators of the economic viability and independence of Black congregations is their ability to purchase their church building. Our findings indicate a clear difference between congregations that are renting their church buildings and those that currently own or are purchasing their church home. Congregations that are renting their buildings are least likely and those that are buying or have purchased their buildings are more likely to offer elderly support programs. Finally, although a variety of faith traditions were included in this study, there were no denominational differences in the likelihood of sponsoring elderly support programs or any other form of outreach program. This finding lends support to the idea that most churches, regardless of denominational affiliation, reflect an orientation and mission that incorporates both spiritual guidance and practical assistance in living for its members and the community at large.

Characteristics of Senior Ministers from Churches

The influence of senior ministers as community leaders in affecting change in African American communities has been documented throughout the history of the Black church (Lincoln and Mamiya, 1990; Harris, 1987; Sullivan, 1978). Given the historic prominence of church leadership, we examined the demographic characteristics and the external church activities of senior ministers of churches who sponsored outreach programs for the elderly (see Table 21.4). Senior ministers from churches with elderly support programs are more likely to have seminary or Bible College training as well as more formal education, compared to senior ministers from churches without elderly programs. We also found that senior ministers of churches that sponsor elderly support programs are more likely to be involved in external community activities than are pastors whose churches are without elderly programs. These community organizations mentioned include (in order of choice) The National Association

TABLE 21.4
Characteristics of Senior Ministers from Churches with Elderly Support Programs

	% Yes	*% No*	*N*	X^2	*Cramer's V/Phi*
Clergy Attributes					
Minister has Seminary or Bible College Training					
No	6.4	93.6	109	13.40***	.15
Yes	21.6	78.4	501		
Education					
<High School	8.8	91.2	57	34.28***	.24
High School	9.2	90.8	109		
Some College	11.8	88.2	93		
College+	18.1	81.9	127		
Masters+	31.9	68.1	188		
Clergy's External Activities					
Involvement in Community Activities					
No	12.2	87.8	221	10.09**	.13
Yes	22.7	77.3	383		

*$p < .05$
**$p < .01$
***$p < .001$

for the Advancement of Colored People, The National Urban League, and local ministerial alliances.

Summary and Conclusions

The results of this study support the contention that the Black church continues to be a vital institution within African American communities. However, as has been demonstrated across several eras and a variety of circumstances, the Black church represents more than a narrowly defined religious institution exclusively concerned with spiritual matters. The Black church functions as a comprehensive and viable support system for its members and the community at large. Several dimensions of support are provided by churches, including those that address the spiritual, emotional, and instrumental needs of the participants. This study focused on the types of assistance that churches provide through their organized outreach efforts to the surrounding community. In this regard, 67 percent of the 635 northern churches in the Black Church Family Project sponsored at least one such outreach program. Although we found that most Black churches actively engage in sponsoring outreach programs for children, youth, and families, few of them targeted the elderly as a focal group to receive church-based services. Only 153 out of the 1,804 programs offered by churches in the sample (about 8 percent) were designed exclusively for the elderly. Programs for families, children, and youth received higher priority than did programs for the elderly. Given the public emphasis on the problems and challenges facing African American youth and the general endorsement of the view that children represent our future, it is not surprising that churches with limited resources tend to address youth and family issues to a greater extent than elderly concerns.

Despite these general trends among Black churches, there were identifiable church characteristics that distinguished those congregations that had assumed the responsibilities of ministering to the needs of elderly adults in their communities. These churches tended to be well established in that they were at least seventy-five years old, possessed large congregations of four hundred or more members, and were perceived as being largely middle-class. In contrast, Caldwell and Greene (1992) found that churches offering general family support programs tended to be much younger and smaller, with an approximate age of forty-one years and average congregation size of 170 members.

Churches with support programs for the elderly also seemed to be more secure financially and were able to provide paid positions for the senior minister and other church staff members, as well as owning their church building. Additionally, churches that participated in outreach programs were recognized as community centers and frequently sponsored nonreligious activities and permitted community groups use of the church building for secular activities. Finally, these churches collaborated with social agencies in operating many of the programs and activities for the elderly. Future research should investigate the nature of this relationship to determine how this type of collaboration could better facilitate services to African American elderly.

The results of this study indicated that the types of services most frequently provided by church-based elderly support programs involved household chores for the home-bound. Activities aimed at keeping senior citizens actively involved in community life were also an important feature of these services. Chatters and Taylor (1990) have discussed the importance of the social integration role of the Black church for aging African Americans. This study demonstrated that church-based programs that address both the instrumental and emotional needs of the elderly help effectively to maintain social involvement. Although churches were often engaged in the provision of direct services to the elderly (e.g., meals-on-wheels, operating housing complexes, providing medical screening), they also functioned as referral agents for the formal system of service delivery. This finding supports the conceptual model described earlier representing the interrelationships among African American families, communities, and the larger society. Specifically, because of its proximity to both the family and the formal system of service delivery, the Black church is in an optimal position to provide direct services and to refer those in need to appropriate professionals.

In general, programs for the elderly were not the first choice of churches that had established outreach programs in the community. Food and clothing distribution efforts were the types of programs offered most often by churches, regardless of church age, size, and financial status. The types of food distribution programs offered included seasonal food distributions, daily meals, and food pantries. Clothing distribution efforts ranged from occasional flea markets to operating thrift stores. Frequently, the food or clothing distribution program was the only community-oriented activity that a church sponsored. However, support programs for the elderly were available only if a church had at least three or more other programs currently in operation. Rarely did we find a church with just one program that was devoted to the needs of the elderly. Finally, as has been demonstrated in previous program development endeavors (e.g., Haber's 1984 experiences in establishing an elderly caregiver awareness project), the support of the senior minister is critical to the survival of church-based programs. In this regard, we examined characteristics of the senior ministers of churches that offered elderly support programs. We found that these ministers were highly educated, with a minimum of at least some college-level training in addition to seminary or Bible College credentials, and were actively involved in the community.

With a conservative estimate of 75,000 Black churches in this country and more than 24 million churchgoers (Lincoln and Mamiya, 1990), Black churches could constitute a natural infrastructure for the delivery of services to the elderly. Most church-based programs are staffed by volunteers, and the potential for regular and continuous contacts with an elderly person is far greater than what is currently being provided by social services or health-care professionals. Church-based support programs for the elderly are a cost-effective alternative strategy for service delivery that should be explored further. One of the several challenges facing the expansion of elderly church-based service programs will be to convince social and health-care agencies, policymakers, and senior clergy that by working cooperatively, the needs of African American elderly, both within and outside the church, can be readily identified and addressed.

BIBLIOGRAPHY

Billingsley, A. (1993) *Climbing Jacob's Ladder: The Enduring Legacy of African-American Families.* New York: Simon and Schuster.

Billingsley, A., and C. H. Caldwell (1991) "The Church, the Family, and the School in the African American Community." *Journal of Negro Education* 60:427–40.

Billingsley, A., C. H. Caldwell, R. Hill, and W. V. Rouse (1991) *Black Churches and Family-Oriented Community Outreach Programs in the Northeastern United States.* Final report submitted to the Ford Foundation and Lilly Endowment, June.

______ (1992) *Black Churches and Family-Oriented Community Outreach Programs in the Northeastern and North Central Regions of the United States.* Final report submitted to the Ford Foundation and Lilly Endowment, April.

Caldwell, C. H., and A. D. Greene (1992) "The Black Church as a Family Support System." In Billingsley et al., 1–24.

Chatters, L. M., and R. J. Taylor (1989) "Age Differences in Religious Participation among Black Adults." *Journal of Gerontology:* 44:S183–89.

______ (1990) "Social Integration among Aging Blacks." In Harel et al., 82–99.

Chatters, L. M., R. J. Taylor, and J. S. Jackson (1985) "Size and Composition of the Informal Helper Networks of Elderly Blacks." *Journal of Gerontology* 40:50–61.

______ (1986) "Aged Blacks' Choices for an Informal Helper Network." *Journal of Gerontology* 41:94–100.

Eng, E., J. Hatch, and A. Callan (1985) "Institutionalizing Social Support through the Church and into the Community." *Health Education Quarterly* 12:81–92.

Frazier, E. F. (1974) *The Negro Church in America.* New York: Schocken Books.

Garland, D., and D. Pancost, eds. (1990) *The Churches' Ministry with Families: A Practical Guide.* Irving, Tex.: Word.

George, L. K., and G. L. Maddox (1989) "Social and Behavioral Aspects of Institutional Care." In Ory and Bond, 116–41.

George, Y., V. Richardson, M. Lakes-Matyas, and F. Blake (1989) *Saving Black Minds: Black Churches and Education.* Washington, D.C.: American Association for the Advancement of Science.

Haber, D. (1984) "Church-based Programs for Black Care-givers of Non-institutionalized Elders." *Journal of Religion and Aging* 1 (1):63–70.

Harel, Z., E. McKinney, and M. Williams, eds. (1990) *Understanding and Serving the Black Aged.* Newbury Park, Calif.: Sage.

Harris, J. H. (1987) *Black Ministers and Laity in the Urban Church: An Analysis of Political and Social Expectations.* New York City: University Press of America.

Jackson, J. S., ed. (1988) *The Black American Elderly: Research on Physical and Psychosocial Health.* New York: Springer.

Jackson, J. S., L. M. Chatters, and R. J. Taylor, eds. (1993) *Aging in Black America.* Newbury Park, Calif.: Sage.

Jacquet, C. H., ed. (1989) *Yearbook of American and Canadian Churches: 1989.* Nashville, Tenn.: Abingdon.

Johnson, C. L., and B. M. Barer (1990) "Families and Networks among Older Inner-City Blacks." *The Gerontologist* 30:726–33.

Letzig, B. (1986) "The Church as Advocate in Aging." *Journal of Religion and Aging* 2:1–11.

Lincoln, C. E. (1973) *The Black Church since Frazier.* New York: Schocken.

Lincoln, C. E., and L. Mamiya (1990) *The Black Church in the African American Experience.* Durham, N.C.: Duke.

Manuel, R. C. (1988) "The Demography of Older Blacks in the United States." In Jackson et al., 25–49.

Mays, B. E., and J. W. Nicholson (1933) *The Negro's Church.* New York: Russell and Russell.

Negstad, J., and R. Arnholt (1986) "Day Centers for Older Adults: Parish and Agency Partnership." *Journal of Religion and Aging* 2 (4):25–31.

Ory, M. G., and K. Bond, eds. (1989) *Aging and Health Care: Social Science and Policy Perspectives.* New York: Routledge.

Payne, W. (1991) *Directory of African American Religious Bodies.* Washington, D.C.: Howard University Press.

Roberts, J. D. (1980) *Roots of a Black Future: Family and Church.* Philadelphia: Westminister.

Smith, E. D. (1988) *Climbing Jacob's Ladder: The Rise of Black Churches in Eastern American cities, 1740–1877.* Washington, D.C.: The Smithsonian.

Steinitz, L. Y. (1981) "The Local Church as Support for the Elderly." *Journal of Gerontological Social Work* 4:44–53.

Sullivan, L. H. (1978) *The Church in the Life of the Black Family.* Valley Forge, Pa: Judson.

Taylor, R. J. (1986a) "Religious Participation among Elderly Blacks." *The Gerontologist* 28:630–66.

______ (1986b) "Receipt of Support from Family among Black Americans: Demographic and Familial Differences." *Journal of Marriage and the Family* 48:67–77.

______ (1988a) "Correlates of Religious Non-involvement among Black Americans." *Review of Religious Research* 30:126–39.

______ (1988b) "Structural Determinants of Religious Participation among Black Americans." *Review of Religious Research* 30:114–25.

______ (1993) "Religion and Religious Observances among Older Black Adults." In Jackson, Chatters, and Taylor, 103–123.

Taylor, R. J., and L. M. Chatters (1986a) "Church-based Informal Support among Elderly Blacks." *The Gerontologist* 26:637–42.

______ (1986b) "Patterns of Informal Support to Elderly Black Adults: Family, Friends, and Church Members." *Social Work* 31:432–38.

______ (1988a) "Church Members as a Source of Informal Social Support." *Review of Religious Research* 30:193–203.

______ (1988b) "Correlates of Education, Income, and Poverty among Aged Blacks." *The Gerontologist* 28:435–41.

______ (1991) "Non-organizational Religious Participation among Elderly Blacks." *Journal of Gerontology: Social Sciences* 46:S103–11.

Taylor, R. J., I. Luckey, and J. M. Smith (1990) "Delivering Service in Black Churches." In Garland and Pancost, 194–209.

Taylor, R. J., M. C. Thornton, and L. M. Chatters (1987) "Black Americans' Perceptions of the Socio-historical Role of the Church." *Journal of Black Studies* 18:123–38.

Tobin, S., J. W. Ellor, and S. M. Anderson-Ray (1986) *Enabling the Elderly: Religious Institutions within the Community Service System.* Albany, N.Y.: State University of New York Press.

Walls, C. T., and S. H. Zarit (1991) "Informal Support from Black Churches and the Well-Being of Elderly Blacks." *The Gerontologist* 31:490–95.

Williams, C., and H. Williams (1984) "Contemporary Voluntary Associations in the Urban Black Church: The Development and Growth of Mutual Aid Societies." *Journal of Voluntary Action Research* 13:19–30.

22 Congregation-Based Health Programs

ANNE MARIE DJUPE
GRANGER WESTBERG

A subtle thing has happened over the past half-century. Christian theology has rediscovered, in the life and teachings of Christ, that he was concerned about whole people—that he was interested in the body as well as the soul. How did the scholarly theologians come upon this "new" insight? It was related at least partly to the tremendous resurgence in understanding of the relationship between the mind and the body. In the 1930s, medicine was just being introduced to the term *psychosomatic illness.* The technically oriented medical profession had resisted the idea that the mind and the body were so integrally related.

Fortunately, there were small groups of progressive Christian lay people and clergy who almost immediately saw in the writings of these early pioneers principles that were congruent with the Christian gospel. These focused on the interrelationship of the body, mind, and soul. Christian scholars began to wrestle with the implications of the healing ministry of Christ. Some called upon the church to take health and wholeness concepts more seriously.

One of the first religiously oriented lay persons to realize the spiritual dimensions of this "whole person" philosophy was the famous statesman-premier of South Africa, Jan Christiaan Smuts. In 1926, while temporarily out of political office, he wrote his remarkably insightful book, *Holism and Evolution.*

Premier Smuts wrote that "this character of wholeness meets us everywhere and points to something fundamental in the universe." He believed that "parts tend to move toward wholes" and that "the whole is greater than the sum of its parts." When parts become whole, he said, "the synthesis affects and determines the parts so that they function towards the whole; and the whole and the parts, therefore, reciprocally influence and determine each other and appear, more or less, to merge their individual characters" (Smuts, 1961, xi).

Smuts's insights have helped many people to grasp what it means to speak of health and wholeness in the same breath. It is the understanding of "everything being interconnected to everything else" that has sensitized people to the remarkable similarity of all this to the message of the Christian gospel and to Christ's insistence on caring for the whole person. What are the implications of this for the ministry of churches today?

THE CHURCH AS A HEALTH PLACE

An increasing number of pastors and congregations are becoming concerned about the physical, mental, and spiritual health of their members. A significant question which arises has to do with their role in health care. When individuals are asked, "What are the health agencies in your community?" most people answer with the names of local hospitals or well-known medical clinics. Technically however, these are not "health" agencies; they are "sickness" agencies. Hospitals and doctors' offices are important, but usually only *after* one gets sick. Then they seek to bring one back to health. They are not basically engaged in teaching people how to become healthy and stay that way. Only recently have hospitals begun to offer seminars for people dealing with stress, grief, etc., and a few doctors' offices have classrooms where they teach their patients how to stay well.

What, then, are the health agencies in a community? What are the institutions in American culture that keep one healthy or, if the institutions are unhealthy, make persons sick? Four come to mind: the home, the school, the church, and the workplace. If any one of these four institutions is unhealthy, long-term negative consequences can result. Where there is a broken home, disease frequently follows. When a school loses its sense of purpose, all sorts of human relational and physical illness results. When a church teaches and preaches a "sick" doctrine, the results can be appalling. When a workplace cares nothing about the human needs of its employees, "sickness" may ensue.

The home and the church are the two institutions concerned about the health of people from birth to death. The church also interacts with all socioeconomic and ethnic groups. The school is interested in persons primarily during the school-age years, and the workplace, as long as one is productive. The church and the home have concern for people throughout their lives. They are in a prime position to influence and motivate people toward healthy living.

How ought the churches of America go about the task of giving the word "health" a much broader and deeper meaning than it now has? There is much confusion about the word "health," and health care usually refers to a delivery system of care to the sick. However, the fact that the word health has "heal" (salvation, wholeness) at its core should call attention to its religious dimension. For many centuries, before the coming of scientific medicine, healing was largely in the hands of the church.

In the 1940s, holism came to the attention of lay persons and clergy, both in and outside the church. The word *holism,* which was coined by Jan Christiaan Smuts, was just beginning to gain attention. It could easily be grasped because of its derivation from the word *holos,* meaning "whole." People seemed to be ready for this word. It expressed what needed to be said about everything being interrelated. That meant that science needed the expanding dimensions of religion, just as religion needed the technological prowess of science.

Finally there was a word that succinctly conveyed the concept of wholeness. Several medical students suggested the spelling of holism with a "w" because it helped people see more immediately the word "wholeness." As a result, there is now an interchange of spelling that, while a bit confusing, in the long run brought unusual attention to the concept. It is in constant use in books and articles referring to wholistic health, wholistic medicine, wholistic psychology, wholistic theology, wholistic architecture, and other areas. The concept belongs to everyone. Health is multidimensional and affects all aspects of an individual's being—physical, psychological, spiritual, and social.

How can the church participate in promoting the health of its congregants and community? In this chapter, three congregationally-based health programs will be described. Each has a slightly different focus and structure, but all attempt to provide a whole-person approach based in congregational settings. These include wholistic health centers, parish nurse programs, and congregational health services. These three programs were developed in conjunction with a university, medical school, or health-care institution, and have provided opportunities for these institutions to be involved in preventive services in their communities. The church provides a key link in the continuum of care and provides the caring and supportive environment to which people return from hospitals and clinics.

Given the chronic nature of most older adult illness patterns, parish nurse and congregational health programs designed to provide wholistic health care are especially appropriate to older people. Haber (1989, 57ff.) has argued that congregations and corporate employment settings could provide a broad range of caregiving and general health services far more economically than they are currently being provided in the U.S.

WHOLISTIC HEALTH CENTERS

The two authors of this chapter have had the opportunity to test out the thesis that local parish churches ought to be more explicitly engaged in whole-person care. In the early 1960s, Westberg opened a wholistic health center in a low-income neighborhood church in Springfield, Ohio on an entirely no-charge basis. Its immediate success led to speculation as to whether middle- and upper-income people would be willing to pay for whole-person health care. In the early 1970s, this pastor, the authors, and a Chicago-area physician opened a wholistic health center in an upper-income neighborhood in the Chicago suburb of Hinsdale, Illinois under the auspices of the University of Illinois College of Medicine. Subsequently, over the next ten years, a number of clinics were established in churches across the country in neighborhoods of all income levels.

In each case, a family practice doctor's office was established in a neighborhood church, a setting where it would be acceptable to talk about God, and prayer, and love, while providing competent medical care. Each center had three key professionals: a doctor, a nurse, and a clinically trained pastoral counselor. Churches provided a natural and friendly setting for the kinds of things that ought to go on in a doctor's office, such as time for explanations, listening, and human interaction.

Churches, when they are functioning at their best, help to keep people well. It was the intention to demonstrate that these three professionals (doctor, nurse, and pastor) ought to be working together as a team and that the parish setting could help make it happen.

Among the first patients were elderly people who had no difficulty understanding the relationship between faith and health. For many of them, the church was already their "health place," although they did not call it that. It was to this church building that they had come weekly, or more often, for worship, Christian education, and human fellowship. The establishment of a wholistic medical clinic in their church did not strike them as being out of character for a congregation already deeply involved in ministry to whole persons in every conceivable circumstance.

Physicians on the staffs of the wholistic centers were, from the beginning, receptive to having counselors available who could take time to listen to the human dimensions of a person's illness history. The intention was to provide a model for other doctors so that they would see the value of spending more time dealing with the spiritual aspects of their patients' lives. One aspect of this whole-person approach was to spend a half-hour with each new patient in a joint "Health Planning Conference," where the staff addressed issues of lifestyle, relationships, and faith, along with a health history. The doctor, nurse, and pastor sat with the patient in a nonmedical setting for the purpose of getting to know each other. In these conversations, the staff became aware of these individuals, each with his or her unique personality. Patients were encouraged to talk about how things were *really* going in their lives. Again and again, the older people expressed amazement that such whole-person concerns were given time for expression and that all three of these health-care professionals were interested in them.

Some very important lessons were learned. Wholistic health care was a movement in which local churches could become part of the healing structure of our present culture. This experience affirmed the belief that churches can play a role in the delivery of health care. Patients responded positively to the clinic staff, who really listened to them and were concerned about their well-being in its totality. This suggested that the staff was concerned about physical health as well as relationships to God, self, family, and others. Patients also appreciated being taught about health and their diseases and treatments, and being treated as colleagues in the process. Patients could return to see the physician, nurse, or counselor as their needs were determined.

The above describes one model of health-care delivery based in a congregational setting. One limitation was that even though these centers utilized space and resources provided by the congregation, they were frequently not fully integrated into the life and mission of the local congregation. However, it was a step forward for churches to incorporate health ministry more intentionally into their teaching, preaching, and activities.

PARISH NURSE

As more and more wholistic health centers revised their pattern of ministry, the question became, "How could this unique relationship with health-care providers be continued?" A new model of care developed as it became increasingly clear that the nurse had played a key role in all of these centers. Nurses were educated in the sciences and humanities and were able to respond to the medical as well as psychosocial and spiritual concerns. Nurses were committed to education and could translate the medical information for the patient. They also seemed to be strongly linked to many other health-care professionals in the community, so it seemed logical that nurses could be placed on the staffs of congregations.

The parish nurse role typically has five components: personal health counselor, health educator, source of referral to the congregation and the community, coordinator of support groups and volunteers, and interpreter of the close relationship between faith and health (Westberg, 1990, 45–49; Djupe, 1991, 5–7). Through a variety of activities in the congregation, including classes, articles in bulletins and newsletters, hospital, home and nursing home visitation, and education regarding medications or treatments, the parish nurse seeks to raise the health awareness of members of the congregation and community.

Judith Ryan has defined parish nursing in the following way: "Parish Nursing is coming to be understood as a non-invasive, nurturing role, focused more on creating the physiologic, psychologic, spiritual, and sociocultural environment in which the client can gain or maintain health or healing than on the diagnosis and treatment of human response to disease" (Ryan, 1990, 4).

Parish nurses focus on health promotion and disease prevention in a variety of creative ways. For example, recently the Self Determination Act was enacted by Congress. Adults over eighteen who are admitted to a health-care facility are being asked about advance directives. Even before this law was enacted, there was an opportunity to prepare people for this law through congregational programs. Educational forums were held, newsletters were written, and bulletin boards developed. Parishioners were also counseled individually. The church provided a unique setting in which to discuss this topic in the context of faith and values. Whether or not individuals chose to implement one of these documents, many were informed in a caring and nonthreatening environment.

Health and wellness committees comprised of lay and health professionals who are members of the congregations are active in assessing the needs within congregations and giving direction and support to health ministries as they develop (Westberg and McNamara, 1981, 8). These committees frequently organize first and then participate in the development of a parish nurse program. In some congregations where there is no parish nurse program, a health and wellness committee develops and directs the health ministry program for the congregation.

Parish nursing is more than the presence of a health professional on the parish staff. It represents the incorporation of the wholistic approach to ministry throughout all aspects of the church's life. Parish nurses also participate in the spiritual life of the church. They have demonstrated involvement in a variety of ways such as attending, planning, and participating in liturgies and funerals, participating in healing services, and training and coordinating volunteers. During home visits of parishioners, the parish nurse may incorporate communion, biblical reflections, music, and prayer.

Kimble discusses the role religion plays in helping the individual confront the aging process. "Three challenges are central to the personal experience of aging: the challenge of the crisis of meaning, the challenge of the crisis of suffering, and the challenge of the crisis of death" (Kimble, 1990, 70). When older adults confront these very difficult challenges, they are also attempting to understand the role of their faith in these experiences (cf. Kimble, chap. 9 this volume). The parish nurse has an opportunity, along with the pastoral staff, to assist parishioners as they address these challenges. For example, a pastor shared the following scenario. A family called and asked to see him. They were struggling with the decision as to whether to take an elderly loved one off the respirator, and they needed help and support. While he felt comfortable with the family and wanted to be of help to them, what about the other factors the family had to face in this high-tech hospital intensive care setting? What questions should the family ask? Was there any hope for their loved one to recover? The pastor was uncomfortable dealing with medical aspects of this situation. Out of this discomfort, he called the parish nurse and asked her to accompany him on this call. The parish nurse had also known the family and had a trusting relationship with them. The parish nurse was able to help translate this complicated medical situation and help the family frame the questions to ask the health-care providers in the hospital. The pastor experienced support and relief because he was freed to be with the family in a pastoral, supportive way. Questions of suffering, meaning, and death were addressed in the context of the family's faith and concern for their loved one.

Parish nurses have also been instrumental in assessing the physical church setting and its impact on the older adult. They have made many recommendations and implemented changes when possible. Examples include good lighting in dark stairwells; replacing small-print Bibles and hymnals with large-print editions; replacing steps with ramps and having hearing devices available at worship and other group gatherings. Much can be done in churches to address these safety concerns and improve the worship environment for older adults. Another area of consideration is the nutritional needs of the elderly. Parish nurses have made congregations more aware of good nutritional habits and have influenced members to serve more nutritious snacks and meals. All aspects of church life contribute to the health of congregations.

As the concept of parish nursing has spread across the country, various models or approaches have developed. Some of the nurses are sponsored by health-care institutions, whereas others are sponsored directly by congregations. Some parish nurses are salaried and others volunteer their services (Solari-Twadell et al., 1990, 59). Parish nurses serve in urban, suburban, and rural settings, in congregations of all sizes, and in a variety of denominations. In fact, a number of denominational leaders have taken the concept very seriously and encouraged various forms of health ministry throughout their congregations.

An example of dramatic success of parish-based nursing services can be found in twenty-seven medically underserved western Iowa counties where more than sixty nurses in over thirty parish nurse services provide a range of health and wholeness services through local congregations. The program was established through a three-year grant from the Kellogg Foundation and local aging and health-care institutions. Over 22 percent of the population in the region is sixty-plus and many of these are clients of the new parish nurse service. The 1990 census revealed that Iowa has the highest proportion of elderly in the nation (over 19 percent). The value of such services in high-density elderly areas seems clear (Northwest Aging Association, 1991).

There has been established a National Parish Nurse Resource Center (NPNRC) which serves as clearinghouse and educational, publishing, and consulting function focused on the development of quality parish nurse programs throughout the country. A self-screened group of 8,000 parish members, health-care administrators, and others receive the NPNRC newsletter quarterly. (ADDRESS: NPNRC, 1800 Dempster St., Park Ridge IL 60068; 708/696-8773). An affiliated resource is the Health Ministries Association, established to provide information, technical assistance and educational resourcing for parish health programs. (ADDRESS: HMA, 1306 Penn Avenue, Des Moines IA 50316; 515/263-8556).

CONGREGATIONAL HEALTH SERVICES

In 1986, the presiding bishop of the former American Lutheran Church invited seven congregations to work in partnership with the ALC Division for Life and Mission in the Congregation and Lutheran General Health Care System to test the model of Congregational Health Partnership. This partnership had three initial objectives: (1) to promote a mindset among members of the faith community to see their congregation as a health place; (2) to strengthen relationships between and among members of the congregation, health-related agencies, and institutions of the church and community; and (3) to identify the needs and resources of the partners and develop responses to those needs.

Through this experience, the partners decided that congregations had a distinct potential to provide health services and to modify and support basic belief systems essential to sustained changes in behavior. Further, they believed that through worship, liturgy, sacrament, and symbol, the church could enable people to draw on their own spiritual resources.

The pilot project, Congregational Health Services, was established in 1991. The services included in this pilot are health risk assessment, clinical screening, health counseling and Christian health education, referral and follow-up with a parish nurse, personal health records, and health-related teaching, preaching, and worship.

Congregational Health Services is a combination of clinical and educational services offered through congregations to address the physical, emotional, and spiritual situations of people. A wholistic approach to human life is modelled through the multimethod, multidisciplinary service delivery of this program.

SUMMARY

Three models have been presented of how congregations play a significant role in providing preventive health-care services to their members. We are witnessing a major revolution in America regarding health care. The costs continue to skyrocket and yet many do not receive care. "The United States spends nearly three times more on healthcare than any other nation but does not, for a variety of reasons, appreciate the best outcomes of any nation" (Shannon, 1991, 5). Consumers are increasingly concerned about their health care. It is clear that traditional approaches are not working. There are, for example, an increasing number of people in America who are uninsured or underinsured. As unemployment rises, the number of uninsured also rises. Many of these people are minority citizens.

> Many of our minority citizens, especially those who are low-income, lack a regular source of comprehensive primary care. At the present time, clients of existing services still encounter roadblocks and dead-ends, largely due to the fragmentation, lack of coordination, and inadequate referral systems. Because they do not receive the preventive services they need, they experience much higher rates of morbidity and mortality. (Illinois Dept. of Public Health, 1991)

In addition to low-income clients, there is a concern for older persons who face multiple chronic illnesses. Several studies, however, including *Healthy People 2000—Healthy Older Adults* (AARP, 1990), have called attention to studies that show that better health, greater longevity, and improved quality of life result from healthier lifestyles and preventive health care. Such benefits should apply to all categories of elderly. Furthermore, it should be recognized that while health promotion is very important for all adults, it has somewhat different effects among older people. "Where disease prevention is not possible, behavioral and lifestyle changes and early treatment may slow the progression of existing chronic diseases and the rate of disability associated with them" (Hickey and Stilwell, 1991, 822).

Chronic illnesses often diminish the functional independence and autonomy of older persons. This can result in reduced ability to participate in the life and activities of churches and may lead to isolation and loneliness. The high level of church/synagogue membership and religious interest among older people suggests that religious groups, through their volunteer resources, financial resources, and other opportunities, could assist the elderly at this critical stage. Many older persons could be helped to overcome the effects of chronic illness in an atmosphere of trust and support while being assisted in practicing their religious faith in ways that are meaningful to them. "The widespread prevalence of religious institutions provides a potentially valuable resource to the older adult in terms of social support (and practical assistance)" (Koenig et al., 1988, 27).

Peterson (1982) offers a number of challenging statements regarding the future role of faith communities and the health of their members. "We do not produce health, but we have the God-given capacity to enable it" (27). Such is the unique and humble framework within which parish health programs can develop.

An excellent opportunity exists in America today for religious groups using one of the above models or some adaptation of them to help address the health and wellness needs of the elderly. Many of our elders are linked to a faith community and look to that faith community for support and assistance (cf. Seeber, chap. 17). Clergy and congregations touch the lives of more older adults on a regular basis than any other social institution except the family. New avenues for cooperation between congregations and formal health-care providers are needed. Continuity of care across the continuum from acute care to prevention and health promotion must be developed. Finally, health-care institutions and faith communities need to be linked in new partnerships to address the health and well-being of older adults.

BIBLIOGRAPHY

American Association of Retired Persons (1990) *Healthy People 2000—Healthy Older Adults*. Washington, D.C.: AARP.

Djupe, A. M., H. Olson, J. A. Ryan, and J. C. Lantz (1991) *Reaching Out: Parish Nursing Services*. Park Ridge, Ill.: Parish Nurse Resource Center.

Haber, David (1989) *Health Care for an Aging Society*. Hemisphere Publishing Corporation.

Hickey, T., and D. L. Stilwell (1991) "Health Promotion for Older People: All Is Not Well." *The Gerontologist* 31 (6):822–28.

Illinois Department of Public Health (1991) "Recommendations and Priorities for Minority Health in Illinois." Report of the Year 2000 Work Group on Minority Health. Springfield, Ill.

Kimble, M. A. (1990) "Religion: Friend or Foe of Aging?" In *Second Opinion* 15:70–79.

Koenig, H. G., J. N. Kvale, and C. Ferrel (1988) "Religion and Well-Being in Later Life." *The Gerontologist* 28 (1):18–28.

Northwest Aging Association (1991) "Parish Nurses: Linking Health, Social, and Religious Institutions, Project Description Booklet." Spencer, Iowa: Northwest Aging Association.

Peterson, R. E. (1982) *A Study of the Healing Church and Its Ministry*. New York: Lutheran Church in America.

Ryan, J. A. (1990) "Liability for Parish Nursing Practice." Paper presented at the Fourth Annual Granger Westberg Symposium. Northbrook, Ill.

Shannon, I. R. (1991) "Healthy People 2000: Challenges and Opportunities." *Journal of Nursing Administration* 21 (12):5, 25.

Smuts, J. C. (1961) *Holism and Evolution*. Compass Books edition. New York: Viking Press.

Solari-Twadell, P. A., A. M. Djupe, and M. A. McDermott, eds. (1990) *Parish Nursing: The Developing Practice*. Park Ridge, Ill.: Parish Nurse Resource Center.

Westberg, G. E., and J. W. McNamara (1981) *The Health Cabinet*. Park Ridge, Ill.: Parish Nurse Resource Center.

______ (1990) *The Parish Nurse*. Minneapolis, Minn.: Augsburg.

23 Congregation-Sponsored Housing

F. ELLEN NETTING

Understanding housing for older adults requires attention to a complex set of issues. First, older adults comprise a highly diverse population with differing needs. Therefore, there must be alternative types of shelter that address the needs and desires of different persons. Second, many older adults want to "age in place," remaining in a familiar environment as they get older. Therefore, housing options must include what can be done to repair, upgrade, assist, and aid older persons in their own homes so that they can "age in place." Third, it is important to recognize the interdependence of housing and long-term care for an aging population. This means that we must consider the unique and changing dimensions of the aging person within a housing environment that can accommodate different social, psychological, and physical needs. These issues focus primarily on the fit of the individual with his or her environment.

There are also multiple macro issues that face those groups and organizations that seek to provide housing options that are sensitive to the needs of older adults. These issues concern the practical implications of how to plan, fund, build, and develop housing, as well as how to respond to regulations and standards within the housing industry. Religious groups have faced these issues whenever and wherever they have sponsored senior housing.

In this chapter we will begin with an overview of housing available for older adults, then focus on what is known about the types of housing provided for the elderly by religious groups. Next we will examine the meaning of religious sponsorship and conclude with a discussion of how congregations can approach housing for elderly persons in their communities.

TYPES OF HOUSING FOR OLDER ADULTS

Over 90 percent of older persons live in their own houses or apartments. This figure includes those who reside in public housing developments as well as those who live in age-segregated retirement communities such as Sun City (Tilson and Fahey, 1990, xx). Therefore, the vast majority of the elderly live in what is often called "independent" living environments.

The remaining 10 percent of the elderly live in more sheltered housing environments. At any one time, approximately 5 percent (1.4 million) are residents in nursing homes. An estimated one million reside in "specialized" housing designed to provide varying levels of supportive services. These include "300,000 in congregate housing, 350,000–700,000 in licensed and unlicensed residential care facilities, and 200,000 in continuing care retirement communities. An unknown number live in miscellaneous residential settings such as hotels, boardinghouses, and shared housing" (Tilson and Fahey, 1990, xx–xxi).

There are many ways to classify and categorize housing for the elderly. In fact, new terms are constantly emerging, some of which are not well defined and others of which mean essentially the same thing. Different states regulate different types of housing, and there is often a great deal of variation in the comprehensiveness of state regulations.

In this chapter, we will examine three broad categories of housing for the elderly: (1) independent living, (2) supportive housing, and (3) nursing home environments. Although this is somewhat of a false trichotomy, the reader will soon see how many variations there are on the themes within each category. For example, independent living encompasses everything from single-family housing to portions of continuing care retirement communities, just as assisted living encapsulates board and care homes for the poor and catered living environments targeted to the more affluent. In short, the housing landscape is varied and its variety is increasing as the senior market expands.

Independent Living

Independent living is somewhat of a misnomer, given the interdependence of persons within societies. However, since the term is often used to denote those environments in which older persons function with minimal assistance, it is used here as an umbrella for discussing home ownership as well as retirement community concerns.

Home Ownership. Most older persons own their own homes and have paid off their mortgages. For many of these persons, their major asset is the equity in their home. State initiatives have been enacted to offer options for home equity conversions, home repair and improvement programs, property tax relief and deferrals, rental assistance, and condominium conversion protection (Tiven and Ryther, 1986). The intent of these various provisions is to assist older persons in remaining in their own homes as long as possible.

The desire to remain within one's own home has led to an increasing interest in the provision of in-home services among the elderly. Consequently, the home as the arena for the provision of social and health-care services has become the focus of more and more research (Gubrium and Sankar, 1990; Ory and Duncker, 1992). In-home services include everything from the use of high-tech medicine, including enteral/parenteral nutrition and chemotherapy, to the use of durable medical equipment and the provision of respite care services (Hughes, 1992). In short, the home environment has been a significant site of accommodation for an aging population. Hughes lists over twenty types of services provided within home settings, noting that "these services are funded by different payers and have different eligibility criteria" (1992, 53).

Continuing to live within one's own home depends upon a number of variables. The first consideration is whether a person lives alone or with others, and whether or not there are available and willing caregivers within the home or nearby. Caregivers may be needed on a temporary or permanent basis to assist with instrumental activities of living such as shopping or doing laundry or with more personal activities such as bathing or dressing. Second, living in one's own home is contingent upon having the financial resources necessary to purchase needed assistance that will substitute for or replace the need for informal caregiving. Third, the required resources must be available within the community in which the person lives. Even with adequate financial means, there must be a provider who can come to the person's home (Tilson and Fahey, 1990).

There is some question as to when living within one's home is no longer considered independent living. For example, if an older widow has a daughter who will serve as caregiver around the clock, then the widow may remain at home. However, for all practical purposes, she is not "independent" even though she is in an environment that is perceived to be on the independent end of the housing continuum. There does not appear to be consensus on when one's own home ceases to be an independent living environment and when it actually becomes equivalent to supportive housing.

Naturally occurring retirement communities (NORCs) are those areas in which a number of persons have aged in place. When they moved into the community (whether it is an apartment building or a neighborhood of single family homes), they were younger and probably in better health. As time has progressed, these communities have become places in which there are large numbers of older persons. They are often seen as "both an opportunity and a challenge" (Tilson and Fahey, 1990, xxii) because they are places where support systems can be developed at the same time that issues can be resolved as residents require assistance.

Retirement Communities. Over the years there have been many attempts to classify and define retirement communities. Hunt and his colleagues (1984) suggest that retirement communities be defined very broadly and that within this definition there are several types. They see these communities as "aggregations of housing units" with minimal services available "planned for people who are predominantly healthy and retired." Their three specific criteria are: "housing, services, and residents" (4–5).

Five types of retirement communities fall within this broad definition. They are "retirement new towns, retirement villages, retirement subdivisions, retirement residences, and continuing care retirement centers" (Hunt et al., 1984,

12). The attributes of size of community population, the health status and age of the residents, the types of services available particularly in terms of the numbers and type of health, recreational, and commercial services, and sponsorship type (for profit and nonprofit) were considered in this classification scheme.

Retirement new towns are privately developed and attract young, active retirees. These towns are self-contained in that they are actually communities designed for the retired with appropriate businesses and services within their domains. Retirement villages are smaller versions of the new towns, with fewer persons and fewer commercial or health facilities available. Retirement subdivisions are residential, not having businesses and services within the division itself. They may even be age-integrated but tend to attract a retired population. Retirement residences offer a number of activities for individuals and groups, but are less focused on outdoor activities that attract persons to towns and villages. Continuing care retirement communities (CCRCs) offer a continuum of housing types, including independent living units, assisted living units, and nursing care (Hunt et al., 1984).

Supportive Housing

A thin line exists between the concept of independent housing and supportive housing. Because older persons are unique and everyone's needs and resources vary, one person's definition of independence will be different from another's. Is the person who lives within his or her own home but has round the clock nursing care considered independent? Obviously not, but the person resides in what is called "independent" housing. This is why it is so important to see housing in the context of long-term care. As the person ages in place and as he or she needs change, there may be attempts to maintain that individual in the least restrictive housing environment.

Congregate Housing. Although the concept of congregate or group housing dates back at least 2,000 years (Nachison, 1985, 34), the first public housing development built exclusively for the elderly in the United States was Victoria Plaza in San Antonio, Texas. This development opened in 1960. Although low-income older persons had been housed in public housing for years, managers realized that buildings designed for younger families did not always accommodate to aging needs. Victoria Plaza was the first in a wave of public housing developments designed to accommodate a lower-income aging population in the United States (Thompson, 1985).

During the 1970s, the United States Department of Housing and Urban Development (HUD) subsidized the development of independent congregate housing and the number of units increased. During the 1980s, the HUD Section 202 program was greatly cut back and current opportunities for affordable housing have not kept pace with demand.

Streib (1990) emphasizes that there is no one concise definition of congregate housing. He does say that generally congregate housing "refers to a multi-unit apartment building in which the apartments all have bathrooms and kitchens or kitchenettes, and where the management provides some supportive services, such as a dining room where residents can obtain at least one main meal a day, optional housekeeping, transportation, and twenty-four hour watch service" (75).

Private sector retirement communities predate federal housing initiatives, although their numbers increased more rapidly when government subsidies became available (Streib, 1990). A number of years ago, the idea "of building two different types of 'retirement' homes: detached houses or garden apartments set in age-segregated communities, such as Leisure World or Sun City" (Tilson and Fahey, 1990, xxii) emerged. These homes were designed to attract the independent, well elderly. Supportive services and recreational opportunities were additional attractions to these communities. The garden apartment type of living became the more modern-day congregate housing in which elderly persons could remain relatively independent but would have some services available should the need arise.

A review of the congregate housing research literature reveals that socioeconomic status is very important to understanding housing the elderly. Streib (1990) identifies three general strata of the aged whose congregate housing needs will vary. First, the affluent are served by private developers. Second, the poor reside in government-subsidized housing. A third group are the middle-income persons who cannot afford private developments but who do not qualify for public housing. These persons typically own their own homes and attempt to stay there as long as possible, given increasing frailty.

Assisted Living. Assisted living has become a buzzword of the housing industry for the 1990s. Often, assisted living is defined as neither independent housing nor nursing care—a vague area between living on one's own and needing around-the-clock care. Regnier (1991) suggests that assisted living is distinctive in that it is built specifically for the purpose of offering certain services that may be needed as persons get older. There are many names used to describe this type of housing, some of which include "residential care facilities, personal care homes, catered living facilities, retirement homes, homes for adults, board and care homes, domiciliary care homes, rest homes, community residents" (ALFAA, 1991, 1), sheltered care, adult congregate living facilities and enriched or residential housing (Hendrickson, 1988).

There are approximately 30,000 to 40,000 assisted living facilities in the United States, according to the Assisted Living Facilities Association of America (ALFAA, 1991, 1). It is believed that there is a favorable growth climate for this type of housing because it offers a bridge between independent living and nursing care for those who can no longer remain in their own homes. Because assisted living is designed for persons who need at least some services, it is not surprising that a typical resident is seventy-five or older, female, and living alone (ALFAA, 1991,1).

Board and Care Homes. "Board and care housing refers to the provision by a nonrelative of food, shelter, and some degree of protective oversight and/or generally nonmedical personal care" (Newcomer and Stone, 1985, 38.) Board and care homes have provided housing for the elderly and disabled for many years in this country. Because there are so many variations on the theme, it is difficult to describe the "typical" home. Often called residential care facilities (RCFs), these homes house between 350,000 and 700,000 frail elderly in different states (Tilson and Fahey, 1990, xxiii).

Nursing Homes

Before the Social Security Act of 1935 became law, poor older persons had few options. They would usually become residents of poorhouses or almshouses if they had nowhere else to go and if they needed long-term care. Even with the passage of the Social Security Act there was still not enough money to cover health-care costs. Without health insurance, a "cottage industry" of private rest homes developed. These facilities were often run by unemployed nurses out of their own homes and were the forerunners of the modern nursing home (Oktay and Palley, 1988).

Nursing homes are often considered health-care institutions and are not described as housing per se. However, for the 5 percent of older persons who reside in nursing homes for months and even years, the nursing home is both "house" and "health-care provider." It may also be the last place some persons will call "home." Therefore, it is important to recognize that nursing homes provide housing just as they provide health care.

RELIGIOUS GROUPS AND SENIOR HOUSING

Homes for the aged as well as hospitals for the poor and incurable emerged on the American landscape during the 1800s, when parishes were unable to support all of their members. These charities were established to supplement what could be provided in the home. During this time, public funded institutions such as the poorhouse also arose. These organizations became the forerunners of today's senior housing (Winklevoss and Powell, 1984).

Housing the elderly has long been a concern for religious groups. When the Bureau of Labor Statistics surveyed homes for the aged in 1929, 80 percent were operated by religious or private organizations. Parent religious bodies had limited or no pension funds for their retired clergy, and these homes served as a refuge for older religious leaders, missionaries, and widows with no other place to go. During the 1930s, as public debate over social security continued, religious groups developed housing that was to become the modern-day continuing care retirement community (CCRC). Of those early homes that had continuing care contracts for their residents prior to the mid-1930s, the majority were sponsored by the Methodists, the Presbyterians, the Church of Christ, and private foundations (Winklevoss and Powell, 1984, 7–8).

The National Council of Churches studied health and welfare organizations under Protestant auspices in 1955. Of the 2,783 organizations surveyed, 494 (18 percent) were homes for the aged. They found that there was no identifiable pattern of what constituted a typical Protestant home. The diversity was surprising (Cayton and Nishi, 1955).

Within the United States, therefore, there are both private and public traditions that have resulted in housing designed for older adults. Lest the reader believe that these traditions are mutually exclusive, housing subsidized by government funds has been initiated, developed, and managed by private nonprofit providers. Many of these have been religious groups. In short, the traditions have been interactive.

An example of how government actually encouraged the growth of senior housing was evidenced in 1959, when the National Housing Act created the Section 231 program. Federal mortgage insurance assisted in the creation of new or greatly remodeled rental housing for the elderly. In the early 1960s, a number of nonprofit continuing care retirement communities were constructed with federal 231 monies (Winklevoss and Powell, 1984, 10).

Similarly, Section 202 housing developments have been developed by church groups, fraternal orders, or other nonprofits. A national survey of Section 202 housing for the elderly and the handicapped indicated that religious groups sponsored 59 percent of all 202 developments for the aged (Special Committee on Aging United States Senate, 1984).

Because of the separation of church and state in the United States, the government does not collect data on religious giving and charitable activity. Therefore, there is no central data base from which one can determine just how many congregational dollars are contributed to senior housing initiatives. Although some denominations collect various data on charitable giving, there is no systematic collection process across congregations for all religious groups (Hodgkinson et al., 1988).

Congregations and Senior Housing

A National Survey. In 1988, the Independent Sector conducted the first national study of the activities and finances of congregations across religious groups. An advisory group of Catholics, Protestants, Jews, Mormons, Muslims, and Buddhists was created in 1986. A sample of 4,205 congregations representing different parts of the country was selected and a detailed survey was conducted (Hodgkinson et al., 1988, 2–3).

The Independent Sector defined a religious congregation as "a community of people who meet together for worship, for fellowship, and for service to their members and the larger community in which they live" (Hodgkinson et al., 1988, 1). In 1986 there were more than 300,000 religious congregations related to numerous religious groups, and 65 percent of adults indicated that they are members of a church or synagogue (Hodgkinson et al., 1988, 1). Many questions were asked about congregation size, composition, expenditures, programs, volunteer time, and activities. Under activities, congregations were asked if they provided housing for senior citizens. A total of 54,755 (18.6 percent) reported affirmatively. Larger congregations (23.4 percent) were more likely to provide housing than were small (12.9 percent) or medium-sized (17.2 percent) congregations (Hodgkinson et al., 1988, 18). Congregation-supported senior housing was fairly evenly spread across urban and rural environments. More liberal congregations (27 percent) were more likely to engage in senior housing activities than were moderate (20 percent), conservative (17 percent), or very conservative (13 percent) congregations (Hodgkinson et al., 1988, 19).

The Independent Sector's study marked a significant beginning to collecting data on religious congregations. Their results emphasized the fact that congregations are actively engaged in human service activities. Although only 18.6 percent reported participating in senior housing activities, 86.9 percent of all respondents were engaged in areas of human services (e.g., preschool day care, family counseling, homeless shelters, meal services, recreation) (Hodgkinson et al., 1988, 18).

Congregations and Affordable Housing. We know that congregations are sponsoring affordable housing for low-income families and the elderly because of the work of an organization based in Washington, D.C. called the Churches' Conference on Shelter and Housing. This organization describes itself as "an ecumenical network of churches, nonprofit organizations, and individuals who believe that the poor have suffered unjustly and too long because of the lack of safe and affordable housing" (Churches' Conference on Shelter and Housing, 1991, 2).

Six models of congregation-sponsored housing ministries have been developed, based on success stories of religious groups who have engaged in these ventures. These models are designed for single congregations that want to do something for persons who are homeless or near homeless. The six models include: (1) eviction prevention, (2) resettling families, (3) temporary church housing, (4) subsidized subleases, (5) developing rental property, and (6) developing housing for sale. Because these models are designed for persons who are homeless, poor, and dispossessed, target populations include all age groups (Churches' Conference on Shelter and Housing, 1990).

In its literature the Churches' Conference on Shelter and Housing offers case examples of successful housing initiatives sponsored by local congregations. They offer Victory Housing, Inc. as an example of denominational, permanent housing alternatives for the elderly. Victory Housing began in 1979, when a facility for the aged was built in the Bethesda parish of the Archdiocese of Washington, D.C. "Most significantly, the original entity has provided high-quality sheltered housing for over 20 frail and elderly citizens in two self-supporting facilities, creating a model of public-private partnership that has attracted favorable attention throughout the nation" (Coates, 1989, 47).

The Churches' Conference on Shelter and Housing's campaign for affordable housing is called "One-Church-One-Home." The Conference reports that three denominations have begun issuing documents and resolutions in support of this campaign. In March 1991, the National Capital Presbytery (118 churches) enacted a comprehensive housing policy urging all Presbyterian congregations to work toward the development of affordable housing in their communities. The Washington diocese of the Episcopal Church created a task force at their 1989 convention that resulted in a working document to engage Episcopal churches in housing ministries. At the denominational level, the General Board of Global Ministries of the United Methodist Church is presenting a resolution at their 1992 General Conference (Kinkannon, 1991, 1). In short, there is movement within the religious community to support the affordable housing campaign at the local and national levels.

Religious Sponsorship of CCRCs

The American Association of Homes for the Aged (AAHA) is a national organization for nonprofit housing for the elderly with a membership of more than "3,400 nursing homes, residential retirement complexes, continuing care retirement communities (CCRCs), low-income rental housing, and community service organizations. Seventy-five percent of its member facilities are sponsored by religious organizations" (AAHA and Ernst and Young, 1989, 1).

Since 1985 AAHA, in conjunction with Ernst and Young, has been developing a database on continuing care retirement communities. Their reports indicate that CCRCs are traditionally long established by religious and fraternal groups. Before World War II, these organizations provided services to the elderly in more institutional-looking settings and "viewed their residents or 'guests' as dependents of the religious sponsor" (AAHA and Ernst and Young, 1988, 7).

It was within the CCRC industry that questions of religious affiliation received serious attention in the late 1970s and early 1980s. In 1978, a chain of United Methodist CCRCs filed bankruptcy. A class action suit against the corporation resulted in an out-of-court settlement of $21 million (Gaffney and Sorensen, 1984). Following this situation, parent religious bodies began to question the nature of religious sponsorship and affiliation. Other denominations began to study the implications of sponsoring this type of senior housing. In October 1984, the American Baptist Homes and Hospitals Association and their Board of National Ministries held a conference on "The Church and Its Affiliate Agencies: Symposium on Sponsorship Liability" (Rasmussen, 1984).

Netting (1987) conducted a study of nine CCRCs to explore the meaning of religious affiliation for these providers of senior housing, given the turmoil that had occurred after the sponsorship liability issues were raised. The diversity of sponsorship models was surprising. Among only nine organizations there were seven distinctive models of religious affiliation: (1) affiliation with a religious order, (2) affiliation with a single congregation, (3) affiliation with multiple congregations of the same denomination, (4) affiliation with multiple congregations from two or more religious denominations, (5) begun by religious leaders but not officially sponsored by any particular church, synagogue, or denomination, (6) sponsored by a denomination, and (7) affiliation with a corporate intermediary. Obviously, the structural arrangements surrounding affiliation varied.

In a followup study, Netting (1991) surveyed 284 religiously affiliated CCRCs in forty-two states. She found that structural relationships between communities and their religious sponsors were difficult to categorize and no identifiable patterns emerged. One hundred and sixty nine (60 percent) respondents indicated that their affiliation with a religious group had never implied financial liability by that group. Another thirty-eight (13 percent) reported that the parent body had been but was no longer responsible financially for debts. Forty-nine (17 percent) communities reported that their religious sponsors were financially liable. Ninety-seven (34 percent) respondents indicated that their denominations were building more retirement communities, while another 182 (64 percent) saw their denominations as making the elderly a high priority. Advantages to religious affiliation were viewed as consumer trust in the community and the opportunity to carry out the church's mission, gain access to residents, and market to seniors.

IMPLICATIONS FOR CONGREGATIONS SPONSORING HOUSING FOR THE ELDERLY

If there are lessons to be learned about senior housing and religious sponsorship, it is that variation and diversity can be expected and that complexity reigns. This makes congregation sponsorship of housing for the elderly a challenge as well as an opportunity for creative thinking.

Variation and diversity means that there is no "one right way" to plan and design senior housing for older adults. There are multiple models, all of which can work, given the aspirations of local congregations and the needs of their communities. We do not have a complete picture of what congregations are doing in terms of senior housing. We do know from the Independent Sector's study that almost 19 percent of congregations in the United States are doing something with senior housing. Exactly what they are doing, we do not know. We do know from efforts of the Churches' Conference on Shelter and Housing that more and more congregations are creating affordable housing alternatives for the poor and the homeless, some of whom are elderly. The Conference provides direction for these congregations in terms of how to proceed to make this happen according to several different models. We do not know the numbers of congregations that are actually providing affordable housing for the elderly.

The complexity of the situation is underscored when religious congregations discover the multitude of issues surrounding what might at first glance appear to be a fairly straightforward concern for shelter. These areas include: (1) selection of target population, (2) aging in place, (3) accommodation and relocation, and (4) regulations and standards. Each of these areas will be briefly examined.

First, congregations will have to determine who the target population is that they want to serve. Today continuing care retirement communities that have traditionally been religiously sponsored often target middle-income retirees. As the for-profit industry embraces the CCRC concept and increasingly targets the "senior market," these communities are often designed to attract affluent elderly. Ironically, CCRCs are often seen as exclusively for the rich, when in actuality there are many church-related homes that serve a middle-income group of elderly who sold their homes and used the equity to buy into the community.

If congregations determine that their priority is serving the low-income elderly, the Churches' Conference on Shelter and Housing may be a resource for providing valuable technical assistance. However, it is important to remember that the low-income family of today may become low-income elders of tomorrow. Because aging is a lifelong process, a congregation that sponsors housing for families may find that they provide opportunities so that these same persons will be in better health and have more chance of success as they age. There is a diverse population in the United States today who do not have adequate shelter. Among these persons is an increasing number of elderly who "are caught in a growing shortage of low-income housing" (Keigher and Pratt, 1991, 2). Therefore, each congregation will have to consider whether it is senior housing that they seek to provide, family housing, or both. In addition, targeting means considering such factors as socioeconomic status, degree of frailty, functional ability, social support (elders living alone), spiritual needs, and health status.

Second, aging in place has become a phrase rampant throughout the gerontological literature. What it means is that persons often want to remain in familiar surroundings, in the place that they call "home," as they get older. This means that congregational members need to balance the autonomy of older persons with their own desires to be beneficent and to provide a safer, more secure living environment. Therefore, congregations may want to consider ways to support older persons within their current housing by developing chore and housekeeping services. These in-home services may be as important as developing alternative housing opportunities, because they may allow older persons to remain in their current housing for a longer period of time. Perhaps congregations will want to address spiritual needs of elders at home, and a chaplaincy outreach program would be appropriate.

Third, questions about accommodation and relocation arise when congregations consider providing senior housing. As one ages, one accommodates to changes that occur. The goal for senior housing, however, is to provide a flexible environment that can accommodate to the aging person's needs. When accommodation is not possible, relocation is a consideration. There are emotional issues, as well as practical concerns, tied to decisions to relocate.

Hofland (1990) suggests four models relevant to living environments for the aged. He calls Model I the Rejection Model. This model is used when independent housing environments will not accommodate to aging needs. As long as the individual is independent, he or she can remain. As soon as he or she cannot be independent, the individual must relocate. Model II is a Social Services Model. This approach fosters dependence in that services are provided to all residents whether they are needed by everyone or not. Model II, therefore, does not respect the individual needs of older persons. A third approach is the Participation Model. There is recognition that older persons are different, and there is an attempt to engage them in deciding what supportive services are needed. A fourth model is an ideal for self-actualization. This last approach would require social reform in that our views of the old would have to be transformed to see the full potential in communities that house the old.

Hofland raises our consciousness in thinking about what senior housing could be—a place where older persons live in fear of being relocated when they become frail *or* an opportunity to live with increasing frailty in an accommodating and caring environment that responds to individual needs. Congregations do not have to sponsor housing in order to contribute to the self-actualization of older residents. Local congregations can develop service projects that support residents within already existing public and private housing developments within their local communities. Local congregations can also advocate for the development of affordable housing.

Fourth, regulations and standards are part of the senior housing industry. Each local community will have its own building codes and zoning requirements. Each state has its own laws and regulations. Some states regulate continuing care retirement communities, others do not. Some states regulate assisted living or board and care homes, whereas others are considering regulation (Netting, Wilson, and Coleman, 1991). If a religious group decides to sponsor housing for the elderly, they will need to recognize the fact that senior housing is a public-private venture. Even if federal or state funds are not used in building the housing, the development of housing will be potentially subject to local, state, and federal oversight.

In addition to public oversight of various types of housing and long-term care facilities, there are developing standards for self-regulation. For example, in "1985 the American Association of Homes for the Aged (AAHA) sponsored the creation of the Continuing Care Accreditation Commission (CCAC) to establish and administer a national accreditation program. . . . Unlike regulation, the process is a voluntary, self-regulatory system of quality assurance that requires a comprehensive self-study and a site visit by a Commission-appointed peer-review team" (Somers and Spears, 1992, 26). The development of standards for various types of housing holds promise for improving the quality of care provided and should be understood by religious congregations eager to embrace various housing models.

SUMMARY

Congregation-sponsored housing for the elderly is a multifaceted challenge offering multiple options. Not only are there many types of housing that can be provided, but there are many subgroups within the elderly population. Determining what target group will be selected, as well as what housing needs will be met for that group, requires careful planning.

Congregations throughout the United States are engaged in senior housing initiatives. These initiatives vary considerably from repair programs for older homeowners to elaborate continuing care retirement communities that have entire denominations sponsoring them. Housing environments include independent living arrangements, a range of supportive housing types, and nursing home environments.

In a time when affordable housing is a pressing national need, there are real opportunities for religious groups to increase their awareness of housing issues and to respond to the needs of a diverse aging population.

BIBLIOGRAPHY

American Association of Homes for the Aged and Ernst and Young (1989) *Continuing Care Retirement Communities: An Industry in Action*. Washington, D.C.: AAHA.

American Baptist Homes and Hospitals Association (1984) *The Proceedings of the Church and Its Affiliated Agencies: Symposium on Sponsorship Liability*. Philadelphia, Pa.: American Baptist Homes and Hospitals Association (ABHHA) and the Board of National Ministries, October 11–13.

Assisted Living Facilities Association of America (ALFAA) (1991) Fact Sheet: Assisted Living.

Cayton, H. R., and S. M. Nishi (1955) *Churches and Social Welfare.* Vol. 2. *The Changing Scene.* New York: National Council of Churches of Christ in the U.S.A.

The Churches' Conference on Shelter and Housing (1990) *One Church: One Home—Six Models of Congregation-sponsored Housing Ministries.* Information from the Conference 1830 Connecticut Avenue, N.W., Washington DC 20009.

______ (1991) Information pamphlet available from the Conference at 1830 Connecticut Avenue, N.W., Washington DC 20009.

Coates, R. (1989) *Building on Faith: Models of Church-sponsored Affordable Housing Programs in the Washington, D.C. Area.* Washington, D.C.: The Churches' Conference on Shelter and Housing.

Gaffney, E. M., and P. C. Sorensen (1984) *Ascending Liability in Religious and Other Nonprofit Organizations.* Macon, Ga.: Mercer University Press.

Gubrium, J. F., and A. Sankar, eds. (1990) *The Home Care Experience: Ethnography and Policy.* Newbury Park, Calif.: Sage.

Hendrickson, M. C. (1988) "Assisted Living: An Emerging Focus on an Expanding Market: Assisted Living Represents a Strategic Interaction of the LTC and Retirement Housing Industries." *Contemporary Long-Term Care* 11:20–23.

Hodgkinson, V. A., M. S. Weitzman, S. Murray, and A. D. Kirsch. (1988) *From Belief to Commitment: The Activities and Finances of Religious Congregations in the United States: Findings from a National Survey.* Washington, D.C.: Independent Sector.

Hofland, B. (1990) "Value and Ethical Issues in Residential Environments for the Elderly." In Tilson, 241–71.

Hughes, S. (1992) "Home Care: Where We Are and Where We Need to Go." In Ory and Duncker, 53–74.

Hunt, M. et al. (1984) *Retirement Communities: An American Original.* New York: Haworth.

Keigher, S. M., and F. Pratt (1991) "Growing Housing Hardship Among the Elderly." *Journal of Housing for the Elderly* 8:1–18.

Kinkannon, K. C. (1991) "Denominational Support for One-Church-One-Home is Developing." *Faith and Action: Newsletter of the Churches Conference on Shelter and Housing* 5 (3):1–6.

Nachison, J. S. (1985) "Who Pays? The Congregate Housing Question." *Generations* 9:34–36.

Netting, F. E. (1987) "Religiously Affiliated Continuum of Care Retirement Communities." *Journal of Religion and Aging* 4:51–66.

______ (1991) "The Meaning of Church Affiliation for Continuum of Care Retirement Communities." *Journal of Religious Gerontology* 8:79–99.

Netting, F. E., and C. C. Wilson (1991) "Accommodation and Relocation Decision Making in Continuing Care Retirement Communities." *Health and Social Work* 16:266–73.

Netting, F. E., C. C. Wilson, and N. Coleman (1991) "Assisted Living: New Term, Old Concept." Unpublished paper presented at the Gerontological Society of America's Annual Scientific Program, San Francisco, November 16.

Newcomer, R. A., and R. Stone (1985) "Board and Care Housing: Expansion and Improvement Needed." *Generations* 9:38–39.

Oktay, J., and H. A. Palley (1988) "The Frail Elderly and the Promise of Foster Care." *Adult Foster Home Journal* 2:8–25.

Ory, M. G., and A. P. Duncker, eds. (1992) *In-Home Care for Older People, Health and Supportive Services.* Newbury Park, Calif.: Sage.

Rasmussen, R. D. (1984) "Autonomy and Independence." In ABHHA, 5–11.

Regnier, V. (1991) "Assisted Living: An Evolving Industry." *Seniors Housing News* (pamphlet):1–5.

Somers, A. R., and N. L. Spears (1992) *The Continuing Care Retirement Community.* New York: Springer.

Special Committee on Aging United States Senate (1984) *Section 202 Housing for the Elderly and Handicapped: A National Survey.* Washington, D.C.: U.S. Government Printing Office.

Streib, G. F. (1990) "Congregate Housing: People, Places, Policies." In Tilson, 75–100.

Thompson, M. M. (1985) "The First Public Housing for the Elderly." *Generations* 9:11–15.

Tilson, D., ed. (1990) *Aging in Place: Supporting the Frail Elderly in Residential Environments.* Glenview, Ill.: Scott, Foresman and Co.

Tilson, D., and C. Fahey (1990) "Introduction." In Tilson, xv–xxxiii.

Tiven, M., and B. Ryther (1986) *State Initiatives in Elderly Housing: What's New, What's Tried, and True.* Washington, D.C.: Council of State Housing Agencies and National Association of State Units on Aging.

Winklevoss, H. E., and A. V. Powell (1984) *Continuing Care Retirement Communities: An Empirical, Financial, and Legal Analysis.* Homewood, Ill.: Irwin.

24 Congregation as a Spiritual Care Community

JANE M. THIBAULT

> Thoroughly unprepared we take this step into the afternoon of life . . . [on] the false presupposition that our truths and ideals will serve us as hitherto. But we cannot live the afternoon of life according to the programme of life's morning—for what . . . in the morning was true will at evening have become a lie. (Jung, 1933, 124–25)

STATEMENT OF PURPOSE

What is the "something different" needed to measure the afternoon and evening of our lives? Does it call for a change of activity, or does it require the transformation of an entire value system? In recent years there have been many attempts to answer this question, and solutions have come from a variety of sources. Groups ranging in interests from health-care providers to real estate developers have promoted such diverse solutions as the concentration on fitness with the enhancement of physical health to the development of increasingly elaborate retirement "communities" that often resemble resorts. Most of these solutions require a change of activity only. What is presented here is the challenge to yet another special-interest group—institutional religion—to transform a value system.

This chapter presents a different model by which to approach and measure life in the later years. It proposes the development of a continuum of small, congregation-based, spiritual care communities in which older adults would support, nurture, encourage, and challenge each other in the domain of the spiritual; they would become intimate spiritual companions for one another in true community. Based on contemplative rather than active values, such communities would serve to enhance the development of meaning in later life through growth in "being" rather than "doing" (Maslow, 1954, 291–99).

DEFINITION OF TERMS

Before discussing the need for such communities and a description of the proposed model, it is first necessary to define the terms *community, spiritual, contemplative,* and *being.* First, what is a true community? We often use the term *community* to describe a collection of loosely related people who have something in common. M. Scott Peck (1987, 59–61) states:

> In our culture of rugged individualism—in which we generally feel that we dare not be honest about ourselves, even with the person in the pew next to us—we bandy around the word "community." We apply it to almost any collection of individuals—a town, a church, a synagogue, a fraternal organization, an apartment complex, a professional association—regardless of how poorly those individuals communicate with each other. It is a false sense of the word. . . . If we are going to use the word meaningfully we must restrict it to a group of individuals who have learned how to communicate honestly with each other, whose relationships go deeper than their masks of composure, and who have developed some significant commitment to "rejoice together, mourn together," and to "delight in each other, make others' conditions our own."

In a similar manner, Jean Vanier (1989, 13–35), founder of the l'Arche communities for the mentally impaired and their caregivers, defines community as an entity where there is "interpersonal relationship, a sense of belonging, and an orientation of life to a common goal and common witness."

In essence, then, for this paper the working definition of a community is a group of individuals who come together intentionally, who share a common purpose, who will honestly enable each other to accomplish that purpose, and who believe that individual purposes can best be accomplished through group endeavor. Relating the above concepts of community to the model presented in this chapter, a spiritual care community is a gathering of older individuals who choose to come together out of a desire to grow spiritually, and who choose to do this in the context of a group because they value the lessons that can be learned from in-depth sharing with one another in an atmosphere of mutual trust, care, concern, and love.

What is meant here by the related words *spirit, spiritual,* and *spirituality?* Various religious groups and denominations have their unique, specific definitions of these terms. In 1971, the White House Conference on Aging attempted to generalize the terms and stated that "all persons are spiritual, even if they have no use for religious institutions and practice no personal pieties" (Moberg, 1971). Conference members then proceeded to clarify their statement by defining the term *spiritual* as: (1) pertaining to one's inner resources, especially one's ultimate concern; (2) the basic value around which all other values are focused; (3) the central philosophy of life—religious, nonreligious, or antireligious—that guides conduct; and (4) the supernatural and nonmaterial dimensions of human nature.

The generic nonreligious term *spirit,* then, is the energy that enables one to reach out to embrace one's basic life-enhancing value, ethic, and ultimate concern, however those are defined. The term *spirituality* flows from that definition and refers to a particular spiritual "style," the way the person seeks, finds or creates, uses, and expands personal meaning in the context of the entire universe (Thibault et al., 1991). In the strictly religious sense, *spiritual* refers to one's search for and growing relationship with God and the values and activities associated with that relationship.

The words *contemplative* and *being* are closely related. *Contemplative* has a very specific theological definition as well as a more philosophical definition. Theologically, the term *contemplative* refers to a person who engages in contemplation, which is a particular mode of prayer. Thomas Merton (1978, 36) defines contemplation as "a supernatural love and knowledge of God, simple and obscure, infused by Him into the summit of the soul, giving it a direct and experimental contact with Him." Webster's Dictionary (1956) defines contemplation as "meditation on spiritual things; the act of considering with attention, musing, study." The term *contemplative* means "devoted to prayer and meditation."

Being and being values have been studied by Abraham Maslow (1954, 291–99). Being values are those values that require one to stop, contemplate, to enjoy leisure, the arts—to be—rather than to be constantly coping, changing, working, acting. Thus, in order to learn to "be," one must learn to be contemplative in the more general sense of that word. When Jung says that the program of life's morning is inappropriate to later life, he is affirming the transition from the active life to the more contemplative life, which is one way to actualize the later years.

BACKGROUND: THE DEVELOPMENT OF WISDOM

Numerous studies of middle-aged and older adult populations indicate that the more interior, experiential, contemplative aspects of religion become increasingly important as individuals shed the roles and responsibilities of an earlier life and approach death (Moberg, 1968; Kivett, 1979; Bianchi, 1985).

The results of the research of gerontologist Bernice Neugarten (1968a) led her to conclude that when individuals become old, their ego functions gradually turn inward, causing a change in the way they master their environment. They become more passive and oriented toward their inner world rather than the exterior world. Neugarten refers to this change as a trend toward "interiority" of personality. This is not a new observation; Eastern cultures have recognized this trend toward interiority for many ages. In an essay Robert Bellah (1978) cites a discussion by Erikson of a Hindu theory of the life cycle. Erikson suggests that in Hindu culture there is a well-conceived distinction between the stage of the early adult householder, who is concerned with reproduction, family relations, power, and productivity, and the last two stages of life, which are defined as "the inner separation from all ties of selfhood, body-boundness, and their replacement by a striving which will eventually lead to renunciation and disappearance."

Erik Erikson speaks of the final stage of life as that which concerns itself with wisdom, the stage at which the individual achieves personal integrity or sinks into despair. The contemplative life is one devoted to the pursuit of wisdom through deliberate detachment from inordinate involvement in physical pleasure, wealth, and attainment through study and meditation. Thus, the contemplative way of living appears to be natural to this stage of life (Neugarten, 1968).

Expanding Erikson's thought, Robert Peck (1968, 88–92) states that the elderly have three tasks to accomplish before the personality can come to full development. These are: ego-differentiation versus work-role preoccupation, body transcendence versus body preoccupation, and ego-transcendence versus ego-preoccupation. He states that the manner of living during the last years of life might be

> to live so generously and unselfishly that the prospect of personal death—the night of the ego, it might be called—looks and feels less important than the secure knowledge that one has built for a broader, longer future than any one ego could ever encompass. . . . It might almost be seen as the most complete kind of ego-realization, even while it is focused on people and on issues which go far beyond immediate self-gratification in the narrow sense.

The work of Carl G. Jung (1933, 95–114) corresponds with that of Erikson and Peck concerning the developmental tasks of the latter part of life. Jung suggests that in the second half of life the person's attention turns inward, and that the person's inner exploration may enable him or her to find a meaning and wholeness in his or her life that makes it possible to accept death. In addition, Jung points out that in most primitive societies the old people are the sources of wisdom and the guardians of the mysteries and the laws in which the cultural heritage of the tribes is expressed.

Else Frenkel-Brunswik (1968) also describes a contemplative style of life as basic to her fifth and last developmental phase, which is characterized by a decrease in socialization, increase in hobbies and concern with animals and plants, and a preference for country rather than urban living. She, too, states that individuals in this last stage are frequently preoccupied with religious concerns.

A factor common to all the above developmental theories is that of increasing interiority. In many individuals this is accompanied by increased religious motivation or spirituality which may serve to prevent the individual from becoming self-preoccupied, isolated, and hypochondriacal.

A significant number of studies have dealt with issues of religion and spirituality in the lives of middle-aged and aging persons. David Moberg (1968, 497–508) identifies five dimensions of religiosity: the experiential, the ideological, the ritualistic, the intellectual, and the consequential dimensions. Moberg asserts that religious experiences, beliefs, and activities appear to be positively related to good socio-personal adjustment in old age. Also, "in all studies examined, with the exception of those relating to church attendance, trends indicate an increased interest in and concern about religion as age increases, even into extreme old age." It appears that despite the fact that older people may not be able to attend services and continue to participate in church activities, their religious beliefs and feelings continue and may even become more intense.

Thus, it can be concluded that older adults for whom religion is a vital aspect of life experience a significant sense of meaning, purpose, and true community with others of the same interest and commitment when participating in liturgical services, group study, charitable work, and other congregation-related activities (Gray and Moberg, 1977). However, it has been well documented that the attendance of older adults at public congregational functions often dwindles involuntarily with their advancing age, due primarily to increasing physical limitations (Heenan, 1972; Bahr, 1970). While these elderly may be "disengaged organizationally but engaged non-organizationally" (Mindel and Vaughan, 1985, 210–15), the withdrawal from active congregation life can also lead to greater levels of social disengagement, a lessening of the sense of purpose and meaning of life, and ultimately, to depression and disability. A recent study by Koenig, Kvale, and Ferrel (1988, 18–28) found strong correlation between levels of morale and the extent of a person's organizational and nonorganizational religious activity and intrinsic religiosity, and concluded that "religious attitudes and activities may influence the complex interactions of health . . . in later life."

THE MODEL: SPIRITUAL CARE COMMUNITY CONTINUUM

Proposed here is the development of a continuum of small, congregation-based, spiritual nurture and growth groups. The purpose of these groups is to foster the wholistic spiritual development of older adults by integrating five components necessary for the growth and development of any small spiritual community: mutual support, study, faith-sharing, outreach, and prayer/meditation (Archdiocese of Louisville, Office of Small Christian Communities, 1989). The following describes the development of the continuum, which is designed to have four levels of intensity of interpersonal interaction and involvement:

Level 1 incorporates information about the potential for spiritual nurture, growth, and development into already-existing congregational subgroups, such as a United Methodist Women's Circle, an Altar Society, or a Sunday School class. Information about aging is provided as the content of a single program.

The purpose is educational and the goal is to raise the consciousness of members of already-existing congregational groups to the fact that aging has its special bio-psycho-socio-spiritual needs and characteristics, not all of which can be met by the congregation as a whole.

Level 2 evolves as a response to a need identified on Level 1 or from another source and is usually both educational and supportive in nature. This group is a small gathering of eight to twelve people who commit to meeting weekly for a limited amount of time, usually no more than six weeks. The purpose is to explore individual and group potential for spiritual caring, growth, and development in later life. Because it is time limited, it enables the older adult to have an experience of intimacy with a group of like-minded people, but does not bring with it the need for a commitment to an ongoing community relationship.

Level 3 is a stable, long-term spiritual care group that develops from among those people in Level 2 who feel energized by the brief experience of community and want to continue at a deeper level and in a spirit of greater interpersonal connectedness. As the number of interactions increases over time, true community can arise within this group. In addition, as intimacy develops, these individuals often choose to meet with increasing frequency for sharing, support and encouragement, study, prayer, and service to society as well as to each other.

Level 4 is a much more radical evolvement of the Level 3 community. It occurs when members of the group desire to commit more fully to their faith journey and decide to covenant with one another for mutual spiritual care and growth in the context of true community. At this level, community members leave their own homes to live together either in one large home or in adjoining apartments in a building designed to have common space.

Precedents for the Spiritual Care Continuum

The model for such a continuum is not new. It has precedents in nearly all religions. Level 4 is representative of all monastic and conventual life as well as the communal lifestyle of groups of adults who live together for ideological purposes. It is very prevalent in the United States in Roman Catholic religious communities, but is also frequently found in Buddhist and other Eastern sects.

Level 3 can frequently be found in the Sunday School class that has had a consistent membership for a long period of time. Cursillo or Emmaus Walk support groups also fall into this category, as *may* United Methodist Womens' groups, Eastern Star, St. Vincent de Paul Societies, B'nai B'rith, Hadassah Sisterhoods, etc. The characteristic variable is that at some level the members have intentionally committed to the sharing of a deeper life experience with one another through one or more of the previously cited five components necessary to the development of community. Long-term small groups appear to fall into four categories: mini-churches, affinity groups, discipleship or growth groups, and recovery groups. Mini-churches are communities within the larger congregation.

Their heterogeneous members come together for worship, study, sharing, and caring. Affinity groups are homogeneous in membership and attract categories of individuals with common interests, such as singles, young marrieds, various categories of professionals, teenagers, retired men, etc. They last as long as there are enough members who need support and remain in that category. Discipleship or growth groups are heterogeneous and convene around an issue or activity such as social action, growth in the spiritual life, scripture study, prayer, etc. Recovery groups such as Alcoholics, Overeaters, or Gamblers Anonymous are also found in Level 3.

One highly organized example of Level 3 is the Roman Catholic Renew Program. In Renew, which is a nationwide program of spiritual renewal in the Catholic Church, each parish is divided into groups of about ten to twelve members who meet weekly to study, share, and pray together around a specified theme. Five six-week sessions are convened over a period of two years and each session lasts six weeks. In a significant number of churches Renew groups have continued to meet in community even after the official end of the program. Thus, Level 3 has very often been the basis for the development of true community within a congregation.

Level 2 groups abound and are found in nearly all congregations. They generally focus on an issue; education of the members around that issue is usually the purpose. True community usually does not have enough time to develop in such a short time, but Level 2 interaction can often create the desire for involvement in a longer-lasting group. Special events revolving around the liturgical calendar are the most common examples of Level 2 groups. Literature currently available for Level 2 groups designed for older adults include *Golden Years: Riding the Crest* (Cutler, 1990) and *A Time For: A Six Session Small Group Discussion Process with Older Adults* (Mulhall and Rowe, 1988).

Level 1 activity is commonly seen in most congregations. It can be a means by which older adults become aware of the potential for spiritual growth which comes with age and a call to those who are potential community members. A special speaker, theme for preaching, or Sunday School topic is an example of Level 1 contact.

The Need for Level 4: The Residential Spiritual Care Community

At this time there exist in the United States a growing number of congregation-related retirement "communities." The primary purpose of these facilities is to provide safe and appropriate levels of housing, meals, assistance with activities of daily living, and opportunities for socialization to large numbers of residents. Their main attraction is the security they provide the older person and the implied high quality of care ensured by the organization's "mission," i.e., the philosophical or theological value base of the congregational sponsor.

When the services such institutions offer are analyzed in terms of Abraham Maslow's hierarchy of human needs, one finds that they are providing quite well for the primary levels of human needs—the need for physiological survival and for safety. However, even at their best, most of these housing situations rarely meet the needs for belonging, self-esteem, self-actualization, and self-transcendence. Very seldom do they become true "communities" in which close and satisfying interpersonal relationships can develop and flourish. Even more rarely do they nurture spiritual growth. At times, friendships among residents and between residents and staff do develop, but little effort is made to establish and nurture the development of truly caring communities among the residents within these facilities.

Level 4 of the Spiritual Care Community Model proposes the development of a communal living situation. Using a community housing model (Brody, 1978), older individuals would not disengage organizationally with advancing frailty, but would strengthen their ties to each other and to the congregation by living together or in close proximity and by sharing their common goal of spiritual growth. In addition, members of such a community would enjoy the opportunity to continue to contribute to the well-being of society by engagement in contemplative living as well as through service or charitable activity when able. The human needs to be met in this type of community include all of the levels of Maslow's hierarchy of needs, from basic security through self-esteem and self-actualization to self-transcendence. Life in such a community would be particularly suited to the development of spiritual integration in later life (McFadden and Gerl, 1990).

At the present time there are no planned, congregation-sponsored retirement communities in this country that have been designed primarily to meet the spiritual needs of older adults. Neither are there religious communities in existence that have been created specifically for this population. The fact that the population of vowed Roman Catholic religious of both sexes is increasing greatly in age is generally regarded as a negative event in light of the orders' active service missions. Some religious orders and seminaries are increasingly willing to accept what are called "late vocations," but they do so with an attitude of great reserve, based on the recognition that the person may not be able to contribute many years of active service in the order and may become a financial burden in his or her last years. Still, vocation directors report that the incidence of request by those over the age of fifty-five to enter Catholic religious communities has increased greatly in the past ten years.

Most of the older people who are interested in joining religious communities have had vocations to marriage, parenthood, or the single life that have enabled them to live spiritual lives of varying intensity throughout adulthood. Many have been active leaders in their congregations. In later life they find themselves becoming even more interested in spiritual life, particularly the experiential and more contemplative aspects of spirituality, while the desire to continue active leadership in the congregation often wanes.

Some individuals seek and find the guidance of spiritual counselors or participate in lay groups associated with religious orders. Most often, the spiritual search in later life is a solitary, unencouraged, and lonely experience. The older person who is very spiritually oriented or "religious" is seldom actively encouraged in his or her quest by friends and family, and her deeper needs may often go unnoticed by her pastor, particularly in youth-oriented church communities (Longino and Kitson, 1985). As long as she can serve the church actively through education or service, she is considered an integral part of the adult congregation. But when she begins to yearn for the more meditative, solitary aspects of religious experience, there is rarely a supportive "community" for her. Sometimes she is not even aware of what she is yearning for, for there are few words to describe the trend towards interiority, especially for people who are theologically and psychologically unsophisticated.

A congregation-based spiritual care community for older adults seeks to accomplish four major goals. *First,* it provides a means by which deeply felt spiritual needs and longings can be met most effectively and efficiently in later life. Such a goal-oriented, meaning-based, "intentional" residential community can enhance the lives of the members by the provision of a daily, ongoing opportunity to share values, ideals, experiences, interests, and commitments in great depth. Participation in a living situation developed specifically for those individuals who yearn to enrich their interior, spiritual lives, and who also desire a support group in which to accomplish this may help to alleviate the problems of isolation and loneliness. This type of housing can foster the sense of true community as defined by Peck and Vanier.

A second goal of such a community is to provide individual members with an opportunity to explore their interior lives and their spiritual dimension in a serious way, with guidance from qualified spiritual counselors.

A third goal is that members continue to contribute in whatever way they can to serve the needs of the society, either by engagement in volunteer activities or by participation in limited part-time work in accordance with health, talents, and interests. This contact with the larger community can provide both young and old with a new image of the aging person as one who is continuing to grow and develop, albeit in a new direction, rather than as one who is biding time or playing bingo until death.

A fourth goal is a sense of connectedness with and concern for God and for all living things. For those who understand and appreciate the value and transformational function of contemplative "work" in the Christian, Jewish, and Buddhist faiths, participation in a community that fosters meditation and contemplative living can provide a unique way in which older adults can contribute to the well-being of all of society and the planet itself, thus providing the individual with a strong sense of meaning and purpose and a growing commitment to social responsibility.

Many devoutly religious people dread the day when they will be forced to give up church attendance or participation in Level 3 group activity. Level 4—the residential spiritual care community—appears to be one solution to this problem of isolation and lack of institutional support.

Level 4: The Design

As previously stated, there are described in the literature no residential communities with a religious or spiritual orientation designed specifically for older adults. The living arrangement that would fit the needs of a residential spiritual care community is the commonly found community housing for the elderly. Called "congregate living sites," the concept of community housing is that of basically independent living with communal aspects. In most of the cases, residents have either their own bedsitting rooms, bath, and small kitchen and share a communal living and dining room, or they have a separate bedroom but share a bath and perhaps a living room and kitchen with one other person and a large dining–living room with the rest of the residents. Many of the community houses are townhouses that have been remodeled to contain efficiency apartments, with provision for some communal space. The essential idea is to provide maximum privacy with maximum opportunity for interrelating, including dining and socializing. Most require that the residents be ambulatory and be able to perform the usual basic and instrumental activities of daily living with minimal, if any, assistance.

In an early review article, Bernard Liebowitz (1976) summarized five characteristics common to community housing: a nonprofit sponsor, fiscal management often supplemented by additional fees; provision of maintenance, housekeeping, and cooking services; and a caregiving staff, which may include a live-in manager, nurse, or social worker. He also stated that the true commune, such as that in which a younger person might choose to live for ecological reasons, has limited potential for the elderly. The problem seems to be that the true commune is spontaneously formed, voluntary, and self-maintaining; this may require too much energy of the old, who do thrive in a community situation where the order is externally imposed and maintained.

SUMMARY

Described above is the development of a congregation-based continuum of spiritual care community for older adults. The intent is to provide an intentional, spiritual community that goes beyond attending merely to the physical needs of older adults for shelter, security, and socialization. Level 4 extends the idea of congregate living to an ideological congregation of elders—the next step in personal and community development for older adults. The time has come for the genesis of such a community. The congregational spiritual care community continuum is truly an example of the way congregations can revise their criteria to encompass the spiritual growth needs of later life. Perhaps such communities can be in place before the year 2000!

BIBLIOGRAPHY

Archdiocese of Louisville (1989) Archdiocese of Louisville, Ky.: Office of Small Christian Communities.

Bahr, H. (1970) "Aging and Religious Disaffiliation." *Social Forces* 49:59–71.

Bellah, R. N. (1978) "To Kill and Survive or to Die and Become: the Active Life and the Contemplative Life as Ways of Being Adult." In Erikson, 61–80.

Bianchi, E. (1985) *Aging as a Spiritual Journey.* New York: Crossroad.

Brody, E. M. (1978) "Community Housing for the Elderly: The Program, the People, the Decision-making Process, and the Research." *The Gerontologist* 18:121–28.

Cutler, W. (1990) *Golden Years: Riding The Crest.* Colorado: Serendipity House.

Erikson, E. H. (1968) "Generativity and Ego Integrity." In Neugarten, 85–87.

Erikson, E. H., ed. (1978) *Adulthood.* New York: Norton.

Frenkel-Brunswik, E. (1968) "Adjustments and Reorientation in the Course of the Life Span." In Neugarten, 77–84.

Gray, R. M., and D. O. Moberg (1977) *The Church and the Older Person.* Grand Rapids, Mich.: Eerdmans.

Heenan, E. (1972) "Sociology of Religion and the Aged: the Empirical Lacunae." *Journal for the Scientific Study of Religion* 40:171–76.

Hofland, B. (1990) "Value and Ethical Issues in Residential Environments for the Elderly." In Tilson, 241–71.

Jung, C. G. (1933) *Modern Man in Search of A Soul.* New York: Harcourt, Brace and World.

Kivett, V. R. (1979) "Religious Motivation in Middle Age: Correlates and Implications." *Journal of Gerontology* 34:106–15.

Koenig, H. G., J. N. Kvale, and C. Ferrel (1988) "Religion and Well-Being in Later Life." *The Gerontologist* 28 (1):18–28.

Kuhlen, R. G. (1968) "Developmental Changes in Motivation during the Adult Years." In Neugarten, 115–36.

Lawton, M. P., E. Brody, and P. Turner-Massey (1978) "The Relationship of Environmental Factors to Changes in Well-Being." *The Gerontologist* 18:133–37.

LeFevre, C., and P. LeFevre, eds. (1985) *Aging and the Human Spirit.* Chicago: Exploration.

Liebowitz, B. (1976) "Implications of Community Housing for Planning and Policy." *The Gerontologist* 18:138–43.

Longino, C. F., and G. C. Kitson (1985) "Parish Clergy and the Aged: Examining Stereotypes." In LeFevre and LeFevre, 200–205.

Maslow, A. H. (1954) "Unmotivated and Purposeless Reactions." In *Motivation and Personality,* 291–99. New York: Harper & Row.

McFadden, S. H., and R. R. Gerl (1990) "Approaches to Understanding Spirituality in the Second Half of Life." *Generations* 14 (4):35–38.

Merton, T. (1978) *What Is Contemplation.* Springfield, Ill.: Templegate.

Mindel, C. H., and C. E. Vaughan (1985) "A Multidimensional Approach to Religiosity and Disengagement." In LeFevre and LeFevre, 210–15.

Moberg, D. O. (1968) "Religiosity in Old Age." In Neugarten, 497–508.

______ (1971) *Spiritual Well-Being* Washington, D.C.: White House Conference on Aging.

Mulhall, D., and K. Rowe (1988) *A Time For: A Six Session, Small Group Discussion Process with Older Adults.* Los Angeles: Franciscan Communications.

Neugarten, B. L. (1968) "Adult Personality: Toward a Psychology of the Life Cycle." In Neugarten, 137–47.

Neugarten, B. L., ed. (1968a) *Middle Age and Aging.* Chicago: University of Chicago Press.

Peck, M. S. (1987) *The Different Drum: Community Making and Peace.* New York: Simon and Schuster.

Peck, R. C. (1968) "Psychological Developments in the Second Half of Life." In Neugarten, 88–92.

Teasdale, W. (1982) "The Mystical Dimension of Aging." In Tiso, 221–48.

Thibault, J. M., J. W. Ellor, and F. E. Netting (1991) "A Conceptual Framework for Assessing the Spiritual Functioning and Fulfillment of Older Adults in Long-Term Care Setting." *Journal of Religious Gerontology* 7 (4):29–45.

Tiso, F., ed. (1982) *Aging: Spiritual Perspectives.* Lake Worth, Fla.: Sunday Publications.

Vanier, J. (1989) *Community and Growth: Our Pilgrimage Together.* Mahwah, N.J.: Paulist Press.

Webster's New Collegiate Dictionary (1956) Springfield, Mass.: G. and C. Merriam.

25 Spiritual Challenges of Nursing Home Life

DAYLE A. FRIEDMAN

SPIRITUAL CHALLENGES OF NURSING HOME LIFE

Older adults who find themselves in a nursing home are most often on a painful journey through loss, change, and disjunction. The spiritual challenges they face are shaped by the dual factors of frailty and institutionalization. Older adults enter long-term care institutions as a result of failing physical and/or cognitive health. Residents often suffer from multiple, chronic illnesses, which together make them unable to perform independently the tasks of daily living. Over 45 percent of nursing home residents have a dementing disorder, such as Alzheimer's disease (National Center for Health Statistics, 1983). These health problems result in the loss of independence and capacity, which prompt the decision to seek placement in the long-term care institution.

Admission to an institution entails giving up one's home and personal environment and living amidst the routines and structures set up by a large organization. Alienation and anomie are frequent concomitants of life in a total institution, as Erving Goffman (1961) has eloquently pointed out. Nursing home residents confront critical spiritual challenges, including empty and burdensome time, meaninglessness, and disconnection.

Time: Routinized and Empty

The Tyranny of Routinized Time. Institutionalized older adults live in an environment characterized by rigid time routines. For the staff of the long-term care facility, time is organized into distinct blocks, comprised of shifts, workdays, and weeks with workdays and weekends. Days are structured by tasks that must be done "to" the residents, such as meals, medications, bed-making, bathing, and toileting. For staff trying to accomplish these demanding tasks in a limited time-frame, it seems there is never enough time.

Like the staff, residents' lives are organized by the institutional routines. Their time is structured by staff schedules, and sometimes staff whim, not by their own needs, desires, or rhythms. When they rise, eat, go to the bathroom, and go to sleep may have little to do with their own personal rhythm or previous habits. Parts of the day may be marked off by meals, as a nursing home resident remarked in Gubrium's study (1975, 166) of a nursing home called Murray Manor: "You go from one meal to the next. That's about it." Other markers in the day are television programs and recreational programs. Unfortunately, the latter often come without warning or anticipation; suddenly, someone swoops down and takes the resident to bingo, to a concert or other program. The resident, however, has not had an opportunity to prepare for this moment, so time seems irrelevant. As another resident in Gubrium's study remarked, "Time doesn't matter here because I don't go out any place unless here for bingo and they always take me up there" (1975, 171).

The Burden of Empty Time. Florida Scott Maxwell (1979, 41) called old age "a desert of time." Paradoxically, despite the degree to which time is structured, to the resident, time seems empty and burdensome. As Kathy Calkins has observed (1990), time in the long-term care institution can seem much like a treadmill—it moves, but nothing happens. The routines of institutional life create a kind of sameness in which days run together; there is little to distinguish Monday from Tuesday or Saturday. One of Gubrium's subjects (1975, 162) said, "You eat, you sleep and sit around."

Much of the institutionalized older person's time is spent *waiting*. Given that residents are dependent on staff to meet many needs, and given that they have little sense of tasks that are theirs to perform, they *wait* . . . for medications, meals, toileting, bedtime, and the recreational activities that break up the routine. "We wait all the time," said one resident of Murray Manor (Gubrium, 1975, 164). Time seems limitless when one is waiting. The resident who waited ten minutes for assistance to return to her room after an activity reports, "I waited forever." A demented woman paces anxiously and approaches staff members asking, "What am I supposed to do now?" Upon being told that she can take a nap, watch television, or wait for dinner, she exclaims in utter exasperation, "This day is *never* going to end!" Time clearly weighs heavily without meaningful markers and momentum toward them. As Renee Rose Shield notes (1988, 185), time is thus "unfillable and fraught with peril."

Now Is All There Is. In a curious way, the present is the only time there is for the resident of the nursing home. The past is absent. There is no one around who shares one's personal history, and there is nothing which evokes it. The resident may cry out to staff in despair, "You don't know who I *am,*" for the staff truly does not know about Mrs. Jones's special reputation as the best cook in the neighborhood, or Mr. Green's status as the pharmacist on whom everyone could rely for help in a pinch. Staff members relate to the impaired older person before them, and the older person experiences a loss of his or her past.

The future for the nursing home resident is, in a way, crystal-clear. Nearly all who enter a nursing home know that this will be their last home. So, the future awaiting the residents is of incapacity and death. Everyone knows the future, yet there is no recognition of it; deaths, when they occur, are often handled in silence and secrecy. Seldom are other residents informed or given an opportunity to respond to deaths in the environment. Thus, in addition to the qualities of routinization and emptiness, time has a disconnected sense about it, as if the present moment were somehow suspended in time (Friedman and Muncie, 1990).

The Loss of Meaning

What Good Am I Anymore? Elderly long-term care residents internalize powerfully negative messages from society and suffer from low self-esteem. This society tends to have an instrumental view of persons' worth, judging them by what they can do or give, not by the value inherent in who they *are* (Heschel, 1966, 81). An older person who is no longer working can feel useless and rejected, for he or she is perceived as a "functionless person, an onus on the majority" (MacDonald, 1973, 272-94). These negative feelings are intensified for the nursing home resident, who is not only not in a "productive" role, but is now in a dependent role. Because American society idealizes independence and abhors dependency, those who find themselves "counting on kindness," as Wendy Lustbader (1991) puts it, feel that they have failed, that they are somehow deficient.

Perhaps the saddest aspect of the self-perception of institutionalized older persons is their feeling of personal insignificance and impotency (Lieberman, 1969, 330–40). As individuals who have ceased to play a role in the community, they lack means of attaining social status or self-respect. Nothing is expected of them, and there is a distinct sense that they are not taken seriously (Shield, 1988, 207; 197).

> Esther, a pious Eastern European–born eighty-three-year-old nursing home resident, remarks, "All my life, I always gave to charity. I used to put money in a charity box every Friday night. I always gave money to the synagogue and to religious schools. Now I'm here, and I can't do anything for anyone. What good am I anymore?"

The sense that one cannot make an impact on one's environment, "the perception of uncontrollability," leads not uncommonly to "learned helplessness" (Hastings, 1985, 1–2), which in turn yields passivity, anxiety, and antisocial behavior.

Given the social stigma regarding aging and dependency, and the lack of meaningful roles, it is not surprising that institutionalized elders have a more negative sense of self-esteem than their noninstitutionalized peers (Mason, 1954, 324–37). Feelings of inferiority and low self-esteem contribute to the prevalence of depression among institutionalized older adults (MacDonald, 1973, 281).

Disjunction and Disconnection

A fundamental feature of life in the long-term care institution is disconnection. The resident is cut off from the past, from familiar surroundings, from past life roles, and from the moorings of home and community. Often, residents have lost significant people in their lives, through death, disability, or distance. Although institutionalization thrusts the older person into a social setting, isolation persists within it. The sense of community one might expect simply does not develop for the older people cast together within the institution, as Shield (1988, 207) notes in her observations of one long-term care facility:

> Instead of *communitas,* residents stay by themselves and try to be "good" patients. Rather than find similiarities among themselves to bind them together, residents emphasize and maintain their differences. Instead of creating the exuberance found in *communitas,* residents often distrust one another, compete with one another, and denigrate one another . . . there seems little reason for the residents to bond together, little reason to help one another and to reciprocate.

Thus, the experience of isolation and discontinuity brings further spiritual challenges to elderly long-term care residents.

THE IMPACT OF RELIGIOUS LIFE IN THE LONG-TERM CARE FACILITY

Religious life can offer elderly nursing home residents a radically different experience of time, personal meaning, and connectedness. While religious life can in no way remove the losses and hardships of institutionalization and frailty, it can provide valuable solace. The description of these experiences is based largely on phenomenological observations, as there has been little empirical research on the impact of religious life upon well-being for frail elders in nursing homes.[1]

A Life of Celebration: Significant Time

Cycles of Significant Moments. In contrast to the routinized, vapid sense of time one has in the long-term care facility, religious life provides a sense of significant time. Religious life offers what Heschel called "a sanctuary in time" (1975). Ritual time gives rhythm and texture to time, as it allows one to live in cycles of significant moments. In religious life, time is divided into cycles of the week (Sabbath to Sabbath), month (in Jewish tradition, new moon to new moon), and year (festival cycle). Each moment has a *location* in time—today is not just Tuesday, which looks just like Monday and Wednesday, but, in a Jewish context, it is the third day after the Sabbath, the eighth day after the New

[1]One exception to the absence of research in this area is work currently under way at Philadelphia Geriatric Center as part of the National Institute on Aging's Collaborative Studies on Special Care Units for Alzheimer's Disease.

Moon, the day after the festival of Shavuot. Today exists *in relationship to* significant moments. There is always something to look forward to and something to savor, so significant moments are actually stretched through what Fred Davis has called the "accordion effect" (cited in Calkins, 1990, 493).

Continuity. Ritual time creates a sense of continuity that is woefully absent from much of nursing home life. This continuity is found on both the personal and the collective levels. A nursing home resident can relive the past in the present through enacting religious rituals in which she participated in the past. For example, a resident lighting Shabbat (Jewish Sabbath) candles exclaims, "Oh, I remember my mother doing this." The past is not lost, and change and discontinuity are muted through the emphasis on what Myerhoff (1984, 325, 322) called the "enduring elements of life that do not pass away"; time is experienced as "flowing duration." Most importantly, the nursing home resident experiences *herself* as the same through time. Linked by these ritual moments, her life is as a continuum, a "single phenomenological reality" (Myerhoff, 1984, 306). In other words, participation in religious life provides a thread of continuity which connects the resident's life in this strange place and time to the whole of her past.

Ritual moments also connect the resident to personal hopes for the future. Participating in the cycle of the week or year prompts a hope that one will be able to do so again, as seen in the frequent statement of residents on leaving religious services, "We should only be well and live to do this again next year!"

The thread of continuity connects the long-term care resident to a past and future much broader than her own. Ritual reenacts one's people's or faith community's past, thereby connecting the participant to deep roots. For example, Passover in the nursing home enables a Jewish resident to be present at the liberation of her people from slavery; Easter enables a Christian to relive the exultation of her people on experiencing the resurrection of her Savior.

Ritual also lends continuity toward the future. When nursing home residents participate in religious ritual, they affirm that "we have been here and we will continue, despite all of the changes in the world around" (Moore and Myerhoff, 1977, 218). When these rituals are continued after their lifetime, something precious will endure; their values, customs, beliefs, and community of faith will be around even when they are not. Participating in ritual helps to ensure that one's faith tradition will continue "from generation to generation." This point is particularly powerful when ritual is shared intergenerationally within the long-term care facility.

A Life of Meaning: A Sense of Significant Being

Religious life offers an institutionalized elder an alternative to experiencing herself as dependent, powerless, and worthless. The message of religious tradition, at least in Christianity and in Judaism, is of the ultimate worth of the human person, for all persons are children of God created "in the image of God" (Gen. 1:27). No matter how incapacitated, no matter how reduced, each nursing home resident has a spark of the Divine within her.

Not only do elderly residents of a long-term care facility have ultimate worth, they have a role to play in the realm of religion. In contrast to secular culture, which teaches that a person's social role is ended when one cannot engage in productive labor or when one becomes disabled, religious tradition teaches that the person has a contribution to make in the community of faith and the service of the Divine. In Jewish tradition, for example, the adult individual's role is to perform the *mitzvot,* the commandments that constitute the content of the Jewish people's covenant with God.

As an obligated person, the Jewish adult has a sense of social significance, for the community depends on the participation of such individuals for its continued functioning (e.g., Jews cannot recite certain key prayers unless ten obligated adults are present to constitute a quorum, called a *minyan*). Moreover, one has a sense of *cosmic* significance as well, for the redemption of the world is seen to depend upon the Jewish people's fulfillment of the *mitzvot.* While there is a clear age of onset of obligation for Jews (Bar or Bat Mitzvah at thirteen years of age), there is no end point for obligation. Consequently, there is no retirement from a life of obligation, nor any senior citizen discount. An older Jew remains obligated to perform the ethical and ritual precepts of her tradition regardless of impairment or incapacity, though the obligation is adjusted to one's capacity in what might be called "sliding-scale obligation" (Friedman, 1987).

Thus, in the nursing home, the service might be abridged, worshipers might participate sitting in a wheelchair instead of standing up at key moments, but while the older adults are present in the service, they are not present as old persons, sick persons, or recipients of care. Rather, they are Jews, members of the *minyan,* who are doing what one does—joining with community to worship God, to mark the Sabbath or the holiday, and to continue the chain of tradition. While this analysis comes from the Jewish context, it could be applied to Christianity and other religious traditions in a similar fashion. Thus, the message to the participant in religious life in the nursing home, whether Jewish, Christian, or another faith, is quite simple: You have a job to do, and you count.

A Life of Connection

Vertical Connection: Continuity through Time. As was discussed earlier, religious life links the nursing home resident to her personal and collective past and future. The present moment is connected to those that came before and to those that will come after. In this way, life has coherence and integration that would otherwise not be possible. As Myerhoff explained (1984, 322), ritual "stresses a timeless transcendent recognition that does not involve change."

Horizontal Connection: Community. For nursing home residents who feel cut off from the outside world and alienated from the other residents with whom they are cast together, religious life offers a unique possibility for experiencing community. Through sharing in religious life, residents who would otherwise view themselves as completely disconnected discover a common bond. The women who sit all day without exchanging a kind word might turn to one another and offer the peace, or wish one another "gut shabbos" (Yiddish for "good Sabbath") after a religious service. The men who want nothing to do with one another during the week find much to talk about in sharing their memories of their congregation. Sharing in worship forges community within the long-term care institution.

Religious life not only creates community within the nursing home, it connects the residents in the institution to the community of faith beyond its four walls. When participating in the cycle of the religious calendar, residents are linked to members of their faith group everywhere who are observing the same holiday at the same time. Furthermore, religious life constitutes a meaningful opportunity for members of the outside community to be involved in the long-term care institution. Intergenerational worship and celebration with community members remind residents that they are part of something larger than the population of the institution—the community of faith—which continues to support them while they are physically separated.

Connection Beyond Dimension: A Link to God's Caring. We have noted religious life's capacity to connect the nursing home resident vertically, through time, and horizontally, to community. Religious life and pastoral care offer the connection whose dimension cannot be characterized: to the Divine Presence. Religious life, particularly pastoral care, affirms for frail elderly nursing home residents the continuance of God's caring for them amidst brokenness and despair. When a person crippled and rendered speechless by a stroke is given an opportunity to participate in religious ritual or activity, she can recall that God loves her. When a chaplain calls on a demented nursing home resident and listens intently to the emotional and spiritual truths embedded in his seemingly incoherent speech, the resident learns anew that he is important in the world and God has not forgotten him.

GUIDELINES FOR BRINGING RELIGIOUS LIFE TO THE NURSING HOME

Religious life can be fostered within the long-term care institution in many different models of service. While it might be carried out by a chaplain on staff of the institution, in most instances, resources for fostering religious life will have to be brought in from the community, ideally in collaboration with staff of the facility. Leadership might come from community clergy; on the other hand, it might be lay volunteers or congregational groups from the community who take the initiative for facilitating religious life within the nursing home. It should be noted that relatively few clergy members are trained in working with the elderly, although specialized programs in aging have been developed in a small number of theological seminaries (Moberg, 1980). The guidelines presented here both describe ideas for religious programming and offer tips for working within the long-term care milieu.

Religious Programming Ideas

Celebration. Religious life can touch nursing home residents through marking the cycles of the religious calendar with celebrations of Sabbaths, festivals, and holy days throughout the year. In addition, ritual can be used to mark significant moments in the lives of residents. In some instances, such as death and bereavement, religious traditions may offer well-established rituals. In others, such as arrival in the institution, receiving a new roommate, or returning from the hospital, new rituals can be created (Kozberg, 1992, 3–4). Rituals create opportunities for residents to articulate the emotions provoked by important transitions and allow them to receive support and acknowledgment from community.

Education. Lifelong learning is a facet of religious life in many traditions. Study of scriptures, text, and tradition enables older adults in the nursing home a chance to continue to grow and to see themselves as participating in the transmission and perpetuation of the faith tradition.

Social Action. Since most religions teach the importance of action in the world to bring spiritual values to fruition, part of the mission of religious life in the nursing home can be to create opportunities for residents to make a contribution to their world. A social action project might involve writing letters to children who have lost their parents through war, contributing money to a school or shelter for the homeless, advocating with elected officials on behalf of a particular cause. In any case, a social action activity will require facilitation and support from more able-bodied others, such as volunteers or staff.

In order for frail elders to experience the impact they can have in reaching out to others in need, someone may need to collaborate, whether to write and send a check using residents' contributions or to serve as scribe for residents wishing to send letters. The result may well be worth any toil involved, for in the end, the residents, individuals frail of body and mind, will discover that they can nonetheless make a difference, as Maggie Kuhn, founder of the Gray Panthers, reflects in her memoir (1991, 212–13):

> What *can* we do, those of us who have survived to this advanced age? We can think and speak. We can remember. We can give advice and make judgments. We can dial the phone, write letters and read. We may not be able to butter our bread, but we can still change the world.

Practical Considerations for Religious Life in Nursing Homes

Timing. In order to facilitate religious life within a long-term care facility, it is necessary to work within institutional rhythms and time-frames. Timing programs means taking into account mealtimes and other established time commitments, as well as staff schedules. Among the challenges facing those who take on this work is balancing the need to program when important resources are available, such as staff, with the desire to be authentic, and to hold observances as close as possible to the "real" time. Because a large proportion of nursing home residents suffer from dementia, and many dementia patients exhibit sundowning behaviors (disorientation increases as night draws near), daytime services and activities may be preferable. Finally, in this setting where attention spans may be quite short, brevity is next to godliness. Abridging a service or celebration to half an hour may result in significant prayers being omitted, but it will also ensure more active participation of worshipers for the time period of the service.

Accessibility. Accessibility is a vital concern in creating religious life in the nursing home. Residents' multiple impairments must be taken into account as programs and services are developed. First, the space needs to be amenable to wheelchairs, walkers, and geri-chairs. Second, residents may need assistance in "transportation" from their rooms to the service. Third, residents may require repeated reminders, verbally and/or in writing, about the event. Fourth, sound amplification should enable the hearing-impaired to participate. Fifth, liturgical materials should be large-type and lightweight; even so, residents may require assistance in turning pages.

Maximize Participation. Attending a religious service or program can be a boost to a resident's sense of spiritual well-being. Active participation provides a further sense of personal significance. For this reason, wherever possible, residents should be encouraged to participate in leading or setting up a service. Calling upon a resident to read or recite or to help others to participate is extremely helpful. In addition, residents can be validated further by the leader's acknowledgment of their experience, knowledge, and perspective.

Involve Families. Visiting loved ones in a nursing home can be a trying experience. When their daily reality has become so removed from the web of family and community life, it can be hard to think of topics for conversation. When cognitive or physical impairments make communication difficult, simply remaining present can be agonizing. When precious relatives have lost significant parts of their functioning, spending time with them can be a painful reminder of the gap between who they were and who they are.

Participating in religious life can be an affirming experience for residents and family members to share. In the context of religious observance, the resident is most connected to that which is whole within her. Often the resident is more expressive and actively participatory in worship than in any other activity in the nursing home. Worshiping, celebrating, or studying provides the visiting family member and the resident with something concrete to do, something in which both can participate and that both enjoy. Finally, family members can be encouraged to participate in religious life within the institution through ritually marking important events in *their* lives, such as marriages, births, and confirmations, within the context of religious observances in the nursing home.

Working with Staff. Staff chaplains, community clergy, or volunteers who take upon themselves the responsibility for facilitating religious life within the nursing home will be effective to the degree that they collaborate with the interdisciplinary team that makes up the nursing home staff. It is essential to work in close coordination and communication with recreational therapists, social workers, and nurses. Sometimes those involved in fostering religious life will act as advocates regarding residents' spiritual needs; on the other hand, often, staff will provide information that will be essential in understanding and serving the residents. Chaplains or community volunteers can come to be seen as a resource for the institution and the staff in caring for the whole person.

Since many nursing homes are multicultural environments, staff may well be from a different religious background than residents. Therefore, education of staff is important to help them to understand residents' religious orientations and needs.

One way of fostering positive collaboration with staff is to acknowledge their religious and spiritual inclinations and to create appropriate opportunities for them to participate in religious life. Residents and staff can find common ground through celebration of more universal holidays, such as Thanksgiving and Martin Luther King Day. Staff's contribution to residents' lives can be acknowledged through ceremonies for times of recognition, such as National Nursing Home Week, Nursing Week, and Social Work Month. Finally, staff can be given important support through opportunities to mourn residents who have died in regular or episodic memorial services.

CONCLUSION

Religious life holds the promise of celebration, meaning, and connection to those who will end their days in nursing homes. Engaging in this work is not only vitally important for the sake of older adults in the faith community, but it is also intrinsically satisfying for those who serve. Ministering to the spiritual needs of institutionalized elders can help to fulfill the vision of the psalmist:

> The righteous flourish like the palm tree,
> and grow like a cedar in Lebanon.
> They are planted in the house of the Lord,
> they flourish in the courts of our God.
> They still bring forth fruit in old age,
> they are ever full of sap and green,
> to show that the Lord is upright;
> he is my rock,
> and there is no unrighteousness in him.
>
> (Psalm 92:12-15)

BIBLIOGRAPHY

Calkins, K. (1990) "Time Perspective, Marking and Styles of Usage." *Social Problems* 17:487–501.

Friedman, D. A. (1987) "The Mitzvah Model: A Therapeutic Resource for the Institutionalized Aged." *Journal of Aging and Judaism* 1 (2):96–108.

Friedman, D. A., and M. Muncie (1990) "Freeing the Captives of the Clock: Time and Ritual in Long-Term Care." Presented at American Society on Aging Conference, San Francisco.

Goffman, E. (1961) *Asylums.* Garden City, N.Y.: Doubleday.

Gubrium, J. (1975) *Living and and Dying at Murray Manor.* New York: St. Martin.

Hastings, R. (1985) "Learned Helplessness." *Geriatric Care* 17 (10):1–2.

Heschel, A. J. (1966) "To Grow in Wisdom." In *The Insecurity of Freedom: Essays on Human Freedom,* 70–84. Philadelphia: Jewish Publications Society.

______ (1975) *The Sabbath.* New York: Farrar, Straus and Giroux.

Kertzer, D. L., and J. Keith, eds. (1984) *Age and Anthropological Theory.* Ithaca, N.Y.: Cornell University Press.

Kozberg, C. (1992) "Let Your Heart Take Courage: A Ceremony for Entering a Nursing Home." *Passages,* Spring: 3–5. Newsletter of the Aging Committee of the Central Conference of American Rabbis.

Kuhn, M., C. Long, and L. Quinn (1991) *No Stone Unturned.* New York: Ballantine Books.

Lieberman, M. (1969) "Institutionalization of the Aged: Effects on Behavior." *Journal of Gerontology* 24:330–40.

Lustbader, W. (1991) *Counting on Kindness: An Exploration of Dependency.* New York: Free Press.

MacDonald, M. L. (1973) "The Forgotten Americans: A Sociopsychological Analysis of Aging and Nursing Homes." *American Journal of Community Psychology* 1 (3):272–94.

Mason, E. (1954) "Some Correlates of Self-Judgment of the Aged." *Journal of Gerontology* 9:324–37.

Maxwell, F. S. (1979) *The Measure of My Days.* New York: Penguin Books.

______ (1984) "Ritual and Signs of Ripening." In Kertzer and Keith, 305–30.

Moberg, D. O. (1980) "Gerontology in Seminary Training." *Theological Education* 16 (3) (Special issue): 283–93.

Moore, S. F., and B. Myerhoff, eds. (1977) *Secular Ritual.* Assen, The Netherlands: Van Gorcum.

Myerhoff, B. (1984) "We Don't Wrap Herring in a Printed Page." In Moore and Myerhoff, 199–224.

National Center for Health Statistics (1983) "Changing Mortality Patterns, Health Services Utilization and Health Care Expenditures: United States, 1978–2003." *Vital and Health Statistics,* Series 3, no. 23.

Shield, R. R. (1988) *Uneasy Endings.* Ithaca, N.Y., and London: Cornell University Press.

26 Older Gay and Lesbian Adults

GARY S. WHITFORD
JEAN K. QUAM

Old people are often considered to be asexual. If one thinks of old people as sexual beings at all, it is almost always as heterosexuals. Although there is some disagreement about the exact numbers, it is widely accepted that about ten percent of older adults are gay or lesbian (terms that are preferred to the more clinical description "homosexual"). This group is one of the most difficult to study and to understand. Those older adults over age sixty-five who are gay or lesbian today grew up during periods in which they were told that being gay was illegal, immoral, sinful, or simply wrong. The majority of these individuals kept their sexuality a secret, as some continue to do today. If their sexual orientation was discovered, they risked being fired from jobs, ostracized by family and friends, and put in a position of hiding their personal lives.

RELIGIOUS VIEWS OF GAYS AND LESBIANS

The relationship between organized religion in the United States and the gay and lesbian population is complicated at best. It has been suggested that organized religion is mostly responsible for the heterosexual majority's negative views toward homosexuality and also responsible for the fact that many gays and lesbians feel alienated from the church (McNeill, 1976). Yet some theologians and lay church members are examining this attitude and looking again at sacred writings and traditions. This has enabled gay persons to engage in dialogue with lay people and religious authorities.

A number of U.S. religious institutions have been engaged in discussion, debate, and conflict about the moral issues of sexuality, with particular interest paid to issues of homosexuality. Members with more conservative views lament what they see as changes in moral standards; progressive members urge new viewpoints. As a result of these differences, institutions sometimes see declines in giving to national offices or at the very least an increase in letters and phone calls to the national office.

During 1994, some major denominations wrestled as they sought to examine their views towards gays and lesbians. The Episcopal Church heard a report at their general convention from a three-year study on sexuality issues. The Evangelical Lutheran Church in America (ELCA) spent the year discussing its human sexuality study, released in the fall of 1993. Two years previous, the Conservative Jews' Rabbinical Assembly engaged in a debate over the ordination of gay and lesbian rabbis. Here again, the assembly asked a task force to frame a report on human sexuality.

The Jewish and ELCA reports agree in some areas. Both uphold the sanctity of heterosexual, long-term marriage while at the same time proposing options for accepting the gay and lesbian lifestyles. These words of acceptance are framed in terms of fidelity and the need for loving, committed relationships. Yet as the discussion proceeds, others come forward with objections. After the church study was released, thousands of negative phone calls were logged at the ELCA national offices in Chicago. Many who objected believed that the church should continue to label homosexuality a sin and not legitimate sexual relationships between persons of the same sex. In fact, many Christians place homosexuality at the top of a list of sins (Scanzoni and Ramey Mollenkott, 1978). Various Christian groups back anti-gay initiatives that are being placed on the ballot around the country.

While some church members threaten to leave a certain denomination if established views on sexuality are changed, many gay and lesbian members have undoubtedly left these churches already. These people have come to expect rejection from churches. Surveys of gays and lesbians give some indication of church affiliation. Berger's study (1982b) of older gay men found that 37% of the respondents were Protestant, 11% Roman Catholic, 14% Jewish, 13% other, and 26% atheist, agnostic, or no preference. Bell and Weinberg (1978) reported that 50% of the white gay males were not at all religious; less than one-third of the black gay males described themselves in such terms. A majority of white lesbians and about a quarter of black lesbians reported that they were not at all religious. Another study found that 34% of gay and lesbian respondents were attending a church which they view as being friendly toward their sexual orientation (Quam and Whitford, 1992). The rest either did not attend church or else attended a mainline church that officially disapproved of their sexual orientation and behavior.

James Nelson (1978) writes that pushing these people away has at the same time pushed them to find community in gay bars, baths, and ghettos. Often when gay persons come out of the closet, they also come out of the church. Speaking from a Christian perspective, John Fortunato (1982) notes that being gay and Christian puts one on the outskirts of the Christian community, exiled, banished. A writer to the magazine *The Other Side* offered this comment: "I'm tired of seeing the gay bars filled with so many youths who once sincerely accepted Christ as Lord and Savior—only to find they hadn't become heterosexual and thus feel excluded from the body of Christ" (Scanzoni and Ramey Mollenkott, 1978, 7). Yet while organized religion may not be providing community for all gays and lesbians, these people are building their own communities, and these communities are contributing toward the achievement of successful aging by this population.

METHODOLOGICAL PROBLEMS

Although the body of research about older gay and lesbian adults has grown, there are serious limitations to the work that has been done. Because it is so difficult to find old gay men and old lesbians who want to talk about their experiences, most research has been done on those adults who are "out" or who tend to be more comfortable about their sexuality. On the other hand, many studies of gay and lesbian adults also draw their subjects from clinical populations such as those who have sought counseling about their sexuality, which gives a skewed view of this group overall.

In addition, most research that purportedly is done on "old" gay and lesbian adults, is, in fact, conducted with individuals who could more accurately be labeled "middle-aged." Newer studies recognize the differences between the various age cohorts and particularly differences between the young-old and the old-old.

All subjects over the age of forty are not lumped together as a sample of old people. Quam and Whitford (1992) particularly found that age was an important factor in feeling that being gay or lesbian hindered one's adjustment to aging.

Another bias in early research was the fact that studies were done on relatively small samples of white, middle-class gay males living in either San Francisco or New York (Berger, 1984; Kimmel, 1978). These results were then generalized to all older gay men and older lesbians. Recent studies have examined the unique needs of older lesbians (Kehoe, 1989) and the unique needs of older gay men (Whitford, 1995) separately.

The vast majority of research that generally looks at the aging process has omitted any questions about a subject's sexual orientation (Berger, 1982) perhaps out of fear of somehow offending the subjects. While most gerontological literature continues to ignore the diversity of sexual orientation among older adults, there is an increasingly large body of literature that is devoted solely to looking at gay and lesbian aging. A recently published resource guide to lesbian and gay aging included more than forty pages of articles, books, and conference papers on the topic (NALGG, 1993).

OLDER GAY MEN

Older gay men are an often overlooked segment of the aging population. In both research and practice older men are usually classified as married or single, without consideration given to the fact that some of these men have unique life experiences that will influence their aging processes. Even the research that does focus exclusively on gay male populations tends to examine younger samples. However, studies in the field of aging can help fill this gap. It has been argued that sexual orientation is a justifiable analytical category in aging studies when same-sexers are institutionalized in heterosexist environments (Kayal, 1984).

Fortunately, the lives of older gay men have begun to receive increased attention during the past two decades. A number of studies have focused on gay men and their life concerns (Bell and Weinberg, 1978; Berger, 1982b; Francher and Henkin, 1973; Gray and Dressel, 1985; Kelly, 1977; Kimmel, 1979; Laner, 1978; Minnigerode, 1976; Quam and Whitford, 1992; Weinberg and Williams, 1975). Much of the current body of research has been successful in countering the negative images of older gay men that are prevalent in our society. These stereotypes view old gay men as depressed, lonely, oversexed, possessing a low self-concept, and having a dread of old age (Berger, 1982b; Francher and Henkin, 1973; Gray and Dressel, 1985; Kelly, 1977). What is emerging is an understanding of the lives of old gay men that can be useful to social service agencies, religious institutions, and other organizations that work with this population.

Aging Process

The current body of research points to ways in which being gay can positively influence the aging process. For example, research has shown that these men may experience less role loss as they age. This occurs when the gay subculture insulates gay males from status role identity and lessens the effects of anxiety inherent in role loss (Francher and Henkin, 1973). In addition, many gay men have developed flexible gender roles. Gender role flexibility can translate into increased independence (Friend, 1980), freedom from role playing (Kimmel, 1978), less likelihood of experiencing role losses, more role flexibility (Berger, 1982a), less need to adjust to new roles, and fewer expectations for having someone care for you (Kimmel, 1978).

The process of coming out of the closet as a gay man can facilitate the aging process. The concept of "mastery of stigma" has been used to explain this phenomenon. A young gay man realizes he is different and must develop the resources to achieve self-acceptance in the face of overwhelming societal disapproval. Older gay men are experiencing a replay of this earlier difficulty, because old age is stigmatized in the same way as homosexuality. The older gay man may thereby be able to maintain self-esteem, in view of his having experienced stigma earlier in life (Berger and Kelly, 1986).

On the other hand, the current cohort of older gay men may be deeply closeted, living in response to a life-long stigmatization (Kimmel, 1979). Such secrecy may have negative effects on adjustment to the aging process. Kimmel wrote that lack of kinship supports may be the most significant issue facing older gay men. Men not involved in gay community groups are more likely to feel that being a gay man hinders their adjustment to aging (Whitford, 1995). Studies have shown, however, that homosexuality per se does not have a negative affect on respondent's adjustment to aging (Kimmel, 1979; Quam and Whitford, 1992). Berger's respondents (1984) also believed there was no difference in adaptation to aging for heterosexuals and homosexuals.

The process of aging may also be different for gay men than it is for lesbians (Quam and Whitford, 1992). Friend (1987) writes that the overall conclusion of the literature is that aging is more stressful and occurs earlier for gay men than for lesbians. Age-related changes in physical appearance have been shown to have a more negative effect for gay men than for lesbians (Minnigerode and Adelman, 1979). But Minnigerode (1976) has found no evidence of accelerated aging for gay men in comparison to the general population. Elsewhere it has been found that older gay men are not seeking to recapture their youth through contact with younger men (Laner, 1978).

Benefits of Community Living

The coming out process that is a part of the development course of many gay men may facilitate a sense of crisis competence that is valuable as one ages (Kimmel, 1978). It has been found that respondents integrated into the gay community are more self-accepting, less depressed, and less fearful of aging (Berger, 1982b). More time spent in the gay subculture means having more gay than nongay friends (Gray and Dressel, 1985) and less likelihood of feeling lonely (Whitford, 1995). Being out to more people in more situations results in better adjustment, especially since gay friends provide more emotional support than does one's family (Friend, 1980).

Despite the mythology surrounding the aging gay male, there is scant evidence that older gay men disengage or are forced to disengage from the gay male community (Bennett and Thompson, 1980). Evidence points to the benefits of being an open, aging gay male in the gay community. Unfortunately, as noted earlier, a number of older men are living closeted lives. The role of integrating these men into their community is a vital one for social service and religious organizations.

Support Networks

There is evidence that most older gay men have established support networks that enhance the experience of growing older. These men have created their own circle of gay friends (Kimmel, 1977) that acts as a surrogate family (Bell and Weinberg, 1978). Some authors note that many gay men could not count on the support of their family of origin and so they learned at an early age to be self-resilient and independent (Berger and Kelly, 1986) and establish their own supports (Kimmel, 1977). Francher and Henkin (1973) also reported that many older gay men cited a loss of family support when they came out. Peers provide supports that others may receive from families. It has been shown elsewhere, however, that older gay men have strong relationships with their families and that a friend-support network reinforces and supplements the family support network (Friend, 1980; Raphael and Robinson, 1980).

This support network is as important to these men as it is to other older people. Psycho-social adaptation is facilitated by integration into a gay community. Being in a relationship has also been shown to be related to higher levels of life satisfaction for gay men (Berger, 1980; Whitford, 1995). Social contacts provide general support or even organized activities for older gay men which address potential problems of isolation, a concern older gay men cite as they age (Whitford, 1995). This association with other gay men is important to self-acceptance, because it exposes a person to beliefs that counter society's negative attitudes (Berger, 1984). Professionals working with this population can be helpful by facilitating the building and reinforcing of this support network and by helping the client meet age peers (Berger and Kelly, 1986). Organizations can assist these men in meeting their basic relationship needs, providing the social contacts, support, and activities that will help their adjustment to aging.

Problems Experienced

Research has also shown that the lives of older gay men are not full of desperation and despair, as was previously conjectured. These men are not trying to recapture their youth (Laner, 1978), and on the average they have stable self-concepts and enjoy satisfactory social and sex lives (Kelly, 1977; Raphael and Robinson, 1980; Weinberg and Williams, 1974). In comparison to their younger gay male counterparts, these men have no greater loneliness, no lower level of happiness, no diminution of self-esteem, and no increased worry about the aging process (Bell and Weinberg, 1974; Bennett and Thompson, 1980; Berger, 1982b).

Gay men experience difficulties, however, some of which are similar to those of nongay older men and some of which are unique. These difficulties include stigmatization of age (Kimmel, 1977), loss of important people, fear of institutionalization (Kelly, 1977), loneliness (Minnigerode and Adelman, 1978), oppression and discrimination (Berger, 1984; Kelly, 1977; Kimmel, 1978; Minnigerode and Adelman, 1978), and changes in health, body, and physical activity (Berger, 1984). Studies have also shown that older gay male respondents report many of the same problems as experienced by all older persons, including poor health, lack of energy, and poor finances in retirement (Berger, 1984; Whitford, 1995).

Old gay men do encounter some unique problems. Old gay men may face discrimination both because of sexual orientation and because of age (Whitford, 1995). The discriminatory impact of certain laws, practices, and rules increase as he ages (Kimmel, 1977). Old gay men face possible legal discrimination when a partner dies (Kimmel, 1977); hospitals and nursing homes may not treat partners as family; a surviving partner may face property ownership problems (Berger, 1982). These unique problems need to be addressed and not ignored.

Programs and Services

Old gay men receive services from all programs designed for elderly population, but their unique needs are seldom addressed. Many studies of older populations have ignored the gay question, and correspondingly, community agencies have been reluctant to admit that some clients may be gay (Kimmel, 1978). It may be that therefore few of these men participate in organized programs. One study found that only 17% of older gay men participated in programs at senior citizen centers. Yet almost 78% of the men expressed interest in a social organization specifically geared towards lesbians and gay men (Whitford, 1995).

Some old gay men are participating in agency programs and services specifically designed to meet their needs. These programs are often self-help based. This approach is useful, because the clients are intimately aware of their own and each other's needs. This helps create useful roles for volunteers who can provide services not found elsewhere (Berger, 1982).

OLD LESBIANS

For the most part, writing and research about lesbians and their needs has focused on younger lesbians. Macdonald and Rich (1984) write poignantly about the invisibility of old lesbians in women's communities. What has been written about older women leaves out the possibility of being homosexual. Thus old lesbians are a relatively unknown and perhaps misunderstood group of women.

Aging Process

Deevey (1990) has described the old lesbian as having a "triple minority status" of being old, female, and lesbian all at the same time. In general, there may be a misunderstanding of what it means to be a lesbian. Kehoe (1989) in thinking particularly about old lesbians stated that "lesbianism is not primarily a sexual relationship at all, but a much wider female interdependence with broader human satisfactions that transcend mere physical attachment." For some older women, there have been strong emotional, social, and financial attachments to other women over a long period of time, and yet they would never consider themselves lesbians. Again, we may begin to see more cohort differences as younger groups of women who have emotional attachments to other women are more comfortable in defining themselves as lesbian and society is more willing to be accepting of that status.

For the most part, old lesbians are concerned about the same issues that concern all older women—loneliness, poor health, and lack of financial resources. Loneliness especially is identified as a serious problem (Quam and Whitford, 1992; Kehoe, 1989). On top of these concerns was another layer of issues that were unique to old lesbians. These include such issues as "coming out" to grandchildren and children, fear of discrimination from health care providers and employers, and difficulty in finding a new partner as one ages. On the other hand, Quam and Whitford (1992) found that some old lesbians believed that being gay helped them face the aging process because they had learned to accept themselves as they are and they had found supportive friends in lesbian community.

Support Networks

Out of the women's movement of the 1970s, women in general learned to seek out other women for support. Many old women and especially old lesbians find support from other women essential as they age. For some old lesbians who may have been ostracized by their family because of their sexual orientation, there has been a trend to form alternative families out of other lesbian friends or lesbian couples. Dorrell (1990) movingly describes an informal support network of seven lesbians who delivered services for an 84-year-old terminally ill lesbian.

Some old lesbians have been in long-term committed relationships for many years. In Kehoe's study of 100 lesbians over the age of sixty (1990), there were ten couples who had been in relationships for more than thirty-five years. Some older lesbian couples worry that they have no legal protection for their relationship. If one partner becomes ill, a lifelong partner may not be acknowledged at all in the decision-making process around treatment or institutionalization. The death of a lifelong partner is rarely recognized in society with the same sympathy that is afforded to heterosexual couples who lose a spouse. Once one has lost a lesbian partner, it is difficult to figure out how to find a new relationship. Kehoe (1989) expressed concern that some older coupled lesbians stay at home and become isolated out of a fear of societal discrimination. This puts old lesbians in this situation at even greater risk of isolation when one partner becomes physically disabled and dependent on her partner.

Several studies have suggested that those lesbians who are active in the lesbian community, such as participating in lesbian social groups or religious organizations, are more likely to have greater self-esteem and accept their own aging (Quam and Whitford, 1992; Raphael and Robinson, 1980). Old lesbians who live in smaller communities or rural areas may be disadvantaged by the lack of services available.

Programs and Services

For the most part, old lesbians say that they want services and programs that are sensitive to the needs of old lesbians without discriminating against them because of their sexual orientation. This can occur in "gay-sensitive" agencies as well as those organizations that serve only a gay and/or lesbian client group. Agencies need to be aware of the kind of programs that they provide and the questions they ask when accepting clients. For example, it is possible to ask, "Who is significant in your life?" or, "With whom do you live?" rather than ask whether a client is married or single. Social activities can be designed that include all participants rather than try to pair up males and females. Literature in waiting rooms can include books or articles about gay and lesbian aging.

One of the most fearful situations for old lesbians is health care that is not sensitive to their needs. When health care providers accept the fact that there is diversity among their patients, disclosure is more likely (Gentry, 1992). However, disclosure also leads to the fear that one's sexual orientation will be recorded in medical records or client progress notes that could be read by many different helping professionals. In one study an old lesbian stated, "I'm afraid of not getting good care if the doctor knew. . . . my biggest fear about getting older is that I will be mistreated when I am too weak or sick to fight back." This leads some old lesbians to say that they would prefer lesbian health care providers or "lesbian only" services such as retirement homes for lesbians or lesbian support groups (Kehoe, 1989).

CONCLUSIONS

A number of national and local organizations serving the old lesbian and gay male population have developed in recent decades. One of the earliest, Senior Action in a Gay Environment (SAGE), began in New York City in 1977. While its original mission was to provide care and support for homebound gay and lesbian seniors, its services have expanded to include education, professional training, social support, and advocacy. Other cities have organizations providing services, support networks, and volunteer opportunities. Survey respondents have stated that these organizations are beneficial and can provide avenues for retired men and women to volunteer their services (Kimmel, 1977; Whitford, 1995). A number of gay religious groups have also developed over the last couple of decades. The Metropolitan Community Church specifically welcomes gay and lesbian members to its fellowship. Other denominations have local congregations which are welcoming, and national organizations exist which serve to work for the interests of gay and lesbian people within certain denominations. For example, Dignity and Lutherans Concerned are groups that serve Roman Catholic and Lutheran gays and lesbians, respectively. Increasingly, more helping professionals will be working with old gay men and old lesbians. It is time to learn more about this group of older adults.

BIBLIOGRAPHY

Bell, A. P., and M. A. Weinberg (1978) *Homosexualities: A Study of Diversity among Men and Women*. New York: Simon and Schuster.

Bennett, K. C., and N. L. Thompson (1980) "Social and Psychological Functioning of the Aging Male Homosexual." *British Journal of Psychiatry,* 137, 361–370.

Berger, R. M. (1980) "Psychological Adaptation of the Older Homosexual Male." *Journal of Homosexuality,* 5 (3): 161–175.

Berger, R. M. (1982a) "The Unseen Minority: Older Gays and Lesbians." Social Work, 27 (3): 236–242.

Berger, R. M. (1982b) *Gay and Gray: The Older Homosexual Man*. Champaign, Ill.: University of Illinois Press.

Berger, R. M. (1984) "Realities of Gay and Lesbian Aging." *Social Work,* 29 (1): 57–62.

Berger, R. M., and J. J. Kelly (1986) "Working with Homosexuals of the Older Population." Social Casework, April, 203–210.

Cain, R. (1991) "Stigma Management and Gay Identity Development." *Social Work,* 36 (1): 67–73.

Deevey, S. (1990) "Older Lesbian Women: An Invisible Minority." *Journal of Gerontological Nursing,* 16 (5): 35–39.

Dorrell, B. (1990) "Being There: A Support Network of Lesbian Women." *Journal of Homosexuality,* 20 (3–4): 89–98.

Fortunato, J. E. (1982) *Embracing the Exile: Healing Journeys of Gay Christians*. Minneapolis: Winston Press.

Francher, J. S., and J. Henkin (1973) "The Menopausal Queen: Adjustment to Aging and the Male Homosexual." *American Journal of Orthopsychiatry,* 43 (4): 670–674.

Friend, R. A. (1980) "Graying: Adjustment and the Older Gay Male." *Alternative Lifestyle,* 3 (2): 231–248.

Friend, R. A. (1987) "The Individual and Social Psychology of Aging: Clinical Implications for Lesbians and Gay Men." *The Journal of Homosexuality,* 4 (1/2): 307–331.

Friend, R. A. (1989) "Older Lesbian and Gay People: Responding to Homophobia." *Marriage and Family Review,* 14 (3/4): 241–263.

Gentry, S. E. (1992) "Caring for Lesbians in a Homophobic Society." *Health Care for Women International,* 13 (2): 173–180.

Gray, H., and P. Dressel (1985) "Alternative Interpretations of Aging among Gay Males." *The Gerontologist,* 25 (1): 83–87.

Johnson, M. T., and J. J. Kelly (1979) "Deviate Sex Behavior in Aging: Social Definition and the Lives of Older Gay People." In O. J. Kaplan, ed., *Psychopathology of aging,* pp. 243–258. New York: Academic Press.

Kayal, P. M. (1984) "Understanding Gay and Lesbian Aging." *Journal of Sociology and Social Welfare,* 11 (2): 409–431.

Kehoe, M. (1990) *Lesbians over 60 Speak for Themselves.* New York: The Haworth Press.

Kelly, J. (1977) "The Aging Male Homosexual: Myth and Reality." *Gerontologist,* 17 (4): 328–332.

Kimmel, D. C. (1977) "Psychotherapy and the Older Gay Man." *Psychotherapy: Theory, Research and Practice,* 14 (4): 386–393.

Kimmel, D. C. (1978) "Adult Development and Aging: A Gay Perspective." *Journal of Social Issues,* 34 (3): 113–130.

Kimmel, D. C. (1979) "Adjustments to Aging among Gay Men." In B. Berzon (ed.), *Positively Gay.* Milbrae, Calif.: Celestial Arts, pp. 146–170.

Kimmel, D. C. (1979) "Life-history Interviews of Aging Gay Men." *International Journal of Aging and Human Development,* 10 (3): 239–248.

Laner, M. R. (1978) "Growing Older Male: Heterosexual and Homosexual." *The Gerontologist,* 18 (5): 496–501.

Lee, J. A. (1987) "What Can Homosexual Aging Studies Contribute to Theories of Aging?" *Journal of Homosexuality,* 13 (4): 43–71.

Lipman A. (1986) "Homosexual Relationships." *Generations,* Summer, 51–54.

Macdonald, B., and C. Rich (1984) *Look Me in the Eye: Old Women, Aging and Ageism.* San Francisco: Spinster's Ink.

McNeill, John J. (1976) *The Church and the Homosexual.* Kansas City: Sheed Andrews & McMeel.

Minnigerode, F. (1976) "Age Status Labeling in Homosexual Men." *Journal of Homosexuality,* 1 (3): 273–275.

Minnigerode, F. A., and M. R. Adelman (1978) "Elderly Homosexual Women and Men: Report on a Pilot Study." *The Family Coordinator,* 27 (4): 451–456.

National Association for Lesbian and Gay Gerontology (1993) *Lesbian and Gay Aging Resource Guide.* San Francisco: NALGG.

Nelson, J. B. (1978) *Embodiment: An Approach to Sexuality and Christian Theology.* Minneapolis: Augsburg.

Quam, J. K., and G. S. Whitford (1992) "Adaptation and Age-Related Expectations of Older Gay and Lesbian Adults." *The Gerontologist,* 32 (3).

Raphael, S. M., and M. K. Robinson (1980) "The Older Lesbian: Love Relationships and Friendship Patterns." *Alternative Lifestyles,* 3 (2): 207–229.

Scanzoni, L., and V. Ramey Mollenkott (1978) *Is the Homosexual My Neighbor?* San Francisco: Harper & Row.

Weinberg, M. S. (1970) "The Male Homosexual: Age-related Variations in Social and Psychological Characteristics." *Social Problems,* 17 (Spring), 527–537.

Weinberg, M. S., and C. J. Williams (1974) *Male Homosexuals: Their Problems and Adaptations.* New York: Penguin Books.

Whitford, G. S. (1995) "Gay Men View Growing Older," *Journal of Gay and Lesbian Social Services,* forthcoming.

Part Five THEOLOGICAL PERSPECTIVES ON AGING

INTRODUCTION

Regardless of their specific theological commitments, all the theologians represented in Part Five agree that the experience of aging inevitably raises religious questions. Because they speak from different faith traditions, they disagree about significant matters such as biblical interpretation, methods of theological inquiry, justifications for a theology of aging, and the lived experience of creation, sin, and redemption in old age. Nevertheless, as humans engaged in the daunting task of reflecting upon God's nature and God's work in the world, they agree about a number of issues. For example, they unflinchingly insist that persons who contemplate aging must also contemplate death. Several of the chapters in this part address the potential for spiritual growth that lies in the diminishment of age; all of them, in one way or another, embrace the dialectic between being and doing that reverberates so profoundly in the lives of aging persons. For some authors, this dialectic points to ancient deliberations about faith and works; for all, the complex and dynamic relation between being and doing forms the foundation for theological reflection on aging.

Taking a chronological approach in chapter 27, *Kerry Olitzky* and *Eugene Borowitz* examine how the convenantal bond between God and the Jewish people shaped views of aging in the biblical, rabbinic, and modern periods. They note the realistic, common sense approach to aging in the Bible and the writings of the rabbis and they assert that the key to understanding these images of old age lies within the context of the relation between parents and children. In the modern period, however, the meaning and purpose of aging has often been obscured by social barriers erected by materialism and reverence for youth. Employing four contemporary models for thinking about aging in the light of

Judaism, Olitsky and Borowitz suggest that the critique of modern culture can reveal a new vision of the possibilities for a covenant between the generations.

Catholic theologian *Drew Christiansen* is also concerned about the way a scientific-technological ethos elicits illusions of complete explanation and total control of the contingencies of human life (chap. 28). Christiansen proclaims an alternative image: the diminishments of age represent an initiation into the mysteries of God and humanity. He asserts that the Christian belief in the triune God gives new meaning to familiar gerontological issues such as dependence, family caregiving, intergenerational relations, and justice in the social commitment to providing care for the old.

Agreeing that aging erodes resources, *Fred Van Tatenhove* cites numerous biblical passages that portray the unity of the life span wherein change and loss are revealed as part of God's plan for human existence (chap. 29). Writing from an evangelical Christian perspective, Van Tatenhove wrestles with the dialectic of being and doing and he concludes that the Bible contains numerous hopeful images regarding fundamental human worth in late life. Like Christiansen, Van Tatenhove believes the aging process guides elders to the heart of the mystery of life.

Sometimes, however, elders lose their way on their spiritual journey. Beset by anxiety about finitude and unable to tolerate the tension between remaining open to life while bringing closure to life, they slip into despair—the negative outcome of the human predicament of self-awareness through time. Further, losses accumulate, impinging on freedom and self-acceptance. For *Omar Otterness* in chapter 30, the challenges to find hope in time and courage in loss represent the central concerns of aging. To elucidate these challenges, he compares Erik Erikson's insights about ego integrity to Paul Tillich's theological reflections on the problem of sin and guilt. Otterness also compares Erikson's notion of generativity and vital involvement in old age with Tillich's doctrine of sanctification and in both he finds possibilities for a restoration of purpose to later life.

Process theology, inspired by the work of Alfred North Whitehead, represents a contrast to theologies that celebrate reason and the intellect as reflections of God in humanity. This theological movement emphasizes emotion and physical embodiment. It offers a wholistic image of the individual—embodied, with feelings, and the cognitive ability to appraise the movement of the self through time. *Thomas Au* and *John Cobb* in chapter 31 discover in the process model what they consider to be the central religious question of aging: How can the human find peace within the seamless fabric of lived time? The challenge for elders is to remain open to God's call to find this peace despite living in a society that expects so little of them and persists in affirming doing while devaluing being.

Social uncertainty about the meaning of aging has produced numerous calls for new metaphors and paradigms of human life and community. In response to the need for a radical restructuring of the ways human beings understand reality and their shared social lives, feminist theologians have provided significant leadership in establishing a mutually critical and constructive dialogue between religious traditions and contemporary social situations. *Mary Knutsen* asserts that redemptive images of aging for both women and men can be found in the recovery of trinity and eschatology. Knutsen forges a feminist theology of aging grounded in the essential relationality of the triune God and in the intersection of the future with the past and present revealed in eschatological understandings of the time. In chapter 32, readers can observe a theologian at work. Knutsen carefully examines the particularities of aging persons today—especially aging women—in light of the enduring significance of the cross, a symbol that radically disconnects old images of human experience from new possibilities for self-understanding and action. She concludes her chapter by calling for rituals that draw people together in order to create fresh perspectives on the transitions of aging. Through such rituals, women and men, old and young, can nurture one another's growth toward a transformed vision of human life and community.

Mark Kolden's approach to theology and Scripture in chapter 33 differs in many important ways from previous chapters yet he, too, finds numerous opportunities for spiritual growth in later life. In what might be termed a post-liberal approach to the theological task, Kolden sets out criteria for the construction of Christian theology. It must be true to tradition, responsive to contemporary life, and morally defensible. Kolden insists that a theological approach to aging counters simplistic dichotomies that stereotype elders either as decrepit, dependent, and demanding, on the one hand, or as vigorous, autonomous, and full of saintly wisdom, on the other. According to Kolden, older persons need redemption as much as younger persons. Experiences of sin and judgment which find no place within social scientific accounts of aging must be addressed by theologians who realize that their enterprise contradicts modern desires to view the ultimate goal of aging as well-being for the self. Well-being is often depicted in the social sciences as a kind of perfect end-state. Kolden presents a different view, arguing that the focus needs to be not on the well-being of the self but on the dynamic relation between being and doing that is revealed in the vocation of the Christian. In old age, as through the rest of the life span, humans are called to serve God and not the self. Simply to be is not enough; being does not supplant doing in later life. Even the most helpless frail elder is doing in the sense of eliciting care from others.

Throughout Part Five, theologians proclaim the possibilities for human life lived long. They take a different approach to the discovery of knowledge about aging than do social scientists; it is hermeneutical, not empirical, epistemology. In their disciplined examination of the light shed by Scripture and tradition upon contemporary life, theologians often discover insights that contradict the modern, therapeutic understanding of the human project. Although social scientists may decry theologians' work—"they have no data"—nevertheless an essential perspective upon the ways the aging process conveys both religious comfort and religious challenge is presented. From Olitzky and Borowitz to Kolden, these chapters assert the moral emptiness of an aged life lived solely in the pursuit of well-being. They counter individualistic biases of modern culture by emphasizing the significance of the aging person's role within the human community. Finally, these chapters offer to social scientists studying aging, spirituality, and religion, a challenge to become more knowledgeable about how the actual beliefs and traditions of older persons shape their experience of the aging process.

Theologians and social scientists rarely engage in dialogue because of their mutual mistrust, vastly different assumptive worlds, and few opportunities to work together to examine a common concern. The volume editors asked *William Clements* to reflect in chapter 34 upon the tensions between theology and science because in his professional life, he has experienced both worlds. As a pastoral caregiver, teacher, and administrator, he has worked in medical schools and seminaries and so has had the unique experience of observing firsthand the chasm between materialistic science and the intuitive-feeling realm of human experience as articulated by theology.

James Birren has written on numerous occasions of the integrative power of metaphor and Clements' work reveals this power. His use of an intriguing metaphor invites readers of all disciplinary backgrounds to consider the ways people structure assumptions about reality according to their own areas of expertise. As a result, each discipline raises questions about the other's legitimacy. Social scientists complain that theologians do not test the predictive accuracy of their models and theologians criticize social scientists for ignoring the fundamental existential concerns of aging persons. As this volume demonstrates, however, the study of spirituality and religion in the aging process requires the convergence of multiple points of view.

The theologians and the social scientists, the academicians and the practitioners all must bring their own expertise to bear upon these important issues. Clements suggests that ample room exists for dialogue between these different approaches to aging processes and persons and his metaphor of the dark warehouse provides a way of beginning that dialogue. Readers of all disciplinary backgrounds should allow Clements to place a flashlight in their hands as they begin to explore unknown domains of inquiry about aging. Clements promises that the adventure will be worthwhile.

27 A Jewish Perspective

KERRY M. OLITZKY
EUGENE B. BOROWITZ

In the course of Jewish history, little can be described as monolithic, especially in regard to the characterization of Jewish thinking. What is presented in this chapter is fairly representative of the general discernible trends in aging throughout Jewish history when viewed through the lens of a particular period or context (Glicksman, 1990; Rosen, 1990). Thus, it is our intention to divide this chapter into two sections along accepted historical standards: (1) the biblical, which merges into the rabbinic and separately, (2) the modern. While the Bible forms a foundation for insight and understanding, there is much more textual material available from the rabbinic period. However, the rabbis introduce very little actual new material regarding "theology," and thus such a merge of material is necessary. The history of Jewish experience is an indispensable ingredient in presenting a theological approach to aging. Entering into a sacred dialogue, each generation adds its own layer of experience to the core of the primary Jewish experience. This historical experience enters into the memory of each Jew through one's ongoing interaction with history (and the sacred literature that records this history).

THE BIBLICAL AND RABBINIC PERIODS

Through the simple accumulation of years, the historical memories of older Jewish adults are deeper and more broad-based and their covenantal bond with the Deity potentially more secure. But the intersection of aging and Judaism does not begin with old age. It really begins with birth, with the growth and development of each human being, fashioned in the image of God. The biblical author saw this quite clearly. Reading the text through a twentieth-century perspective, Rachel Dulin has pointed out:

> The ancient Israelite writers viewed aging as the last part of an ongoing developmental process. Each phase of life was marked by physical and psychological changes as maturity set in and old age approached. . . . Aging is an inescapable part of the human experience. Congruent with the multiplication of our cells and the growth and maturity of our bodies, genetically programmed biological clocks are counting

> our finite years. Slowly, but inexorably, deterioration and weakness become the dominant symptoms of life. Biblical man [*sic*] observed that old age was that stage in which decline was most visible. (1986, 50, 51)

Hence, the locus classicus of the biblical view of aging found in Leviticus is: "You shall rise before the aged and show deference to the old. You shall fear your God. I am Adonai" (Lev. 19:32). Recognizing the need to raise the weakened elderly for God's protection, the law requires one to rise when an old person approaches and not speak before the elder had spoken. For example, in the Talmud (Kiddushin 33a), we read that Rabbi Yohanan rose up in the presence of an aged ignoramus out of respect for the suffering endured in the course of a long life. Indeed, the text implies a direct and necessary relationship between respect for the elderly and reverence for God. Ecclesiasticus, the apocryphal Wisdom of Ben Sira (25:4–6), makes this line even stronger. Ben Sira wrote: "How beautiful is the wisdom of old people and thoughtful advice of individuals who are honored. Much experience is the crown of old people. Their enhancement is reverence for Adonai." Later, in the Talmud (Berachot 8b), this respect is even demonstrated for the one who has lost his learning (e.g., wisdom): "Respect even the old person who has lost his learning for there were placed in the ark of the Covenant not only the two perfect tablets of the Law but also the fragments of the tablets that Moses shattered when he saw the people dancing before the Golden Calf." Yet, in the treatment of the biblical material many find a tendency to overstate the "golden age syndrome" and underplay what is better classified as biblical realism. The hope for a good old age is ever present in the text, but it may be more of a reaction to the reality of young deaths and difficult living than theological speculation. As Shlomo Balter has pointed out,

> One should not be lulled by these passages into believing that Judaism viewed aging with either equanimity or anticipation. It must not be forgotten that these passages and attitudes emerged within the context of the world in which the average life expectancy was limited and the rate of infant mortality very high. Understandably, in such a society those who survived and grew old were granted a special status. (1978, 9)

Long life was seen by many as a reward for righteous living. This was probably more wishes and hopes, a sense of God's special gifts, than the reality of most lives. As Benjamin Blech has shown, old age thus became both a blessing and a curse. While being alive is itself considered good, there was never a guarantee that the maladies of old age would be prevented, even among those "blessed" by old age (1977, 65–78). The twelfth chapter of Ecclesiastes spells it out graphically, if metaphorically:

> So appreciate your vigor in the days of your youth, before those days of sorrow come and those years arrive of which you will say, "I have no pleasure in them;"

before sun and light and moon and stars grow dark, and the clouds come back again after the rain:

> When the guards of the house become shaky,
> And the men of valor are bent,
> And the maids that grind, grown few, are idle,
> And the ladies that peer through the windows grow dim,
> And the doors to the street are shut—
> With the noise of the hand mill growing fainter,
> And the sound of the bird growing feebler,
> And all the strains of music dying down;
> When one is afraid of heights
> And there is terror on the road.—
> For the almond tree may blossom,
> The grasshopper be burdened,
> And the caper bush may bud again;
> But humans set out for their eternal abode,
> With mourners all around the street.—
> Before the silver cord snaps
> And the golden bowl crashes,
> The jar is shattered at the spring,
> And the jug is smashed at the cistern.
> And the dust returns to the ground
> As it was,
> And the lifebreath returns to God
> Who bestowed it.
> Utter futility—said Koheleth—
> All is futile!
>
> (Eccles. 12:1-8, adapted from Ginsberg, 1982, 399–400)

In the Midrash Rabbah to this chapter, the author identifies each metaphor as a specific reference to a part of the body which deteriorates and seeks to function properly in old age. While one may read the chronological years of many of the long-lived biblical personalities as metaphors as well, it is patently clear that the author intends the reader to understand that ancestors were given long lives as rewards for their righteousness. Rachel Dulin further indicates:

> Four conditions were illustrated by the Biblical text to describe blessed old age: lack of infirmity, presence of children, economic success, and being accorded respect. The Biblical heroes who achieved blessed old age were endowed with at least one of these attributes in addition to long life. Although each hero was blessed in a different way and to a different degree, each became a symbol of God's blessing. (1988, 79–80)

Therefore, if persons are blessed with old age, then they are the veritable embodiment of holiness. Having lived so long, elderly Jewish persons then intensify their level of covenant through living righteously and through the performance of *mitzvot*.

Rachel Dulin notes:

> Regardless of what biblical people knew about the debilitating nature of the aging process, they still wished to live long. With the yearning to hold on to life, the reality of growing old was altered and the concept of old age at times was given an extended meaning. It was transferred, theologically, to a higher plane in which old age lost its physical dimension, its debilitating nature and became a symbol of reward. By ignoring the races of the imprint of time, by overlooking decrepitude and suffering, biblical people projected their wish to live long into old age with dignity as a reward given by God to the righteous. . . . And once old age with dignity was conceptualized as one of God's rewards for humans, appropriate projection, not living into old age, was realized as part of God's retribution for wrongdoing. (1986, 77–78).

Aging associated with dying and death is, however, not a joy. For the biblical authors, all one had to anticipate was Sheol, the great pit under the earth to which the shades of the dead were gathered. While a theology of aging without a serious concern with death is denial, the rabbis eventually transcended this challenge when they introduced the notion of eternal soul and resurrection. It is well to keep in mind the dialectic of the biblical view. As the psalmist wrote,

> Do not cast me off in old age; when my strength fails, do not forsake me. I come with praise of your mighty acts, O Adonai. I celebrate your beneficence, yours alone. You have let me experience it, God, from my youth. Until now, I have proclaimed your wondrous deeds, and even in hoary old age, do not forsake me, God, until I proclaim your strength to the next generation. (Psalms 71:9, 16-18)

This psalm indicates the classical Jewish realism and separates the other streams of thought as ideals and hope. While the value of the latter should not be underestimated, much of their glorification of Jewish attitudes may never have happened. Even the phrase *all tashliheni*—"do not forsake me" is repeated in the liturgy and has become part of folk Judaism, an indication that everyone was not engaged in a communal effort to treat the elderly with respect.

In general, the Jewish notion of reverence for parents reinforced the laws commanding deference for the aged. This attitude helped to establish the basis for what would eventually become a social system of caring for the elderly. While the rabbinic views of aging—including those that believe that the age at death is determined by individual acts of goodness and evil—are fraught with theological challenges, reverence for those who live to old age then becomes representative of all later Judaism. With the rabbis, this theme of reverence for old-age wisdom becomes institutionalized. As the rabbinic way of being a Jew becomes more accepted, a major social form in which age counts is introduced.

The question of how long one lives is a major theological issue. The rabbis discussed it on numerous occasions. In Megillah 27b–28a, for example, a group of teachers in the academy are asked, "Why have you merited long life?" While no real conclusions are drawn, it is implicit that the premise of the statement is, as Richard Sarason points out, that "lifespan is a function of proper conduct, and that a life lived in study and observance of God's revealed Torah will *ipso facto* be lengthened" (Chernick, 1989, 101–6; Bayme, 1989, 107–8; Ben Sorek, 1989, 109–110; Sarason, 1989, 111–12).

Sociologist Allen Glicksman sees respect for the elderly as tied to the more dominant issue of authority in the Jewish community, a salient theme that literally shapes the development of the Jewish community throughout its history. But since the Talmud saw learning as the sine qua non for community authority, somewhat of a compromise seems to have been reached. The assumption was made that if one lived a long time, that person learned a great deal about Jewish tradition and was consequently deemed wise (Glicksman, 1990, 5). The ideal state, of course, was combination of wisdom and old age. A Yiddish proverb says it best: "Old age to the unlearned is winter. To the learned, it is harvest time."

Beyond the general notion of inspiring reverence, Jewish tradition views the aged as a group imbued with a special purpose: to pass on traditional wisdom and sound advice to the young. The rabbis viewed the past as a guide to the present. "Remember the days of old," the Bible taught them. "Consider the years of ages past. Ask your parents, they will inform you. Your elders, they will tell you" (Deut. 32:7). Given the choice between listening to the old or heeding the impetuous voices of the young, the rabbis almost invariably went with experience and listened to the elders. A famous rabbinic text (Tosefta Avodah Zarah 1:19) referring to the rebuilding of the Temple in Jerusalem in Hadrian's time explains why: "If young people advise you to build a Temple, and old people say destroy it, listen to the latter. The building of the young is destruction while the tearing down by the old is construction." While this sounds like a formula for community conflict, the traditional Jewish ideal was actually far more harmonious. The goal remains a world where young and old might work together for common ends, earlier envisioned by the prophet Joel (2:28): "And it shall come to pass afterward that I will pour out My spirit on all flesh. Your sons and daughters shall prophesy; your elders shall dream dreams and your young see visions."

Human beings are created in the image of God. This does not refer to a physical representation. Rather, it goes beyond the corporeal by definition. Like God, the human species is creative, albeit on a significantly more limited basis. As a matter of fact, in every case where the imitation of God is apparent, the limitations are also made clear. God is eternal. Human beings are mortal. However, they approximate or imitate immortality and the ability to create through the act of procreation. Thus, the relationship between young and old is necessarily tied to our relationship with God. And all Jewish attitudes toward the elderly are refractions of the guidance of the Jewish tradition in regard to the idealized relationship between adult children and their parents. By comparison, little is really said by the rabbis about the elderly per se, unless it is placed in the context of the relationship between parents and children. In the mouth of Malachi (4:5) God speaks: "Behold. I will send you Elijah the prophet before the great and terrible day of Adonai comes. He will turn the hearts of parents to their children and the hearts of children to their parents, *lest I come and smite the land with a curse.*" Jewish tradition argues that such lack of regard for the elderly is an outright rejection of God as the Source of life and law in the universe.

Such an analysis is particularly poignant if Robert Katz's notion that old age may be the "sabbath" of human life is accepted (Katz, 1975; Olitzky, 1988). If one assumes that among the many functions and purposes of the Jewish Sabbath is to force the individual from "creating" and be reminded of her or his mortality (in contradistinction to the eternal creative ability of God), then this notion has profound theological consequences. It is the day that moves the individual to a higher plane where mind and soul can take precedence over body and flesh. Old age thus becomes the period in which our active energies are transformed into spiritual energies that sustain the soul more than the body. This is to say that the focus of this creativity, as in the focus of Shabbat, is on a higher plane of existence. Old age—because of the wisdom of experience and the consequent growth of knowledge—leads the individual to this higher plane.

Jewish tradition, which speaks of the aged in lofty terms, also evidences a commonsense approach to old age (Reuben, 1976). The frank realism that was expressed in both biblical and rabbinic literature can be summarized by this text from Genesis Rabbah 69: "There is old age without the glory of long life and there is long life without the ornament of age. Perfect is that old age which has both." Like the authors of the Bible, the rabbis were not blind to the frailties of the human condition. In their book of wisdom for everyday living, Pirke Avot (4:20), they ask, "What is one like who learns in old age?" The answer: "To ink written on erased paper." They also wrote in the same *mishnah:* "What is one like who learns from the old?" This time the answer was, "To one who eats ripe grapes and drinks old wine." These attitudes can be considered synthesized by Rabbi Meir who suggested later in the same text: "Do not look at the flask. Rather look at what is in it. There may be a new flask full of old wine and an old flask that has not even new wine in it." They understood the need to offer incredibly profound sage advice, based on a lifetime of living, but they also knew what it was like to face the physical limitations of the body. Old age, according to this view, is dark and dull, without music or the sounds of the world. They proclaimed in the Babylonian Talmud (Shabbat 152a) that the intelligence of the aged is dissipated. The speech of the old is faltering. The ears of the elderly are unreliable. To an older person even a little hill seems like the greatest of mountains. They even urged the individual (in Midrash Tanhuma Miketz 10) to pray that "in his older years his eyes may see, his mouth eat, and his legs work, because in old age, all powers fail."

From reading texts like the following from Avodah Zarah (17b), we know that the inspired instructions of the rabbis were not always kept by the people. In this passage, Elazar ben Prata is asked why he had not been to the house of study lately. His reply, "I am too old and was afraid that I would be trampled down under the feet of the crowd." A similar sentiment is expressed in Bava Kamma (92b): "Now that we are old, we are treated like infants." This last stage of life is described by so many as pathetic and without hope. Consider this selection from Midrash Tanhuma:

> Apelike, his disposition changes. Childlike, he asks for everything, eating, drinking and playing like a child. There he sits, even with his children and the members of his house mocking him, disregarding and loathing him. When he utters a word, he hears "let him alone. He is old and childish." Yet, when the angel of death arrives, he starts to weep and his cry pierces the world from one end to the other.

The perspective of the rabbis on old age, both positive and negative, was not just filtered through the protracted lenses of the academies or through the leisure of theological speculation. Instead, they learned from the people, sharing their joy as well as their pain. One text from the Jerusalem Talmud (Beitzah 1) says it so poignantly: "Stones which we sat on in our youth make war against us in our old age." In this respect, things have not changed greatly. While medical advances have brought life expectancy in closer proximity to lifespan potential for the human species, the fear of finitude and dependency among human beings that permeated the rabbinic mindset resonates with contemporary attitude as well, a reflection of the human condition.

Perhaps the balance of rabbinic views should be read as a juxtaposition of a Jewish ideal to a human reality. Persons often find themselves in the situation described immediately above. This is the reason why Jews are commanded and exhorted to treat the elderly with respect. In one way or another, as much as persons must face the unavoidable reality of death, none among them truly wants to die.

THE MODERN PERIOD

In turning to contemporary Jewish life, a paradox immediately suggests itself. As a thoroughly modernized, secularized community, Jews rarely approach practical issues of living by directly reflecting on what their people's religious teachings might have to say about them. On the practical level they tend to operate out of their own sense of what they consider right. Being generally more affluent than their grandparents were and living longer than prior generations did, possibilities open up for them that were unknown in the past. The many positive aspects of this development are offset by the obstacles our culture particularly creates for the elderly. These problems include: segregation and separation from family, no clear place in the social scheme, and the threat that respect for privacy will become abandonment, among others. All of these problems plague the Jewish community as much as they do non-Jewish society.

Yet, one also sees a certain skewing of the statistics and a general ethos which can be distinguished from what is operative in the general society. The latter emerges most clearly in the way in which organized Jewish communities in the United States have moved to create special residences and services for the elderly. If that indicates the continuing power of the classic Jewish ethos, one can then see its further effect on the many Jews who consider respect for and care of their parents a major indicator of their humanity—and, by extension, of the community's treatment of the aged.

It is the theologian's or philosopher's task to try to give some cognitive insight into the religious bases of this ongoing commitment, often to strengthen or redirect it. And it is a sign of the relative newness of this issue that there has been almost no direct treatment of the theme. In a sanguine mood that might be attributed to the adequacy of Jewish tradition on this topic, it did not really require any academic reconsideration even in the changed modern circumstances. To some extent, this is the position of many traditionalists, stressing the primacy of Jewish action over abstract reflection. Perhaps the problems of aging have intensified, or human and Jewish resources now seem less self-evident than they once did. This sense makes it desirable to provide a more abstract reflection on the Jewish religious attitude toward aging. Perhaps, too, one can gain new insight into the present duty by such an exercise. This chapter will proceed by an exploration of four contemporary models of Jewish thinking and seek to draw out their implications for aging (Borowitz, 1983).

The oldest still effective pattern of thinking about Judaism is ethical rationalism, exemplified most fully in the neo-Kantianism of Hermann Cohen (Borowitz, 1983, 29–52). In a typical Kantian shift of emphasis from traditional religion's concern with what God had instructed people to do, to what the modern mind could itself teach us about proper human duty and aspiration, Cohen continued the classic Jewish concern with deeds. But he gave this activism a special interpretation that has left its mark upon much Jewish self-understanding: Rational people ought to be self-legislating and need to make their universal ethical regard the center of their existence. Both themes invested personal agency with an intensity they had not had in prior generations. This becomes particularly evident when one keeps in mind Cohen's liberal shift from (rabbinic Judaism's) this-and-otherworldly faith to one that needed to be lived in this world alone.

The resulting emphasis on ethical action as the telltale sign of true Jewishness has dominated much of popular thought about Judaism. Equally, it has had its effect on specifically Jewish action. The astonishingly disproportionate involvement of Jews in the various causes for human betterment in recent generations is tribute to the widespread appeal of this reinterpretation of Judaism. As a result, much of the Jewish concern for the aged must be seen in the context of this fundamental yardstick of Jewish faithfulness. In an academic sense, this can be taken a step further. The Kantian emphasis on the universal horizon of rational ethics means that one must extend dignity to *every* moral agent—a notion that still has revolutionary implications for the further humanization of our society and planet. But that means that one cannot simply "cast off" the elderly regardless of how "unproductive," infirm, or troublesome they appear to be. As moral agents they must be treated to the extent we possibly can as "ends in themselves" and not as "means to an end."

The dark side of this doctrine is connected with its easy conflation to the capitalistic notion of individuals shaping their own destiny, of "making a life for themselves," as social-cultural entrepreneurs, or economically, in providing for themselves, preferably well. The ethical activism of the Cohenian self was quickly assimilated to the American practical bent while, of course, also modifying it. But it is this emphasis on the self's usefulness, on what one does or can do, and, at its worst, on what goods are yielded, that creates a special problem for becoming old in America. Too often, humanity is identified with a need to be in control rather than simply with the ability to initiate. Action is no longer enough; effectiveness has become critical. Fully being a person means not being dependent upon anyone else, always being able to do for oneself.

This concept surely has its own promise. It encourages persons, at whatever age, to try new things, to see what they might yet become, to undertake such long-deferred dreams as they might now reasonably seek to make reality. Doing often brings great joy and satisfaction. But what happens when one tires, and would simply like to be, not having to prove by actions that one still retains one's humanity?

Productive action is a futile standard even for the young. How many can fully take advantage of all their abilities or of the opportunities that present themselves to them? But it is a devastating challenge for most of the elderly who cannot hope to do what they once did physically, emotionally, or economically. And it is the threat of losing such areas of control that one has established for oneself that depresses persons as the years lengthen. As long as one cannot simply be, as long as one feels one must continually do and by the doing demonstrate one's humanity, old age devolves rather than dignifies.

The Jewish ethical rationalists should not be blamed for this degradation of their teaching. There is nothing in what they said to demean whatever capacity a person has to be a moral agent. It is not difficult to argue that years and experience can bring moral insight. But in the way that this theory has been coopted by the productive genius of our society, it has been an unwitting accomplice to the transformation of youth and vigor to the honored age of our society.

A second model of contemporary Jewish philosophy has emphasized the social over the individual. As elaborated in the naturalism of Mordecai Kaplan,

Judaism is the evolving religious civilization of the Jewish people (Borowitz, 1983, 98–120). Critical of the exaggerated individualism of the Kantians and impressed with the way in which individuals are shaped by their culture, Kaplan argued for reconstructing a full ethnic existence for Jews in order to remedy the ills brought into Jewish life by patterning modern Judaism in terms of the Protestantism that dominated the democratic countries. Instead of individual faith and ethics being the ground of a Jewishness worked out through religious institutions, Kaplan called for a Jewish life in which the social whole rather than just the synagogue shaped the character of Jews. Hence the land of Israel, the Hebrew language, the Jewish calendar, folk traditions and lore, Jewish art, music, and dance, and a full range of communal institutions to support these variegated aspects of Jewish civilization (as Kaplan called it) would now give Jewishness its vitality. It is easy enough to see how these cultured components would transmit Jewish values, particularly with the survival of the folk itself as a major criterion of Jewish duty. However, following Emile Durkheim, Kaplan argued that religion and personal spirituality would result from a vigorous ethnic existence rather than being its cause.

Kaplan said nothing special about the elderly in his philosophy of Judaism, but several of its themes suggest a special approach to the topic. Honoring the people and its traditions, imbued with a strong sense of how individual existence is the result of fold creativity, he would probably argue that the years one lives form a prominent part of Jewish existence and thus express an appreciation of the aged, the bearers of the tradition. As a result of the explicit humanism of this approach, its insistence on the humane values Jews have inherited from their premodern forebears would make the historical teachings about honoring the hoary head a living part of contemporary Judaism. Finally, with the group and its creativity central to the continuity of Judaism and vitality of individuals in contradistinction to the notion of individual initiative, it would be easier for people to see themselves as dignified, even if increasingly passive, in the ongoing life of the fold. And, if it needs adding, the community's own responsibility to all the constituencies within it would, in this reading of the centrality of the folk, lead to a vigorous, respectful concern with the aged.

The very strengths of this position have, however, also led to its limited effectiveness as providing a new conceptualization of aging. When the ethnic group becomes the generator of one's norms—with the exception of the moral law that Kaplan asserts is inherent in the universe—one has little basis on which to chide the folk for the ethos they have come to accept. That is particularly true in this case, as Kaplan enthusiastically spoke of living in two civilizations. Of course, he anticipated that one would take what he pointed to as the humane best of both cultures: American and Jewish. But with regard to the elderly, the Jewish community, as it has increasingly acculturated, has often come to be as youth-dominated and as action-oriented as has much of America with much the same result. The Jewish tradition once honored the aged because God instructed to do so. It believed that the wisdom of the past or of accumulated years was better than that of the present or of the young. A philosophy committed to change as people react to new situations, for all that it seeks to remain loyal to its ethnic roots, is far more likely to honor the recent and the new and have no independent basis for dignifying the elderly.

In a striking address to the White House Conference on Aging in 1961, Abraham Joshua Heschel produced the only sustained Jewish theological treatment of the topic of aging (Heschel, 1981). Typically, it was not a systematic analysis. Instead, it was academic in frame and abstract in approach. Heschel assumed that a systematic statement would concede too much power to human reason in its contemporary technical, impersonal mode, as if detachment from a concern as human as aging were the proper way in which to confront it. Rather, here as elsewhere, Heschel's concern was to transmit or even evoke a new vision, one that would alone make it possible for us to change our society's pervasive, pernicious attitude toward the elderly. He did this in two ways that were closely related. The first was polemical: an insistent, persistent critique of the style our culture teaches about relating to the aged or to thinking of oneself as old. The second was visionary: giving us tantalizing glimpses of what we might yet do and be. Both lines of his thought were carried out in his uncommon gift for the striking phrase, the telling aphorism, the stunning reversal of the anticipated. Quite consciously, he reached for the heart as well as the mind, knowing that if he did not affect the whole person then no amount of intellectual brilliance would accomplish his purpose (Borowitz, 1983, 165–83).

Not only did Heschel express broadscale generalities with incredible insight, but he also exposed a steady stream of specific follies for judgment. In large part, his extraordinary perceptiveness must be attributed to the different standard that he confidently brought to bear on secular American life. On the simpler level it had to do with the fatal preference for space over time. Americans want time to serve them as a means to conquer one or another manifestation of space. They seek to use time efficiently or, when that cannot be done, to kill it pleasantly. So years have to do with productivity. When the elderly cannot any longer compete with the more vigorous time-users, they are considered a burden and consider themselves "useless." Society then recommends that the elderly play or otherwise amuse themselves since, by this standard, there is nothing serious for them to do.

The root of this insidious vision of existence is the exaltation of the thing, another way of saying idolatry. The clear and present measure behind Heschel's view of living is the God of the Bible, the One whom no thing can represent although to whom anything might awaken one. Knowing God is real, more real than any human theory of reality could explicate, and concerned with each person, in a dignity conferring relationship that nothing, not even sin, can obliterate, Heschel knew time was given as an incomparable endowment of humanity. In some sense persons are things and certainly can be said to occupy space.

However, in neither aspect can they be said to be most truly what their relationship to God discloses them to be.

Consider, for example, persons' pressing concern with their needs, or their need to be needed by others. It builds their lives on themselves or their society as the source of their worth and significance. It is a bloated humanism which takes their justifiable recognition that they are not isolates but social animals and turns it into a compulsive way of life. And then come the years when persons feel that no one needs them anymore and one difficulty or another makes it impossible for them to fulfill what for so long they took to be their rightful needs. Their problem is not, therefore, essentially one of better techniques or arrangements but of a functioning spirituality. In Heschel's memorable closing words, "It takes three things to attain a sense of significant being: God, a Soul and a Moment. And the three are always here. Just to be is a blessing. Just to live is holy" (1968, 75).

Heschel called for conversion, for giving up the false gods that gave persons false standards. Instead, he urged persons to confront the living God who calls them to sanctify time, whatever time is given them.

Something of this recognition that human value is not self-bestowed or earned in social usefulness is carried over into the fourth model of a Jewish theological reflection on aging, the postmodern covenant theology of Eugene B. Borowitz (1991). Only in his view, God, the real and independent One, mysteriously but lovingly gives people a substantial measure of self-determination, making them capable of being full, if subordinate, covenant partners. Relationship rather than hierarchy becomes the instructive model here, allowing God's uniquely normative quality to yoke itself to the free, self-making power of humans while thus keeping it, ideally, from self-worship and its inevitable dehumanization.

Once relatedness becomes the heart of spirituality and the finest mode of a person's service of God, the elderly attain enhanced dignity and continuing power. For with the self forever unable to satisfy itself or its needs except in relation to others, the covenant between the generations takes on its commanding power. Persons would never have come to be or been the selves they now are without the forebears who had the faith to bring them into being and nurture their selfhood. How much of what they take to be their very individuality they owe to their relationships with those older than them. And how much more of themselves have they gained as they risked relationships with those younger than themselves. Rather than lives being measured in terms of an eternal present or compared to some idealized, vigorous youthfulness, it is faithfulness over the years—the model of God's involvement with humans—that provides such glory as a human being can accomplish. And even when debility makes it difficult or even impossible for persons actively to carry on their relationships, they remain those whose partnerships over time exercise their proper demands on others.

Increasingly, individualism carried to extremes shows its destructiveness. Borowitz would give the individual more room in contemporary religiosity than would Heschel, for Borowitz recognizes the spiritual benefits involved in reasonably autonomous living. But he insists on persons exercising their autonomy in relationship to God as part of a humanity covenanted to God. It is a far more social and theological vision of existence than many in the Jewish community are ready for. But in the stubborn insistence of so many Jews to affirm their ethnic roots and freshly open themselves up to their people's historic relationship with God, a new theological possibility of refreshing and enhancing the old Jewish esteem for the aged makes itself presently manifest.

While there are those in the modern Jewish world, primarily right-wing or orthodox, who would still hold that there is a necessary relationship between righteous living and old age as a blessing by God, most Jews would argue that righteous living is important but not the primary cause for old age. Nature and nurture play indispensable roles, and the human species is limited in both life-span and life expectancy (Kushner, 1981, 1986). The major reason for the abrupt change in the theology of aging from rabbinic to modern times is the loss of faith in the system of a tight reward and punishment. Jews observe that things do not happen as they were taught in the rabbinic period; they are not rewarded in years for their good deeds. Thus, rather than searching for an understanding regarding the years of their lives, they work to increase the life of their years through their relationship with God, the Source of all life.

BIBLIOGRAPHY

Balter, S. (1978) *Helping Aging to Come of Age*. New York: United Synagogue of America Commission on Jewish Education.

Bayme, S. (1989) "Longevity." *Journal of Aging and Judaism* 4 (2):107–8.

Ben Sorek, E. (1989) "Reflections on the Text." *Journal of Aging and Judaism* 4 (2):109–10.

Blech, B. (1977) "Judaism and Gerontology." *Tradition* 16:65–78.

Borowitz, E. B. (1983) *Choices in Modern Jewish Thought: A Partisan Guide*. New York: Behrman.

______ (1991) *Renewing the Covenant, a Theology for Postmodern Jews*. Philadelphia: Jewish Publications Society.

Chernick, M. (1989) "Megillah 27b–28a." *Journal of Aging and Judaism* 4 (2):101–6.

Dulin, R. Z. (1986) "The Elderly in Biblical Society." *Journal of Aging and Judaism* 1 (1):50–51.

______ (1988) *A Crown of Glory*. New York: Paulist Press.

Ginsberg, H. L., ed. in chief (1982) *The Writings . . . Kethubim*. Translation of the Holy Scriptures. Philadelphia: Jewish Publications Society.

Glicksman, A. (1990) "The New Jewish Elderly: A Literature Review." *The Journal of Aging and Judaism* 5 (1):7–21.

Heschel, A. J. (1981) "The Older Person and the Family in the Perspective of Jewish Tradition." In LeFevre and LeFevre, 35–44.

Hiltner, S., ed. (1975) *Toward a Theology of Aging*. New York: Human Sciences Press.

Katz, R. L. (1975) "Jewish Values and Sociopsychological Perspectives on Aging." In Hiltner, 135–50.

Kushner, H. S. (1981) *When Bad Things Happen to Good People*. New York: Schocken Books.

______ (1986) *When All You Ever Wanted Wasn't Enough*. New York: Summit Books.

LeFevre, C., and P. LeFevre (1981) *Aging and the Human Spirit: A Reader in Religion and Gerontology*. Chicago: Exploration Press.

Olitzky, K. M. (1988) "Old Age as a Sabbatical Transformation of Life: A Model for All Faiths." *Journal of Aging and Judaism* 2 (4):210–20.

Reuben, S. C. (1976) "Old Age: Appearance and Reality." Rabbinic Thesis. Hebrew Union College—Jewish Institute of Religion, New York.

Rosen, S. (1990) "The New Jewish Elderly: A Symposium." *Journal of Aging and Judaism* 5 (1):7–21.

Sarason, R. (1989) "Rabbinic and Contemporary Reflections on Old Age." *Journal of Aging and Judaism* 4 (2):111–12.

28 A Catholic Perspective

DREW CHRISTIANSEN, S. J.

> The real high point of my life is still to come. I mean the abyss of the mystery of God, into which one lets oneself fall in complete confidence of being caught up by God's love and mercy forever.
>
> Theologian Karl Rahner at eighty (1990, 38)

It often appears that technological society so insulates modern-day people from the contingency of human life that they come to lose the capacity for wonder that moved earlier generations to search for God and surrender in worship. They have become accustomed to wonders. Summiting Mt. Everest, which only decades ago seemed an extraordinary feat, has now become a high-priced tourist event. For many people the miracle of birth itself has been "demystified," turned into "a matter of choice." Coronary bypass surgery, organ transplants, corneal implants, bionic joints have become commonplace, easing much of the anguish of old age.

There is very little space in this technological world where humans do not seem supremely in control. As a result, the sense for primal religious experience has been dulled. The occasions in which the intuition arises that humans participate in a vast, complex world not of their making, one in which they play an exceedingly minor role but in which they are nonetheless highly valued, seem to have become year by year more rare. Technology need not obscure the mystery at the heart of human life. Gilkey has persuasively demonstrated that scientific activity itself can be an occasion to experience religious mystery (1970). Interpreters of culture such as Steiner also show the sacred presence in artistic enjoyment (1989). The point is simply that many of the life experiences that offer an occasion to experience mystery have been so altered to make it less easy to apprehend them in a religious way, and that old age, by contrast, is shared human experience that still holds that power. But the technological advances that relieve many of the complaints of aging notwithstanding, old age remains the one phenomenon shared by most people that opens up sensibilities to the contingency of human existence and the transcendent mystery.

It is not just that old age brings one face to face with mortality. The religious virtualities of old age are of a more subtle and intimate nature. Unlike death, which is a one-time event and can overtake a person quite suddenly, aging is a process that transpires over a long period of years, comprising a succession of transitions and crises that over time force attention to ultimate realities and profoundly change the self-understanding of the elderly. Traditional views of preparation for death as an essentially religious activity have generally regarded death as the end of a process of aging or illness. Aging in contemporary times has been altered in that a long period of active life is followed by another long period of declining health and disability for many older adults (Christiansen, 1990).

Aging restricts mobility, diminishes senses, and impairs speech and thinking. It leads to a withdrawal from active public life, and forces one in time to rely on the help of others to carry out the most basic daily activities. The loss, suffering, and diminishment of old age, its disengagement, isolation, and dependence are opportunities to experience the precariousness of human existence, the graciousness of human life, and the transcendent greatness of being. To some gerontologists, this analysis may seem to place excessive emphasis on the negative, debilitating aspects of an infirm, late old age and neglect the changing demographics of an extended life expectancy which allows for a long period of active aging before final decline (Neugarten, 1986). The emphasis is a conscious one, because it is the diminishment and dependence in old age which existentially is most likely to pose ultimate questions (Christiansen, 1990).

What's more, aging also draws those who love and care for old people into new and deeper engagement with human existence. In the decline of their loved ones they may experience the fragility of their own existence, and in their inability to care for loved ones as they would like, they may come to know the limits of human action and, indeed, the impuissance of human love. Thus, in the midst of the spiritual dullness of a technicist culture, old age remains perhaps the one universal experience that opens hearts and minds to the mystery "in which we live and move and have our being" (Acts 17:28).

OLD AGE: THRESHOLD OF MYSTERY

"[Man's] ground," wrote the twentieth century's leading Roman Catholic theologian, Karl Rahner, "lies in the abyss of mystery, which accompanies him always throughout life. The only question is whether he lives with mystery willingly, obediently and trustingly, or represses it and will not admit it, 'suppressing' it, as Paul says" (Rahner, 1969, 135). Whether persons are themselves growing old or are simply companions to the elderly, old age affords in a special way the opportunity to overcome the temptation to deny the mystery at the heart of their lives and instead to accept, embrace, and affirm it.

The name ordinarily given to this mystery is "God." Employing the word "mystery" reminds persons that divine presence exceeds every limit they would place on it (Rahner, 1969, 135). Rahner speaks of "mystery" rather than of "God," then, to encourage individuals to encounter the wonder and the terror that a genuine encounter with God entails.

First, the gradual physical decrement associated with old age opens the human spirit to mystery by demonstrating in the most intimate way how profoundly people's very lives escape their control. Indeed, it invites appreciation of how their lives are mysterious, wrapped in mystery, penetrated through and through with mystery. Second, the steady accumulation of losses which is the process of aging can result (sometimes after detours into denial, anger and self-pity) in a quiet turn to interiority where elders can appropriate for themselves the spirit's yearning for the mysterious God who exceeds every expectation. Third, the diminishment, which is the inward experience of loss undergone in old age, awakens the soul to the giftedness of life and make it receptive to grace. Finally, the personal acceptance of limitation and even more of diminishment awakens the peculiar virtue of aging that Erik Erikson calls "wisdom" (1976) and Ronald Blythe "benignity" (1975), the willingness to bless life in the face of one's own suffering and mortality.

MYSTERY AND REVELATION

The awakening to mystery in old age described above, however, points to the God of natural theology, a presence available to all as a common grace of creation. It is not the God of Christian revelation, the one who without ceasing to be mystery "gives himself to us without intermediary" and "becomes the innermost reality of our being" (Rahner, 1969, 135). For of themselves, human hearts are overawed by God's mystery, and even when intimating God's transcendent goodness, as if blinded by light, are unable to fathom that this presence which both exceeds their grasp and yet penetrates everything without exception has turned its face toward them and invites them to communion. It is only through the divine self-disclosure in Christ that persons can come to understand that "God is love" (1 John 4:8) and not an obscure force governing "our lives in remote detachment and judgment" (Rahner, 1969, 136). The privileged understanding of the exposure to mystery in old age receives its positive meaning through the historical revelation in which God communicates the divine life to humanity. The mysterious God recognized in the aging process is, as Rahner has written, the "God who has given himself so fully in his absolute self-communication" to human creatures that the God who is the ground of their being becomes the God of salvation history (1966, 69).

Salvation history, as Rahner points out, is the revelation of God's self-giving to humanity as Creator, Redeemer, and Gracegiver. Through the mystery of salvation, the triune God—Father, Son, and Spirit—is revealed in relation to humanity's existence in history (Rahner, 1969, 136). The Christian belief in the triune God, therefore, holds implications for understanding old age as an initiation to the mystery of God.

The whole of human life, of course, is wrapped around with this mystery and penetrated by it. Old age is only one of many points at which the immersion of human life in mystery becomes evident. The same Christian doctrines examined here with respect to old age could equally be examined for their applicability to other stages of human life. But, because old age is a privileged moment for appropriating involvement in that mystery, Christian faith offers an opportunity to integrate the personal, familial, and social experience of aging in ways that post-modern society appears to be incapable of doing. For, in the absence of faith, the relentless diminishment which is aging becomes, as Jean Paul Sartre wrote, "an irrealizable," an undeniable phenomenon of which humans are a part but which they are both intellectually and affectively loath to make their own (de Beauvoir, 1973). Only in faith that the mystery in which they live is love itself can they begin to fathom the mystery which is their own aging.

To consider old age from the perspective of Christian faith, this essay will organize itself around the trinitarian symbols of Father, Son, and Spirit (Creator, Redeemer, Gracegiver). The doctrine of Creation (Father) leads to consideration of (1) dependence, (2) filial obligation, and (3) justice in eldercare; the doctrine of Redemption (the Son) to (1) forgiveness, (2) humility, and (3) spiritual friendship; and the doctrine of Grace (the Spirit) to (1) sanctification and (2) mystery and the end of life.

"MAKER OF HEAVEN AND EARTH"

Creation and Dependence in Old Age

Old age is haunted by twin fears: fear of abandonment and fear of dependence. These are ancient fears. The biblical writer Sirach admonished his disciples, "Do not make a boast of disgrace overtaking your father." He went on to counsel, "My child, support your father in his old age. Even if his mind should fail, show him sympathy, do not despise him in your health and strength" (3:10; 12-13). The psalmist cries out that the God of his youth will not abandon him in old age. "Do not reject me now I am old/ nor desert me now my strength is failing" (Ps. 71:9).

As in biblical times, people today loathe the dependence which comes with old age only less than the alternative: abandonment and neglect. The fear of dependence and the fear of abandonment are opposite sides of the same reality. As a result of increasing physical and sometimes mental loss, elders grow increasingly vulnerable and so dependent on others for support. Abandonment is the worse fate. It means not only enduring infirmity and disability without the resources needed to cope, but also living on in disgrace, being unable to care properly for oneself, without the help and companionship of loved ones.

Dependence seems, however, only less desirable than abandonment. Dependence, especially familial dependence, which is the condition of 90 percent of chronically infirm elderly in the United States today, while it promises to assure reliable support and companionship, carries with it the loss of independence and the special risks of abuse that come with intimate but unequal relations (Lewis, 1988). Americans possess an inordinate fear of dependence (Clark, 1972), so much so that one psychologist describes American culture as "counterdependent" (Rogers, 1974). But, from the point of view of Christian theology, dependence in old age, whether it takes the form of reliance on family members, on a network of friends, or on professional helpers, is an instance of the profound dependence at the heart of created existence. When, in the Creed, Christians confess their faith in "the Maker of Heaven and Earth," they are declaring that all God's creatures are dependent on the Divine Goodness for their existence (Gustafson, 1977 and 1983; Evans, 1979). All creatures owe their being to God. Their very existence, all that sustains them, everything that helps them flourish, all they are and can be comes from the Divine Hand. The accumulation of losses persons suffer in old age, the deepening vulnerability advanced aging carries with it, opens the mind and heart to the sense of "absolute dependence"—the intuition of the shear gratuitousness of existence—which discloses the mystery of their lives as creatures of God. Even at their most active, humans are still receiving and being made. A person attains spiritual maturity when he or she comes to realize that existence is not in one's own hands.

For Christians who truly believe their lives are in God's hands, it is possible to accept assistance, to deal trustingly with others, to receive their kindnesses, and to find satisfaction in their companionship, because Christians understand that their very lives come from and are sustained by a Source beyond their control. They are able to trust in their caregivers because they have a fundamental trust in God. The "basic trust" they exhibit in these relationships proceeds from the trust they have in the providential care of the Father which Jesus revealed.

Created Order and Family Piety

When Christians profess a belief in "God Almighty," they do not simply affirm that God is greater than any other force. Rather, they express a belief that God is "the orderer and governor" of life who disposes and shapes all the forces of life. The ancient Greek term *Pantokrator,* the one who governs all things, captures the meaning more appropriately than the English "God Almighty." God is the source of the patterns that create reliable order and meaningful structure in things. One part of the created order God has constituted is the family. Old age is one of the recurrent problems in the human life cycle, and family ties provide the primary means of predictably meeting the needs of infirmity in late life.

In the biblical tradition, the fourth commandment of the Decalogue, "Honor thy father and thy mother . . . ," was not, as later tradition was inclined to suppose, intended in the first instance as an instruction for children to heed their parents, but rather as an obligation laid on adults to look after their parents in their old age (Harrelson, 1980; Collins, 1986a). Such caregiving necessarily involved physical or financial support, as can be seen from Jesus' chiding of the Pharisees for exempting big donors from their filial obligations (Matt. 15:1-7). But it also, as in the Sirach text cited above, involved showing them respect by maintaining their standing in society.

Contemporary exegetes argue that the filial obligation enjoined by the fourth commandment was, in effect, a guarantee of the human rights of the elderly (Harrelson, 1980). Similarly, in the view of one moralist, Roman Catholic social teaching regards various support systems for the elderly as means of upholding their human dignity (Curran, 1985). Thus, intergenerational family ties constitute one of the natural regularities by which the divine governance of creation provides for elders in their time of need.

It is worth noting that while conventional wisdom has projected "a myth of abandonment" (Shanas, 1981), i.e., a decline in family caregiving to the elderly in the period since World War II, according to sociological studies, levels of direct caregiving by family members in the United States remained relatively constant, at about 65 percent, from 1945 through 1980, but have climbed to as much as 90 percent in the period from 1980 to 1990 (Lewis, 1988). What once appeared to be traditionalist family ties have proven durable even in the crowded days of postmodernity, illustrating the way in which a divinely created order continues to rule lives at a time of life when every utilitarian standard would find no reason to provide support.

Traditional authors, like Aquinas, wrote of two sorts of duties to parents, namely, service (*obsequium*), which includes support or physical care (*sustenatio*), and respect (*reverentia*), but the accent fell on respect (Aquinas, 1972, 2a IIae, 101). By contrast with older generations of moralists, contemporary authors are disposed to emphasize the material aspects of eldercare. To be sure, the physical and material facets of caregiving contribute to the dignity of the elderly in that such services preserve seniors from neglect and establish a ring of privacy that shelters the enfeebled and senile from the public derision that comes with isolated living, neglect, and abandonment. But emphasis on the material deeds of caregiving obscures the importance of expressions of esteem and affection, of such activities as visiting, giftgiving, and listening to reminiscences, for the well-being and self-respect of old people, practices whose value older commentators understood.

Justice and Eldercare

The biblical tradition regarded care of widows as paradigmatic of justice (Harris, 1987). Jesus rebuked the Pharisees for hypocritical rulings that allowed people to avoid contributing to the financial support of parents when they made donations to the Temple treasury (Matt. 15:1-9). John's Gospel depicts Jesus entrusting his mother to "the beloved disciple's" care (19:25-27). The Letter of James teaches that "pure, unspoiled religion" consists in "coming to the help of orphans and widows . . ." (1:27). In keeping with the same tradition, the early Jerusalem community instituted the office of deacon to oversee the distribution of bread to widows who had no adult son to care for them (Acts 6:1-6; Laporte, 1981).

In our own time, Catholic social teaching identifies eldercare as an element of the common good, which the several units of society (family, local community, public authority) ought to supply according to *the principle of subsidiarity,* i.e., with the most immediate social unit, in this case the family, taking responsibility for eldercare, but receiving assistance from or being relieved of direct responsibility by larger social units when its resources prove insufficient to the task (Curran, 1985).

The first place, then, to consider contemporary issues of justice in eldercare lies with the family itself. The relevance of familial justice in caregiving is underscored by the dramatic rise in the incidence of family care of the elderly in the last decade. While larger numbers of mostly retired men, moreover, are undertaking the role of caregivers, the responsibility still falls largely to women. But with the majority of women now also in the workforce, it becomes increasingly important that spouses and siblings as well as teenage and young-adult grandchildren join in the tasks of supporting infirm elders.

Family resources, however, are limited, and they can be overtaxed by prolonged support of a chronically ill loved one. While the principle of subsidiarity assigns responsibility to the smallest unit capable of exercising it effectively, it equally demands that larger social units, particularly government, intervene when the smaller units, in this case the family, can no longer shoulder a problem satisfactorily.

Modern welfare states have largely met the demand for social responsibility to the elderly, making significant progress in overcoming elderly poverty and securing financial independence for elders through social security programs and more recently protecting families against financial ruin by guaranteeing health-care provision to seniors with programs like Medicare in the U.S. (Wolfe, 1989).

In the 1980s, however, growth in numbers of the elderly combined with escalating health-care costs led to debates in many nations over limiting support to the elderly (Wolfe, 1989). Proposals included: (1) making social security a need-based program rather than an age-based entitlement, eliminating or heavily taxing awards to wealthier recipients (Longman, 1988); (2) rationing healthcare for people over eighty (Callahan, 1987); (3) restricting all government health-care support to particular sorts of interventions (public health, preventative care, and chronic palliative care) (Callahan, 1989); and (4) providing a system of support for family caregivers (Kingson et al., 1986; Lewis, 1988).

With its stress on *the common good,* Catholic social teaching enjoins advantaged individuals and groups voluntarily to restrict their enjoyment of entitlements until most people can enjoy similar levels of benefits (Christiansen, 1989; Curran, 1985). On that basis, the common good may be invoked to restrict social security to needy recipients, to tax wealthy old people for support of the poor, as the rescinded 1988 Catastrophic Healthcare Bill tried to do, and to limit the types of health care available at public expense. In addition, the social teaching's *option for the poor* would test all proposals for health-care reform in terms of their affects on poor people (National Conference of Catholic Bishops, 1986; Catholic Health Association of America, 1991). Thus, in the created order, intergenerational obligations belong not only to family members but to the society as a whole, and they embrace the obligations of the well-to-do, including wealthy seniors, to the elderly poor.

In summary, the doctrine of creation helps people appreciate the reality of dependence in their lives, underscores the role of family structures in maintenance of the dignity of seniors, and establishes the basic structures of intergenerational justice.

JESUS CHRIST REDEEMER AND LORD

Forgiveness and the Intergenerational Family

In the created order, adult children should be available to care for their aging parents when they decline and parents should be ready to accept their children's adult roles. But, in fact, parents and adult children are often estranged, and both generations find it difficult to accept the role reversals that come about in the mature family. The adjustments and negotiations attendant on new stages in family relationships bring strain and conflict. The uncertainties of these transitions are natural ones, but they can give rise to misunderstandings and resentment; they can call up long forgotten grievances and lead to struggles for dominance.

From the perspective of theology, family relations in late life, as at any other period, are marked by sin. A theology of aging must take account not only of the sinfulness that can mark family life but also of the forgiveness and redemption that empower family members to make new beginnings. The doctrine of redemption in Christ embraces both these mysteries.

Abandonment is the fundamental sin in intergenerational relations. Along with its variations—perfunctory shows of concern, emotional indifference, purchasing care as a substitute for personal involvement, "dumping" elderly family members on public institutions—abandonment discloses the depth of sin and the absence of genuine love between the generations. It shows how "unnatural," in the sense of uncaring, men and women can become. Elder abuse and exploitation likewise show the basic distortion of human relations which is sin.

Abandonment and abuse constitute intergenerational sin in its most corrupt form, but even in its venial or minor expressions sin places a special burden on relations between the generations. Precisely because family relations are intimate and perduring, alienation, resentment, distorted relations, and simple unresolved problems can take on a history that is hard to overcome. Because infirm old age brings with it new intimacies and role reversals, because both generations become mutually vulnerable in caregiving situations, the risk is great that a family's sinful past will insinuate itself in the late stages of family life. This tendency to prolong the distortions in human action is what traditional theology described as *concupiscence,* an inclination to repeat and magnify inherited patterns of sin. The weight of the past seems to make it impossible to make a new beginning.

From the point of view of Christian faith, however, new beginnings are possible, even in late life, because of the redemptive life, death, and resurrection of Jesus. Jesus died for humanity's sins, and Christians buried with Christ in baptism rose "to walk in newness of life" (Matt. 26:28; Rom. 6:4). The implication drawn by the early church from Jesus' redemptive work is mutual forgiveness. The exhortation of the Letter to the Colossians is typical: "Bear with one another; forgive each other as soon as a quarrel begins. The Lord has forgiven you, now you must do the same" (Col. 3:13). In their new life in Christ, Jesus' disciples are called to replicate the pattern of divine forgiveness and mutual service (Luke 6:36-37; 22:24-27). Christ's humility in (life and) death warrants the disciples' deference to one another (John 13:1-15; Phil. 2:1-11).

Thus, confession of sin, repentance, and mutual forgiveness are preconditions for the new taxing relations the generations are asked to undertake in late life. Forgiveness is likewise a virtue necessary for everyday living in situations of dependent care so fraught with tensions and disappointments for both generations. "How often ought I forgive my brother?" Peter asked. "Seven times?" "No," Jesus answers, "seven times seventy" (Matt 18:21-22). Thus, the gospel preached by Jesus announces a forgiveness that is as salient to late-life families as to any stage of human life.

Humility in Aging

From a normative point of view, human relations, whether in the family or in society at large, ought to be arranged so as to sustain the dignity of the elderly. The natural course of advanced aging, however, is frequently a cause for humiliation. Infirm and chronically ill elders lack the strength to assert themselves as they once did, they require assistance in the tasks of daily living, and they may even be unable to exercise functions such as walking, speaking, or grooming which are essential to a sense of personal competence and self-worth. Physical decline, moreover, is compounded by increasing social isolation and dependence. Thus, even as normative arrangements attempt to preserve the dignity of the elderly against the impact of decline, old age may be personally perceived as a humiliation. Indeed, where a loving family is absent or social programs deficient, decrepit old age may also be occasion for actual humiliation by others. In any case, advanced old age is a time of diminishment and suffering which invites serious religious reflection (Christiansen, 1993). For the Christian living under the horizon of the cross, however, the natural humiliations of aging become the occasion to develop the virtue of humility on the model of Christ.

The prophecy of Peter's passion in John's Gospel may be applied to all infirm elderly:

> . . . when you were young
> you put on your own belt
> and walked where you liked;
> but when you grow old
> you will stretch out your hands,
> and someone else will put a belt around you
> and take you where you do not want to go. (21:18)

The infirmity of old age takes everyone down a road where they "do not want to go." For the disciple of whom Peter is the type, accepting the diminishment of aging is the way "to follow" the Lord (John 22:19). As Jesus "emptied himself" and humbled himself "even to accepting death, death on a cross," so the aged in accepting diminishment in their physical decline and dependence share in the sufferings of Christ.

Thus, the Jesuit philosopher-scientist Pierre Teilhard de Chardin prayed of the stages of loss in old age,

> [I]n all those dark moments, O God, grant that I may understand that it is you . . . who are painfully parting the fibres of my being in order to penetrate the very marrow of my substance and bear me away within yourself. (1960, 90)

For Teilhard, old age is a primary opportunity for "the divinisation of passivities" through which one attains communion with God. The humble consent to diminishment and suffering in old age, "when all my strength is spent," brings one to the threshold of encounter with the God of mystery. But, for the Christian this consent to mystery gives rise to a joy and peace that transfigures even the pained-wracked, broken body because Christ himself gave an example of humility in undergoing the passage from death to risen life.

Spiritual Friendship

While Christian discipleship entails forgiveness, humility, and mutual service, it contains another dimension that, while found in other stages of life as well, is associated in a special way with old age, namely, spiritual friendship. In the farewell discourse in the Gospel according to John, for example, Jesus says to his disciples:

> I shall not call you servants any more,
> because a servant does not know his master's business;
> I call you friends,
> because I have made known to you
> everything I have learnt from my Father. (John 15:15)

In Acts, Luke describes the early Christian community in terms reminiscent of the classical ideal of friendship, a "brotherhood" living as with "one heart," "united heart and soul" (2:42, 46; 4:32) in a life of mutual support and prayer.

In later centuries, this ideal became the basis of a long tradition of spiritual friendship in which men and women together sought wisdom through a life of the study of Scripture, prayer, and contemplation. The classic topos for this shared religious experience is Monica and Augustine's shared vision at Ostia recorded in Book IX of *The Confessions* (Augustine, 1963, 200–202). A later, medieval tradition viewed such communion in knowledge and love as the essence of Christian charity. In their shared love of God, according to this tradition, spiritual friends grow in love of one another and of humankind (Aquinas, 1975, 2a IIae, 25).

Old age, and especially late old age, provide a special occasion for spiritual friendship and, as in the case of Monica and Augustine, for spiritual friendship between the generations. Much of "the work" of late old age is of a moral and spiritual nature: integrating one's life experience, coping with disengagement and loss, suffering with diminishment, and meeting death. These are experiences that pose questions of life's meaning, test faith, and lead one to prayer. While much of this activity is solitary—and deepening and enriching solitude is a continuing task of the spiritual life—the elderly naturally seek validation, companionship, and guidance in their spiritual quest. For that reason, old age offers a special opportunity for spiritual friendship.

Often housebound or bedfast, having outlived many of their contemporaries, men and women in late old age sometimes desire companionship even more than physical care. But friends who are ready to share their deepest fears and hopes offer the possibility of truly bringing their lives to a happy end. By listening to their stories, sharing their feelings, and praying with them, family members and other caregivers can assist frail and sick old people in meeting these psychological and spiritual needs and so enriching their last years together. Encountering together the mystery of the God who meets them in old age, the elderly and their spiritual friends attain a degree of intimacy rare at any time of life. Thus, for the elderly, the experience of redemption leads to the practice of forgiveness, stimulates a growth in Christlike humility, and opens the opportunity of spiritual friendship.

HOLY SPIRIT: GIVER OF LIFE

Sanctification

In the economy of salvation, the work of the Spirit is to make real, personal, and inward the life of grace won for humanity in Christ. As a liminal experience, old age is an occasion to experience the grace of God actively transforming individual lives. Often this takes the form of a deepening of lifetime fidelity to

God. The biblical sources are replete with references to the lifelong fidelity of pious individuals. Psalm 71, for example, declares, "God you taught me when I was young/ and I am still proclaiming your marvels" (v. 17). Eleazar's martyrdom in fidelity to the Jewish dietary laws (2 Macc. 6:18-31) "proves him worthy of his years." Simeon and Anna, in Luke's infancy narrative, are models of fidelity (2:25-38), and Peter's martyrdom in old age is testimony to his love of the Lord (John 21:15-23). Finally, the widows of the early church are assisted in view of their proven devotion to prayer and good works (1 Tim. 5:3-16).

Such fidelity comes at a cost. The psalmist's faith that "God will give me life again" follows a struggle with the fear of divine abandonment. Eleazar and Peter suffer martyrdom for their faith. Widows are tested by poverty and the lack of supportive families. Old age is no guarantee of fidelity. The elderly must face crises and challenges: from the weakening of their bodies, their isolation in society, and the fear of death. In this context, the Spirit is a comforter who sustains a new life of virtue in imitation of Christ.

Fidelity is only one of many virtues that may manifest themselves in old age. "The fruits of the spirit" (Gal. 5:22) are diverse, but together they represent the growing conformity of the Christian to Christ. Indeed, the call, as with Peter, can be a very personal one: "You are to follow me" (John 21:22). But, the gift of the Spirit gives the elderly the assurance that they can continue to grow in holiness even as they suffer diminishment in their bodies.

Mystery and the End of Life

At the extreme limit, old age seems to outrun even the devotion that gives life meaning and integrity. When individuals become senile, fall into a coma, or must be sustained by complex medical instrumentation, they are once again brought face to face with the mystery that penetrates and sustains life. Nature in its course seems ultimately to frustrate human beings. At this point, nothing is left but, on the pattern of Christ, to trust that the mystery that envelops them is indeed the God of love. Here faith, hope, and love are indistinguishable as the elderly are called to surrender themselves, in Rahner's words, to "the abyss of the mystery of God, into which one lets oneself fall in complete confidence of being caught up by God's love and mercy forever" (Rahner, 1990, 38).

BIBLIOGRAPHY

Aquinas (1972) *Virtues of Justice in the Human Community.* Summa Theologiae, Vol. 41 (2a2ae. 101–22). Edited by T. C. O'Brien. New York: McGraw-Hill.

______ (1975) *Charity.* Summa Theologiae, Vol. 34 (2a2ae. 29–33). Edited by R. J. Batten. New York: McGraw-Hill.

Augustine (1963) *The Confessions of St. Augustine.* Translated by Rex Warner, Introduction by Vernon J. Bourke, IX.10, 200–202. New York: New American Library/ Penguin.

Blythe, R. (1979) *The View in Winter: Reflections on Old Age.* New York: Harcourt, Brace, Jovanovich, 235–46.

Callahan, D. (1987) *Setting Limits: Medical Goals in an Aging Society.* New York: Touchstone Books.

______ (1989) *What Kind of Life?: The Limits of Medical Progress.* New York: Simon and Schuster.

Catholic Health Association of America (1991) *With Justice for All? The Ethics of Healthcare Rationing.* Catholic Health Association.

Christiansen, D. (1990) "And Your Elders Will Dream Dreams: Aging, Liminality and the Church's Ministry." In Coleman and Sanks, 123–35.

______ (1993) "The Common Good and the Politics of Self-Interest." In Gelpi, 54–86.

Clark, M. (1972) "Cultural Values and Dependency in Later Life." In Cowgill and Holmes, 263–74.

Clements, W. M., ed. (1981) *Ministry with the Aging.* San Francisco: Harper & Row.

Coleman, J. A., and T. H. Sanks, eds. (1993) *Reading the Signs of the Times.* New York: Paulist Press.

Collins, R. (1986a) "The Fourth Commandment: For Children or Adults?" In 1986b, 82–97.

______ (1986b) *Christian Morality: Biblical Foundations.* Notre Dame, Ind.: Univ. of Notre Dame Press.

Cowgill, D. O., and L. D. Holmes, eds. (1972) *Aging and Modernization.* New York: Appleton-Century-Crofts.

Curran, C. E. (1985) "Filial Responsibility for an Elderly Parent." *Social Thought* 11 (2):40–52.

de Beauvoir, S. (1973) *Coming of Age.* Translated by Patrick O'Brien. New York: Warner.

Erikson, E. H. (1976) "Dr. Borg's Life Cycle." *Daedalus* 15 (2):1–28.

Evans, D. (1979) *Struggle and Fulfillment: The Inner Dynamic of Religion and Morality.* Philadelphia: Fortress.

Gelpi, D., ed. (1989) *Beyond Individualism: Toward a Retrieval of Moral Discourse in America.* Notre Dame, Ind.: Univ. of Notre Dame Press.

Gilkey, L. (1970) *Religion and the Scientific Future.* New York: Harper & Row.

Gustafson, J. M. (1977) *Can Ethics be Christian?* Chicago: Univ. of Chicago Press.

______ (1983) *Ethics from a Theocentric Perspective.* Vol. 1. Chicago: Univ. of Chicago Press.

Harrelson, W. J. (1980) *The Ten Commandments and Human Rights.* Philadelphia: Fortress.

Harris, J. G. (1987) *Biblical Perspectives on Aging: God and the Elderly.* Philadelphia: Fortress.

Kingson, E. A., B. A. Hirshorn, and J. M. Cornman (1986) *Ties that Bind: The Interdependence of Generations.* Cabin John, Md.: Seven Locks.

Laporte, J. (1981) "The Elderly in the Life and Thought of the Early Church." In Clements, 37–55.

LeFevre, C., and P. LeFevre, eds. (1981) *Aging and the Human Spirit.* Chicago: Exploration.

Lewis, M. A. (1988) "The Parish and the Elderly." *Church* 4 (2):18–22.

Longman, P. (1988) *Born to Pay: The New Politics of Aging in America.* New York: Simon and Schuster.

National Conference of Catholic Bishops (1986) *Economic Justice for All.* U.S. Catholic Conference.

Neugarten, B. L., and D. A. Neugarten (1986) "Age in the Aging Society." *Daedalus* 115 (1):31–50.

Rahner, K. (1966) "The Concept of Mystery in Catholic Theology." *Theological Investigations.* Vol. IV. Translated by Kevin Smyth, 36–73. Baltimore: Helicon Press.

______ (1969) "Mystery." *Sacramentum Mundi: An Encyclopedia of Theology.* General editor Adolf Darlap; vol. 4, Edited by Karl Rahner et al., 133–36. New York: Herder.

______ (1990) *Faith in a Wintry Season: Conversations and Interviews with Karl Rahner in the Last Years of His Life.* Edited by Paul Imhof and Hubert Bullowans. Translated and edited by Harvey D. Egan. New York: Crossroad.

Rogers, W. R. (1974) "Dependency and Counterdependency in Psychoanalysis and Religious Faith." *Zygon* 9 (3):190–201.

Shanas, E. (1981) "Social Myth as Hypothesis: The Case of the Family Relations of Old People." In Lefevre and Lefevre, 128–36.

Steiner, G. (1989) *Real Presences.* Chicago: Univ. of Chicago Press.

Teilhard de Chardin, P. (1960) *The Divine Milieu.* New York: Harper.

Wolfe, A. (1989) *Whose Keeper? Social Science and Moral Obligation.* Berkeley, Calif.: Univ. of California Press.

29 Evangelical Perspectives

FRED VAN TATENHOVE

Aging is a fact of life. From the moment one comes from "the dust of the ground" to the moment one returns to "the ground" (Gen. 2:7; 3:19), the process of aging is present. Growing older cannot be postponed. Thus, aging influences all aspects of life and must be considered in any attempt to understand the meaning of life.

The purpose of this chapter is to present a theological reflection of aging that represents an "evangelical" perspective. One aspect of this perspective is the belief that human beings are part of an interrelated, holistic order, created by God. Thus, theological reflections about aging cannot be confined to one area of human existence and experience. As theologian Martin Heinecken says, ". . . there can be no separate 'theology of aging,' set apart from the theological orientation as a whole" (1981, 76). Though it may be true that there is no separate theology of aging, it does not mean that the Christian community has intentionally excluded the human experience of aging from its theological task. Rather, theological inquiry has tended to focus upon other areas of human experience. Only recently has aging been viewed as a human condition worthy of special attention and as a human phenomenon that raises critical questions for theology. The intent is "not to separate aging from the broader ongoing theological task" . . . but "to recognize aging . . . in such a way that a concern with aging will become an intentional component of the broader theological inquiry" (Maldonado, 1985, 1–2).

Theological reflections about aging from an evangelical tradition are not based upon a common emotional experience or on human reason (though both are valid sources for doing theological reflection). Rather, they are biblically based and confessionally believed, and applied to any particular aspect of life. Evangelicals base theology primarily upon a commitment to study the biblical text as the inspired word of God. From this commitment to the Bible as the primary source of authority for faith and practice, clear doctrinal positions are formed. The Bible is accepted as God's inspired written word, the fall in the Genesis account explains the destruction and sin in the world, the death and resurrection of Christ is the fulfillment of God's plan to redeem a fallen world, faith in Christ is vital for salvation, and heaven and hell are realities.

However, the label "Evangelical" describes a community that encompasses a wide variety of religious expressions and beliefs. The intent of this chapter is not to describe an "evangelical agenda;" rather, it is a perspective about aging from one person's description who moves within that community.

A central emphasis in evangelical theology is the biblical teaching that human beings are unique (Genesis 1:27). Each person is created to be in relationship with God. This understanding was given special attention by the Apostle Paul, whose one goal was to proclaim Christ as "the Son of God" (Acts 9:20) and to call people to live a life "in Christ" (Gal. 2:20; Eph. 3:17; Col. 1:27). The message that he preached was inclusive; Christ's sacrificial death was offered so that every human being, Jew or Gentile, slave or free, would have the opportunity to become one in the unity of the body and spirit of Christ (1 Cor. 12:12-13). Aging, then, must be understood from the biblical position that all persons, of any age, are included in God's redemptive grace.

From a biblical perspective, several considerations are important for understanding the aging process. First, life is not static. Development, growth, and change are everywhere in God's created universe. The writer of Ecclesiastes states, "For everything there is a season, and a time for every matter under heaven: a time to be born, and a time to die;" (3:1-2). The inherent and inevitable presence of change and aging in the universe is one characteristic that differentiates the creature from God as Creator. Browning supports this biblical understanding: "From the broadest possible perspective, aging refers to the simple process of moving from the beginning to the end of life" (1975, 154).

Second, aging is God's intentional plan for human existence. It is part of what it means to be created as a human being. Adam and Eve were to "be fruitful and multiply, and fill the earth and subdue it" (Gen. 1:28). This implies a sequence of conception, birth, and growth. Aging, then, is not to be viewed as another negative outcome of the fall. However, the fall does indeed influence the aging process.

Third, the concepts of "age," "aging," and "ageism" are not synonymous. "Age," which is often equated with old age, is more correctly used to identify the chronology of a person's life. "Aging," then, refers to the ongoing process which influences every living creature. "Ageism," describes any form of discrimination on the basis of age. Although it is usually associated with older people, youth can also experience such prejudice and bias, as illustrated by Paul's counsel to Timothy, "let no one despise your youth" (1 Tim. 4:12).

This chapter will focus upon a number of theological considerations that relate to the meaning of aging: (1) the image of God in human nature, (2) the stages and temporality of life, and (3) the experience of hope derived from spiritual maturity and a faith in the redemptive work of Christ. First, because human beings are created in the image of God, aging is part of human experience. Second, successfully to negotiate change through the stages of life, each individual must accept and participate in God's created order. Third, adjustment to the later years of aging must include the development of hope rooted in spiritual maturity and experienced in the acceptance of one's own finality.

AGING AS A PROCESS WITHIN CREATION

The Bible contains numerous statements that the world and all that is in it has purpose and value because each facet is created by a just and loving God. The Genesis account of creation is clear; the world matters because God created it and declared that "indeed, it is very good" (Gen. 1:31).

Aging and the *Imago Dei*

The view that human life is created in the image of God is central to biblical teaching. This means that aging, although not part of God's nature or experience, is included in God's intended plan for human beings. From a theological perspective, the acceptance of aging as a part of the created order means that individuals are to be valued at any age. People are important because they are a special creation of God and have a covenant relationship with God. This exclusive relationship is affirmed in a number of biblical passages. The opening chapter of Genesis describes human beings as created according to God's likeness and given the right of dominion over the rest of creation (Gen. 1:26-28).

The Bible does not give a complete and clear description about how those characteristics which reflect God in human nature are developed. However, the biblical authors unanimously agree that human beings occupy a special relationship to the Creator. This formation in the image of God sets human beings apart from the rest of God's creation (Ps. 8:5-6). This is especially true when the Bible refers to older individuals. The writer of Leviticus calls us to "rise before the aged and defer to the old" (19:32). Job said that "wisdom is with the aged, and understanding in length of days" (12:12).

The biblical understanding of the *imago Dei* emphasizes human qualities or characteristics that correspond to divine attributes. Theologians have not always agreed uniformly about how and where these attributes are resident in each person. Irenaeus understood *imago Dei* as human rationality and freedom (Roberts and Donaldson, 1896, I:518). Augustine assumed that the image was represented by the soul, where memory and intelligence was assigned (Augustine, 1963, 417–19; 425–28).

Calvin took a less restrictive position, believing that the soul was indeed the center of the image of God, but that God's image was reflected in every area of one's being: ". . . yet there was not part of man, not even the body itself, in which some sparks did not glow" (Calvin, 1960, XX:188). Luther also included Adam's humanness as part of God's image, but argued that the Fall so corrupted it ". . . that we cannot grasp it even with our intellect" (Luther, 1955, 1:65).

While Luther believed that the image was lost in the Fall, he also affirmed the special relationship human beings had in their initial state, which God did not forget after the Fall. Therefore, even after the Fall, all life is to be respected and reverenced (2:141).

John Wesley stated that the image of God in human nature not only contains a rational and immortal dimension and dominion over other creatures, but also includes "actual knowledge, both of God and of his works; in the right state of his intellectual powers, and in love, which is true holiness" (Wesley, 1979, 4:293). Although the moral image was lost in the Fall, "political" (dominion) and "natural" (understanding, free will) aspects of the image remained, even though they were seriously marred (6:223).

Wesley also emphasized the active role of prevenient grace in human experience. This means that after the Fall, God did not abandon creation. Clearly, the value and sanctity of human life cannot be denied. Human beings possess, in varying degrees (at least potentially), the divine qualities such as intelligence, will, and rationality by which they relate to God and others.

Furthermore, the author of Genesis understood *tselem* (image) as something more vigorous and dynamic than simply the possession of certain divine qualities. Old Testament scholar Cline writes, ". . . according to Genesis 1 man [*sic*] does not have the image of God, nor is he made in the image of God, but is himself the image of God" (1968, 80). He supports the view that image is not something humans *have;* image is what they *are.* Thus, the Hebrew concept of life was holistic (physical and spiritual). It included both the corporeal, animated part of human life and the spirit. The whole being was involved: body and soul/spirit (89).

The significance of the biblical and theological teaching about the image of God in human nature is that each individual is to be accepted and respected as a creation of God. This means that people created in the image of God do not diminish in worth or sanctity as they move through the aging process. To be human is to represent God. Therefore, the image of God is not something people achieve or something people do. Rather, it is what one is to be in God's intended plan.

Being versus Doing

The tension between "being" and "doing" is not new. The biblical writers recount how God attempted to call his people to a quality of life that would shape their inner character. Psalm 119 implies that the value of life rests upon deeper foundations and more abiding relationships than chronological age or personal accomplishments (119:97-104). The teachings of Jesus suggest that the best response to the aging process is to seek fullness of life at every stage. To desire "to be" the people of God at every stage of life enables a person to experience what Jesus implies in his words, "I came that they may have life, and have it abundantly: (John 10:10).

"Abundantly" does not imply the accumulation of chronological age. Merely to accumulate years does not guarantee quality of character. Solomon is a clear illustration of this fact. Like Saul, he reflected a better character in his youth than in his old age. When one's life is moving in the wrong direction, the accumulation of years does not change its quality. What is called for is a change of character, a change in what constitutes the "beingness" of the person's life. The direction of a person's inner life determines destiny. Jesus implies this in his response to the Pharisee's question about the disciples not keeping the traditional Jewish customs and rituals. "Listen and understand: it is not what goes into the mouth that defiles a man, but what comes out of the mouth that defiles a man" (Matt. 15:10-11). Carlyle Marney is correct: "The Christian faith rests on neither doing nor having. Salvation by faith is salvation by grace—an affirmation of being as being" (1974, 45).

Although the New Testament writers emphasized that the quality of the inner life was central to "being in Christ," they did not overlook that "doing" is to be the natural expression of the inner nature. To take out of biblical context either James's statement, "So faith by itself, if it has not works, is dead" (James 2:17), or Paul's statement, that we are ". . . justified not by the works of the law, but through faith in Jesus Christ" (Gal. 2:16), results in a distorted understanding of the meaning of Christian experience. Faith in Christ provides the motivation and the capacity to produce good works.

While it is clear in the biblical texts that the ultimate worth of an individual is not based upon human achievement, doing, working, and achieving usually score the highest in a culture that is success-driven. What Katz observed in the 1970s still lingers today (although with "early retirements" this may be changing): "We associate status with productivity. We believe everyone must work as long as possible, moonlight if necessary, achieve, and strive" (1975, 146). However, productivity is not always possible for the elderly. Aging eventually erodes the resources and energies of a person's life. Desirable as it may be to remain active and productive until death, this is not the criterion for determining the worth of a person.

To link personal value to accomplishments in the marketplace is to measure individual worth in terms of occupation, income, social approval, and production. This can result in the community regarding individuals whose external capacities have been severely limited as if they have no intrinsic value. They are now judged on their inability to occupy a position of status and productivity in the economy.

This is not the biblical teaching about how to measure the value of a human life at any age. One day Jesus was overtaken on a journey by a prosperous young man who wanted to know what he must *do* to inherit eternal life. Informing Jesus that he had been faithful in observing the commandments, the young man wondered what he lacked (Matt. 19:16-22). Jesus spoke to him about the disposition of what he *had,* so that the young man might come to terms with what he *was.* Nicodemus, a leader of the Jews, came to Jesus by night to ask what he must *do* to merit eternal life (John 3:1-21). Note again that Jesus chose not to relate to him on the level of *doing,* but led Nicodemus to talk of birth—and *being.*

The capacity to *do* is not the measure for determining the worth or value of a human being. God's redemptive plan, fulfilled in the death and resurrection of Jesus Christ, is offered to all persons. Furthermore, even the quality of one's life is not achieved by "good works." Paul writes, "For by grace you have been saved through faith, and this is not your own doing; it is the gift of God—not the results of works, so that no one can boast" (Eph. 2:8-9).

God calls all people to be in a redemptive, dynamic relationship with himself. This relationship shapes life and influences all other relationships. The worth and sanctity of each individual is intrinsic to being formed in the image of God. Aging does not diminish the gift of God's redemptive grace given to those who "hunger and thirst for righteousness" (Matt. 5:6). When this truth is central, a biblical understanding of aging is possible.

AGING AS A PROCESS ABOUT LIVING

Change and growth are inherent in the aging process. In its broadest definition, aging is the process of moving from the beginning to the end of life, through an unfolding series of changes. The aging process of the infant is not unlike that of the elderly. Each represent the opposite extremes of the process and are individually unique, but not disconnected. Individuals in either of these periods are not morally or socially superior to those in the other. They are both part of the same process.

The Stages of Life

Life moves through temporal transitions from the past to the present to the future. Shakespeare describes seven stages from infancy to the elderly years. He characterizes the last stage as a "second childishness" and portrays it with diminishing images:

> "All the world's a stage,
> And all the men and women merely players:
> They have their exits and their entrances:
> And one man in his time plays many parts,
> His acts being seven Ages. At first the infant,
> Mewling and puking in the nurse's arms . . .
> . . . Last scene of all,
> That ends this strange eventful history,
> Is second childishness, and mere oblivion,
> Sans teeth, sans eyes, sans taste, sans everything.
>
> (Shakespeare, 1901, Act II, sc.7)

The biblical writers hold a more hopeful view of persons at the closing season of life. Old Testament images portray life as a journey, a "sojourning" or "pilgrimage" that spans a person's life (Gen. 47:9; Pss. 39:12; 119:54). The writer of Ecclesiastes states that there is a time or season for everything (3:1-8). Leviticus (27:1-8) describes different chronological age groups, assigning marketplace type values to each age group. The psalmist describes his life as a "passing guest, an alien (sojourner), like all my forebears" (Ps. 39:12).

Stages of life are reflected in the Hebrew terms that describe persons of different ages, several of these appearing together in Jeremiah 6:11 and 51:22. Richards suggests that there are more than a dozen terms referring to persons of different ages. (1988, 22–23). Jeremiah describes three to five stages to the seasons of life, such as children, young men, husbands/wives, old folks, and the very aged (6:11). In Deuteronomy 32:25 and Psalm 148:12 four phases seem to be suggested—sucking children, virgins/maidens, young men, and those of gray hairs. These verses suggest that aging is part of the experience of the child as well as that of the adult.

Some excellent contemporary resources discuss how individuals experience various stages in life. One of the most familiar and quoted descriptions of the stages of life is Erikson's "Eight Stages of Man" (Erikson, 1950). David Levinson (1981) based his book *The Seasons of a Man's Life* largely on Erikson's work. James Fowler adapted Erikson's psychosocial development ideas to faith development in his book *Stages of Faith* (1981).

Basic to Erikson's assumptions about the stages of life is his definition of epigenesis: "Everything that grows has a ground plan and out of this ground plan the parts arise, each part having its time of special ascendancy, until all have arisen to form a functioning whole" (Erikson, 1968, 92). Besides his focus upon the psychological, Erikson gives attention to the biological, social, and cultural dimensions of human development. He is sensitive to the importance of value issues related to human growth and experience. His eight stages include the entire life process from birth to death.

His model is compatible with a holistic view of human nature and the aging process, in which no stage is less important than another. From the first stage of life (Trust vs. Mistrust) to the last stage (Integrity vs. Despair), the human person is still alive to thoughts, feelings, and actions. The experience of ego-integrity is closely linked to acquiring basic trust. From the beginning to the end, to trust life and to accept the aging process without remorse enables a person in the final stage of life to answer with affirmation the question, "What has become of me?"

When an elderly person can experience what Erikson describes as integrity, that person is ready to step out of the center of life with a feeling of value and worth. This makes it more possible to resolve closure issues or unfinished business that often confronts an individual in the final years of the aging process (Richter, 1986).

Reviewing one's past life with integrity is represented in the life of Moses, when he recounts his leadership efforts on behalf of the people of Israel. After surveying God's acts and covenant with them, he concludes by reciting a poem about Israel's history and then pronouncing a blessing (Deut. 32–33). Paul is much more concise in the review of his life when he proclaims, "I have fought the good fight . . ." (2 Tim. 4:7). Both men came to the closing chapter of their lives with a sense of personal integrity.

The Temporality of Life

The "temporality" of life, states David Tracy, is not merely a series of disconnected experiences or "nows" that exist only for the moment and "then perish to yield to yet another 'now'" (1975, 123). All the stages of life are linked and interrelated. Aging is but one expression of the temporality and brevity of this life.

The transitory nature of life is evident in the biblical writings as well as in other sources. The Bible does not exhort people to seek, like Ponce de Leon, the fountain of youth, but to recognize that life moves towards a culmination.

The Old Testament clearly describes the passing of the years. Although "length of days" is often desired, the days of one's life pass quickly. "As for mortals, their days are like grass; they flourish like a flower of the field; for the wind passes over it, and it is gone, and its place knows it no more" (Ps. 103:15-16). Life moves rapidly "like a passing shadow" (Ps. 144:4).

The New Testament clearly indicates that human beings are not created for this world alone. The whole creation is "groaning" for redemption (Rom. 8:22), a realization of another life prepared by God for all who have been redeemed through the sacrificial death and resurrection of Jesus Christ (Gal. 1:4; Titus 2:14).

The aging process is one of the clearest expressions of the temporal existence of physical life. This biblical truth is reflected in the words of a gospel song, "This world is not my home I'm just a passing through." The Christian's hope is not anchored in this world. The psalmist suggests that this present fleeting life should lead all to pray, "So teach us to count our days that we may gain a wise heart" (90:12). The aging process cannot be resisted. Job provides an example of one who in his elderly years openly accepted his "autumn days" (29:1-6).

Browning points out that the transience of life is especially evident in Erikson's model. The last two stages of his model, generativity versus stagnation and integrity versus despair confront each person with the temporal nature of life (Browning, 1975, 157–59).

Generativity is expressed in concern for others. An inner quest to create and maintain the resources for the next generation reaches its most active expression in the mid-life period of the adult stage. When some measure of success can be achieved in this endeavor during the middle years, a person can then experience integrity in the later years. To achieve integrity is to make peace with one's life history, without regret. Integrity enables the elderly person to have an active concern about life in the presence of declining vitality and approaching death. As Browning suggests, integrity in the closing years of human life "makes it possible for a person to live with what he has been and what he has brought into this world that is likely to survive him" (159).

AGING AS A PROCESS TOWARD SPIRITUALITY

Human beings are more than biological and emotional. Created in the image of God, each person possesses a spiritual dimension that lives for eternity. From the moment of conception, the child is created to grow, to be a whole person, to become an adult. Both in physical-emotional development and in spiritual growth, maturity and spirituality are the goals. From a biblical perspective, the plan for every human being is to be in a redemptive relationship with God and to achieve eternal life. The psalmist describes this quest: "As a deer longs for flowing streams, so my soul longs for you, 0 God" (42:1). Augustine was correct—the human spirit is restless until it finds rest in God.

The aging experience, in spite of a diminishing physical vitality and health, can include an increasing spiritual maturity and readiness for a life after death. This is the biblical message and the hope of every Christian.

Growth toward Spiritual Maturity

Biblical teaching relates spiritual maturity to a faith commitment in Jesus Christ. Personal faith in Jesus Christ results in a redemptive relationship with God. This personal faith, with its hope in eternal life, is the ultimate comfort in the aging process. The spiritual journey of those in Christ influences all areas of human activity, including physical, social, emotional, and psychological needs.

Spiritual maturity is the capacity to identify and affirm what is ultimately sacred and to yield increasingly to that affirmation. Like aging, spiritual growth occurs over a period of time. The Apostle Peter exhorts his readers to "grow in the grace and knowledge of our Lord and Savior Jesus Christ" (2 Pet. 3:18). Paul declares the importance of spiritual growth in his letter to the believers at Ephesus: "We must grow up in every way into him who is the head, into Christ" (Eph. 4:15). It is growth by which the mind, spirit, character, and work of Jesus Christ is reproduced within a person. To experience spiritual maturity is to be "in Christ."

As a person moves towards the elderly years, the finality of life becomes more central. This gradual movement toward confronting the end of the aging process has spiritual implications. Carl Jung observed that persons beyond midlife inevitably come to an awareness of a religious dimension.

Confining as the aging process may eventually be, it does allow a type of independence that frees many elderly to take a more active role in shaping their ultimate destiny. Many persons in their advanced years write and talk more openly about their personal beliefs. They have a new candor and feel less inhibition. With the redefining of status, vocation, and identity, there comes a freedom to express the inner values and principles that have been developing.

The maturing process is like a spiritual mentor guiding one toward the deeper issues of life and the meaning of existence. As self-centeredness diminishes with the reduction of defensiveness, energy can be channelled to the deeper and more eternal issues of life. Describing this change from a psychological perspective, Pruyser suggests, "With greater and more profound knowledge of the inevitable ambiguities of life and acceptance of irreducible ambivalence of one's own feelings, unpleasant realities can be faced with less denial, and negative affects or dubious propensities are no longer so prone to lead to reaction formation" (1975, 114).

Growth toward Death with Hopefulness

Aging means ultimately preparing for death. A person's age is never fixed until the time of death, and death can come at any point in the aging process. The answer to the question, "Can any of you by worrying add a single hour to your span of life?" (Luke 12:25) is relevant. Although being free of tension may prolong a person's life, death is inevitable.

The journey of life includes identifiable stages of physical development, ongoing experiential learning, and gradual exchange of vitality for wisdom, although not every person will experience these components of aging the same way. From the biblical perspective the conclusion of this temporal life releases each person to experience hope of eternal life. One purpose of life is to live in such a manner that when death comes, one is prepared for eternal life. Each person is responsible for determining how he or she reacts and responds to the natural law of aging. The capacity and courage to face the inevitable conclusion of the aging process is found in a personal faith in the redemptive act of Jesus Christ. As Marney concludes,

> And above all, the Christian being is a *hope,* a hope of having not yet arrived. A hope that the last word is not "frustration," that "more to follow" still goes at the end of every page. This hope is the confidence that my obedience and hungry unfilledness, my fears and causes do matter and do participate in a coming and a kingdom that matters. (1974, 47)

The Christian faith enables the believer to live and not grow weary and to face death with hope. Paul set the tone when he described his readiness to accept death or to accept life. As he contemplated his concluding years, his crowning statement was, "For to me, living is Christ, and dying is gain" (Phil. 1:21). The process of living for Paul was not locked in this life, nor was he out of touch with the meaning of his aging. He was open to both realities and was willing to accept each in its proper time.

Hope is the thread that runs through the biblical teachings. Throughout life, the challenge for each person is to embrace the ongoing aging process with a firm conviction that there is more to come, like "an open door which no one is able to shut" (Rev. 3:8). With this faith and hope for the future, an individual can live in a youth-oriented culture affirming the process of aging, unashamed of growing older. From a biblical view, life moves towards a climax and it is hopeful, recognizing that each chapter has something to offer. The Christian hope enables one to prepare for the inevitable (Heb. 9:28).

Addressing the 1961 White House Conference on Aging, Rabbi Abraham Heschel said

> They who live with a sense for the Presence know that to get older does not mean to lose time but rather to gain time. And they also know that in all their deeds, the chief task of humanity is to sanctify time. All it takes to sanctify time is God, a soul, and a moment. And the three are always there. (1981, 41–42).

The hope of the Christian is that God is always present to sanctify time and life and aging.

BIBLIOGRAPHY

Augustine (1963) *The Trinity*. Translated by Stephen McKenna. Washington, D.C.: Catholic University of America Press.

Browning, D. S. (1975) "Preface to a Practical Theology of Aging." In Hiltner, 154.

Calvin, J. (1960) *Institutes of the Christian Religion*. Edited by J. T. McNeill. Translated by F. L. Battles. Philadelphia: Westminster.

Chadwick, O. (1964) *The Reformation*. Baltimore: Penguin Books.

Clements, W. M., ed. (1981) *Ministry with the Aging*. San Francisco: Harper & Row.

Cline, D. J. A. (1968) "The Image of God in Man." *Tyndale Bulletin*. 19:53–103.

Erikson, E. H. (1950) *Childhood and Society*. New York: Norton.

______ (1968) *Identity: Youth and Crisis*. New York: Norton.

Fowler, J. W. (1981) *Stages of Faith: The Psychology of Human Development and the Quest for Meaning*. San Francisco: Harper & Row.

Heinecken, M. J. (1981) "Christian Theology and Aging: Basic Affirmations." In Clements, 77–90.

Hendrickson, M. C. (1986) *The Role of the Church in Aging*. New York: Haworth.

Heschel, A. J. (1981) "The Older Person and the Family in the Perspective of Jewish Tradition." In LeFevre and LeFevre, 35–44.

Hiltner, S., ed. (1975) *Toward a Theology of Aging*. New York: Human Sciences Press.

Katz, R. L. (1975) "Jewish Values and Sociopsychological Perspectives on Aging." In Hiltner, 135–150.

LeFevre, C., and P. LeFevre (1981) *Aging and the Human Spirit: A Reader in Religion and Gerontology*. 2nd ed. Chicago: Exploration.

Levinson, D. J. (1981) *Seasons of a Man's Life*. New York: Knopf.

Luther, M. (1955) "Lectures on Genesis," *Luther's Works*. ed. Jaroslav Pelikan, St. Louis: Concordia.

Maldonado, D., Jr. (1985) "Towards a Theology of Aging." *National Interfaith Coalition on Aging* vol. XI, No. 4, Winter.

Marney, C. (1974) *Priests to Each Other*. Valley Forge: Judson.

Powers, E. A., ed. (1988) *The Aging Society: A Challenge to Theological Education*. Washington, DC: AARP Publications.

Pruyser, P. (1975) "Aging: Downward, Upward, or Forward?" In Hiltner, 102–18.

Richards, K. H. (1988) "Biblical Studies: Old Testament," in Powers, 21–27.

Richter, R. L. (1986) "Attaining Ego Integrity Through Life Review." In Hendrickson, 1–12.

Roberts, A., and J. Donaldson, eds. (1896) *Ante-Nicene Fathers*. Vol.I, Buffalo: The Christian Literature.

Shakespeare, W. (1901) *As You Like It*. New York: The University Press.

Skaggs, F. (1981) *The Bible Speaks on Aging*. Nashville: Broadman.

Tracy, D. (1975) "Eschatological Perspectives on Aging." in Hiltner, 119–34.

Wesley, J. (1979) "The Doctrine of Original Sin." In *The Works of John Wesley*, 3rd ed. Letters and Essays. Grand Rapids: Baker Book House.

30 A Neo-Orthodox Perspective

OMAR OTTERNESS

Does the Christian tradition have something meaningful to say about the issues raised by the aging experience? The realities of aging and the negative stereotypes ascribed to old age in our culture provide a challenge to any belief system that would claim an authentic structure of meaning for the later years. Thus, it is important to explore the insights into life's journey that come through the Christian witness. What does it mean to grow old under the promises of the gospel? What are the challenges? What are the opportunities? Are there resources within the Christian tradition to make the later years of life an adventure of grace?

The purpose of this essay is to seek answers to these questions through an exploration of the Christian faith as interpreted by the Protestant tradition. To limit the scope of this search, the primary resource will be the theology of Paul Tillich. Although the metaphysical presuppositions of his theology do not conform to Protestant orthodoxy, he maintains that the organizing principle of his theology is the Protestant theme of justification by grace through faith (1963, 223). He wanted to be understood as one who sought to give new forms of expression to the Protestant tradition.

Tillich did not write an explicit theological interpretation of aging. Thus, the procedure will be to locate the problematic issues of aging as identified by Erik Erikson, a social scientist, and then seek in the writings of Tillich a theological response to them. This procedure will require an eclectic use of the writings of Tillich. Without any claim to giving a comprehensive or critical study of his thought, the purpose of this chapter is simply to seek insight into the experiences of aging in whatever context it appears.

Erikson first developed his theory of the eight stages of human development when he was in his forties (Erikson, 1950). He returned to reflect on it in his later years and reaffirmed it with some reservations (Erikson, 1982). The theory is helpful for our purposes because it does not consider aging simply as a physical process, but places it in its social context and recognizes the important role played by religious values.

It should not be surprising that aging issues have a fundamental religious dimension. They deal with what is essential to being fully human. How are people to understand their finite contingency and mortality? How are they to cope with the limits and suffering that erupt in life? How are they to affirm the meaning of life in the face of boredom and despair? While these questions are common to every stage of life, they become more urgent in old age when time is running out and there is an inevitable decline in life energies.

Three aging issues identified by Erikson and recognized by other gerontologists will be considered. The first is the need for the aged to claim what Erikson calls integrity when they seek to bring closure to life. The second is the need to affirm autonomy when faced with increased limits on their freedom due to physical, mental, and social changes. The third issue relates to the need for generativity throughout the lifespan. The three issues are closely related in that they are basic to maintaining a sense of meaning in life. It will become evident that these issues raise questions of religious significance and are open to theological interpretation.

INTEGRITY

According to Erikson, human development proceeds through eight stages from infancy to old age. At each stage there is a crisis due to a tension between opposing forces that must be successfully negotiated if one is to move on to the next stage. For example, in infancy there is a tension between mistrust and trust out of which must emerge a basic trust if the development is to be positive. The virtues to be developed (trust, autonomy, initiative, industry, identity, intimacy, generativity, and integrity) are critical at a certain chronological stage and become essential components of all the later stages. Thus, if one is to come to old age with an integrated self, it is necessary to negotiate successfully each stage of life and to renew its virtue throughout life.

At the stage of old age, Erikson describes the crisis as a tension between integrity and despair. If the crisis is successfully encountered, the outcome is wisdom. Because this stage is not a transition to a following stage, it is a time when one must confront the question: Can the meaning of who I have become be sustained and provide integrity for this final stage of life?

Erikson describes integrity as "a sense of coherence and wholeness" when one reviews past life (1982, 65). It involves the essentially religious task of being able to affirm the meaning of one's life. This life-review seeks to identify and confirm the goals of one's life and to relate them to present values and relationships. He explains that this "cannot mean only a rare quality of personal character" but must include "a timeless love for those few 'Others' who have become the main counter players in life's most significant contexts" (1982, 65). There are threads of meaning and relationships that are needed to give coherence to life.

Erikson contends that the goal of integrity in old age is not easily achieved because of the "loss of linkages" in the fundamental life processes: physical strength, mental acuity, and social interaction (1982, 65). The encounter with these forces can lead to despair and a disdain of life. It is a conflict that cannot be avoided because it is "a natural and necessary reaction to human weakness and to the deadly repetitiveness of depravity and deceit" (1982, 64). According to Erikson, this negative dimension of the aging experience can be "denied only at the danger of indirect destructiveness and more or less hidden self-disdain" (1982, 64). If these forces dominate, however, the result is the despair of confusion and loss of purpose.

What is required at the last stage of life is a "philosophical" construction of myth and ritualization which in "maintaining some order and meaning in the disintegration of body and mind" can still "advocate a durable hope in wisdom" (1982, 64). Erikson warns that this must not be a false escape into some form of dogmatism rooted in a form of "coercive orthodoxy."

The wisdom that emerges from integrity rightly claimed is described as "the acceptance of one's one and only life cycle . . . as something that had to be and that by necessity, permitted no substitutions" (Erikson, 1964, 131). Wisdom is the virtue that gives one "the ability to sustain our sameness and continuity in the face of changing fate" (Erikson, 1950, 42).

In the writings following his first introduction of the theory, Erikson placed greater emphasis on the virtue of hope at the last stage in life. This is the fruition of the quality of trust first developed in infancy. In adulthood it becomes faith. It is important because "an adult who has lost all hope, regresses into as lifeless a state as a living organism can sustain" (Erikson, 1964, 42).

From Psychosocial to Theological Perspective

Erikson has introduced a psychosocial perspective on old age with its challenge to attain integrity over despair. In contrast to Freud, he recognizes that there is a religious dimension to successful aging. Although there are neurotic expressions of religion, Erikson views it as the main channel for constructing a symbol system by which one seeks to make sense of one's experience and to integrate it into a meaning structure that can have a positive relationship to the development of the ego (1964, 103). He also credits religion with having a deeper insight into alienation and evil than found in a humanistic analysis (1964, 153).

Although Erikson as a clinician does not attempt to elaborate a religious basis for successful aging, he does correlate the virtues of his cycle theory with the theological virtues of faith, hope, and charity (1964, 111–12). His theory can be interpreted as a normative vision of the good person and of the ideal old age (Browning, 1976, 25).

When his understanding of religion was described as a form of projection, Erikson rejected the analysis as inadequate. He responded: "Man does not just project something on to nothing. He is probably projecting something onto some reality that is actually there. There may even be an interaction between man's projection and this reality" (Browning, 1976, 26).

It is clear that Erikson's concern for values and meaning structures moves his analysis into the realm of religion, and thus, it is not necessary to place it in opposition to a theological perspective. He has realized that it is important to go beyond the social and psychological analysis, but his scientific and humanist approach does not allow him to give content to that further quest. It is necessary to turn to a specific religious tradition to find an adequate response to those issues. Religion does not appear in the abstract but is embodied in particular religious traditions and communities. Thus, the next task is to turn to the writings of Tillich to explore the ways the Christian tradition understands the experiences of integrity and despair that Erikson has described.

Tillich's Theological Response

Tillich's theological method is to correlate the questions raised by an existentialist and phenomenological analysis of the human condition with answers that come from Christian revelation. Because Tillich claims that his analysis of the human condition is based on observations independent of Christian revelation, it is not surprising that it is similar to the analysis made by Erikson on the basis of social psychological data. Both Erikson and Tillich describe the negative and positive polarities of human existence. They both describe despair as the potential tragic result of the human journey, and they both see the need for an integrity or wholeness that goes beyond physical and social well-being.

Although Tillich is giving an analysis of the human condition without special reference to old age, it has significance for this study because the religious questions he considers are most likely to emerge into full consciousness in old age. As Erikson recognizes, it is often possible to bury such issues through the active years, but in the life-review that takes place at the last stage they move to the forefront.

Finitude and Anxiety. According to Tillich, the threat to integrity has its deepest root in the anxiety common to all finite creatures. Tillich writes: "Anxiety is finitude, experienced as one's own finitude. This is the natural anxiety of man as man, and in some way of all living beings. It is the anxiety of nonbeing, the awareness of one's finitude as finitude" (1952, 35–36).

Although the metaphysical presuppositions of Tillich's ontology are beyond the purview of this chapter, it is necessary to state his basic worldview in order to understand his use of such terms as *nonbeing* in the above quotation. Tillich maintains that all existence resides in "Being itself," his nonsymbolic term for God. Finite beings, however, are estranged from that reality and therefore live under the threat of nonbeing. The crucial issue is how the estranged human being can overcome estrangement from "Being itself."

Tillich maintains that the anxiety of human existence is not caused by sin, but it is an inevitable concomitant of finitude. This anxiety should not be confused with fear, which has definite objects that can be removed. Anxiety is a faceless undercurrent of all life which may emerge into full consciousness at any stage of life.

It is the human capacity for self-transcendence which makes finitude the cause of anxiety. Human beings look at their own finitude in a way that transcends it. According to Tillich, "the power of infinite self-transcendence is an expression of man's belonging to that which is beyond non-being, namely being itself" (1951, 212).

The aging process that ends in death is the most concrete evidence that the human being is tied to the natural finite order. Whereas all animal life experiences death, it is only the human animal who can project its own death and choose suicide over life. Tillich writes: "Temporality means for man the anxiety of having to die; this hangs over every moment and characterizes the whole of human existence" (1951, 212). The awareness of one's finitude is a sign both of self-transcendence and of the threat of nonbeing. The anxiety is not caused by the suffering involved in death, but by the realization that one cannot preserve one's own being.

The category of space as another dimension of finitude is also related to anxiety. Physical space such as home, country, etc., and social space such as vocation, social standing, etc., which are positive values in life, are under the sentence of finally being lost. The experience of these losses as one ages are the little deaths that precede the final death.

The most important aspects of anxiety are the experiences of sin and guilt which have a complex relationship to finitude. Guilt is the result of sin, but it is finitude that makes sin possible. In what appears as a paradox, Tillich says that sin is inevitable because of finitude, and yet it is not a fate independent of the role played by human freedom. The basic human problem is not to overcome the finitude and the anxiety that accompanies it, but to overcome the sin and guilt that flow from them.

Sin is the attempt to exist independently of God. It is the attempt to be one's own god. One seeks to center the meaning of life in the finite self. One can do this because the human being is created in the image of God with the capacity for self-transcendence and freedom. This attempt cannot succeed because it is a denial of one's finitude. The guilt that results is more than the bad conscience because of an immoral act. It is an awareness that one's personhood is threatened by judgment and self-hatred. Guilt is beyond the human capacity to overcome. In Tillich's terms, it brings with it the threat of nonbeing.

Tillich describes the negative outcome of the human predicament as despair. This despair has the two elements of self-hatred and the realization that one cannot escape from the self. The nature of despair is described as follows:

> Despair is the state of inescapable conflict. It is the conflict, on the one hand, between what one potentially is and therefore ought to be and, on the other hand,

> what one actually is in the combination of destiny and freedom. The pain of despair is the agony of being responsible for the loss of the meaning of one's existence and unable to recover it. One is shut up in one's self and in conflict with one's self. One cannot escape, because one cannot escape from one's self. (Tillich, 1957, 75)

It is remarkable how similar this description is to Erikson's understanding of despair as the tragic result of not being able to claim integrity in review of one's life.

The basic presupposition for Tillich's analysis of the human predicament is evident in this description of despair: "The experience of separation from one's eternity is the state of despair. It points to the limits of temporality and to the situation of being bound to the divine life without being united with it in the central act of personal love" (1957, 78). When the quest to overcome despair and estrangement becomes one's ultimate concern, it raises the question of God.

After this analysis of the human predicament, Tillich turns to Christian revelation for his answer. This is found in the historical manifestation in Jesus as the Christ, described by Tillich as "the New Being" who makes possible a "New Creation." Tillich writes: "The New Creation is the reality in which the separated is reunited. The New Being is manifest in Christ because in Him the separation never overcame Him and God, between Him and mankind, between Him and Himself" (1955, 25). He describes the heart of the Christian witness in this way: "We want only to show you something we have seen and to tell you something we have heard: That in the midst of the old creation there is a New Creation, and that this New Creation is manifest in Jesus who is called the Christ" (1955, 25). Under the conditions of history you have in Jesus as the Christ a human life in which all forms of anxiety were present, but from which all forms of despair were overcome. Jesus is the Christ because in him the break between estranged existence and essential being was overcome. His surrender of his selfhood to God, the universal, was done without losing his selfhood.

In the interpretation of the significance of Jesus as the Christ, Tillich seeks to give a contemporary statement of the central Reformation doctrine of justification by grace through faith and thus show how one participates in the New Creation. At the center of this doctrine is the affirmation that one does not achieve integrity or wholeness on one's own, but that life is restored to health by the free gift of a gracious God who meets one with forgiveness in Jesus Christ. As a theologian of the Protestant "Gestalt of Grace," Tillich points to the divine love as the source of self-acceptance.

In response to Erikson's call for integrity in old age as the basis for the self-acceptance essential to it, Tillich would claim that the ability to accept one's life as whole and complete is not available apart from the grace of God. He writes:

> He who is accepted ultimately can also accept himself. Being forgiven and being able to accept oneself are one and the same thing. No one can accept himself who does not feel that he is accepted by the power of acceptance which is greater than he, greater than his friends and counselors and psychological helpers. (1955, 12)

Yet, as Tillich emphasizes, it is difficult for self-centered human beings to "accept that they are accepted." They want to be independent and self-sufficient—to be their own god rather than finite beings made in the "image of God." It is only when faith breaks through this primal sin of pride that one realizes the courage to live as a finite creature in the face of life's anxieties.

Courage is not a self-generated virtue but results from faith. Tillich writes:

> Faith in the almighty God is the answer to the quest for a courage which is sufficient to conquer the anxiety of finitude. Ultimate courage is based upon participation in the ultimate power of being. . . . Neither finitude nor anxiety disappears, but they are taken into infinity and courage. (1951, 304)

Implications for the Aging Experience

It remains to consider the ways Tillich's theology sheds light on the need for integrity in old age as described by Erikson. Whereas Erikson recognizes the religious dimensions of the issues he has raised, the most he has to propose in the face of the threat of despair in old age is a guarded optimism which states: "We must allow for the human being's potential capacity, under favorable conditions, more or less actively to let the integrative experiences of earlier stages come to fruition—the gradual maturation of integrity" (Erikson, 1964, 65).

Tillich would most likely agree with Erikson that self-acceptance of one's life as lived is essential to a creative old age. However, he would maintain that this is never a human achievement. The realities of sin and guilt are still powerful when one reviews one's life in old age. Robert Butler states:

> There are those who refuse to admit that old people, like all people, suffer from past guilt and acquire new guilt for their misdeeds. They pretend that old age is as innocent as childhood. This is wholly invalid. Old people have made and continue to make their own contribution to their own fate. I am quite certain that I have never seen anyone at any age who did not have a sense of guilt, and, in some measure, a legitimate basis for it. (1975, 414)

If this analysis is correct, then Tillich's contribution to the understanding of the quest for integrity is not only to recognize guilt as a central issue but also to point to the grace of God as a basis for self-acceptance. Tillich writes: "Man can love himself in terms of self-acceptance only if he is certain that he is accepted. Otherwise his self-acceptance is self-complacency and arbitrariness. Only in the light and power of 'love from above' can he love himself" (1954, 121–22).

In Tillich's thought, courage born of faith is the virtue that plays a similar role to integrity in Erikson's thought. Erikson recognized that in the last stage of life there is a need for a "philosophical stance" as the basis for "a durable hope" in the face of the disintegration of the body and mind (1982, 64). What Tillich is able to do from within the circle of Christian faith is to articulate a mythos that provides a basis for such a hope.

THE LOSSES AND LIMITS OF OLD AGE

A second challenge in old age is the increased experience of losses and of new limits on one's freedom. These are recognized by Erikson when he states that in old age there is

> the loss of linkages in all three organizing processes: in the Soma, the pervasive weakening of tonic interplay in connecting tissues, blood-distributing vessels, and the muscle system; in the Psyche, the gradual loss of mnemonic coherence in experience, past and present; and in the Ethos, the threat of a sudden and nearly total loss of responsible function in generative interplay. (1982, 65)

All of these factors make the achievement of integrity difficult.

Erikson recognizes the social stigma that is attached to growing dependence and lack of freedom. He writes:

> In a country that has prided itself on independence rather than interdependence, on fresh zest and enthusiasm rather than cautious deliberation, and on agility and buoyancy rather than forthright firmness, the predominant value is, of course, youthfulness. . . . It is not surprising then, that ageism poses such a problem for all older people. (Erikson et al., 1986, 301)

Tillich on Destiny and Freedom

The point where finite freedom reaches its limits is what Tillich calls the "boundary situation" which is unique to human beings. It is the point where the finite human relates to the transcendent. Tillich responds to the issues it raises in a discussion of the themes of destiny and freedom (1951, 184–86).

The self-transcendence which Tillich has described as the evidence for the human relationship to God is also the source of freedom. It permits one to stand above the natural flow of events and in some small way to shape them. Tillich states that "freedom is experienced as deliberation, decision, and responsibility" (1951, 184).

This freedom, however, stands "in polar interdependence with destiny" (1951, 185). Destiny includes all the genetic inheritance, natural and social forces that shape one's existence, and all one's past decisions that impact one's present position in life. Tillich says destiny "is not a strange power which determines what shall happen to me. It is myself as given, formed by nature, history and myself. My destiny is the basis of my freedom; my freedom participates in shaping my destiny" (1951, 185).

Tillich maintains that the freedom of the transcendent self in its past history has had some power to shape the present with its limits and possibilities. The place one stands in the present is both a product of one's genetic and social inheritance and the decisions one has made in the past. One's present situation is not the result of a blind fate. It also follows that one's future destiny, although it does have limits set by our past, is not outside of our freedom and responsibility. Tillich writes: "Our destiny is that out of which our decisions arise; it is the indefinitely broad basis of our centered self-hood; it is the concreteness of our being which makes all our decisions our decisions" (1951, 184).

Although Tillich emphasizes personal responsibility for one's destiny, he recognizes the ambiguity of living under conditions beyond one's control. There are powerful forces at work, both in the natural order and the social order that leave the finite being powerless. Finitude means that one does not have total control of one's fate, and that gives rise to an anxiety intrinsic to human life. Tillich writes:

> Everyone carries a hostility toward the existence into which he has been thrown, toward the hidden powers which determine his life and that of the universe, toward that which makes him feel guilty and that which threatens him with destruction because he has become guilty. . . . Below this, at a deeper level, there is self-rejection, disgust, and even hatred of one's self. (1955, 21)

It is at this "boundary situation" that one can surrender to a fatalistic despair. The result is the loss of a meaningful destiny and also the loss of freedom (1951, 223). According to Tillich, "our present situation is characterized by a profound and desperate feeling of meaninglessness. . . . The question, 'What for?', is cynically dismissed. Man's essential anxiety about the possible loss of his destiny has been transformed into an existential despair about destiny as such" (1951, 223).

It is central to Tillich's theology that a courage born of faith is necessary to overcome the threat of meaninglessness. At the heart of that faith is the affirmation of the grace known through Jesus as the Christ. "Grace transforms fate into a meaningful destiny; it changes guilt into confidence and courage" (Tillich, 1948, 156). Such a courage supports a responsible self in the face of life's losses and ambiguities. It makes possible a meaningful destiny and a continued exercise of freedom within the limits imposed by outside forces. The next task is to explore the implications of this analysis for issues related to the aging experience.

Implications for the Aging Experience

There are three implications for the understanding of the losses and limits of freedom that accompany old age. The first observation is simply to recognize that at every stage in life there are limits on the exercise of freedom—this is part of the finite human condition. It is not unique to old age as such. The challenge in life is to exercise freedom within the limits that life imposes. This recognition should encourage one not to deny, hide, or disguise the losses and limits that come with aging. There is no truth to the quest for the fountain of youth. Anyone who has visited or worked in a nursing home recognizes that the losses and limits are real and cannot be dismissed with a Pollyanna optimism. The question remains as to how one responds to the losses and limits.

A second implication for the aging experience is the recognition that we are created, not for independence, but for interdependence. The honest recognition of limits brings one to the realization that no one can have complete control of his or her destiny or live in self-sufficiency. The American ideal of independence that avoids dependency at all costs is a false ideal. Tillich maintains that as finite creatures people are dependent upon both God and one another. Within a community of faith it should be possible both to give and to receive help without destroying the dignity of the other.

The third implication is to observe that Tillich points to the Christian faith as a way of maintaining both freedom and meaningful destiny in the face of life's losses and limits. Tillich does not suggest that one is to celebrate or seek out the losses, but he claims that when they are encountered with courage they can be occasions for personal growth. This courage "is rooted in faith in God as its creative ground" (1951, 300). Tillich maintains that God even participates "in the negativities of creaturely life as the ground of being and meaning" (1951, 300).

According to Tillich, belief in providence is not the expectation of divine intervention to change one's condition. Rather, it is a faith that "when the conditions of a situation are destroying the believer, the divine condition give him a certainty that transcends the destruction" (1951, 300). There is a sense of transcendent security in the face of life's vicissitudes. It is a faith that "accepts 'in spite of'; and out of the 'in spite of' faith the 'in spite of' of courage is born." (1952, 172).

Tillich maintains that there is no point in life where complete control of one's destiny is lost. One can recognize the ambiguity of control and lack of control that pervades all of life and yet have the courage to claim responsibility for one's destiny. This may be only the freedom to determine the attitude with which one responds to the circumstances beyond one's control. In the revelation of God, Tillich finds a basis for a hope that overcomes despair and restores a measure of freedom.

CONTINUED GENERATIVITY

The first two issues have dealt with negative dimensions of the aging experience. They were issues faced in bringing a closure to life. It was only in his later years that Erikson acknowledges that with the great increase in life expectancy there needs to be a consideration of how the bonus years are to be lived. He asks if his earlier analysis still holds "when old age is represented by a quite numerous, fast-increasing, and reasonably well-preserved group of mere 'elderlies'" (1982, 62). He recognizes the tremendous differences between the retirees of age sixty-five and the over-eighty-five age group and suggests that a ninth stage be added to his theory. The younger retiree is not primarily concerned about bringing closure to life when there may be another fourth of life to be lived. Many find, however, that the leisure endorsed by society for this stage of life does not provide a fulfilling meaning to life.

It is because of this new breed of retirees that Erikson suggests a need to emphasize that the generativity prescribed for the earlier stage needs to be continued. He writes: " . . . old people need to maintain a *grand*-generative function" (1982, 63). They have the potential for years of continued engagement with life. He points to examples of failure to achieve this. From his clinical experience he has observed many that "lack in old age that minimum of vital involvement that is necessary for staying really alive" (1982, 63). They have succumbed to the despair of stagnation with "a mourning for autonomy weakened, initiative lost, intimacy missed, generativity neglected, not to speak of identity potentials by passed or, indeed, in all too limiting identity lived" (1982, 63).

According to Erikson, generativity stands in conflict with self-absorption. When the tension is successfully overcome, the virtue of care emerges. The generative person is one who is able to go beyond self-preoccupation to an active concern for others. The generative person is characterized by trust in the world and hope for the future. There is the capacity for meaningful work, intimacy, and love (Browning, 1973, 181–92).

Tillich on Sanctification

It is in Tillich's doctrine of sanctification that we find an understanding of the Christian life that parallels Erikson's understanding of generativity (Tillich, 1963, 228–37). Sanctification is the process of growth in the Christian life. Although the earlier exposition of Tillich's thought focused on justification, the purpose was to provide a basis for a more positive understanding of the Christian life. The person who finds the basis for integrity and self-acceptance in the gift of grace is set free from self-concern for a creative love for others. "In the midst of our futile attempts to make ourselves worthy, in our despair about the inescapable failure of these attempts, we are suddenly grasped by the certainly that we are forgiven, and the fire of love begins to burn" (Tillich, 1955, 13).

The doctrine of sanctification holds that the inner life of the spirit need not conform to the laws that govern the physical body. Paul writes: "So we do not lose heart. Even though our outer nature is wasting away, our inner nature is being renewed day by day" (2 Cor. 4:16). Tillich ascribes this renewal to the work of the Spiritual Presence (1963, 228). According to Tillich there are four aspects of the process of sanctification (1963, 228–37).

Increased Awareness. The "increased awareness" described by Tillich is similar to the wisdom that Erikson understands as the outcome of integrity. It recognizes the ambiguities of life but does not succumb to despair. "One becomes increasingly aware of his actual situation and of the forces struggling around him and his humanity but also becomes aware of the answers implied in this situation" (Tillich, 1963, 231). It can lead to a different set of priorities, the realization that relationships are more important than material accumulations. It allows for the honest recognition of failures and frailties of human existence by those whose identity and destiny are secure under the promises of grace.

Increased Freedom. The second aspect of sanctification is increased freedom. Tillich interprets this as a freedom from the binding power of law upon the conscience. Life need no longer be lived by the rules from the past. To live under the law, according to Tillich, is to be confronted by threats and demands. Although the Christian is never outside the law, the Christian has the freedom "to judge the given situation in the light of the Spiritual Presence and to decide upon adequate action, which is often in seeming contradiction to the law" (1963, 233).

This freedom gives rise to the courage to take risks. There is no longer the pressure to conform to the norms of society. According to David Maitland, older adults are called to be part of the counterculture (1991, 13–23).

Increased Relatedness. A third characteristic of sanctification is the power to "break through the wall of self-seclusion" and establish new and better relationships with others. This corresponds closely with the virtue of care which Erikson relates to generativity. Tillich does not claim that all human relationships become perfect; they remain subject to estrangement and hostility. However, the "vertical relationship" and the reconciliation that comes with forgiveness restores the horizontal relationship.

The process of sanctification, according to Tillich, results in a humility and "a mature self-relatedness in which self-acceptance conquers both self-elevation and self-contempt" (163, 234). It makes it possible for one to live at peace with the self and in openness with others in the midst of the ambiguities of existence.

Although Tillich does not refer to the concept of Christian vocation which is central to Luther's thought on sanctification, he affirms the essential truth of Luther's position (1963, 274). This holds that the freedom to love is born out of the experience of the love of God. The call to vocation for every Christian who has experienced the acceptance of God is to make one's life available to neighbor needs out of gratitude for the gift of grace. This call to vocation does not end with retirement from one's occupation. It gives purpose and meaning to the later years.

The Principle of Self-Transcendence. The fourth aspect of sanctification is the recognition that the goals of increased awareness, freedom, and relatedness are only possible when the self continues in relation to the divine source of its being. Tillich states that "sanctification is not possible without a continuous transcendence of oneself in the direction of the ultimate—in other words, without participation in the holy" (1963, 235).

Without prescribing what form it should take, Tillich emphasizes the importance of a devotional life. He writes:

> The self-transcendence which belongs to sanctification is actual in every act in which the Spiritual Presence is experienced. This can be in prayer or meditation in total privacy, in the exchange of Spiritual experiences with others, in communications on a secular basis, in the creative works of man's spirit, in the midst of labor or rest, in private counseling, in church services. It is like breathing in another air, an elevation above average existence. It is the most important thing in the process of spiritual maturity. (1963, 236)

Implications for the Aging Experience

In contrast to the first two issues which are concerned with bringing a closure to life, both Erikson and Tillich see the need to affirm the present by a continued involvement in life. They both hold out the prospect for continued growth and a movement toward maturity. In contrast to those who interpret aging as the experience of the cross (Sapp, 1987, 141), Tillich would maintain that every age is one in which there can be the positive experiences of growth, service, joy, and gratitude. This is not to deny that there will be many crosses along the way, but it is to affirm that they are not to have the last word.

It is important to note that the goal of sanctification for Tillich is not the achievement of perfection. One continues to need to live under the promise of justification by grace through faith. Nevertheless, there is real growth. "The Christian life never reaches the state of perfection—it always remains an up-and-down course—but in spite of its mutable character it contains a movement toward maturity, however fragmentary the mature state may be" (Tillich, 1963, 237).

In an age when society has adopted negative stereotypes of aging and has not found a creative role for the older adult, the Christian concepts of sanctification and vocation can become the means for restoring purpose to the later years. The motivation for such a transformation does not need to wait for the transformation of society's values, but is already available to those older adults who live under the promises of the gospel. There is grace for graceful and affirmative aging.

CONCLUSION

In addition to the statements on the implications for aging at the end of each section of the chapter, there are three additional conclusions that follow from this study. The first is to affirm that any wholistic study of aging must include the role of religion. The social-psychological analysis of Erikson and the phenomenological-existential analysis of Tillich both affirm that religion is an inescapable dimension of human existence. It is not an optional concern for those who happen to be interested. It therefore follows that any study of aging that ignores the religious dimension is guilty of reductionism.

Second, Tillich has illustrated how theology can contribute to creating a structure of meaning. Theology is to be understood as a second-order discipline that seeks to give a coherent account and interpretation of primary human experiences. Langdon Gilkey describes the function of theology as follows:

> By thematizing experience into understanding and so in part conquering the terrors to which life is subject, it brings into awareness those sacral elements of human existence that are celebrated in joy, and gives creative guidance for action, and provides intelligible, credible ground for hope in the future. (1975, 11)

If Robert Butler is correct in identifying the question of meaning as the primary issue for the elderly (1975, 14), then theology can play a significant role. However, it is important to note that theology remains powerless unless it also finds expression in a community of faith that lives under the promises of God.

Tillich points to the resources within the Christian tradition that address the issues of aging. Insofar as the Christian community embodies and articulates that message, it can help meet the quest for meaning. Although Tillich's theology needs to overcome the barrier of its philosophical language in order to speak in the language of the lay person, it does respond to the issues of integrity, limits on freedom, and the need for generativity. To a culture that both denies and fears the aging process, the faith community needs to bear witness to the God of grace who gives courage for the living of our days.

Finally, this study illustrates how the questions of meaning are best met through the exploration of the resources of specific historical religious traditions and communities of faith. There is no claim that Tillich's theology provides the only viable structure of meaning; it does not even exhaust the resources with the Protestant Christian tradition. It demonstrates, however, that religion does not live in the abstractions of religion in general. It therefore follows that those who minister to the elderly in any setting should do so in terms of their specific historical tradition. It also follows that all of the faith communities should probe their traditions to respond to the issues of aging. This should be the religious community's contribution to a wholistic understanding of aging. It will be an important contribution, because in the experience of aging the religious questions are unavoidable.

BIBLIOGRAPHY

Browning, D. (1973) *Generative Man*. New York: Dell.

______ (1976) "Conference on Erikson and Religion." *Criterion* 15 (2):25–26.

Butler, R. N. (1975) *Why Survive? Being Old in America*. New York: Harper & Row.

Erikson, E. H. (1950) *Childhood and Society.* New York: Norton.

______ (1964) *Insight and Responsibility.* New York: Norton.

______ (1978) "Introduction: Reflections on Aging." In Spicker, Woodward, and Van Tassel, 1–8.

______ (1982) *The Life Cycle Completed: A Review.* New York: Norton.

Erikson, E., J. Erikson, and H. Kivnick (1986) *Vital Involvement in Old Age: The Experience of Old Age in Our Time.* New York: Norton.

Gilkey, L. (1975) *Catholicism Confronts Modernity, A Protestant View.* New York: Seabury.

Maitland, D. J. (1991) *Aging as Counterculture: A Vocation for the Later Years.* New York: Pilgrim Press.

Sapp, S. (1987) *Full of Years, Aging and the Elderly in the Bible and Today.* Nashville: Abingdon.

Spicker, S. F., K. M. Woodward, and D. D. Van Tassel, eds. (1978) *Aging and the Elderly, Humanistic Perspectives in Gerontology.* Atlantic Highlands, N.J.: Humanities Press.

Tillich, P. (1948) *The Shaking of the Foundations.* New York: Charles Scribner's Sons.

______ (1951) *Systematic Theology.* Vol. 1. Chicago: University of Chicago Press.

______ (1952) *The Courage To Be.* New Haven: Yale University Press.

______ (1954) *Love, Power, and Justice.* London: Oxford University Press.

______ (1955) *The New Being.* New York: Charles Scribner's Sons.

______ (1957) *Systematic Theology.* Vol. 2. Chicago: University of Chicago Press.

______ (1963) *Systematic Theology.* Vol. 3. Chicago: University of Chicago Press.

31 A Process Theology Perspective

THOMAS AU
JOHN B. COBB, JR.

THE RELEVANCE OF THE PROCESS MODEL

Process theology is often cast in the language of youth. It associates God with that which makes for life and growth. It emphasizes the role of anticipation and of constituting ourselves moment by moment for the sake of the future. It is associated with the activistic, pragmatic strain in American thought. It emphasizes adventure, zest, and transformation. What can such a theology say to the aging?

It can, of course, point out that in healthy aging, all those notions continue to have relevance. But to say only that would miss the point. These qualities of youth do continue throughout life, but they do not constitute what is distinctive about aging. Emphasizing the ways in which the aged can still be youthful blocks attention to what is most important about aging. If process theology is limited to these themes, then it has quite limited relevance to the aging.

When Alfred North Whitehead wrote the books that have most inspired process theologians, he was himself already aging. He published *Process and Reality* at the age of sixty-eight and *Modes of Thought* when he was seventy-seven (1978; 1938). Charles Hartshorne has continued to publish in his nineties (1991). It would be surprising if they gave expression only to the values of youth.

Whitehead understood his task to be to discern the general structures or patterns that are true of all things whatsoever. For him all "things" are events, and the unit events are acts of experience. Hence we can say that Whitehead sought, through the particularity of every experience, to discern its universal character. This must be exemplified equally in "experience drunk and experience sober, experience sleeping and experience waking, experience drowsy and experience wide-awake . . ." (Whitehead, 1933, 290–91). For purposes of this essay, the universal structure is to be found alike in the experience of children and the experience of the aging.

The account of what is universal to all experience is far from irrelevant to the study of particular types of experience. Whitehead understands all experiences whatever, human and nonhuman, to be occurrences of the many becoming one and being increased by one. This is quite different from viewing them as the thinking of a mental substance, or as the reception and organization of sense data. When process theologians adopt Whitehead's model, they focus on how human experience grows out of the human body, out of its past, out of relations with the wider world, human and nonhuman, and out of God. Visual and auditory experience, as well as thinking, are viewed as important parts of what comes to be in some experiences. But these are by no means the basis of all experience.

Whitehead described the way each one of the many participates in constituting the new "one" as a "prehension" or "feeling." Experience is made up of these prehensions. Each prehension consists in an objective datum—that is, what is felt, such as some occurrence in the body—and a subjective form, that is, "how" it is felt, which is usually an affective tone. All experience is experience of something, and all experience is affective. This affective aspect of experience is best thought of as emotion. And this "how" of feeling is the base of experience so far as it is subjective. For those who follow this model, the reality of experience is very much determined by what is felt, including the body and the body's environment, both physical and social. But the value of experience is finally to be found in its affective tone, its emotions. The many become one, and the one cannot be abstracted from the many. But what is new in the one is the unique way it clothes the many in emotional tone.

In other words, the bodily condition and the immediate environment are of immense importance in shaping what an experience is. They provide its basic content. But experience is never finally determined by them. There is always some act of self-determination in how this is felt and how it is interpreted.

By this act of self-determination an experience becomes the new "one" as a response to the "many." It is directed to attaining a particular definiteness in the moment in which it occurs. Whitehead says that it aims at a definite, immediate satisfaction. But he also proposes that it aims at this satisfaction with some view as to how this satisfaction will affect the future. In the human case, individuals constitute themselves moment by moment in ways that will produce results they favor in the future. Part of that future can be quite remote, but in all cases some of it will also be quite immediate. For example, one would not start a word without the intention of finishing it.

The extreme generality of this model, its applicability to experience drunk and experience sober, to experience infantile and experience aging, does not render it irrelevant to more concrete analysis. Process theologians have found it illuminating and helpful. But simply to see how a particular experience exemplifies the model does not tell all one needs to know. It tells how one experience is like all the others, and that every experience is unique. But it does not tell *how* each differs from all the others.

It tells that a human experience grows out of a human body just as a mouse's experience grows out of a mouse's body. But it does not tell what growing out of a human body makes possible that growing out of a mouse's body does not. It tells that there will be a difference between experiences growing out of an aging body and those growing out of the bodies of children, but it does not tell what those differences will be. In short, it tells that most of what we need to know can only be learned by empirical study of the particulars.

To begin with a model, even a metaphysical one, does not entail approaching particulars deductively. The model influences the selection and formulation of questions and the interpretation of the data. But the model itself calls one to be open to the evidence. Indeed, if one finds that using the model leads to misleading selectivity in treating the evidence or to distorting the interpretation, then the model should be changed. The model should be kept only as long as it unveils what is there and allows the evidence to address without restriction.

The model leads one to expect that the condition of the body will have an important effect on experience. It leads one to expect that the body's physical environment will be important, and that the emotions as well as the actions of people in that environment will be important. It suggests that one's personal past will be important. It suggests that all these factors will interact with each other in complex and partly unpredictable ways. And it suggests that the individual is not simply the product of all these influences, but responds to them with some small element of freedom in every moment.

If there is reason to think that what is really going on is obscured by these expectations, or if it turns out that no such influences are at work, then the model of the many becoming one and being increased by one should be modified. But if the model provides guidance in the process of concrete analysis and explanation, then it should be kept and used. The claim of process theologians is that the model helps them understand what is going on, opens them to the evidence, and assists them in its interpretation. The invitation to write this paper provides another occasion, and another context, to test the fruitfulness of the model.

An essay on process theology and aging will be the product of the interaction of the model and the evidence. It will aim to formulate some generalizations about the evidence that are suggested by the model. But no one set of generalizations can ever constitute *the* process view of aging. From the perspective of the model, these generalizations can only constitute one set of hypotheses for further testing.

THE EMPIRICAL EVIDENCE

The process model leads one to expect that changes in the body will lead to changes in experience. It does not identify what those changes will be. Only from observation can one learn that. Based on such observation, five stages can be distinguished through which aging proceeds when it is not interrupted by death from accident or disease. These stages are: the active older adult, the slowing older adult, the frail older adult, the assisted older adult, and the immobile older adult. The physiology of the aging process over time is characterized thus by reduced mobility.

The process model also tells one that emotions are of fundamental importance to the value of existence. It does not tell whether the emotional life declines with mobility. Observation indicates that it need not. Emotions do not diminish proportionately with bodily functioning or even with mental alertness. The capacity for emotional response to warmth, anger, touch, or abuse remains throughout life.

That emotions continue even when persons have lost their faculties of communication is illustrated in a recent experience that one of the authors had. He had asked all but one of the persons in a ward how they were feeling. The one he omitted was a woman who had not spoken for two years. As he walked past her she said: "I'm okay too!" She never spoke again, but at that moment she registered very poignantly that she, too, still had emotions that needed recognition.

The process model also leads one to expect that the accumulation of experience over the years will affect the character of new experience. But it does not tell what the effect will be. It leads one to expect that there will be interaction between the accumulated experience and bodily changes. But it does not tell which will be more important in shaping the resultant experience.

In other words, the model suggests that the experience of the aged will differ from that of the young both by virtue of having a longer history of personal experience behind it and by virtue of bodily changes. It leads one to expect that the bodily condition will be affected by the personal history and that the present state of the personal history will be affected by the bodily condition. But what features of bodily health will be most affected by personal history and what bodily changes will have what effects on the continuity of cumulative experience can be learned only from empirical investigation.

The process model leads one to expect that there will be continual change in personal experience, that this change will in general be gradual and cumulative, and that there will be considerable continuity throughout. It will not exclude dramatic shifts, such as those that might result from brain damage or drastic environmental change, but in the absence of these, it anticipates continuity through continuous change. It leads to skepticism about any clearcut developmental shifts occurring in all people at the same time and dividing the life cycle neatly into periods. But it suggests that some common patterns can be found. Some generalizations can be made about people in their seventies and eighties that do not apply equally to those in their twenties and thirties. It is these generalizations that will be considered here.

THE RELIGIOUS QUESTION FOR THE AGING

Because this is being written by theologians, key questions selected are: What is the basic religious issue or challenge for the aging? Is this the same as that for the young, or are there differences?

The process model introduces such questions. Over against a view that assumes there must be one basic spiritual need for all people at all times, such as being forgiven for one's sins, process thought sees large scope for differences. Paul Tillich described how the religious question and answer has changed for Christians through history (1990). Matthew Fox has shown that alongside the fall-redemption paradigm for understanding the religious need, there is also a creation-fulfillment one (1991). Rita Brock has proposed that we see the deepest human problem as damage rather than sin, and salvation more as healing than as forgiveness (1988). From the process perspective there is no reason to suppose that one model expresses the most pressing need of all people at all times. This openness does not preclude the possibility that there is some unity of ultimate need. But if there is, that should be shown and not announced on the basis of some supposedly objective authority. Actually, the Christian's primary authority, the Bible, uses the word *salvation* with quite a variety of meanings.

But how can such a question be investigated? It is an empirical question, in the sense of being a factual one. But even the simplest empirical investigations have to be guided by some hypothesis involving some presuppositions and ways of ordering thought. And the investigation of the spiritual need and opportunity of the aged is not a simple empirical question. It can be approached through interviews and questionnaires or through quite subtle observation of behavior. But none of this will yield any result except as this inquiry is shaped and directed by insightful hypotheses.

It is at this point that process theology may be able to contribute. Does the model as initially confronted suggest any hypotheses for testing? It is the authors' contention that it does, or perhaps more exactly, that it refines and clarifies an hypothesis that arises initially out of experience with the aging.

The process of aging is, in a special way, being-toward-death. Some regard the inevitability of death and the diminishment that precedes it as a cynical trick played on a captive humanity by a trickster God. As death approaches, they will make themselves and those about them miserable. Others will find the adjustment to death the final challenge. Having passed through the other stages of maturation successfully, they can deal with this one also with inner serenity. Yet what is required in this final stage is unique. This chapter will discuss it in terms of two ways of being-in-the-world: the way of "doing" and the way of "being."

Most people derive meaning and satisfaction from doing things. It is often commented that this doing is quite future-oriented, so that people are always preparing for the future without much ability to enjoy it when it comes. There is something quite unsatisfactory about this kind of life, and many practice meditation as a way of collecting themselves in the immediacy of the present, just to "be," to enjoy what is, without reference to its use, its meaning, or how it might profitably be changed. One can think of this as a shift from the ethical to the aesthetic mode of being in the world.

Given these alternatives, it is proposed that whereas the dominant mode of being-in-the-world for those who are younger is "doing," the primary mode for the aging is "being." To shift from the mode of doing to the mode of being may be the great spiritual task of aging. Many of the aging find life meaningless because they have derived their meaning entirely from kinds of doing of which they are now incapable—caring for children, earning a living, serving the community in active public ways, perhaps simply attending church. Their task is to find satisfaction in a life that is not oriented to achievement and service in these ways.

DOING AND BEING

Thus far the hypothesis has been presented in a way that requires no assistance from the process model. But if it is to be tested, it requires more precision. Does "being" involve complete immersion in the moment with no reference to past or future? Is "doing" defined by a future-orientation, or is playing a game of tennis also an act of "doing"? Is the "being" into which the aging need to move contrasted with being physically and mentally active? Or is it to be contrasted with finding the meaning of the present in relation to its future consequences?

This hypothesis needs refinement. First, as people age and their physical energy and dexterity decline, they must reduce the level of their activity, at least physically. In this sense "doing" declines. But many of them are able to find other tasks to perform that do not require as much energy and dexterity. This is a healthy and desirable adjustment in the process of aging.

Second, the kinds of activity that most aging people can perform and are allowed by our society to perform rarely have much public visibility. Social recognition is likely to have provided much of the incentive to act in earlier years, and this declines markedly. A healthy adjustment of the aging is to finding satisfaction in the doing itself, without regard to its recognized public importance.

Third, in the aging process, the time comes for many when, in their own eyes, none of their activity is important. This is a further and more challenging change. They must now find meaning without any expectation that they can perform acts that help others. The meaning must be found simply in the experiences themselves. This is the fullest sense of "being" versus "doing."

Portraying matters in this way, however, suggests that this shift is a last desperate expedient. As long as one can perform any act of service, one properly finds one's meaning in that. Only when that is impossible, this seems to say, does one fall back on "being."

Actually, one can find in the literature quite the opposite depiction. Buddhism, for example, takes enlightenment as a pure mode of being in somewhat the sense discussed. It is incomparably more meaningful than the performance of social duties. One will perform those duties both before and after enlightenment, but it is the pure being of enlightenment that gives them meaning.

If "being" is understood in this radical sense, however, it can hardly be the task of the aged. Although it is said to be attained causelessly and apart from striving for attainment, this happens in Zen practice only in the context of physically stressful sitting or the puzzling wrestling with *Koans.* What is proposed is not that near the end of life one should undertake this. Yet, it is not that the importance and value of "being" is absent from earlier stages of life and appears only when all "doing" becomes impossible.

At this point, finally, the process model may be helpful in the clearer formulation of the hypothesis. In this model every experience constitutes itself with a double aim. It aims to attain some immediate satisfaction in itself. It aims also to contribute to subsequent satisfactions. Stating this in more ordinary language, people are always aiming to enjoy life as it comes, and they are always concerned about the effects of what they do.

One could dispute this by saying that some of what people do is only for immediate enjoyment and some is only for future advantage. If this is true, then the model must be changed. But it is important to think carefully and reflect attentively on experience. One might give, as an example of an action that is purely present-oriented, indulging oneself in food or drink or sex in a way that can only be enjoyed by shutting out all consideration of future consequences. In analyzing this, one can assume, probably beyond the evidence, that the longer-term future of the next day—or even two minutes away—plays no role at all in the present experience. One is simply absorbed in the immediate enjoyment of eating, drinking, or sex. The model allows for that as an extreme case. But the model focuses analysis on what is happening moment by moment. In the moment when one lifts the glass from the table, is there no intention of moving it to the lips? As one tilts it, is there no intention of having the liquid enter the mouth? As one swallows, is there no intention of enjoying its effects? Obviously the immediate future plays a large role at each stage.

Perhaps a more promising example would be the experience of one who is absorbed in activity such as playing the piano. Consider the case when there is no conscious control of bodily movements. The hands, the arms, the feet, all act in perfect coordination without the intervention of conscious purposes. In such moments there is deep enjoyment, even ecstasy. Still, if one analyzes the successive moments of ecstatic experience, they do not appear to be cut off from relations to one another. The enjoyment of the moment is enhanced by the immediate memory of the past moments and by the expectation that the present moment is not the last. The state may be maintained almost effortlessly, but one cannot deny that there is a desire that it continue. The present experience forms itself so as to allow for that continuation.

The claim that there are experiences that order themselves only for the sake of future consequences is similarly exaggerated. Persons do many things they do not enjoy in order to avoid trouble in the future. They go to the dentist, submit themselves to surgery, take bad-tasting medicines, force themselves to study for an upcoming examination when they are tired, and on and on. The role of future consequences in determining how they constitute themselves can be enormous. But does it ever exclude the role of a preference for whatever satisfaction may still be possible in the present? Persons make themselves as comfortable as they can in the dentist's chair; they seek ways to minimize the bad taste of the medicine; and they may drink coffee to feel better while they study. All of this is too obvious to deserve elaboration.

It is more important to point out that the two elements in all experience are intertwined. A major element in present satisfaction in most cases is the anticipation of its future consequences. In the extreme case when persons are doing something that is painful for the sake of a better future, they may take some satisfaction from feeling that they are doing their duty or that they can get it over with. In more ordinary cases, the two are not disconnected. Persons enjoy conversing with a friend and simultaneously enjoy the sense that by conversing in a certain way they are deepening their friendship and increasing the chances for its continuation. As they bite into food that they relish, they are enjoying the immediate taste but also the prospect that for at least a few more seconds that taste will continue.

How can one relate the implications of this model to the distinction of "doing" and "being"? First, these can be understood and defined more precisely. The element of doing is the aspect of experience that is attentive to the consequences of what is happening in the immediate now. The element of being is the aspect of experience that is oriented to immediate satisfaction. Both are present in all experience, and the anticipation of the future always affects the satisfaction in the present. There is no pure doing or being, but there are instances in which one predominates drastically over the other.

The dialectic of doing and being affects people at every stage of life. The authors cannot think of a period in life when overwhelming preoccupation with doing at the expense of being is healthy or when total preoccupation with being is desirable. Nevertheless, this does not invalidate the hypothesis that is being explored and refined. It is important that young people find great enjoyment in life hour by hour. But it is also important that much of this enjoyment come from their sense of how they are readying themselves for the tasks of maturity. The effort of many youth to shut out anticipation of the future for the sake of immediate highs is obviously unhealthy.

For the aging, the situation is different. They are not preparing themselves in order to *do* something in the future that they are not yet ready to do. They cannot derive present satisfaction from that. They are not now able to *do* some of the things they once did that bring recognition and the immediate sense of accomplishment. They may not be able to *do* anything that in their own estimation contributes significantly to others; so the immediate satisfaction in the moment cannot be enhanced by that kind of expectation. They may not even be able to anticipate that the satisfactions they presently enjoy can continue much into the future. To whatever extent one has in the past found present satisfaction enriched by anticipations of this sort, a change is inevitable. This will mean either that the absence of such expectation troubles and spoils present satisfaction or that the immediacy of that satisfaction will be enjoyed untroubled and may even become purer and fuller. It is proposed that the challenge of aging is to find this untroubled satisfaction in being.

As the personal future fades in importance, often the past rises. This can mean living in the past, and that is not healthy. It can mean guilt for past failures and resentment for what life has denied one, and that poisons the experience of the aging. But it can also mean acceptance of what has been, as it has been, with all its failures and limitations, as good. Even if one cannot accomplish much more, one takes satisfaction in the accomplishments of the past. Without belittling one's sins and shortcomings or the suffering and loss one has experienced, one affirms it all as worthy of having been. One senses that although it is past, it has not lost its reality and importance. It is a living past.

If the primacy of being is accepted and enjoyed, then the results will be a contentment and peace almost impossible to those who live with the burdens of multiple responsibilities and obligations. The irony is that this shift to being can also be a great blessing to others. That is, when the aging person accepts the inability to act for the benefit of others, this acceptance in fact becomes a benefit for them.

At a crude level, it is a great relief to children and other caretakers when an aging person becomes free of the frustration of trying to do what he or she cannot do and becomes contented. But more than that is meant here. To be in the presence of one who has found peace is not a mere relief from the obligation to try harder to meet that person's felt needs. It is also an immediate blessing. According to the process model, people feel one another's feelings. To be with someone who is truly at peace communicates peace. When a pastor who has visited such a person says that more has been received than given, this may be quite literally true. Even if the aged person says little, a spirit is felt.

Most of us know older people who have blessed others in this way. One example is a woman who entered a retirement community at eighty-six and died two years later. She had breast cancer when she entered, but she chose not to attribute her declining mobility to that. In her case this denial enabled her to remain cheerful and giving to those around her. She had been in the nursing unit less than a month when she died, but her death caused a real sense of loss. All who had served her felt that she was always giving them more than they had been able to give to her.

THE ATTAINMENT OF PEACE

According to this hypothesis, the primary task of the aging is to find peace. That task has been explained in terms of the process model. This is a clearly religious task. The process model also suggests a theistic element in the explanation of how success and failure occur.

In the process model, alongside the personal past, the body, and the wider environment, there is also one other reality included in experience. This is God. It is the inclusion of God that makes it possible for the experience to be something more than the purely determined product of the other elements. God is the source of alternative possibilities for the subjective self-constitution of the experience. God is the source both of freedom and of direction. God calls persons in each moment, offering them the possibility to respond to just that situation in the most creative way and empowering them to decide to just what extent they will realize this possibility—how close they will come to hitting the mark. That mark is never exactly the same in two moments of experience, and over longer periods of time it changes drastically. It has been suggested in this chapter that for youth the call of God is to find present satisfaction in preparing for future responsibilities, and that God's call to the aging is to find peace in the enjoyment of what is as it happens.

Now one can ask why some devout Christians enter into this peace and others do not. Is there a theological explanation? According to the process model there are always many factors entering into the outcome, but the authors believe that among these the way one has understood God and God's call is important.

According to the process model, God's call is unique in every moment. The ideal for the believer is openness to that call and spontaneous responsiveness. Nevertheless, in socializing persons into the faith, it is inevitable that they be given guidance about the general structures of God's call. They are not to rule their lives by hunches and chaotic feelings. It is not easy to discern the Spirit, and the churches have all felt the need to give moral guidance through precepts and examples. Most of these place a major emphasis, quite rightly, on service of others even at a cost to oneself. Most of them discourage seeking satisfaction in immediate pleasures at the expense of such service.

For many Christians the pattern of life proposed in these precepts is internalized and identified as the call of God. Instead of facilitating attention to God's direct and immediate call, it too often replaces this. Some Christians have no other effective way of understanding what God calls them to do and be. As a result, when obedience to the call, understood in this way as active service of others, becomes impossible, they feel worthless and can find no alternative way to live with dignity and self-respect. The theological teaching that has worked fairly well in earlier years becomes for them, in their aging, an obstacle to meeting their greatest need and realizing their finest possibility.

Fortunately, this is not true for all Christians. Some know that all the precepts of the church are no more than helpful guides to the Christian life. Life is a life of loving God and other creatures. Love transcends precepts and is moved with a sensitivity to the needs of others that can never be captured in rules and generalizations. Love can express itself in deeds of service, but it is not limited to that expression. It has its value in itself and not only in the acts to which it gives rise. It makes one sensitive to what the other is feeling. And, as love of God, it opens one to the ever-changing divine call. For Christians who understand themselves in this way, their faith passes naturally into peace.

THE CONTRIBUTION OF WISDOM

One reason for beginning, as this chapter has, with the movement from being to doing is that in this culture so little is expected of the aged. This distinguishes this culture from traditional cultures. In those cultures, the cumulative experience of the aged was an important source of knowledge for the whole society. The young respected the old, not out of a sense of duty or pity, but because the old possessed the knowledge they lacked. This gave to the aged a role in doing. In this culture, on the other hand, it is generally said that change is so rapid that the cumulative experience of the old is irrelevant to the young. They must learn from one another or from those only a little older.

When the focus is on information, the likelihood in many fields is that most of the aged have little to contribute. Only a few of them keep up with the rapid changes in the many fields. Their information is soon outdated.

If knowledge is not simply the possession of information but also the cumulative experience of processing it, the situation is somewhat different. Even if the older persons do not have all the latest information at their fingertips, they may have an understanding of what is going on that can continue to make a distinctive and important contribution. The insights derived from long experience are not quickly superseded by new data.

In many fields, this kind of knowledge is more important than currency with rapidly changing information. Many older people do keep alert and are able to bring their longer experience to bear in ways that are fully relevant. Not all aging senators and Supreme Court justices are inferior to their younger colleagues. Profoundly original and influential books have been written by persons in their eighties. If social expectations were different, many other older persons would be able to contribute greatly from their longer experience and different knowledge. The shift from doing to being could be postponed.

However matters may stand with respect to knowledge, there is something different suggested by the word *wisdom,* something that has a more religious cast. Not all the aging are wise, but there is a unique possibility for wisdom among the aging. Here, too, is a challenge and opportunity for the aging.

Through youth and the middle years, most thinking is ordered by ambitions and responsibilities. Individuals try to see how they can best attain their goals and fulfill their responsibilities. These ambitions may be laudable, and their responsibilities may be well selected. But every set of ambitions and responsibilities orients a person's thought in one way rather than another. Those with other goals will see things differently. Persons may be able to learn from one another and come to terms with one another, but their continuing commitments will also keep them apart. Their Christian faith will give them some guidance as to how to live in the midst of these tensions, turning conflicts into occasions for learning, and helping them to expand their horizons. But one's experience of others will be deeply affected by how *the other persons'* gifts and commitments and interests relate to *one's own* projects.

In healthy aging, ambitions and responsibilities lessen. As one shifts from doing to being, the element of competitiveness declines. One can experience the other for just what that other is rather than in terms of how that other relates to one's own projects. Much that once seemed terribly important seems less so. Other matters, whose importance has been obscured by one's interests, loom larger. The measure of importance is shaped less by one's own needs and hopes.

The wisdom that comes with healthy aging, even when cumulative knowledge is discounted, is the recognition of how things are in themselves rather than how they relate to oneself and one's projects. More of the reality can be acknowledged with less judgment. Wisdom is, then, a judgment of importance that is disinterested without being uninterested. It is accepting of much that those oriented to accomplishment must reject. It accepts that orientation too, with understanding, but not as the last word.

It is sometimes commented that children turn to the aged for something their parents cannot give them. This is not something better, only different. Parents cannot and should not separate their love from their concern about preparing their children to meet the expectations of the world. For the healthily aging those expectations no longer loom so large. They can appreciate the children as they are. The children need that, too. It is another gift that grows out of the turn from doing to being.

There is no guarantee of such wisdom simply with the passing of the years. Those who cannot separate their self-esteem from doing are likely to project their goals on others, demanding that these others fulfill them when they themselves no longer can. Instead of complementing parental love with their acceptance of what is, they will complain, criticize, and meddle, leaving the children confused and troubled. The question of whether the aging fulfill their special calling and realize their special potentialities is important not only for them but also for all who come into relation with them.

DYING

One can hardly discuss aging without considering dying itself. In the process model, dying is a part of all living. No sooner does a momentary experience come into being than it perishes. One can distinguish the act of becoming from its passing, but they are not separable. For process thought, this continual dying is of greater religious import than the last breath or heartbeat. Hence the discussion of dying belongs with every phase of life and not only with the last.

Nevertheless, there are important differences. For the child, the dying of one moment is succeeded by the coming into being of another in which we can hope for some greater depth and fullness. In other words, it is expected that a child grows. The death of one experience is the seedbed for the birth of another, and in some important sense, the character of the later ones justifies the perishing of the earlier ones.

With the aging, matters are somewhat different. By many measures, the later experiences are often impoverished in comparison with earlier ones. There may be loss of memory, loss of vision, loss of hearing, and a general decline in alertness to what is going on. This is a second level of dying.

Part of the spiritual task of aging is to accept the new experiences as they are rather than to deplore this dying. If one bemoans the decline of quality, the quality of what still occurs is worsened. On the other hand, there is, even in this context, the possibility of growth, growth in acceptance and in peace. That is a part of the spiritual triumph possible in aging, but by no means an inevitable part of the aging process.

The third level of dying comes when no new experience succeeds the old ones. One moment of living experience perishes, and there are no more. If one has not accepted the dying that is a part of all life and the dying that is the diminishment of experience, then it is not likely that one will gracefully accept this final dying either. But if one has accepted the others, then the end of life can be accepted too—even welcomed.

It is not the case that those who find peace in the process of dying are preoccupied with questions of life after death. Indeed, such preoccupation belongs to a mode of future-oriented thinking from which they are freed. But this does not mean that they do not believe in such life, or that questions of what happens after death are not important. Many have a strong assurance that they will be reunited with those they have loved most, and this assurance is part of their peace. Others think of moving on to a deeper union with God than has been possible in this life. The woman described above, whose spirit blessed those around her, gained some of her serenity and was able to continue to express her love, at least in part, because of her assurance of the life to come.

PROCESS THEOLOGY AND DYING

Process thought addresses the different levels of dying in different ways. For it, most fundamental is the perishing that is part of all coming to be. For some thoughtful people, this becomes a source of deep sadness, even meaninglessness. If the past is no more, if all that exists of the past is occasional fading memories, then of what worth has all the effort been? Can this fleeting, dying moment justify all that has been and is no more? Or did past efforts find their justification in those earlier fleeting moments that were so much oriented to their future?

Most people, of course, do not worry about this consciously. Their reflection on what once was and is no more sometimes gives rise to melancholy, but for the most part, they pick up and move on, setting aside these sentimentalities. The present is felt to gain its meaning from its anticipated future, not from its past.

Still others, noticing the frantic efforts of people to achieve goals and to believe that this accomplishment is lasting, suspect that the underlying sense of the dying of all things lies at the bottom of this hopeless quest. Sartre thought that we all craved for the union of presentness with endurance—an ontological impossibility—and that this leads to much that is destructive in relations with one another (1956).

In any case, in the description of what is involved in the achievement of peace by the aging, it is suggested that this includes a certain satisfaction in the past, accepted as real, with all of its limitations and disappointments. If this is correct, then especially for these older people, the sense of meaning is bound up with the assumption, usually not articulated, that perishing is not the last word, that what happened is not drained of importance simply because it is past and remembered by so few.

The process model proposes that indeed the past lives on, not only in fragmentary ways in the present, but fully and wholly in God. God is not outside the world, but includes it. All that persons do, they do for God and to God. The sense of the reality of the past, of its intrinsic importance, that can give them satisfaction as they come to the completion of their lives is justified.

With respect to life after death in the conventional sense, the process model is open. This is one of those factual questions that can only be answered on the basis of evidence, not by deduction from the model. The authors' judgment is that the evidence, from the resurrection of Jesus to what is now called near-death experiences, combined with the deep conviction of God's love, allows persons to support those who are dying in peace in their expectation of reunion with loved ones who have died, and also in their hope for a new closeness to God. For those who are at peace, this suffices.

But among those who are not at peace, this does not suffice. Some, for example, cannot come to terms with death because they fear a punitive God. This may not be as common today as it once was, but even where the church's explicit teaching has not encouraged such fears, the presence of guilt and the projection of a judgmental father can produce them. It may help to offer some reflections on what assurances can honestly be given.

From the point of view of most Christian theologians, including process theologians, one cannot simply assure everyone that everything will be perfect once they die. That is not part of this tradition. Judgment is also part of inherited teaching. Differences in this life will not prove simply irrelevant to whatever mode of being there may be beyond the grave. For those who have attained peace, the issue of judgment does not arise. There is no reason to suppose that their peace will be taken from them. But for those who are not at peace, the issue must be taken seriously.

On the other hand, most Christian theologians today find many of the classical images of judgment incompatible with the God they know in Jesus Christ. These images suggest that God imposes on sinners a punishment that is not inherently entailed by their sin, that is, that God causes suffering that is not necessary. It is suggested, in contrast, that judgment is like the burning of the hand of a child who touches a hot stove. God's judgment is not like that of a parent who adds to the suffering caused by the burning by whipping the child. This is not to trivialize judgment. The burn from the stove can be painful indeed.

Images of this kind of judgment can be offered. One may think, for example, that at death defenses against God are stripped away, and persons stand naked in the divine presence. For some this is the beatific vision for which they have longed. For others it is an occasion of humiliation and shame that puts an end to all their self-deceptions and efforts to deceive others.

The best image in literature is that of C. S. Lewis in *The Great Divorce* (1946). Lewis describes in a convincing way the openness of heaven to all, but also the discomfort some feel in being there. They prefer hell, not because they are happy there, but because they are incapable of the love apart from which there is no happiness.

Many theologians also like the image of the Hound of Heaven in Francis Thompson's poem (Hopkins, 1949). The point here is that God's desire for salvation never ends, no matter how long individuals resist. There may be no guarantee that hell will ultimately be emptied, but if persons remain there, it will not be because of sins they have committed here on earth alone, but because they continue to insist on rejecting God's love everlastingly.

These are not necessarily comforting images. Some may recognize themselves among those who will be made miserable by the vision of God or unable to enjoy the heavenly happiness. But the fear of cruel treatment by a vindictive God can and should be vigorously and confidently countered. This should be part of the church's work throughout life, but for those who are not at peace, it may be particularly important as death approaches.

THE ROLE OF THEOLOGY

This essay has attempted not only to speak theologically about aging and dying, but also to make the role of theology, and specifically process theology, explicit. The authors have tried to show in what ways their insights and affirmations have been shaped by the perspective of process thought. Since one major way in which process thought informs people is to open them to empirical observations, it is evident that without the benefit of process thought many can come to similar conclusions. Indeed, it is hoped that these conclusions will commend themselves to others apart from any commitment to process theology. Features of reality that are most clearly discerned from one point of view should be visible to others once they are pointed out.

Nevertheless, it is hoped that this essay shows how theology in general, and process theology in particular, can inform the way persons look at human life. It can help them ask appropriate questions and can introduce useful distinctions. It can add rigor to the formulations suggested to them by observation. It can open them to dimensions of the situation that are not often noticed by those who lack such perspective. And it can speak a responsible word of comfort and assurance.

The authors also hope that this essay can help to alleviate the fear of some that the introduction of a theological perspective involves the heavy-handed imposition of ideas that are not justified by the evidence. Theology has gotten a bad name by its association with a dogmatic approach. In the authors' view, the Christian faith should justify itself in every case by its actual ability to illuminate the situation rather than by an authority claimed to be independent of the evidence. It is their conviction that it can do so. That is why they are Christians.

BIBLIOGRAPHY

Brock, R. N. (1988) *Journeys by Heart: A Christology of Erotic Power.* New York: Crossroad.

Fox, M. (1991) *Creation Spirituality: Liberating Gifts for the Peoples of the Earth.* San Francisco: HarperSan Francisco.

Hartshorne, C. (1991) *The Philosophy of Charles Hartshorne.* Edited by L. E. Hahn. La Salle, Ill.: Open Court.

Hopkins, G. M. (1949) *Poems.* Mount Vernon, NY: Peter Pauper.

Lewis, C. S. (1946) *The Great Divorce.* New York: Macmillan.

Sartre, J. P. (1956) *Being and Nothingness: an Essay on Phenomenological Ontology.* Translated by Hazel E. Barnes. New York: Philosophical Library.

Tillich, P. (1990) *The Encounter of Religions and Quasi-religions.* Edited by T. Thomas. Lewiston, N.Y.: E. Mellen.

Whitehead, A. N. (1933) *Adventures of Ideas.* New York: Macmillan.

______ (1938) *Modes of Thought.* New York: Free Press.

______ (1978) *Process and Reality: An Essay in Cosmology.* New York: Free Press.

32 A Feminist Theology of Aging

MARY M. KNUTSEN

A feminist theology of aging emerges at the intersection of three distinct scholarly disciplines and social movements: (1) feminist scholarship and feminism as a sociopolitical movement in contemporary U.S. society; (2) the scholarly study of human aging and the broader reality of an aging U.S. society; and (3) theology as a discipline committed to a mutually critical, mutually illuminating, and mutually enlivening dialogue between the classic texts and practices of a religious tradition and the distinctive characteristics and issues of contemporary life, for the sake of the enhancement of life in community with God, each other, and creation.

What is feminism? Despite the extraordinary variety of feminist scholarly disciplines and movements, feminism and feminist scholarship could be said to be rooted in a single simple, albeit profound, affirmation: Women are fully human. The humanity of women is not defective or derivative from our roles in relationship to men and children, but embodies the fullness of what it is to be a human being (Farley, 1985, 44–47). Consequently, feminist scholarship, including feminist theology, has undertaken both the critical task of exposing the ways in which our institutions and ideologies ignore, distort, or demean the humanity of women and the constructive task of generating new, fuller visions of humanity, society, cosmos, and God.

Within feminism and feminist scholarship different models of what it is to be human have resulted in several distinct approaches to scholarly and sociopolitical activity. In her introductory essay to a volume of essays on contemporary feminist scholarship, Stanford law professor Deborah Rhode points out that feminism and feminist scholarship since 1960 can be understood in terms of three distinct models of human gender relations (Rhode, 1990). The first and earliest model, which might be called the "equal rights" model, is concerned to oppose the notion of a mysterious "eternal feminine" and to deny that there are any essential differences between men and women. Women are essentially the same as men in human aptitudes and capabilities and should be given equal access to educational and employment opportunities as well as equal pay for equal work. While noting the significant contributions of this model, Rhode also notes its limitations: It carries the danger of reinforcing the normativity of the male and of obscuring the actual inequalities of power and position between men and women in contemporary U.S. society. The second model, which might be called the "revaluing difference" model, emphasizes by contrast the differences between men and women. This model undertakes to specify and socially revalue the distinctiveness of women's values and experience, especially the characteristics of nurturing and care for interpersonal relationships historically associated with women (Chodorow, 1978; Gilligan, 1982). While again noting the positive contributions of this model, Rhode also notes its limitations: We have "been too much concerned with gender difference, too little with gender disadvantage" (Rhode, 1990, 197). A focus on "difference," and specifically a focus on women's essentially "nurturing" character, not only has the danger of subtly legitimating women's subordination, but also lifts up a largely white, middle class value and so obscures both the reality of disadvantageous power structures and their differential impact on women of a variety of races, classes, familial situations—and ages. Perhaps this accounts for the strange fact that although "what really caused the women's movement was additional years of human life" opening up new vocations for women (Friedan, 1993, 16), the women's movement until recently has paid very little attention to older women or to the problem of ageism (Lewis and Butler, 1984; Saiving, 1988, 117; Friedan, 1993).

The third and most recent model, which might be called the "common good" model, begins precisely with this recognition of the structures of domination as they differentially affect diverse women's—and children's and men's—situations and experiences. This model calls for a move beyond sameness or difference from a male norm and, more broadly, beyond the whole framework of Lockean individualism and individual rights rooted in that male norm. Rather, its aim is both to expose the multiple intersecting forces of domination and exploitation concretely at work in U.S. society and to begin to articulate a richly textured vision of a common good which could engage the contributions and serve the needs of a widely diverse population of women, children, and men (Rhode, 1990; Fox-Genovese, 1991; cf. Sapp, 1992).

Recent studies of aging are also addressing the root question of what it is to be human, and the need to develop a fuller vision of human life in society. These authors stress the need to move beyond the "medical model" of aging toward new metaphors of human life in time (Birren, 1985–6; Kimble, 1990; Kenyon, Birren, and Schroots, 1991; Simmons, 1990) including a recovery of the profoundly spiritual dimensions of the human experience of aging (Bianchi, 1983; Birren, 1990; Kimble, 1989, 1990, 1991; Lefevre and Lefevre, 1981; Maitland, 1991; Nouwen and Gaffney, 1976; Seeber, 1990; Sittler, 1986). What these often wise and even deeply moving works propose is not merely an addendum on "spirituality" to a dominant medical model, but a paradigm shift in our understanding of human life which can transform both the experience of aging itself and the public perception and roles of older persons in church (Becker, 1986; Tilberg, 1984) and society (Bianchi, 1993, 175–224; Maitland, 1991,

117–146). To date, however, a large majority of these authors and the majority of their case studies and examples have been male, a limitation which several of them acknowledge explicitly. While studies on and voices of older women have begun to emerge (Alexander et al., 1991; Brody, 1990; Buchanan, 1987; Finger, 1991; Friedan, 1993; Martz, 1991; Saiving, 1988), much work remains to be done before the creative possibilities for a shared new paradigm of human life in time can be glimpsed.

As a discipline engaged in a mutually critical and constructive dialogue between a specific religious tradition and a specific contemporary situation, theology is involved with a double particularity: the particularity of the contemporary situation it seeks to engage—here, women, aging, and notions of the normatively human in contemporary U.S. society—and the particularity of the specific religious texts and traditions which it brings to the dialogue. A recognition of this doubly particular, deeply "local" character of theology has increasingly marked contemporary theology, and has been particularly evident in the vigorous expression of previously unheard women's voices in feminist, womanist (African-American), mujerista (Hispanic), Asian, and African theologies (Thistlethwaite and Engel, 1990). Not only are these exciting new theologies explicitly involved in the particularities of their cultures and social worlds, they are also marked by the particularities of their religious traditions (e.g., Christian, Jewish, Native American), their particular movements within those traditions (e.g., Roman Catholic, Lutheran, National Baptist, Reformed, Pentecostal) and by the particular theological approaches they engage (e.g., liberation theologies, process theologies, theologies of hope).

In rejecting ersatz claims to an abstract universality, however, such theologies need not succumb to a sheer relativism (Bernstein, 1983). Rather, it is precisely in and through their enactment of a mutually critical, mutually illuminating, and mutually enlivening dialogue between the particularities of their situation and the particularities of their religious traditions that such theologies open persons to the possibility of an enriched awareness of the ultimate context of all life: the encompassing reality of God.

As a theologian, I believe that the search for new paradigms of human life and human community in contemporary feminism and studies of aging must also finally engage critically and constructively with our deepest "root metaphors" for ultimate reality, for God, because these root metaphors shape profoundly both our perceptions of reality and our patterns of social interaction (Lakoff and Johnson, 1980). As a Christian, and specifically as a Lutheran, and even more specifically a trinitarian theologian, I believe that the reality of God's own life as a trinitarian community in which the whole of history is enhanced and will finally be transformed provides the ultimate context for all life and can richly enhance the understanding and experience of human life in time and community. The test of any such claim, however, is its ability to illumine the particulars. And so we turn to engage in theological dialogue with four particularities of women's lives and aging in contemporary U.S. society: (1) economic and social situation; (2) psychosocial development; (3) experience of embodiment; and (4) experience of time. The chapter closes with a discussion of the ways ritual can enact the creative dialogue of aging and religion by actually transforming the shape of our shared human lives in time.

THE ECONOMIC AND SOCIAL SITUATION OF OLDER WOMEN: A QUESTION OF JUSTICE

It is helpful to begin with some basics. First, U.S. society is aging. Although people over 65 in 1790 constituted just 2% of the U.S. population, in 1990 they constituted 12.6% of the U.S. population, and it is expected that by 2030 people over 65 will constitute 20–23%—nearly a quarter—of the U.S. population (Famighetti, 1993). People over 65 are the fastest growing group in the U.S. Moreover, today more than ten million are over 75 years old: we are also experiencing the "aging of the aged." While only 5% of the over-65 population are hospitalized or in nursing homes at any given time, there is nonetheless a widespread view of age as a time of decline (Lyon, 1985, ch. 2).

Second, since women live approximately seven to eight years longer than men, the majority of the elderly are female, and many live alone. As Kimble reports (Kimble, 1985), the average age of widowhood in the U.S. is 56. Of surviving spouses, 85% are female. Hence, while ¾ of men over 65 are married, ⅗ of women are not, and ⅔ of all widows over 65 live alone. Of all nursing home residents, ¾ are women.

Third, women over 65 are not only the fastest growing—and arguably the most isolated—group in American society. They are also among the poorest. The poverty rate for older women is nearly twice that for older men. Private pensions are not available to over 80% of retirement age women, and only 2% of widows receive benefits from their husbands' pensions. In fact, one-third of all widows live below the official poverty level (Kimble, 1985). When the data on women of color is isolated from these group statistics, the situation is even worse. In 1989 over half of black and Hispanic elderly females not living with their families were living at or below poverty level (Carstensen and Pasupathi, 1993, 75).

Finally, the situation is not likely to get any better for "baby boomer" generation women—who will reach 65 beginning in 2010—despite their entry into the workplace in large numbers. While media and advertising have lifted up the image of the well-paid "career woman," the reality is that 80% of all full-time working women today make less than $20,000 a year, are twice as likely as men to have no pension whatever, and far more likely than men to have no health insurance (Faludi, 1991, xiii). Moreover, even while working full-time, women still bear the major responsibility for primary childcare and for care of elderly parents, and so have difficulties in obtaining and keeping high-paying jobs. Indeed, single, divorced, and widowed women with their dependent children represent the largest and still rapidly growing group of poor people in U.S. society, a phenomenon which contemporary scholars have named the "feminization of poverty" (Sidel, 1992, 15–26). It is estimated that 25% of young women today will live at or near the poverty level in old age (Carstensen and Pasupathi, 1993).

Many voices have now begun to address some of the major public policy changes needed to alleviate some of the injustice manifest in these statistics and ultimately to reshape the political and moral economy of aging in U.S. society (Minkler and Estes, 1984; 1991). It has been pointed out, for instance, that current Medicare policy, requiring substantial diminishment of a couple's resources before providing for nursing home care, often leaves the surviving spouses—almost always women—with inadequate resources to sustain their own older years and so contributes to the disproportionately high levels of poverty among older women (England et al., 1991; Carstensen and Pasupathi, 1993). Yet, more than such reform is needed, as evidenced by the defeat of several proposals to modify Medicare's long-term care provisions and by the even more tragic spectacle of politicians forcing conflict between the needs of the two poorest, and two largely female populations in the U.S.—the elderly and children of single-parent women.

What is needed, Sapp argues in his analysis of American public policy on aging (Sapp, 1992), is a move beyond a political society envisioned as a battle of competing intergenerational interests for a share of a limited set of designated resources—a "zero-sum game"—toward a political society rooted in a larger vision of the common good shaped by the biblical and humane values of love for others, community, mercy and justice, spirituality, recognition of our dependence and mortality, and the beneficence of God. What Sapp points to is the need for a basic shift in the "root metaphor" of society and of justice. The biblical vision of a just society is not that of a blindfolded figure holding scales, blindly balancing competing claims, but that of a community characterized above all by its care for widows and fatherless children (e.g., Exodus 22:22-24)—precisely the two groups often pitted against each other. Regarding the need for a larger vision of society and the common good, analysts of aging policies, Biblical scholars, and third wave feminism converge. What is needed is a fundamental change in the root metaphors that shape basic moral, political and economic values and practices.

The root metaphor that has long shaped the U.S. political and social imagination has its origins in the Enlightenment. In particular, the impact of Newton's science of mechanics led to the envisioning of the universe as a vast machinery of interacting forces, while Locke's treatises on government extended this mechanistic metaphor into political life as well. Accordingly, as theologian Robert Jenson observes, the U.S. Constitution envisions political life as itself a kind of machine, a mechanism of "checks and balances" between competing forces that "would grind out liberty and justice mechanically, that is, independently of the personal dedication to liberty and justice of those who at any moment are the polity's cogs and levers" (Jenson, 1988, 8). Indeed, Michael Kammen entitled his book on the U.S. Constitution in terms of what the constitutional framers hoped the American political process might become under the constitution: *A Machine that Would Go of Itself* (Kammen, 1986). That politics is not a matter of public discourse engendering a shared vision of a common good, but is a matter of "power politics"—the clashing of competing forces and interests in a machinery of checks and balances—is all too deeply ingrained into our very sense of what it is to engage in politics and policy-making.

The Enlightenment not only generated a distinctive—and deeply problematic—image of cosmos and polis, however. It also generated a distinctive understanding of ultimate reality, of God: the deist god who sets the machine going and then, in the words of Bette Midler's Emmy award-winning song, "watches from a distance" as we battle it out below, the weakest and poorest continually losing.

If both church and culture are to move toward more life-giving root metaphors of cosmos, community, and the common good which can shape new approaches to public discourse and policy, a reimagining of the ultimate context and horizon of human life must occur. This ultimate context and horizon is the reality of God. Here Christian theology has a powerful proposal to make: that ultimate reality is not a machinelike thing or a distant watcher, but is personal, indeed tri-personal: three personal identities in a community of divine life. Ultimate reality—God's own life—is itself relational, a giving and receiving of divine life, in which all creation has its ultimate ground and horizon.

One of the most exciting developments in Christian theology in the past thirty years is the broad recovery of a trinitarian understanding of God rooted in biblical narrative and patristic theology (see Peters, 1987 a,b; Moltmann, 1981). The biblical and Christian God is not a distant, unchanging singularity, but in Jesus Christ and the Holy Spirit God is deeply involved in shared historical and human life. The community of divine life among Father, Son, and Holy Spirit embraces into itself and will finally transform the whole of history and creation in the resurrection from the dead inaugurated in Christ and his Spirit. God's life with humanity is profoundly historical, social, and eschatological.

What this recovery of a trinitarian understanding of God promises for both church and culture is a powerful reshaping of the understanding and experience of human life in time and community within the life of God, and so a powerful new framework for our moral and political economy.

In his study of the ways a trinitarian understanding of God could transform approaches to the economy, property, work, and justice, Meeks points out that people have also imagined the economy as a kind of machine, operating by fixed laws of the market, in which human beings are individual cogs and consumers—

a view of the human which has been called "possessive individualism." A very different vision of political and economic life is opened up by understanding that ultimate reality, God's own life, is a community of persons united in self-giving love.

> The ancient Cappadocian doctrine of perichoresis or the 'mutual coinherence' of the persons of the Trinity is a model of interrelationships of the members of the household that God intends. All the persons of the triune community have their own characteristics and their own tasks. Yet they are constituted as persons precisely by their relationships with the other persons of the community. (Meeks, 1989, 11-12)

"The same should be said for human economic community," Meeks continues:

> There is in reality no such thing as a radically individual and isolated human being. We are what we are as a result of being constituted by our relationships with the other members of the communities in which we live. All social goods are given to us communally. Such communal coinherence should be the presupposition of distributive justice. (Meeks, 1989, 12)

I would make only one major change in Meeks's proposal: the community of divine life in the triune God is not a "model" for persons to imitate but the very ground of life together in creation and community: God's communal life embraces into itself the whole of history and creation. Catherine LaCugna states this well in her recent book on the trinity: "There are not two sets of communion—one among the divine persons, the other among human persons, with the latter supposed to replicate the former. The one perichoresis, the one mystery of communion includes God and humanity as beloved partners in the dance" of communal life (LaCugna, 1991, 274).

IDENTITY AND RELATIONALITY: GENDER AND PSYCHOSOCIAL DEVELOPMENT

A common and influential image of human development in aging is that of an upward and then downward curve centered on work and economic productivity and characterized by a "mid-life crisis" (the beginning of the downward curve) and finding its final denouement in retirement. Now, however, there is growing evidence of the depressive and even deathly effect this construal of the pattern of life can have on many older men, whose suicide rates are the highest in the country (Miller, 1979, 11–12; Kimble, 1991, 71). What is desperately needed is not only a spiritual construal of this downward curve (Bianchi, 1993), but a new, more life-giving model for what it is to be a man. As a changing economy increasingly makes life-long job security a thing of the past, and as evidenced by these devastatingly high suicide rates, an image of manhood rooted in autonomy, work, and the "breadwinner" role has become increasingly deadly for many men. Important resources for this vital task of reimaging manhood can be found in the new men's studies that have appeared since 1970 (see Brod, 1987, for a review). The best of these studies both trace shifting paradigms of manhood in American history, and so give a far richer sense of the variety of models of manhood in the past, and creatively explore new models of manhood, lifting up ways men can be freed for a richer, more fully relational experience of their identity, callings, and value (Gerzon, 1982; Pleck and Pleck, 1980; Osherson, 1992; and especially Rotundo, 1993).

There is also growing evidence that this work-centered upward and downward curve simply does not apply to many women. The so-called "empty nest syndrome," once posited for women as analogous to the crises of mid-life and retirement in men, does not exist for many women, sociologist Lillian Rubin discovered more than a decade ago. "Almost all the women I spoke with," she disclosed, "respond to the departure of their children, whether actual or impending, with a decided sense of relief" (Rubin, 1979, 15). Rather than being a time of facing mortality and decline, mid-life is for many women a time of exploration and development of long deferred personal goals and new vocations (Block, Davidson, and Grambs, 1981). Hence, for many women, "aging offers new freedoms from the constraints of childrearing and homemaking, new opportunities, and even some degree of liberation from traditionally defined sex-role behavior" (Buchanan, 1987, 182). Both men and women need a new set of images for the shape of lives in time and for what it is to be a gendered human being.

As attention has turned in the last twenty years to the study of women's distinctive psychosocial experience and development, more and more studies have disclosed that psychological models of human development have tended to eclipse women's distinctive developmental journeys and values. One of the most influential of these studies of women's distinctive psychological identity and development is Nancy Chodorow's *The Reproduction of Mothering* (1978). Chodorow begins her work with the observation that most primary childcare is done by women. The differences in male and female psychology and values, she argues, emerge from the fact that both male and female children develop their most elemental sense of themselves, their gender identities, and their patterns of relationship with others, out of their primary relationship with a female caretaker. The male child, in order to achieve a male gender identity, does so by a process of separation and individuation over against the mother, while the female child achieves her gender identity and sense of value through a process of identification with and preservation of relationship with the mother. From this matrix emerge quite distinct forms of self-identity, values, and patterns of relating to others: for boys, independence and autonomy; for girls, nurturing and preserving relationship. From this matrix emerge as well the distinctive pathologies of each: males can become so negative and preoccupied with separation as to have difficulty forming or sustaining relationship, while females can become so identified and even fused with others as to fail to become a distinct self.

The even more influential work of Carol Gilligan (1982) extends into the arena of moral development and ethics this idea that male identity and values are premised on separation and female identity and values are rooted in preservation of relationship . Gilligan's book addresses in particular Kohlberg's theory of moral development which posits six stages marked by an increasingly autonomous self-identity and growing capacity to abstract relevant moral values out of situations and to assess their comparative weight. In Kohlberg's schema, women are most often placed at stage three: Rather than autonomously evaluating abstract goods, women tend to seek compromise solutions that will keep everyone involved in the sustaining community of relationships.

In contrast to Kohlberg's schema, and in implicit contrast to a broader Enlightenment idealization of autonomous man (Benhabib, 1987), Gilligan argues for the revaluation of the distinctive "ethic of care" exemplified in many girls' and women's lives: a conviction that life itself is sustained through the preservation of caring personal and social relationships. Susan Moller Okin points out that Kohlberg's stage three (where most women are placed) confuses the idea that moral behavior is what pleases or is approved by others (characteristic of children's thinking) with the notion that moral behavior is what helps others, and so simply fails to recognize the moral significance of an ethic of care (Okin, 1990). Indeed, others argue, within such an ethic of relationality and care lies a crucial resource for reimagining the whole of social and political life, beyond the morass created by all too pernicious individualism (Cole and McQuin, 1992; Noddings, 1984; 1990; Tronto, 1993).

The work of the Stone Center at Wellesley College (Jordan et al., 1991) develops even more carefully and fully both a critique of the emphasis on autonomy in many psychologies—including a critique of Erik Erikson's developmental psychology—and a constructive alternative. The human developmental process, they argue, is not paradigmatically to be understood as a process of separation and individuation, but rather as a process of developing increasing capacities for mature and complex interrelationships with others. At every stage of development, the human being is fundamentally a "self-in-relation," and assessment of psychological growth and health should be normed by capacities for increasingly mature and complex interrelationships. Such a paradigm, they argue, both would be a richer one for men (Jordan et al., 1991, 7) and would enable the recognition and revaluing of women's experience of their self-identity and self-value. Women's core sense of self and of self-value, they argue, is rooted in their sense of their capacity empathically to relate to and care for others—a capacity too often denigrated as inadequate individuation or even as "co-dependency"—and to receive reciprocal empathic responses and care from others. They then explore the implications of this for counseling relationships with women, understanding and treating depression in women, education, and the workplace.

What is the significance of all of this for a feminist theology of aging? First, both the new men's studies and these studies of women's development and values help provide a critical perspective on the normative model of what it is to be human that is embedded in psychological theories of aging. In the logotherapy of Victor Frankl, for instance, although there is much that is important and helpful, it is not difficult to discern an emphasis on autonomous self-definition and heroic striving rather different from the paradigm of the self-in-relation and an ethic of community and care. In his analysis of Frankl's work and its significance for aging (Kimble, 1990), Kimble points to three central values in Frankl's work which help highlight this: (1) a conviction the "'man is ultimately self-determining'" and "'always decides what his existence will be, what he will become in the next moment'" (Frankl cited in Kimble, 1990, 118); (2) a sense of integrity is achieved in the "eternalization of the past" in memory, a past that cannot be taken away (121); and (3) the "defiant power of the human spirit" as a reflection of the very image of God in each human individual (123–4). A model of the "self-in-relation" and an "ethic of care" at least raise questions about whether such a view of human life could speak to the lives of women, whether it is finally the most potentially fruitful resource even for men, and what its implications might be for a larger vision of community and society.

Biblical and theological perspectives might helpfully be brought into this conversation (Dulin, 1988; Harris, 1987; Knierim, 1981; Sapp, 1987; Stagg, 1981). While there is certainly a variety of vividly wrought human characters in the Bible, and so a rich variety of portraits of human life—Job is quite a "defiant spirit," for instance—the renewal of a rich web of communal relationships seems to be a major biblical value, even in the book of Job. To be sure, Job's defiant spirit and insistent self-definition as a righteous man (over against both his "friends" and God) are important and even creative, and ultimately contribute to God's unleashing of a wildly more inclusive creation (Job 38-41) and community (Job 42). Job's defiant spirit and insistent self-definition may well speak with particular power to those who, like Job, are in the midst of the crisis of experiencing the wrongful loss of their former public role, status, and power in the community, and so perhaps particularly to postretirement men. But defiant self-definition is not finally the whole story. Where does Job most fully "image" God—only in his act of individual defiance, or in the final role he plays bringing his erstwhile "friends" and previously nameless daughters into a vastly expanded new creation and community (Job 42:7-17)?

Other studies of aging and religion have relied on the developmental "stages of faith" developed by James Fowler (Fowler, all) in conversation with the developmental studies of Piaget, Kohlberg, Erikson, and others. In the introductory essay in *Faith Development in the Adult Life Cycle* (Stokes, 1982)—a report on research on adult faith development—Bruning and Stokes explicitly note that most of the researchers and subjects were men, and that caution is needed in drawing conclusions about women, especially if judged by a male standard, as

Gilligan's studies suggest (Stokes, 1982, 26–27). Yet no critical reconstruction of the normative "stages" is undertaken, and in his 1990 summary of the data, Stokes simply reports that most women define faith as "a relationship with God" and are found to be in the (relatively low) developmental stage three, "characterized by socialization and dependency," in contrast to higher stage men, who define faith as "a set of beliefs" and who tend to be more "internalized and independent" (Stokes, 1990, 175–176). Once again, a question may at least be raised: Why is relationality with God and others less "developed" than independence?

Many of the schools of "family therapy" that are so influential in social work training and practice—and so also for many older and elderly persons—are also open to question about their implicit norms of human being and value. In her intelligent and careful critical analysis of eight distinct schools of family therapy, including those of Murray Bowen, Salvador Minuchin, and Carl Whitaker, Deborah Luepnitz points out the presence in them of an Enlightenment model of "autonomous man" and the multiple ways in their therapeutic strategies undervalue, demean, or even attack women's relational self-identities and values (Luepnitz, 1988). In many of these psychologies and in the broader society, she argues, there is a pervasive tendency toward the blaming and depersonalization of mothers. Mothers tend to appear only as engulfing presences to be negated and controlled for proper separation and individuation to take place—not as persons whose own personhood needs to be recognized and built up. Indeed, she writes, "one might say that the institution of family therapy, like the institution of the family itself, has built deep into its foundations a forceful denial of maternal subjectivity" (Luepnitz, 1988, 154). The object-relations theory of D. W. Winnicott and others provides a better resource, she and others argue, because it recognizes that the most basic of human needs is for relationships of mutual empathic responsiveness and recognition. For Winnicott, genuine identity—for both mother and child—is not premised on the negation of the mother, but is constituted through a developing reciprocal recognition and appreciation of the personal uniqueness of each other in the "intersubjective space" of play. Once again, it is important to move beyond models of "autonomous man"—whose often hidden subtext is the negation and depersonalization of caretaking women—toward a more life-giving model of "selves-in-relation."

There are dangers in identifying women too exclusively with caretaking and relationality, dangers of overgeneralization that obscure the realities of race and class (Spelman, 1988), and the danger of legitimating exploitation. As sociologist Rosabeth Moss Kanter points out, common observations about women—they are more relationally oriented than achievement oriented, more concerned with friendships developed in the workplace than with the work itself—are true of both men and women in positions of blocked opportunity or limited power and responsibility. Dead-ends lead people to focus their commitments and sources of self-esteem elsewhere, to focus on work relationships and social situations rather than on task accomplishment or achievement: being well-liked itself becomes a form of success. Indeed, Kanter's work suggests, the whole idea of women's greater capacity for interpersonal relationship may be more an effect of blocked opportunities than of a natural propensity (Kanter, 1977). For too long, the roles of relational caretaking or work achievement have been assigned only to women and men, respectively, to the detriment of the lives of both. All human beings—at every age—need both mutually empathic relationships and socially and economically supported aspirations and achievements.

What difference does all this make for a feminist theology of aging? Emerging new models of human life in men's and women's studies not only provide a critical perspective on the psychological models employed in studies of religion and aging and so resources for theological anthropology, they also help provide a critical and constructive resource for a theological account of the dynamics of life together in God.

Consider, for example, the theology of sin and grace. In a 1960 article entitled "The Human Situation: A Feminine View," which is now widely acknowledged to have inaugurated contemporary Christian feminist theology, Valerie Saiving argues that theology's omission of women's voices and experience results in a skewed account of the human situation and of the realities of sin and grace (Saiving, 1960). Theologians such as Reinhold Niebuhr and Paul Tillich understand sin fundamentally as rooted in an overly separated, self-enclosed self—pride—while grace is understood as a shattering of the self which opens one to new community with others and with God. Yet for many women, Saiving argues, the problem is an overly diffuse existence spread out endlessly into everyone else's feelings and needs. Sin also needs to be understood as a failure to value and actualize one's own self-identity and grace needs to be articulated as an empowering of authentic selfhood, not the further shattering of an already centerless existence. Both men's and women's experience are needed, she concludes, for a fuller account of the human situation and the dynamics of sin and grace.

Consider as well the reality of God. The Enlightenment model of "autonomous man" and the deist conception of God as a distant, self-enclosed "one," are clearly parallel, and doubly wrong. The recovery from biblical and patristic sources of an historical understanding of God's life allows the recognition that first, God and humanity are not parallel images of each other, but that God's life opens out in Jesus Christ and the Holy Spirit to include the whole of human history and creation within itself. The triune God is not a distant mirror image of humanity, but the encompassing ground and horizon of all of history and creation. Second, the recovery as well from biblical and patristic sources of a social understanding of the relationality within the triune God underscores the ultimacy of relationality in the constitution of reality. Within the life of the triune God, and among all created life in God, relationality generates each personal identity, and the personal identities thus generated in turn constitute and transform the dynamics of their relationality. In short, as John Zizioulas puts it in the title of his book on trinity, it is essential to understand *Being as Communion* (Zizioulas, 1985). Moreover, as we shall see in the next two sections, the triune life of God is both at its heart profoundly incarnational and, in its telos, wildly inclusive.

EMBODIMENT AND SHAME: GOD "DEEP IN THE FLESH"

Too often in American culture, the realities of human bodiliness and the bodily changes of aging are feared and repressed, and hence are sources of one of the most searing of human experiences: a deep sense of shame about the very body that gives each one of us our particular and only means of participation in life. Anyone who has worked with older persons undergoing diminished control of bodily functions knows how devastatingly shame-filled this experience can be and the importance of preserving a sense of dignity and integrity through such losses. The elderly are not alone, however, in this fear of exposure and shame. As a growing number of both popular and scholarly books attest, a debilitating fear of exposure and sense of shame seem increasingly to be replacing both guilt and low self-esteem as the presenting problems in psychologists' and pastors' offices all over the country (Kaufman, 1980; Nathanson, 1987; Smedes, 1993). The problem at root is not a sense of having violated an internalized norm (guilt), but a sense of shamefulness and fear of exposure which rend the very core of the self and call for new kinds of healing pastoral response (Albers, 1985).

A sense of shame related to bodiliness may be particularly powerful among women, exacerbated by media representations of women's bodies and by centuries of religious and cultural misogynism. As Margaret Miles points out in her study of images of women's bodies in the history of Christian art (Miles, 1989), women's bodies have been represented for centuries to the popular religious imagination as dangerously entrapping, loathsome and even grotesque objects rather than as locations of unique, and often uniquely vulnerable, human life and personal subjectivity. Several centuries of the persecution, torture, and murder of possibly millions of aging women as witches lie hidden deep in our collective history and consciousness. Rather than being portrayed only as objects, Miles proposes, women's bodies—including women's aging bodies—need to be publicly represented in art and the popular media as bearers of human subjectivity, as locations of distinctively human voices. Only in this way, she argues, will it be possible to "limit the projection of male fears and longings and, ultimately, reassure men that, in Calypso's words, "'the heart within me is not of iron, but yearning, like yours'" (Miles, 1989, 168).

Although there is some evidence of this needed public representation of older women in shows like "Golden Girls," "Murder She Wrote," the movie "Fried Green Tomatoes," and popular books like *When I Am An Old Woman, I Shall Wear Purple* (Martz, 1991), Miles and other Christian feminists point to the need for an even deeper transformation in the understanding and experience of embodiment and aging. More than a quarter of a century after she wrote the inaugural article in contemporary Christian feminist theology, Valerie Saiving has now published a theological reflection on human bodiliness and aging which may well have a similar epochal significance for Christian feminist theology (Saiving, 1988). "As an older woman," she begins, "I sometimes wonder whether the women's movement is made up exclusively of women between the ages of 16 and 45, for so little is ever said about what it means to be human after the later age" (Saiving, 1988, 117).

The neglect of older women and of aging in the women's movement is but a part of a larger phenomenon in Western religious history, Saiving argues: a persistent opposition of bodiless, formless Spirit to bodily particularity. At the heart of this, she argues, is a peculiarly Western nihilism, a hatred of the actual:

> To exist, to be in the full sense is to be something concrete, definite, limited; it is to be finite. . . . Potentiality becomes ecstasy only when it becomes actuality, that is, when it becomes finite. It seemed . . . that the long history of hatred of the body and idealization of an impossible bodiless Spirit was, in the final analysis, the history of human rebellion against the finitude of the human creature, the finitude of everything actual. (Saiving, 1988, 120)

Growth into actuality is growth into the increasing particularity of bodies with age, bodies which are the very medium of communion with God, with others, and with the earth—and so the medium of all joy. Saiving recounts that since her youth she experienced herself and her body as essentially one and was glad this was so: "Every ecstatic moment, every experience of beauty, love, or peace I had known had come to me through my human body" (Saiving, 1988, 119). Even now, after many years of struggling with crippling arthritis, heart disease, and depression, she affirms the need to recognize that even these "are simply more extreme expressions of that same finitude which is our bodiliness and the indispensable ground of joy" (122).

Saiving's persuasive and moving article enriches a sense of the concrete actuality and bodily diversity in all creation, without developing any explicitly Christian themes. Consistent with her observations, however, is "the hint half-guessed, the gift half-understood" that lies at the heart of Christianity and indeed at the center of God's own triune life: the incarnation of God in Jesus Christ, God "deep in the flesh" of bodily, finite, cruciform human life. For Christians, growth into the actuality of particular, finite bodies with age is an ever deepening journey into God "deep in the flesh" in Jesus Christ, an ever deepening actualization of our baptism into the corporeal and communal body of Christ. Hence aging and death need to be seen not just as part of the "downward slope" of human life but in light of the paschal mystery of Christ (Curran, 1981). In this light, death can be seen (1) as a natural, bodily event, what Saiving might call the completing moment of finite particularity and actuality, and (2) as taking place in Christ, in whom even the chasm of death is taken into God's life. Yet also, death can be seen (3) as intimately connected with sin, which crucified Christ and which violates and rips life with each other and God and, finally, (4) in light of Christ's triumph over sin and death in the resurrection, promising the bodily transformation of all earthly existence.

Saiving concludes her article with three suggestions for an approach to aging. First, she argues, Western civilization is a "complex, tortuous, partly unconscious series of efforts" to deny bodiliness and finite actuality, efforts which have "paradoxically created ever more terrible forms of aging and death," including torture, war, and the exploitation of the earth; we need "to undo a social order based on denial of the living body and to create a new order based on its affirmation" (123–124). Second, the affirmation of bodily existence also entails the ability to affirm old age, sickness, and death as part of the journey into actuality. As it is, there seems to be no room in this society for the aged, and the chronically ill, crippled, and dying seem to be "an embarrassment to everyone, including themselves," thus compounding the bodily pain of aging with the even greater pain of shame and isolation. We need an "imaginative vision of the kind of human community in which we might be able to affirm life in its totality" so that "others might be truly with us" in our experiences of illness, loss, and death (124). Finally, she concludes, we need "to place ourselves in a larger whole" of community, cosmos, and the life of God in which "the self participates and finds itself affirmed" (124).

THE GIFT OF THE FUTURE: THE SHAPE AND PURPOSE OF OUR LIVES IN TIME

The experience of aging is integrally interrelated with human efforts to develop a sense of the shape and purpose of lives in time. Many have pointed out, for instance, the importance of a process of "life review": the creative, healing work of generating a sense of the shape, coherence, and meaning of lives in time in story form. This process of life review is inseparable, however, from larger societal, cultural, and religious construals of the shape of shared life in time as human beings. And today, unfortunately, U.S. society and culture provide little that is life-giving in this regard. Not only the elderly, but also increasing numbers of youth and young adults seem to have been given no view of the future except as a time of lowered expectations, decline, and death.

Martin Luther long ago pointed out that everyone has a "god" of some sort—something or someone to rely on to be the ultimate source of help in times of need. More recently, Lutheran theologian Robert Jenson has argued that what all people ultimately rely on includes some provision of a sense of the shape and purpose of their lives in time (Jenson, 1982, 1–5). There are many such gods—

many different patternings of time—represented in the world's religions, he observes (see also Sokolovsky, 1990). In some religious traditions, sacrality is located in the past, in the ancestors, and time is understood as a continual repetition of that sacred past—a continual repetition of 'the way it's always been done.' In other religious traditions, both past and future disappear into a timeless nirvana, while Western existentialism eclipses every past and future with the "now" of existential decision. In Christianity, however, the resurrection of Jesus Christ as the first-fruits of a general resurrection of the dead decisively transforms the ultimate shape of time, Jenson argues. For Jesus is alive, the victor over death, and in the Spirit of his resurrection life comes bearing the promise and foretaste of his final future for all humanity. Humanity need not work toward an endlessly deferred future; rather, an astonishingly gracious future comes toward humanity in the risen Jesus. For Christianity, in short, the center of gravity for shared human life in time is not an eternalized past or timeless now, but the promise and power of an astonishingly gracious new future already coming toward humanity and all creation in the risen Jesus.

I would modify Jenson's proposal only by stressing that both the cross and the resurrection of Christ decisively transform time. What is effected in the cross and resurrection is a radical discontinuity in the very heart of human life in time. The son of God on the cross, Paul proclaims, effects an apocalyptic shattering of the old creation and its structures and powers, while the resurrection of Christ is the first fruits of a radically new creation, a volcanic upsurging of life out of death which will finally spill out to transform even past lives, to raise the dead. Thus the cross also has tremendous significance for the experience of time and aging. God is with humanity in Jesus Christ, right down to the depths of suffering, sin, and death: nothing can separate people from the love of God in Christ Jesus. Even more, however, God in Christ's entry into the depths of sin, death, and the demonic is not simply to have persons all stay there, but to expose, judge, and explode open those powers: to engage in a terrible battle. Far from legitimating or endorsing the suffering that sin and death bring into the world, the cross exposes and condemns it and calls for participation in the battle, sure of the victory promised in the risen Jesus. The poverty, isolation, shame, suffering and death in the world—including that experienced by the aging and elderly, most of them women—is not endorsed but exposed by the cross, which also incorporates the faithful into the battle and creates a radical discontinuity between old and new creation.

This new creation is already approaching from the future. The recovery of eschatology is, with trinity, one of the two most important developments in Christian theology in the modern period. Here, eschatology is not just an exploration of far off, distant "last things"—a final appendix to Christian faith and theology—but has to do with the reality of a radically new future already begun in the risen Jesus and approaching humanity in him. The future comes to human beings, and it comes as gift.

What is the significance of such a sense of the shape of time for the experience of aging? Perhaps, first, it could help replace the sense of time as endless decline to open up a sense of the possibilities in each new future, and so change both the experience of life in the present and the ways one understands and narrates the past. As the historian Arthur Danto has pointed out, the future does reshape the understanding of the past: the people who were in the Thirty Years' War didn't know they were in the Thirty Years' War. Further experience of life in time involves mourning and loss, but it also continually opens people to understand anew the significance of past events in light of the dawning future, and so presents new possibilities of understanding and action in the present. Life review need not only be an event of closure, of letting go, but can also be a continual process of understanding and telling stories anew, opening people up to new possibilities of self-understanding and action in the present, however limited these might be. Both individually and collectively, people need not finally cling to an eternalized past but are opened by and to an ever new future.

Second, such a construal of life in time might well nurture greater interrelationship between generations. The eschatological symbols of Judaism and Christianity, reveal that time is not "a series of atomic moments that tends to coopt the young, imprison the mature, and forget the old" but that life is a continually creative interaction of future, past, and present (Tracy, 1975, 132). Too often aging and elderly persons get assigned to a remote and irrelevant past, while youth are pushed out toward a shapeless, formless, yawning future. What a difference it might make if youth could be brought together with the aging and elderly so as to see there the coming toward them of a future with a richly human face; and both young and old could work together to reshape a sense of the promise as well as the perils of their lives in time.

Finally, such a reshaping of the basic sense of life in time might well help shape a powerful sense of just how wildly encompassing is the larger whole. God in the resurrection of Christ has opened up all the graves of history to await a word which will finally raise all the dead and give new life to the whole of creation. The community of this new creation extends across all the eons of human time and into the farthest reaches of the universe.

GRACE AND RITUAL

So far this paper has presented a theological discussion of (1) the character of a just society, (2) human beings as selves-in-relation, (3) human bodiliness, and (4) the shape of human lives in time. Throughout, I have proposed that the reality of God's own life as a trinitarian community in which the whole of history is embraced and will finally be transformed critically illumines and is illumined by each of these four dimensions of human aging.

Theological discussion, however, is not enough. Bodily and communal—"corporate" in a double sense—rituals are needed through which the grace of

God is actually communicated and enacted in and among persons to shape a new public reality in their relational, bodily, and temporal lives together. For the Christian church, these powerful ritual means of grace include the proclamation of the Word, baptism, confession and absolution, and holy communion; means through which God actually embraces people into God's triune life. These rituals are the foundation and life-blood of Christian community.

Rituals are not only enacted in churches, however. Rituals occur in daily lives—in the realm that Lutherans call the "left hand of God"—to order time and to connect people with each other and the world in reliable and meaningful ways: bedtime stories, birthday parties, rituals of greeting and parting, even conventions about which way to face in elevators, and many others. God is working silently in these rituals as well, through the left hand, continually ordering created life, shaping life in community, restraining chaos and evil.

A great deal of the isolation, loneliness, poverty, and sense of shame in the human experience of aging in American society has to do with the fact that there are virtually no rituals through which people corporately enact and celebrate the major transitions in life, nor celebrate the reality and presence of the aging and elderly among us. Rather, the process of aging is privatized, hidden away, and even rendered shameful, depriving all persons of any sense that their own futures might have a richly human face.

Consider, for example, a life transition which has a devastating impact on many elderly: moving from one's home into a nursing care facility. How much different might that transition be were people from the person's family and friends from the neighborhood, church, and work convened by a pastor or other leader to enact with that person a beautifully planned double ritual: a ritual walk through each room of the house, recounting the story of a particular event or events in the family's life which happened in each room and ritually consecrating that room and that memory to God, followed by carrying to the new residence some objects evocative of those stories and a ritual of blessing for the new residence. How much richer might be the lives of *all* who participated in such an event.

There are many other possibilities for rituals of life transition, for instance a communal rite of retirement (Simmons, 1990, 162–164) or a ritual to celebrate the new possibilities for a mother and new relationship for the parents and family on the departure from home of the last child. Moreover, rituals of transition are not the only possibilities. Rituals should be developed that celebrate and enact new realities of community life, for instance involving youth and elderly together. Shared socio-political life also has a ritual dimension, and could benefit from actualizing this ritual dimension more carefully and fully so as genuinely to open up a public space for civil discourse—not just a battle of competing interests. As Keifert argues in his book on ritual and the creation of public space, an "ideology of intimacy" exacerbates fear of exposure and shame. Ritual simultaneously respects the inviolable boundaries of personal identity and integrity and joins people together in a new public space, a new creation (Keifert, 1992).

There is no pat formula for developing such rituals. What is important is for the pastor or other leader to engage with the person, family, and community to discern the narrative and ritual patterns already nascently at work in the situation and to use a creative ritual imagination in developing an appropriate and effective rite. There is now a growing number of books which help prompt more creative ritual imaginations (Imber-Black and Roberts, 1988, 1992; Myerhoff, 1992; Nelson, 1986; Ramshaw, 1987).

Care is needed. As Barbara Myerhoff observes, ritual done badly is worse than no ritual at all, for it threatens to uncover everything as mere play-acting, as sham. Ritual done well, however, may not only transform the shape of shared human lives, but even bring people unexpectedly into the presence of the living God (Myerhoff, 1992, 159–190). And that is something no theology can ever do.

BIBLIOGRAPHY

Albers, R. H. (1995) *Shame: A Faith Perspective.* New York: Haworth.

Alexander, B. B. et al. (1991) "Generativity in Cultural Context: The Self, Death and Immortality as Experienced by Older American Women." *Aging and Society* 11:417–42.

Atkinson, C. W., C. H. Buchanan, and M. R. Miles (1987) *Shaping New Vision: Gender and Values in American Culture.* Ann Arbor, Mich.: UMI Research Press.

Becker, A. H. (1986) *Ministry With Older Persons: A Guide for Clergy and Congregations.* Minneapolis, Minn.: Augsburg.

Benhabib, S. (1987) "The Generalized and the Concrete Other: The Kohlberg-Gilligan Controversy and Feminist Theory." In Benhabib and Cornell, 77–95.

Benhabib, S., and D. Cornell, eds. (1987) *Feminism As Critique.* Minneapolis, Minn.: University of Minnesota.

Bernstein, R. J. (1983) *Beyond Objectivism and Relativism: Science, Hermeneutics, and Praxis.* Philadelphia: University of Pennsylvania.

Bianchi, E. C. (1993) *Aging as a Spiritual Journey.* 2d ed. New York: Crossroad.

Birren, J. E. (1985) "Aging as a Scientific and Value-Laden Field of Inquiry." *Journal of Religion and Aging* 2:29–39.

______ (1990) "Spiritual Maturity in Psychological Development." *Journal of Religious Gerontology* 7:41–54.

Block, M. R., J. L. Davidson, and J. D. Grambs (1989) *Women Over Forty: Visions and Realities.* Rev. ed. New York: Springer.

Brod, H. (1987) *The Making of Masculinities: The New Men's Studies.* Boston: Allen and Unwin.

Brody, C. M. (1990) "Women in a Nursing Home: Living with Hope and Meaning." *Psychology of Women Quarterly* 14:579–92.

Buchanan, C. H. (1987) "The Fall of Icarus: Gender, Religion, and the Aging Society." In Atkinson, Buchanan, and Miles, 169–90.

Carstensen, L. L., and M. Pasupathi (1993) "Women of a Certain Age." In Matteo, 66–77.

Chodorow, N. (1978) *The Reproduction of Mothering: Psychoanalysis and the Sociology of Gender.* Berkeley: University of California Press.

Clements, W. M., ed. (1981) *Ministry With the Aging.* San Francisco: Harper and Row.

Cole, E. B., and S. C. McQuin, eds. (1992) *Explorations in Feminist Ethics: Theory and Practice.* Indianapolis: Indiana University.

Curran, C. E. (1981) "Aging: A Theological Perspective." In LeFevre and LeFevre, 68–82.

Dulin, R. Z. (1988) *A Crown of Glory: A Biblical View of Aging.* New York: Paulist.

England, S. E. et al. (1991) "Community Care Policies and Gender Justice." In Minkler and Estes, 227–44.

Faludi, S. (1991) *Backlash: The Undeclared War Against American Women.* New York: Crown.

Famighetti, R., ed. (1993) *The World Almanac and Book of Facts, 1994,* p. 363, from U.S. Bureau of the Census; 1990 Census. Funk & Wagnalls: Mahwah, NJ.

Farley, M. A. (1985) "Feminist Consciousness and the Interpretation of Scripture." In Russell, 41–51.

Finger, R. H. (1991) "A New Wrinkle on Time: Women and Aging." Daughters of Sarah 17:2–21.

Fowler, J. (1981) *Stages of Faith: The Psychology of Human Development and the Quest for Meaning.* New York: Harper and Row.

Fox-Genovese, E. (1991) *Feminism Without Illusions: A Critique of Individualism.* Chapel Hill: University of North Carolina.

Friedan, B. (1993) *The Fountain of Age.* New York: Simon and Schuster.

Gerzon, M. (1982) *A Choice of Heroes: The Changing Face of American Manhood.* Boston: Houghton Mifflin.

Gilligan, C. (1982) *In a Different Voice: Psychological Theory and Women's Development.* Cambridge, Mass.: Harvard University Press.

Hall, D. J. (1986) *Imaging God: Dominion as Stewardship.* New York: Friendship.

Harris, J. G. (1987) *Biblical Perspectives on Aging: God and the Elderly.* Philadelphia: Fortress.

Hiltner, S., ed. (1975) *Toward a Theology of Aging.* New York: Human Sciences Press.

Imber-Black, E., J. Roberts, and R. Whiting, eds. (1988) *Rituals in Families and Family Therapy.* New York: Norton.

______ (1992) *Rituals For Our Times: Celebrating, Healing, and Changing Our Lives and Our Relationships.* New York: HarperCollins.

Jenson, R. W. (1982) *The Triune Identity: God According to the Gospel.* Philadelphia: Fortress.

______ (1988) *America's Theologian: A Recommendation of Jonathan Edwards.* New York: Oxford University.

Jordan, J. V. et al. (1991) *Women's Growth in Connection: Writings From the Stone Center.* New York: Guilford.

Kammen, M. (1986) *A Machine That Would Go of Itself: The Constitution in American Culture*. New York: Alfred A. Knopf.

Kanter, R. M. (1977) *Men and Women of the Corporation*. New York: Basic.

Kaufman, G. (1985) *Shame: The Power of Caring*. Cambridge, Mass.: Schenkman.

Keifert, P. R. (1992) *Welcoming the Stranger: A Public Theology of Worship and Evangelism*. Minneapolis, Minn.: Fortress.

Kenyon, G. M., J. E. Birren, and J. F. Schroots, eds. (1993) *Metaphors of Aging in Science and the Humanities*. New York: Springer.

Kimble, M. A. (1985) "The Surviving Majority: Differential Impact of Aging and Implications for Ministry." *Word and World* 5:395–404.

______ (1989) "The Nurture of the Elderly: Aging and the Crisis of Meaning." *Word and World* 9:154–65.

______ (1990) "Aging and the Search for Meaning." In Seeber, 111–29.

______ (1991) "Religion: Friend or Foe of the Aging?" *Second Opinion* 15:70–81.

Knierim, R. (1981) "Age and Aging in the Old Testament." In Clements, 21–36.

LaCugna, C. (1991) *God For Us: The Trinity and Christian Life*. San Francisco: Harper.

Lakoff, G., and M. Johnson (1980) *Metaphors We Live By*. Chicago: University of Chicago.

LeFevre, C., and P. LeFevre, eds. (1981) *Aging and the Human Spirit: A Reader in Religion and Gerontology*. Chicago: Exploration Press.

Lewis, M. I., and R. N. Butler (1984) "Why is Women's Lib Ignoring Old Women?" In Minkler and Estes, 199–08.

Luepnitz, D. A. (1988) *The Family Interpreted: Psychoanalysis, Feminism, and Family Therapy*. New York: Basic.

Lyon, K. B. (1985) *Toward a Practical Theology of Aging*. Philadelphia: Fortress.

Mackinnon, C. A. (1990) "Legal Perspectives on Sexual Difference." In Rhode, 213–25.

Maitland, D. J. (1991) *Aging as Counterculture: A Vocation for the Later Years*. New York: Pilgrim.

Martz, S. (1991) *When I Am An Old Woman I Shall Wear Purple*. Watsonville, Calif.: Papier-Mache.

Matteo, S., ed. (1993) *American Women in the Nineties: Today's Critical Issues*. Boston: Northeastern University.

Meeks, M. D. (1989) *God the Economist: The Doctrine of God and Political Economy*. Minneapolis, Minn.: Fortress.

Miles, M. R. (1989) *Carnal Knowing: Female Nakedness and Religious Meaning in the Christian West*. New York: Beacon.

Miller, M. (1979) *Suicide After Sixty*. New York: Springer.

Minkler, M., and C. L. Estes, eds. (1984) *Readings in the Political Economy of Aging*. Farmingdale, NY: Baywood.

______ (1991) *Critical Perspectives on Aging: The Political and Moral Economy of Growing Old*. Amityville, NY: Baywood.

Moltmann, J. (1981) *The Trinity and the Kingdom*. New York: Harper and Row.

Myerhoff, B. (1992) *Remembered Lives: The Work of Ritual, Storytelling, and Growing Older.* Ann Arbor, Mich.: University of Michigan.

Nathanson, D., ed. (1987) *The Many Faces of Shame.* New York: Guilford.

Nelson, G. M. (1986) *To Dance With God: Family Ritual and Community Celebration.* New York: Paulist.

Noddings, N. (1984) *Caring: A Feminine Approach to Ethics and Moral Education.* Berkeley, Calif.: University of California Press.

______ (1990) "Ethics from the Standpoint of Women." In Rhode, 160–73.

Nouwen, H. J. M., and W. J. Gaffney (1976) *Aging: The Fulfillment of Life.* New York: Doubleday.

Okin, S. M. (1989) *Justice, Gender, and the Family.* New York: Basic.

______ (1990) "Thinking Like A Woman." In Rhode, 145–59.

Osherson, S. (1992) *Wrestling With Love: How Men Struggle with Intimacy.* New York: Fawcett Columbine.

Peters, T. (1987a) "Trinity Talk: Part 1." Dialog 26:44–48.

______ (1987b) "Trinity Talk: Part 2." Dialog 26:133–38.

Pleck, E.H., and J. H. Pleck, eds. (1980) *The American Man.* New Jersey: Prentice-Hall.

Ramshaw, E. (1987) *Ritual and Pastoral Care.* Philadelphia: Fortress.

Rhode, D. L., ed. (1990) *Theoretical Perspectives on Sexual Difference.* New Haven, Conn.: Yale University.

Rotundo, E. A. (1993) *American Manhood: Transformations in Masculinity from the Revolution to the Modern Era.* New York: Basic.

Rubin, L. B. (1979) *Women of a Certain Age: The Midlife Search for Self.* New York: Harper and Row.

Russell, L. M., ed. (1985) *Feminist Interpretation of the Bible.* Philadelphia: Westminster.

Saiving, V. (1960) "The Human Situation: A Feminine View." *Journal of Religion* 40:151–70.

______ (1988) "Our Bodies/Our Selves: Reflections on Sickness, Aging, and Death." *Journal of Feminist Studies in Religion* 4:117–25, Fall.

Sapp, S. (1987) *Full of Years: Aging and the Elderly in the Bible and Today.* Nashville: Abingdon.

______ (1992) *Light on a Gray Area: American Public Policy on Aging.* Nashville: Abingdon.

Seeber, J. J., ed. (1990) *Spiritual Maturity in the Later Years.* New York: Haworth.

Sidel, R. (1992) *Women and Children Last: The Plight of Poor Women in Affluent America.* New York: Viking Penguin.

Simmons, H. C. (1990) "Countering Cultural Metaphors of Aging." In Seeber, 153–66.

Sittler, J. (1986) *Gravity and Grace: Reflections and Provocations.* Minneapolis, Minn.: Augsburg.

______ (1986) "Aging: A Summing Up and a Letting Go." In Sittler, 119–27.

Smedes, L. B. (1993) *Shame and Grace: Healing the Shame We Don't Deserve.* San Franciso: Harper.

Sokolovsky, J., ed. (1990) *The Cultural Context of Aging: Worldwide Perspectives.* New York: Bergin and Garvey.

Spelman, E. V. (1988) *Inessential Woman: Problems of Exclusion in Feminist Thought.* Boston: Beacon.

Stagg, F. (1981) *The Bible Speaks on Aging.* Nashville: Broadmen.

Stokes, K., ed. (1982) *Faith Development in the Adult Life Cycle.* New York: W. H. Sadlier.

______ (1990) "Faith Development in the Adult Life Cycle." In Seeber, 167–84.

Thistlethwaite, S. B., and M. P. Engel, eds. (1990) *Lift Every Voice: Constructing Christian Theologies from the Underside.* San Francisco: Harper and Row.

Tilberg, C. W. (1984) *Revolution Underway: An Aging Church in an Aging Society.* Philadelphia: Fortress.

Tracy, D. (1975) "Eschatological Perspectives on Aging." In Hiltner, 119–34.

Tronto, J. C. (1993) *Moral Boundaries: A Political Argument for an Ethic of Care.* New York: Routledge.

Zizioulas, J. D. (1985) *Being As Communion.* New York: St. Vladimir's Seminary.

33 Constructive Theology

MARC KOLDEN

INTRODUCTION

In modern times, when the authority of both the scriptures and the church can no longer be taken for granted, the definition of theology itself has become a central topic for theology (Gilkey, 1979, 7–20). To speak of *constructive* theology is already to acknowledge the loss of traditional authority. All theology today is constructive theology, which is simply to say that theology must take responsibility for constructing its own formulations in terms of appealing for its conclusions using criteria that are intelligible in public discussion (Hodgson and King, 1985, 1–27).

The present chapter is an attempt at a constructive *Christian* theology of aging, which is to say that the understanding of faith in God and of humans in relation to God that is explored and commended is concerned with the triune God, the God who became flesh in Jesus of Nazareth, the one who Christians claim was crucified for the sins of the world. As the diversity within the Christian churches might suggest, there is no single Christian theology of aging or anything else. Every Christian theology is *a* Christian theology, not *the* Christian theology, and therefore its "Christian" character is also part the constructive task of theology.

Three areas of concern or three different criteria seem to emerge most often in approaching the theological task today. The first requires that theology deal with the biblical and churchly witness in a way that is *faithful*. The second insists that theology must be *intelligible* in the present situation, both in terms of how it retrieves the tradition and in relation to the insights of other disciplines. And the third claims that theology must lead to ways of thinking and acting that are *morally responsible* (Tracy, 1975, 43–87; Miguez Bonino, 1975, 86–105). These three areas of concern—faithfulness to the Christian tradition, contemporary intelligibility, and moral responsibility—are intended to be reminders and guideposts in constructing a Christian theology of aging that will honor the experience of persons as they age, that will take into account the expertise and data learned by those who work with the aging, and that will draw on the insights of the Christian tradition in ways that illuminate the topic and nourish faith and ministry.

Little has been said explicitly about aging so far in these introductory reflections on theology and method. The point has been to make sure that a theology of aging is constructed in a critical fashion, aware of how ideas and data from a variety of sources are being used. As has been well said, the theological task with regard to aging demands that we "think through the claims of the tradition in mutually critical dialogue with contemporary interpretations of experience and the claims of contemporary theological disciplines" (Lyon, 1985, 14). While there may be no single correct way to think theologically about aging, there may be more or less fruitful and responsible ways to think. What follows is one proposal that is intended to be both substantive and open to correction and conversation in that it seeks to make the approach to thinking obvious, explicit, and appropriately qualified.

THEOLOGICAL REFLECTION ON THE BIBLICAL TRADITION

A Christian Proposal

> We do not live to ourselves and we do not die to ourselves. If we live, we live to the Lord, and if we die, we die to the Lord; so then, whether we live or whether we die, we are the Lord's. For to this end Christ died and lived again, so that he might be Lord of both the dead and the living. (Romans 14:7-9)

These words of the apostle Paul, tucked away in a lengthy passage about Christian obedience, offer a horizon for understanding the whole of Christian life (Käsemann, 1980, 371–72). The focus of such a life is on the God of Jesus Christ, the source and the goal, the whence and the whither. Neither life nor death is ultimate; what is ultimate is that "we are the Lord's." Christians do not live to themselves, they do not die to themselves, even if those are commonly held notions. In truth, they live to the Lord and they die to the Lord and this reorients everything. While these verses could sound casual or even flippant, their point is rather to underscore the *freedom* that faith in Christ grants, even and perhaps especially for the elderly, because in all things they are the Lord's.

Unpacking the Christian Understanding of Life

Because the biblical tradition is so radically God-centered in its treatment of human life, and to the extent that this is related to aging, it is important to attempt to be comprehensive, even in a summary fashion. A framework is needed for making sense of particular issues and data (Lyon, 1985, 21). It is not sufficient simply to cull out commandments about treatment of the elderly or examples of ways of living in ancient times without relating these to the overarching biblical themes of the God who creates, provides, rules, judges, and redeems.

Nor will it do to read back into the Bible modern views of what humans are as if there were no gap between ancient and modern assumptions.

In brief, a Christian understanding of the biblical tradition regarding human beings may be expressed in the following threefold pattern. The first part of the pattern and the most important thing to say about humans is that they are *creatures* of God. This means, above all, that humans are "very good" (Gen. 1:31). As this creatureliness is delineated, humans are portrayed first as being "in the image of God" (Gen. 1:26-27; 1 Cor. 11:7). Christian tradition has taken this to refer to human freedom and the capacity for self-transcendence, qualities that distinguish humans from other creatures. For humans to be creatures also indicates that they are of "the dust of the ground" (Gen. 2:7; 3:19), finite and mortal, limited and dependent, though even in this "very good," for this is part of God's ordering: theirs is a finite freedom. It is one of both growth and loss, of both progress and regress. (There is a certain ambiguity to life even apart from any mention of sin.) Linked to these two characteristics of being both free and finite is another, namely, that human life is life in community with God and with other humans. In the Bible no one is an autonomous individual just as no one is independent of God. God's creative work is ongoing: where there is breath, there God's Spirit is at work (Ps. 104:29-30), and where there is a person there is a person-in-community. H. R. Niebuhr referred here to the "triadic" form of human existence, in which each person is always in relation both to God and to others (1963, 79–84; see also Wingren, 1981, 18–25, 37–43). It should be noted that this understanding of what it means to be human suggests a certain moral shape to life and offers norms for judging one's goals and means for achieving them. The relevance of these should not end as one grows older.

A second part of the pattern or framework by which the Bible portrays humans is the doctrine of *sin*. In Genesis sin is introduced in the chapter following the creation story, although the full force of a Christian understanding of sin is not articulated until after the time of Christ—initially by Paul and fully by Augustine four centuries later. Several points must be noted. Distinguishing the idea of sin from that of creation says that sin did not originate with God: to be human, finite, and mortal is not yet to be identified with sin. Sin is foreign to God's creative work (R. Niebuhr, 1941, 178–207). Sin is first portrayed as disobedience, but upon further reflection that becomes *unbelief*: unbelief in God's original word that it is good to be a creature, that being both free and finite, both self-transcendent and limited, is the way God intends humans to be. Sin is seeking to flee God-given creatureliness, either by trying to rise above it (to be "like God," as the serpent promises in Gen. 3:5) or to sink beneath it, becoming one with the animals and abdicating all responsibility (Gen. 3:12-13; Bonhoeffer, 1959, 64–82).

It should be added at this point that ever since the Bible was read historically (i.e., critically) in the Christian church, beginning in the late eighteenth century among Protestants, the biblical stories both of creation and of the origin of sin have been read not as literal reports of events in the past but in symbolic ways as parables or myths conveying something that is true for all ages. There are examples in the Bible itself of such ways of understanding (see Romans 5:12, where Adam's sin is a pattern for the sin of all, and 1 Corinthians 15:21-22, where it is said that "all die in Adam"), and modern interpreters of scripture have tended to agree with Reinhold Niebuhr's dictum that the symbolic parts of scripture must be taken "seriously but not literally" (1943, 50). Among other things, this means that created goodness and sinful defection are to be understood as being continually true of every person. The "fall" into sin does not annul the reality that life in every moment is God's good gift, even though sin qualifies that goodness. The doctrine of sin intensifies and makes more complex a view of human life as ambiguous (Westermann, 1974, 89–112). For example, while human wisdom or expertise may well be greater for many older people, the fear of death or insecurity about financial well-being may also increase with age. No view of aging will be adequate that sees it in terms of either simple progress or regress.

A third part of the pattern by which the Christian tradition understands humans beings has to do with Jesus the savior. He is understood to be the one sent by God, who is one with the Father, who comes to reconcile humans and the world to God. Jesus is portrayed in the New Testament as the "new Adam" (Rom. 5:12-21; 1 Cor. 15:45-49), as the one who is the very "image of God" intended for all people (Col. 1:15; 3:10). Jesus reenacts and reverses the pattern of Adam's sin (Phil. 2:5-11), taking the sin of all people upon himself and bearing the punishment for it (Rom. 3:21-6:11). Jesus' resurrection both reveals his triumph over death (the "last enemy," 1 Cor. 15:26) and establishes him as the living Lord of all. Because of this, people are "set right" with God—their sins are pardoned, God's Spirit is given to them, and they are "new creatures" and members of a new community, the "body of Christ" (Rom. 5:1-11; 8:1-17; Acts 2; 1 Cor. 12–14; 2 Cor. 5:14-21). All this is a free gift of God, given by sheer promise and received in faith (trust), effectively restoring persons to be creatures again—creatures who trust God's word rather than those who seek to live apart from it (Wingren, 1981). Such persons are those who know that whether they live or whether they die, they are the Lord's. They are joined to the risen Christ, they participate in him, they share in his death and resurrection in the sense that they have already died in his death and now live eternally with him by faith and hope, if not yet by sight (Rom. 6; Gal. 2:20; Heb. 11:1-3; Sittler, 1972, 23–50, esp. 34–35). Clearly, this emphasis on a divinely promised future will affect how Christians understand the meaning of life and death, and this will be different from purely secular perspectives.

Using this Pattern as a Paradigm for Understanding Aging

Nearly all Christian traditions have taken this threefold biblical pattern of divine creation, human bondage to sin, and divine redemption to be in some way paradigmatic for understanding human life in the world. Using some version of this paradigm, Christians have sought to account for the ambiguities of present life and the reality of authentic life with God available now by faith through Word and Sacrament and promised in fullness beyond this life.

To see the radical implications of this paradigm, which often are blurred in contemporary Christian practice and thus may not be seen by those who think about religion and aging, it is crucial to see that the focus on redemption through Jesus Christ is not only or even primarily on eternal life after death, but on being set free in this life from the fear of death and eternal separation from God in order to be able to live now as faithful creatures. Divine redemption through incarnation affirms creation and leads to notions of humans as "stewards" of creation and as persons with divine "callings" precisely in their worldly responsibilities (Wingren, 1957). This paradigm hangs on both to the biblical insistence on the goodness of creation and to the pervasive influence of sin, which results in a paradoxical understanding of Christian existence as being at the same time fully righteous through faith in Christ and yet still affected by sin. Such a view takes both human creativity and human capacity for evil with full seriousness, so that it is at once both hopeful and realistic. The extent to which such a view can he made intelligible today is one of the tasks of what follows in this chapter, although it should be noted that theologians as diverse as Karl Barth, Hans Küng, Jürgen Moltmann, Reinhold Niebuhr, Paul Tillich, and Gustaf Wingren as well as novelists such as John Updike (see Kort, 1970) have addressed these issues with considerable force in relation to many areas of life.

CHRISTIAN THEOLOGY AND AGING

One of the problems in some literature on aging and theology is that much attention is given to the various aspects of aging as a biological, psychological, sociological, and economic phenomenon and only superficial connections are made to theological concerns. The result is that theology is used to endorse conclusions drawn for other reasons rather than to contribute to or illuminate the discussion. Also, when this happens, much that might be of theological importance is omitted, as the other disciplines do not introduce it. Death and human limitations might appear in such treatments, but sin and judgment will not. Likewise, human well-being and sources of meaning might be addressed, but the relation of these to divine creativity or the hope for eternal life with God will not be. Especially in the consumer societies of the North Atlantic, with their emphases on rights, security, achievements, and individual comfort, the honest recognition of human sinfulness and pettiness, the need for repentance, the claim of God on each person, and each one's responsibility for the neighbor will be easily ignored. By beginning with a theological perspective centered on living to the Lord and dying to the Lord, on Christian vocation and stewardship, which stands in some opposition to much of what society takes for granted, it is intended that a more fruitful and more fully theological understanding of aging will result.

Death and Judgment. Perhaps the starkest theological contribution will be the insistence on the Christian notion that as persons who are created good but are also sinful, they go through judgment and are in need of salvation in the form of resurrection and transformation (1 Cor. 15:35-58). Looking at aging through this lens, rather than seeing it primarily as a journey toward fulfillment or authentic existence, leads to quite different conclusions as well as different evaluations of circumstances in life. Rather than achieving their "destiny" seen as the goal of life, the notion of divine judgment means that there is no straightforward move possible toward some sort of eternal destiny; reaching their eternal destiny is something that comes instead as a gift of God in Jesus Christ. In addition, if life is seen primarily not under the image of a pilgrimage to somewhere else but under the notions of stewardship and vocation, the ideas of the hope for resurrection and transformation (both as actions of God) set people free to devote their energy and love to life in the present (Fowler, 1984, 107–26; Kolden, 1990, 202–5).

A key aspect of the conversation may be the way that Christian theology deals with life and aging because of its understanding of death. For the Christian there are several dimensions to death. Consider first these two: death as an end of historical life and death as potential condemnation or eternal separation from God. (1) Christian theology knows of "natural" death, which occurs for all people, though it thinks of it not chiefly in biological terms but as part of God's creative ordering of life. Thus, death is not to be either denied or treated with contempt. (2) Christians also think of death in relation to condemnation or eternal separation from God ("the wages of sin," Rom. 6:23). While all persons know of the first dimension of death, theology would suggest that unbelievers also have some inkling of the second dimension, as Reinhold Niebuhr wisely warned when he observed that people are correct to "discern an accent of the fear of judgment in the fear of death" (1943, 294; see also Lyon, 1985, 19–20). Without such a distinction, neither life nor death will be adequately understood. Is life to be preserved at all costs? Not if death is a normal part of God's ordering of creation. Is the goal of life simply longevity? Not if judgment applies to all. Yet most people live as if life itself is the highest good, at least when it comes to their own life. Such a view is subject to criticism from all three criteria: appropriateness to the tradition, current intelligibility, and moral responsibility.

The Christian claim that God, not life, is the highest good and that God is not only revealed but incarnate in Jesus the crucified one adds still another dimension. Not only is death both part of the natural process of life and also the "wages of sin," but in addition it is the way of the righteous: those who follow

Jesus, who was obedient unto death, will die with him—and in at least two senses. By baptism and faith they will already in this present life be joined to his death (Rom. 6:3-6); this is the death of the "old self" (or the sinful self) that sets them free to live not for that self but to walk in newness of life, no longer enslaved to sin. In the New Testament, this death is both an eschatological or anticipatory reality, known now only in faith, and yet it is considered to be more real or true than the continued presence of sin in them. It is the final judgment already put behind them; the forgiveness of sins spoken now in Jesus' name is the last judgment ahead of time, that pronounces them both guilty and therefore dead and pardoned and therefore alive for eternity. It is this gospel (the good news) that people need to hear not only at the time of death but each day (Thielicke, 1970, 105–14, 150–61, esp. 189–202; Forde, 1984, 463–66).

A final dimension of death for the Christian is that of spending one's life for the love of the neighbor, following Christ in his obedience as a servant. In the penitential piety of the medieval church, "taking up one's cross" had become a form of morbid self-discipline designed to mortify the flesh as a way of meriting salvation. But Jesus in the New Testament speaks of bearing the cross rather in terms of following him in his mission (Luke 14:26-27). At the time of the Reformation, Martin Luther rejected religious "crosses" aimed at seeking one's own reward when he saw that justification by faith apart from works meant that works have nothing to do with salvation but everything to do with our earthly neighbors in need. Therefore, he directed people to obedience in their earthly callings—to spend their lives there. And when devout believers worried that they were not "bearing their crosses," Luther assured them that there would always be a cross in their calling. That is, in carrying out the sorts of loving service demanded by a person's many places of responsibility, the old sinful self that still persists in this age would get disciplined and "mortified" (put to death) while doing useful works for others. This was not a counsel by Luther to glorify suffering, but simply a way of reassuring that God was taking care of both the believer's own sanctification and the neighbor's well-being through faithful acts in one's earthly calling (Wingren, 1957, 50–63). As Christians die with Christ in the sense of spending their lives in his service, which (it has been said) is "perfect freedom," they also have their old sinful self put to death.

These dimensions taken together have many implications for human life, not least for matters relating to aging. The need throughout life for repentance, forgiveness, and amendment of life will need to help shape ministry and worship. The legitimate fear of death and judgment will need to be confronted and neither minimized nor addressed with something less than the gospel. The truth that "whether we live or whether we die, we are the Lord's" will assist people in accepting death as part of life, on the one hand, and in seeing Christ's triumph over death as his overcoming the judgment of death, on the other hand. The understanding that their death has already occurred in baptism into Christ and their faith in him will free persons to treat life as something good and valuable and as part of God's will for them because they look forward to eternal life with God rather than to death as only loss and separation.

In addition, all of these comments on the dimensions of death relate to the more general areas of vocation and being good stewards. Here, theology must be careful, however, because a faulty understanding of Christian vocation that relates it only to occupation may seem to suggest that upon retirement one no longer is called to serve God, but only to serve oneself. Yet, as the sixteenth-century reformers spelled out their view of vocation, it was clear that it applied to people in whatever circumstances they found themselves: they could serve God wherever they were because the whole world was God's and the neighbor in need provided the focus for such service. This included one's occupation, of course, if one were employed, but it was much more inclusive than that, involving family, community, educational, and citizenship responsibilities (Kolden, 1983). These latter roles and duties do not cease upon retirement, but in some cases may even become more important, especially if they are guided by an understanding of stewardship as the wise use of all they have been given. Indeed, even at the final stages of life in extreme frailty or illness, one may still find a vocation in prayer for others or in being a recipient of the love of family and caregivers—if life is from God and they are the Lord's. Such an understanding would question the attitude rampant in society concerning the right to a secure and even luxurious retirement. Clearly, the "gods" of society, such as money and self, lead all in this direction. And the point here is not to deny the importance of an adequate standard of living for all elderly persons, but to challenge on theological and moral grounds the excessive pursuit of pleasure which becomes the focus of retirement for many. Such a focus forgets that "if we live, we live to the Lord," for "we are the Lord's."

Fulfillment or Vocation? It is frequently suggested in literature on aging that as one gets older the emphasis should be placed more on *being* than on *doing* because to continue the emphasis on doing (achievement, success, making something of oneself) that dominates earlier periods of life will undermine human dignity at a time when the capacity for doing is diminished or lost altogether. The truth of this on one level is both obvious and important, but perhaps it ought to lead to a more thorough examination of the relation of being and doing from a theological perspective. In the terms of classical theological polemics, this could be seen as related to the debate about faith and works.

Which is more important, faith or works? The tendency in the tradition has been to answer, "Faith, but not at the expense of works," indicating that there is a perennial tendency to choose one or the other. If *doing* is connected with works and *being* with faith, then it might seem as if the first five or six decades of life would be most concerned with works, to be followed by retirement years concerned for faith. When it is stated that way, the problems are obvious. The proposed relation between doing and being is too simple—theologically, but also psychologically: it will not work if a person has spent sixty-five years creating self-worth by what he or she does to suppose that such a person can suddenly shift to an emphasis on simply being and find it satisfactory.

Christian theology suggests that in speaking of faith and works one must distinguish between "this age" and the "age to come" or between that which relates to things of this life and that which relates to the eternal God (Wingren, 1957). Faith is always (properly speaking) faith in *God* (Tillich, 1957). It is better understood in its biblical meaning as "trust" rather than belief. In this sense it is a state of being, a trusting relationship created and nourished by a trustworthy God. Faith is necessarily related to that which is eternal; and it is always focused on the "age to come," even as it exists very much in the midst of "this age." Works, on the other hand, are the actions appropriate to the present age: the actions that people do and that in turn "make them who they are." But this latter sense reveals the problem.

While, to some extent, it is true in this age that their works make them who they are, if persons make this into their total understanding of what is true about themselves, they are destined to lose who they are—at death and in many smaller diminishments prior to death. Worse yet, if they seek to establish their value with respect to *God* by their works, they will be condemned because they will never be as good or as pure or as worthy as God expects. (This topic was explored in the first century in Paul's epistles to the Romans and the Galatians, in the fourth century in the disputes between Pelagius and Augustine, and above all in the Reformation of the sixteenth century in the writings of Luther and Calvin and their opponents).

The resolution of this issue as it may pertain to the matter of doing and being regarding the elderly might be as follows. Distinctions must be made between works and faith, this age and the age to come, so that each finds its proper role and neither emphasis is lost or misused. In this life the need for works (doing) is obviously important, both in terms of the "works" of the growing child (learning to walk and talk and mature in all the ways necessary for being an adult) and in terms of the necessary work and activity expected by society of all people (granting that those with special needs must be treated appropriately). Here, in society, as Luther said (perhaps to our surprise), a person is justified by works (1963, 117). As it is said, persons who do good are good and those who do evil are evil—and these distinctions are very important for this age and this society.

Yet, as people make these judgments, they realize that even the best among them are not truly good: great political leaders have sexual and financial sins, wonderful relatives have chemical addictions or marital problems. Presumably, even Mother Teresa is not perfect. On this matter the Christian tradition has said there is another point of reference, another basis for reality than what individuals make of themselves by what they do. And it is not, as might be supposed, that after they have done their part, then God moves in to supply what is lacking—although some Christian theology and piety have said or implied that. Rather, when it comes to their ultimate worth, their being right with God, God does it all. That is what the saving work of Christ is all about. That is what salvation "by faith alone" means (Forde, 1984, 406–12). God "sets persons right," justifies them (makes them righteous), by declaring them to be so, by pardoning them.

The image of "pardon" is very appropriate here because it acknowledges that people in themselves are guilty, but that they are nevertheless not condemned but let off, as when President Ford pardoned former President Nixon (who, presumably, was guilty). Some have suggested that this amounts to a "legal fiction," both with regard to Nixon and for the Christian. But this depends upon what is truly "real"—our doings and misdoings or God's declarations. The Christian tradition has said that God's declaring individuals righteous *makes* it so (just as Ford's pardon made it so in the legal realm) in a way that is "more real" than the ambiguous mix of good and evil in each one of them in "this age."

The purpose of all this is to allow the judgment of the age to come to affect life in this age: to set people free from the program of making something of themselves by what they do both so that what they do can be directed instead to the good of their neighbor and society and so that they can rest secure throughout life in the understanding of who they are—beloved creatures of God. That knowledge, that they are the Lord's, cannot wait for old age without diminishing all life up until that point. Being does not merely supplant doing, as might be supposed when it is recommended as an alternative for older people. In terms of faith in God, being precedes, accompanies, and concludes doing and in the process gives doing direction, freedom, value, and forgiveness. If there is to be the dignity and security of being for people in old age, it will have to come from the source of all being, and it will be more likely to come about if it begins as early in life as possible. Most churches have baptized infants in acknowledgement of that fact, and the nearly universal insistence by Christians on the centrality of regular worship not only as a human activity but as the arena of divine activity testifies to the importance of human beings coming to know, above all, that "we are the Lord's."

Worship and Mission. If the task of theology, finally, is to transmit the tradition, albeit critically, this is also very close to the task of ministry. The chief arena in which the tradition is transmitted is corporate worship, where, through the reading of scripture, prayers, hymns, liturgy, sermon, sacraments, and the physical gathering of the body of believers the faith of the community is not only expressed but handed on. The major Anglican, Catholic, Lutheran, and Orthodox traditions have insisted that God works to create saving faith in people through "external means": the gospel and the sacraments. Their point is that because of the distinction between Creator and creature, trustworthy God and unbelieving human, holy and righteous Lord and unrepentant sinner, people need to be given new life from outside themselves. The proclaimed word and the material sacraments are "objective" gifts from God as opposed to the ambiguous and unreliable subjectivity of humans; the spoken gospel, baptism, and the Lord's Supper are tangible means of encounter with the God who is external to their often confused inner selves. The point is not that faith is not internal and subjective, but that faith is not generated in people's inner selves or by their subjectivity. Faith as trust is created or evoked in them by the trustworthiness of God. The external gospel and sacraments in the setting of corporate worship are to this way of thinking essential for each individual as well as for the church as a whole.

Rabbi Abraham Heschel once replied to a young man who had complained about the irrelevance of the traditional liturgy because it did not say what he meant by pointing out that the purpose of participating in the liturgy is not that it will say what we mean but that we will come to mean what it says (quoted by Neuhaus, 1979, 127). It takes time for the realization to set in that "if we live, we live to the Lord, and if we die, we die to the Lord." Worship is a key aspect of living to the Lord. Among other things, this means that worship needs to be familiar and repetitive even as it is an encounter with the God whose mercies are new every morning and who is always doing new things. It is in the retelling and the remembering of the saving works of God by word, song, symbol, gesture, water, bread, wine, and posture that the God who is Spirit, Truth, Life, Light, Love, and above all the Word made flesh can meet us in ways that we can grasp. If the paradigmatic acts of God are creation and incarnation, then the suggestion by Urban Holmes that good worship ought to be vulgar in the sense of being "earthy," of the common people, related to the totality of human experience, is exactly on target (1981, 94).

Worship for all ages, but especially for the elderly and above all for those in the final stages of frailty, should be symbolically rich in terms of both sound and sight and should be sacramental both in the more abstract sense of emphasizing the "direction" of worship as being from God to them and in the concrete sense of celebrating the sacraments. When hearing begins to fail or minds begin to wander, sermons and lessons and novel forms of prayer will not be sufficient, but familiar forms of prayer and song that already have an echo inside the worshiper from long experience will still serve. Symbols, vestments, altars, crosses, gestures (the sign of the cross, the laying on of hands, the "passing of the peace") will convey even to those who see and hear only partially the presence and reassurance of God. The reception of holy communion and perhaps even the reaffirmation of baptism (utilizing the pouring of water, as in the Easter Vigil) as regular parts of worship are important to believers of all ages, according to this way of thinking, but will surely be crucial for the elderly. In contrast, the typical Protestant nursing home worship, with few symbols, little or no liturgy, no sacraments, banal hymns, and too much talk, mostly by the worship leader (wearing casual attire), not surprisingly does not minister to the needs of most residents.

Finally, if familiarity over time with both life's ambiguities and the promises of the Christian gospel is normally a part of coming to live life and face death in the assurance that "we are the Lord's," then who better to bear witness to the truth of Christ than the older members of the community? Persons who in faith have known joy and sorrow, meaning and meaninglessness, self-sacrifice and undeserved blessing, the deaths of loved ones and the births of new family members—and who have reflected on this as worshipers and learners with divine vocations as stewards of God's good creation—will transmit the tradition with integrity and effectiveness. Churches need to concentrate not only on their ministry to and for the elderly, but increasingly on their ministries by and with such members.

There is no assumption in any of this that living equals growth, but there is a belief in what has been written above that the Christian life may be one of growth in grace. As one goes through life trusting in the undeserved and utterly dependable grace of God in Jesus Christ, the greatness of this gracious God will become ever more apparent, even and especially in the midst of life's contingencies. In the passage from Romans, the contingencies are obvious: "whether" we live or "whether" we die. But the unconditional affirmation is even clearer: no matter what, we *are* the Lord's. This message is one that can sustain Christians in every situation in life but above all in death. "For to this end Christ died and lived again, so that he might be Lord of both the dead and the living." One of the chief tasks of theology is to explore the meanings of this and the ways that it is true in relation to the varieties of human experience, not least of all that of aging.

Truth Claims. If one grants that constructive theology with regard also to aging should give a certain priority to the Christian tradition, there will be much more intellectual give-and-take than might be true if the emphasis were on the phenomenon of aging examined first in itself and then with selected "relevant" religious beliefs added. Some scholars or practitioners from other disciplines might see the present proposal as an example of the imperialism of theology, intruding its categories into what would otherwise be an empirical or phenomenological approach. Yet, if the aging persons themselves are Christian believers, the fact of their being such means that to study their reality without full-fledged theological considerations would itself be less than fully empirical or true to the phenomena.

It is also the case for the theologians, ministers, and chaplains who think about working with people in older age groups that the faith of the church they serve makes truth claims about *all* of reality and not only for those who happen to be participants in their faith. In this regard, ministry can never be simply giving people what they want: a little religion to some, a bit of humanistic encouragement to others. The Christian message (and also the message of other religious groups) claims to be true regardless of whether it is believed or not. With all people, and perhaps especially with the elderly, who may have both greater capacity and experience to reflect on matters of faith, it is important to express the message as something that is true and matters ultimately precisely so that it can be tested against other ways of making sense of life.

Here Paul Ricoeur's notion (1967, 347–57) that religious symbols amount to a "wager" that they offer a better understanding of humans and reality than alternative views is suggestive. "That wager then becomes the task of verifying my wager and saturating it, so to speak, with intelligibility . . . by its power to raise up, to illuminate, to give order to that region of human experience" (355). In other words, while theology should play an active role in this process of making sense of life and aging, theology should not be imperialistic or authoritarian precisely because it invites *reflective* assent (and, of course, acknowledges the possibility of dissent). This is true both at the level of scholarly reflection and in the daily lives of persons; and in each case, all these meanings need to be tested by all three criteria: appropriateness to the Christian tradition, contemporary intelligibility, and moral responsibility. Theology, as with Christian life itself, ought to be able to live with such contingencies, since that is an implication of what it means to believe that "whether we live or whether we die, we are the Lord's."

BIBLIOGRAPHY

American Association of Retired Persons (1988) *Aging Society: A Challenge to Theological Education*. Washington, D.C., AARP.

Bonhoeffer, D. (1955) *Ethics*. New York: Macmillan.

______ (1959) *Creation and Fall*. New York: Macmillan.

Braaten, C., and R. Jēnson, eds. (1984) *Christian Dogmatics*. Philadelphia: Fortress.

Clements, W. M., ed. (1981) *Ministry with the Aging*. San Francisco: Harper & Row.

Forde, G. (1984) "Christian Life." In Braaten and Jenson, 2:391–469.

Fowler, J. W. (1984) *Becoming Adult, Becoming Christian: Adult Development and Christian Faith*. San Francisco: Harper & Row.

Gilkey, L. (1979) *Message and Existence*. New York: Seabury Press.

Hodgson, P., and R. King, eds. (1985) *Christian Theology*. 2d ed. Philadelphia: Fortress Press.

Holmes, U. T. (1981) "Worship and Aging: Memory and Repentance." In Clements, 91–106.

Käsemann, E. (1980) *Commentary on Romans*. Grand Rapids, Mich.: Eerdmans.

Kolden, M. (1983) "Luther on Vocation." *Word & World* 3:382–90.

______ (1990) "Ministry and Vocation for Clergy and Laity." In Nichol and Kolden, 195–207.

Kort, W. (1970) "John Updike's Fiction: Cross and Grace in Beruf." *Anglican Theological Review* 52:151–67.

Luther, M. (1963) "Lectures on Galatians." 1535. In *Luther's Works*. Edited by J. Pelikan and H. T. Lehmann. Vols. 26–27a. St. Louis: Concordia.

Lyon, K. B. (1985) *Toward a Practical Theology of Aging*. Philadelphia: Fortress Press.

Miguez Bonino, J. (1975) *Doing Theology in a Revolutionary Situation*. Philadelphia: Fortress Press.

Moltmann, J. (1967) *Theology of Hope*. New York: Harper & Row.

Neuhaus, R. (1979) *Freedom for Ministry*. San Francisco: Harper & Row.

Nichol, T., and M. Kolden, eds. (1990) *Called and Ordained*. Minneapolis, Minn.: Fortress Press.

Niebuhr, H. R. (1963) *The Responsible Self*. New York: Harper & Row.

Niebuhr, R. (1941) *The Nature and Destiny of Man*. Vol. 1. New York: Scribner's.

______ (1943) *The Nature and Destiny of Man*. Vol. 2. New York: Scribner's.

Pannenberg, W. (1991) *Systematic Theology*. Grand Rapids, Mich.: Eerdmans.

Ricoeur, P. (1967) *The Symbolism of Evil*. Boston: Beacon Press.

Sittler, J. (1972) *Essays on Nature and Grace*. Philadelphia: Fortress Press.

Thielicke, H. (1970) *Death and Life*. Philadelphia: Fortress Press.

Tillich, P. (1951) *Systematic Theology*. Vol. 1. University of Chicago Press.

______ (1957) *Dynamics of Faith*. New York: Harper.

Tracy, D. (1975) *Blessed Rage for Order*. New York: Seabury Press.

______ (1987) *Plurality and Ambiguity*. San Francisco: Harper & Row.

Westermann, C. (1974) *Creation*. Philadelphia: Fortress Press.

Wingren, G. (1957) *Luther on Vocation*. Philadelphia: Muhlenberg.

______ (1981) *Credo*. Minneapolis, Minn.: Fortress Press.

34 Science and Religion in Dialogue

WILLIAM M. CLEMENTS

The way science and religion relate to and interpenetrate each other in the larger world of scholarship and discourse is of importance to gerontology as the boundaries of gerontology expand. Once religion and the liberal arts become full partners within gerontology, the dialogue becomes crucial to the emergence of a new synthesis that is more inclusive of the human experience of aging. In addition, the constituent disciplines found within science and religion are in no way static enterprises, but are ever changing and modulating as they move through time. This chapter, therefore, represents an initial, impressionistic step in the emerging discussion between science and religion within gerontology. It will employ a metaphor to address the potential for dialogue between science and religion in two academic domains: medical education and theological education.

Whether theological or medical, the two domains look monolithic when gazed at from a distance. The approaching stranger who is based in a discipline or profession outside the indexed model and is coming from a distant professional land probably has radically different basic assumptions about reality from those found within the discipline. From the outside, it is fairly easy to talk about either "science" or "religion." From the vantage point of the entry gate to the discipline, the stranger is likely to see faint outlines of traits and tendencies. While still dimly perceived, the faint outlines can become generalities and then even slogans. Prematurely the outsider is sorely tempted to lift up these faint outlines as reality without due regard for the many internal complexities found in the particular model.

To the insider, the newly arrived outsider might seem like a disoriented stranger with a flashlight who has just entered a dark warehouse for the first time. The stranger, standing at the door of the dark warehouse, does not know what is important inside the warehouse and shines the flashlight randomly around the strange space, illuminating first one, then another shape. These shapes are actually boxes and other containers that hide their contents from direct observation by the stranger standing at the door. The contents of each container far surpass the cryptic written message observable on the outside. In this scenario "trivial" shapes and outlines are focused upon to the detriment of "core issues" defined by the regular inhabitants of the warehouse.

The internal complexities, which usually become apparent only when one functions within the model, contain many contradictions and nuances. These subtleties that are usually only apparent to the insider serve to inhibit that insider from painting with a broad brush and reaching general observations and conclusions. For one who is already inside the model, one who perhaps has never even ventured outside the model, it may sometimes be easy to understand the role that internal inhibitions play, not all of them positive. At the same time, however, obvious relationships and blind spots might be overlooked by the insider. From the vantage point of the insider, who has a tendency to forget or who never becomes aware of the inherent limitations of particular disciplinary tools, blind spots and chauvinism can become commonplace. These tendencies, hidden to the insider, may be glaringly obvious to the outsider.

Thus, to describe another discipline one runs the risk of merely being able to describe the few shapes that one's flashlight has managed randomly to illuminate, without getting inside the mystery boxes. In other words, the descriptive tools of one's primary discipline limit one's ability to describe another discipline, sometimes because important traits and attributes are simply not seen and sometimes because they are seen but assumed to be insignificant. A third possibility always exists that what is observed defies description in the stranger's primary disciplinary language. In describing shapes from the darkened warehouse, however adequately or completely, the stranger is also likely to use terms that are largely unfamiliar to the inhabitants of the discipline being described. All of this sounds terribly complicated, even frustrating—and it is—but it holds enormous promise for exciting growth on the part of both the "stranger" and the "inhabitant."

Medical education and theological education, from the fields of science and religion respectively, largely function as two darkened warehouses with only the very occasional stranger traveling from one to the other. This state of affairs seems likely to continue indefinitely, despite the fact that both health and religion are known to be vitally important in the lives of elderly people.

PARALLELS—THE SPLIT BETWEEN THEORY AND PRACTICE

All cannot be summed up as two dark warehouses, however. There are many parallels, as might be expected, between medical education and theological education. One parallel is the tendency to split theory and practice. In medical education this is seen most clearly when comparing the "basic scientist" and the "clinician." The basic scientist might be a biochemist or an anatomist whose major activity is research and who grudgingly teaches only the occasional section of a course to first-year medical students. This basic scientist is most probably not a physician, does not hold the M.D., and never examines patients or makes patient-care decisions. On the other hand, the physician-educator, or physician-scientist, is the clinician who teaches and conducts research based primarily upon patient-care concerns. In medical education, the division between the academic and the applied is thus quite real and very observable, with the overwhelming preponderance of power resting with the clinician. This physician-scientist might spend long hours in the laboratory or peering at computer print-outs, with motivation for the work based largely upon a desire to deal with a concrete problem experienced by patients. By contrast, the basic scientist is usually not concerned with the applications of completed research, leaving applications, if any, for others to figure out. The basic scientist's style of research is almost totally intellectually driven, with one question leading to another as the solution to the intellectual puzzle is pursued.

The division between the theoretical and the applied is equally apparent in theological education. Those professors who teach in the classic theological disciplines, such as theology and history, are usually more concerned about intellectual dialogue than they are about making concrete applications in the day-to-day life of an individual or community. Major exceptions are drawn for liberation theologians, who are trying to bridge the gap between theory and practice at every opportunity.[1] Like the basic scientist in medical education, the theologian does not devise the practical question "How do I help this person or church in need?" but asks the theoretical one, "How might my variant of the theological enterprise (neo-orthodox, process, etc.) speak to this intellectual problem of human understanding?" The way in which the resulting answer is applied to the concrete human condition is taken up, if at all, by others. The professor from the classic theological disciplines might not be an ordained clergyperson and might not have received a seminary education. This means that, like the basic scientist in medical education, the classic theologian would not be dealing with "the human document" directly. The theologian and the basic scientist both live in a world of abstractions. Unlike medical education, however, the classic disciplines in theological education are in the power positions within religious education. The parallel in theological education to the physician-scientist would be the practical theologian whose professional identity is that of the pastoral counselor, the homiletician, the religious educator, the liturgist, etc. The intellectual question being asked by these practical theologians is likely to flow from a pastoral concern involving human experience. The intellectual question is often quite concrete and is usually imbedded in a unique set of life circumstances and cultural meanings and assumptions. The motivation to undertake the particular research is likely to be based on the desire to help someone in particular or persons experiencing similar problems or dilemmas. Although there is an intellectual dialogue that is vitally important to the process, the desire to ease suffering

[1]Many thanks to Kathleen Greider, M.Div., Ph.D., Assistant Professor of Pastoral Care and Counseling at Claremont, who pointed this out and made many helpful suggestions at other junctures.

or improve life can never be discounted in the work of either the physician-scientist or the practical theologian.

MUTUAL SELF-DECEPTIONS

There are numerous ways to proceed with this discussion. One might be to present and analyze what the scientific and religious models report that they do. This approach would depend on the self-conceptualization of each model and would produce two "inside" representations of reality in dialogue with each other. Another approach might be to have a series of monologues in which "religion," for example, discusses those matters and approaches that "science" says are characteristic of itself, without a substantive dialogue taking place, and vice versa. An even richer tapestry of interrelated meanings is more likely to appear as a result of careful attention to what is actually observed in each discipline, in addition to what is said about what is observed. This approach gradually enables one to reach some "as-if" hypotheses about each discipline.

Medicine (Science)

One "as-if" conclusion about clinical medicine is that it only attends to those matters about which it expects to intervene effectively. "Intervening effectively" in this case means to alter the course of a particular process in the direction of a more desirable outcome. Barring serious illness, what is seen and recorded are, for the most part, only those conditions for which effective (pharmacological) treatment exists. Much of the rest is simply ignored as irrelevant, because the pharmacologically-oriented physician does not have the means to alter the outcome.

It also seems "as if" in medicine the only things that are "real" are those things that can be measured or otherwise quantified. The human dimension of the medical equation rarely fits into the measurement or quantification mode. As a result, the human dimension is largely ignored unless it becomes strong enough to threaten the other measurements that are capable of being made. At that point it is attended to, not because the human dimension is understood as inherently important, but because the unattended human dimension has the power to jeopardize the scientific process that might lead to "real" improvement or healing.

Psychiatry has suffered because of this taste for the tangible and concrete. No reliable laboratory tests exist for most psychiatric conditions, for example. As a result, psychiatric diagnosis and treatment appear subjective to the physician-scientist because measurements do not exist to quantify the misery or the rate of recovery. Because it is "soft" and does not entirely fit the "hard" measurement model, psychiatry is equated with "voodoo" and "head-shrinking." Treatable psychiatric conditions are frequently ignored by the nonpsychiatrist until they reach the point of interfering with the ongoing process of hard, scientific diagnosis and treatment. At this point of jeopardy, and frequently not before, the psychiatrist is called in.

"Progressive" health-care institutions have ancillary staff to attend to the human elements that accompany the scientific procedures. Social workers, psychologists, candy stripers, and chaplains are viewed in this fashion. There is a hierarchical pyramid, and at the top is the physician, with everyone else fitting in down below. Despite the physician's orientation to patient care (as compared with the basic scientist's), each scientific advance has seemingly pulled the physician further and further away from physical and emotional contact with patients. At one time the physician would place her hands on the forehead of the patient and then on his back to check for fever. Then the thermometer was invented and the physician used that instrument instead of touching the patient. More accurate temperatures were ascertained, undoubtedly, but something else was lost—human touch. Now the physician rarely checks the patient's temperature directly, and probably would not know how to use one of the temperature or thermometer machines without instruction. Instead, there is a technician who moves from one hospital room to another, checking and recording the results. Routine temperatures are not even checked by nurses in many hospitals. Today, temperatures are read by the physician from the medical chart in another room outside of the patient's awareness. Just about every scientific advance has led to a decrease in human contact between physician and patient. This process of bifurcation between the quantifiable and the humanistic has become widespread in our society far beyond this sole example from medicine.

The chasm between quantification (science) and feeling (art, literature, and religion) appears to be widening as the fruits of the scientific model are harvested and utilized. This widening chasm between science (mechanistic materialism) and feeling (the affective, artistic, and intuitive realm) appears to be a general pattern that applies to broader Western society and is not merely isolated within the medical arena. The scientific paradigm is so strong and pervasive that dualistic thinkers place in opposition to it anything that represents a different approach to reality from mechanistic materialism. Either it is scientific (materialistic, or quantifiable) or it is frivolous or soft or not based in "facts."

Theology (Religion)

Unlike most other countries, the United States is a pluralistic society fragmented along a multitude of ethnic and religious lines. Culture has been transmitted from generation to generation by family, religion, and the arts. The United States is a culture of cultures, with islands of cultural meaning and identity forming archipelagoes that stretch over the horizon in all directions. Thus, being Armenian in America is, in part, defined as participation in the Armenian community, and this in turn usually means participating in the festivals and worship of the Armenian Orthodox Church, where the scattered community gathers. Science neither transmits nor fosters this sort of cultural identity and meaning.

When talking about "religion," one needs to be conscious of the three hundred or so denominational bodies that exist in the United States and the approaches to religion (liberalism, fundamentalism, orthodoxy, neo-orthodoxy, ultramontanism, etc.) that cross-cut these denominational lines. There are many fundamental differences between religions that are culturally, historically, and ethnically based, with theological differences being mere manifestations of these variations. Theology at its best should be able to talk about "what is" in descriptive terms and not merely in proscriptive terms when communicating with the broader public. Every religious (and scientific, one should not forget) statement is located somewhere and is relative to other approaches to reality. Christian scripture is full of this sort of discussion as divergent local religious communities began to talk to each other as the church emerged in experience and histories began to be written.

Earlier in this discussion, medical education (an example of a scientific model) was described as being mechanistic and materialistic. Theological education (an example of a religious model), by way of contrast, tends to be paradigmatic. Abstract classifications of reality that organize and classify ideas and perceptions of reality are more important than the concrete referents to which the classifications and perceptions eventually refer on some level. Theology tends to operate (liberation theology excluded) "as if" there were no concrete reality that could be at variance with the paradigm under discussion, with very little effort being expended to "test" the accuracy of the model being promulgated.

Just as the scientific model does not adequately address the human need for existential meaning, aesthetic pleasure, or an ethical ideal, so the theological model fails to address the measurable or concrete. Both models are partial and incomplete while harboring hegemonistic impulses. These omnipotent tendencies or impulses ignore the need for completion. Thus, science ignores religion and religion ignores science.

OBSERVATIONS ON MEDICINE AND THEOLOGY FROM THE WAREHOUSE

Moving back to the image of the darkened warehouse for a moment, imagine that both medicine and theology have received reports of damage to contents of their respective warehouses. Medical persons, being preoccupied with fixing things, would tend to rush to the scene and open immediately the first carton that appeared to be damaged. They would unpack everything from the damaged carton right there on the floor and ponder how to fix the contents that had been damaged. They would forget to ask the question of whether the carton was likely to be damaged again unless the conditions that led to the original damage were altered, how many more seriously damaged cartons might already exist in a forgotten corner of the warehouse, etc. The theologians, on the other hand, feeling little or no need to view the actual damage, would argue among themselves about the best way to determine the nascent plan that had been used to design and arrange the warehouse. They would be preoccupied with understanding the nature of "warehousedom" and discovering the many unstated assumptions that had been instrumental in the minds of those who had originally stacked and arranged the cartons. Medicine would get involved with repairing the contents of one damaged carton, never looking at the whole. Theology, with its preoccupations with antecedents and patterns, would busy itself with considering the whole problem and never actually open a single box. Both the warehouses would still remain full of unexamined and unusable cartons. How much better things might be if the two disciplines, medicine (science) and theology (religion), could actually communicate with each other and thereby begin to influence eventual outcomes in each area with some reference to the other.

On the popular level, religion tends to be artistic, intuitive, affective, and value-seeking, while on the level of theological education it tends to be cognitive, rational, and paradigmatic. Every student in theological education is expected to be grounded in the historical development of certain ideas and ideals that have shaped the particular tradition. In the context of theological education, how someone approached a problem or issue five hundred years ago might be valued as more relevant and significant than the latest theory or approach hot off the press. In medical education, however, a mere decade ago is considered ancient history in a paradigm that is assumed to move only in one direction—forward. Medical education is largely ahistorical in that students are not expected to learn the history of medicine, just as theological education is largely antimaterialistic in that students are rarely expected to measure or quantify anything. Thus, educational traditions force students into an "either-or" paradigm of reality. Either reality is scientific—materialistic and quantifiable—but without existential meaning and incapable of transmitting personal or cultural values that do not fit the scientific paradigm, or it is religious—rationalistic, aesthetic, affective, and paradigmatic—but without possibility of quantification or establishing itself as factually based. What a choice!

GERONTOLOGY

Most of gerontology would find itself solidly within the scientific paradigm but would perhaps be frustrated at times because so many of its issues are clearly affective, value-laden, aesthetic, and rationalistic at the core. How does the scientific gerontological model address euthanasia, ethical suicide, or a war between the generations from the standpoint of mechanistic cause-and-effect materialism?

How do measurement and quantification contribute to wisdom (the ability to make mature, sensible decisions) on these points? On what philosophical or theological basis do gerontologists make value recommendations? Can the paradigms and historical developments that have illuminated value decisions be described with the precision that has come to be expected of scientists? Gerontologists operating from a scientific point of view need to be aware of the limitations of their expertise, just as gerontologists employing a religious perspective need to acknowledge their limitations.

For example, it is embarrassing, within the medical model, for a professional colleague to assume to have a working knowledge of medicine based on a few Dristan and Preparation H advertisements on TV or on a childhood visit or two to the physician. Likewise, it is just as embarrassing for a colleague to enter the religious domain with the same level of sophistication based on having watched a television evangelist, or having attended a Sunday school for a few sessions as a child, or having shed a dissatisfying religious heritage and assumed that all religion would be equally dissatisfying, all religion being pretty much the same as that which was discarded.

In order to communicate effectively within a discipline, one must use the symbolic paradigms characteristic of that discipline. Thus far in the evolution of gerontology, the discipline has drunk deeply at the well of scientific quantification and measurement. This has helped the discipline to gain a toehold as a scientific enterprise on graduate school faculties. Yet, this measure of success has come at a price—a price that has largely gone unrecognized and unacknowledged. The price extracted for entering the scientific discussion more or less as an equal has been that gerontology does not adequately or effectively address the aesthetic, affectional, or religious domains in the lives of people. Yet, this is the point at which individual and cultural meanings are constructed. As a result of the cultural bargain to function monoparadigmatically, gerontology has had relatively little to say in the professional literature that deals with existential meaning construction, that uses the rich language of religion, the arts, and so forth. When gerontology has entered the religious domain, it has not used theological tools as a means of communication, but has tended to view religious people as research subjects and studied them with the tools of quantification and measurement. Thus far, the result has been that gerontology has had little influence, one must say, on either theological education or on the experiential lives of the subjects studied.

Theological education, for its part, has almost totally ignored human aging as a paradigm because within the tradition aging was not historically an issue that was lifted up and reflected upon by the classic disciplines. A strategy of introducing "scientific" gerontology into the theological curriculum attempts to mix two models, essentially unself-consciously. Unfortunately, this approach is destined to end in failure, if success is gauged by having an impact on the discipline of theological education. The theological professor, who has spent decades mastering a liberal arts approach to studying reality, is simply not going to throw all of this preparation overboard and adopt a new language ("gerontospeak") that cuts one off from meaningful dialogue with professional peers within the theological academy. Nor is the introduction of a visiting scientist "mole" (to borrow a term from the shadow world of espionage) likely to have any greater degree of success in affecting theological education.

Instead of "moles" and "gerontospeakers," what is needed is a strategy that, on the one hand, involves gerontology deeply in consulting roles within theological education, and, on the other hand, utilizes practical theological consultants appropriately when "religious" research is undertaken within gerontology. With this strategy both disciplines maintain their own academic integrity, and yet the process of cross-fertilization can be carried forward to a new level of development and sophistication. The chasm between science and religion becomes unbridgeable only when either science or religion loses sight of the elderly person. When the focus of attention is so weighted toward internal disciplinary dialogue, the reality of aging can receive short shrift. The vision of the stranger with a flashlight entering warehouses and beginning to talk with the insiders about the odd shapes and boxes that are stacked about is exciting and holds promise for both insiders and outsiders—but most of all it holds promise for gerontology.

As an academic and applied discipline, gerontology is uniquely suited to serve as a bridge between the scientific and the religious approaches to reality. It does seem to be true that the essential unity of human beings becomes increasingly obvious with age, to both the theologian and the scientist.[2]

Recognizing this, gerontology needs to move further in the direction of a more inclusive model of study and reflection—a model that is more wholistic and better able accurately to describe and illuminate the range of human experiences, dilemmas, and opportunities connected with aging. If gerontology is to actualize its full potential to study and shape the aging experience in a wholistic sense, then it must accelerate the move toward academic pluralism. As research tools from the liberal arts (historical, literary, philosophical, ethical, and theological, to name only a few) are more broadly utilized in gerontology, research will become even more diverse. The gerontological impact will begin to permeate academia more broadly, so that "gerontologists" will be as likely to be historians or theologians as they are now social or psychological scientists.

If gerontology moves in these directions in future decades, then it will be in a powerful position to challenge seriously the exclusivistic "either/or-ness" of both the scientific and the religious models of reality. In this sense, gerontology would then begin to repay the great debt that is owed to its parental or constituent disciplines and fully enter the intellectual dialogue of the academy.

[2]Marjorie Suchocki, Ph.D., Ingraham Professor of Theology at Claremont, made this suggestion and others in reading a draft version of this chapter.

Part Six SOCIAL SCIENTIFIC PERSPECTIVES ON AGING

INTRODUCTION

The guiding epistemological assumptions of gerontology have constrained the study of religion, spirituality, and aging. Long wedded to a positivistic worldview, the behavioral and social sciences of aging have largely failed to note expressions of elders' multifaceted spirituality and the outcomes of their apprehensions of mystery and numinosity. In addition, the gerontological literature contains few insights about older adults' commitments to religious institutions nor does it acknowledge their private, prayerful expressions of faith, hope, trust, and even doubt. The core beliefs about what ultimately grants meaning to a long life are seldom revealed in answers to the myriad survey questions posed by gerontologists. Presently, however, this well-established pattern of neglect is yielding to new theories and methods appearing on the horizon of gerontology. The chapters in Part Six indicate that the current theoretical and methodological ferment is producing a greater acceptance of the study of spirituality and religion. By providing a historical perspective, several of these chapters also challenge the temptation to claim that this study is entirely new. Together, these chapters demonstrate the enormous potential for behavioral and social scientific inquiry into older adults' efforts to maintain a meaningful sense of the self, others, the world, and God while adapting to significant biological, psychological, and social changes.

Jackie Lanum and *James Birren* begin chapter 35 by examining theories that address the influence of biological determinism on longevity and the way social determinism shapes the interchange between aging individuals and the social world. They present a detailed discussion of the reciprocal interactions of changing biological resources, social conditions, and psychological responses of behavioral control and self-regulation. Using Birren's counterpart theory, they explain how the nervous system, with its power to represent the self symbolically through time, can maintain self-regulation in light of different rates of change in biological and social conditions. Students of spirituality, religion, and aging can find within counterpart theory a wholistic explanation of aging. This theory incorporates biological insights at both an evolutionary and a physiological level; it demonstrates the mutuality between the embodied aging self and changing social conditions; it asserts that both intellectual and emotional resources contribute to psychological adaptation to the aging process. Counterpart theory has the potential to explain how spirituality and religion support the self-regulatory responses of older persons; it also points to ways the spiritual and religious growth of elders can positively affect the adaptation of younger persons to the exigencies of human life.

The next three chapters are written by persons who were pioneers in the study of spirituality, religion, and aging. Earl Brewer, David Moberg, and Barbara Payne wrote and conducted research about older adults' public and private religious lives at a time when few other gerontologists recognized the significance of such work. They persisted in presenting their empirical observations for peer review by fellow social scientists; they advocated for elder concerns with religious judicatory bodies; they insisted that professional organizations recognize the urgency they felt about the need to study the spiritual and religious dimensions of aging. In their chapters, the reader will learn about the history of the gerontological study of spirituality and religion from individuals who in large measure created that history.

Earl Brewer outlines in chapter 36 three theoretical perspectives on the sociology of religion that have implications for the study of aging. Like the theologians in Part Five, Brewer points out how religion can provide a sense of continuity, identity, and affirmation to aging persons living in the midst of social change that often contributes to the denigration of the old.

Research on the role of religion in older adults' lives has revealed its effects upon psychological and physical well-being, as noted in earlier chapters. *David Moberg* catalogs in chapter 37 such research efforts dating back to the 1940s. He describes the various research methods employed and cites both the accomplishments and the limitations of a positivistic approach to the study of religion, spirituality, and aging.

Gerontology has been slow to acknowledge the legitimacy of this research as *Barbara Payne* notes (chap. 38). Following an examination of the history of research efforts by persons primarily identified as sociologists of religion, Payne expresses hopefulness that gerontology may now be ready to include the study of religion and spirituality and she asserts that the future holds great promise for further developments in this area.

If Brewer, Moberg, and Payne represent the first generation of gerontologists concerned about sources of meaning and purpose in older adults' lives, then the final two authors in Part Six could be said to represent the second generation. Gary Reker and Steven Weiland write and conduct research in a climate different from that encountered by the first generation. Gerontology is beginning to expand its boundaries to include theories and research methods that invite rather than reject the study of spirituality and religion.

Gary Reker argues in chapter 39 that all persons who work in any capacity with older persons need to become informed consumers of research information and he presents a straightforward explanation of empirical and phenomenological models of inquiry. He examines research approaches grounded in positivism-operationism and those grounded in interpretive social science. He compares the ways they dictate how data are obtained and analyzed, their views of the persons who contribute the data, and their assumptions about the interpretive role of the researcher. In straightforward, non-technical language Reker lays out the defining characteristics of quantitative and qualitative research. He notes the amount of energy consumed by those who would argue the merits of one over the other and he urges gerontologists to view these approaches as complementary.

In chapter 40, *Steven Weiland* looks to the future of gerontology when there will be an increased tolerance of diverse research methods. Like Reker, he calls for pluralism in theory and method. If indeed gerontologists are seeking new meanings in aging—some of which will be found in spiritual experience and religious beliefs and practice—then they will have to recognize the limitations of traditional scientific paradigms. Interpretive social science questions the assumptions underlying much gerontological research. Through its analysis of culture, its respect for narrative, and its interpretations of acts of meaning, this emerging model of social scientific inquiry holds much promise for gerontologists concerned about recovering the spiritual, religious, and moral dimensions of later life.

Part Six reveals that gerontology is in the midst of a struggle between maintaining continuity with its scientific heritage while at the same time being open to changes advocated by the phenomenological perspective. If gerontology is successful in allowing these different approaches to be complementary and not antagonistic, then the future is bright for the continuing study of spirituality and religion. The practitioners in Part Two have clearly indicated the significance of both the spiritual motivation to seek meaning and the religious responses of many older persons to this need. The theologians in Part Five prod students of aging with questions that reframe late twentieth century assumptions about well-being in later life. Now it remains for behavioral and social scientists in cooperation with gerontologists trained in the humanities to use their resources to illuminate the spiritual and religious journeys of aging. Perhaps guidance and inspiration for this undertaking will come from elders whose tolerance of ambiguity and paradox functions in the service of genuine growth. By continuing and expanding the study of spirituality and religion, gerontology will mature and find new ways to understand how human beings—bound by biology and living in community with others—respond to the mystery of life and time.

35 Adult Development Theories and Concepts

JACKIE C. LANUM
JAMES E. BIRREN

A BRIEF HISTORICAL INTRODUCTION TO THE PSYCHOLOGY OF AGING

Aging has been a topic of concern since the beginning of recorded history (see Woodruff-Pak, 1988). Long before research on human aging began in natural science, the mystery of aging and long life was addressed through myth and religious beliefs. Gruman (1966) identified three themes that occur in historical myths and that may be latent if not apparent in modern thinking.

The first of these themes is the *antediluvian* theme that people lived longer in the past and that this power was lost through some sin or fall from grace. The story of Adam and Eve illustrates this theme in Western religion, but this myth appears in some form in almost all cultures. Contemporary Christians who interpret the Bible literally can point to Adam as living 930 years, Seth for 912 years, Noah for 950 years, and Methuselah for 969 years.

The *hyperborean* theme, attributed to the Greeks, is that there are people in some distant part of the world favored by the gods who have the secret of immortality or at least of youthful longevity. Contemporary hyperboreans claim that there are very long-lived individuals in remote areas of the Himalayas, the Andes, and the Georgian region of Russia.

Third is the *rejuvenation* theme that there exist special waters, substances, or activities that will restore youth and vigor. King David was given a virgin to sleep with (1 Kings: 1-3), and Ponce de Leon discovered Florida in his search for the fountain of youth. Of the three myths, the rejuvenation myth is most persistent in modern times as various vitamins, enzymes, and hormones are touted as at least partial "cures" for aging. Comfort (1964) cites the rejuvenation experiments of seventy-three-year-old French physiologist Charles Brown-Sequard as the beginning of experimental gerontology. Brown-Sequard reported in an 1889 public lecture that he had injected himself with extracts from monkey testicles.

The Belgian M. A. Quetelet is more commonly considered the first gerontologist (Birren, 1961). In 1835, he published a book titled *On the Nature of Man and the Development of His Faculties* in which he used statistical techniques and measured the averages and distributions of many human traits. Among these, he looked at variations in birth and death rates and the distribution of the productivity of English and French playwrights by age. Quetelet (1835/1969) was the first to make a clear statement of the lawfulness of aging. "Man is born, grows up, and dies, according to certain laws which have never been properly investigated, either as a whole or in the mode of their mutual reactions" (5).

Darwin (1859) gave a further rationale for studying human development as a part of the natural world. Natural selection emphasized variation and individual differences as well as a continuity between species. It was his belief in natural selection that led Darwin's cousin Galton (1883) to measure up to two hundred characteristics in 9,337 males and females aged five to eighty to quantify variability in the population and changes across the lifespan. Slowly, natural determinism replaced predestination or mystical forces as an explanation for longevity.

Following Quetelet's 1835 publication, it was 1922 before the publication of another book-length monograph. Toward the end of his life, G. Stanley Hall, a psychologist who coined the term *adolescence* and is considered the father of developmental psychology, wrote *Senescence, the Last Half of Life*. Hall challenged the idea, current at the time, that old age was a regression back through the stages of childhood. He also studied religious beliefs and fears of death by means of a questionnaire and concluded that people did not necessarily show an increase in religious interest, nor did they become more fearful of death as they grew older (Hall, 1922). Despite Hall's stature as one of the founders of modern psychology, his work on aging was largely ignored. Even into the 1970s, most of the history and systems books, general texts, and handbooks of psychology do not mention aging as a subject, even though the *Handbook of Aging and the Individual* was published in 1959 (Birren, 1959; Birren and Birren, 1990).

Birren and Lanum (1991) metaphorically describe aging as psychology's last elephant, using the parable of the blind Indians each grasping a part, then trying to describe the beast. There are several implicit points in this metaphor. First, at present, the psychology of aging is characterized by islands of information with no unifying theories. Psychologists have specialized in particular subtopics such as learning, personality, and perception and then have investigated them in people of different ages. Second, aging has a taboo nature. It has threatening associations with death and existential questions about the meaning of life, and is burdened by a moral view of what is the appropriate role of aging individuals. The study of aging also has elephantine qualities of being big and complex. Whereas the task of general psychology is to describe how behavior is organized, the psychology of aging must address a dynamic system describing how behavior comes to be organized, how it changes over time, and the conditions under which it becomes disorganized (Birren and Lanum, 1991).

Psychologists have taken as their purview the behavior of the individual and have long recognized that the individual responds both to internal, physiological influences and to external, environmental influences. Social and cultural factors play a unique and profound role as environmental influences on human behavior. In broad overview, the individual with cognitions, personality, affect, and previous experience is sandwiched between a biological and social world. Moment-to-moment behaviors are determined by the unique interactions of these three worlds. The fact that in aging, psychologists must simultaneously consider the interactions of the biological, behavioral, and social aspects of the person across time gives this area unusual theoretical potential to influence other areas within psychology and the life sciences.

BIOLOGICAL AND SOCIAL DETERMINISM

Having made the point that biological and social factors are of utmost importance to the psychology of aging, it is unfortunate that the limits of space do not allow us to elaborate. However, we have summarized the major theories in these areas for the reader to reference for further information.[1]

Given the number of obvious physical changes that accompany aging, it is not surprising that the oldest and still most prominent theories of aging refer to biological factors. Biological theories are ultimately interested in longevity and have typically addressed themselves to variation in the length of life in different species, individual differences in human life expectancy, age and the susceptibility to disease, and changes in functional capacity with age (see Table 35.1). The increase in disease with age, along with the current high regard for the medical establishment, has resulted in the biomedicalization of aging (Estes and Binney, 1989). However, the relationship between aging and disease remains obscure, as does the relationship between aging and mortality. Both disease and death, though increasing in probability with age, may or may not be related to age (Cristofalo, 1988). The mechanisms of biological aging are still not understood and, once they are, the possibility of technical intervention in the aging process will raise ethical and moral questions that modern cultures are unprepared to meet. This is an area in which religion and ethics might make a significant contribution.

The central questions addressed by social theories concern the way roles, norms, and socialization prescribe the interactions between individuals and between individuals and society (see Table 35.2). Age is one of the major attributes of the individual that determine the eligibility and appropriateness for various social positions; age also modifies the behavior of an individual in a specific position (Atchley, 1991).

[1]The authors are indebted to Susan McFadden for summarizing this information into Tables 35.1 and 35.2.

TABLE 35.1
Theories of Aging Based upon Biological Determinism

Theory	*Central Questions*	*Key Assumption(s)*	*Theorist(s)*
Evolution	Do differentiation and adaptation continue in the postreproductive phase of life?	The force of natural selection declines with age and there may be direct, selective pressure for senescence.	Darwin (1872) Rose (1991)
	Is longevity genetically determined?	1) Longer-lived parents have longer-lived children 2) Nearly universal sex differences favor the female 3) Longevity is related to species 4) Deaths of identical twins occur close in time	Rockstein (1974)
Genome	Is aging genetically programmed?	1) Certain genes may alter physiology in later life, leading to death 2) Cells contain certain programs determining the number of times they can reproduce	Hayflick (1977)
Wear-and-tear	Does metabolic rate affect longevity?	Rate of energy expenditure in metabolism affects longevity	Rubner (1908)
Running-out-of-program	Do genes that produce positive outcomes in early life produce negative outcomes later?	Genes may no longer be able to correct for problems or reduce wear-and-tear on the body	Enesco & Kruk (1981) Masaro (1984)
Subtheories			
Gene mutation	Do gene mutations accumulate?	Genetic mutation causes functional loss in cells, leading to lowered resistance to diseases such as cancer	Sinex (1974)
Accumulation-of-errors	Do changes in the body's proteins affect aging?	Problems with protein synthesis result in cellular damage	Cutler (1982) Bjorksten (1974)
Neuro-endocrine	What role do the hypothalamus and the pituitary play in aging?	They may be the body's "master timekeepers"; their changes reduce the function of homeostatic mechanisms	Finch & Landfield (1985) Dillman (1981)
Autoimmune	Does the immune system change?	1) The immune system may develop antigens to the body's proteins 2) There may be a reduced efficiency in recognizing and destroying foreign proteins	Walford (1969) Adler (1974)

TABLE 35.2
Theories of Aging Based upon Social Determinism

Theory	*Central Questions*	*Key Assumption(s)*	*Theorist(s)*
Disengagement	Are elders excluded from roles by social forces in agreement with their desires?	A mutual process of disengagement of the individual and the social world is normative	Cumming & Henry (1961)
Activity	How do various types of activity contribute to elder's adaptation?	1) Meaningful activities are defined by the interaction of the individual and the society	Caven et al. (1949) Burgess (1960)
		2) Informal activity contributes to well-being; highly structured activity may hinder well-being; solitary activity has little effect	Longino & Lipman (1982)
Continuity	What is the effect of stability of social roles?	1) Those who maintain role stability adapt most successfully to aging	Atchley (1971)
		2) Stability of personality contributes to role continuity and well-being	Neugarten et al. (1977)
Social competence/ breakdown	How do individual conditions and social expectations interact dynamically?	1) Negative feedback cycles occur when individual dysfunction is socially reinforced	Kuypers & Bengtson (1973)
		2) Non-normative behavior is negatively labeled, leading to its continuation when the individual accepts the role label	Matras (1990)
Age stratification	How does cohort affect aging?	1) Characteristics of old age will vary according to cohort	Foner (1974, 1986)
		2) Older people develop a subculture that redefines essential assumptions about health, work, status, etc.	Rose (1965)
Dependency	How does the distribution of political/economic power affect older people?	1) Political and economic status determine the outcomes of aging, especially for women	Wallerstein (1979) O'Rand & Henretta (1982)
		2) Government programs for elders give jobs to service providers but do not substantially change life conditions	Estes (1979)
Social exchange	What maintains social interaction among different age groups?	1) Interaction occurs and continues if it is perceived as mutually beneficial	Blau (1964) Emerson (1976)
		2) Older people do not have socially valued characteristics to offer in exchange relations and thus have fewer social interactions	Dowd (1975, 1978, 1980)
Social phenomeno-logical	How is the meaning of age and aging socially constructed?	Everyday social life influences how people subjectively evaluate their life circumstances	Gubrium & Lynott (1983)

The major difficulty in addressing social determinants of aging is that of simultaneously considering the influences of the society on aging and the individual's experience of aging, both of which have social origins. Researchers have tended to get stuck in either a macro- or microanalysis which has considered neither the relationship between the two nor the mechanisms by which one is transformed into the other. Furthermore, there is a reciprocal interaction that makes it difficult to specify independent and dependent variables. For example, an individual's sense of satisfaction and well-being may derive from her activity or disengagement (as the case may be), but her sense of well-being may also determine her activities. The sociologist has typically chosen the social structure of the group as the determining variable, whereas psychologists look more at components of the individual and how they relate to behavior.

PSYCHOLOGICAL DETERMINISM

Research in psychology has come from two very different perspectives. There is the classical academic perspective where psychologists attacked questions handed down to them from philosophers, using scientific research techniques. These were primarily questions of epistemology concerned with perception, learning, memory, attention, and problem solving. These have become major research areas of psychology and are dominated by experimenters interested in particular component processes that affect individual functioning. For these researchers, age is a source of variance that needs to be addressed. Many experimenters in these areas have extended their studies to include older subjects, and much of the experimental aging literature is an attempt to explain the differences in performance of the old relative to the young. Questions of development are secondary to this perspective.

The second perspective has come from a clinical concern and can trace its origins to medicine. Here research centers on what is normal and abnormal; development is a more central concern. Individual differences are not merely sources of variance but a topic of major interest.

It is impossible to summarize all of the relevant research and theory in the psychology of aging, so selected areas of cognitive theory will be reviewed as representative of the first perspective; personality theory will be examined as representative of the second.

Cognitive Theories

Although theory is not emphasized in the content areas of cognitive psychology, the acquisition of data is directed by hypotheses derived from miniature theories related to the particular topic. These miniature theories come from larger traditions within psychology. The most pervasive conceptual frameworks come from either associationism or information processing.

Associationism derives historically from the Newtonian conception of the universe as a machine. In this view, the human is not spontaneously active but reacts to external forces and undergoes increments in the behavioral repertoire by the addition of new machinery or decrements by the wearing out of component parts. All behavioral phenomena except a few determined by reflex reactions and inborn associations are thought to be reducible to learning phenomena. The stimulus (S) represents the environment and the response (R) the behavior. Learning is the accumulation of S-R connections through experience and is inferred to exist within the organism (O). Learning, though it is an inferred central construct, results from contiguous occurrences of previously unrelated Ss and Rs. Practice either leads to an increment of associative strength or an increment in the ability to utilize associations. Images or other cues may be used as mediators to bridge the gap between S and R in order to facilitate associations. Changes in perception, attention, or memory influence the ability to make associations or the strength of the stimulus needed to arouse the association. For example, the sensory changes that occur with aging may make the strength of the stimulus insufficient to activate the association.

Very little recent work in aging has derived directly from associationism, although it was a very popular approach until the 1960s. Deficits in learning S-R associations appear in the elderly due primarily to fewer rehearsal Rs being made by older persons in the same length of time (Korchin and Basowitz, 1957; Canestrari, 1963; Witte and Freund, 1976). In the rehearsal process for S-R learning, older subjects are less likely to use images as mediators or spontaneously invent mediators (Hulicka, 1965; Hulicka and Grossman, 1967). The latter finding may be because older people are no longer in educational settings. Treat et al. (1978) showed that the elderly begin to use mediators spontaneously after practice, although some true loss of mediational ability is also likely (Kausler, 1991).

The intellectual antecedents of the information processing approach are communication theory and computer science. Communication theory considers information anything that reduces uncertainty; it assumes that all information-processing channels have limited transmission capacity.

In information processing, structures are of two types: an operative structure with a limited storage capacity within which processes are conducted, and a large capacity storage structure for holding information permanently. Mental operations may be viewed as a sequence of stages that take resources of energy, space, and time. Because the operations of each stage take time to complete, reaction time becomes a measure of mental time.

The general resource model utilizes a theory that addresses the sources of age differences in cognitive abilities (Salthouse et al., 1988). Here it is assumed that either processing capacity or storage capacity is diminished in the elderly, and that a single pool of resources is called upon by all cognitive activities. There are two general versions of the resource theory: the spatial model and the temporal model. Limited spatial capacity is often assumed by researchers interested in models of working memory, attention, and problem solving, but there is no agreed-upon measure of storage capacity and different estimates do not correlate highly.

The most pervasive and well-documented finding in the scientific literature on aging is that there is a general slowing in the rate of processing with age across a large number of tasks. Numerous studies have shown that slowing with age cannot be accounted for by peripheral changes resulting in longer response times (Birren and Fisher, 1992). The pervasiveness with which age-related slowness is exhibited across tasks and even species suggests that a fundamental property of the central nervous system is involved.

The generalized slowing hypothesis has been elaborated to explain deficits in processing by Cerella et al. (1980), Cerella (1985), and Salthouse (1982, 1985a, 1985b). Time is viewed as an indirect measure of spatial resources and strategic efficiency. A quantitative change in speed may result in qualitative changes because the slowing of operations means that some strategies are no longer effective.

Slowing is greater on complex tasks than on simple tasks. This slowing may be attributable to reduced levels of arousal (Birren, 1970) or to a decrease in the signal-to-noise ratio (Salthouse, 1985a). Salthouse (1985a, 1985b) invoked a computer analog with increased cycle times.

The neural network hypothesis (Cerella, 1991; Greene, 1983) makes several simple assumptions. The brain is composed of links and nodes that a signal must transverse between input and output. Response latency is a function of the number of links that must be traversed. If a link is broken, a detour is taken which adds time by increasing the number of links between input and output. The hazard rate for losing links is constant over the lifespan but accumulates so that there is a greater decrease in efficiency with age. Equations modeling this process predict age outcomes over a wide range of information processing conditions (Cerella, 1991). A few notions about degeneration in the central nervous system seem to explain a myriad of task-specific effects and eliminate the need to appeal to disuse, cautiousness, attentional deficits and the like.

The major strength of the generalized slowing hypothesis and network theory is the realization that age deficits can be distributed throughout the nervous system rather than localized in particular processing stages. However, there are several weaknesses that limit its generality. First, there are some obvious exceptions to generalized slowing. Reading and verbal reaction time seems to be less affected (Waugh, 1980; Nebes and Andrews-Kulis, 1976; Nebes, 1980), and tasks that are highly practiced to the point of automatic processing are spared (Kausler, 1991). Second, most cognitive psychologists are not willing to give up task-specific analyses. Such a general model does not address individual variability and the effects of different problem-solving strategies.

An interest in individual variability and ways of enhancing performance have characterized recent studies in intelligence and aging. In general, mental activities that are practiced continue to develop, while those that are not exercised tend to deteriorate (Denney, 1982; Cornelius, 1984). The importance of work environment as well as education is stressed in the maintenance of intellectual functioning. Kohn and Schooler (1983) found that those whose work involved breadth and diversity and who had autonomy in determining their own priorities were advantaged.

Instruments used to measure intellectual function were developed for younger populations in educational settings and are not ecologically valid for older adults. An ecologically valid test is one that measures what is important in the context of adult functioning. Schaie et al. (Schaie, 1977–78; Schaie and Schooler, 1989) have examined aging in the context of social structure to determine what is relevant. The acquisition of knowledge is emphasized for youth. In the context of work and family, the young adult is called upon to apply the cognitive skills acquired earlier. While young adulthood emphasizes acquisition and flexibility, middle and later adulthood focus on stability, responsibility, and commitment. The older adult must face additional demands of physical and context losses for which he or she must compensate.

Indeed, the thinking of an adult may be qualitatively different because it demands an integration of social dimensions involving a knowledge of self and others as well as of the specific dimensions of a given task (Labouvie-Vief and Blanchard-Fields, 1982). Several studies have found a greater correlation or interrelatedness among intelligence subtests (e. g., Baltes et al., 1980; Cunningham and Birren, 1980) which has been variously interpreted as "dedifferentiation" or "neointegration" (Baltes et al., 1980). Empirical evidence exists for a more integrative classification strategy in older adults (Kramer and Woodruff, 1984). More valid tests may be generated for understanding the intellectual functioning of older adults following the development of a better concept of "wisdom."

Personality Theories

While most other psychologists are specialists working with miniature theories about limited behavioral domains, personality theorists are integrative. They are interested in how the various psychological processes work together as a functional whole. Personality theorists have been concerned with two major developmental issues: to what extent is personality stable across the lifespan, and to what extent is personality change a consequence of developmental stages that unfold in some natural sequence versus being subject to the influence of random experience, environmental events, and other variables such as health?

Early developmental theory was dominated by stage theorists who believed that the personality developed in a stepwise fashion in concert with changing biological capacity and environmental demands. Freud was the premier stage theorist but had no contributions to make to adult development, as he believed that most of the important changes occurred before age five and that development was essentially completed by adolescence. Psychoanalysis was a retrospective analysis conducted in a surrogate parental environment for adults who had not resolved residual conflicts of the childhood stages. Freud (1924) held that psychoanalysis was not useful for individuals past age fifty because the mass of accumulated material was too great ever to be reviewed and resolved, and shrinking intellectual abilities rendered individuals no longer educable.

Jung, in contrast, preferred to treat patients who were middle-aged or older, for they had begun to comprehend the complexities of life (Butler and Lewis, 1977). Although Jung was not a strict stage theorist, he spoke of life's seasons, each with its own particular character, values, and tasks (see Staude, 1981). He described a transition between each season when one looks for new values and ways of being, the previous ones having become unsatisfactory. Jung personally had a very difficult midlife transition about which he wrote extensively, but he also postulated a late-life transition characterized by a search for spiritual values.

In Jung's system there were four basic functions of personality: sensation, feeling, thinking, and intuition. Each function existed on a dimension of introversion/extroversion that characterized the individual. There were other polarities of the psyche such as female/male, light/dark, and individual/collective. In early life, one personality function could develop to a greater extent than the other functions, but in the second half of life the task was to achieve balance and wholeness by developing the less developed functions. Extroversion was favored in early life, when the major task was adaptation to the external world. The second half of life favored introversion, where continued individuation involved finding one's spiritual center. Also, to achieve inner harmony and balance, men needed to develop the neglected feminine aspects of their psyche and females the masculine.

Erikson (1959) was the first to extend the stage concept of psychoanalytic theory from childhood to adulthood. Erikson, however, placed much more importance on social forces than Freud and characterized stages according to the psychosocial crises that needed to be resolved at each time period. While success in one stage of life is built on successful resolution of previous stages, resolution is not permanent. Development becomes more complex with age, and when a later crisis is severe, earlier crises are likely to be revived. In particular, the adolescent identity crisis may be revisited in different ways but hopefully resolved more easily once the initial resolution is accomplished.

For Erikson, later adulthood centers around ego-integrity versus despair and is the point at which an individual reviews his or her life and finds it is a meaningful whole or looks back with regret on its failures. Successful resolution results in the acceptance of life and culminates in wisdom. Despair centers on what might have been and the dim prospects for the future. At this point no studies have systematically investigated Erikson's ideas.

There are a number of other theories of change across the lifespan that do not use the concept of stages. Robert Havighurst proposed that different developmental tasks occur at different ages based on biological development and social expectations. A developmental task is one whose successful achievement leads to happiness and success in later tasks, while failure results in unhappiness, disapproval by society, and difficulty with later tasks (Havighurst, 1972). The tasks of late maturity (age sixty-plus) are to adjust to health changes, adjust to retirement, adjust to deaths of spouse and friends, affiliate with one's age group, and accept one's own death.

Loevinger (1976) identified conformist, conscientious, autonomous, and integrated personality traits which were roughly correlated with age. Integration represents the highest level and is more likely found in later adulthood. Similarly, Vaillant (1977) used a model of coping and adaptation and found more mature defense mechanisms with age.

Neugarten is one of the best-known of the non-stage lifespan theorists and has been credited with a life-course perspective from which much research has been generated. She, Havighurst, and a number of associates (Neugarten and Associates, 1964) undertook a large cross-sectional study of the residents of Kansas City. They tested the disengagement hypothesis of Cumming and Henry (1961), finding that a number of different activity patterns may result in life-satisfaction. Personality factors maintain considerable stability across ages. The lifespan is viewed as a developmental whole with age norms affecting the timing of adult role transitions (e.g., marriage, career, retirement) and the perceptions a person has of him- or herself (e.g., "middle-aged," "elderly") (Hagestad and Neugarten, 1985). People check their activities against the norms they perceive for their age group. Their behavior and self-concept is influenced by whether they perceive themselves as "on time" or not.

Fiske (1980) sought to classify commitments and determine if they change in predictable ways. She found interpersonal, altruistic, mastery, and self-protectiveness as key types of commitments. These change in somewhat idiosyncratic ways over time, but there is a shift from mastery to interpersonal commitment that characterizes more men and from interpersonal commitment to achievement (mastery) that characterizes more women. She describes this as "balancing out." In another study, Fiske and Chiriboga (1990) find older men and women seeking a balance between peace and quiet and boredom. Boredom is a potent stressor, and neither men or women appeared to desire withdrawal.

Many empirical studies of changes in various personality traits have not been part of large theoretical endeavors. These shed light on the question of whether there is change versus stability across the lifespan. Specifically, introversion-extroversion, rigidity, cautiousness, depression, and hypochondriasis will be reviewed.

The first cross-sectional study testing extroversion versus introversion found that older men showed greater introversion than younger (Brozek, 1955). Slater and Scarr (1964) found similar results longitudinally but attributed it to a higher dropout rate from death of the extroverts. No further studies have tested to see whether introversion may be related to longevity. Schaie and Parham (1976) attributed the higher level of introversion to cohort effects. Those who are presently elderly were raised in an era that did not encourage as much individual expressiveness as is encouraged in the current younger generations. However, Neugarten (1977) consistently finds that people become more introspective with age. What appears to be introversion may instead be reflectiveness.

Heglin (1956) reported that rigidity increased with age. Schaie (1958) qualified these results by looking at different types of rigidity and correlated them with results on an intelligence test. When Chown (1961, 1972) statistically controlled for differences on intelligence test performance, age differences in rigidity disappeared. It is possible that age differences in rigidity and performance on intelligence tests are related to the slowing in the central nervous system that is basic to aging (Birren, 1964). Rigidity is also a factor sensitive to cohort effects. The elders of tomorrow will likely be less rigid because of continued exposure to complex environments with continued opportunities for intellectual growth (Botwinick, 1978).

Cautiousness is another trait that may be a natural response to slowing in the central nervous system (Birren, 1964). Elderly subjects generally show a preference for withholding a response rather than producing an incorrect one. Young subjects will guess much more readily and produce errors of commission. Alternatively, errors of omission may be due to a different criterion of performance adopted by the older cohort or to a reduced sensory acuity.

Depression is the most common psychiatric disorder in the elderly and is a concomitant of the many types of loss that may be experienced. However, epidemiological studies show no higher incidence of depression in the elderly than in the general population (Blazer, 1982; Boyd and Weissman, 1982; Craig and Van Nata, 1979; Hirschfield and Cross, 1982).

Hypochondriasis is an abnormal preoccupation with bodily symptoms and illness and is a trait often attributed to the elderly. Although Costa and McCrae (1985), in a ten-year longitudinal study, found no differences in the health concerns of older adults, cross-sectional studies find that older adults score higher on this scale of the MMPI (Calden and Hokanson, 1959; Swenson, 1961). Although exaggerated concerns for physical well-being may be a consequence of health changes, it may also be a consequence of this cohort's aversion to expressing psychological distress directly. Because psychological problems have been equated with character defects and are not socially acceptable in the current generation of older Americans, they may come out as excessive health concerns.

What can one conclude about personality change and age? The major conclusion is that there is both consistency and change, but changes that take place do so in a context of remarkable continuity within the individual (Neugarten, 1977). People have the subjective opinion that they have changed to a greater extent than measures indicate (Woodruff and Birren, 1972). Overall life neither improves nor worsens, and there is neither growth nor decline in psychological well-being (McCrae and Costa, 1984; Costa et al., 1987).

Against this background of stability, a few changes do occur with regularity. Older men decline in general "masculine" activity and become more affiliative and emotional; older women are willing be more aggressive and egocentric than when they were younger. There is more reflectiveness or interiority with age, but this does not indicate social withdrawal.

What can one conclude about developmental stages in personality and aging? This question cannot be answered by looking at average scores on cross-sectional inventories. Instead, comprehensive longitudinal studies are required that examine how individuals change. Unfortunately, longitudinal studies have either tended to cover fairly short time spans or involve very select populations. Only those studies conducted with in-depth interviews have shown the qualitative changes implied by stage theories, and these are subject to the researchers' subjective interpretation. At this point, the tentative conclusion can be made that gender-linked variables and cohort variables are better predictors than developmental stages (Rossi, 1985; Lowenthal, 1975; Schaie and Geiwitz, 1982). For most people, aging means continuing familiar activities in familiar environments. Changes in health, finances, and marital status are more important influences in adaptation than changes in personality.

AN ECOLOGICAL THEORY OF AGING: THE COUNTERPART THEORY

Focusing on the individual, psychology is strategically placed between biology, which considers the cells and organs, and sociology, which considers group and cultural interactions. Bronfenbrenner (1977) calls for an ecological orientation in which the behavioral tendencies of an organism are viewed as resulting from the biological background of the organism and its interactions with a particular environment. A theory of aging also needs to include time course, change, and the changing organization of the behavior across the lifespan.

The first difficulty encountered by a global theory of aging is that the biological, social, and psychological processes do not age at the same rate (Birren and Schroots, 1984). A person's biological age is his or her current position relative to potential lifespan and is functionally defined by the loss of vital capacities and physiological regulatory processes that increase the probability of dying. The social age refers to a person's role and habits relative to others in the particular culture of which he or she is a member. Psychological age refers to the person's capacity to adapt behaviorally to situational or environmental demands. "Clearly psychological age is influenced by the biological and social factors, but the concept goes further in that it involves the use of adaptive capacities of memory, learning, intelligence, skills, feelings, motivations, and emotions for exercising behavioral control or self-regulation" (Birren and Cunningham, 1985, 8).

Aging is not a mirror image of earlier development but a transformation. Because different systems age at different rates, the relationships do not remain the same, so that the old person may be phenomenologically different from the younger self. Birren and Renner (1977) sought a definition of aging that recognized concurrent incremental as well as detrimental functions across the lifespan.

In the counterpart theory of aging, Birren (1964) uses an ecological approach and attempts to resolve the difficulties caused by the divergent time courses of the various aspects of aging. The counterpart theory postulates an active organism whose late-life state may not be directly programmed but is an indirect consequence of earlier programming and current environmental experiences which require new behavioral adaptations.

As a starting point, counterpart theory points out that biological aging seems to be more than a random process of depletion. For example, there is a characteristic length of life that is species specific. Also, there is a relationship between one's longevity and that of one's parents and grandparents. Although there is evidence for genetic programming, the further one moves past reproduction, the less likely it is that genetic programming will be well organized because late-life, postreproductive characteristics cannot be directly subject to selective pressure. Although the genetic program for aging may be less well coordinated than that of early development, the genetics that are finely tuned to produce a fit organism for reproductive success continue to influence the later state of the organism. There are a number of ways this can happen. The simplest is fairly direct but with the late-life consequences being different from the early ones. Smith (1957) used the example of blood pressure: in order to reach an optimal mean arterial value at an early age, the deleterious effects of high blood pressure may be more likely in old age. Another way in which programming can be expressed later is through pleiotropism, where genes with multiple effects may code for late characteristics different from those of early development. The consequence is an increased number and variety of genetic diseases in late life. Developmental programming may also be disrupted or compromised by environmental effects such as exposure to hazardous chemicals or malnutrition.

An important observation is the fact that across species longevity is correlated with brain size. In particular, the brain-body weight ratio with encephalization is a key factor in length of life (Sacher, 1977). Not only is the brain a key organ of adaptation for the individual, but an increased likelihood of survival may accrue to the young of those having long-lived elders. In hunter-gatherer societies, elders are important agents of cultural transmission—progenitors of information to the young as to how to survive and function in a particular environment. The key point is that natural selection for longevity may have been coupled with favorable behavioral characteristics. The counterpart theory embraces the potential of both psychological and biological "wisdom" increasing with age as part of the aging transformation.

Physiological subsystems are arranged in a vital hierarchy so that the failure of one can have a cascading effect on those lower in the hierarchy. The systems uppermost in the hierarchy are those that are able to incorporate experience or "memory" into their functioning: the nervous system and the immune system. The brain is the most critical of the two, containing a "master clock" with effects expressed through neurons that control hormonal flow and information to all parts of the body. "As the major integrating system of the body as well as its archive, the nervous system is in a key position to disseminate influences to other organs" (Birren, 1988, 167).

Birren (1988) proposes that the human sense of the self as a psychological being with a sense of direction through time derives from the storage of the past. It is this accumulated experience which enables an organism to be strategic. Not only do people adapt to new events, but they have goals and a self-consciousness about their position in the flow of events. The long-lived, postmitotic neurons of the brain remain for a lifetime and contain within them an information system that allows accumulation of experience and its processing so that new situations are perceived and acted on in different ways across the lifespan.

Social experience is one of the programmers of the nervous system so that beliefs and behaviors reflect not only individual experience but that of the cultural milieu. How people age is a reflection not only of physiology but of societal age norms. Because of its dual role in regulating both behavior and metabolic processes, the complex nervous system is the ultimate organ of adaptability both behaviorally and physiologically. The brain, then, is that link sought by theorists trying to understand the relationship between the social, psychological, and biological domains of aging.

The organism functions as if it has purpose, and that purpose is self-regulation. The probability of survival after birth increases as the organism becomes biologically self-regulating. The probability of survival also increases as behavioral adaptation allows the organism to control its environment. It is behavioral self-regulation which allows the aging individual continued functioning even as physical capacity is diminished.

Wisdom may involve metastrategies that take an account of present circumstances, integrate them with previous experience, and process information to extend the capacity of self-regulation beyond its previous limits. Birren and Lanum (1991) use the metaphor of the captain of an aging ship, who continues to navigate successfully. Despite the disadvantages of an older craft, he has a superior knowledge of his ship's capacities, the route he needs to take, the sea and weather conditions, and can develop novel strategies to reach port.

In the view of the counterpart theory, development continues throughout the lifespan. Encephalization is positively correlated with longevity, and the brain is the organ of integration between the biological, psychological, and social domains of aging, enabling new strategies in the face of changing environments. The older organism is a transformation of the younger organism. This transformation is both an indirect consequence of evolutionary forces expressed in genetic programs and a consequence of strategies developed by an active and goal-oriented organism. The counterpart theory places the organism in an ecological context in which the passage of time can have concurrent positive and negative consequences that affect the organization of the organism's abilities.

Parting Concerns

A valuable critique of aging research by Dannefer (1988) points out the frequency with which the increasing heterogeneity of people with age is acknowledged but remains unstudied. First, there is the assumption that science is searching for a normative view of the world that emphasizes generality not differences. Underlying this may be the individual researcher's conviction that his or her theory most adequately describes the actual situation and also the situation as it should be. There is the unhappy tendency to equate normativity with normality. A second major influence is the concept of development itself, which emphasizes sequentiality, unidirectionality, irreversibility, qualitative-structural transformation, and universality. While this may adequately describe growth of lower biological organisms, it does not adequately deal with human aging, which is a dialectical process in which the activities of the human act back on the aging of the biological organism in many ways.

The nonpsychologist tends to frame questions about aging less in terms of behavioral capacities than in terms of the experience of living or the patterns of life and their effects. Research in psychology has not dealt with questions regarding the experience of life. The compartmentalization of behavior by process or content increases the efficiency of research, but does not address the way an individual perceives or feels about the quality of life and alternative goals. Questions about the dynamics of the aging person, the goals, motivations, decision-making, and satisfaction about life require tapping into the inner views of the older person. Although emotions, feelings, and the experience of the quality of life are more difficult to measure, one might expect to see more research on life as it is experienced in addition to continued research on cognitive capacities.

There are also questions about the significance of behavior patterns over the course of life that need to be addressed. What difference do earlier behavior patterns have on late-life outcomes? This question brings the psychologist out of preoccupations with methodological issues into facing broad issues of greater significance for humankind.

It is possible that early development is more organized than is adult life and aging, but it is most unlikely that later adult life is only entropy or noisy disorganization of the adult following the time of optimum reproductive competence. In the next century one might anticipate that psychologists will be able both to pose and to answer more powerful questions about what makes the differences in the ways people grow up and grow old. The answers to such questions will help to maximize the number of productive, contented lives and minimize tortured and destructive ones.

BIBLIOGRAPHY

Adler, W. H. (1974) "An 'Autoimmune' Theory of Aging." In Rockstein, Sussman and Chesky, 33–42.

Atchley, R. C. (1971) "Retirement and Work Orientation." *The Gerontologist* 11:29–32.

______ (1991) *Social Forces and Aging.* 6th ed. Belmont, Calif.: Wadsworth.

Baltes, P. B., S. W. Cornelius, A. Spiro, J. R. Nesselroade, and S. L. Willis (1980) "Integration versus Differentiation in Fluid/Crystallized Intelligence in Old Age." *Developmental Psychology* 16:625–35.

Binstock, R., and E. Shanas, eds. (1985) *Handbook of Aging and the Social Sciences.* 2d ed. New York: Van Nostrand Reinhold.

Birren, J. E. (1959) *Handbook of Aging and the Individual.* Chicago: University of Chicago Press.

______ (1961) "A Brief History of the Psychology of Aging." *Gerontologist* 1:67–77.

______ (1964) *The Psychology of Aging.* Englewood Cliffs, N.J.: Prentice-Hall.

______ (1970) "Toward an Experimental Psychology of Aging." *American Psychologist* 25:124–35.

______ (1988) "A Contribution to the Theory of the Psychology of Aging: As Counterpart of Development." In Birren and Bengtson, 153–76.

Birren, J. E., and V. L. Bengtson, eds. (1988) *Emergent Theories of Aging.* New York: Springer.

Birren, J. E., and B. A. Birren (1990) "The Concepts, Models, and History of the Psychology of Aging." In Birren and Schaie, 3–20.

Birren, J. E., and W. R. Cunningham (1985) "Research on the Psychology of Aging." In Birren and Schaie, 3–34.

Birren, J. E., and L. M. Fisher (1992) "Speed of Behavior as a Reflection of Health and Aging." ERGO. Amsterdam, The Netherlands.

Birren, J. E., and J. C. Lanum (1991) "The Metaphors of Psychology and Aging." In Kenyon, Birren, and Schroots, 103–29.

Birren, J. E., and V. J. Renner (1980) "Concepts and Issues of Mental Health and Aging." In Birren and Sloane, 3–33.

Birren, J. E., and K. W. Schaie, eds. (1977) *Handbook of the Psychology of Aging.* New York: Van Nostrand Reinhold.

______ (1985) *Handbook of the Psychology of Aging.* 2d ed. New York: Van Nostrand Reinhold.

______ (1990) *Handbook of the Psychology of Aging.* 3d ed. New York: Academic Press.

Birren, J. E., and J. F. Schroots (1984) "Steps to an Ontogenetic Psychology." *Academic Psychology Bulletin* 6:177–90.

Birren, J. E., and R. B. Sloane, eds. (1980) *Handbook of Mental Health and Aging.* Englewood Cliffs, N.J.: Prentice-Hall.

Bjorksten, J. (1974) "Crosslinkage and the Aging Process." In Rockstein, Sussman, and Chesky, 43–59.

Blau, P. M. (1964) *Exchange and Power in Social Life.* New York: Wiley.

Blazer, D. G. (1982) "The Epidemiology of Late Life Depression." *Journal of the American Geriatrics Society* 30:581–92.

Botwinick, J. (1978) *Aging and Behavior.* 2nd ed. New York: Springer.

Boyd, J. H., and M. M. Weissman (1982) "Epidemiology." In Paykel, 109–25.

Bronfenbrenner, U. (1977) "Towards an Experimental Ecology of Human Development." *American Psychologist* 32:513–31.

Brozek, J. (1955) "Personality Changes with Age: An Item Analysis of the MMPI." *Journal of Gerontology* 10:194–95.

Burgess, E. W. (1960) "Aging in Western Culture." In Burgess (ed.), 3–28.

Burgess, E. W., ed. (1960) *Aging in Western Societies.* Chicago: University of Chicago Press.

Butler, R. N., and M. I. Lewis (1977) *Aging and Mental Health.* 2d ed. St. Louis: C. V. Mosby.

Calden, G., and J. E. Hokanson (1959) "The Influence of Age on MMPI Responses." *Journal of Clinical Psychology.* 15:194–95.

Canestrari, R. E., Jr. (1963) "Paced and Self-Paced Learning in Young and Elderly Adults." *Journal of Gerontology.* 18:165–68.

Cavan, R. S., W. Burgess, R. J. Havighurst, and H. Goldhammer (1949) *Personal Adjustment in Old Age.* Chicago: Science Research Associates.

Cerella, J. (1985) "Information Processing Rates in the Elderly." *Psychological Bulletin* 98:67–83.

______ (1991) "Aging and Information-Processing Rate." In Birren and Schaie, 201–21.

Cerella, J., L. W. Poon, and D. M. Williams (1980) "A Quantitative Theory of Mental Processing Time and Age." In Poon, 332–40.

Chown, S. M. (1961) "Age and the Rigidities." *Journal of Gerontology* 30:216–24.

______ (1972) "The Effect of Flexibility-Rigidity and Age on Adaptability in Job Performance." *Industrial Gerontology* 13:105–21.

Comfort, A. (1964) *Ageing: The Biology of Senescence.* San Francisco: Holt, Reinhart and Winston.

Cornelius, S. W. (1984) "Classic Pattern of Intellectual Aging: Test Familiarity, Difficulty, and Performance." *Journal of Gerontology* 39:201–6.

Costa, P. T., and R. R. McCrae (1985) "Hypochrondriasis, Neuroticism, and Aging: When Are Somatic Complaints Unfounded?" *American Psychologist* 40:19–28.

Costa, P. T. Jr., A. B. Zonderman, R. R. McCrae, J. Cornoni-Huntley, B. Z. Locke, and H. E. Barbano (1987) "Longitudinal Analyses of Psychological Well-Being in a National Sample: Stability and Mean Levels." *Journal of Gerontology* 42:50–55.

Craig, T. J., and P. A. Van Nata (1979) "Influence of Demographic Characteristics on Two Measures of Depressive Symptoms: The Relation of Prevalence and Persistence of Symptoms with Sex, Age, Education, and Marital Status." *Archives of General Psychiatry* 36:149–54.

Cristofalo, V. J. (1988) "An Overview of the Theories of Biological Aging." In Birren and Bengtson, 118–27.

Cumming, E., and W. E. Henry (1961) *Growing Old: The Process of Disengagement*. New York: Basic Books.

Cunningham, W. R., and J. E. Birren (1980) "Age Changes in the Factor Structure of Intellectual Abilities in Adulthood and Old Age." *Educational and Psychological Measurement* 40:271–90.

Cutler, R. G. (1982) "The Dysdifferentiative Hypothesis of Mammalian Aging and Longevity." In Giacobini et al., 1–19.

Dannefer, D. (1988) "What's in a Name? An Account of the Neglect of Variability in the Study of Aging." In Birren and Bengtson, 356–84.

Darwin, C. (1859) *On the Origin of the Species by Natural Selection*. London: John Murray.

Denney, N. W. (1982) "Aging and Cognitive Changes." In Wolman, 37–66.

Dillman, V. M. (1981) *The Law of Deviation of Homeostasis and Diseases of Aging*. Boston: J. Wright/PSG.

Dowd, J. J. (1975) "Aging as Exchange: A Preface to Theory."*Journal of Gerontology* 30:584–94.

______ (1978) "Aging as Exchange: A Test of the Distributive Justice Proposition." *Pacific Sociological Review* 21:351–75.

______ (1980) *Stratification Among the Aged*. Monterey, Calif.: Brooks-Cole.

Emerson, R. M. (1976) "Social Exchange Theory." *Annual Review of Sociology* 2:335–62.

Enesco, H. F., and P. Kruk (1981) "Dietary Restriction Reduces Age Pigment Accumulation in Mice." *Experimental Gerontology* 16:357–61.

Erikson, E. H. (1959) "Identity and the Life Cycle." *Psychological Issues* 1:18–164.

Estes, C. L. (1979) *The Aging Enterprise*. San Francisco: Jossey-Bass.

Estes, C. L., and E. A. Binney (1989) "The Biomedicalization of Aging: Dangers and Dilemmas." *The Gerontologist* 29 (5):587–96.

Finch, C. E., and L. Hayflick, eds. (1977) *Handbook of the Biology of Aging*. New York: Van Nostrand Reinhold.

Finch, C. E., and P. W. Landfield (1985) "Neuroendocrine and Automatic Functions in Aging Mammals." In Finch and Schneider, 567–94.

Finch, C. E., and E. L. Schneider, eds. (1985) *Handbook of the Biology of Aging*. New York: Van Nostrand Reinhold.

Fiske, M. (1980) "Changing Hierarchies of Commitment in Adulthood." In Smelser and Erikson, 238–64.

Fiske, M., and D. A. Chiriboga (1990) *Change and Continuity in Adult Life*. San Francisco: Jossey-Bass.

Foner, A. (1974) "Age Stratification and Age Conflict in Political Life." *American Sociological Review* 39:1081–1104.

______ (1986) *Aging and Old Age: New Perspectives*. Englewood Cliff, N.J.: Prentice-Hall.

Freud, S. (1924) *Collected Papers*. Vol. 1. London: Hogarth Press.

______ (1924) "Sexuality in the Aetiology of the Neuroses." In Freud, 220–48.

Galton, F. (1883) *Inquiries into Human Faculty and Its Development*. London: Macmillian.

Giacobini, E. et al., eds. (1982) *The Aging Brain: Cellular and Molecular Mechanisms of Aging in the Nervous System.* New York: Raven.

Greene, V. L. (1983) "Age Dynamic Models of Information-Processing Task Latency: A Theoretical Note." *Journal of Gerontology* 38:46–50.

Gruman, G. J. (1966) "A History of Ideas About the Prolongation of Life: The Evolution of the Prolongevity Hypothesis to 1800." *The American Philosophical Society Transactions* 56: Part 9.

Gubrium, J. F., and R. J. Lynott (1983) "Rethinking Life Satisfaction. *Human Organization* 42:30–38.

Hagestad, G. O., and B. L. Neugarten (1985) "Age and the Life Course." In Binstock and Shanas, 35–61.

Hall, G. S. (1922) *Senescence, the Second Half of Life.* New York: Appleton.

Havighurst, R. J. (1972) *Developmental Tasks and Education.* 3d ed. New York: McKay.

Hayflick, L. (1977) "The Cellular Basis for Biological Aging." In Finch and Hayflick, 159–86.

Heglin, H. J. (1956) "Problem Solving Set in Different Age Groups." *Journal of Gerontology* 11:310–17.

Hirschfield, R. M. A., and C. K. Cross (1982) "Epidemiology of Affective Disorders: Psychosocial Risk Factors." *Archives of General Psychiatry* 39:35–46.

Hulicka, I. M. (1965) *Age Group Comparisons for the Use of Mediators.* Paper presented at the Annual Meeting of the Southwestern Psychological Association, Oklahoma City, Okla.

Hulicka, I. M., and J. L. Grossman (1967) "Age-Group Comparisons for the Use of Mediators in Paired Associate Learning." *Journal of Gerontology* 22:46–51.

Kausler, D. H. (1991) *Experimental Psychology, Cognition, and Human Aging.* 2d ed. New York: Springer.

Kenyon, G. M., J. E. Birren, and J. J. F. Schroots, eds. (1991) *Metaphors of Aging in Science and the Humanities.* New York: Springer.

Kohn, M. L., and C. Schooler (1983) *Work and Personality: An Inquiry into the Impact of Social Stratification.* Norwood, N.J.: Ablex.

Korchin, S. J., and H. Basowitz (1957) "Age Differences in Verbal Learning." *Journal of Abnormal and Social Psychology* 54:64–69.

Kramer, D. A., and D. S. Woodruff (1984) "Breadth of Categorization and Metaphoric Processing: A Study of Young and Older Adults. *Research on Aging* 6:271–86.

Kuypers, J. A., and V. L. Bengtson (1973) "Social Breakdown and Competence: A Model of Normal Aging." *Human Development* 16:181–201.

Labouvie-Vief, G., and F. Blanchard-Fields (1982) "Cognitive Aging and Psychological Growth." *Aging and Society* 2:183–209.

Loevinger, J. (1976) *Ego Development: Conception and Theories.* San Francisco: Jossey-Bass.

Longino, C. F., and A. Lipman (1982) "The Married, the Formerly Married and the Never Married: Support System Differentials in Planned Retirement Communities." *The International Journal of Aging and Human Development* 15:285–97.

Lowenthal, M. F. (1975) "Psychosocial Variations Across the Adult Life Course: Frontiers for Research and Policy." *The Gerontologist* 15 (1):6–12.

Masaro, E. J. (1984) "Food Restrictions and the Aging Process." *Journal of the American Geriatric Society* 32:296–302.

Matras, J. (1990) *Dependency, Obligations, and Entitlements: A New Sociology of Aging, the Life Course, and the Elderly.* Englewood Cliffs, N.J.: Prentice-Hall.

McCrae, R. R., and P. R. Costa, Jr. (1984) *Emerging Lives, Enduring Dispositions: Personality in Adulthood.* Boston: Little.

Nebes, R. D. (1980) "Vocal versus Manual Responses as a Determinant of Age Differences in Simple Reaction Time." *Journal of Gerontology* 33:884–89.

Nebes, R. D., and M. E. Andrews-Kulis (1976) "The Effect of Age on the Speed of Sentence Formation and Incidental-Learning." *Experimental Aging Research* 2:315–31.

Neugarten, B. L. (1977) "Personality and Aging." In Birren and Schaie, 626–49.

Neugarten, B. L., & Associates (1974) *Personality in Middle and Late Life.* New York: Atherton.

O'Rand, A. M., and J. C. Henretta (1984) "Delayed Career Entry, Industrial Pension Structure, and Early Retirement in a Cohort of Unmarried Women. *American Sociologist* 47:365–73.

Paykel, E. S., ed. (1982) *Handbook of the Affective Disorders.* New York: Guilford Press.

Poon, L. W., ed. (1980) *Aging in the 80's: Selected Contemporary Issues in the Psychology of Aging.* Washington, D.C.: American Psychological Association.

Quetelet, A. (1969) *A Treatise on Man.* (1835) New York: Franklin.

Renner, V. J. (1977) "Research on the Psychology of Aging: Principles and Experimentation." In Birren and Schaie, 3–38.

Rockstein, M. (1974) "The Genetic Basis of Longevity." In Rockstein, Sussman, and Chesky, 1–10.

Rockstein, M., M. L. Sussman, and J. Chesky, eds. (1974) *Theoretical Aspects of Aging.* New York: Academic Press.

Rose, A. M. (1965) "The Subculture of Aging: A Framework for Research in Social Gerontology." In Rose and Peterson, 3–16.

Rose, A. M., and W. A. Peterson, eds. (1965) *Older People and Their Social World.* Philadelphia: Davis.

Rose, M. R. (1991) *Evolutionary Biology of Aging.* New York: Oxford University Press.

Rossi, A. S., ed. (1985) *Gender and the Life Course.* New York: Aldine de Gruyter.

Rubner, M. (1908) "Probleme des Wachstums und der Lebensdauer." *Gesellschaft für Innere Medizin und Kinderheilkunde* 7:58–81.

Sacher, G. E. (1977) "Life Table Modification and Life Prolongation." In Finch and Hayflick, 582–638.

Salthouse, T. A. (1982) *Adult Cognition: An Experimental Psychology of Human Aging.* New York: Springer.

______ (1985a) *A Theory of Cognitive Aging.* Amsterdam: Elsevier.

______ (1985b) "Speed of Behavior and Its Implications for Cognition." In Birren and Schaie, 400–26.

Salthouse, T. A., D. H. Kausler, and J. S. Saults (1988) "Utilization of Path-Analytic Procedures to Investigate the Role of Processing Resources in Cognitive Aging." *Psychology and Aging* 3:29–37.

Schaie, K. W. (1958) "Rigidity-Flexibility and Intelligence: A Cross-Sectional Study of the Adult Life Span from 20 to 70 Years." *Psychological Monographs: General and Applied.* 72, no. 9.

______ (1977–78) "Toward a Stage Theory of Adult Cognitive Development." *International Journal of Aging and Human Development* 8:129–36.

Schaie, K. W., and J. Geiwitz (1982) *Adult Development and Aging.* Boston: Little.

Schaie, K. W., and J. A. Parham (1976) "Stability of Adult Personality: Fact or Fable?" *Journal of Personality and Social Psychology* 9:151–66.

Schaie, K. W., and C. Schooler, eds. (1989) *Social Structure and Aging: Psychological Processes.* Hillsdale, N.J.: Erlbaum Associates.

Sinex, F. M. (1974) "The Mutation Theory of Aging." In Rockstein, Sussman, and Chesky, 1–10.

Slater, P. E., and H. A. Scarr (1964) "Personality in Old Age." *Genetic Psychology Monographs* 70:229–69.

Smelser, N. J., and E. H. Erikson, eds. (1980) *Themes of Work and Love in Adulthood.* Cambridge, Mass.: Harvard University Press.

Smith, J. M. (1957) "Genetic Variations in Ageing." In Yapp and Bourne, 115–22.

Staude, J. R. (1981) *The Adult Development of C. G. Jung.* Boston: Routledge and Kegan Paul.

Swenson, W. M. (1961) "Attitudes toward Death in an Aged Population." *Journal of Gerontology* 16:49–52.

Treat, N. J., L. W. Poon, J. L. Fozard, and S. J. Popkin (1978) "Toward Applying Cognitive Skill Training to Memory Problems." *Experimental Aging Research* 4:305–19.

Vaillant, G. E. (1977) *Adaptation to Life.* Boston: Little.

Walford, R. L. (1969) *The Immunologic Theory of Aging.* Copenhagen: Munksgaard.

Wallerstein, E. (1979) *The Capitalist World-Economy.* New York: Cambridge University Press.

Waugh, N. C. (1980) "Age-related Differences in Acquisition of a Verbal Habit." *Perception and Motor Skills* 50:435–38.

Witte, K. L., and J. S. Freund (1976) "Paired-Associate Learning in Young and Old Adults as Related to Stimulus Concreteness and Presentation Method." *Journal of Gerontology* 31:186–92.

Wolman, B. B., ed. (1982) *Handbook of Developmental Psychology.* Englewood Cliffs, N.J.: Prentice-Hall.

Woodruff, D. S., and J. E. Birren (1972) "Age Changes and Cohort Differences in Personality." *Developmental Psychology* 6:252–59.

Woodruff-Pak, D. S. (1988) *Psychology and Aging.* Englewood Cliffs, N.J.: Prentice-Hall.

Yapp, W. B., and G. H. Bourne, eds. (1957) *The Biology of Ageing.* London: Institute of Biology.

36 Sociological Theories

EARL D. C. BREWER

INTRODUCTION

Sociology is a relatively new discipline in the human sciences. The roots of modern sociology lie in the ideas of Enlightenment social philosophers of the eighteenth and nineteenth centuries. Emile Durkheim (1947) in France and Max Weber (1963) in Germany were among the scholars who first investigated the religious behavior of people as sociocultural activities rather than as theological ones. Early sociologists following Durkheim and Weber recognized the importance of religion in providing a sense of identity for individuals and a sense of social solidarity in society.

Sociology lacks a single dominant theory by which human behavior can be explained. However, dating from the early period of sociological thought, there have emerged three major theoretical paradigms that have had great influence. These are structural-functionalism, conflict theory, and symbolic-interactionalism.

Although sociology has heavily influenced the study of aging during the current century, the newly emerging field of religion, spirituality, and aging has not been carefully addressed by any of the human sciences. The present paper will review some of the tenets of the major sociological theories with special emphasis on their applicability to religion and aging. It will specifically consider two major content areas in sociological research: demographic studies and social change.

MAJOR THEORETICAL PERSPECTIVES

Structural-functionalism as an overarching pattern of explanation is premised on the idea that human society is like a huge organism in which actions of individual actors express the status, roles, and norms established within the society. It presumes that any behavior that continues across time serves some value or function in society. Otherwise, it would not persist (Parsons, 1951). Early studies of role loss among older people was based on a functionalist set of understandings about human life. It was assumed that life is largely shaped by the roles and expectations to which persons are assigned in society. A number of scholars have noted the role losses that typically occur in later life and have equated these with significant loss of prestige and power in the society. Scholars have suggested that older people, dealing from a diminishing status and role base, often try to exchange prestige and power for security (Dowd, 1980).

Religious groups, too, are structured by the expected behaviors of people in prime roles and positions. Customs or structured sets of role behaviors might persist just because they are believed to serve some useful purpose for society and/or the individual. In addition, functionalism expects that societies tend to seek stability instead of change or innovation. Religious practices, which often involve a revering of past events or persons, are viewed as helping to stabilize society and to discourage change. Religious institutions are seen as helping to inculcate a common basic set of values that help to hold society together (Weber, 1963). The theoretical struggles in searching for a social system theory have been reinvigorated in the emergence of general systems theory (von Bertalanffy, 1968; Buckley, 1967).

By sharp contrast, conflict theory, sometimes referred to as power theory, is premised on the assumption that both conflict and change in society are inevitable and normal. In any society there will occur two broad classes of people: those who have significant power and those who lack such power (Coser, 1956). Conflict between these groups is continuous. Karl Marx (1904), from whom these ideas are derived, analyzed the division of power between those who own the means of production and those who are essentially laborers, that is, those who must earn their way by the labor of their hands instead of the earnings of their capital. Marx assumed that the world would always face a relative scarcity of valued things and that competition for goods, services, and other valued things would ensure the continuation of conflict. The major institutions of society were controlled by the dominant class, the one with power, and would be used to keep those less powerful in their (subordinate) places. Even religion was seen as a pawn of the dominant class and an opiate of the masses that discouraged persons from challenging the order of society. Religion might offer comfort to the poor and elderly as part of the promise of a better life in the world to come.

Older Americans were perceived by the culture as a needy and power-deprived group in the 1960s when the Older Americans Act and Medicare were passed to assist these "deserving old people." This suggests that an implicit power base for the elderly existed since commitments for the poor elderly were made. Certainly by the late 1970s politicians viewed the elderly as a potential voter block, as the American Association of Retired Persons (AARP) and other interest groups emerged in Washington. Despite the burgeoning membership of AARP, that expectation has not, as of the 1990s, ever materialized. However, even in the 1960s, the elderly were seen as a group to be carefully served due to the rising cost of nursing home care for them and the spiraling number of older citizens.

The one theory indigenous to American culture is symbolic-interactionism. It was first taught by social philosopher George Herbert Mead (1934) at the University of Chicago. Mead and colleagues John Dewey and Albion Small taught a view of human behavior that is in many ways a mirror of American pragmatism, that tradition of thought focused on action rather than rules, morals, or ideas. Mead suggested that people develop a sense of self-identity through their interaction with the important persons in their lives. Individuals' judgements of themselves are seen as a product of the imagined judgements about them made by the several significant other people in their lives. From that socially-based sense of self emerged a recognition of the reciprocal nature of the roles and relationships each person experiences. Such patterns are continually in the process of renegotiation as persons interact. Both the meaning of these interactions and the reflexive social process followed in understanding the interactions will affect how persons choose to act (Payne, 1990, 30). Society is largely shaped by the common meanings and significant symbols that people develop between themselves in the processes of interaction.

Chappell and Orbach (1986) point out that, although it has been studied very little, not only present but past meanings affect our sense of meaning and our behavior. Clearly, groups that help to shape and express the symbolized meanings that people share in society are important in shaping the society. Religious groups are powerful sources of such meaning. The regular participation of older persons in religious groups allows them to be participants in the evolving meaning system of society. Nonaccess or limited access to such groups would undercut the sense of meaning for older persons (Mead, 1934).

Any of the above theories can be used to examine the importance of religion in the lives of older people. In turning to two major content areas in sociological study, the theoretical perspectives will be assumed to explain much of the behavior of older persons.

DEMOGRAPHY OR POPULATION STUDIES

> One widely used definition of demography is as: the study of the size, territorial distribution, and composition of the population, changes therein, and the components of and changes which may be identified as natality, mortality, territorial movement (migration) and social mobility (change of status). (Hauser and Duncan, 1959, 2)

Demography is related to several disciplines in the academic world. Population studies are important aspects of sociology, especially in helping to group, analyze, and make comparative statements about categories of people in a society. Demography allows separate comparison of people by social characteristics such as age, education, sex, income, and so on. Theories related to demography are of central importance to gerontology, as demographic studies include changes in the age structure of a society. Thus, demography defines the older age groups and their social characteristics, and these become a central focus of gerontology. Demographic theory also aims to identify recurring patterns of population, to study variations in such groups, and to formulate generalizations dealing with such variations and their consequences in population composition, dynamics, and relationships (Matras, 1973).

Demographic study has revealed that one of the most dramatic changes in the latter part of the twentieth century has been the rapid increase in the proportions of older and especially the very old population. While the population sixty-five-plus increased from 4 percent to 9 percent of the population between 1900 and 1960, it is expected to increase from 9 percent to 18 percent of the population by 2020. The eighty-five-plus population, in the meantime, increased by sevenfold in that same sixty years and will increase sevenfold more in the next sixty years (U. S. Senate Special Committee on Aging, 1986).

Perhaps the most dramatic increase is coming in terms of 100-year-olds. Compared with only 15,000 in 1980, there will be 100,000 by 2000, 250,000 by about 2025, and nearly 1,000,000 centenarians in the U. S. by 2080 as the baby-boomers reach the century mark (NIA and Bureau of the Census, 1987). In sharp contrast to these rapidly escalating numbers of elderly is the lack of personal, social, and cultural structural changes to serve meaningfully the needs of a massive older population. This represents a clear challenge brought about by the social changes of the twentieth century.

Many population studies have focused on a comparison between older adults and younger adults in the United States. An excellent summary of research findings several years ago was presented in *Aging and Society* (Riley and Foner, 1968). The authors emphasized the relationships between younger and older people and other aspects of population structure and dynamics as well. This can be seen in their review of studies concerning social roles. Among social role studies was a review of data relating to the older population and religion.

Some of the general findings relating to religion and aging are summarized below. It should be noted that while *Aging and Society* presents an adequate summary of the research literature in this field, much of the research is inadequate because it is only cross-sectional in nature and/or was based upon local or limited samples. As a result, generalization is very problematic to any group other than the one studied. More appropriate use of theories and improved methods of inquiry utilizing longitudinal and cross-sequential techniques are greatly needed in following up on these earlier studies. According to the data reported in Riley and Foner, women tend to be more actively involved in organized religious life than men. Membership in religious organizations tends to increase with age. Participation in organized religious activities appears to be related to a variety of life-satisfaction measures more consistently than any other variables except perceived health status. Participation in religious groups remains a part of many older peoples' lives longer than any other voluntary activity. Despite the more active involvement of older women in religious groups, leadership in religious organizations is dominated by men (Riley and Foner, 1968, 484).

A variety of statistical data about religious groups and aging exists. One source is *The Yearbook of American and Canadian Churches* (Bedell, 1993). A more accurate source are different surveys and polls conducted by groups like the Gallup Organization. For instance, *The People's Religion* (Gallup and Castelli, 1989) contains a summary of information about religious practices, some of which is noted below.

More than other age groups, older adults believe that religion was very important in the past (while growing up) and also in the present. Persons sixty years of age and over had the highest proportion of any age category claiming never to have doubted the existence of God. Seventy-two percent of those over fifty believe in life after death. Older persons attend charismatic services more regularly than any other group. They also report the highest proportion (48 percent) of religious TV viewing. Nearly half of those sixty-five and over support an amendment to restrict abortion. Sixty percent thought it possible to develop values courses in public schools. At least 26 percent of the fifty-plus population group listed the church/synagogue as excellent in meeting personal and family needs, while 43 percent rated it as good with very few thinking it only fair or poor.

This supportive perspective on religion is the view of the present cohort of older people. Evidence is not yet available as to whether it reflects a life change or period effect. For that, longitudinal studies will be required (Brewer, 1986).

SOCIAL CHANGE

Another major content area in sociology that helps in understanding the aging experience is that of social change processes. For the early Greek philosopher Heraclitus, the only constant was change (Wheelwright, 1959, 29). The twentieth century has been a time of continuous change. Yet, it is through change that repose comes, claimed Heraclitus. To understand that idea, change must be seen in tension with stability and continuity. Thus, change and resistance to change are twin processes that fit together. The adage that the more things change, the more they stay the same can also be reversed, i.e. the more things stay the same, the more they change.

At the macro level of sociological theory, there are broad stage theories of change that are understood as evolutionary. Toennies, for example, developed the concepts of community (*gemeinschaft*) and society (*gesellschaft*). The first was communal and traditional while the second was organizational and modern (Toennies, 1963). Toennies posited as universal a change or shift from rural to urban and from traditional to modern. Similar patterns were described by Durkheim in a shift from mechanical solidarity to organic solidarity as societies modernized

(Durkheim, 1964). More recent theories of social change have focused on the processes of change as traditional societies appear to move toward Western industrial societies in what is considered modernization (Moore, 1963). Part of the change often noted in such times is that of a shift from spiritual or religious customs to sensate or secular customs. Cowgill has argued that the elderly under conditions of modernization experience severe losses of status and prestige (1972).

The micro level of change examines the processes of change affecting individuals and small groups. Individuals experience life-course changes from birth to death with many shifts in roles, interaction patterns, family and group relations (Brewer, 1979). The current cohort of elderly began life in a society of limited change and have lived through periods of rapid social change.

In contrast to the sharp emphasis on change in human experience noted above is Atchley's theory of continuity and spiritual experience in aging (see Atchley, chap. 4). Atchley's theory presents the discovery that despite living in an age of change, older people have learned to maintain both internal and external continuity in their lives. Both individual and social or societal change contribute to the perpetuation of dysfunctional roles and behavior among many of the elderly. Labels such as the "roleless role of the elderly" and stereotypes of mental and physical decline with age have mirrored these roles, while older individuals at times have accepted and followed them.

Religious life and faith have been major coping mechanisms in the lives of many elderly, virtually a lifeboat for many elderly in a sea of social change (see Pargament et al., chap. 3). Payne (1990) tells of one such case in which religion provided an older woman with the basis for a continuity of identity and hope amid a world of social changes. Patty (Boyle, 1983) began a new life in late middle age by relocating to Washington, D.C. from Virginia, where she had taught in a university for many years. She lived in a new setting, having chosen a number of new life interests, including a dynamic ecumenical church which she believed would be stimulating. In this new world, however, many saw not the progressive Patty but an old woman and acted accordingly. Desperately needing some positive affirmation in her life as she tested out many new relationships, Patty soon moved to a church familiar to her denominational past. She was welcomed into the church community, but people there, too, tended to see her as an old woman and not the creative, competent Patty. There followed a time of pure disillusionment. The one place in her world where Patty expected to find encouragement treated her as an outsider, and she felt helpless and betrayed. The reconstruction that followed amounted in symbolic-interactionist terms to a change in the generalized-other images of self and of meanings in her "definition of the situation" (Thomas, 1928, 572). She accepted the inappropriate images some chose to hold of her but proceeded to displace other such images. Through continuing education classes in the area, she demonstrated that she was quite capable of learning and of success as a student. She developed friends in the church through her listening skills and interest in others. In becoming a caregiver for an aging cousin, she found the love returned to her that she needed and was willing to give if someone wanted to receive it.

Payne has pointed out that Patty went through several stages of change in developing a new identity and that the religious roles and religious social context were especially important in the process (Payne, 1990, 32–34). They in fact constituted a large part of her "generalized other" which changed in the course of developing a new identity. Payne believed that the interactive process model used by symbolic-interaction scholars offered the best way to understand the experiences Patty faced.

> In terms of professionals and other institutional members, the case of Patty indicates the need for a deeper understanding and appreciation of the dynamic plasticity of the self—even into old age; that self-development and changes do occur. They must also understand and appreciate the significance that the symbolic meanings of the church as a family—the beliefs, rituals and practices—have for older persons. Such an understanding could provide direction in counseling older persons, in affirming their personhood, and in helping older persons find new, appropriate and contributing roles in the church. (Payne, 1990, 37)

BIBLIOGRAPHY

Bedell, K., ed (1993) *Yearbook of American and Canadian Churches.* Nashville: Abington Press.

Birren, J. E., and V. L. Bengston (1988) *Emergent Theories of Aging.* New York: Springer.

Boyle, S. P. (1983) *The Desert Blooms: A Personal Adventure in Growing Old Creatively.* Nashville: Abingdon.

Brewer, E. D. C. (1979) "Life Stages and Spiritual Well-Being." In Moberg, 99–111.

______ (1986) "Research in Religion: An Unlikely Scenario." *Journal of Religion and Aging* 3:91–102.

Buckley, W. (1967) *Sociology and Modern Systems Theory.* Englewood Cliffs, N.J.: Prentice-Hall.

Chappell, N. L., and H. L. Orbach (1986) "Socialization in Old Age: A Median Perspective." In Marshall, 75–106.

Coser, L. A. (1956) *The Functions of Social Conflict.* New York: Free Press.

Cowgill, D. O., and L. D. Holmes, eds. (1972) *Aging and Modernization.* New York: Appleton-Century-Crofts.

Dowd, J. J. (1980) *Stratification Among the Aged.* Monterey, Calif.: Brooks-Cole.

Durkheim, E. (1947) *The Elementary Forms of Religious Life.* Glencoe, Ill.: Free Press.

______ (1964) *The Division of Labor in Society.* New York: Free Press.

Gallup, G., Jr., and J. Castelli (1989) *The People's Religion: American Faith in the 90's.* New York: Macmillan.

Hauser, P. M., and D. Duncan (1959) *The Study of Population*. Chicago: University of Chicago Press.

Marshall, V. W. (1986) *Laterlife: The Social Psychology of Aging*. Beverly Hills: Sage.

Marx, K. (1904) *A Contribution to the Critique of Political Economy*. New York: International Library.

Matras, J. (1973) *Populations and Societies*. Englewood Cliffs, N.J.: Prentice-Hall.

Mead, G. H. (1934) *Mind, Self and Society*. Chicago: University of Chicago Press.

Moberg, D. (1979) *Spiritual Well-Being: Sociological Perspectives*. Washington, D.C.: University Press of America.

Moore, W. E. (1963) *Social Change*. Englewood Cliffs, N.J.: Prentice-Hall.

National Institute on Aging, and Bureau of the Census (1987) *America's Centenarians: Data from the 1980 Census*. U.S. Dept. of Commerce, Bureau of the Census. Washington, D.C.: U.S. Government Printing Office.

Parsons, T. (1951) *The Social System*. Glencoe, Ill.: Free Press.

Payne, B. P. (1990) "Spiritual Maturity and Meaning-Filled Relationships: A Sociological Perspective." In Seeber, 25–39.

Riley, M., and A. Foner (1968) *Aging and Society*. New York: Russell Sage.

Seeber, J. J., ed. (1990) *Spiritual Maturity in Later Life*. New York: Haworth.

Thomas, W. I., and D. S. Thomas (1928) *The Child in America*. New York: Knopf.

Toennies, F. (1963) *Community and Society*. New York: Harper & Row.

Turner, J. H. (1978) *The Structure of Sociological Theory*. Rev. ed. Homewood, Ill.: Dorsey.

U.S. Senate Special Committee on Aging, AARP, FCA, and AoA (1986) *Aging America: Trends and Projections*, 1985–86 ed. Washington, D.C.: U.S. Government Printing Office.

von Bertalanffy, L. (1968) *General System Theory*. New York: George Braziller.

Weber, M. (1963) *The Sociology of Religion*. Boston: Beacon Press.

Wheelwright, P. (1959) *Heraclitus*. Princeton, N.J.: Princeton University Press.

37 Applications of Research Methods

DAVID O. MOBERG

This chapter provides examples of research, mainly from the social and behavioral sciences, that illustrate major methods used to study religion and aging and some of their findings. It includes a variety of methods for describing religious behaviors, beliefs, and attitudes, analyzing their relationships with other aspects of human life, and determining their consequences for well-being. The work reported is but a sample of research that has been done; much more is presented in other chapters.

INCIPIENT PIONEERING EFFORTS

Modern research on religion, spirituality, and aging has emerged relatively recently out of ancient and medieval scriptural, literary, philosophical, and inspirational sources. As an interdisciplinary subject, gerontology draws upon the methods and findings of all its component disciplines.

The innovative semiautobiographical work of psychologist G. Stanley Hall (1922) on senescence as "the last half of life" includes one of the first surveys about aging. He sent a questionnaire to "a few score of names of mostly eminent . . . old people" who were all "cultivated Americans" (321). Open-ended questions asked about their long life, experiences, and feelings. He combined the responses with his own perspectives. Except for a question on the church and clergy and one on dying and the hereafter, there was no explicit focus upon religion. Yet, he reported that comments from an unspecified number of respondents included the reaction that their parents had imposed too strict a religious and moral regimen upon them (330), that they became increasingly skeptical about religious beliefs and churches over the years (354), that most were agnostic and had no connection with any church (354–55), and that old women were almost always more religious than old men (350).

Although Hall mentioned the social class bias of his respondents and refrained from using percentages because of their small number, his personal biases, religious skepticism, and reduction of religion to psychological variables are evident in casual comments on religious topics sprinkled throughout his book.

For example, he interprets Christian faith as "only a hope-wish born of the unspent momentum of the will-to-live" (364). "Hymns have given the Western world ideas of death that the scientific descriptions of it show to be utterly false to fact" (144). Christianity "is not the religion for old men, and the revival of its attitudes, which we often see in them, is a phenomenon of arrest or reversion and not one of the advance that senescence should mark . . ." (83).

A similar antireligious bias is reflected in Covalt's (1960) assertion based on twenty-five years of medical practice that religion is not important to older people. Her evidence is the failure of patients to discuss religion with their physicians and to call out to God or pray audibly when they are dying.

CHALLENGES AND PROBLEMS IN RESEARCH ON RELIGION

The temptation among gerontologists to allow private prejudices to color their allegedly objective descriptions and interpretations of religion and aging has continued (Moberg, 1983). Yet, despite the tendency of gerontologists to ignore religion, coincidental findings about it occasionally emerge as subsidiary "aha" findings of research that focuses upon other topics. For example, Landis (1942) asked a random sample of 450 persons aged sixty-five to ninety-eight questions about past and present happiness and found that church attendance is related to happiness. When Lawton (1943) interviewed "about 50" persons with an average age of sixty to determine their satisfactions compared to those enjoyed in their youth, he found that only good health exceeded health of the spirit or trust in God in rank order of importance as a source of contentment in later life.

Some studies centered around other subjects have casually included religion as a secondary topic of interest. The pioneering work of Cumming and Henry (1961) in the Kansas City Study of Adult Life that developed disengagement theory, for example, had but a single question about belief in life after death as its measure of "religious piety" among persons aged seventy to eighty. They equated it with four questions about the meaning of life among those over eighty (254–56). Their religious activity score was based upon frequency of church attendance and membership in "any auxiliaries, committees, (teach Sunday school), or anything like that."

Orbach (1961) analyzed statistics for 6,911 adults aged twenty-one and over from five Detroit Area Study probability surveys during 1952 to 1957. The cross-sectional data did not show any general trend toward increased religiosity as measured by church attendance in old age. There was a fairly constant rate of attendance for the four age groups of 21–39, 40–59, 60–74, and 75-plus, except for a large increment in nonattendance among the oldest group. This finding has sometimes been used erroneously to support the claim that people become "less religious" in the later years. Orbach wisely warned about the logical limitations of such cross-sectional data. They cannot demonstrate whether or not there have been actual changes in the religious participation of specific persons or groups during their lifespan, nor about whether social differences among the elderly are more or less important than chronological age alone.

Age differences in religion-related characteristics that regularly emerge from public opinion polls provide only cross-sectional data as of the time of the survey; they cannot provide longitudinal evidence of changes with age over the human lifespan, although repeated findings of similar differences over long periods of time suggest the possibility of such a trend. These comparisons persistently show that the elderly have been the most religious age category for at least half a century and that this is not simply a cohort or period effect. It most probably is a correlate or result of both the aging process and differential survival by which the less religious people die earlier on average than the more religious (Moberg, 1990a, 179–87).

Longitudinal studies are necessary to determine life-cycle changes in people's religion, but none of the 212 projects in the comprehensive inventory of longitudinal social science studies (Young, Savola, and Phelps, 1991) are on religion, and its extensive subject index does not list such concepts as religion, faith, church, and spirituality. Analyses of retrospective life-reviews can help to fill that gap, even though they reflect problems of defective, incomplete, distorted, and selective recall and reporting. The majority of subjects in the Durham Veterans Administration Hospital Mental Health Survey, for example, reported that religion increased in importance as they grew older, only 5 percent reporting that it had decreased (Koenig, 1994, 168).

The importance of distinguishing between various potential measures of religion was brought out directly and forcefully in research on elderly persons in Central Missouri by Mindel and Vaughan (1978). They found that about 55 percent did not attend religious services regularly and thus had low levels of "organizational religiosity" [if above-national-average attendance is low!], but they nevertheless had high levels of "nonorganizational religiosity." They listened to religious services on radio and TV, prayed, listened to religious music, and gained help in understanding their lives from ideas learned through their religion, so religion remained salient for them.

Far too much current gerontological research and education, and particularly that which pertains to religion, still depends upon "thin descriptions and interpretations." This etic approach imposes an outside investigator's views on the topics and people under investigation. It contrasts sharply with "thick description" that is based upon the emic perspective of attempting to understand and appreciate the subjects' own interpretations of their actions, thoughts, and feelings (Denzin, 1989, 34, 39, 159–62, 200).

Whenever one applies or examines the findings of any research, it is important to note the explicit components used to identify the concepts of the study. "Religion" has many dimensions, each of which can be manifested in diverse ways (Glock, 1962; Moberg, 1967), and the same is true of most, if not all, other research variables. Therefore, the use of but one or a few of its indicators can produce misleading as well as incomplete results. The sample of people surveyed also needs attention, for differences in religious behavior are often evident by age (even among the elderly), gender, social class, ethnicity, religious identity, region, and other characteristics.

PERSONAL ADJUSTMENT AND LIFE-SATISFACTION STUDIES

The circumstances and characteristics that influence whether people are "aging successfully," adapting appropriately to their circumstances, feeling satisfied, experiencing quality of life, and having a sense of well-being or happiness has been a central concern of many gerontologists. When religion is included, it is one of the wholesome influences. Thus, a thesis by Oles (1949) reported findings from interviews and a questionnaire given to thirty-eight Orthodox Jews over age sixty-five. All of the well-adjusted persons were intensely or fairly religious, compared to 75 percent of the fairly adjusted and only 35 percent of the poorly and very poorly adjusted. Analysis of 553 case studies by Pressey and Simcoe (1950) similarly found that the "successful" were more likely than the "problem old people" to attend church.

A flurry of studies emerged under the influence of Cavan et al. (1949) at the University of Chicago. Their Chicago Activities and Attitudes Inventory was widely used to analyze "personal adjustment" in old age. Thus, J. H. Britton's (1949) study of 444 retired school teachers found that church membership, frequency of reading the Bible or prayer book, and belief in an afterlife were related to good adjustment for both men and women. J. O. Britton's (1949) study of 161 retired YMCA secretaries similarly found that frequency of church attendance and of reading the Bible were associated with adjustment. Albrecht's (1951) research on one hundred persons past age sixty-five showed that a combination of eight characteristics was required for good adjustment, among them regular church attendance.

Additional studies that found church attendance related to happiness or personal adjustment were by Pan (1951), Schmidt (1951), and Shanas (1949). The latter two also mentioned that reading the Bible or other religious books and listening to radio church services were associated with good adjustment, as also was belief in a life after death in the research of Shanas and both Brittons. Religion was not a primary focus of attention in these and other adjustment studies, or it would have been mentioned in many more research reports.

Whenever church membership was included among the variables in these early studies, it was associated with good adjustment with but a few minor exceptions. An exploratory study of sixty-eight elderly persons (Moberg, 1950), however, found that matching individual church members with nonmembers by use of nine control variables (similar characteristics) *decreased* the differences in the mean personal adjustment scores of the two groups, although the members still had higher scores. This suggested the possibility that complete control of all factors influencing personal adjustment in old age might eliminate the differences between the groups. The same study also defined Christian fundamentalists as those who believed the Bible to be infallible and the final authority for faith and practice and who believed Jesus is truly God and the Savior who shed his blood for our sins. It found that they had higher adjustment scores than the nonfundamentalists and that the differences *increased* when individuals were matched by using eleven control variables.

Multidimensional Research

Those findings led to Moberg's (1951) research project that focused explicitly upon religion. Because experiments on this subject are impossible, he used quasi-experimental designs (see Reker, chap. 38, this volume). These systematically study the relationships between variables by making observations under conditions of control that neither manipulate nor exert force upon people. Instead, they select and compare an experimental group of persons who already have been exposed to some type of treatment, social program, or natural force in the environment (in this case religion) with a control group who have not been or have been only to a lesser degree (Chapin, 1947).

A lengthy interview schedule gathered data from 219 persons aged sixty-five and over who resided in five retirement homes, a veteran's home, and a county home. A fully representative sample of all guests in the homes was impossible because some were difficult to locate, senile, physically ill, or mentally deficient. The main concern, however, was with relationships among variables, not with sampling some larger universe.

The chief method used in analyzing the data was matching each individual in the experimental group of the more religious people with a similar less or nonreligious person in the control group (see Greenwood, 1945, 81–120). The control variables used for matching were those found relevant in previous studies: gender, education, marital status, family status, social organizations, self-rating of health, present employment, and closeness in age. Whenever there was doubt as to which person to select for matching, additional secondary controls (Moberg, 1954) of nativity, place and length of residency, occupation, means of support, and father's occupation were used to increase the similarities of the matched persons. The Chicago Attitudes Inventory (E. W. Burgess et al., 1948) was used to measure personal adjustment.

The 132 church members had a mean personal adjustment score of 28.4, compared to 23.3 for the 87 nonmembers, a statistically significant difference. When seven control variables were used, it was possible to match only fifty-three pairs; this reduced the members' scores to 26.8 and increased the nonmembers' to 24.9.

Addition of two more controls brought the scores of the remaining nine pairs to 24.1 and 24.2, respectively.

Case studies made it apparent that religion had significantly influenced the lives of many nonmembers. Only twenty-three of the eighty-seven nonmembers had never been members; their mean adjustment score was 21.5, while the former members' was 24.0. Matching with seven controls left eleven pairs of current members and never-members with mean scores of 25.5 and 21.5, a nonsignificant difference.

Analysis of one hundred early returns revealed that religious beliefs and activities were not a single meaningful frame of reference, so they were analyzed separately. A religious activities score was compiled for each respondent on the basis of current and past church membership, present attendance at religious services, attendance change since age fifty-five, attendance at age twelve, present and past offices held in the church, and frequencies of reading the Bible, private prayer, family worship or prayers, and grace at meals during most of the adult life. The scores correlated positively ($r = .593$) with personal adjustment scores.

The eighty-six persons with the seven highest religious activity scores had a mean adjustment score of 31.1, while the forty-one with the seven lowest had a mean score of 18.3. Matching them with seven control variables resulted in nineteen pairs with adjustment scores of 28.7 and 16.3, respectively, a highly significant difference. Further analysis revealed that those who formerly were leaders in their churches had higher adjustment scores than nonleaders, a difference that remained in the matched pairs.

A religious belief score was similarly calculated on the basis of sacred vs. secular attitudes toward the future and beliefs about prayer, sin and forgiveness, the Bible, and Jesus. It correlated .660 with the religious activities scores and .462 with the personal adjustment scores. The 155 "believers" (persons in the four highest score categories) had an average adjustment score of 28.0 compared to 19.9 for the 35 "nonbelievers" (the five lowest belief scores). Matching with seven control variables reduced the numbers to twenty-two pairs with statistically significantly different scores of 27.2 and 19.9 respectively.

This research showed that the relationship between church membership and good personal adjustment is spurious. Membership per se is not a cause of good adjustment. Instead, good adjustment is more basically a reflection of the religious activities and beliefs associated with membership. However, this study does not definitively establish a causal connection in either the direction of religion's contributing to good adjustment or of adjustment's contributing to religiosity. Neither does it reveal whether persons with low adjustment who begin to participate in religious activities and adopt religious beliefs become better adjusted.

Replications of Moberg's (1951) research on fifty-seven older institutionalized persons (A. Burgess et al., 1960) and on fifty-five elders who lived independently in a middle-class urban community (Renfrew et al., 1961) reached similar conclusions.

Recent Life-Satisfaction Studies

In 1988 Moberg (1990b) attempted an empirical and conceptual replication of his 1951 research by adapting the interview schedule to fit conventional modes of precoding and recording data for computer analysis. The threefold "Agree ____, Disagree ____, ? ____" response pattern of the Chicago Attitudes Inventory (E. W. Burgess et al., 1948) was modified to the sixfold "Strongly Agree, Agree, Tend to Agree, Tend to Disagree, Disagree, Strongly Disagree." Interviews were completed for one hundred mobile elders residing in congregate-living and public housing facilities in the Milwaukee, Wisconsin, metropolitan area.

The findings were similar to those of the 1951 study. Persons who had never been church members had the lowest personal adjustment scores (18.0), former members next (26.2), and those who still were members the highest (33.4). The correlation between adjustment and religious activities scores was .403 (significant at the .000 level) and that with the religious beliefs score was .224 (significant at the .025 level).

Instead of matching individuals from the experimental (church members) and control (nonmembers) groups, multiple regression was employed. Of the eight independent variables in the equation, the religious activities score and self-rating of health accounted for almost all of the observed variance in personal adjustment scores. Despite or because of its correlation of .536 with the religious activities score, the religious belief score did not contribute significantly to the variance in adjustment. This may result partly from ceiling problems, for respondents were very religious. They were predominantly Christian; 84 percent prayed at least several times a week; 92 percent believed in the concept of sin; only 4 percent did not believe their own sins had been forgiven; 76 percent believed Jesus was the Savior who shed his blood for our sins; 63 percent believed the Bible is the perfect Word of God. Only 2 percent had "no religion," so even those with relatively "low" belief scores had high levels of religiosity. The belief scale failed to differentiate between moderate and high levels of belief. Furthermore, the multiple regression technique included all respondents, while the 1951 experimental designs accentuated differences by omitting people in the middle categories of beliefs and activities.

Further evidence, however, suggests that religious activities are more significantly related to personal adjustment and similar concepts such as morale and life satisfaction than are the beliefs and attitudes presumed to be their roots. A study of 156 retired professionals by Alexander and Duff (1991) found that social religious activity is significantly related to life-satisfaction, but private devotional behavior and intensity of religious commitment do not predict well-being. They concluded that "the primary function of religion for promoting feelings of personal well-being is in integrating the individual into a moral community" (20).

Coke's (1991) survey of 166 elderly African Americans also found that only family roles explained more variance in life-satisfaction than hours spent in church participation. Ortega et al. (1983) similarly discovered in research on 4,522 Alabamans that elderly blacks were significantly more satisfied or happy than elderly whites. Relationships with their church friends were far more important than those with kin and non-church-related friends; the "community of faith" was a focal point for community activities and a pseudo-extended family.

Reviews of several studies by Witter et al. (1985) and by Cox and Hammonds (1988) similarly conclude that activities are more significant to life-satisfaction than are religious beliefs. On the other hand, Steinitz's (1980) secondary analysis of 1,493 elders in National Opinion Research Center surveys showed that belief in life after death was a much stronger and more discriminating predictor of both well-being and Weltanschauung than frequency of church attendance. Hence, the particular beliefs and activities analyzed, as well as the types of people sampled, may significantly influence findings on relationships between religious variables and life-satisfaction.

The Duke Longitudinal Study of Aging has indicated that religious activities decline gradually in late old age, while religious attitudes tend to remain unchanged. Religion becomes an increasingly important factor in the adjustment of older persons as they age despite declining church attendance. Religious behavior is correlated more strongly than religious attitudes with various measures of adjustment (Blazer and Palmore, 1976).

CLINICAL HEALTH RESEARCH

Religiously attuned members of the helping professions, as well as clergy and other church leaders, often share anecdotes and experiences about the role of prayer, faith, and spiritual support in various therapies, as well as about the importance of their own religious commitment as an aid in dealing with the trauma of illness, accidents, and disabilities of clients and patients (see, e.g., Fish and Shelly, 1988 and Carson, 1988 on religion in therapy). Most of the reports are purely descriptive, and claims by advocates of various types of spiritual healing tend to be exorbitant, but systematic research is beginning to lay a more solid foundation for generalizations about the role of religion in health and healing (see Koenig et al., 1988; Koenig, 1993).

More than thirty studies of health-care utilization have examined the effects of religious variables (Schiller and Levin, 1988). Over three-fourths report significant differences in utilization rates even though the measure of religion in most is simply Protestant, Catholic, or Jewish affiliation.

An analytic survey of research on religion in four major psychiatric journals noted that a religious variable was included in only 59 of 2,348 quantitative articles between 1978 and 1982 (Larson, Pattison et al., 1986). Of these 49

(83 percent) used only a single static measure of religion (usually denomination) rather than multiple dynamic measures, and available religious research reports were seldom cited. It concluded that the academic knowledge and skills needed to evaluate religion have not been absorbed into psychiatric research. The samples of people studied in most of the research also are skewed, with significant overrepresentations of Jewish and other/none affiliations and underrepresentations of Protestants (Larson, Donahue et al., 1989). Similar patterns of neglect and distortion of religion are found in the research related to clinical practice and research in family medicine (Craigie et al., 1988; see also Craigie et al., 1990), despite the fact that "family physicians generally recognize the important role of faith and trust as an ally in the healing process" (Foglio and Brody, 1988, 473).

Larson, Koenig, et al. (1989) examined the relationship between blood pressure, self-perception of the importance of religion, and frequency of church attendance in a rural sample of 407 white men who were free from hypertension and cardiovascular disease. Those who rated religion as important and attended church at least weekly had significantly lower diastolic blood pressure than those who were low on either, and even more so on both, of those religion measures. The differences persisted among those aged fifty-five and over, even when adjustments were made for age, socioeconomic status, smoking, and the Quetelet index of the weight-height ratio.

Thirty female patients aged sixty-five and over with no psychiatric history or current cognitive impairment who were on the orthopedic units of a large midwestern teaching hospital for hip fractures and surgical repair were examined by Pressman et al. (1990) for geriatric depression, ambulation status, and religiosity (religious services attendance, self-perceived religiousness, religion or God as a source of strength and comfort). Religiousness scores were not correlated with initial depression scores, but at discharge they were significantly negatively related and the scores were significantly correlated also with better ambulatory status. Both relationships were even more significant when the severity of illness was controlled, but when depression was controlled, religiosity was no longer significantly correlated with ambulation status, perhaps because of the small size of the sample. Ambulation and lower depression, however, were significantly associated with church attendance. The research data, theories, and interpretive conclusions of research reported by Pargament et al. (1992) similarly point to the positive role of religion as a preventive of mental illness.

Koenig's (1990) overview of research on the prevalence of religious behaviors, attitudes, and coping behaviors among community-dwelling elders and those seeking attention for medical illness found that for older adults, "religion appears to convey and reflect anything but maladjustment, instability or mental illness" (50) and that no studies demonstrate a significant negative correlation between religion and well-being. He concluded that "because of its widespread prevalence and the depth of permeation into the psychic processes of older adults, religious issues should be addressed by the therapist or counselor" (50). In spite of these and other important findings, the geriatric and psychiatric research reported in pastoral counseling journals often is methodologically deficient, failing to state hypotheses and sampling methods, use control groups, report response rates, evaluate at two or more points in time, and discuss limitations of findings (Gartner et al., 1990).

Regardless of the difficulties of experimentation with people, a very significant experiment relevant to religion and aging was conducted at San Francisco General Hospital (Byrd, 1988). All patients admitted to the coronary care unit over a nine-month period were invited to enter a prospective double-blind randomized protocol to assess the therapeutic effects of intercessory prayer. After explaining the project and obtaining informed consent, 393 cooperated (57 refused for personal reasons, religious convictions, and/or unwillingness to sign the consent form). The patients were randomly assigned by a computer to receive or not receive intercessory prayer; neither they, the staff, physicians, nor the project director knew who was in which group. The average age of the experimental group was 58.2 ± 14.8 years, and that of the control group was 60.1 ± 15.0. There were no significant differences in the primary diagnoses of the two groups at the time of entry.

The intercessors were "born again" Catholic and Protestant Christians who engaged in daily devotional prayer and Christian fellowship in a local church. Each patient in the experimental group was randomly assigned to from three to seven intercessors, who were given the patient's first name, diagnosis, general condition, and pertinent updates. Daily until discharge from the hospital they prayed to God for rapid recovery, prevention of complications and death, and whatever else they believed beneficial to the patient. No personal contacts were made; their praying occurred outside of the hospital.

During hospitalization, the group prayed for had significantly fewer instances of congestive heart failure, cardiopulmonary arrest, pneumonia, intubation/ventilation, diuretics, and antibiotics than the control group. The comparative hospital course after admission was graded as follows on the basis of careful criteria:

	Experimentals	Controls
Good	85%	73%
Intermediate	1	5
Bad	14	22

These differences are significant at the one percent level.

The results show measurable beneficial effects of intercessory prayer, even without accounting for conditions beyond control of the study, such as prayers on behalf of both groups by persons outside the research, religious convictions of the patients, and whether they prayed for themselves.

At California's Camarillo State Hospital, Gonzales-Singh (1977) established therapy groups for elderly mentally ill or impaired Jewish and Catholic patients who had been religiously active in the past. He found that the use of familiar religious rituals, symbols, and worship patterns had significant therapeutic results that far outshone the conventional treatment that did not incorporate religion (see also Ellor et al., 1987).

Experimental research on people is limited by ethical values, especially the need to protect their autonomy and civil liberties (see Kimmel, 1988). These restrictions are even greater in studying religion than on many other topics. To impose experimental conditions related to religious commitment upon research subjects removes or reduces the voluntary nature of faith commitment that is central to intrinsic or "genuine" religiosity. Experiments with such activities as presenting different programs, styles, or patterns of worship, religious education, counseling, and value clarification, however, are often feasible, and "natural experiments" of comparing or contrasting instances that occur without the intrusion of a researcher seldom are objectionable.

LIFE AFTER LIFE STUDIES

In the U.S.A. and other "developed nations," most deaths occur among the elderly. The reports of near-death experiences by people who have been revived from clinical death by cardiopulmonary resuscitation (CPR) or other means have emphasized pleasant experiences such as seeing a bright light at the end of a dark tunnel, meeting deceased loved ones, and having an out-of-body experience of watching oneself from a distance. Moody (1976, 184) concluded from his study that "we cannot fully understand this life until we catch a glimpse of what lies beyond it," thus encouraging the belief that his and similar reports (e.g., Kübler-Ross, 1969) depict everyone's experiences at death.

Rawlings (1978, 1980), a teacher of CPR in medical schools who has had extensive personal experience in resuscitating clinically dead people, has warned against undue reliance upon reports of revived persons that are given subsequent to the experience. He was startled to discover that immediately upon recovery there are approximately equal incidents of patients who report blissfully happy and horrendously hellish experiences while "dead." Altogether only about one-fifth (20 percent) of all who are resuscitated report about any "life after life." However, those who report terrifying experiences immediately after recovery tend to repress them completely. As little as twenty minutes later, they can no longer share them even with the attending physician who heard their accounts. They do not want to admit their failures, much less to "being in hell" during their life beyond. (See also, Rawlings, 1994.)

Most psychologists and psychiatrists who have studied this subject have not resuscitated anyone. They interrogate volunteers who are eager to report their "good" experiences but not the "bad" ones, and they do so days, weeks, or months after the clinical death (Rawlings, 1980, 21, 187). To generalize from such a biased sample is misleading enough, but to ignore the unpleasant half is even worse. Furthermore, those who are revived after near-death experiences are very few compared to those who die without returning. To assume they are a valid sample of all deaths, even if the half with terrifying experiences is included, is existential as well as statistical folly.

FUTURE DIRECTIONS FOR RESEARCH

The dominant data gathering technique in studies of religion and aging persistently remains the use of questionnaires and interview schedules. Like all other methods, these always reflect the specific purposes of the research and the special interests and biases of the investigators.

All of the techniques and methods of the social and behavioral sciences can be used effectively in the study of religion and aging. We have sketched examples of survey research, experiments and experimental designs, longitudinal studies, and applications of measuring tools and techniques. They, along with such other methods as case studies, participant observation, ethnomethodology, grounded theory, historical analyses, use of personal documents, ideal-type taxonomies, games, and computer simulations, all have their respective strengths and weaknesses. The faults of each can be corrected in part by the complementary use of additional and different methods. Neither quantitative statistically-based studies nor intensive qualitative analyses are sufficient by themselves alone to provide a full and clear understanding of the broad and significant scope, implications, and consequences of religion in the lives of older people and its important role in local, regional, national, and global society.

Numerous instruments to measure such concepts as intrinsic and extrinsic religion, spiritual maturity, and Christian lifestyle are at various stages of development and validation (Bassett et al., 1991; Benner, 1991; Kirkpatrick, 1989; Moberg, 1984, 1986), and techniques such as the life-review (Hateley, 1985), reminiscence (Georgemiller and Getsinger, 1987), and the spiritual lifeline (Gross, 1985) are widely used in therapy for older people. Supplementing the clinical applications with research can be highly beneficial to our understanding of the relevance of religion and spirituality to personal and collective well-being. The extensively used and solidly validated Spiritual Well-Being Scale (Paloutzian and Ellison, 1982; Ellison, 1983), for example, has shown that religious well-being is positively related to personality integration (Ellison and Smith, 1991; Ledbetter et al., 1991). The Scale's ceiling problems make it impossible to distinguish between different degrees of high spirituality, thus skewing group scores negatively (toward lower levels), but it has seldom revealed significant differences that seem attributable to age alone (Bufford, Paloutzian, and Ellison, 1991).

Replicating past research to confirm or modify findings of what already has been done is very important. In the psychology of religion much work has been devoted to developing measuring instruments but far too little to using and reusing them. As a result, the scientific understanding of religious phenomena and their relationships to other variables is developing much more slowly than it ought (Gorsuch, 1990). The same certainly applies to other disciplines and domains of research related to religion and aging.

Gerontological studies of religion need the triangulation (Denzin, 1989) that applies numerous research methods to divergent types of people under varying sets of circumstances by researchers from many disciplines and professions who have various worldviews and diverse sets of values and who use many theoretical models, measuring instruments, analytical tools, and conceptual approaches. Research methods textbooks, handbooks on the unique issues and problems confronted in gerontological studies (Lawton and Herzog, 1989; Schaie et al., 1988; Fry and Keith, 1986) and a well-grounded understanding of both religion and aging are invaluable resources for these studies. All the evidence to date indicates that such research will continue to reveal significant contributions by religion and spirituality to the well-being of older people.

BIBLIOGRAPHY

Albrecht, R. (1951) "The Social Roles of Old People." *Journal of Gerontology* 6:138–45.

Alexander, F., and R. W. Duff (1991) "Influence of Religiosity and Alcohol Use on Personal Well-Being." *Journal of Religious Gerontology* 8 (2):11–25.

Bassett, R. L., W. Camplin, D. Humphrey, C. Dorr, S. Biggs, R. Distaffen, I. Doxtator, M. Flaherty, P. J. Hunsberger, R. Poage, and H. Thompson (1991) "Measuring Christian Maturity: A Comparison of Several Scales." *Journal of Psychology and Theology* 19 (1):84–93.

Benner, D. G., ed. (1991) "Special Issue—Spirituality: Perspectives in Theory and Research." *Journal of Psychology and Theology* 19 (1):1–117.

Blazer, D. B., and E. Palmore (1976) "Religion and Aging in a Longitudinal Panel." *The Gerontologist* 16 (1):82–85.

Britton, J. H. (1949) "A Study of the Adjustment of Retired School Teachers." Dissertation, University of Chicago.

Britton, J. O. (1949) "A Study of the Adjustment of Retired YMCA Secretaries." Dissertation, University of Chicago.

Bufford, R. K., R. F. Paloutzian, and C. W. Ellison (1991) "Norms for the Spiritual Well-Being Scale." *Journal of Psychology and Theology* 19:56–70.

Burgess, A., K. Jessup, and C. Tenove (1960) "The Relationship Between Religion and Personal Adjustment in Old Age." Bethel College, St. Paul, Minn.: (unpublished paper).

Burgess, E. W., R. S. Cavan, and R. J. Havighurst (1948) *Your Activities and Attitudes.* Chicago: Science Research Associates.

Byrd, R. C. (1988) "Positive Therapeutic Effects of Intercessory Prayer in a Coronary Care Unit Population." *Southern Medical Journal* 81 (7):826–29.

Carson, V. B. (1988) *Spiritual Dimensions of Nursing Practice.* Orlando, Fla.: Saunders.

Cavan, R. S., E. W. Burgess, R. J. Havighurst, and H. Goldhamer (1949) *Personal Adjustment in Old Age.* Chicago: Science Research Associates.

Chapin, F. S. (1947) *Experimental Designs in Sociological Research.* New York: Harper and Bros.

Coke, M. M. (1991) *Correlates of Life Satisfaction among the African-American Elderly.* New York: Garland.

Covalt, N. K. (1960) "The Meaning of Religion to Older People." *Geriatrics* 15:658–64.

Cox, H., and A. Hammonds (1988) "Religiosity, Aging, and Life Satisfaction." *Journal of Religion and Aging* 5 (1-2):1–21.

Craigie, F. C., Jr., D. B. Larson, and I. Y. Liu (1990) "References to Religion in *The Journal of Family Practice.*" *Journal of Family Practice* 30 (4):477–80.

Craigie, F. C., Jr., I. Y. Liu, D. B. Larson, and J. S. Lyons (1988) "A Systematic Analysis of Religious Variables in *The Journal of Family Practice,* 1976–1986." *Journal of Family Practice* 27 (5):509–13.

Cumming, E., and W. E. Henry (1961) *Growing Old: The Process of Disengagement.* New York: Basic Books.

Denzin, N. K. (1989) *The Research Act: A Theoretical Introduction to Sociological Methods.* 3d ed. Englewood Cliffs, N.J.: Prentice-Hall.

Ellison, C. W. (1983) "Spiritual Well Being: Conceptualization and Measurement." *Journal of Psychology and Theology* 11 (4):330–39.

Ellison, C. W., and J. Smith (1991) "Toward an Integrative Measure of Health and Well-Being." *Journal of Psychology and Theology* 19 (1):35–48.

Ellor, J. W., J. Stettner, and H. Spath (1987) "Ministry with the Confused Elderly." *Journal of Religion and Aging* 4 (2):21–33.

Ferraro, K. F., ed. (1990) *Gerontology: Perspectives and Issues.* New York: Springer.

Fish, S., and J. A. Shelly (1988) *Spiritual Care: The Nurse's Role.* 3d ed. Downers Grove, Ill.: InterVarsity Press.

Foglio, J. P., and H. Brody (1988) "Religion, Faith, and Family Medicine." *Journal of Family Practice* 27 (5):473–74.

Fry, C., and J. Keith (1986) *New Methods for Old-Age Research.* Westport, Conn.: Bergin and Garvey.

Gartner, J., D. B. Larson, and C. D. Vachar-Mayberry (1990) "A Systematic Review of the Quantity and Quality of Empirical Research Published in Four Pastoral Counseling Journals: 1975–1984." *Journal of Pastoral Care* 44 (2):115–23.

Georgemiller, R. J., and S. H. Getsinger (1987) "Reminiscence Therapy: Effects on More and Less Religious Elderly." *Journal of Religion and Aging* 4 (2):47–58.

Glock, C. Y. (1962) "On the Study of Religious Commitment." *Religious Education* 57 (Research Supplement): S98–110.

Gonzales-Singh, E. E. (1977) "The Comfort of the Known in the Unknown World of the Elderly's Mental Illness." Paper presented at the National Intra-Decade Conference on Spiritual Well-Being of the Elderly, Atlanta, Ga. (April).

Gorsuch, R. L. (1990) "Measurement in Psychology of Religion Revisited." *Journal of Psychology and Christianity* 9 (2):82–92.

Greenwood, E. (1945) *Experimental Sociology: A Study in Method.* New York: King's Crown.

Gross, G. D. (1985) "The Spiritual Lifeline: An Experiential Exercise." *Journal of Religion and Aging* 1 (3):31–37.

Hall, G. S. (1922) *Senescence: The Last Half of Life.* New York: Appleton.

Hateley, B. J. (1985) *Telling Your Story, Exploring Your Faith.* St. Louis, Mo.: Chalice.

Kimmel, A. J. (1988) *Ethics and Values in Applied Social Research.* Newbury Park, Calif.: Sage.

Kirkpatrick, L. A. (1989) "A Psychometric Analysis of the Allport-Ross and Feagin Measures of Intrinsic–Extrinsic Religious Orientation." In M. L. Lynn and D. O. Moberg, eds., *Research in the Social Scientific Study of Religion.* Greenwich, Conn.: JAI Press, 1–31.

Koenig, H. G. (1990) "Research on Religion and Mental Health in Later Life: A Review and Commentary." *Journal of Geriatric Psychiatry* 23 (1):23–53.

______ (1994) *Aging and God: Spiritual Pathways to Mental Health in Midlife and Later Years.* New York: Haworth.

Koenig, H. G., M. Smiley, and J. A. P. Gonzales (1988) *Religion, Health, and Aging: A Review and Theoretical Integration.* Westport, Conn.: Greenwood.

Kübler-Ross, E. (1969) *On Death and Dying.* New York: Macmillan.

Landis, J. T. (1942) "Hobbies and Happiness in Old Age." *Recreation* 35:607, 641–42.

Larson, D. B., M. J. Donahue, J. S. Lyons, P. L. Benson, M. Pattison, E. L. Worthington, Jr., and D. G. Blazer (1989) "Religious Affiliations in Mental Health Research Samples as Compared with National Samples." *Journal of Nervous and Mental Disease* 177 (2):109–11.

Larson, D. B., H. G. Koenig, B. H. Kaplan, R. S. Greenberg, E. Logue, and H. A. Tyroler (1989) "The Impact of Religion on Men's Blood Pressure." *Journal of Religion and Health* 28 (4):265–78.

Larson, D. B., E. M. Pattison, D. G. Blazer, A. R. Omran, and B. H. Kaplan (1986) "Systematic Analysis of Research on Religious Variables in Four Major Psychiatric Journals, 1978–1982." *American Journal of Psychiatry* 143 (3):329–34.

Lawton, G. (1943) "Happiness in Old Age." *Mental Hygiene* 27:231–37.

Lawton, M. P., and A. R. Herzog (1989) *Special Research Methods for Gerontology.* Amityville, N.Y.: Baywood.

Ledbetter, M. F., L. A. Smith, J. D. Fischer, W. L. Vosler-Hunter, and G. P. Chew (1991) "An Evaluation of the Construct Validity of the Spiritual Well-Being Scale." *Journal of Psychology and Theology* 19 (1):94–102.

Mindel, C. H., and C. E. Vaughan (1978) "A Multidimensional Approach to Religiosity and Disengagement." *Journal of Gerontology* 33:103–8.

Moberg, D. O. (1950) "The Influence of Religion on Personal Adjustment in Old Age." Unpublished manuscript.

______ (1951) "Religion and Personal Adjustment in Old Age." Dissertation, Univ. of Minnesota.

______ (1954) "Two Problems of Experimental Designs." *The Midwest Sociologist* 16 (1):10–12.

______ (1967) "The Encounter of Scientific and Religious Values Pertinent to Man's Spiritual Nature." *Sociological Analysis* 28:22–33.

______ (1983) "The Ecological Fallacy." *Generations* 8 (1):12–14.

______ (1984) "Subjective Measures of Spiritual Well-Being." *Review of Religious Research* 25:351–64.

______ (1986) "Spirituality and Science: The Progress, Problems, and Promise of Scientific Research on Spiritual Well-Being." *Journal of the American Scientific Affiliation* 38:186–94.

______ (1990a) "Religion and Aging." In Ferraro, 179–205.

______ (1990b) "Religion and Personal Adjustment in Old Age: Replication and Explication." *RIE: Resources in Education* No. ED320062 RIENOV90. Ann Arbor, Mich.: ERIC/CAPS Clearinghouse, Univ. of Michigan.

Moody, R. A. (1976) *Life after Life: The Investigation of a Phenomenon—Survival of Bodily Death*. New York: Bantam Books.

Oles, E. S. (1949) "Religion and Old Age: A Study of the Possible Influence of Religious Adherence on Adjustment." Thesis, Bucknell Univ. Dept. of Psychology.

Orbach, H. L. (1961) "Aging and Religion: Church Attendance in the Detroit Metropolitan Area." *Geriatrics* 16:530–40.

Ortega, S. T., R. D. Crutchfield, and W. A. Rushing (1983) "Race Differences in Elderly Personal Well-Being: Friendship, Family, and Church." *Research on Aging* 5 (1):101–18.

Paloutzian, R. F., and C. W. Ellison (1982) "Loneliness, Spiritual Well-Being and Quality of Life." In Peplau and Perlman, 224–37.

Pan, J. S. (1951) "Factors in the Personal Adjustment of Old People in Protestant Homes for the Aged." *American Sociological Review* 16:379–81.

Pargament, K. I., K. I. Maton, and R. Hess, eds. (1992) *Religion as a Resource for Preventive Action: Conceptual and Empirical Foundations*. New York: Haworth.

Peplau, L. A., and D. Perlman, eds. (1982) *Loneliness: A Sourcebook of Current Theory, Research and Therapy*. New York: Wiley Interscience.

Pressey, S. L., and E. Simcoe (1950) "Case Study Comparisons of Successful and Problem Old People." *Journal of Gerontology* 5:68–175.

Pressman, P., J. S. Lyons, D. B. Larson, and J. J. Strain (1990) "Religious Belief, Depression, and Ambulation Status in Elderly Women with Broken Hips." *American Journal of Psychiatry* 147 (6):758–60.

Rawlings, M. (1978) *Beyond Death's Door*. Nashville: Nelson.

______ (1980) *Before Death Comes*. Nashville: Nelson.

______ (1994) *To Hell and Back*. Nashville: Nelson.

Renfrew, K., J. R. Svendsen, M. Valdas, and J. E. Williams (1961) "Religion and Personal Adjustment in Old Age." Unpublished paper, Bethel College, St. Paul, Minn.

Schaie, K. W., R. T. Campbell, W. Meredith, and S. O. Rawlings, eds. (1988) *Methodological Issues in Aging Research*. New York: Springer.

Schiller, P. L., and J. S. Levin (1988) "Is There a Religious Factor in Health Care Utilization?: A Review." *Social Science and Medicine* 27 (12):1369–79.

Schmidt, J. F. (1951) "Patterns of Poor Adjustment in Old Age." *American Journal of Sociology* 57:33–42.

Shanas, E. (1949) *The Personal Adjustment of Recipients of Old Age Assistance.* Dissertation, Univ. of Chicago.

Steinitz, L. Y. (1980) "Religiosity, Well-Being, and Weltanschauung Among the Elderly." *Journal for the Scientific Study of Religion* 19:60–67.

Witter, R. A., W. A. Stock, M. A. Okun, and M. J. Haring (1985) "Religion and Subjective Well-Being in Adulthood: A Quantitative Synthesis." *Review of Religious Research* 26:332–42.

Young, C. H., K. L. Savola, and E. Phelps (1991) *Inventory of Longitudinal Studies in the Social Sciences.* Newbury Park, Calif.: Sage.

38 The Interdisciplinary Study of Gerontology

BARBARA PITTARD PAYNE

Gerontology provides an appropriate framework for the study of religion in the aging experience because both gerontology and religious studies are interdisciplinary and multidisciplinary fields of study. Most gerontologists have a specialization within a discipline such as sociology, psychology, or biology. In like manner, the scientific study of religion includes specialization within a discipline such as sociology of religion, psychology of religion, or philosophy of religion. Each of these disciplinary approaches to aging and to religion exists within an interdisciplinary and multidisciplinary context. No one discipline explains the aging process. Likewise, no one discipline explains religious behavior.

This chapter begins with a very brief review of the history of gerontology and its contributions to the study of religion and aging. A major section focuses on social gerontological perspectives on religious beliefs, practice, and experience among older adults. It includes a brief statement on the implications of theoretical plurality in the study of religion and aging. The final section suggests some future directions for the relationship between gerontology and the study of religion.

A BRIEF HISTORY OF GERONTOLOGY

Interest and curiosity about long life is not new, but the scientific study of aging is a product of the twentieth century. Birren and Clayton (1975) note that historically old age was not unknown; it was simply uncommon. Furthermore, contemplation of longevity belonged to the domain of religious writings and theology and was not considered a subject for scientific investigation. The increase in longevity and related advances in medical technology in the twentieth century stimulated scientific approaches to the processes of aging.

It was not until the mid-twentieth century that gerontology became established as an area of scientific study and was included in academic disciplines. Although there were a number of significant publications on the processes of aging in the 1920s, especially the work of psychologist G. Stanley Hall (1922) on senescence, the ground work for gerontology began in the 1930s with two unrelated events: advancements in medicine and the Great Depression. The consequences of the former resulted in a shift from research concern about infectious diseases to chronic degenerative diseases often experienced in later life. At the same time, improvements in medical care led to growing numbers of persons over age sixty-five.

During the Great Depression, the first publicly supported old age assistance program was enacted with the passage of the Social Security Act in 1935. This marked the beginning of planned retirement as a socially expected and approved time of life. Hendricks and Hendricks (1986) observe that at a time when the United States had more workers than jobs and industry was in major need of capital and a stable labor force, no better solution could have been found. The Social Security program also relieved families of major economic responsibility for older parents.

By the 1940s, interest in degenerative and chronic diseases had grown, an interdisciplinary volume on the problems of aging (Macy Foundation, 1937) was published, and professional conferences on aging began to be held. One of these conferences, sponsored by the National Institute of Health in 1941, dealt with topics that continue to be of concern: the significance of aging as a public health problem, intellectual changes with age, and management of an aging work force. Gerontology was becoming an independent and important field, but this momentum was interrupted by World War II (Birren and Clayton, 1975; Payne, 1990).

After the war, the Gerontology Unit within the National Institute of Health was staffed, the Gerontological Society of America was founded in 1945, and the Southern Conference on Gerontology was organized in 1950. These organizations encouraged discussion among professionals from all disciplines who were conducting research in aging.

The 1958 annual meeting of the Southern Conference on Gerontology was the first national conference to focus on religion and aging. Scudder's (1958) report on the conference theme—Organized Religion and the Older Person—was the first collection of articles on religion and aging viewed from research, theoretical, and theological perspectives (Payne, 1990).

After the first White House Conference on Aging, held in 1961, the next major federally funded program was enacted: the Older Americans Act of 1965. Title IV of the Act stimulated a proliferation of academic programs, research, publications, and organizations by providing funding for research and training in aging. The spread of gerontology programs in higher education led to the organization of the Association for Gerontology in Higher Education (AGHE).

In the 1970s, the humanities joined the disciplinary areas in gerontology. In his recent work, Achenbaum (1992) traces the history of integrating the humanities into gerontology research, training, and practice. He identifies the breakthrough as the funding of projects between 1974 and 1978 by the National Endowment for the Arts. With greater visibility of the humanities in gerontological study, the study of religion and aging began to attract more attention.

In 1976, an ad-hoc committee on the humanities was proposed to the Gerontological Society of America (GSA). By the early 1980s, the Arts and Humanities luncheon had become an annual event at GSA, and editors of *The Gerontologist* included a historian, a philosopher, and a literary critic. In 1990, the first historian joined the board of the *Journal of Gerontology*. These developments have particular significance for the integration of religion and spirituality into gerontology, as they add visibility and substance to the study of the role of religion in the aging process.

TRENDS AND THEMES IN SOCIAL GERONTOLOGY

Studies at the University of Chicago in the 1940s introduced themes that persisted for decades. The Kansas City Study of Adult Life (Cumming and Henry, 1961) and Cavan's and colleagues' (1949) studies of successful aging set the emphasis on disengagement and activity as indicators of adaptation to aging/retirement. These studies were the first of any magnitude to investigate the new retirement lifestyle introduced by the Social Security Act in 1935. Much attention was devoted to role losses, retirement as the roleless role, and the search for work role replacements (Burgess, 1960b).

These issues and themes influenced the focus of the Duke University studies of normal aging (Busse and Maddox, 1985; Palmore, 1970, 1974). These investigators chose to study older persons in the community where most older people were found. The limitations of cross-sectional studies soon became apparent, especially in the studies of cognitive functioning, and this led the Duke researchers to adopt a longitudinal design for their study of normal aging. Since the interviews conducted as part of the Duke study of normal aging included questions about religion, it represents one of the few sources of longitudinal data on the role of religion among older people.

During this period, aging (or long life) was viewed as a social problem for society and the individual, especially because of the high rate (17 percent) of poverty among those over sixty-five years of age. Atchley (1972) reported that in the 1960s, the

> White House Conference on Aging drew attention to the majority of older Americans who were poor in the midst of plenty. . . . 60 percent of older people in 1965 had incomes below or near the poverty level and . . . 80 percent had no income apart from Social Security. (139)

The introduction of private pensions and other supports resulted in a reduction of the poverty problem by the 1980s. Indeed, success in attacking this problem moved gerontologists to shift from focus on the needy to an effort to challenge the "greedy geezer" theme introduced by the March 28, 1988 issue of *The New Republic*. Gerontologists have responded by reporting research to refute claims that older people are selfish and threaten the economic security of younger persons (Atchley, 1988; Binstock, 1983; Pollack, 1988). Increasingly, gerontologists are examining public policy issues in light of intergenerational relationships. The largest lobbying organization in the United States, the American Association of Retired Persons (AARP), has also mounted a major effort aimed at emphasizing intergenerational concerns.

Major current societal and individual issues revolve around the cost of health care, long-term care, caregiving, and the burden of caregiving. With the growing numbers of persons age eighty-five and older, such issues have taken on particular urgency. Other significant themes found in gerontological research and public policy debate include wellness and disease prevention and extension of the human health span as well as the maximum lifespan.

Issues related to minorities and gender, especially the older woman, began to be explored in the 1970s. During this period of the Civil Rights and feminist movements, Susan Sontag (1972) pointed out the double standard of aging for those who are old and female. Lewis and Butler (1972) questioned the absence of feminist attention to aging issues, and Payne and Whittington (1976) examined popular stereotypes about older women. The longer life expectancy of women and the higher incidence of widowhood received research attention from Lopata (1973, 1979). Gender differences continue to be investigated in work roles (Belgrave, 1988; O'Rand and Henrietta, 1982), retirement (Atchley, 1982), and religion (Alston and Alston, 1980; Payne and Whittington, 1976; Payne, 1993). Alston and Alston (1980) reported that the older woman is far more likely to be a church attender than her male counterpart or younger women. Furthermore, their data indicate that:

> women are more religiously active at all ages and that the more frequent attendance of women is highly correlated with their greater identification with their religious affiliation. (276)

Current knowledge on minority differences in the aging process was the focus of the 1986 Workshop sponsored by the National Institute on Aging, American Association of Retired Persons, and the Health and Human Resources Minority Health Office. Four major areas addressed were: (1) demography; (2) epidemiology; (3) biomedical research; and (4) social and behavioral sciences. Included in the review of current knowledge about African Americans was the role of the church and religious beliefs (Jackson, 1988).

TRENDS AND THEMES IN GERONTOLOGY AND RELIGION

Although gerontology has grown rapidly since World War II, interest in religious themes and issues has lagged behind other topics. Some have argued that lack of government research funds has produced this situation, while others have noted the historical tensions between science and religion. Whatever the reasons, and they are complex and historically rooted, handbooks, textbooks, and journals devoted to the study of aging have given little attention to religion. Beginning in the mid-1980s, however, professional gerontological societies began to take notice of religious issues, and research on aging and religion has attracted increasing attention as the twentieth century draws to a close.

The earliest studies of religion and aging were efforts to determine if religious faith increases in importance as one ages (Starbuck, 1903). The common assumption was that it does. This issue seemed to be resolved by the work of Alston and Wingrove (1974) which showed that there is no difference in religiosity by age, and the findings of Blazer and Palmore (1976), which demonstrated that attendance at church declines with age, but private religious practices do not.

Other researchers continued to seek more definitive explanations of the relation between religious faith and age (Ainlay and Smith, 1984; Mindel and Vaughn, 1978; Young and Dowling, 1987). These later investigators questioned the measures used in earlier studies to determine religiosity among older people, and their critiques led them to develop multidimensional measures. For example, Mindel and Vaughn (1978) added questions about attitudes about the helpfulness of religious ideas to surveys of religious behavior, and they investigated organized religious activities as well as nonorganizational religious activities. They reported that regardless of level of organizational participation, older respondents described themselves as being religious very often.

Ainlay and Smith (1984) took another step and established as an additional characterization of religiosity older peoples' desire to participate in the life of the church. They found that religious organizational participation does not cease in later life but decreases and is compensated for by nonorganizational religious activities and participation.

Young and Dowling (1987) surveyed members of five AARP chapters, using a modified version of the scales developed by Mindel and Vaughn. They found some variation by membership in a liberal or conservative church. Also, the more active older people are, the more actively they participate in organized religion. Younger older people participate in organized religious activities and the older persons participated more in nonorganizational activities. Not surprisingly, both organized and nonorganized participation increased with strength of religious conviction. An unexpected finding concerned the importance of interaction with family and friends in continued nonorganizational religious participation. One suggested interpretation is that these networks contribute to one's spiritual well-being and provide support for nonorganizational participation.

Markides's (1983) four-year longitudinal study of religiosity and adjustment showed that church attendance and practice of private prayer remained stable and that self-rated religiosity increased with age. However, there was no evidence of an overwhelming turn to religion in older persons.

The relation of religiosity and adaptation among the oldest-old has been studied by the researchers involved in the Georgia Centenarian Longitudinal Study (Courtenay et al., 1992). Preliminary findings from this research begun in the late 1980s show that religiosity does not change significantly as one ages. The authors report a significant relationship between religion and physical health, but not between religiosity, mental health, and life-satisfaction. Religion was found to be strongly related to coping with health and family problems. These oldest-old report reliance on prayer and beliefs. Future research from this study will provide longitudinal evidence to confirm or challenge assumptions about the use of religion as a coping mechanism. At this point in the research, Courtenay and his colleagues find that a significant number of centenarians agree with one of the 101-year-old subjects who stated: "I don't worry about the future; it's in God's hands" (000).

Research by Koenig and his associates (chap. 1) on religion, health, and health care brought renewed attention to these themes. They found that older people rely on religion as a coping behavior especially during events over which they have little control (Koenig et al., 1988). The most frequently reported coping behaviors were: trust and faith in God, prayer, help and strength from God, church friends, church activity, clergy help, and Bible reading. Koenig cautions that these data were collected from older adults living in the south, where there is a high degree of religious commitment, and he notes the need for other researchers to gather data in different parts of the country. Taylor (1988) reported similar findings among Blacks, but he noted a stronger reliance on the church as a social organization for identity and support. He reported that older Blacks considered God a protector of health, the giver of good health, and they do not hold God as responsible for ill health.

In a study of religious involvement and health among the elderly, Idler (1987) found that greater religiousness is associated with lower levels of functional disability and depressive symptomology. Idler also reported a difference in health status and the type of religious involvement. Among women, the more they attended religious services and the more they knew other members of the congregations, the less physically disabled or depressed they were likely to be. Among men, the more they were engaged in private religious practices, the less disability and fewer feelings of depression they experienced.

It is interesting to note that many of the themes explored in research on religion and aging have been generated by popular interest and historical accident. For example, the 1971 White House Conference on Aging's religious section was labeled "spiritual well-being" to avoid the church and state issue. This became the catalyst for the shift from a focus on religiosity to spiritual well-being and to the current themes of spirituality and aging being explored by gerontologists. This shift coincides with attention to the intensified search for meaning in life by all age groups and an increasing interest among persons in different age cohorts in the spiritual dimension of human life (Gallup, 1991; Payne, 1990).

THEORETICAL PLURALISM

Although some have suggested the desirability of developing a single multidisciplinary theory of aging, one obstacle is that there is no unity about theoretical perspectives within the disciplines (Passuth and Bengston, 1988). To date, there is no one theory in sociology, psychology, or biology that claims to explain fully the complex, dynamically interactive processes of aging.

The study of religion has the same disciplinary diversity and lacks a unified theory to explain religious behavior. This does not mean that theories from the various disciplines (such as sociology, psychology, and philosophy) cannot be employed to explain aging religious behavior in defined areas. Instead of straining for one unified gerontological theory, it is more appropriate to call for theories within the disciplines that analyze the social, psychological, and physical contexts of aging behavior, including religious behavior.

For example, gerontological theories derived from sociology can be applied to religiosity in later life in a number of ways. The disengagement/activity concepts are relayed to the sociological theory of structural functionalism. One can utilize this theoretical structure to understand how older persons disengage from past roles and develop new volunteer/service roles within the religious community. The concepts of interiority and disengagement provide the framework for articulating the meaning of religious aloneness and the development of creative solitude and the meditative life. Activity theory can be used to explain the value of new roles within religious organizations that provide social identity, meaningful social roles, and the development of social networks.

Exchange theory (Dowd, 1973) is also derived from the sociological theory of structural-functionalism. It emphasizes role losses and negative meanings of relationships between the elderly and other age groups. It can also be used to emphasize the positive contributions, resources, skills, and services that older people can make and are making to the faith community.

Another rich source of theoretical insight derives from the work of Durkheim (1897/1951) and Weber (1922/1964) on social cohesiveness. To these great sociological thinkers, religion is an element of culture that provides access to a system of symbols, rituals, and beliefs that structure personal and social life. This work is replete with stimulating ideas that constitute an appropriate theoretical framework for the study of religion and aging.

Theoretical pluralism in gerontology should not occasion despair on the part of researchers. Rather, it provides a rich tapestry that enables the person interested in religion and aging to view the topic from many varied perspectives, as these examples from sociology demonstrate. Theories do not, after all, proclaim truth. They only provide a relatively useful way of organizing and interpreting observations about human experience and interactions with the social world.

PROJECTIONS ABOUT THE FUTURE OF GERONTOLOGY AND RELIGION

The interest and momentum in the study of aging, religion, and spirituality can be expected to continue to escalate. This will translate into research that asks new questions, probes for depth, and employs different methodologies. The return to scientific favor of qualitative methods is a sign of this trend (see chaps. 38 and 39). These methods are highly appropriate for studies of the meaning of life and religious/spiritual experiences. Both qualitative and quantitative studies of religious organizations can be expected to increase in response to the graying of congregations and to the societal need for collaboration between the religious community and the service community to provide social support for older adults in their communities.

The humanities, including theology, will contribute to the understanding and interpretation of the aging experience and the meaning of long life. A major effort will be made to relate the knowledge and issues about aging processes to religious behavior, spirituality, and religious institutions. Spirituality studies will expand to focus on faith development among older men and women.

Current research on organizational and nonorganizational practices among older people will be expanded to include the responses organizations make to the changing religious needs and practices of their increased older adult membership. It will be important for researchers to employ sequential research designs so that they can control for cohort and time of measurement effects. The data available today about religion and aging may not reflect the life experience of the baby-boomer cohort as they enter later life.

In summary, efforts to integrate gerontology and religion can be expected to continue. There is much work to be done. Fortunately, a new climate of legitimacy for seeking answers to these questions awaits researchers willing to explore the interface between religion and aging.

BIBLIOGRAPHY

Achenbaum, W. A. (1992) "Afterword: Integrating the Humanities into Gerontologic Research, Training, and Practice." In Cole, Van Tassel, and Kastenbaum, 458–72.

Ainlay, S. C., and D. R. Smith (1984) "Aging and Religious Participation." *Journal of Gerontology* 39 (3):357–63.

Alston, J., and L. Alston (1980) "Religion and the Older Woman." In Fuller and Martin, 262–78.

Alston, J. P., and C. R. Wingrove (1974) "Cohort Analysis of Church Attendance." *Social Forces* 53 (2):324.

Atchley, R. C. (1972) *Social Forces and Aging: An Introduction to Social Gerontology.* Belmont, Calif.: Wadsworth.

______ (1982) "The Process of Retirement: Comparing Women and Men." In Szinovacz, 153–56.

______ (1988) "Retiree Bashing: No Good Deed Goes Unpunished." *Generations* 13 (2):21–22.

______ (1991) *Social Forces in Late Life.* Belmont, Calif.: Wadsworth.

Belgrave, L. L. (1988) "The Effects of Race Differences in Work History, Work Attitudes, Economic Resources, and Health in Women's Retirement." *Research on Aging* 10 (3):383–98.

Binstock, R. H. (1983) "The Aged as Scapegoat." *The Gerontologist* 23 (2):136–43.

Birren, J. E., and V. L. Bengtson, eds. (1988) *Emerging Theories of Aging.* New York: Springer.

Birren, J. E., and V. Clayton (1975) "History of Gerontology." In Woodruff and Birren, 15–27.

Blazer, D. G., and E. Palmore (1976) "Religion and Aging in a Longitudinal Panel." *Gerontologist* 16 (1):82–85.

Burgess, E. W. (1960) "Aging in Western Culture." In Burgess, 3–28.

Burgess, E. W., ed. (1960b) *Aging in Western Societies.* Chicago: Univ. of Chicago Press.

Busse, E. W., and G. W. Maddox (1985) *The Duke Longitudinal Studies of Normal Aging: 1955–1980.* New York: Springer.

Cavan, R. S., E. W. Burgess, R. J. Havighurst, and H. Goldhammer (1949) *Personal Adaptation to Old Age.* Chicago: Science Research Associates.

Cole, T. R., D. D. Van Tassel, and R. Kastenbaum, eds. (1992) *Handbook of the Humanities and Aging.* New York: Springer.

Courtenay, B. C. et al. (1992) "Religiosity and Adaptation in the Oldest-Old." *The International Journal of Aging and Human Development* 34 (1):47–56.

Cowdry, E. V., ed. (1939) *Problems of Aging.* Baltimore: Walhams and Wilkins.

Cumming, E., and W. Henry (1961) *Growing Old.* New York: Basic Books.

Dowd, J. J. (1973) "Aging as Exchange: A Preface to Theory." *Journal of Gerontology* 30:534–94.

Durkheim, E. (1951) *Suicide: A Study in Sociology.* (1897) Translated by J. A. Spaulding and G. Simpson. Glencoe, Ill.: Free Press.

Fuller, M. M., and C. A. Martin (1980) *The Older Woman: Lavender Rose or Gray Panther.* Springfield, Ill.: C. Thomas.

Gallup, G. Jr. (1991) "What Every Pastor Should Know about the Average American." *Emerging Trends* 13 (2):4–5.

Hall, G. S. (1922) *Senescence, the Second Half of Life.* New York: Appelton.

Hendricks, J., and C. D. Hendricks (1986) *Aging in Mass Society: Myths and Realities.* Boston: Little, Brown and Co.

Idler, E. L. (1987) "Religious Involvement and the Health of the Elderly: Some Hypotheses and an Initial Test." *Social Forces* 66:226–37.

Jackson, J. S., ed. (1988) *The Black American Elderly: Research on Physical and Psychological Health*. New York: Springer.

Koenig, H., M. Smiley, and J. A. P. Gonzales (1988) *Religion, Health and Aging: A Review, and Theoretical Integration*. Westport, Conn: Greenwood.

Lewis, M., and R. Butler (1972) "Why Is Women's Lib Ignoring Older Women?" *International Journal of Aging and Human Development* 3:223–31.

Lopata, H. (1973) *Widowhood in an American City*. Cambridge, Mass.: Schenkman.

______ (1979) *Women as Widows: Support Systems*. New York: Elsevier.

Markides, K. S. (1983) "Aging, Religiosity, and Adjustment: A Longitudinal Analysis." *Journal of Gerontology* 38 (5):621–825.

Mindel, C. H., and C. E. Vaughn (1978) "A Multidimensional Approach to Religiosity and Disengagement." *Journal of Gerontology* 33:103–8.

O'Rand, A., and J. C. Henrietta (1982) "Midlife Work History and Retirement Income." In Szinovacz, 25–44.

Palmore, E., ed. (1970) *Normal Aging: Report from the Duke Longitudinal Study, 1955–1969*. Durham, N.C.: Duke University Press.

______ (1974) *Normal Aging II: Reports from the Duke Longitudinal Studies, 1970–1973*. Durham, N.C.: Duke University Press.

Passuth, P. M., and V. Bengtson (1988) "Sociological Theories of Aging: Current Perspectives and Future Directions." In Birren and Bengtson, 333–55.

Payne, B. P. (1990) "Spirituality and Aging: Research and Theoretical Approaches." *Generations* 14 (4):11–14.

Payne, B. P., and F. J. Whittington (1976) "Older Women: An Examination of Popular Stereotypes and Research Evidence." *Social Problems* 23:488–504.

Pollack, R. F. (1988) "Serving Intergenerational Needs: Not Intergenerational Conflict." *Generations* 12 (3):14–18.

Sontag, S. (1972) "The Double Standard of Aging." *Saturday Review of Society*, September 23, 29–38.

Starbuck, E. D. (1903) *The Psychology of Religion: An Empirical Study of the Growth of Religious Consciousness*. 3d ed. New York: Charles Scribner's Sons.

Szinovacz, M., ed. (1982) *Women's Retirement*. Beverly Hills, Calif.: Sage.

Taylor, R. J. (1988a) "Correlates of Religious Non-involvement among Black Americans." *Review of Religious Research* 30:126–39.

______ (1988b) "Structural Determinants of Religious Participation among Black Americans." *Review of Religious Research* 30:114–25.

Weber, M. (1964) *The Sociology of Religion*. (1922) Boston: Beacon Press.

Woodruff, D. S., and J. E. Birren, eds. (1975) *Aging: Scientific Perspectives and Social Issues*. New York: Van Nostrand Reinhold.

Young, G., and W. Dowling (1987) "Dimensions of Religiosity in Old Age: Accounting for Variations in Types of Participation." *Journal of Gerontology* 42 (4):176–80.

39 Quantitative and Qualitative Methods

GARY T. REKER

Readers of this book might wonder why it is important to include a chapter on quantitative and qualitative methods in a compendium devoted almost entirely to religion and aging. Two good reasons come to mind. First, a comprehensive understanding of religion, spirituality, and aging can only be achieved when one has an awareness of the way in which social scientists conduct research. It enables scholars in fields other than the behavioral and social sciences to conduct their own research, thereby contributing to the knowledge base of their discipline. Second, for scholars not engaged in research, a basic grasp of scientific methods empowers them to critically analyze, review, and evaluate the quality of the research reported in scholarly journals and the popular media.

This chapter will present an overview of the quantitative and qualitative methodologies used in the behavioral and social sciences. The first section gives a brief introduction to two major theoretical approaches and indicates how they influence the choice of research methods. The second section discusses a number of issues relevant to an understanding of developmental research. Two subsequent sections describe and evaluate the major descriptive and explanatory research designs of human development. The fifth section introduces and evaluates the major contemporary methods of qualitative research, citing appropriate examples from the empirical literature. The final section discusses common issues in the application of quantitative and qualitative methods and highlights the important contribution of each in advancing an understanding of human behavior.

Methodology refers to a set of procedures by which problems are approached and answers are found. In the behavioral and social sciences the term applies to how research is conducted. A variety of methods are available. The method chosen is strongly influenced by the theoretical perspective, assumptions, interests, and goals of the investigator. Consequently, methods differ in terms of the kind of data collected, the way in which data are collected, and the means of analysis.

The behavioral and social sciences have been dominated by two major theoretical perspectives: positivism/operationism and phenomenology/interpretive social science. Positivism is a philosophical position that holds that knowledge is limited to experiences and to observed facts with little regard for the subjective states of individuals (Comte, 1896). In psychology, positivism is associated with operationism, reductionism, statistical analysis, and rejection of mentalistic constructs.

On the other hand, phenomenology/interpretive social science is concerned with understanding human behavior from the person's own frame of reference (Rabinow and Sullivan, 1979). It is largely descriptive, utilizing nonmathematical analytical procedures that require theoretical and social sensitivity, acute observational skills, and good interactional abilities on the part of the researcher (Strauss and Corbin, 1990).

Adherents of positivism/operationism and phenomenology/interpretive social science differ in the problems they pose and the answers they seek. Positivists seek "facts" through a variety of methods (e.g., questionnaires, inventories, behavioral observations, etc.) that operationalize the variables of interest. Operationalization produces *quantitative* data that can be analyzed statistically to prove relationships between the variables. The underlying assumption is that the important factors in human behavior can be isolated and studied independently (Hesse, 1980). Phenomenologists, on the other hand, seek understanding through methods (e.g., autobiography, personal documents, life history, in-depth interviews, etc.) that yield descriptive data on how the individual experiences the world and the meanings he or she ascribes to those experiences. Description produces *qualitative* data that can be content-analyzed, thematized, or taxonomized, examined for recurring patterns, and related to other relevant variables. The assumption is that human behavior is the product of complex, mutually dependent factors that must be studied in natural contexts.

Traditional research in the social and behavioral sciences conceptualized research methods as on a continuum, anchored by quantitative methods on the one end and qualitative methods on the other. Such a unidimensional perspective suggests that quantitative and qualitative methods are diametrically opposed. Over the years, heated debate on the merits of quantitative versus qualitative methods have ensued, culminating in polarized positions and a strong preference for the quantitative approach. More recently, renewed interest in psychological research on the "inner" development of the whole person has led to increasing acceptance of qualitative methods as a legitimate form of scientific inquiry (e.g., Kaufman, 1986; Reker and Wong, 1988; Rennie et al., 1988). This chapter attempts to demonstrate that an alternate, equally plausible perspective, in which quantitative and qualitative methods are seen as operating jointly and in complementary fashion, can enrich our understanding of subjective phenomena such as religiosity and spirituality. Given the traditional preference for quantitative methods, we will first turn to a discussion of their use in lifespan developmental research.

DEVELOPMENTAL RESEARCH ISSUES

Major Effects

The lifespan developmental perspective provides the framework for the discussion of research methods in this chapter (see, e.g., Baltes et al., 1977). Within this framework, the basic research questions are in terms of *what* happens (description), *why* it happens (explanation), and *how* it can be changed (optimization). In the study of adult development and aging, three major effects that explain differences between and within individuals are age, cohort, and time of measurement (Schaie, 1984; Schaie and Hertzog, 1985).

Age Effects. Most people think of age as an index of the length of time since birth, referred to as chronological age. Chronological age provides a convenient shorthand index to organize events and data based on calendar time. It is particularly useful for developmental researchers who wish to describe individuals falling within specified age groups. Chronological age is also useful when the processes under investigation are time-dependent, such as biological growth.

In actual fact, age is considered a proxy or surrogate variable representing the complex underlying biological, psychological, and social processes that influence people over time (Birren and Cunningham, 1985). Age does not directly cause anything; it is merely a marker of the occurrence of many things. More precisely, developmental researchers study phenomena *related* to age; hence it is more appropriate to talk about age-related effects. While alternative conceptualizations of age in terms of specific processes have been proposed (e.g., biological age, psychological age, social age [Birren and Cunningham, 1985]), most developmental researchers prefer chronological age as the primary variable of interest.

Cohort Effects. Cohort effects are differences due to the experiences unique to a particular generation. Cohorts can be specific or general. For example, all people born in a specified year constitute a "birth cohort"; thus, all people born between 1946 and 1962 belong to the "baby boom cohort." Each generation is influenced by different kinds of historical or social events such as educational opportunities, wars, the Great Depression, hippie movement, AIDS epidemic, etc. These unique experiences may shape the attitudes, values, or behavior of the cohort in profound ways that need to be taken into account.

Time of Measurement Effects. Time of measurement effects reflect differences due to social, environmental, historical, or other events occurring either at the time that the data are collected or between periods of data collection. These events affect an entire society, independent of age or cohort. For example, data gathered on religiosity during the 1960s and 1970s when the "God is dead" debate and later the "Jesus movement" were prominently featured in the national media could have been shaped by the particular events of that time of measurement.

Practice effects are a special type of time of measurement effect. In situations where performance is the primary variable, any increases between two or more time periods may reflect the benefit of previous exposure to the task.

Confounding. Unfortunately, the effects of age, cohort, and time of measurement are interrelated, posing a real challenge for developmental researchers searching for unambiguous explanations. For instance, if one is interested in studying the extent of religious activity of sixty-year-olds, it is necessary to select the cohort that was born sixty years ago. However, one cannot know whether the religious activity reported is due to the fact the subjects are sixty years old or due to the specific life experiences they have had as a result of being born in a particular historical period. In effect, age and cohort vary simultaneously or are totally *confounded.* Other sources of confounding are age with time of measurement and cohort with time of measurement. The next section discusses developmental research designs containing these confounds and how to minimize their effects.

Age Changes and Age Differences

Developmental researchers are mainly interested in the general question of what happens as people grow older. There are two fundamental ways in which this question can be broached. One can study the same individuals over time and document *age changes,* or one can compare individuals of different ages and document *age differences.* The former focuses on change within the same individuals (intraindividual change); the latter focuses on differences between individuals (interindividual difference). For example, the study of the religious involvement of individuals seventy years old compared to their religious involvement fifty years earlier when they were twenty years old reflects an age change. The study of the religious involvement of twenty-year-olds compared to that of seventy-year-olds reflects an age difference.

It is important to distinguish between age changes and age differences because they clearly imply different things. Many researchers use methods that yield information on age differences, but make the assumption that such differences are valid estimates of age changes. The assumption may not always be tenable, particularly when extreme age groups (young versus older adults) are compared, leaving the results subject to misinterpretation (i.e., claiming age effects when in reality they are cohort differences).

There are at least three related issues that developmental researchers must deal with when attempting to measure age change or age differences. First, the meaning or personal significance of a construct may undergo revision over time. In that case, observed change may simply reflect changed meaning. One way to control for such change is to demonstrate empirically that the structural properties of the measured construct remain invariant across age. A second issue is the possibility that the standard for self-assessment may change. For example, self-report measures of health might shift from an absolute or "personal" standard in the young to a relative "comparison with others" standard in the elderly. Shifting standards confound true developmental change and need to be taken into account. A third issue relates to the differential applicability of some items within a measuring instrument when administered to younger and older adults. Items not relevant to older cohorts can contribute to distortions in developmental profiles. Careful selection of scales containing items that are equally applicable to a broad age range can guard against such distortions.

DEVELOPMENTAL RESEARCH METHODS

It is useful to distinguish between two major types of developmental research methods: descriptive and explanatory. Descriptive methods focus on the relationships among the time-related variables of age, cohort, time of measurement, and other variables of interest. The task is to identify and describe the nature of age changes and age differences. A feature intrinsic to descriptive methods is that cause-effect relationships cannot be inferred. This should not be seen as a shortcoming, as the goal is not systematic manipulation and isolation of conditions, but rather systematic observation of what occurs "naturally."

Explanatory methods involve the specification of the antecedents or causes of change within and between individuals. Explanatory methods attempt to simulate developmental processes in controlled, artificial settings (Baltes et al., 1977). Variables are manipulated and subjects are randomly assigned to various groups or conditions. Thus, cause-effect relationships can be inferred.

Descriptive Research Designs

The major ways in which developmental researchers gather data on age changes and age differences include the cross-sectional, longitudinal, and sequential designs.

Figure 39.1 depicts a matrix of age, cohort, and time of measurement effects. Birth cohort is represented by the years down the left column. Time of measurement is represented by the year across the bottom. Age is represented by the numbers in the body of the half matrix. Also shown in Figure 39.1 are the two developmental designs that can be constructed from the half matrix. A third design, called a time-lag design, is also possible (any single diagonal line). However, in time-lag designs age is held constant; thus, age-related effects cannot be measured. Because of their nondevelopmental nature, time-lag designs will not be discussed further in this chapter.

FIGURE 39.1
Age, Cohort, and Time of Measurement Effects in Developmental Research Designs

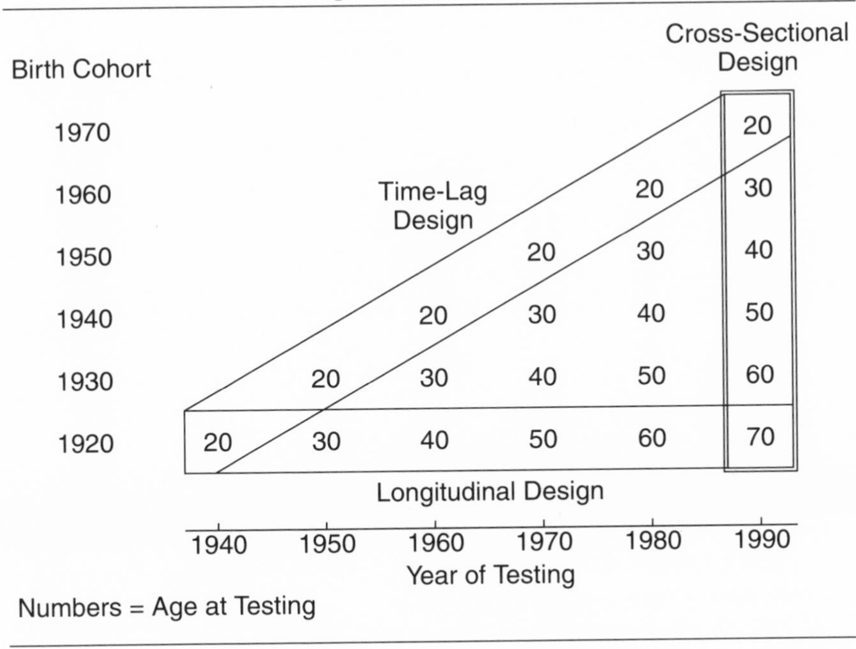

Simple Cross-Sectional Designs. In a cross-sectional design, subjects of different ages are tested and compared at one point in time. Any single vertical column in Figure 39.1 represents a cross-sectional design. Cross-sectional designs allow for the recording of age differences. Since time of measurement is held constant, differences between groups can be due either to age differences or to cohort differences. This confounding of age and cohort is the major problem with cross-sectional studies.

For illustrative purposes, suppose that a researcher was interested in the relationship between age and religious conviction. A cross section of individuals of ages 20, 30, 40, 50, 60, and 70 years is obtained and asked to report on their degree of involvement with religious beliefs and practices. The hypothetical data might show that as age increases, so does the percentage of people who become involved with religious activities. What interpretation can be placed on these findings? There are two possibilities. Either people become more religious as they age, or the increase in religious activities reveals a cohort difference. That is, it may be that older people today held stronger religious convictions when they were members of a younger generation. In a simple cross-sectional design, the two interpretations cannot be disentangled. More powerful designs are needed to determine whether the findings reveal a cohort or age effect.

The above example may be hypothetical, but the dilemma of confounding exists in the real world of science. The early cross-sectional research on the development of intelligence across the lifespan, showing a large drop as a function of age, was due to a misinterpretation of the findings. What was interpreted as an age effect was really a cohort effect indexed by a lack of educational opportunities for the progressively older cohorts in the studies (Schaie and Strother, 1968).

In addition to the problem of confounding, cross-sectional designs pose a number of potential limitations. The key indicator of developmental change in cross-sectional designs is the average score on a variable obtained for several cohorts. Unless the samples studied are truly representative of the general population, group averages may not adequately represent the individual case. As well, distortions in the developmental profile can occur as individual differences increase. This is particularly problematic in older adults who show increasing heterogeneity on a number of variables with advancing age (Dannefer, 1988).

Despite the problems and limitations, cross-sectional designs remain the most popular because data can be collected quickly, efficiently, and inexpensively. Unless retesting is required, subjects are seen only once. Results can be used as norms against which other subjects can be compared. Verification of findings can be achieved instantaneously by drawing new samples.

Simple Longitudinal Designs. In a longitudinal design, the same individuals are observed at two or more different times. Any single horizontal row in Figure 39.1 represents a longitudinal design. Longitudinal designs allow for the recording of age changes. In this case, only one cohort is studied, effectively eliminating cohort effects as an explanation of change. However, in longitudinal designs, confounding occurs between age and time of measurement.

For illustrative purposes, imagine that a researcher had been able to chart the attitudes toward religious leaders (trusting versus mistrusting) for a 1920 cohort who were assessed at six different times: 1940, 1950, 1960, 1970, 1980, and 1990, when they were 20, 30, 40, 50, 60, and 70 years old, respectively. The results of such a hypothetical inquiry might show a change toward more mistrusting attitudes as a function of time. Again, two possible interpretations are tenable. Either true developmental change in attitudes toward religious leaders has occurred over time or the change is due to social-historical events, such as scandals about television evangelists and media attention to sexual abuse by clergy. In a longitudinal study it is not possible to tell which of these interpretations is most appropriate.

Longitudinal designs have a number of additional problems associated with them: single cohort assessment, subject attrition, practice effects, time factor, cost factor, and use of outdated measures. In longitudinal designs, only one cohort is studied. The developmental pattern observed in one cohort may not hold up for another. Thus, one needs to be cautious in generalizing results to another cohort. Longitudinal studies run the risk of attrition or subject dropout. Subjects drop out for various reasons, including loss of interest, moving away, illness onset, or death. Systematic attrition can lead to selective sampling of the more competent, highly educated, healthier cohorts who are not representative of those who began the study. As a result, the developmental pattern of the "survivors" is likely to reveal a positivity bias. Inherent in longitudinal designs is the need to conduct repeated measurements on the same individuals using the same measures. Under these conditions, performance may actually increase over time because participants have the opportunity to become familiar with the measures or to "practice." Such practice effects contribute to misinterpretation. Lastly, longitudinal studies of long duration are very time-consuming, costly, and require the researcher to continue to use procedures and measuring instruments that may be outmoded.

Despite their limitations, longitudinal studies are appearing more frequently in the gerontology literature, presumably in recognition of the need to observe intraindividual change directly.

In summary, simple cross-sectional designs involve different cohorts, one-time assessment, and measure age differences. Age and cohort effects are confounded. Simple longitudinal designs involve one cohort, repeated assessments, and measure age changes. Age and time of measurement are confounded. These confoundings create problems in the interpretation of changes within and between individuals.

Fortunately, more complex extensions of the simple designs, known as *sequential designs,* are available to help separate the three major sources of variation in developmental research. Unfortunately, a detailed discussion of these complex designs is beyond the scope of this chapter. The interested reader should consult Baltes et al. (1977) and/or Schaie and Hertzog (1985). It is important to note, however, that although sequential designs are extremely powerful, they are costly and time-consuming, requiring a lifetime effort. They are not the method of choice for the majority of developmental researchers. Given this reality, a stage approach to methodology may be more appropriate. That is, one first conducts simple cross-sectional studies, controlling in systematic fashion for as many extraneous variables as possible. Once reliable age differences on the phenomena of interest are isolated, longitudinal, sequential, and experimental studies can be conducted to identify the specific underlying mechanisms contributing to the observed differences.

Explanatory Research Designs

Three familiar explanatory research strategies are the experimental, quasi-experimental, and nonexperimental designs. While not central to the study of development, explanatory designs can help narrow the many rival explanations of age-related effects found in developmental research.

Experimental Designs. In the true experiment, the researcher manipulates one or more variables (independent) and observes the effect on one or more variables (dependent). Participants are randomly assigned to groups or conditions, thus exerting control over a number of subject and environmental characteristics.

To illustrate how the experimental method can help explain age-related effects, take the often-cited finding of a decline in memory performance as a function of age. There are several possible explanations of this pattern: It could reflect changes in the central nervous system; it could reflect differences in practice at memory tasks; it could reflect a cohort difference due to educational opportunities; or it could reflect differences in motivation because the stimuli to be remembered are not that meaningful to the person. To eliminate the latter as an explanation, a researcher could select groups of young, middle-aged, and older adults and randomly assign half of each group to a memory task containing meaningful stimuli (e.g., the names of movie stars). The other half of the subjects in each group might be given a memory task containing meaningless stimuli (e.g., nonsense syllables). All subjects would then be assessed for memory retention. A significant decline in the retention scores of older adults for meaningless stimuli with no corresponding drop in the retention scores for meaningful stimuli would provide support for the "lack of motivation" explanation.

Quasi-Experimental Designs. In quasi-experimental designs, subjects are *not* assigned randomly to groups or treatment conditions, often for ethical reasons. Thus, preexisting groups are studied. For example, suppose that the administrators of two newly constructed nursing homes are contemplating using the drug physostigmine as a treatment for memory loss in early-onset Alzheimer's patients. One of the nursing homes is chosen at random to be the control home (Nursing Home A); the other is the experimental home (Nursing Home B). In Nursing Home A, an intact group of fifteen early-onset Alzheimer's patients are identified; twenty are identified in Nursing Home B. All thirty-five patients are pretested on a memory test. Nursing Home B patients are administered the drug, physostigmine, on a daily basis for three months. Nursing Home A patients receive either no drug or a placebo (some inert agent that looks like the drug). At the end of three months, patients in both nursing homes are retested on the memory test. Significant improvements in memory for Nursing Home B patients compared to Nursing Home A provides support for the hypothesis that physostigmine improves memory performance in early-onset Alzheimer's.

One drawback of quasi-experimental designs is that alternative explanations are possible. For example, differences in nursing care practices, involving more frequent interaction with Nursing Home B patients, could account for the observed improvement in memory performance, independent of drug effects.

Thus, one needs to be cautious in the interpretation of findings when quasi-experimental designs are used. In any event, such designs provide useful information in situations where manipulation of variables is not feasible.

Nonexperimental Designs. In nonexperimental designs, subjects are not randomly assigned to groups or conditions and no distinction is made between independent and dependent variables (although the variables are often renamed as the predictor and criterion variables). Comparisons are made of intact groups and grouping is often on the basis of organismic (e.g., sex, race) or experiential (e.g., health status, educational level) variables. Because such designs measure the co-relationship among variables, they are also referred to as *correlational designs.*

To illustrate, suppose researchers were interested in studying the role of religious beliefs and practices in predicting the well-being of a sample of older adults. They would obtain a fairly large sample (N > 100) of older adults and administer measures of the strength of religious beliefs and practices (e.g., church attendance, private prayer, Bible study, etc.), morale, life-satisfaction, depression, and happiness. They could simply compute the correlations between religious beliefs/practices and the well-being measures, but a more powerful strategy is to use regression analyses. In regression analysis, the individual (unique) and the overall contribution of the components of religious beliefs/practices in predicting positive and negative well-being outcomes can be assessed.

Strictly speaking, nonexperimental designs are not explanatory in the sense of addressing cause-effect relationships. However, they offer some explanatory power when used in conjunction with the more powerful statistical procedures currently available, such as multiple regression, causal modeling, or LISREL. At the very least, nonexperimental designs are useful for descriptive information and offer lead-ins for generating research hypotheses.

QUALITATIVE RESEARCH METHODS

While quantitative methods have dominated the traditional scientific approach to data collection and analysis, there is a growing interest in questions that focus on subjective experiences and on naturally occurring social interactions among individuals. A number of nonquantitative approaches, known collectively as qualitative methods, are deemed more appropriate for such inquiries and are cited with increasing regularity in the social and behavioral sciences. Qualitative methods are descriptive, discovery-oriented, language-based, and address the meaning of human experience. Meaning is embodied in text or deciphered from text and is derived through the act of interpretation. Qualitative methods have been effectively employed in psychotherapy process research (Rennie et al., 1988); studies of student life (Kuh and Andreas, 1991; Patton,

1991); health psychology (Pennington, 1988); counseling (Koziey and Anderson, 1990); nursing (Knafl and Howard, 1984; Knafl and Webster, 1988); and caregiving (Farran et al., 1991). In psychology and gerontology, qualitative methods are most sensitive to the investigation of various types of meaning in life (personal, experiential, social, cultural) and existential topics that center on spirituality and religiosity.

Organizational Framework

Qualitative research needs to be viewed as a separate and distinct approach with its own set of standards of scientific rigor. In contrast to the deductive focus of quantitative research, qualitative research is more analytical and inclusive, focused on building the categories and inducing them.

Qualitative methods, because of their descriptive nature, are content and labor intensive. The methods vary in terms of the degree of precision and rigor in the analyses, ranging from very simple coding of data into categories to the use of multiple recursive steps involving several raters working independently.

No researcher approaches his or her subject matter in a vacuum. The qualitative researcher's conceptual framework, theoretical interest, and specific focus will influence the choice of the organizing construct or system for coding the large amounts of information collected from individuals. The most commonly cited organizing systems for coding life histories and open-ended interviews include the use of metaphors (Thomas et al., 1990), prototypes (Wong, 1991), phenomenal patterning (Koziey and Anderson, 1990), or themes (Allen and Chin-Sang, 1990; Kaufman, 1986).

An extant problem in qualitative research is the lack of systematic procedures for data management and data analyses. Few guidelines actually exist to direct qualitative researchers. In addressing this need, Knafl and Webster (1988) provide a useful organizational framework for conducting qualitative research. They identify four purposes of qualitative research: illustration, instrumentation, sensitization (description), and conceptualization (theory building). Each of these purposes has associated with it specific techniques for data collection, data management, and data analysis. Data collection refers to how the data are obtained. Qualitative researchers use materials collected from naturally occurring social interactions by means of field notes, open-ended interviews, audio- or videotaped recordings, and transcripts. Data management involves the indexing of descriptive data into smaller units for later retrieval and communication. Knafl and Webster (1988) offer a number of "tagging" or "coding" techniques for this purpose (e.g., colored markers, colored paper clips, colored index cards, etc.). Data analysis involves extracting the meaning from the coded data and constructing thematic, taxonomic, or conceptually relevant categories. An additional feature of data analysis involves constructing summary statements of the coded data, tabulating frequencies, and/or relating the emergent themes to other qualitative or quantitative variables.

A useful strategy in explicating the methods of qualitative research is to draw on the existing literature for examples of each of the four major research purposes outlined by Knafl and Webster (1988). This should give the reader a more comprehensive understanding and appreciation of how qualitative research is conducted. A detailed account of the step-by-step operating procedure for conducting qualitative research is beyond the scope of this chapter. The reader interested in these details should consult Glaser and Strauss (1967), Strauss and Corbin (1990), or Taylor and Bogdan (1984).

Illustration

Research Example. Wong (1991) examined the adaptive role of reminiscence through a qualitative analysis of Stewart Alsop's narrative account of his past life and battle with terminal cancer (Alsop, 1973). Wong (1991) introduced the prototypical approach to qualitative analysis and illustrated the "mastery-oriented" prototype through numerous illustrations from Alsop's autobiography.

Data Collection Technique. Wong relied on the personal narrative or life story as presented in Alsop's (1973) *Stay of Execution.*

Data Management Task. Wong proposed the prototype approach to classifying life histories. A prototype is an ideal exemplar of a conceptual category. An ideal exemplar is highly typical or representative of a category. In Wong's study, the prototypical analysis focused on lifelong patterns of adaptation or coping. In the first step of prototypical analysis, recurrent themes and salient images are identified and coded. In the second step, one must decide on whether the cluster of themes is prototypical of any pattern of adaptation. The dominant and common attributes in the cluster then determine the prototype label. On the basis of prior knowledge and observations of common patterns of coping, Wong identified what he called the "mastery-oriented" prototype. The dominant attributes include the tendency to deal directly with problems, confidence in one's competence, and courage in the midst of adversity. The recurrent themes identified in Alsop's life story were self-mastery, cognitive control, courage, Winston Churchill as his icon, overcoming mortality through procreation, and acceptance. According to Wong, these themes are consistent with a larger body of knowledge on mastery and self-efficacy and provide empirical evidence that Alsop is a prototype of mastery.

Data Analytic Task. Since the collection of qualitative data was solely for the purpose of illustration, there is no need for further data analysis.

Contribution. Wong's study demonstrates the merits of the prototype approach to qualitative research. The mastery prototype is effectively illustrated in ways that lend scientific credibility (verifiability and generalizability) to qualitative methods. Evidence is provided to support the hypothesis that the mastery prototype is an effective coping mechanism in adapting to unfortunate life circumstances. The findings highlight the rich nature of autobiographical data and capture the uniqueness of a personality not revealed through traditional methods of data collection.

Instrumentation

Research Example. Farran et al. (1991) worked within an existential paradigm to identify existential themes in the caregiving experience. One of the goals was to develop a quantitative instrument to measure aspects of the identified themes.

Data Collection Technique. Data from ninety-four family caregivers of dementia patients were obtained. Caregivers participated in a two-hour interview about caregiving conducted in their homes. Seven open-ended questions provided data for the qualitative analysis. Responses were recorded verbatim. Quantitative data were also obtained.

Data Management Task. One person on the research team independently identified and defined categories based on the responses to each of the seven questions. Two additional persons independently assigned caregivers' responses to these categories. All three persons compared response assignments and worked toward consensus.

Data Analytic Task. The response categories for the seven questions were grouped into four major themes: (1) loss and powerlessness, (2) values, choices, provisional and ultimate meaning, (3) caregiving resources, and (4) responsibilities of caregiving. Each theme included subcategories and specific responses.

The percentage responding was calculated for themes and subcategories. Multiple responses to themes and subthemes was allowed. Themes were related to the quantitative measures of number of years caregiving, caregiver effort, caregiver support, and level of burden.

Contribution. The researchers identified existential themes in the caregiver experience that led to the development of an interactive model for finding meaning through caregiving (Farran and Keane-Hagerty, 1992) and a quantitative instrument to measure aspects of the identified themes (Farran, 1992).

Sensitization

Research Example. Thomas, Kraus, and Chambers (1990) worked within the interpretative social science paradigm to conduct a crosscultural study of meaning and purpose in the lives of elderly men. Their organizational construct was the metaphor, defined as figurative language that points beyond itself. Their primary goal was to tap the nuances and connotations of beliefs about the lives of the elderly that gave rise to a sense of meaning and purpose.

Data Collection Technique. Fifty Indian and fifty English men seventy years of age or older participated in the study. Subjects were encouraged to respond to open-ended questions about themselves, their past, and their present situation. Responses were tape-recorded and subsequently transcribed. The reported findings, however, are based on an intensive qualitative analysis of ten Indian and ten English randomly selected protocols.

Data Management Task. A team of three researchers independently content-analyzed the interview protocols for metaphors. Consensus was reached through a "group hermeneutic process" whereby individual input is viewed in light of a larger group understanding and group understanding is modified in light of individual textual analyses. The process continued until no new metaphoric themes could be identified (saturation).

Data Analytic Task. Explicit metaphors were grouped into relevant categories (e.g., family, career, health, etc.) for each respondent. Emerging themes across respondents were noted and a generalized description was provided for each sample. A second level of metaphoric analysis sought to identify underlying or implied metaphors. At this stage, focus was on groups of interviews, not individual protocols. Care was taken to overcome rater bias at all steps of the data analysis. Marked differences were found in the psychological worlds of English and Indian men. English men were more privatized and stoic, with an underlying nature metaphor. Indian men expressed strong achievement concerns and concerns for family and society, with an underlying metaphor of building up and completing duty to family, society, and God.

Frequency counts of the major themes within each sample were obtained to assess the salience of the emergent metaphors.

Contribution. This study suggests that metaphors provide a unique way of looking at psychological states and underlying assumptions. The metaphors identified in the interviews tend to be robust and provide insight into the lived experiences of men in widely differing cultures. The authors suggest that metaphors may be thought of as a person's stable "accent" through which levels of experiencing can be revealed.

Conceptualization

In the previous examples of illustration, instrumentation, and sensitization, the task of data collection, management, and analysis proceeds in a sequential manner. When the study purpose involves conceptualization or theory building, these same tasks are carried out simultaneously (Knafl and Webster, 1988). Thus, there is an immediate interplay between data management and analysis of emerging concepts. This results in coding categories that differ in levels of conceptualization, some being very descriptive, others much more abstract. Throughout the process, the descriptive data is continuously reviewed for conceptual relevance. The end result is a conceptual model that remains "grounded" in the data that gave rise to it. Among the variety of qualitative methods (for a comprehensive listing, see Patton, 1990), the grounded theory approach of Glaser and Strauss (1967) has received the most attention. Grounded theory can be considered the prototype of qualitative methods and stands as the best example of the theory building purpose.

Research Example. Rennie et al. (1988) and Rennie (1992), working within a psychotherapeutic context, applied the grounded theory method to investigate the client's subjective experience of therapy. This approach stands in sharp contrast to traditional conceptualizations of the psychotherapeutic process conducted from the vantage point of the therapist. The psychotherapeutic context, because of its interactive nature, is considered ideal in explicating the interplay between data management and data analysis.

Data Collection Task. Rennie (1992) obtained the client's tape-recording of an hour of therapy and replayed the experience to the client immediately following the session. The client was encouraged to comment freely and spontaneously on any aspect of the therapy experience. Client responses were tape-recorded and transcribed, producing between forty to eighty pages of text for each of sixteen inquiries.

Data Management Task. Rennie and associates chose "meaning units" as their unit of analysis. Meaning units were defined as passages of transcript that convey a main concept or that "stand out." Meaning units varied in length from one line to a half a page of text. Meaning units were sorted into clusters on the basis of the meaning embedded in the items. Clusters were symbolized by descriptive categories; descriptive categories were grouped under main categories; and main categories were grouped under a conceptualized "core category."

Data Analytic Task. Over 3,000 meaning units were assigned to 51 clusters, 11 descriptive categories, 4 main categories, and 1 core category. The four main categories are (1) client's relationship with personal meaning, (2) client's perception of the relationship with the therapist, (3) client's experience of the therapist's operations, and (4) client's experience of outcomes. When the interrelationships of the four main categories were examined, the qualities of self-awareness and self-control emerged as attributes of the core category. The core category was conceptualized as "client's reflexivity," a broad concept encompassing both self-awareness and agency (Rennie, 1992).

Contribution. Rennie (1992) identified a new construct, client's reflexivity, as central to the psychotherapeutic process. In that process, clients are agents as well as patients. Qualitative analysis of the inner experience of therapy makes overt what is often left unexpressed, leading to greater congruence between what one is thinking and what one is saying in therapy. The inductively derived construct and its intercorrelations with lower-order categories provide the organizational structure for a therapeutic perspective in which the "challenge of therapy is to control sensitively what clients cannot control and to work productively with the ways in which they assume control" (Rennie, 1992, 230–31).

To summarize, it is clear from the four study purposes that qualitative methods contribute substantially to the investigation of phenomena over and above that provided by traditional quantitative approaches. Qualitative methods can be used to clarify and illustrate quantitative findings, build research instruments, develop basic knowledge, and create new theories. Their primary contribution lies in the process of making subjective phenomena more explicit, thereby allowing phenomenological experiences to be accorded the status of empirical facts (see Reker and Wong, 1988, 216–20). Furthermore, the research examples clearly demonstrate that contemporary qualitative methods utilize procedures that meet the widely accepted canons for conducting "good" science, including precision, rigor, reproducibility, theory-data compatibility, generalizability, and verification (Strauss and Corbin, 1990).

QUANTITATIVE AND QUALITATIVE METHODS: TOWARD COMMON GROUND

The emphasis in this chapter has been on the complementary nature of quantitative and qualitative methods, not on the relative merits of the two approaches. The ultimate goal is to conduct good science, in terms of both theory creation and theory verification. Both quantitative and qualitative methods are necessary to achieve this common goal. Each enriches and augments the discoveries of the other. The concurrent use of quantitative and qualitative methods provide more complete answers to research questions and may add new and deeper insights and understanding of human development.

Common Goals, Complementary Ways. Qualitative research methods differ from the traditional quantitative approaches in a number of important ways. Specifically, qualitative methods rely on the *inductive* mode of scientific inquiry. Instead of using data to verify existing theory (hypothetico-deductive), qualitative researchers generate theory based on the data. In practice, while quantitatively and qualitatively oriented researchers make use of similar data collection techniques (e.g., interviews, observations, etc.), they differ in the way the techniques are structured and employed. Quantitative researchers use techniques that are highly structured and elicit information from respondents based on predetermined conceptualization and instrumentation (e.g., existing questionnaires, preestablished codes). Qualitative researchers attempt to avoid preconceptions about the phenomena under investigation and let the data "speak for themselves." In this way, the "true" nature of phenomena will be revealed and allowed to emerge through systematic codification of descriptive material.

Thus, the main distinction between quantitative and qualitative methods is with the *way* in which the data are derived and analyzed. A qualitative method can be used on data that has already been quantified (e.g., census data), but it remains a qualitative analysis. In addition, data derived through qualitative methods can be summarized quantitatively by means of frequency counts, percentage responding, or by indices of central tendency and deviation. The latter retains its identity as a qualitative analysis, even though a quantitative aspect has been added.

A second important difference is with the nature of the *focus* of the inquiry. Inductive inquiries place emphasis on the subject's perspective or view of the world, as opposed to the perspective of the researcher. Thus subjects become informants, not respondents. Subjects are assumed to occupy the most privileged position vis-à-vis personal awareness of psychological states and experiences. Their input informs, illuminates, and infuses meaning into phenomena. In that context, the qualitative approach is characterized by reflexivity in that the informant becomes both the subject and the object of the investigation in a process of "turning back on the self" (Lawson, 1985).

A third important difference stems from the implicit acknowledgment by qualitative researchers that all facts are interpretive facts and remain so independent of the methodology used to discover the "facts." Even the most sophisticated quantitative researcher must eventually "make sense" of the data.

Common Concerns. Despite their documented contribution, qualitative methods have been and continue to be criticized. Most criticism focus on researcher-subject interactions and how this affects data collection. Some of the most salient criticisms are summarized below.

1) *Qualitative researchers selectively screen and analyze nonrepresentative data.* This problem is inherent in all forms of research. The qualitative researcher is aware of the potential biases in data collection and analysis and uses special techniques to minimize them. In quantitative research, questionnaires are chosen on the basis of what is considered important by the researcher. Thus, reality is forced into a predetermined structure, yielding distant and reflective

representations of experiences. A quantitative researcher controls for bias in response sets and styles, such as the tendency to respond in a socially desirable manner, by assessing the degree of such influence.

2) *Qualitative researchers elicit data confounded by their own presence in the research setting.* While such researcher-subject reactivity cannot be avoided, there are checks and balances by which such effects can be minimized. Qualitative researchers can observe and weigh their potential effects on subjects and report them in enough detail to allow for independent verification. By the same token, quantitative instruments are equally problematic, influencing data collection in uncertain ways. For example, items occurring early in a questionnaire can lead the respondent to react in systematic, but unspecified ways to subsequent items.

3) *The findings of qualitative research are not generalizable to other subjects or settings.* Generalizability refers to the question of whether subjects or settings are at all representative of the population. Ideally, a wide and varied sample of subjects should be studied but because of the intensive, time-consuming nature of qualitative research, available resources only allow the study of a few. In the limiting case, it is an N of 1. Is this at all problematic? The problem may be more apparent than real. Quantitative researchers, in search of general laws, see generalizability as applying only to persons. Thus, the "average" of many individuals is seen as typical or representative of the phenomena under study. Consequently, single-subject designs are regarded as having little relevance for science. However, it can be argued that single-subject studies are a logical prerequisite for discovering general laws. General laws should be those that hold for *each* of *many* individuals (Hooker, 1991).

While the criticisms of qualitative research may have some merit, it must be recognized that all research methods contain biases and distortions. The main point is that researchers of all persuasions need to be aware of the potential biases and distortions inherent in their methods with the goal of minimizing their influences.

It is becoming increasingly evident that qualitative methods are receiving widespread recognition in the behavioral and social sciences. In a recent editorial published in *The Gerontologist,* Gubrium (1992) notes that qualitative research has come of age in gerontology. He states:

> Qualitative research is a way of knowing, a way of documenting the aging experience and making its distinct contribution to the field. There are many equally acceptable and scientific ways of doing gerontology, just as our humanistic colleagues reveal the aging experience in their ways. Broadly, qualitative research does what all of us aim to do: understand what it means to grow or be older, how that varies in time and place, and what is particular and general about the process. (582)

SUMMARY

A comprehensive understanding of issues in religion, spirituality, and aging requires an appreciation of the methods used in the conduct of scientific research. The purpose of this chapter was to highlight the important contributions of the traditional quantitative methods and the contemporary qualitative approaches to advancing our knowledge of human development. Central to the chapter is the conviction that quantitative and qualitative methods are necessary to achieve the goals of good science, those of theory creation and theory verification. In the field of religion and spirituality, methods that allow us to objectify highly subjective experiences may be more appropriate to our understanding of the complexities of human development. In the final analysis, concurrent reliance on both quantitative and qualitative methods will enrich and augment our scientific discoveries.

BIBLIOGRAPHY

Allen, K. R., and V. Chin-Sang (1990) "A Lifetime of Work: The Context and Meanings of Leisure for Aging Black Women." *The Gerontologist* 30:734–40.

Alsop, S. (1973) *Stay of Execution: A Sort of Memoir.* Philadelphia: Lippincott.

Baltes, P. B., Reese, H. W., and J. R. Nesselroade (1977) *Life-Span Developmental Psychology: Introduction to Research Methods.* Pacific Grove, Calif.: Brooks-Cole.

Birren, J. E., and V. L. Bengtson, eds. (1988) *Emergent Theories of Aging.* New York: Springer.

Birren, J. E., and W. Cunningham (1985) "Research on the Psychology of Aging: Principles, Concepts, and Theory." In Birren and Schaie, 3–34.

Birren, J. E., and K. W. Schaie, eds. (1985) *Handbook of the Psychology of Aging.* 2d ed. New York: Van Nostrand Reinhold.

Chinn, P. L., ed. (1992) *An Anthology of Caring.* New York: National League for Nursing.

Comte, A. (1896) *The Positive Philosophy.* Translated by Harriet Martineau. London: George Bell and Sons.

Dannefer, D. (1988) "What's in a Name? An Account of the Neglect of Variability in the Study of Aging." In Birren and Bengtson, 356–84.

Farran, C. J. (1992) "Finding Meaning through Caregiving: Pilot Test of an Instrument for Family Caregivers of Persons with Alzheimer's Disease." Provisional Procedures Manual, Rush University, Chicago.

Farran, C. J., and E. Keane-Hagerty (1992) "An Interactive Model for Finding Meaning through Caregiving." In Chinn, 225–37.

Farran, C. J., E. Keane-Hagerty, S. Salloway, S. Kupferer, and C. S. Wilken (1991) "Finding Meaning: An Alternative Paradigm for Alzheimer's Disease Family Caregivers." *The Gerontologist* 31:483–89.

Glaser, B. G., and A. Strauss (1967) *The Discovery of Grounded Theory: Strategies for Qualitative Research.* Chicago: Aldine.

Gubrium, J. F. (1992) "Qualitative Research Comes of Age in Gerontology." *The Gerontologist* 32:581–82.

Hesse, M. (1980) *Revolutions and Reconstructions in the Philosophy of Science.* Bloomington, Ind.: Indiana University Press.

Hooker, K. (1991) "Change and Stability in Self during the Transition to Retirement: An Intraindividual Study Using P-technique Factor Analysis." *International Journal of Behavioral Development* 14:209–33.

Kaufman, S. R. (1986) *The Ageless Self: Sources of Meaning in Late Life.* New York: Meridian.

Knafl, K. A., and M. J. Howard (1984) "Interpreting and Reporting Qualitative Research." *Research in Nursing and Health* 7:17–24.

Knafl, K. A., and D. C. Webster (1988) "Managing and Analyzing Qualitative Data: A Description of Tasks, Techniques, and Materials." *Western Journal of Nursing Research* 10:195–218.

Koziey, P. W., and T. Anderson (1990) "Phenomenal Patterning and Guided Imagery in Counseling: A Methodological Pilot." *Journal of Counseling and Development* 68:664–67.

Kuh, G. D., and R. E. Andreas (1991) "It's About Time: Using Qualitative Methods in Student Life Studies." *Journal of College Student Development* 32:387–405.

Lawson, H. (1985) *Reflexivity: A Post-Modern Predicament.* LaSalle, Ill.: Open Court.

McClusky, K. A., and H. W. Reese, eds. (1984) *Life-Span Developmental Psychology: Historical and Generational Effects.* New York: Academic Press.

Patton, M. J. (1990) *Qualitative Evaluation and Research Methods.* Newbury Park, Calif.: Sage.

______ (1991) "Qualitative Research on College Students: Philosophical and Methodological Comparisons with the Quantitative Approach." *Journal of College Student Development* 32:389–96.

Pennington, S. (1988) *Healing Yourself: Understanding How Your Mind Can Heal Your Body.* Toronto: McGraw-Hill Ryerson.

Rabinow, P., and W. M. Sullivan, eds. (1979) *Interpretive Social Science: A Reader.* Berkeley, Calif.: University of California Press.

Reker, G. T., and P. T. P. Wong (1988) "Aging as an Individual Process: Toward a Theory of Personal Meaning." In Birren and Bengtson, 214–46.

Rennie, D. L. (1992) "Qualitative Analysis of the Client's Experiences of Psychotherapy: The Unfolding of Reflexivity." In Toukmanian and Rennie, 211–33.

Rennie, D. L., and L. Brewer (1987) "A Grounded Theory of Thesis Blocking." *Teaching of Psychology* 14:10–16.

Rennie, D. L., Phillips, J. R., and G. K. Quartaro. (1988) "Grounded Theory: A Promising Approach to Conceptualization in Psychology?" *Canadian Psychology* 29:139–50.

Schaie, K. W. (1984) "Historical and Cohort Effects." In McClusky and Reese, 1–45.

Schaie, K. W., and C. Hertzog (1985) "Measurement in the Psychology of Adulthood and Aging." In Birren and Schaie, 61–92.

Schaie, K. W., and C. R. Strother (1968) "A Cross-sequential Study of Age Changes in Cognitive Behavior." *Psychological Bulletin* 70:671–80.

Strauss, A., and J. Corbin (1990) *Basics of Qualitative Research.* Newbury Park, Calif.: Sage.

Taylor, S. J., and R. Bogdan (1984) *Introduction to Qualitative Research Methods.* 2nd ed. New York: Wiley.

Thomas, L. E., P. A. Kraus, and K. O. Chambers (1990) "Metaphoric Analysis of Meaning in the Lives of Elderly Men: A Cross-Cultural Investigation." *Journal of Aging Studies* 4:1–15.

Toukmanian, S. G., and D. L. Rennie, eds. (1992) *Psychotherapy Process Research: Paradigmatic and Narrative Approaches.* Newbury Park, Calif.: Sage.

Wong, P. T. P. (1991) "Aging, Dying and Reminiscence: The 'Mastery' Prototype and Resilience." Unpublished manuscript, Trent University, Peterborough, Ontario.

40 Interpretive Social Science and Spirituality*

STEVEN WEILAND

Does the study of aging always bring knowledge of what it means to grow old? With gerontology's growth have come questions about priorities and perspectives for inquiry. This chapter first summarizes problems of method in gerontology that yield doubts about its status as a conventional science. There follows a review of the perspective known as "interpretive social science," beginning with recognition of its advantages by a leading theorist of adult development and aging. The next section offers a highly selective account of the interpretive stance based on the views of some of those who have made it influential across the disciplines. Finally, there is a discussion of an exemplary inquiry into aging—an "encounter" as defined below—that highlights the significance of spirituality and religion in gerontology.

The terms *spirituality* and *religion* often appear together in this chapter for reasons that are plain: Their uses are joined in history, in common and professional usage, and in the ambiguities of language. Religion reflects formal or institutional idioms of belief in God and concern with ultimate problems and questions of human life. Spirituality may be understood as "intrinsic" religiosity (Bianchi, 1982, 176); it may or may not be experienced or expressed as part of traditional religious practice. But religion is typically spiritual in at least some sense of that term. Scholars interested in both and in aging have favored *spirituality* to designate the timeless and universal human search for "meaning" and the desire for "wholeness" or an integrated self thinking, feeling, and acting in the presence of the "numinous" (Seeber, 1990). No scholar insists on a choice between religion and spirituality; but spirituality is often used to signify the more inclusive human practice. "[It] is not without focus; rather its lines mark a wider canvas" (Bianchi, 1982, 177).

*I wish to acknowledge Melvin Kimble's encouragement to a relative newcomer to gerontology to write on the broad subject of interpretive social science. Susan McFadden has been a perceptive reader and has guided me toward a more coherent presentation. Faults that remain are entirely my own.

CROSSROADS OF GERONTOLOGY

In a scholarly and scientific environment of increasing specialization, workers in the same field often have difficulty understanding each other, much less those in adjacent and remote disciplines. Nevertheless, perhaps the one theme on which there is now widespread agreement is the uncertain status of traditional scientific paradigms in the social and behavioral sciences. The "Paradigm Dialog," as it has been called (Guba, 1990), represents the gathering together of questions about the foundations of the academic disciplines, especially the recent prominence of models of inquiry based on the natural sciences. To be sure, as the latest editions of the widely cited *Handbooks* on aging demonstrate, major projects of inquiry base on empirical, experimental, and measurement-based methods continue to produce beneficial results (Achenbaum, 1991). Fresh empirical studies are welcomed, as are theoretical and analytic approaches, because of the availability of new and increasingly sophisticated techniques of quantitative analysis (Streib and Binstock, 1990). But scholars in gerontology have now registered their skepticism about reigning paradigms and have proposed the reformulation of the study of aging with greater attention to themes such as spirituality and religion that cannot be fitted to strict scientific methods (Birren and Bengtson, 1988; Cole and Gadow, 1986; Cole, Van Tassel, and Kastenbaum, 1992; Reinharz and Rowles, 1987). Some of these skeptics and critics are affiliated with mainstream approaches; others have come to gerontology from other domains, activating the field's multidisciplinary character. Appropriately enough, the fact of "generations of gerontology," or self-consciousness about relations between cohorts of scholars, is contributing to interest in new approaches such as interpretive social science (Seltzer, 1992).

Interpretive social science takes the social practices of disciplinary inquiry to be central to the work of science and scholarship, including the social and institutional roles of scholars and scientists. It attends to the many disciplinary rhetorics. It is a stance toward inquiry that brings forward questions scholars have about the academic norms of objectivity and subjectivity, about the social construction of ideas and beliefs, and about the ideologies shaping scholarly, scientific, and other practices. Fields of inquiry and practice that cannot quite be called independent disciplines but borrow from older forms of study tend to reflect (and sometimes reflect upon) these problems. Education is one such field, preoccupied with a seemingly interminable debate over qualitative vs. quantitative methods. Nevertheless, controversy of this kind can make scholars more critically reflective about their methods and can open up new subjects for inquiry.

Gerontology is now showing signs of institutionalizing such a debate, and this has many implications for understanding the roles of spirituality and religion in mid- and late life. When the historian of aging W. Andrew Achenbaum asked, "Can gerontology be a science?" he mixed a bit of timely skepticism into his question. In effect, he was also asking, "*Should* gerontology be a science?" at least in the sense that we understand conventional science to operate: dominated by rigid standards of evidence, measurement, and logical inference, and solely interested in what can be investigated on such terms.

> Ideally, a science of gerontology should provide an appropriate rationale and method to help us to describe the patterns and explain the design inherent in the interactive processes of otherwise seemingly chaotic bits of information. Typically, scientists rely on paradigms to guide them in gathering empirical data and to devise research strategies which distinguish between those independent and dependent variables necessary to test the falsifiability of a given set of propositions. Gerontologists, however, have thus far been unable to formulate such a framework. The very phenomena we assume have an impact on the nature and dynamics of senescence often prove to be part of the heuristic problem we want to solve. (Achenbaum, 1987, 7–8)

In other words, the objects of gerontological inquiry are not in the form needed for representing findings with the confidence of the experimental sciences. Indeed, narrow empirical studies can distract gerontologists from the elements of aging that give it such social and personal urgency, such as its role in the recovery of particular social values (see Achenbaum, 1985). In addition, demographic change, having prompted significant attention to the problems of adulthood and aging, has tempted specialists in these subjects to focus on age-segmented studies in the manner of child psychology, which is parochial in its own way despite its contributions to theories of cognitive and personality development.

By the very nature of its subject, gerontology must include attention to measureless themes in human experience, even as it is also accountable as a science to testable propositions. Studying aging means looking closely at loss, suffering, and death, even as older people experience new kinds of growth and even personal transformation. Aging prompts thought about life's meanings and personal fate. Speaking directly to other gerontologists, Achenbaum stated the problem of this new vocation:

> To acknowledge all of the complexity and paradoxes intrinsic to senescence threatens to render any theory empirically unfalsifiable. Yet to limit our focus to solving puzzles in a sharply restricted manner because it builds on the latest work done by one's colleagues is to lose sight of the larger forces and hitherto underappreciated anomalies that cumulatively might make one's findings mere artifacts. Until it comes to grips with basic questions of definition and scope, appropriate levels of analysis, and a consensus concerning the most suitable way to measure and (re)interpret data, gerontology cannot be a comprehensive science. (1987, 11)

There is room for negotiation in the ambition to be "comprehensive," one option being the simultaneous development of several gerontological specialties (but probably with familiar consequences for those not legitimized by the standard scientific method).

In the past few years, other critics of gerontology have shown less hospitality than Achenbaum to the prospect of a gerontological science. A central goal of the field in understanding adulthood and late life, they argue, should be the "critical" and even the deliberately unscientific perspective (e.g., Baars, 1992; Estes et al., 1992; Moody, 1988; Tornstam, 1992). There is, however, a consensus among such critics about the need for even more pluralistic methods for a field that suffers, it sometimes seems, from the conflict of disciplines and approaches. Achenbaum proposes that gerontologists employ a "pliable vocabulary" that may not only increase understanding but also prompt more collaboration. Nancy Datan (1987) did this when she demonstrated the continuity between themes in the social and behavioral sciences and the study of literature and myth. She urged the cultivation of "methodological heresies" that can direct us toward the way adults themselves interpret or give meaning to their experience. She anticipated the increasing popularity of narrative for such purposes and conveyed, in her focus on myth, the durability of ancient and spiritual meanings in modern lives.

With a few exceptions in the social sciences (e.g., Payne, 1990), interest in spirituality, religion, and aging has been a part of the effort to give the humanities a larger role in gerontology (Cole and Gadow, 1986; Cole, Van Tassel, and Kastenbaum, 1992; Moody, 1988). However, limiting these themes to humanistic domains of inquiry would also limit recognition of how social gerontology has been too narrowly defined. A "pliable" vocabulary for inquiring into relations among spirituality, religion, and aging would reach across the disciplines so that crucial areas of social policy and practice (especially those remote from humanistic study) would reflect new theoretical integrations.

Although gerontology is essentially a post-World-War-II enterprise, it has many features of an established scholarly and scientific institution. Accordingly, Achenbaum noted that "gerontologists have reached a stage of intellectual maturity wherein to understand our knowledge and its basis we must be more self-reflective about what we do" (1987, 14). When a group of influential gerontologists joined in such a project (Estes et al., 1992; Hendricks, 1992; Hickey, 1992; Schaie, 1992; Seltzer, 1992) they demonstrated how, in the field's development over the past few decades, pluralistic intentions and recognition of the significance of contexts came to compete with scientific specialization. Hence, there is a trend toward attention to smaller and smaller questions (Hickey, 1992) at the same time that there is recognition that "cohort and period may have more interesting explanatory properties than age" (Schaie, 1992). Paradoxically, although there is great theoretical ferment in the social sciences, proponents of "the gerontological imagination" are not optimistic about the widening of professional interest to include spirituality, religion, and other themes deriving from a more critical view of gerontology's research domain. "The present environment is decidedly less favorable to the social sciences than in past decades, and is overtly hostile to critical perspectives and competing paradigms challenging the dominant ones of today. Uneven development and intellectual stagnation threaten the social sciences and the social gerontology that is built upon them" (Estes et al., 1992, 60).

Although it is important to acknowledge the gap between gerontological aspirations for a new and timely science (with humanistic overtones) and what gerontologists can claim from traditional disciplinary resources, it is also important not to overstate it. Given the ferment in the academic disciplines today, it is hard to see how they are stagnant, unless one blames the collection of disagreements over historical, epistemological, and political themes for making it difficult to apply findings from the social sciences to urgent public problems. The historical development of gerontology has taken place as social scientific inquiry itself has been transformed. Hence, the urgency deriving from demographic change and from internal disagreements in gerontology about its direction and purposes is matched (if not inspired) by the intensity of change in the many academic pursuits constituting this multidisciplinary field (Diesing, 1991; Rosenau, 1992).

Even the oldest academic disciplines (at least their versions as "departments" for research and teaching) date only from the end of the last century. They represent part of the modernization of experience that has secularized everyday life as well as the way people think and speculate about its structure and meaning. In the ancient, medieval, and early modern worlds, religion was the primary forum for contemplating adulthood and aging as distinctive parts of human experience (Cole, 1992; Erikson, 1978). As it came to compete with other new forms of disciplined study, religion as a form of developmental understanding was displaced by science and then social science. They have gained in influence despite their general neglect of the traditional ways in which older people give meaning to their lives. Now, as the social sciences come to reflect the problems of intellectual postmodernism—including a strong strain of "antifoundationalism" reflecting suspicions about the epistemology of the sciences—there is a crisis of confidence in their ability to explain fundamental meanings in human experience (Rosenau, 1992).

Gerontology can be understood as a crossroads and at a crossroads: it is a place where disciplines meet, collaborate, and conflict in their contributions to this multidisciplinary field. As the interpretive movement in the social sciences shows, the concept of "multidisciplinarity" carries as much potential for conflict as it does for collaboration. In addition, there is a second crossroads of gerontology. It is a field with complementary and competing possibilities, where inquiry is the subject of increasing self-consciousness, especially concerning how the durability of spiritual and religious themes may be reconciled with the achievements and promise of the sciences of aging. A crossroads presents and forecloses choices. The many forms of gerontological inquiry and practice show signs of promise and strain. The very character of spiritual and religious themes highlights gerontology's utility, even its urgency, while making significant projects of inquiry appear irreconcilable in assigning meaning to old age.

THEORIES OF THE MIDDLE RANGE

The problem of theorizing about gerontology in a way that would make it more hospitable to the roles of spirituality and religion has been addressed largely indirectly. For example, in a brief but important essay Bernice Neugarten (1985) welcomed the rejection of positivism (or "rational empiricism") as the source of methods for the social sciences. In doing so, she invited the potential transformation of a field of inquiry she helped to invent. Her pathmaking work of the 1960s (e.g., 1968) largely reflected (if in moderate form) many of the scientific and intellectual habits about which she later expressed some skepticism. She relied on a widely read collection of essays assembled by the anthropologist Paul Rabinow and political scientist William Sullivan (*Interpretive Social Science,* 1979) to register her agreement with a group of critical ideas, now recognizable as close to mainstream ones: (1) the social sciences have suffered from futile attempts to imitate the natural sciences with their assumptions about the knowable world and the possibility for a completely detached or objective viewpoint for inquiry into it; (2) inquiry into the world of human experience always reflects subjectivity and contexts; and (3) findings in the behavioral and social sciences cannot be verified definitively; instead, we make interpretations.

> In this framework, there are no immutable laws; no reductionist models that are securely based in logical self-evidence; no "received" truths; and surely no value-free social science. Change is fundamental; change is dialectical; meanings are multiple and inexhaustible. The aim is understanding, within the limits of our cultural and historical present. The goal is not to discover universals, not to make predictions that will hold good over time, and certainly not to control; but instead, to explicate contexts, and thereby to achieve new insights and new understandings. (Neugarten, 1985, 292)

The consequences are ambiguity and indeterminacy, but these amount to methodological advantages, "a more open world for social scientists" who can now practice more diverse forms of inquiry, borrow from other fields, choose subject matter with greater freedom, and represent more self-consciously their own role in research.

Even so, Neugarten asserted that the adoption of the interpretive approach does not mean the triumph of scientific and intellectual relativism in which arguments and findings stand on their own, justified merely in terms of their stated purposes and self-determined standards. Even those working in the spirit of the newly open world of inquiry will want to adhere to criteria of evidence and to seek agreement with suitable representations of inquiry. "We attempt to build theories of the middle range, even if theories are themselves interpretations. . . . We can attempt to represent the world that can be known to us, if not the 'true' world" (Neugarten, 1985, 293). Just how difficult it will be to locate the middle range is apparent from Neugarten's expression of ambivalence about the uses of quantitative methods and their inability to help the researcher break out of the "hermeneutic" (or interpretive) circle. Such methods do not, she said, reflect the real world, but have the danger of reductionism and offer always the temptation of (misleading) clarity. Worse yet, they can be superficial and neglectful of the most important questions about human experience. In gerontology this is apparent in the popularity of cross-sectional analyses, where research often stops just when it should begin: with inquiry into the inner experience of membership in a cohort or of living in a period. Neugarten suggested that the goals of anthropologist Clifford Geertz' model of "thick description" be added to the study of aging (see Climo [1992] for a general account of the uses of anthropology for gerontology). Certainly this is familiar scholarly advice in contemporary social science—it is discussed in the next section—but it is necessary because methods in gerontology have been parochial. The field's conventional empiricism is a constraint on its potential for finding new meanings in aging.

Neugarten's search for the "middle range" signifies the durability of traditions in social science that rely on empirical inquiry and the need for conceptual frameworks that are relativist and adaptive without abandoning the claims of knowledge in addressing social problems. But the study of aging itself is a social activity, as the sociology of science (in reflecting the famous work of Thomas Kuhn on "paradigms" and disciplinary change) has now demonstrated for science and scholarship generally. In the study of aging, individual disciplines present their own developmental dynamics, varying in their hospitality to spirituality and religion as significant or even legitimate domains of inquiry, while they seek to join them to more inclusive projects of inquiry. In this light, theories of the middle range also reflect the accommodations disciplines make in sustaining and reformulating (and then, in the Kuhnian formulation, sustaining again) agendas for research and practice. As political scientist Paul Diesing states in his account of practices in the social sciences:

> We do not produce knowledge by testing hypotheses or predictions against observable data; such tests can neither confirm nor disconfirm theories or hypotheses. There is no instant truth or falsity. Instead, knowledge is produced by a community or tradition which develops the possibilities of some initial text, paradigm, method, or concepts. Communities diversify, form branches, combine or intermingle, and disappear. Community members develop their theory by using it to produce data which then change the theory. They also develop theory by shifting to a new area requiring a different interpretation of the theory. (Diesing, 1991, 325)

Religion and spirituality are gaining in significance in the interpretation of aging through the internal dynamics of the disciplines constituting gerontology and through diversification in the major gerontological communities (The

Gerontological Society of America, the American Society on Aging, and the Association for Gerontology in Higher Education), often as new branches of inquiry reflecting the adaptation of disciplinary perspectives to these themes. Accordingly, the middle range should demonstrate thematic, theoretical, and methodological variety in the study of aging. And, as will be proposed below, "initial texts" can be identified to prompt specific attention to spirituality and religion.

MOTIVES AND MEANINGS

Interpretive social science is not by itself a theory of human action and meaning making and it is more than a single method for studying them. A convenient analogue—because it derives from the study of aging—is the conception of a "family of methods or theoretical orientations," as Paul Baltes (1987) designates those that make up the "lifespan" approach in developmental psychology. Indeed, Baltes's model itself may be taken as a sign of the impact on gerontology of the interpretive social sciences, as they seek to promote reconfigurations of disciplinary practice that highlight the dialectical relations between traditions and innovations. In doing so, the descriptive function of social inquiry is not abandoned but problematized by new epistemological concerns. In addition, the representational capacity of the traditional social sciences is now understood within recognition of the contingencies (historical and personal) of disciplinary rhetorics. Finally, even as traditional ideas of the subject—the coherent and observable identity of the person—are destabilized, individualism is strengthened in the self-reflexive imperatives of contemporary discourses.

Pauline Rosenau concluded her synthesis of the conflict of interpretive stances by noting that "post-modern social science is in its infancy, and thus, like many incipient paradigms, its overall shape and character is vague, its substantive contribution still shadowy and fragmentary, mixed and uneven" (1992, 169). Even as a relatively young discipline, gerontology can be said to have made a permanent place for itself in science and scholarship. Through its "interpretive" practitioners it gains in potential utility by recognition of its still open character, its hospitality to skepticism and criticism, and its willingness to inquire into its scientific premises as a part of its theory building. However, the problem is not only the need for greater flexibility or variety in methods. What is also needed is a change in the motives for the study of aging generally, from the preoccupation with biomedical mastery of the body's and the mind's decline to recognition of the uses of representations of aging reflecting life's contingent and unknowable dimensions.

Restoring attention to the largest questions of human experience (what Achenbaum termed the need for "scope") is certainly one objective of the theoretical frameworks represented in the work of Rabinow and Sullivan (1979,

1987). There is no consensus about a common program for research or theory building. No one but the editors use the precise phrase "interpretive social science," and the uses of interpretation vary according to whether, for example, reference is make to the political philosopher Charles Taylor or to Clifford Geertz, the interpretive social scientist who has perhaps been most influential across the disciplines.

Writing in the early 1970s (significantly enough, for the subject of this chapter, in the *Journal of Metaphysics*), Taylor contemplated the Western political environment—including the rebellious youth and university cultures—and found a cultural crisis of "frightening proportions." It was secular and scientific but also spiritual: "There is no relation to the absolute where we are caught in the web of meanings which have gone dead for us" (Taylor, 1987, 73). The historical project of representing such meanings in the forms of intersubjective experience in which they developed derives from the belief (Taylor claims this to be essential to any work in the human sciences) that human beings are "self-defining," making it impossible to predict and presumably to control human behavior according to models of the natural sciences.

> With changes in his self-definition go changes in what man is, such that he has to be understood in different terms. But the conceptual mutations in human history can and frequently do produce conceptual webs which are incommensurable, that is, where the terms cannot be defined in relation to a common stratum of expressions. . . . Each will be glossed in terms of practices, institutions, ideas in each society which have nothing corresponding to them in the other. (Taylor, 1987, 79)

Geertz also believes in "self-definition" as the core of human experience, and he is fond of the metaphor of the web. Perhaps the most widely cited assertion in scholarly projects adopting the "interpretive" perspective is his declaration that "believing . . . that man is an animal suspended in webs of significance he himself has spun, I take culture to be those webs, and the analysis of it to be therefore not an experimental science in search of law but an interpretive one in search of meaning" (Geertz, 1973b, 5).

With these general guidelines Geertz has inspired a line of inquiry based (as Neugarten acknowledged) on the complementary principle of "thick description" or the untangling of the complex "structures of signification" making up human culture(s). Anthropology is the model, but its implications for inquiry into human meaning generally derive from Geertz's belief that the "data" of social science are "really our own constructions of other people's constructions of what they and their compatriots are up to" (1973b, 9). Penetrating deeply into the ways that people make meaning for themselves and their communities is the essential task, because "most of what we need to comprehend a particular event, ritual, custom, ideas, or whatever is insinuated as background information before the thing itself is directly examined" (1973b, 9). What is most worth knowing—like the role of religion in human development—cannot be reached by what Geertz calls "size-up-and-solve" social science. By focusing on the "complex specificity" of human behavior, more can be learned about it in order to produce more skepticism about completely understanding it. There is no choice but interpretation, "guessing at meanings, assessing the guesses, and drawing explanatory conclusions from the better guesses" (1973b, 20).

In one of Geertz's own interpretive studies of religion he proposes just how the problem of spirituality or religiosity would disturb the routines of gerontological study:

> The religious perspective . . . differs from the scientific perspective in that it questions the realities of everyday life not out of an institutionalized skepticism which dissolves the world's givenness into a swirl of probabalistic hypotheses, but in terms of what it takes to be wider, nonhypothetical truths. Rather than detachment, its watchword is commitment, rather than analysis, encounter. (Geertz, 1973c, 112)

Geertz himself is generally quite restrained in his work, but his idiosyncratic prose style and his experiments in format (e.g., 1981) reflect his belief, as he finally came to express it in a study of a group of famous predecessors (1988), that the "life" and the "work" of interpretive inquiry run together in the form of an "encounter." As the discussion below of Thomas Cole's *The Journey of Life* suggests, such encounters are essential to the integration of spirituality, religion, and the study of aging.

The interpretive stance is part of the potential for the transformation of academic work, opening space for greater reflexivity and the drawing together of private and public (or scientific) meanings. Even as Neugarten was urging greater subjectivity in research in adult development, scholars in her own and in the next generation of experimentalists and theorists were revealing breaches in their own scientific experience: the intrusion of subjectivity into scientific objectivity and of the stories of human experience into the sciences of prediction and control. These point to an interpretive science of human development that can display and explain "acts of meaning," as Jerome Bruner calls them in his account of how continuities in the behavioral and social sciences are revealed in the need to revise our forms of inquiry into personal identity:

> The Self, like any other aspect of human nature, stands both as a guardian of permanence and as a barometer responding to the local cultural weather. The culture, as well, provides us with guides and stratagems for finding a niche between stability and change: it exhorts, forbids, lures, denies, rewards the commitments that the Self undertakes. And the Self, using its capacities for reflection and for envisioning alternatives, escapes or embraces or reevaluates and reformulates what the culture has on offer. Any effort to understand the nature and origins of the Self is, then, an interpretive effort akin to that used by an historian or an anthropologist trying to understand a "period" or a "people." (Bruner, 1990, 110)

Bruner (1991) has now added narrative to the essentials of cognitive inquiry. His belief in the uses of autobiography as a primary source of human meaning likely derives in part from the effort to account for his own life and career (1983).

THE HUMAN WHOLE AND THE LIFESPAN PERSPECTIVE

As Birren and Bengtson (with many colleagues; 1988) have proposed, there are now several "emergent theories" of adult development and aging, several of which reflect elements of the "interpretive" approach. Interpretive social science itself has evolved as Rabinow and Sullivan acknowledged in a second version of their influential book. The success of the "interpretive turn" in the human sciences and the growing popularity of hermeneutics as a method has presented new problems. In effect, the "textualizing" of all human experience (via the influence of Ricoeur [1981b], for example) invited the conversion to interpretivism of many scholarly practices that, while displaying procedural sophistication, could not convey a sufficient range of contexts and applications, places in which new knowledge would matter for individuals and communities.

Indeed, Rabinow and Sullivan now express uneasiness over the assimilation of the interpretive or hermeneutic approach as merely another method in the toolkit of social and behavioral science. "It is hardly surprising that hermeneutics should also fall victim to our society's obsession with technical procedures and formalistic organization of knowledge" (1987, 2). Hence, they reassert the significance of the reformation in science and scholarship to challenge our practices of knowing.

> Interpretive social science seeks to replace the standing distinction between the social sciences as descriptive disciplines and the humanities as normative studies with the realization that all human inquiry is necessarily engaged in understanding the human world from within a specific situation. This situation is always and at once historical, moral, and political. It provides not just the starting point of inquiry but the point and purpose for the task of understanding itself. But if this is so, interpretation is not simply a dimension of science. Rather, it means that science, like all human endeavors, is rooted in a context of meaning which is itself social reality, a particular organization of human action defining a moral and practical world. (20–21)

Rabinow and Sullivan struggle to find a "middle range" within the complex intellectual dynamics of postmodern discourses and theorizing. Hence, they write: "Our aim has been to argue for an interpretive position which seeks to defend critical inquiry and debate without reifying what can legitimately be called reason's claims and to open an understanding of tradition as a set of possible, but not infinite, resources for meaningful action" (21).

A program for the application to gerontology of interpretive social science is plain in Rabinow and Sullivan's work, even if the problem of aging is never specified. They lament the separation, in the university curriculum and the practices of research, of cognitive analysis and normative judgment. The result is the putative independence of the natural or behavioral scientist from the historical, moral, or political meaning of research (its "practical" elements, in their view). And they state ruefully: "Politicians and our academic experts find it easier to talk about the standard of living than about what a society might be living for. In social technocracy as in scientism, analytic reason has cut itself off from *the human whole* that could give some sense to its formal operations" (Rabinow and Sullivan, 1987, 16; emphasis added). Here is the core of the idea of meaning, an interpretive standard conveyed in an image representing the object of gerontological inquiry and the potential place of spirituality and religion within it. It supplies the moral tone Rabinow and Sullivan would make part of science and scholarship and the developmental goal specified in 1975 by the National Interfaith Coalition on Aging: "Spiritual well-being is the affirmation of life in a relationship with God, self, community, and environment that nurtures and celebrates wholeness" (cited in Payne, 1990, 13).

Not surprisingly, in the academic social sciences interest in "wholeness" is expressed in a secular vocabulary, even if its manifestations include many implications for understanding the role of spirituality and religion in human development. The search for "wholeness" in the study of adult development and aging can be seen in the "lifespan perspective" as that has come to define authoritative work in the social and behavioral sciences (Baltes, 1982). The interpretive stance is reflected in the "family" of methods identified by Baltes (1987) as representing, in effect, the "pliability" of developmental psychology in recognizing pressures from other fields (including the humanities) and the salience of themes, such as creativity and wisdom, that science itself cannot fully explain. Meanings in adulthood and old age can only be identified with greater attention to subjectivity within the interpretive formats people themselves invent, adopt, and adapt (and behavioral and social scientists explain). For example, psychologists Bertram Cohler (1982) and Carol Ryff (1986) each show how the personal construction of meaning in turn structures the life-course, especially efforts to give it wholeness—an overall form representing an individual's interpretation of her or his experience.

Ryff, who works more in the empirical and experimental tradition than Cohler (who relies generally on the psychoanalytic method), has struggled with the arguments for and against stage-structured approaches as part of her research into the ways adults perceive lifespan transitions. "Those who continued to endorse stage models were deemed naive and had to suffer the embarrassment of advocating theories that were uncommonly neat and tidy" (Ryff, 1985, 99). But she acknowledged the durability of her own commitment to the stage-structured view, like Erik Erikson's famous one, and rejected the idea that it was her and her colleagues' orderliness (i.e., the scientific method) that mattered most. Ryff revealed a motive outside the scientific norms of gerontological science.

> The attraction was that [stage-structured theories] formulated spiraling progressions of improvement for the individual. Each theorist had formulated ways in which the individual could continue to develop, become more differentiated, and function at a higher level. It was this quality, these spiraling progressions of improvement, that captured and sustained my interest. Admittedly, such conceptions of personal improvement are likely to be sprinkled with individual differences, cohort effects, and cultural variability, but such effects do not discount the impact these models have as guiding ideals that influence what people become and how they develop. Such images of human fulfillment are central to understanding how we conceive life-span development. (1985, 99)

Can a science of adult development and aging be built on the study of such "images"—including religious and spiritual ones—rather than on the conventional data of the behavioral and social sciences? Ryff believes so and says so directly in her own voice, an important gesture itself in gerontological research. But her theoretical commitments are tempered by her empirical projects. While the results suggest that people see themselves changing in ways suggested by the major stage-structured developmental theories, cohort particularities and personality idiosyncrasies will always need to be recognized. Stage theory can neither be vindicated nor refuted. Ryff calls for a theoretical model and research lying between the false ideal of orderliness and the view that there is no underlying developmental structure of personality and cognition in adulthood. In like manner, another dynamic should define interpretive inquiry in gerontology: the meeting of the inside, or phenomenological, and the outside, or sociological realms (Ryff, 1986).

These versions of the middle range define an ideal hard to meet, especially where the object of inquiry is something as seemingly obscure as human "fulfillment." James Fowler's well-known model of faith development, and its debt to Erikson's theory, is a case in point in revealing the tension between orderliness and the mysteries of religious belief. But no developmental theory appears be able to account for what prompts and sustains faith across the lifespan, or at least to convince social and behavioral scientists that religion merits a place in their theories (Reich, 1992).

Inevitably, perhaps, lifespan theorists have found routes to the modification of stage-structured determinism in the study of the growth of such capacities as creativity and wisdom. The latter especially, as depicted in a recent account (Birren and Fisher, 1990), appears to share many features of the religious or spiritual life. Ryff's version of the psychology of aging (like Cohler's and Baltes's, to name but two other influential figures in a rapidly growing area of inquiry) comes to the border of aging, spirituality, and religion without actually specifying the latter as compelling variables, even when investigating "well-being" (Ryff, 1991). Nevertheless, the vocabularies of psychological science (a constraint for Ryff, as revealed by the personal breach in an otherwise conventionally detached method) cannot obscure the overlap of these domains.

ENCOUNTER, COMMITMENT, AND NARRATIVE IN INTERPRETIVE GERONTOLOGY

Gerontology is now pliable enough to house the explicit quest for spiritual and religious meanings in the experience of aging. In a typically postmodern paradox, the recovery of such meanings for social gerontology as a field of inquiry and as a social practice can be observed in the workings of scholarship, in resistances to its own traditions, and in assertions about its role within the study of aging's scientific paradigm. The results of innovative projects of interpretive social science will come to displace the theoretical argument about its origins and goals. Interpretive social science can be seen not merely as a technique—what Rabinow and Sullivan feared—but as an "encounter," as Geertz uses the term to distinguish between religious and scientific perspectives. But the binary approach may conceal how scientific and scholarly projects can be understood as "encounters" framed by, in Geertz's terms, "wider truths." These do not necessarily compromise "detachment," but signify its relation to the "commitments" of scholars.

As a field at the border of the biological, behavioral, and social sciences and the humanities, gerontology poses complex choices in defining the vocation of inquiry. It also shares in post-World-War-II developments in scholarly life which make academic work remote from public discourse on urgent questions of social policy and individual meaning (Jacoby, 1987). However, the scope of gerontological inquiry—or the advantage of its multidisciplinary burden—presents opportunities for fresh approaches to the meaning of inquiry itself as part of the project of identifying the meanings of aging.

We can see in an exemplary work—Thomas Cole's *The Journey of Life* (1992)—how an interpretive stance can revive the spiritual and religious meanings of aging even as it meets the formal requirements of disciplinary discourse. For Cole, the interpretation of aging is first an historical project. He shows that until the nineteenth century, attitudes toward adult development and aging were shaped by religious beliefs. People accepted aging and dying as part of the eternal or cosmic order of life, as mysteries that cannot be explained. The secular, scientific, technological, and individualist tendencies of the modern period displaced this ancient and medieval view. Victorian and then-modern ambitions for mastery overcame centuries-old acceptance of mystery.

In Cole's view, aging cannot be understood apart from its spiritual meanings: "Aging, like illness and death, reveals the most fundamental conflict of the human condition: the tension between infinite ambitions, dreams, and desires on the one hand, and vulnerable, limited, decaying physical existence on the other—the tragic and ineradicable conflict between spirit and body" (Cole, 1992, 239). The search for understanding directs us to interpret aging in several domains. The conflict is revealed only most recently in a set of American historical and social conditions, for it also shapes dramatic and narrative traditions (e.g., in the story of Oedipus): "Aging is a moral and spiritual frontier because its unknowns, terrors, and mysteries cannot be successfully crossed without humility and self-knowledge, without love and compassion, without acceptance of physical decline and mortality, and a sense of the sacred" (243).

By focusing on meaning—the record of how people experienced and understood aging—Cole situates his inquiry quite deliberately within the philosophical and methodological framework of interpretive social science. The interpretive stance helps in overcoming the "dissociation" of images and attitudes from scientifically understood facts of aging. Although Cole acknowledges the difficulties in defining meaning, he recognizes that a crucial distinction between forms of inquiry reflects the ways in which the study of aging may be organized. "The scientific questions about meaning are part of the human attempt to develop logical, reliable, interpretable, and systematically predictive theories. The *existential* questions about meaning are part of the human quest for a vision within which one's experience makes sense" (xviii). Just as these questions cannot be neatly separated into discrete projects of inquiry—manifestations of C. P. Snow's (in)famous "Two Cultures"— they are joined in the human paradox. Cole welcomes the benefits of science and medicine even as he expresses skepticism about the hegemony of biomedical approaches to the study of aging. However, it is the scientism of social inquiry that has impoverished understanding of aging by displacing existential questions. In the matter of religion particularly, the secular academic professions have neglected or even resisted religious themes out of principles of "scholarly distance" (Gorsuch, 1988).

Cole is aware that conventional forms of inquiry into aging, even those with qualitative or humanist aspirations, will not prompt the recovery of spiritual, religious, and moral themes. Hence, he makes his version of interpretive social science (or interpretive or critical gerontology) part of the "narrative quest" for the meaning of aging in its cultural settings. As Ronald Manheimer (1989) argues, any such inquiry into aging is an approach to "the unavoidable question" about life's purposes, the recognition of the meanings of mortality. Narrative has represented the aging person (in literature and film) and also guided thinking about the life course. Aging can be seen as a form of narrative understanding of life's meanings; narrative as a cultural institution reflects how the meanings of human development are understood (Cohler, 1992). Narrative may have an inclusive cognition function: the organization of experience into "acts of meaning" (Bruner, 1990, 1991). Such narrative responsibilities fall naturally to history, and Cole accepts them in the multiple roles prompted by the interpretive stance. That is, he provides a narrative of aging embedded in its cultural context, the sequence of historical situations in which ideas and ideals of aging have changed. This historical narrative includes the present, particularly as it is defined by Cole's own experience. Indeed, Cole's insertion of himself into the scholarly narrative—a bold innovation in a young field seeking scholarly and scientific legitimacy—is central to his interpretive stance, giving it a distinctive narrative form of authority in its effort to overcome "dissociation."

The Circle Is Broken

In his account of the history of ideas about adult development and aging, Cole focuses on the essential transitions in the European and American middle class, "a historical evolution from communal ideals of transcendence through societal ideals of morality to individual ideals of health" (xxx). He finds the gradual displacement of the idea of aging as a spiritual journey by the framework of life's ages and stages. The transformation is represented in popular iconography of the life cycle, which Cole displays and interprets. These forgotten images—quite literal ones in relation to Ryff's—show how cultural representations reflect and direct individual experience. Their changes over the course of four centuries indicate how belief in longevity within secular time displaced faith in eternal time. "The old Protestant vision of life as a voyage, with its emphasis on introspection, on receiving experience as well as actively molding it, on reconciling past and future in the present, on yielding one's life up to its Maker, provided an inwardly viable ideal of continuity and meaning" (158). Carefully rationalized, predictable stages offering opportunities for intervention and control replaced the image of the journey, with its obscure destination.

During the nineteenth century, social and economic forces helped Americans to see their lives as their "property" whose value could be enhanced (i.e., one could live longer) through appropriate behavior. Victorian spiritual leaders unwittingly secularized their own traditions by acquiescing. "Leaving behind traditional ideas about human imperfection and divine omnipotence, they adopted a hygienic utilitarianism that had little room for either the vicissitudes of old age or the glory of God" (78). The new "civilized" morality was organized around the mutually reinforcing virtues of independence, health, and worldly success. The aging body was seen merely as a vessel of failure and sin. "The devastating implications of ageism lay not in negative images alone but in the splitting apart of positive and negative aspects of aging, along with the belief that virtuous individuals could achieve one and escape the other" (91).

In abandoning the view of aging in which inevitable loss was unified with the hope for redemption, the American middle class established a new psychological structure for growing old.

> Acknowledgement of the intractable sorrows and infirmities of age remained culturally acceptable as long as men and women lived in families, churches, and communities

> regulated by principles of hierarchy, dependency, and reciprocal obligation. But how could the ideology and psychology of self-reliance be squared with decay of the body? Only by denying its inevitability and labeling it as failure. (104)

The story of aging is brought into our own time with the further decline of the journey as the symbol for the life-course and the institutionalization of age- and stage-structured views of adult development. Although Cole would probably acknowledge that some include a strong religious and spiritual component—Erikson's, most prominently (e.g., 1982)—the "images of human fulfillment" they present are decidedly secular. The emergence of gerontology and geriatrics as forms of professional expertise has further isolated the study of adult development and aging from its prescientific traditions.

"Standing Between my Daughter and my Grandmothers"

Cole tells the story of the transformation of American ideas about aging largely through accounts of the lives and work of clerics, scientists, and others who played crucial roles in determining the new norms of adult development. For example, his report of the pioneering psychologist G. Stanley Hall's (1922) early-twentieth-century effort to give new meaning to old age shows how it sealed off science from religion and reflected its author's own disappointment with the fruits of old age. While he saw the need for aging to provide an "outlook tower to guide the human race" (Hall cited in Cole, 220) he could not see beyond the model of mastery and the worldly and practical judgment it brought. Hall's personal struggle helped advance the science of gerontology without establishing how a critical part of the meaning of the new enterprise was irreconcilable with the modern organization of such inquiry. Although Cole terms Hall's vision of wise old age "hollow and unconvincing" (for its functional bias), his account of the pioneer gerontologist ends in a compelling human paradox: "By attacking religious belief systems that were already compromised in their efforts to nourish and redeem aging and death, Hall unwittingly deepened the cultural void surrounding the end of life. But in spite of himself, Hall did not allow the scientific search for explanation and control to suppress his human search for meaning" (226).

The biographical approach is a clue to Cole's own interpretive stance. There is a second narrative in *The Journey of Life,* one that can be called a narrative of authorship. The conventional narratives of aging and of the development of the science and social sciences of gerontology are brought together in Cole's implicit and explicit account of his own career, made into a calling by his family experience and its relation to professional responsibilities. Few other works of academic scholarship begin as his does, with an account of aging and death in his own family. "The rock of old age no longer seems so secure. . . . But if old age looks more frightening now, it still symbolizes the spiritual integrity and wisdom that have attracted me since childhood. . . . I sense its possibilities for wholeness and self-transcendence" (xvii). Cole is candid about the events of his own career, not for purposes of self-display but to make plain what is at stake in his interpretation of the history of aging. In an historical irony, his study approximates the work of the famous Victorian "sages" who recognized while living through the changes he describes how the powers of a strong personal voice needed to be wedded to the analytical or critical disposition (Holloway, 1953). They also complained of the trends Cole, from the other side of modernism, identifies as antithetical to the human spirit. "We are living through the search for ideals adequate to a postmodern culture, in which the recovery of cosmic and collective sources of meaning may enable us to appreciate the spiritual and moral aspects of aging without devaluing individual development" (xxx).

Cole offers an interpretation of historical experience and of the uses of his own text reflecting the pressures on today's scholars to situate their work within a complex theoretical environment. But his interpretation (if you will) of the uses of interpretive social science prompts him to incorporate the individual case he knows best, his own. His story—as son and parent, scholar and citizen—is part of the historical development of gerontology. Bruner has asserted that "all narrative environments are specialized for cultural needs [and] all stylize the narrator as a form of Self" (1990, 84). By expanding the narrative environment for social scientific inquiry into aging, Cole has shown how scholars and scientists can respond to cultural needs within adaptive forms of discourse, recognizable within disciplinary traditions but straining at rhetorical and expressive boundaries that extend meaning. Hence, the "form of Self" displayed in the Journey of Life is a narrator stylized by the dialectic of his vocation, one which has as its subject the "unavoidable question(s)."

Geertz cautioned against a "general theory" of cultural interpretation, even one that would explain the role of religion and spirituality. "The essential task of theory building . . . is not to codify abstract regularities but to make thick descriptions possible, not to generalize across cases but to generalize within them" (1973b, 26). In effect, Cole has made his own life and career such a case, as meaningful for our time as Hall's (at least in Cole's interpretation of it) was for his. His text satisfies Neugarten's (and others', e.g., Hendricks [1992]; Seltzer [1992]) challenge to gerontologists to bring forward their own experience as part of their work, giving it a new form of self-conscious authority. It also responds to her strategic interest in a theory of the "middle range" for coordinating the study of aging with the transformation of the social sciences. Cole's own version is specialized for his particular interest: "All societies establish systems of meaning that help people orient themselves toward the intractable limits of human existence. Religion dominated such social meaning systems in the past; science and medicine dominate them today. In the future we will need a rapprochement between ancient wisdom and modern science, between mystery and mastery" (xxii).

CONCLUSION: BOUNDARY CONDITIONS AND PROBLEMS OF BEING

Other interpretive social scientists treat the relations between religion and aging quite differently from Cole. Although the middle-class Californians studied by anthropologist Sharon Kaufman (1986) identify themselves as Jews or Christians, their religious identity is fragile: "The organized practices or philosophies of their faiths hold no special meaning as they tell their stories now. . . . Religion is not a direct source of meaning . . . though the Judeo-Christian heritage shared by this group is an important part of their cultural context" (102). Accordingly, Kaufman sees the modern dilemma—"the importance of living by religious principles in a world defined by secular standards and ambitions"—as an historical artifact. Although she reported that her subjects still looked to "religious teachings" and "higher truths" for guidance, she asserted that "the tension between religious and secular lifestyles and the need to live by religious truths are no longer compelling facts of American life, and they have lost their meaning as vital pathways" (187).

Can this view be reconciled with Cole's? Certainly, he agrees that religion is not now the force it was in shaping an individual's experience of old age. But he understands his role in gerontological inquiry differently—as an advocate for reestablishing the priority of the spiritual and moral dimensions of late life. Meaning can be understood as what an interpretive social scientist brings to a text as well as what he or she finds in order to produce it. Theoretical positions and disciplinary practices provide both constraints and opportunities; they may chasten the instincts or wishes of the author and they may prompt resistance to convention. There is room, as psychiatrist and historian Robert Jay Lifton (1976) has argued, for "the Person in the Paradigm."

Methodological innovation in the study of aging derives from attention to new "boundary conditions" (Schaie, 1992). These can include, as Ryff (1986) insists, the meeting of the inner and outer realms in the domains of scholarship—as indeed it appears to be right now in demonstrations of scholarly subjectivity, a cornerstone of "postmodern" academic inquiry (Heller, 1992). Ryff names activities at other boundaries as indispensable to providing "images of human fulfillment": "As social scientists we are plagued or blessed, depending on one's point of view, with having to look outside our own disciplines to understand change and transformation in our own variables. Our knowledge of the inner and outer realms advances through acknowledgement of this interdependence" (1986, 69).

Understanding comes from interpreting some interpretations as, what Diesing (1991) calls the "initial texts" of a new field, the ones that define new (or renewed) forms of thought and practice. Resolving the conflict between scientific and interpretive gerontology does not mean agreement *within* the latter. Kaufman finds personal "integration" among the aged independent of religious consciousness. Cole sees the possibility for "wholeness" only in the recovery of traditional habits of spirituality. Paradoxically, the interpretive perspective underlies both views. But the expansion of "boundary conditions"—as Cole's "encounter" demonstrates—will redefine how scientists, scholars, and practitioners in gerontology confront the most meaningful of professional and personal dilemmas.

Gerontologists can demonstrate how understanding human experience may be constrained by the very terms often used to describe it. That is what Erikson proposed when he urged attention to what we "cannot fathom" with our theories of "anxiety," "guilt," and "identity." For "these are all problems of Being, the open or disguised presence of which we must learn to discern in the everyday involvements of old people" (1984, 163). Erikson himself gradually brought spirituality and religion near to the center of his work. In adopting the stance of "interpretive social science," the vocations of gerontology can study human experience from the point of view of a small boy who once helped Erikson to express the meaning of "integrality" or the need to "keep things together" in late life. The child had asked his mother what would happen when he died. "'Your soul will go to heaven,' she said, 'and your body into the ground.' 'Mommy,' he said, 'if you don't mind, I'd like to keep my stuff together'" (164).

BIBLIOGRAPHY

Achenbaum, W. A. (1985) "Religion in the Lives of the Elderly: Contemporary and Historical Perspectives." In Lesnoff-Caravaglia, 98–116.

——— (1987) "Can Gerontology Be a Science?" *Journal of Aging Studies* 1:3–18.

——— (1991) "The State of the Handbooks on Aging in 1990." *The Gerontologist* 31:132–34.

Baars, J. (1992) "The Challenge of Critical Gerontology: The Problem of Social Constitution." *Journal of Aging Studies* 5:219–43.

Baltes, P. (1982) "Life-Span Developmental Psychology: Observations on History and Theory Revisited." In Lerner, 79–111.

——— (1987) "Theoretical Propositions of Life-Span Developmental Psychology: On the Dynamics between Growth and Decline." *Developmental Psychology* 23:611–26.

Baltes, P. B., and O. G. Brim, Jr., eds. (1982) *Life-Span Development and Behavior.* Vol. 4. New York: Academic Press.

Bianchi, E. (1982) *Aging as a Spiritual Journey.* New York: Crossroad.

Binstock, R. H., and L. K. George, eds. (1990) *Handbook of Aging and the Social Sciences.* 3d ed. San Diego: Academic Press.

Birren, J. E., and V. L. Bengtson, eds. (1988) *Emergent Theories of Aging.* New York: Springer.

Birren, J. E., and L. M. Fisher (1990) "The Elements of Wisdom: Overview and Integration." In Sternberg, 317–32.

Bruner, J. (1983) *In Search of Mind.* New York: Basic Books.

______ (1990) *Acts of Meaning.* Cambridge: Harvard University Press.

______ (1991) "The Narrative Construction of Reality." *Critical Inquiry* 18:1–21.

Climo, J. J. (1992) "The Role of Anthropology in Gerontology: Theory." *Journal of Aging Studies* 6:41–55.

Cohler, B. J. (1982) "Personal Narrative and Life Course." In Baltes and Brim, 206–43.

______ (1992) "Aging, Morale, and Meaning: The Nexus of Narrative." In Cole, Achenbaum, Jacobi, and Kastenbaum, 107–33.

Cole, T. R. (1992) *The Journey of Life: A Cultural History of Aging in America.* New York: Cambridge University Press.

Cole, T. R., W. A. Achenbaum, P. Jacobi, and R. Kastenbaum, eds. (1992) *Voices and Visions of Aging: Toward a Critical Gerontology.* New York: Springer.

Cole, T. R., and S. Gadow, eds. (1986) *What Does it Mean to Grow Old? Reflections From the Humanities.* Durham, N.C.: Duke University Press.

Cole, T. R., D. D. Van Tassel, and R. Kastenbaum, eds. (1992) *Handbook of Aging and the Humanities.* New York: Springer.

Datan, N., D. Rodeheaver, and F. Hughes (1987) "Adult Development and Aging." *Annual Review of Psychology* 38:153–80.

Diesing, P. (1991) *How Does Social Science Work? Reflections on Practice.* Pittsburgh: University of Pittsburgh Press.

Erikson, E. H. (1982) *The Life Cycle Completed: A Review.* New York: Norton.

______ (1984) "Reflections on the Last Stage—and the First." *Psychoanalytic Study of the Child* 39:155–65.

Erikson, E. H., ed. (1978) *Adulthood.* New York: Norton.

Estes, C. L., E. A. Binney, and R. A. Culbertson (1992) "The Gerontological Imagination: Social Influences on the Development of Gerontology, 1945–Present." *International Journal of Aging and Human Development* 35:29–65.

Featherman, D. L., R. M. Lerner, and M. Perlmutter, eds. (1992) *Life-Span Development and Behavior.* Vol. 11. Hillsdale, N.J.: Erlbaum Associates.

Geertz, C. (1973a) *The Interpretation of Cultures.* New York: Basic Books.

______ (1973b) "Thick Description: Toward an Interpretive Theory of Culture." In Geertz 1973a, 3–30.

______ (1973c) "Religion as a Cultural System." In Geertz 1973a, 87–125.

______ (1981) *Negara: The Theater State in Nineteenth Century Bali.* Princeton, N.J.: Princeton University Press.

______ (1988) *Lives and Works: The Anthropologist as Author.* Stanford, Calif.: Stanford University Press.

Gorsuch, R. L. (1988) "Psychology of Religion." *Annual Review of Psychology* 39:201–21.

Guba, E. (1990) *The Paradigm Dialog.* Newberry Park, Calif.: Sage.

Heller, S. (1992) "Experience and Expertise Meet in New Brand of Scholarship." *Chronicle of Higher Education* May 6:A7–9.

Hendricks, J. (1992) "Generations and the Generation of Gerontology." *International Journal of Aging and Human Development* 35:31–47.

Hickey, T. (1992) "The Continuity of Gerontological Themes." *International Journal of Aging and Human Development* 35:7–17.

Holloway, J. (1953) *The Victorian Sage*. London: Macmillan.

Jacoby, R. (1987) *The Last Intellectuals: American Culture in the Age of Academe*. New York: Basic Books.

Kaufman, S. R. (1986) *The Ageless Self: Sources of Meaning in Late Life*. Madison: University of Wisconsin Press.

Lerner, R. M., ed. (1982) *Developmental Psychology: Historical and Philosophical Perspectives*. Hillsdale, N.J.: Erlbaum Associates.

Lesnoff-Caravaglia, G., ed. (1985) *Values, Ethics, and Aging*. New York: Human Sciences Press.

Lifton, R. J. (1976) *The Life of the Self: Toward a New Psychology*. New York: Simon and Schuster.

Manheimer, R. J. (1989) "The Narrative Quest in Qualitative Gerontology." *Journal of Aging Studies* 3:231–52.

Marshall, V., ed. (1986) *Later Life: The Social Psychology of Aging*. London: Sage.

Moody, H. R. (1988) "Toward a Critical Gerontology: The Contribution of the Humanities to Theories of Aging." In Birren and Bengtson, 19–40.

Neugarten, B. (1985) "Interpretive Social Science and Research on Aging." In Rossi, 291–300.

Neugarten, B. L., ed. (1968) *Middle Age and Aging*. Chicago: University of Chicago Press.

Payne, B. P. (1990) "Research and Theoretical Approaches to Spirituality and Aging." *Generations* 14 (4):11–14.

Rabinow, P., and W. M. Sullivan, eds. (1979) *Interpretive Social Science*. Berkeley, Calif.: University of California Press.

______ (1987) *Interpretive Social Science: A Second Look*. Berkeley, Calif.: University of California Press.

Reich, K. H. (1992) "Religious Development Across the Life Span: Conventional and Cognitive Developmental Approaches." In Featherman et al., 145–88.

Reinharz, S., and G. Rowles (1987) *Qualitative Gerontology*. New York: Springer.

Ricoeur, P. (1981a) *Hermeneutics and the Human Sciences: Essays in Language, Action, and Interpretation*. Cambridge, Mass.: Cambridge University Press.

______ (1981b) "The Model of the Text: Meaningful Action Considered as a Text." In Ricoeur 1981a, 197–221.

Rosenau, P. M. (1992) *Post-Modernism and the Social Sciences: Insights, Inroads, and Intrusions*. Princeton, N.J.: Princeton University Press.

Rossi, A. S., ed. (1985) *Gender and the Life Course*. New York: Aldine de Gruyter.

Ryff, C. (1985) "The Subjective Experience of Life-Span Transitions." In Rossi, 97–114.

______ (1986) "The Subjective Construction of Self and Society: An Agenda for Life-Span Research." In Marshall, 32–74.

______ (1991) "Possible Selves in Adulthood and Old Age: A Tale of Shifting Horizons." *Psychology and Aging* 6:286–95.

Schaie, K. W. (1992) "The Impact of Methodological Changes in Gerontology." *International Journal of Aging and Human Development* 35:19–29.

Seeber, J. J., ed. (1990) *Spiritual Maturity in the Later Years.* New York: Haworth.

Seltzer, M. M. (1992) "Continuity and Change Revisited." *International Journal of Aging and Human Development* 35:67–82.

Sternberg, R. J., ed. (1990) *Wisdom: Its Nature, Origins, and Development.* Cambridge, Mass.: Cambridge University Press.

Streib, G. F., and R. H. Binstock (1990) "Aging and the Social Sciences: Changes in the Field." In Binstock and George, 1–16.

Taylor, C. (1987) "Interpretation and the Sciences of Man." In Rabinow and Sullivan, 33–81.

Tornstam, L. (1992) "The Quo Vadis of Gerontology: On the Scientific Paradigm of Gerontology." *The Gerontologist* 32:318–26.

Name Index

Subject Index